THE CONDUCT OF AMERICAN FOREIGN POLICY DEBATED

Herbert M. Levine
and
Jean Edward Smith

McGRAW-HILL PUBLISHING COMPANY

New York St. Louis San Francisco Auckland Bogotá Caracas Hamburg Lisbon
London Madrid Mexico Milan Montreal New Delhi Oklahoma City
Paris San Juan São Paulo Singapore Sydney Tokyo Toronto

**THE CONDUCT OF
AMERICAN FOREIGN POLICY DEBATED**

1 2 3 4 5 6 7 8 9 0   DOCDOC   8 9 4 3 2 1 0 9

ISBN 0-07-037489-9

This book was set in Palatino by the College Composition Unit in
cooperation with Monotype Composition Company.
The editors were Bert Lummus and John M. Morriss;
the production supervisor was Denise L. Puryear.
The cover was designed by Karen Quigley.
Project supervision was done by The Total Book.
R. R. Donnelley & Sons Company was printer and binder.

Library of Congress Cataloging-in-Publication Data

The conduct of American foreign policy debated / [edited] by Herbert
   M. Levine and Jean Edward Smith.—1st ed.
      p.   cm.
   Includes bibliographies.
   ISBN 0-07-037489-9
   1. United States—Foreign relations—1945   2. United States—
Foreign relations administration.   3. Treaty-making power—United
States.   I. Levine, Herbert M.   II. Smith, Jean Edward.
JX1417.C625   1990
353.0089—dc20   89-12141

ABOUT THE EDITORS

HERBERT M. LEVINE is a political scientist, who taught at the University of Southwestern Louisiana for twenty years. He is the author or editor of several debate books in political science. His recent books include *World Politics Debated* (McGraw-Hill, 1989) and *Political Issues Debated* (Prentice-Hall, 1990). He is based in Chevy Chase, Maryland.

JEAN EDWARD SMITH is Professor of Political Science at the University of Toronto. He is the author of *The Defense of Berlin* (Johns Hopkins, 1964), *Germany Beyond the Wall* (Little, Brown, 1969), and *The Constitution and Foreign Affairs* (West, 1989). He is editor of *The Papers of General Lucius Clay*, 2 vols. (Indiana University Press, 1974), and is working on a biography of General Clay.

To Professor James Barros—
an indefatigable foe of easy generalizations.

CONTENTS

LIST OF CONTRIBUTORS   xi

PREFACE   xv

PART 1 CONSTITUTIONAL AND HISTORICAL FOUNDATIONS   1

1   Is the President Primarily Responsible for U.S. Foreign Policy?
    (The Supreme Court's Interpretation of the Constitution?)   17

    YES. George Sutherland, *United States v. Curtiss-Wright
          Corporation*, Opinion of the Court   18
    NO.   Robert H. Jackson, *Youngstown Sheet and Tube v.
          Sawyer,* Concurring Opinion   22

    Questions for Discussion   27
    Suggested Readings   27

2   Should Congress Leave Foreign Policy to the President? (The
    View of the Framers)   29

    YES. Alexander Hamilton ("*Pacificus*"), *The Nature of the
          Foreign Relations Power*   30
    NO.   James Madison ("*Helvidius*"), *The Nature of the Foreign
          Relations Power*   33

    Questions for Discussion   37
    Suggested Readings   37

3   Does the Supreme Court Have a Role in Foreign Policy?   39

    YES. William J. Brennan, Jr., *Baker v. Carr*, Opinion of the
          Court   40
    NO.   Felix Frankfurter, *Baker v.* Carr, Dissenting Opinion   42

Questions for Discussion   43
Suggested Readings   43

4   Is the Separation of Powers an Impediment to Conducting
    Effective Foreign Policy?   45

    YES. John Norton Moore, *The Constitution, Foreign Policy,
          and Deterrence: The Separation of Powers in a
          Dangerous World*   46
    NO.   Ted Galen Carpenter, *Global Interventionism and a New
          Imperial Presidency*   51

    Questions for Discussion   69
    Suggested Readings   70

5   Should Politics Stop at the Water's Edge?   71

    YES. Charles H. Percy, *The Partisan Gap*   72
    NO.   Fred Charles Iklé, *Beyond the Water's Edge:
          Responsible Partisanship in Foreign Policy*   79

    Questions for Discussion   82
    Suggested Readings   82

6   Is a System of Permanent Alliances in America's National
    Interest?   83

    YES. John Foster Dulles, *Challenge and Response in United
          States Policy*   84
    NO.   George Washington, *Farewell Address to the People of
          the United States*   88

    Questions for Discussion   90
    Suggested Readings   90

Part 2   THE PROCESS OF FOREIGN POLICY   92

7   Is an Active Foreign Policy Compatible with Democracy?   111

    YES. Leon Wieseltier, *Democracy and Colonel North*   112
    NO.   Charles Krauthammer, *The Price of Power*   118

    Questions for Discussion   122
    Suggested Readings   123

8   Are Covert Operations Ever Appropriate in a Democracy?   125

    YES. Angelo Codevilla and Roy Godson, *Covert Action*   126
    NO.   Lewis H. Lapham, *A Wish for Kings*   132

Questions for Discussion   135
Suggested Readings   135

9   The War Powers Resolution: Is the Cure Worse Than the
     Disease?   137

     YES. Robert F. Turner, *The War Powers Resolution:
           Unconstitutional, Unnecessary, and Unhelpful*   138
     NO.   Daniel P. Franklin, *The War Powers Resolution: An
           Efffective Mechanism of Congressional Control*   154

     Questions for Discussion   162
     Suggested Readings   163

10   Are Treaties More Binding Than Executive Agreements?   165

     YES. Edwin Borchard, *Treaties and Executive Agreements—
           A Reply*   166
     NO.   Myres S. McDougal and Asher Lans, *Treaties and
           Congressional-Executive or Presidential Agreements:
           Interchangeable Instruments of National Policy*   173

     Questions for Discussion   179
     Suggested Readings   179

11   Should the State Department (Rather Than the National
     Security Council) Lead in Foreign Policy?   181

     YES. I. M. Destler, *State: A Department or "Something
           More"?*   182
     NO.   Duncan L. Clarke, *Why State Can't Lead*   193

     Questions for Discussion   201
     Suggested Readings   201

12   Should More U.S. Ambassadors Be Drawn from the Foreign
     Service?   203

     YES. Charles S. Whitehouse, *The Case for Career
           Appointments*   204
     NO.   John Krizay, *The Case for Political Appointments*   207

     Questions for Discussion   209
     Suggested Readings   209

PART 3 **THE POLITICAL CONTEXT OF FOREIGN POLICY**   **210**

13   Is the Relationship between the Military and Industry in the
     United States a Threat to the Democratic Political System?   223

YES. New Times, *Alliance of the Forces of Adventurism and Aggression*   224

NO. James P. Mullins, *What Is So Wrong with the Military-Industrial Complex?*   232

Questions for Discussion   237
Suggested Readings   237

14   Do the Media—Particularly Television—Undermine American Support for Military Operations?   239

YES. Cass D. Howell, *War, Television, and Public Opinion*   240

NO. Wallace B. Eberhard, *A Familiar Refrain But Slightly out of Tune*   247

Questions for Discussion   251
Suggested Readings   251

15   Does Governmental Secrecy Conflict with Constitutional Rights?   253

YES. John Shattuck and Muriel Morisey Spence, *The Dangers of Information Control*   254

NO. Michael A. Ledeen, *Secrets*   264

Questions for Discussion   271
Suggested Readings   272

16   Is the Israeli Lobby in the United States Too Powerful?   273

YES. Eric Alterman, *Pumping Irony*   274
NO. Mitchell Bard, *Israeli Lobby Power*   283

Questions for Discussion   286
Suggested Readings   287

17   Should Greater Grass-Roots Participation in Foreign Policy be Encouraged?   289

YES. Michael H. Shuman, *Dateline Main Street: Local Foreign Policies*   290

NO. Peter J. Spiro, *Taking Foreign Policy away from the Feds*   302

Questions for Discussion   313
Suggested Readings   313

PART 4   THE CONSEQUENCES OF FOREIGN POLICY   **314**

18   Should Containment Continue To Be U.S. Policy toward the Soviet Union?   329

YES. Francis P. Sempa, *Geopolitics and American Strategy: A Reassessment* 330
NO. Earl C. Ravenal, *An Alternative to Containment* 344

Questions for Discussion 361
Suggested Readings 361

19 Do Arms Control Agreements Serve U.S. Security Interests? 363

YES. Defense Monitor, *The Unravelling of Nuclear Arms Treaties: Another Step toward Nuclear War* 364
NO. Charles Krauthammer, *The End of Arms Control* 374

Questions for Discussion 381
Suggested Readings 381

20 Should the United States Devolve Its Frontline Defensive Role in Europe to Its NATO Allies? 383

YES. David P. Calleo, *NATO's Middle Course* 384
NO. Colin S. Gray, *NATO: Time To Call It a Day?* 392

Questions for Discussion 406
Suggested Readings 406

21 Is Free Trade Good for the United States? 407

YES. Steven E. Daskal, *Free Trade and Prosperity: A Global Approach* 408
NO. John M. Culbertson, *The Folly of Free Trade* 414

Questions for Discussion 423
Suggested Readings 423

22 Should the United States Take Active Measures against All Dictatorships? 425

YES. Roy Lechtreck, *Let's Treat All Dictators Alike* 426
NO. Ted Galen Carpenter, *The United States and Third World Dictatorships: A Case for Benign Detachment* 431

Questions for Discussion 447
Suggested Readings 447

23 Is the United States in Relative Decline? 449

YES. Paul Kennedy, *The (Relative) Decline of America* 450
NO. Joseph S. Nye, Jr., *Understating U.S. Strength* 461

Questions for Discussion 474
Suggested Readings 474

LIST OF CONTRIBUTORS

ERIC ALTERMAN, a political journalist, is the Washington Fellow of the World Policy Institute.

MITCHELL BARD is a foreign policy analyst in Washington, D.C., specializing in Middle East affairs.

EDWIN BORCHARD was Justice S. Hotchkiss Professor of Law at Yale Law School.

WILLIAM J. BRENNAN, JR., is an Associate Justice of the United States Supreme Court.

DAVID P. CALLEO is Professor of European Studies at the Johns Hopkins University School of Advanced International Studies.

TED GALEN CARPENTER is the Director of Foreign Policy Studies at the Cato Institute in Washington, D.C.

DUNCAN L. CLARKE is Professor of International Relations at American University's School of International Service.

ANGELO CODEVILLA served as a professional staff member of the Senate Intelligence Committee from 1977 until 1985 and is now Senior Research Fellow at the Hoover Institution.

JOHN M. CULBERTSON is Professor of Economics at the University of Wisconsin at Madison. He has been an economist with the Board of Governors of the Federal Reserve System.

STEVEN E. DASKAL of Annandale, Virginia, is a defense systems analyst and writer.

DEFENSE MONITOR is published by the Center for Defense Information, a private organization concerned with U.S. national security matters.

I. M. DESTLER is a professor in the School of Public Affairs at the University of Maryland.

JOHN FOSTER DULLES was the Secretary of State from 1953 to 1959.

WALLACE B. EBERHARD, Colonel, U.S. Army Reserve, Retired, is Professor of Journalism at the University of Georgia, Athens, Georgia.

FELIX FRANKFURTER was an Associate Justice of the United States Supreme Court from 1939 to 1962.

DANIEL P. FRANKLIN is an Assistant Professor of Political Science at Colgate University. He is currently doing research and writing on the legislative veto and the limits of presidential prerogative.

ROY GODSON is Associate Professor of Government at Georgetown University and a consultant to the National Security Council.

COLIN S. GRAY is President of the National Institute for Public Policy in Fairfax, Virginia.

ALEXANDER HAMILTON was Secretary of the Treasury in the administration of President George Washington. He was also one of the three authors of *The Federalist Papers.*

CASS D. HOWELL, Major, U.S. Marine Corps, is an intelligence officer on the Commander in Chief, Pacific, Airborne Command Post, Hickam Air Force Base, Hawaii.

FRED CHARLES IKLÉ served as Under Secretary of Defense for Policy in the Reagan administration. He was director of the U.S. Arms Control and Disarmament Agency from 1973 to 1977.

ROBERT H. JACKSON was an Associate Justice of the United States Supreme Court from 1941 to 1954.

PAUL KENNEDY is the J. Richardson Dilworth Professor of History at Yale University. He is the author of *The Rise and Fall of British Naval Mastery* (1976) and *Strategy and Diplomacy, 1870–1945* (1983).

CHARLES KRAUTHAMMER is a syndicated columnist.

JOHN KRIZAY is a former Foreign Service Officer.

ASHER LANS was former Comment Editor, *Yale Law Journal* and University Fellow in the Faculty of Political Science, Columbia University.

LEWIS H. LAPHAM is editor of *Harper's Magazine*.

ROY LECHTRECK is Associate Professor of Political Science at the University of Montevallo in Montevallo, Alabama.

MICHAEL A. LEDEEN, a national security analyst, is President of ISI Enterprises, Inc., of Chevy Chase, Maryland.

JAMES MADISON was the President of the United States from 1809 to 1817. He was also one of the three authors of *The Federalist Papers*.

MYRES S. McDOUGAL is Sterling Professor Emeritus of Law at Yale Law School.

JOHN NORTON MOORE is Walter L. Brown Professor of Law and Director of the Center for Law and National Security at the University of Virginia.

JAMES P. MULLINS, General, United States Air Force, served as commander of the Air Force Logistics Command.

NEW TIMES is a Soviet weekly of world affairs. The editors include EVGENY BUGROV, ANATOLY CHAPIS, PAVEL IVANOV, ALEXEI NIKOLIN, and ANATOLY RASSADIN.

JOSEPH S. NYE, JR., is Director of the Center for Science and International Affairs at Harvard University's John F. Kennedy School of Government.

CHARLES H. PERCY served as a U.S. Senator from Illinois from 1967 to 1985. He was a member of the Senate Foreign Relations Committee and held the post of chairman.

EARL C. RAVENAL is Distinguished Research Professor of International Affairs at Georgetown University's School of Foreign Service and a Senior Fellow of the Cato Institute.

FRANCIS P. SEMPA is Assistant District Attorney of Lackawanna County, Pennsylvania.

JOHN SHATTUCK is Vice-President for Government, Community, and Public Affairs at Harvard University and a Lecturer at Harvard Law School.

MICHAEL H. SHUMAN, an attorney, is President of the Center for Innovative Diplomacy in San Francisco, California.

MURIEL MORISEY SPENCE is the Director of Policy Analysis at Harvard University's Office of Government, Community, and Public Affairs.

PETER J. SPIRO is Special Assistant to the Legal Adviser, U.S. Department of State.

GEORGE SUTHERLAND was an Associate Justice of the United States Supreme Court from 1911 to 1938.

ROBERT F. TURNER is Associate Director of the Center for Law and National Security at the University of Virginia.

GEORGE WASHINGTON was the first President of the United States, holding that office from 1789 to 1797.

CHARLES S. WHITEHOUSE is Assistant Secretary of Defense for Special Operations. He is the former President of the American Foreign Service Association.

LEON WIESELTIER is Literary Editor of The *New Republic*.

PREFACE

The conduct of U.S. foreign policy has become one of the central issues of the age. There is scarcely a classroom, newspaper, or television newscast in which some matter relating to international affairs does not figure prominently. Even the most mundane economic matters are charged with serious global implications.

Until the Second World War, the United States was on the periphery of world politics. International issues aroused little attention from most Americans. The United States devoted itself to internal development, and political debate focused on domestic issues. The few exceptions—such as the future of Spain's overseas empire in the 1890s or American participation in World War I—were invariably followed by a retreat into isolation and a renewed concern with state, local, and purely national matters.

But with the defeat of Germany and Japan in 1945, the United States found itself thrust to the center of the international arena. The following decades witnessed enormous international problems and tensions, including the advent and proliferation of nuclear weapons, important advances in technology, the conquest of space, and the growth of crusading ideologies. America's position as a superpower compels it to lead or respond to all these developments, and its status has thus influenced virtually every aspect of American life. One indication is the amount of money the United States spends in the international arena. The U.S. defense budget (which is exceeded only by that of the Soviet Union) amounts to $300 billion in fiscal year 1989. That is 6.5 percent of the gross national product and more than one-fourth of all federal expenditures. An additional $26 billion was allocated for diplomatic activities, foreign aid, and military assistance.[1]

---

[1] *Congressional Quarterly Almanac* (Washington, D.C.: Congressional Quarterly, 1987), pp. 163, 169, 190; International Monetary Fund, *International Financial Statistics*, 41, no. 4, (1988): pp. 524–25; U.S. Department of State, *Treaties in Force on January 1, 1987* (Washington, D.C.: Government Printing Office, 1987), pp. 239–40.

The scope of America's international commitments is worldwide. From the Persian Gulf to Central America, from the Pacific Rim to Western Europe, American forces stand deployed in a high state of combat readiness. The United States maintains more than 330 military installations overseas. Mutual defense treaties link the United States with thirty-nine countries. And the American military arsenal provides a guarantee against foreign aggression for many countries of the nonCommunist world.

The complexity of managing American foreign policy has grown apace. For more than a hundred years, the entire diplomatic and military establishment of the United States was housed in a single structure—the old State, War, and Navy Building adjacent to the White House. Today, that building houses merely the executive spillover from the president's personal staff. The Department of Defense employs as many people in the Pentagon as worked for the entire federal government in Washington, D.C. fifty years ago. Nearly seven million Americans are engaged in defense activity, either on active duty in the armed forces (2.2 million), as Defense Department employees (1.1 million), or as defense industry employees (3.3 million).[2]

President Dwight D. Eisenhower commented on the impact of this vast national security apparatus in his Farewell Address in 1961. He noted that "the total influence—economic, political, even spiritual—is felt in every city, every State house, every office of the Federal government. We recognize the imperative need for this development. Yet we must not fail to comprehend its grave implications."[3]

Almost two hundred years ago, James Madison expressed a more foreboding view in a letter to Thomas Jefferson. Madison observed that the "management of foreign relations appears to be the most susceptible [to] abuse of all [the] trusts committed to a Government because they can be concealed or disclosed, or disclosed in such parts and at such times as will best suit particular views." The foreign relations power was particularly subject to abuse, said Madison, because "the body of the people are less capable of judging, and are more under the influence of prejudices, on that branch of their affairs than any other. *It is a universal truth that the loss of liberty at home is to be charged to provisions against danger, real or pretended, from abroad.*"[4]

Madison's words have a contemporary ring. Revelations that high officials of the Reagan administration had secretly entered into arrangements with Iranian officials and international arms dealers to sell U.S. arms to Iran

---

[2] *Defense Monitor*, 15, no. 3 (1986); *Washington Post*, May 12, 1988, p. 1; U.S. Department of Commerce, Bureau of the Census, *Statistical Abstract of the United States, 1933* (Washington, D.C.: Government Printing Office, 1933), p. 153; *ibid.*, 1988, p. 317; *Soldiers*, 43, no. 2 (February 1988), pp. 28–31.

[3] *Public Papers of the Presidents: Dwight D. Eisenhower, 1960–61* (Washington, D.C.: Government Printing Office, 1961), p. 1038.

[4] *Letters and Other Writings of James Madison*, ed. Philip R. Fendall (Philadelphia: Lippincott, 1865), 2: 142, italics added.

in exchange for the release of American hostages held captive in Lebanon startled many in the United States. These revelations, combined with the disclosure that profits from the sale were diverted illegally to finance the Contra guerrilla war against the Sandinista government in Nicaragua, produced one of the stormiest encounters between the president and Congress since World War II.

The controversy generated by those revelations raised a number of issues concerning the conduct of American foreign policy. Should the United States engage in covert activities? How much secrecy in foreign policy should be permitted to a democracy? What are the constitutional limits of the president in the conduct of foreign policy? Has Congress become too assertive in the conduct of foreign policy?

Such questions are not new in American history. Some go back to the Constitutional Convention in 1787; others have been prominently discussed since the United States became a world power in the twentieth century. In recent decades, many questions about the conduct of American foreign policy have been sparked by specific events, such as the extraordinary actions taken by Franklin D. Roosevelt as the United States moved closer to war with Germany, the use of armed forces by Harry S. Truman in Korea, the Bay of Pigs failure of John F. Kennedy, and military decisions on Vietnam by Lyndon B. Johnson and Richard M. Nixon. Some of the questions concern the proper functioning of a constitutional democracy. Others involve the rationality of decision making in government. Still others deal with the societal influences on foreign policy and the wisdom of specific policy outcomes.

The purpose of this book is to provide the student with a deeper insight into these various issues. Each subject is treated in a debate context. The format lends itself particularly to a discussion of foreign policy issues. One of the earliest and most famous debates in American history was between Alexander Hamilton ("Pacificus") and James Madison ("Helvidius") in 1793 over the respective roles of the president and the Congress in the conduct of U.S. foreign policy (see Debate 2). Indeed, there were few issues raised in the recent Iran-Contra affair that had not been anticipated by Hamilton and Madison almost two hundred years ago.

The central theme of this book is the stress that threats to national security place on democratic institutions. Three hundred years ago the democratic philosopher John Locke observed that there could be no liberty at home unless a nation was protected from its enemies abroad. Locke's solution was to place primary responsibility for the nation's defense—what he called "federative power"—in the hands of the chief executive. And because of the unpredictability of foreign affairs, the "federative power" depended not so much upon statutory authority as on "the prudence of these who have this power committed to them, to be managed by the best of their skill for the advantage of the commonwealth."[5]

---

[5] John Locke, *Second Treatise on Civil Government*, 2d ed. (London, 1694), sec. 143–48.

The American constitutional system has for the most part followed Locke's prescription. It has worked well or poorly, depending on the skill and prudence of various chief executives. But it has worked. And the traditional restraints on executive authority, such as the separation of powers, checks and balances, judicial review, and the written Constitution, come into play far less often in foreign affairs than when domestic issues are involved.

Yet many of the debates in this book focus on the tension between the protection of the United States from potential enemies abroad (what we call *national security*) and the preservation of our traditional liberties at home. In the quest for the former, to what extent must the latter be compromised? In a penetrating essay written on the eve of World War II, Harold Lasswell postulated the rise of the "garrison state" in which continuing international tension, combined with vast technological progress, would produce a society concerned primarily with national survival.[6] Have fifty years of superpower status and global insecurity altered the fundamental nature of American democracy?

The book is divided into four parts: constitutional and historical foundations, the process of foreign policy, the political context of foreign policy, and the consequences of foreign policy. The part introductions provide a general discussion of the topics involved as well as specific comments to put each debate into context. Each debate is preceded by a specific question. That question is answered by a Yes and a No essay. Questions for discussion and a brief list of suggested readings follow each debate.

The purpose of the debate format is to enliven interest in the subject matter. But such a format has disadvantages. First, while it aids in highlighting the issue and articulating alternatives, it leaves no issue resolved. Second, the debate approach suggests that there are only *two* sides to a given issue; shades of gray are eliminated. Third, the relative skill of the particular author sometimes determines the outcome. In assembling a book of this nature the editors did not always find it possible—regardless of the effort—to select two authors of equal ability on each question.

Finally, the book betrays no ideological or substantive bias. The editors have no hidden agenda. The concern has been to raise contemporary issues in the most challenging manner possible. The purpose is to stimulate the student to recognize that there are *at least* two points of view on the major issues pertaining to the conduct of American foreign policy.

ACKNOWLEDGMENTS

We would like to express our thanks for the many useful comments and suggestions provided by colleagues who reviewed this text during the course of its development, especially to Deborah J. Gerner, Northwestern University; Joseph S. Lepgold, Lawrence University; Thomas Magstadt,

---

[6] Harold Lasswell, "The Garrison State," *American Journal of Sociology,* 46 (Jan. 1941), pp. 455–66.

Kearney State University; Mark Miller, University of Delaware; James A. Rhodes, Luther College; and Mark M. Sawoski, Roger Williams College.

McGraw-Hill editors provided expert assistance at every stage of the project. Jim Anker and Bert Lummus were the political science editors; Annette Bodzin was the project supervisor; and Ann Hofstra Grogg was the copy editor.

Herbert M. Levine

Jean Edward Smith

PART ONE

Constitutional and Historical Foundations

American foreign policy does not take place in a vacuum; nor do those who make policy write on a clean slate. The ineluctable factors of geography and population provide broad limits that constrain action and sometimes dictate response. The history of American economic development provides additional constraints, as do the ideals of Western democracy which underlie that development. The peculiarities of the American character—a character formed by immigration and a frontier—often place strict limits on the options available to policy makers. The relative wealth, technology, and educational achievements of the United States set obvious limits to the policies that can be pursued, as do the political attitudes that those factors have produced.

Perhaps even more important, foreign policy, by definition, takes place in a realm beyond the limits of U.S. control. The international arena is a world of sovereign states: independent, not always predictable, and sometimes hostile. Each of these states pursues its individual policies based on what it perceives as its unique *national interest*. Those policies may be friendly or unfriendly to the United States. But U.S. ability to affect them is limited.

An equally important variable pertains to the instruments of foreign policy. What are the means—political, military, economic, and cultural—available to the United States to affect policy abroad? And above all, where does the responsibility lie for the conduct of U.S. foreign policy?

The U.S. Constitution divides the foreign relations power between the president and the Congress. Professor Edward S. Corwin of Princeton University, the late dean of constitutional law scholars, once referred to this division as "an invitation to struggle for the direction of American foreign policy."[1] The president is commander in chief of the armed forces; he is the chief executive; and he enjoys broad discretion to protect the nation's security. As the Supreme Court stated in 1863 (upholding President Abraham Lincoln's imposition of a blockade on southern ports during the Civil War), "He shall determine the degree of force the crisis demands."[2] But at the same time, Congress controls the appropriations process (it may or may not provide the funds the president requests); it passes the laws that govern executive action; it enjoys the exclusive authority to declare war, to raise an army and maintain a navy, to establish the rules and regulations for the conduct of the armed forces, and to draft men and women into the military service should that be required. The Senate participates jointly with the president in the treaty process and must confirm all executive appointments in the military and the diplomatic service.

This divided authority makes the conduct of American foreign policy exceedingly complex. But that is deliberate. As James Madison noted, "The complexity of our federal government and the diversity of interests among the members of it" make offensive measures against foreign nations "*improbable in Council, and difficult in execution.*"[3] Professor Joseph W. Bishop, Jr., expressed the same thought somewhat differently when he observed that:

> a good case can be made out for the proposition that the present imprecise situation is, in fact, reasonably satisfactory. Neither the executive nor the Congress is very sure of its rights, and both usually evince a tactful disposition not to push the assertion of their rights to obsessive extremes. Of such is the system of checks and balances.[4]

The Framers of the Constitution were well aware of the importance of foreign affairs. Indeed, as the debates at the Constitutional Convention in 1787 made clear, national security was uppermost in the minds of those who met at Philadelphia to draft the Constitution. The United States was no bucolic republic in 1787 but was, rather, a revolutionary state that imperiled the stability of Europe's dynastic order. Great Britain threatened immediate military intervention against the newly independent colonies if the terms of peace were not complied with; Spain was entrenched in Florida and controlled the mouth of the Mississippi River at New Orleans, blocking navigation and commerce into the midsection of the continent; France still fretted over the loss of Canada; while both France and Britain pressed their claims to the vast region of the trans-Ohio. Rather than being protected by the Atlantic Ocean, the United States was at the vortex of the struggle for political control of

---

[1] Edward S. Corwin, *The President: Office and Powers,* 4th rev. ed. (New York: New York University Press, 1957), p. 171.

[2] *The Prize Cases,* 2 Black (67 U.S.) 635, 682 (1863). See also *Martin v. Mott,* 12 Wheat. (25 U.S.) 19 (1827).

[3] James Madison, *The Papers of James Madison,* ed. Charles F. Hobson and Robert A. Rutland (Charlottesville: University Press of Virginia, 1981), 8: p. 106, italics added.

[4] Joseph W. Bishop, Jr., "The Executive's Right of Privacy: An Unresolved Constitutional Issue," 66 *Yale Law Journal* 477, 491 (1957).

North America. And in that situation, the men who drafted the Constitution were determined not to hobble the government in its conduct of foreign affairs.

The result is a curious anomaly. The domestic powers of the national government, powers that were carved from those already belonging to the states, were strictly enumerated and tightly limited by the Constitution. But the foreign relations power was nowhere specified or described. To some extent, that power exists outside the constitutional framework.

In the first place, the authority of the United States to act in foreign affairs is an *inherent* power, one attributable to the national government simply because the United States is a sovereign state under international law. In that sense, the foreign relations power is not simply a compendium of powers enumerated in the Constitution.[5]

More important, *the United States existed before the Constitution was written*. It was already endowed with full authority to act in international affairs. As an independent nation, the United States, under the Continental Congress, successfully waged the War of Independence and concluded a series of international treaties, including the treaty of peace with Great Britain in 1783. Consequently, the power of the United States to act in foreign affairs existed before the Constitution. It does not depend on any affirmative grant contained in that document, although, quite obviously, the government cannot do what the Constitution forbids.

The result is that the power of the American government to act in international relations is far greater than its power to act domestically. This arrangement was not an unfortunate oversight or careless omission on the part of the Framers, but an approach traditionally adopted by all nations. The security of the nation is paramount.

The Constitution, therefore, did not deal at length with the foreign relations power. It gave certain responsibilities to the president and others to Congress and directed that some be shared, such as the treaty power and the war power. But it placed no limits on those powers. As a result, the constitutional evolution of the authority to conduct foreign relations differs fundamentally from the constitutional development of domestic authority. Not only do the president and Congress enjoy much greater discretion, but the Supreme Court has been extremely reluctant to intervene in matters of foreign policy. Beginning with Chief Justice John Marshall in 1801, the Court has held frequently (though not invariably) that foreign policy questions are "more political than legal" and has deferred to the judgment of the president and Congress.[6] For example, despite the clear reference in Article I, section 8 of the Constitution to Congress's power to declare war, the Supreme Court consistently refused to hear any challenge to the constitutionality of the war in Vietnam.

The broad discretion that the president and Congress enjoy permits the

---

[5] *Chinese Exclusion Case*, 130 U.S. 581, 604 (1889).
[6] *Foster v. Neilson*, 2 Peters (27 U.S.) 253, 308 (1824).

United States to act quickly and decisively when national security is at stake. Rather than an eighteenth-century relic, the Constitution has proved surprisingly well fitted for a modern superpower. As Professor William Y. Elliott of Harvard University observed:

> The machinery for integrating and controlling foreign policy in the United States may seem cumbersome, not always logical, and certainly one calculated to multiply the impact of special interests. But the striking fact is that so far the boldest and most radical changes in the history of the United States have won sweeping support.... Somehow, the machinery works.[7]

The six debates that constitute Part I deal with the constitutional, ideological, and economic context of U.S. foreign policy. The first debate examines the constitutional role of the president. Is the president primarily responsible for the conduct of American foreign policy? In separate landmark decisions, two justices of the Supreme Court came down on different sides of the issue. The second debate looks at the role of Congress. In a classic confrontation, Alexander Hamilton and James Madison dispute whether the initiative lies with Congress or the president. The issues raised by these two Framers have recurred in virtually every administration since George Washington, but the clarity and persuasiveness of Hamilton and Madison have rarely been duplicated. The third debate considers the Supreme Court. The Court is the ultimate arbiter of the Constitution, yet it has rarely intervened when foreign policy was at stake. The fourth debate deals with the overall structure of the American government: Is the separation of powers an impediment to conducting effective foreign policy? On the other hand, is it an essential ingredient in the preservation of American liberty? Debate 5 focuses on the American foreign policy consensus. It asks, Should foreign policy issues be the subject of partisan debate? Does politics stop "at the water's edge"? If so, how can we be certain the best policy has been adopted? Is there an adequate articulation of policy alternatives? The final debate in Part I studies two traditional U.S. attitudes toward foreign policy—isolationism and internationalism. Is a system of permanent alliances in America's national interest?

IS THE PRESIDENT PRIMARILY RESPONSIBLE FOR U.S. FOREIGN POLICY? (THE SUPREME COURT'S INTERPRETATION OF THE CONSTITUTION)

The power of the president is described in Article II of the Constitution. But the phraseology of the article is terse and leaves many questions unanswered. "The executive Power [whatever that is] shall be vested in a President of the United States of America." The president is made commander in chief of the armed forces and is authorized to send and receive ambassadors and to make treaties, provided that two-thirds of the Senate concur. From

---

[7] William Y. Elliott, "The Control of Foreign Policy in the United States," *Political Quarterly,* 20, no. 4 (Oct.–Dec. 1949): p. 351.

that cryptic language, reinforced by numerous Supreme Court decisions,[8] the tradition has evolved that the president is the sole representative of the United States in foreign affairs. That tradition reflects ancient ideas of royal prerogative; foreign relations were a monopoly of the Crown. But it was reinforced early in U.S. history by such diverse political antagonists as Thomas Jefferson and John Marshall. It was Jefferson who, as America's first secretary of state, refused to accept the credentials of the French envoy in 1790 because they were addressed to Congress, not the president. Jefferson told the envoy (Citizen Genêt) that "The transaction of business with foreign nations is Executive altogether."[9] John Marshall expressed the same sentiment to the House of Representatives in 1800 when he stated:

> The President is the sole organ of the nation in its external relations, and its sole representative with foreign nations....The demand of a foreign nation can be made only on him. He possesses the whole Executive power. He holds and directs the force of the nation.[10]

Congress itself appeared to share that view when, in 1799, fearing that individual American citizens were meddling in foreign affairs, it passed the so-called Logan Act "to Prevent Usurpation of Executive Functions."[11] The act, which is still on the statute books, makes it a federal crime for individuals to engage in diplomatic negotiations with foreign countries.

So strong is the tradition that the president directs foreign policy that in 1987 the Tower Commission investigation into the activities of President Ronald Reagan's National Security Council (NSC) focused its findings on presidential responsibility. According to John Tower, the former U.S. senator from Texas who headed the commission, "The President is the ultimate decision-maker in national security. No one can or should pretend otherwise....A strong Executive with the flexibility to conduct foreign and diplomatic affairs is an essential feature of our form of government."[12]

But the views of Jefferson, Marshall, and, more recently, Senator Tower, do not tell the whole story. The president's role is not exclusive. Congress enjoys an equally if not more important policy-making role through its legislative authority and ultimate control of federal spending. The final report of the Tower Commission puts the matter in a more objective perspective, ob-

---

[8] *Martin v. Mott,* 12 Wheaton (25 U.S.) 19 (1827); *The Prize Cases,* 2 Black (67 U.S.) 635 (1863); *Ex Parte Vallandigham,* 1 Wallace (68 U.S.) 243 (1864); *Ex Parte Quirin,* 317 U.S. (1942); *Korematsu v. United States,* 323, U.S. 214 (1944).

[9] Opinion on the Question Whether the Senate Has the Right to Negative the Grade of Persons Appointed by the Executive to All Foreign Missions, April 24, 1790. Thomas Jefferson, *The Writings of Thomas Jefferson,* ed. Paul Leicester Ford (New York: G.P. Putnam's Sons, 1895), V, pp. 161–62.

[10] 10 *Annals of Congress* 613 (1800).

[11] Acts of the Fifth Congress, statute III, chapter 1, Jan. 30, 1799; 18 U.S.C. 5; 72 Stat. 126 (1932).

[12] Televised press conference remarks of former Sen. John Tower, Feb. 26, 1987, reprinted in *New York Times,* Feb. 27, 1987.

serving that "Ours is a government of checks and balances, or shared power and responsibility. The Constitution places the President and the Congress in dynamic tension. They both cooperate and compete in making national policy."[13] In fact, one could argue that while the president is indeed *the sole representative* and spokesperson of the United States in international affairs, *the formulation of policy* is much more of a joint endeavor.

No Supreme Court decision discusses the foreign relations power with greater clarity than *United States v. Curtiss-Wright Corporation.*[14] The case involved an arms embargo imposed by President Franklin D. Roosevelt during the Chaco War between Bolivia and Paraguay. In 1934, Congress had delegated broad powers to the president to prevent the sale of arms to the belligerents. The Curtiss-Wright Corporation violated Roosevelt's embargo and shipped machine guns to Bolivia. When the company was indicted, it challenged the constitutionality of the president's action. Note that in this instance the president was acting in accordance with Congress's expressed wishes. But the decision of the Supreme Court, which upheld the president, goes far beyond the issue of delegated power.

Written by Justice George Sutherland of Utah, the *Curtiss-Wright* decision represents a ringing reaffirmation of the power of the president in foreign relations. One of the enduring curiosities about the decision is that it was handed down by the very same Supreme Court that was in the process of overturning much of the New Deal's domestic economic program. In fact, Justice Sutherland was the leader of the conservative justices on the Court who opposed Roosevelt and the author of some of the most conservative economic decisions ever rendered by the Supreme Court.[15] But Sutherland was also an ardent American nationalist. In 1918, while president of the American Bar Association, he had delivered a series of lectures at Columbia University that supported vigorous presidential leadership in foreign affairs.[16] Many of the phrases and expressions that Sutherland used in those lectures reappear in the *Curtiss-Wright* decision.

Why did the Supreme Court grant such enormous powers to the president in foreign relations while restricting presidential authority at home? The answer may lie in Sutherland's own conservatism and a reluctance to embarrass the nation abroad. The Court recognized that occasions might arise in foreign affairs when the United States would have to act quickly and decisively. Sutherland was determined to ensure that the president would be able to do so.

An alternative view of presidential authority is provided by Justice Robert H. Jackson, concurring in the Supreme Court's decision in *Youngstown Sheet*

---

[13] John Tower, Edmund Muskie, and Brent Scowcroft, *The Tower Commission Report* (New York: Bantam Books, 1987), p. 6.

[14] *United States v. Curtiss-Wright Corporation,* 299 U.S. 304 (1936).

[15] *Adkins v. Children's Hospital,* 261 U.S. 525 (1923); *Tyson Brothers v. Banton,* 273 U.S. 416 (1927); *Rybnik v. McBride,* 277 U.S. 350 (1928); *Carter v. Carter Coal Co.,* 298 U.S. 238 (1936).

[16] George Sutherland, *Constitutional Power and World Affairs* (New York: Columbia University Press, 1919).

and Tube v. Sawyer, a steel seizure case during the Korean War.[17] In 1952, President Harry S. Truman issued an executive order taking possession of the nation's steel mills in order to avert an industrywide strike that he believed would jeopardize national security. Truman based his action on the "inherent" powers of the president as commander in chief and chief executive. Note that in this instance, unlike the situation in *Curtiss-Wright,* Congress had not authorized the president's action. In fact, as Justice Jackson pointed out, President Truman was acting *contrary* to the will of Congress.

In some respects, Jackson's views in *Youngstown* were as surprising as Sutherland's in *Curtiss-Wright.* Robert H. Jackson was appointed to the Supreme Court by Franklin D. Roosevelt in 1941. As Roosevelt's attorney general, Jackson had authored a controversial 1940 opinion permitting the president to provide beleaguered Britain with fifty American destroyers to protect British shipping from German U-boats, and he was widely regarded as one of the most liberal justices on the Court. Yet he joined five of his colleagues to hold that the president had no implied emergency power that would permit him to seize the nation's steel mills.

Jackson's opinion in the steel seizure case is especially noteworthy because of the three categories of presidential action he describes. When the president acts with the support of Congress, "his authority is at its maximum." When he acts in the absence of a congressional mandate, the president must rely upon his own authority. But when he acts contrary to the will of Congress, "his power is at its lowest ebb."

It is of more than passing interest that Justice Sutherland, one of the most conservative justices ever to sit on the Supreme Court, should write the Court's opinion most supportive of broad presidential discretion in matters pertaining to national security, while Justice Jackson, a noted liberal, should author one of the most restrictive.

SHOULD CONGRESS LEAVE FOREIGN POLICY TO THE PRESIDENT? (THE VIEW OF THE FRAMERS)

The division of authority between the president and Congress in American foreign policy has been both an asset and a liability. When the Senate delayed ratification in 1988 of the Intermediate-range Nuclear Forces Treaty with the Soviet Union until important verification issues were resolved, it applied a necessary brake to executive momentum. But when the Senate declined to give its consent to the Versailles Treaty after World War I, it undermined peace and stability in Europe and, it can be argued, helped pave the way for World War II.

The respective roles of the president and Congress in the formulation of American foreign policy have never been precisely defined. Instead, they coexist in amorphous uncertainty. At times the president dominates; at other

---

[17] *Youngstown Sheet and Tube v. Sawyer,* 343 U.S. 579 (1952).

times, the Congress. And both can marshal impressive constitutional and historical arguments to justify their authority.

One of the earliest such disputes occurred shortly after George Washington was inaugurated for his second term in 1793. Washington sought to keep the United States out of the war then waging between Great Britain and France, and he issued a neutrality proclamation for that purpose.[18] The proclamation was immediately attacked by those in the United States who supported France, and Washington was charged with exceeding his authority.

In what became a spirited exchange, Alexander Hamilton undertook to defend Washington's action in a series of eight articles published in the *Gazette of the United States* under the pseudonym "Pacificus." James Madison replied to Hamilton's arguments in a series of letters signed "Helvidius," which were also published in the *Gazette*. The "Pacificus-Helvidius" debate ranks as one of the most eloquent expositions of the respective powers of the president and Congress in foreign affairs. And because it pitted two of the most prominent Framers against one another, it revealed the inherent ambiguity of the Constitution as to which branch was intended to control.

Hamilton argued that the conduct of foreign affairs belonged exclusively to the president and that the broad grant of authority given to the president in Article II of the Constitution was unlimited, unless the Constitution *specifically* said otherwise. Madison contended that Congress was the principal organ of the national government and possessed full authority over foreign affairs, except for that *specifically* given to the president. Madison maintained that the control of foreign relations rested with Congress under the Articles of Confederation and that the Constitution, by omission, had left it there. In Madison's view, the president was merely the executive agent of Congress. The will of Congress, not that of the president, should determine American policy.

DOES THE SUPREME COURT HAVE A ROLE IN FOREIGN POLICY?

Since the landmark case of *Marbury v. Madison* in 1803,[19] the Supreme Court of the United States has emerged as the ultimate interpreter of the Constitution. Yet in foreign policy issues, many of which have profound constitutional implications, the Court has rarely intervened. The constitutionality of U.S. involvement in the war in Vietnam between 1965 and 1973, President Jimmy Carter's decision to terminate America's defense treaty with Taiwan in 1979, as well as President Reagan's use of military force in Latin America and Lebanon in the 1980s have all been held to be *political questions*, not legal issues, and therefore to be beyond the jurisdiction of the courts.

The *doctrine of political questions*, as it is called, is a judicial invention. It

---

[18] For the text of the proclamation, see *Documentary Source Book of American History: 1606–1926*, ed. William MacDonald, 3d ed. (New York: Macmillan, 1937), pp. 243–44.

[19] *Marbury v. Madison*, 1 Cranch (5 U.S.) 137 (1803).

holds that the Constitution is a *political* document as well as a *legal* document and that not all constitutional issues are legal issues. Some—such as most foreign policy questions—are political. This doctrine allows the Court to step aside gracefully from matters not properly within its ken. The doctrine traces to John Marshall, the great chief justice, who observed in *Marbury v. Madison:* "By the Constitution of the United States, the President is invested with certain important political powers, in the exercise of which he is to use his own discretion, and is accountable only to his country in his political character, and to his own conscience." Marshall added:

> Whatever opinion may be entertained of the manner in which executive discretion may be used, still there exists, and can exist, no power to control that discretion. The subjects are political: they respect the nation, not individual rights, and being entrusted to the executive, the decision of the executive is conclusive.[20]

The result is that the Supreme Court has declined to rule on such questions as which competing faction is the proper government of a foreign country;[21] what are the boundaries of the United States;[22] which country is sovereign over disputed territory;[23] whether a treaty is in force or has expired;[24] whether the president can terminate a treaty;[25] the proper duration of a military occupation;[26] the level and status of military training;[27] military promotion policies;[28] and whether the United States was at war or peace.[29]

During the early 1960s it appeared that the Supreme Court might be prepared to reconsider the application of the doctrine of political questions to foreign policy issues. In *Baker v. Carr*, the fundamental case involving legislative reapportionment, the Court abandoned the doctrine insofar as most domestic issues were concerned.[30] In writing the decision for the majority, Justice William J. Brennan, Jr., implied that foreign policy issues would also come under greater judicial scrutiny. The pertinent extract of Justice Brennan's opinion is reprinted as the affirmative answer to the question of whether the Supreme Court has a role in foreign policy. It is a vigorous argument for judicial involvement and restricts the doctrine of political questions to very narrow circumstances. The negative answer is provided by Justice Felix Frankfurter, dissenting in *Baker v. Carr*. This was Frankfurter's last written

---

[20] Ibid, at 164.
[21] *United States v. Palmer*, 3 Wheaton (16 U.S.) 610 (1818); *Oetjen v. Central Leather Company*, 246 U.S. 297 (1918).
[22] *Foster v. Neilson*, 2 Peters (27 U.S.) 253 (1829).
[23] *Williams v. Suffolk Insurance Co.*, 13 Peters (38 U.S.) 415 (1839); *Jones v. United States*, 137 U.S. 202 (1890).
[24] *Doe v. Braden*, 16 Howard (57 U.S.) 635 (1853).
[25] *Goldwater v. Carter*, 444 U.S. 996 (1979). The reasons for the holding varied among the justices.
[26] *Neeley v. Henkel*, 180 U.S. 109 (1901).
[27] *Gilligan v. Morgan*, 413 U.S. 1 (1972).
[28] *Schlesinger v. Ballard*, 419 U.S. 498 (1974).
[29] *Ludecke v. Watkins*, 335 U.S. 160 (1948).
[30] *Baker v. Carr*, 369 U.S. 186 (1962).

opinion in a long judicial career, and, as he notes, decisions pertaining to foreign policy traditionally have been committed "not to courts but to the political agencies of government for determination by criteria of political expediency." As a result, said Frankfurter, there is no ascertainable judicial standard by which "a political decision...can be judged."

Baker v. Carr was decided in 1962. It was followed shortly by American involvement in Vietnam. For whatever reason, the Court abandoned the position articulated by Justice Brennan and retreated to its traditional deference to the president and Congress in foreign policy matters.

IS THE SEPARATION OF POWERS AN IMPEDIMENT TO CONDUCTING EFFECTIVE FOREIGN POLICY?

On April 2, 1798, Madison wrote in great alarm to Vice-President Jefferson about the "violent passions and heretical politics" of President John Adams, which he believed were pushing the nation inexorably toward war with France. "The Constitution," Madison noted, "supposes what the History of all governments demonstrates, that the Executive is the branch most interested in war, and most prone to it." As a result, Madison reminded Jefferson that the Constitution has "with studied care, vested the question of war with the Legislature." If President Adams disregarded Congress, said Madison, the American people would be "cheated out of the best ingredients of their Government, the safeguards of peace, which is the greatest of their blessings."[31]

Madison spoke with authority. The Framers had been determined to provide for the nation's defense, so they concentrated responsibility to respond to sudden attacks in the hands of the president. But they also sought to make the initiation of offensive war extremely difficult. Similarly, given the fear of some states that the federal government might conclude international agreements at their expense, the Constitution required the agreement of two-thirds of the Senate (in which each state had two votes) to all treaties. This sharing of the war power and the treaty power (it is not actually a *separation* of power) unquestionably has complicated the conduct of American foreign policy. But it is consistent with the intent of the Framers. It has prevented any one branch, or one faction, from becoming dominant for an extended period.

Unlike the separation of powers in the domestic context—where the president and Congress have clear-cut and distinctively separate roles—the foreign affairs responsibilities tend to be shared. The president makes foreign policy by his actions as "sole organ" in foreign relations or as commander in chief; by executive agreements (that is, by international compacts that are not submitted to the Senate for its advice and consent); by public statements an-

---

[31] James Madison, *The Writings of James Madison*, ed. Gaillard Hunt (New York: G. P. Putnam's Sons, 1902), II, pp. 131–33.

nouncing U.S. intentions; and by his constitutional duty to send and receive ambassadors—the function of diplomatic recognition. Congress makes foreign policy by regulating foreign commerce (the Trade Act passed by Congress in 1988 is a good example); by its control of federal spending; and by its general legislative and oversight responsibility. But for the most part, these are joint functions. The president carries out the foreign policy he makes as well as that made by Congress, and the Congress "executes" the president's policies by the passage of implementing legislation and the appropriation of funds.

The absence of a precisely defined boundary between the authority of the president and that of Congress in foreign affairs has led to inevitable disputes between the two branches. And since the Supreme Court has rarely spoken in foreign affairs,[32] these disputes remain unresolved in principle and unsettled in practice. Forceful presidents, such as Lincoln and the two Roosevelts, effectively took powers from Congress; on the other hand, the Vietnam War stirred Congress to confront the president and reassert congressional authority. One of the curiosities of the American system that continues to baffle foreign observers is this continued ebb and flow of power between the two political branches. This *dual legitimacy*, as political scientists call it, has been criticized as unworkable in many countries,[33] but in the United States it has provided a reassuring stability. As Baron Montesquieu suggested while defending the separation of powers in his famous passage in Book XI of *The Spirit of Laws* (1748), political stalemates have been avoided by the very necessity for action.

In the debate that follows, Professor John Norton Moore, director of the Center for Law and National Security at the University of Virginia, argues that the separation of powers in foreign affairs has not only outlived its usefulness but is outright dangerous in a world of nuclear confrontation. In Moore's view, the tendency of Congress to "micromanage" foreign policy diminishes the credibility of the American nuclear deterrent and hobbles U.S. ability to respond quickly to threats abroad. Ted Galen Carpenter of the Cato Institute presents the counterargument. He suggests that the very possibility of nuclear war necessitates that decision making be broadly based and that the abdication of congressional responsibility to the president threatens the nature of American democracy. "An unfettered chief executive in foreign affairs does not merely heighten the danger of unwanted and unnecessary wars," he writes, "it poses a potentially lethal threat to our entire system of checks and balances, thereby jeopardizing domestic liberties."

---

[32] But compare, *Youngstown Sheet and Tube v. Sawyer*, 343 U.S. 579 (1952).

[33] For example, the shared power between President Paul von Beneckendorff und Hindenburg and the Reichstag in the Weimar Republic has often been suggested as a contributing factor in Adolf Hitler's rise to power. On the other hand, the Fifth Republic in France appears to have prospered under such a system.

SHOULD POLITICS STOP AT THE WATER'S EDGE?

It is axiomatic in American politics that foreign policy should be bipartisan. That view is grounded in the necessity for the fifty states to speak with one voice when dealing with foreign nations. In the brief years of independence before the Constitution was framed, this was not always the case. The various states did not feel bound by commitments made by the Continental Congress, and even U.S. treaties were subjected to varying state interpretations. The supremacy clause of the Constitution remedied that defect insofar as the states were concerned.[34] And Article I, section 10, specifically forbids the states from engaging in foreign affairs.

But the substance of American foreign policy has remained a divisive issue. The French Revolution, in particular, divided Americans sharply. The Federalists, led by President John Adams, opposed the French Revolution; Jefferson and his supporters embraced it. As president, Adams spoke for the United States. But his policy was bitterly contested and figured prominently in Jefferson's electoral victory in 1800.

The same was true of the War of 1812, the Mexican War, and the Spanish-American War. All were opposed by significant and highly vocal constituencies within the American population, while the Civil War, by definition, pitted American against American in the most extreme form of partisan dispute. Of these wars, only the Civil War threatened national survival. And only in the Spanish-American War did the United States enter onto the stage of world politics. Nevertheless, the idea that foreign policy should be bipartisan found little support in the United States in the nineteenth century. Foreign policy, for the most part, was seen as an expression of domestic politics. And many Americans, particularly in the Democratic party, believed with Jefferson and Madison that the United States should shun international involvement.

In what may seem to be a paradox, America's rise to superpower status in the twentieth century eroded political partisanship in foreign policy. The battles over isolation continued to be fought, but with declining intensity and not along party lines. The First World War did not engender uniform national support, but the opposition tended to form on an ethnic and sectional basis rather than by party. The Republican party led the opposition to the Versailles Treaty, but much of the opposition was personally directed at President Woodrow Wilson, and many Democrats joined in. Similarly, America's entry into World War II was strongly opposed by large segments of the population until the Japanese attack on Pearl Harbor. (The extension of the Draft Act in June 1941 passed the House of Representatives by only one vote.)

The true birth of bipartisanship in foreign policy traces to World War II.

---

[34] Article VI, paragraph 2: "This Constitution, and the Laws of the United States which shall be made in Pursuance thereof; and all Treaties made, or which shall be made, under the Authority of the United States, shall be the supreme Law of the Land; and the Judges in every State shall be bound thereby, any Thing in the Constitution or Laws of any State to the Contrary notwithstanding."

For the first time since the Civil War, America's survival was threatened directly. Patriotism transcended political party, and the country united behind the leadership of Franklin D. Roosevelt, who brought prominent Republicans (such as Henry Stimson as secretary of war and Frank Knox as secretary of the navy) into his administration. When World War II ended, the tradition of bipartisanship continued. The United States found itself the leader of the noncommunist world, and national survival was threatened once more. The arguments over the redeployment of U.S. troops to Europe in 1948 and the use of U.S. troops in the Korean War in the early 1950s (particularly in its latter stages) witnessed a brief revival of partisanship, but the benign transition from the Democratic Truman administration to that of Republican President Dwight D. Eisenhower solidified bipartisanship's hold. Since 1952, it has often been considered unpatriotic, if not un-American, to dissent from the foreign policy consensus. That consensus has entailed resistance to communist expansion and support for a strong defense establishment and for America's allies.

To be sure, partisan differences have appeared since the end of the Truman administration. Some notable examples include the continuation of U.S. involvement in the Vietnam War in the late 1960s and early 1970s, ratification of the Strategic Arms Limitation Treaty II in 1979, and U.S. aid to the Contra forces fighting the Marxist government in Nicaragua in the 1980s. These differences have been of a tactical nature, however, and were for the most part argued within the context of the national consensus on foreign policy.

It is important to note that bipartisanship in foreign policy is a relatively recent innovation. It traces to the emergence of national security as a national concern and the growth of a consensus that supports extensive U.S. involvement in world affairs. Its advantages lie in the support it provides to the president to lead from a position of strength when dealing with foreign governments. Not only does the president speak for the United States in a constitutional sense but in a popular sense as well. An often-overlooked disadvantage of bipartisanship, however, is that it retards the development of policy alternatives. When it becomes disloyal to dispute policy or to criticize U.S. leadership, the nation is deprived of one of the essential strengths of democracy. The Vietnam War is a useful case in point. The passage of the Tonkin Gulf Resolution in 1964,[35] which initiated massive U.S. involvement in Vietnam, was scarcely debated in either chamber of Congress and passed with but two dissenting votes in the Senate. If foreign policy had been fair game for political partisanship, a more thorough airing of the issue undoubtedly would have taken place.

In the debate that follows, former Sen. Charles H. Percy of Illinois argues the necessity for a bipartisan foreign policy from his vantage point as chair-

---

[35] Tonkin Gulf Resolution, Aug. 10, 1964, Public Law 88–408, 78 stat. 384. Repealed Jan. 1, 1971.

man of the Senate Foreign Relations Committee. (Senator Percy was defeated for reelection in 1984.) A strong advocate of congressional-executive cooperation, Percy bases his case on the perils America confronts and the urgent necessity for the United States to stand behind the president. An alternative view is provided by Fred Charles Iklé, former director of the U.S. Arms Control and Disarmament Agency and most recently under secretary of defense for Policy in the Reagan administration. Iklé argues that a responsible opposition on foreign policy matters "can help open up the...bureaucracy to ideas and criticism from the outside." In his view, "Without responsible partisanship in foreign affairs, the American people are denied the opportunity to express a choice and make a commitment."

IS A SYSTEM OF PERMAMENT ALLIANCES IN AMERICA'S NATIONAL INTEREST?

The ideological context of American foreign policy is sometimes referred to as a tension between two opposing foreign policy orientations—isolationism and internationalism. From the *isolationist* perspective, the U.S. national interest is best served by maintaining a healthy sense of detachment from events elsewhere. Isolationism permits the United States to concentrate on domestic development and avoids U.S. entanglement in the quarrels of other nations. This orientation draws its inspiration from President Washington's Farewell Address, in which he urged Americans to "steer clear of permanent alliance with any portion of the foreign world" and asserted that "the nation which indulges towards another an habitual hatred, or an habitual fondness, is in some degree a slave. It is a slave to its animosity or to its affection, either of which is sufficient to lead it astray." In Washington's view, "The great rule of conduct for us, in regard to foreign nations, is, in extending our commercial relations, to have with them as little *political* connection as possible."

Throughout the nineteenth and much of the twentieth century, Washington's admonitions dominated U.S. foreign policy. The Monroe Doctrine, the refusal of the United States to join the League of Nations, the neutrality legislation of the 1930s, and to some extent the fear of future Vietnams reflect that perspective.

The *internationalist* view holds that events abroad inevitably impinge upon U.S. interests and that any policy based on a denial of their relevance is self-defeating. The events leading to World War I, Adolf Hitler's rise to power, Japanese aggression in China, the outbreak of the Second World War, and above all, the menace of communism in the postwar world suggest that Washington's advice is no longer appropriate. Such widely divergent undertakings as U.S. membership in the United Nations, the North Atlantic Treaty Organization, and the Alliance for Progress; treaty obligations in Southeast Asia, the Middle East, and Latin America; military assistance for the Contras; as well as the conflicts in Vietnam and Korea can be traced to an internationalist view in general, and, more recently, a vigorous anticommunist attitude in particular.

Perhaps the leading postwar advocate of the view that American interests are best served through a system of military alliances and *collective security* was John Foster Dulles. Dulles was the principal foreign policy spokesman for the Republican party after World War II and became President Eisenhower's secretary of state in 1953, a position he held until shortly before his death in 1959. Dulles viewed the international situation as fraught with peril for the United States and saw the world locked in a moral struggle between communism and democracy. "In our modern world no nation, however powerful, can find safety in isolation," said Dulles. "Security for one is only to be achieved through cooperation with other like-minded nations."

In the debate that follows, Secretary Dulles's view in 1957 is pitted against that of President Washington in 1796. The chronological context is, of course, important, but the ideas in each argument address eternal problems for American foreign policy. Washington's Farewell Address was not an actual speech but was first published in the Philadelphia *Daily American Advertiser* on September 19, 1796. Washington's main purpose was to announce his retirement from public life (and avoid a third term as president). But Washington also presented his views about the nature of the Union, the pursuit of domestic tranquility, and the conduct of foreign relations. It is the latter section of Washington's address that is reprinted. Dulles's presentation is selected from an article he wrote on the thirty-fifth anniversary of the founding of the journal *Foreign Affairs,* a publication that over the years has been a major advocate of the internationalist view of American foreign policy.

1 Is the President Primarily Responsible for U.S. Foreign Policy? (The Supreme Court's Interpretation of the Constitution)

YES

George Sutherland

United States v. Curtiss-Wright Corporation, *Opinion of the Court*

NO

Robert H. Jackson

Youngstown Sheet and Tube v. Sawyer, *Concurring Opinion*

United States v. Curtiss-Wright Corporation, Opinion of the Court

George Sutherland

The broad statement that the federal government can exercise no powers except those specifically enumerated in the Constitution, and such implied powers as are necessary and proper to carry into effect the enumerated powers, is categorically true only in respect of our internal affairs. In that field, the primary purpose of the Constitution was to carve from the general mass of legislative powers *then possessed by the states* such portions as it was thought desirable to vest in the federal government, leaving those not included in the enumeration still in the states. That this doctrine applies only to powers which the states had, is self evident. And since the states severally never possessed international powers, such powers could not have been carved from the mass of state powers but obviously were transmitted to the United States from some other source. During the colonial period, those powers were possessed exclusively by and were entirely under the control of the Crown. By the Declaration of Independence, "the Representatives of the United States of America" declared the United [not the several] Colonies to be free and independent states, and as such to have "full Power to levy War, conclude Peace, contract Alliances, establish Commerce and to do all other Acts and Things which Independent States may of right do."

As a result of the separation from Great Britain by the colonies acting as a unit, the powers of external sovereignty passed from the Crown not to the colonies severally, but to the colonies in their collective and corporate capacity as the United States of America. Even before the Declaration, the colonies were a unit in foreign affairs, acting through a common agency—namely the Continental Congress, composed of delegates from the thirteen colonies. That agency exercised the powers of war and peace, raised an army, created a navy, and finally adopted the Declaration of Independence. Rulers come and go; governments end and forms of government change; but sovereignty survives. A political society cannot endure without a supreme will somewhere. Sovereignty is never held in suspense. When, therefore, the external sovereignty of Great Britain in respect of the colonies ceased, it immediately passed to the Union....

The Union existed before the Constitution, which was ordained and established among other things to form "a more perfect Union." Prior to that event, it is clear that the Union, declared by the Articles of Confederation to be "perpetual," was the sole possessor of external sovereignty and in the Union it remained without change save in so far as the Constitution in express terms qualified its exercise....

It results that the investment of the federal government with the powers of external sovereignty did not depend upon the affirmative grants of the Constitution. The powers to declare and wage War, to conclude peace, to make treaties, to maintain diplomatic relations with other sovereignties, if they had never been mentioned in the Constitution, would have vested in the federal government as necessary concomitants of nationality....As a member of the family of nations, the right and power of the United States in that field are equal to the right and power of the other members of the international family. Otherwise, the United States is not completely sovereign. The power to acquire territory by discovery and occupation, the power to expel

Excerpted from George Sutherland, Opinion of the Court, *United States v. Curtiss-Wright Corporation*, 299 U.S. 304 (1936). Footnotes have been omitted.

undesirable aliens, the power to make such international agreements as do not constitute treaties in the constitutional sense, none of which is expressly affirmed by the Constitution, nevertheless exist as inherently inseparable from the conception of nationality.…

Not only…is the federal power over external affairs in origin and essential character different from that over internal affairs, but participation in the exercise of the power is significantly limited. In this vast external realm, with its important, complicated, delicate and manifold problems, the President alone has the power to speak or listen as a representative of the nation. He *makes* treaties with the advice and consent of the Senate; but he alone negotiates. Into the field of negotiation the Senate cannot intrude; and Congress itself is powerless to invade it. As Marshall said in his great argument of March 7, 1800, in the House of Representatives, "The President is the sole organ of the nation in its external relations, and its sole representative with foreign nations." The Senate Committee on Foreign Relations at a very early day in our history (February 15, 1816), reported to the Senate, among other things, as follows:

> The President is the constitutional representative of the United States with regard to foreign nations. He manages our concerns with foreign nations and must necessarily be most competent to determine when, how, and upon what subjects negotiation may be urged with the greatest prospect of success. For his conduct he is responsible to the Constitution. The committee consider this responsibility the surest pledge for the faithful discharge of his duty. They think the interference of the Senate in the direction of foreign negotiations calculated to diminish that responsibility and thereby to impair the best security for the national safety. The nature of transactions with foreign nations, moreover, requires caution and unity of design, and their success frequently depends on secrecy and dispatch.

It is important to bear in mind that we are here dealing not alone with an authority vested in the President by an exertion of legislative power, but with such an authority plus the very delicate, plenary and exclusive power of the President as the sole organ of the federal government in the field of international relations—a power which does not require as a basis for its exercise an act of Congress, but which, of course, like every other governmental power, must be exercised in subordination to the applicable provisions of the Constitution. It is quite apparent that if, in the maintenance of our international relations, embarrassment—perhaps serious embarrassment—is to be avoided and success for our aims achieved, congressional legislation which is to be made effective through negotiation and inquiry within the international field must often accord to the President a degree of discretion and freedom from statutory restriction which would not be admissible were domestic affairs alone involved. Moreover, he, not Congress, has the better opportunity of knowing the conditions which prevail in foreign countries, and especially is this true in time of war. He has his confidential sources of information. He has his agents in the form of diplomatic, consular and other officials. Secrecy in respect of information gathered by them may be highly necessary, and the premature disclosure of it productive of harmful results. Indeed, so clearly is this true that the first President refused to accede to a request to lay before the House of Representatives the instructions, correspondence and documents relating to the negotiation of the Jay Treaty—a refusal the wisdom of which was recognized by the House itself and has never since been doubted. In his reply to the request, President Washington said:

> The nature of foreign negotiations requires caution, and their success must often depend on secrecy; and even when brought to a conclusion a

full disclosure of all the measures, demands, or eventual concessions which may have been proposed or contemplated would be extremely impolitic; for this might have a pernicious influence on future negotiations, or produce immediate inconveniences, perhaps danger and mischief, in relation to other powers. The necessity of such caution and secrecy was one cogent reason for vesting the power of making treaties in the President, with the advice and consent of the Senate, the principle on which that body was formed confining it to a small number of members. To admit, then, a right in the House of Representatives to demand and to have as a matter of course all the papers respecting a negotiation with a foreign power would be to establish a dangerous precedent.

The marked difference between foreign affairs and domestic affairs in this respect is recognized by both houses of Congress in the very form of their requisitions for information from the executive departments. In the case of every department except the Department of State, the resolution *directs* the official to furnish the information. In the case of the State Department, dealing with foreign affairs, the President is *requested* to furnish the information "if not incompatible with the public interest." A statement that to furnish the information is not compatible with the public interest rarely, if ever, is questioned.

When the President is to be authorized by legislation to act in respect of a matter intended to affect a situation in foreign territory, the legislator properly bears in mind the important consideration that the form of the President's action—or, indeed, whether he shall act at all—may well depend, among other things, upon the nature of the confidential information which he has or may thereafter receive, or upon the effect which his action may have upon our foreign relations. This consideration, in connection with what we have already said on the subject, discloses the unwisdom of requiring Congress in this field

of governmental power to lay down narrowly definite standards by which the President is to be governed. As this court said in *Mackenzie v. Hare*, 239 U. S. 299, 311, "As a government, the United States is invested with all the attributes of sovereignty. As it has the character of nationality it has the powers of nationality, especially those which concern its relations and intercourse with other countries. *We should hesitate long before limiting or embarrassing such powers.*" (Italics supplied.)

In the light of the foregoing observations, it is evident that this court should not be in haste to apply a general rule which will have the effect of condemning legislation like that under review as constituting an unlawful delegation of legislative power. The principles which justify such legislation find overwhelming support in the unbroken legislative practice which has prevailed almost from the inception of the national government to the present day. . . .

Practically every volume of the United States Statutes contains one or more acts or joint resolutions of Congress authorizing action by the President in respect of subjects affecting foreign relations, which either leave the exercise of the power to his unrestricted judgment, or provide a standard far more general than that which has always been considered requisite with regard to domestic affairs. . . .

While this court may not, and should not, hesitate to declare acts of Congress, however many times repeated, to be unconstitutional if beyond all rational doubt it finds them to be so, an impressive array of legislation such as we have just set forth, enacted by nearly every Congress from the beginning of our national existence to the present day, must be given unusual weight in the process of reaching a correct determination of the problem. A legislative practice such as we have here, evidenced not by only occasional instances, but marked by the movement of a steady stream for a century and a half of time, goes a long way in the direction of proving the presence of unassailable ground for the constitutionality of the practice, to be found in the origin and history of the power involved, or in its nature, or in both combined....

The uniform, long-continued and undisputed legislative practice just disclosed rests upon an admissible view of the Constitution which, even if the practice found far less support in principle than we think it does, we should not feel at liberty at this late day to disturb.

We deem it unnecessary to consider, *seriatim,* the several clauses which are said to evidence the unconstitutionality of the Joint Resolution as involving an unlawful delegation of legislative power. It is enough to summarize by saying that, both upon principle and in accordance with precedent, we conclude there is sufficient warrant for the broad discretion vested in the President to determine whether the enforcement of the statute will have a beneficial effect upon the reëstablishment of peace in the affected countries; whether he shall make proclamation to bring the resolution into operation; whether and when the resolution shall cease to operate and to make proclamation accordingly; and to prescribe limitations and exceptions to which the enforcement of the resolution shall be subject.

Youngstown Sheet and Tube v. Sawyer, Concurring Opinion

Robert H. Jackson

That comprehensive and undefined presidential powers hold both practical advantages and grave dangers for the country will impress anyone who has served as legal adviser to a President in time of transition and public anxiety. While an interval of detached reflection may temper teachings of that experience, they probably are a more realistic influence on my views than the conventional materials of judicial decision which seem unduly to accentuate doctrine and legal fiction. But as we approach the question of presidential power, we half overcome mental hazards by recognizing them. The opinions of judges, no less than executives and publicists, often suffer the infirmity of confusing the issue of a power's validity with the cause it is invoked to promote, of confounding the permanent executive office with its temporary occupant. The tendency is strong to emphasize transient results upon policies—such as wages or stabilization—and lose sight of enduring consequences upon the balanced power structure of our Republic.

A judge, like an executive adviser, may be surprised at the poverty of really useful and unambiguous authority applicable to concrete problems of executive power as they actually present themselves. Just what our forefathers did envision, or would have envisioned had they foreseen modern conditions, must be divined from materials almost as enigmatic as the dreams Joseph was called upon to interpret for Pharaoh. A century and a half of partisan debate and scholarly speculation yields no net result but only supplies more or less apt quotations from respected sources on each side of any question. They largely cancel each other. And court decisions are indecisive because of the judicial practice of dealing with the largest questions in the most narrow way.

The actual art of governing under our Constitution does not and cannot conform to judicial definitions of the power of any of its branches based on isolated clauses or even single Articles torn from context. While the Constitution diffuses power the better to secure liberty, it also contemplates that practice will integrate the dispersed powers into a workable government. It enjoins upon its branches separateness but interdependence, autonomy but reciprocity. Presidential powers are not fixed but fluctuate, depending upon their disjunction or conjunction with those of Congress. We may well begin by a somewhat over-simplified grouping of practical situations in which a President may doubt, or others may challenge, his powers, and by distinguishing roughly the legal consequences of this factor of relativity.

1. When the President acts pursuant to an express or implied authorization of Congress, his authority is at its maximum, for it includes all that he possesses in his own right plus all that Congress can delegate. In these circumstances, and in these only, may he be said (for what it may be worth) to personify the federal sovereignty. If his act is held unconstitutional under these circumstances, it usually means that the Federal Government as an undivided whole lacks power. A seizure executed by the President pursuant to an Act of Congress would be supported by the strongest of presumptions and the widest latitude of judicial interpretation, and the burden of persuasion would rest heavily upon any who might attack it.

2. When the President acts in absence of either a congressional grant or denial of author-

Excerpted from Robert H. Jackson, Concurring Opinion, *Youngstown Sheet and Tube v. Sawyer*, 343 U.S. 579 (1952). Footnotes have been omitted.

ity, he can only rely upon his own independent powers, but there is a zone of twilight in which he and Congress may have concurrent authority, or in which its distribution is uncertain. Therefore, congressional inertia, indifference or quiescence may sometimes, at least as a practical matter, enable, if not invite, measures on independent presidential responsibility. In this area, any actual test of power is likely to depend on the imperatives of events and contemporary imponderables rather than on abstract theories of law.

3. When the President takes measures incompatible with the expressed or implied will of Congress, his power is at its lowest ebb, for then he can rely only upon his own constitutional powers minus any constitutional powers of Congress over the matter. Courts can sustain exclusive presidential control in such a case only by disabling the Congress from acting upon the subject. Presidential claim to a power at once so conclusive and preclusive must be scrutinized with caution, for what is at stake is the equilibrium established by our constitutional system.

Into which of these classifications does this executive seizure of the steel industry fit? It is eliminated from the first by admission, for it is conceded that no congressional authorization exists for this seizure. That takes away also the support of the many precedents and declarations which were made in relation, and must be confined, to this category.

Can it then be defended under flexible tests available to the second category? It seems clearly eliminated from that class because Congress has not left seizure of private property an open field but has covered it by three statutory policies inconsistent with this seizure. In cases where the purpose is to supply needs of the Government itself, two courses are provided: one, seizure of a plant which fails to comply with obligatory orders placed by the Government; another, condemnation of facilities, including temporary use under

the power of eminent domain. The third is applicable where it is the general economy of the country that is to be protected rather than exclusive governmental interests. None of these were invoked. In choosing a different and inconsistent way of his own, the President cannot claim that it is necessitated or invited by failure of Congress to legislate upon the occasions, grounds and methods for seizure of industrial properties.

This leaves the current seizure to be justified only by the severe tests under the third grouping, where it can be supported only by any remainder of executive power after subtraction of such powers as Congress may have over the subject. In short, we can sustain the President only by holding that seizure of such strike-bound industries is within his domain and beyond control by Congress. Thus, this Court's first review of such seizures occurs under circumstances which leave presidential power most vulnerable to attack and in the least favorable of possible constitutional postures.

I did not suppose, and I am not persuaded, that history leaves it open to question, at least in the courts, that the executive branch, like the Federal Government as a whole, possesses only delegated powers. The purpose of the Constitution was not only to grant power, but to keep it from getting out of hand. However, because the President does not enjoy unmentioned powers does not mean that the mentioned ones should be narrowed by a niggardly construction. Some clauses could be made almost unworkable, as well as immutable, by refusal to indulge some latitude of interpretation for changing times. I have heretofore, and do now, give to the enumerated powers the scope and elasticity afforded by what seem to be reasonable, practical implications instead of the rigidity dictated by a doctrinaire textualism.

The Solicitor General seeks the power of seizure in three clauses of the Executive Article, the first reading, "The executive Power shall be vested in a President of the United States of America." Lest I be thought to exaggerate, I quote the interpretation which his brief puts upon it: "In our view, this clause constitutes a grant of all the executive powers of which the Government is capable." If that be true, it is difficult to see why the forefathers bothered to add several specific items, including some trifling ones.

The example of such unlimited executive power that must have most impressed the forefathers was the prerogative exercised by George III, and the description of its evils in the Declaration of Independence leads me to doubt that they were creating their new Executive in his image. Continental European examples were no more appealing. And if we seek instruction from our own times, we can match it only from the executive powers in those governments we disparagingly describe as totalitarian. I cannot accept the view that this clause is a grant in bulk of all conceivable executive power but regard it as an allocation to the presidential office of the generic powers thereafter stated.

The clause on which the Government next relies is that "The President shall be Commander in Chief of the Army and Navy of the United States...." These cryptic words have given rise to some of the most persistent controversies in our constitutional history. Of course, they imply something more than an empty title. But just what authority goes with the name has plagued presidential advisers who would not waive or narrow it by nonassertion yet cannot say where it begins or ends. It undoubtedly puts the Nation's armed forces under presidential command. Hence, this loose appellation is sometimes advanced as support for any presidential action, internal or external, involving use of force, the idea being that it vests power to do anything, anywhere, that can be done with an army or navy.

That seems to be the logic of an argument tendered at our bar—that the President having, on his own responsibility, sent American troops abroad derives from that act "affirmative power" to seize the means of producing a supply of steel for them. To quote, "Perhaps the most forceful illustration of the scope of Presidential power in this connection is the fact that American troops in Korea, whose safety and effectiveness are so directly involved here, were sent to the field by an exercise of the President's constitutional powers." Thus, it is said, he has invested himself with "war powers."

I cannot foresee all that it might entail if the Court should indorse this argument. Nothing in our Constitution is plainer than that declaration of a war is entrusted only to Congress. Of course, a state of war may in fact exist without a formal declaration. But no doctrine that the Court could promulgate would seem to me more sinister and alarming than that a President whose conduct of foreign affairs is so largely uncontrolled, and often even is unknown, can vastly enlarge his mastery over the internal affairs of the country by his own commitment of the Nation's armed forces to some foreign venture. I do not, however, find it necessary or appropriate to consider the legal status of the Korean enterprise to discountenance argument based on it.

Assuming that we are in a war *de facto*, whether it is or is not a war *de jure*, does that empower the Commander in Chief to seize industries he thinks necessary to supply our army? The Constitution expressly places in Congress power "to raise and *support* Armies" and "to *provide* and *maintain* a Navy." (Emphasis supplied.) This certainly lays upon Congress primary responsibility for supplying the armed forces. Congress alone controls the raising of revenues and their appropriation and may determine in what manner and by what means they shall be spent for military and naval procurement. I suppose no one would doubt that Congress can take over war supply as a Government enterprise. On the other hand, if Congress sees fit to rely on free private enterprise collectively bargaining with free labor for support and maintenance of our armed forces, can the Executive, because of lawful disagreements incidental to that process, seize the facility for operation upon Government-imposed terms?

There are indications that the Constitution did not contemplate that the title Commander in Chief *of the Army and Navy* will constitute him also Commander in Chief of the country, its industries and its inhabitants. He has no monopoly of "war powers," whatever they are. While Congress cannot deprive the President of the command of the army and navy, only Congress can provide him an army or navy to command. It is also empowered to make rules for the "Government and Regulation of land and naval Forces," by which it may to some unknown extent impinge upon even command functions.

That military powers of the Commander in Chief were not to supersede representative government of internal affairs seems obvious from the Constitution and from elementary American history. Time out of mind, and even now in many parts of the world, a military commander can seize private housing to shelter his troops. Not so, however, in the United States, for the Third Amendment says, "No Soldier shall, in time of peace be quartered in any house, without the consent of the Owner, nor in time of war, but in a manner to be prescribed by law." Thus, even in war time, his seizure of needed military housing must be authorized by Congress. It also was expressly left to Congress to "provide for calling forth the Militia to execute the Laws of the Union, suppress Insurrections and repel Invasions...." Such a limitation on the command power, written at a time when the militia rather than a standing army was contemplated as the military weapon of the Republic, underscores the Constitution's policy that Congress, not the Executive, should control utiliza-

tion of the war power as an instrument of domestic policy. Congress, fulfilling that function, has authorized the President to use the army to enforce certain civil rights. On the other hand, Congress has forbidden him to use the army for the purpose of executing general laws except when *expressly* authorized by the Constitution or by Act of Congress.

While broad claims under this rubric often have been made, advice to the President in specific matters usually has carried overtones that powers, even under this head, are measured by the command functions usual to the topmost officer of the army and navy. Even then, heed has been taken of any efforts of Congress to negative his authority.

We should not use this occasion to circumscribe, much less to contract, the lawful role of the President as Commander in Chief. I should indulge the widest latitude of interpretation to sustain his exclusive function to command the instruments of national force, at least when turned against the outside world for the security of our society. But, when it is turned inward, not because of rebellion but because of a lawful economic struggle between industry and labor, it should have no such indulgence. His command power is not such an absolute as might be implied from that office in a militaristic system but is subject to limitations consistent with a constitutional Republic whose law and policy-making branch is a representative Congress. The purpose of lodging dual titles in one man was to insure that the civilian would control the military, not to enable the military to subordinate the presidential office. No penance would ever expiate the sin against free government of holding that a President can escape control of executive powers by law through assuming his military role. What the power of command may include I do not try to envision, but I think it is not a military prerogative, without support of law, to seize persons or property because they are important or even essential for the military and naval establishment.

The third clause in which the Solicitor General finds seizure powers is that "he shall take Care that the Laws be faithfully executed...." That authority must be matched against words of the Fifth Amendment that "No person shall be...deprived of life, liberty or property, without due process of law...." One gives a governmental authority that reaches so far as there is law, the other gives a private right that authority shall go no farther. These signify about all there is of the principle that ours is a government of laws, not of men, and that we submit ourselves to rulers only if under rules.

The Solicitor General lastly grounds support of the seizure upon nebulous, inherent powers never expressly granted but said to have accrued to the office from the customs and claims of preceding administrations. The plea is for a resulting power to deal with a crisis or an emergency according to the necessities of the case, the unarticulated assumption being that necessity knows no law.

Loose and irresponsible use of adjectives colors all nonlegal and much legal discussion of presidential powers. "Inherent" powers, "implied" powers, "incidental" powers, "plenary" powers, "war" powers and "emergency" powers are used, often interchangeably and without fixed or ascertainable meanings.

The vagueness and generality of the clauses that set forth presidential powers afford a plausible basis for pressures within and without an administration for presidential action beyond that supported by those whose responsibility it is to defend his actions in court. The claim of inherent and unrestricted presidential powers has long been a persuasive dialectical weapon in political controversy. While it is not surprising that counsel should grasp support from such unadjudicated claims of power, a judge cannot accept self-serving

press statements of the attorney for one of the interested parties as authority in answering a constitutional question, even if the advocate was himself....

...Contemporary foreign experience may be inconclusive as to the wisdom of lodging emergency powers somewhere in a modern government. But it suggests that emergency powers are consistent with free government only when their control is lodged elsewhere than in the Executive who exercises them. That is the safeguard that would be nullified by our adoption of the "inherent powers" formula. Nothing in my experience convinces me that such risks are warranted by any real necessity, although such powers would, of course, be an executive convenience.

In the practical working of our Government we already have evolved a technique within the framework of the Constitution by which normal executive powers may be considerably expanded to meet an emergency. Congress may and has granted extraordinary authorities which lie dormant in normal times but may be called into play by the Executive in war or upon proclamation of a national emergency. In 1939, upon congressional request, the Attorney General listed ninety-nine such separate statutory grants by Congress of emergency or wartime executive powers. They were invoked from time to time as need appeared. Under this procedure we retain Government by law—special, temporary law, perhaps, but law nonetheless. The public may know the extent and limitations of the powers that can be asserted, and persons affected may be informed from the statute of their rights and duties.

In view of the ease, expedition and safety with which Congress can grant and has granted large emergency powers, certainly ample to embrace this crisis, I am quite unimpressed with the argument that we should affirm possession of them without statute. Such power either has no beginning or it has no end. If it exists, it need submit to no legal restraint. I am not alarmed that it would plunge us straightway into dictatorship, but it is at least a step in that wrong direction.

As to whether there is imperative necessity for such powers, it is relevant to note the gap that exists between the President's paper powers and his real powers. The Constitution does not disclose the measure of the actual controls wielded by the modern presidential office. That instrument must be understood as an Eighteenth-Century sketch of a government hoped for, not as a blueprint of the Government that is. Vast accretions of federal power, eroded from that reserved by the States, have magnified the scope of presidential activity. Subtle shifts take place in the centers of real power that do not show on the face of the Constitution.

Executive power has the advantage of concentration in a single head in whose choice the whole Nation has a part, making him the focus of public hopes and expectations. In drama, magnitude and finality his decisions so far overshadow any others that almost alone he fills the public eye and ear. No other personality in public life can begin to compete with him in access to the public mind through modern methods of communications. By his prestige as head of state and his influence upon public opinion he exerts a leverage upon those who are supposed to check and balance his power which often cancels their effectiveness.

Moreover, rise of the party system has made a significant extraconstitutional supplement to real executive power. No appraisal of his necessities is realistic which overlooks that he heads a political system as well as a legal system. Party loyalties and interests, sometimes more binding than law, extend his effective control into branches of government other than his own and he often may win, as a political leader, what he cannot command under the Constitution.

But I have no illusion that any decision by this Court can keep power in the hands of Congress if it is not wise and timely in meeting its problems. A crisis that challenges the President equally, or perhaps primarily, challenges Congress. If not good law, there was worldly wisdom in the maxim attributed to Napoleon that "The tools belong to the man who can use them." We may say that power to legislate for emergencies belongs in the hands of Congress, but only Congress itself can prevent power from slipping through its fingers.

QUESTIONS FOR DISCUSSION

1. What are the advantages in having the president exercise strong powers in the conduct of foreign policy?
2. What are the disadvantages?
3. What does the Constitution say about the powers of the president in the conduct of foreign policy?
4. How have the development and deployment of nuclear weapons affected the president's powers in foreign affairs?
5. How do the president's powers in foreign affairs compare to the president's powers in domestic matters with respect to the separation of powers?

SUGGESTED READINGS

Adler, David Gray. "The Constitution and Presidential Warmaking." *Political Science Quarterly*, 103 (Spring 1988), pp. 1–36.

Barilleaux, Ryan J. *The President and Foreign Affairs: Evaluation, Performance, and Power.* New York: Praeger, 1985.

Corwin, Edward S. *The President: Office and Powers, 1787–1984: History and Analysis of Practice and Opinion.* 5th ed. rev. by Randall W. Bland, Theodore T. Hindson, and Jack W. Peltason. New York: New York University Press, 1984.

Crovitz, L. Gordon. "Presidents Have a History of Unilateral Moves." *Wall Street Journal*, Jan. 15, 1987, p. 22.

Jordan, Kent A. "The Extent of Independent Presidential Authority to Conduct Foreign Affairs Activities." 42 *Georgetown Law Review* 1855 (1984).

Lea, James F. "The President's Military Power under the Constitution." *USA Today Magazine*, 116 (Sept. 1987), pp. 12–15.

Marcus, Maeva. *Truman and the Steel Seizure Case: The Limits of Presidential Power.* New York: Columbia University Press, 1977.

Morris, Bernard S. "Presidential Accountability in Foreign Policy: Some Recurring Problems." *Congress and the Presidency,* 13 (Autumn 1986), pp. 157–76.

Paust, Jordan J. "Is the President Bound by the Supreme Law of the Land? Foreign Affairs and National Security Revisited." 18 *Hastings Constitutional Law Quarterly* 719 (1982).

Rockman, Bert A. "The Modern Presidency and Theories of Accountability: Old Wine *and* Old Bottles." *Congress and the Presidency,* 13 (Autumn 1986), pp. 135–56.

Rose, Gideon. "When Presidents Break the Law." *National Interest,* no. 9 (Fall 1987), pp. 50–63.

Tower, John, Edmund Muskie, and Brent Scowcroft. *The Tower Commission Report.* New York: Bantam Books, 1987.

See also Suggested Readings for Debates 2, 4, 7, and 9.

2 Should Congress Leave Foreign Policy to the President? (The View of the Framers)

YES

Alexander Hamilton ("Pacificus")

The Nature of the Foreign Relations Power

NO

James Madison ("Helvidius")

The Nature of the Foreign Relations Power

The Nature of the Foreign Relations Power

Alexander Hamilton ("Pacificus")

It will not be disputed, that the management of the affairs of this country with foreign nations is confided to the government of the United States.

It can as little be disputed, that a proclamation of neutrality, when a nation is at liberty to decline or avoid a war in which other nations are engaged, and means to do so, is a *usual* and a *proper* measure. *Its main object is to prevent the nation's being responsible for acts done by its citizens, without the privity or connivance of the government, in contravention of the principles of neutrality;* an object of the greatest moment to a country whose true interest lies in the preservation of peace.

The inquiry then is, what department of our government is the proper one to make a declaration of neutrality, when the engagements of the nation permit, and its interests require that it should be done?

A correct mind will discern at once, that it can belong neither to the legislature nor judicial department, and of course must belong to the executive.

The legislative department is not the *organ* of intercourse between the United States and foreign nations. It is charged neither with *making* nor *interpreting* treaties. It is therefore not naturally that member of the government, which is to pronounce the existing condition of the nation, with regard to foreign powers, or to admonish the citizens of their obligations and duties in consequence; still less is it

charged with enforcing the observance of those obligations and duties.

It is equally obvious, that the act in question is foreign to the judiciary department. The province of that department is to decide litigations in particular cases. It is indeed charged with the interpretation of treaties, but it exercises this function only where contending parties bring before it a specific controversy. It has no concern with pronouncing upon the external political relations of treaties between government and government. This position is too plain to need being insisted upon.

It must then of necessity belong to the executive department to exercise the function in question, when a proper case for it occurs.

It appears to be connected with that department in various capacities:—As the *organ* of intercourse between the nation and foreign nations; as the *interpreter* of the national treaties, in those cases in which the judiciary is not competent, that is, between government and government; as the *power* which is charged with the execution of the laws, of which treaties form a part; as that which is charged with the command and disposition of the public force....

The second article of the Constitution of the United States, section first, establishes this general proposition, that "the EXECUTIVE POWER shall be vested in a President of the United States of America."

The same article, in a succeeding section, proceeds to delineate particular cases of executive power. It declares, among other things, that the president shall be commander in chief of the army and navy of the United States, and of the militia of the several states, when called into the actual service of the United States; that he shall have power, by and with the advice and consent of the senate, to make treaties; that it shall be his duty to receive ambassadors and other public ministers, *and to take care that the laws be faithfully executed.*

Excerpted from Alexander Hamilton ("Pacificus"), in the *Gazette of the United States* (Philadelphia), June 29, 1793, Hamilton's italics.

It would not consist with the rules of sound construction, to consider this enumeration of particular authorities as derogating from the more comprehensive grant in the general clause, further than as it may be coupled with express restrictions or limitations; as in regard to the co-operation of the senate in the appointment of officers, and the making of treaties; which are plainly qualifications of the general executive powers of appointing officers and making treaties. The difficulty of a complete enumeration of all the cases of executive authority, would naturally dictate the use of general terms, and would render it improbable that a specification of certain particulars was designed as a substitute for those terms, when antecedently used. The different mode of expression employed in the Constitution, in regard to the two powers, the legislative and the executive, serves to confirm this inference. In the article which gives the legislative powers of the government, the expressions are, "All legislative powers herein granted shall be vested in a congress of the United States." In that which grants the executive power, the expressions are, "*The executive power* shall be vested in a President of the United States."

The enumeration ought therefore to be considered, as intended merely to specify the principal articles implied in the definition of executive power; leaving the rest to flow from the general grant of that power, interpreted in conformity with other parts of the Constitution, and with the principles of free government.

The general doctrine of our Constitution then is, that the *executive power* of the nation is vested in the President; subject only to the *exceptions* and *qualifications,* which are expressed in the instrument.

Two of these have been already noticed; the participation of the senate in the appointment of officers, and in the making of treaties. A third remains to be mentioned; the right of the

legislature "to declare war, and grant letters of marque and reprisal."...

If on the one hand, the legislature have a right to declare war, it is on the other, the duty of the executive to preserve peace, till the declaration is made; and in fulfilling this duty, it must necessarily possess a right of judging what is the nature of the obligations which the treaties of the country impose on the government; and when it has concluded that there is nothing in them inconsistent with neutrality, it becomes both its province and its duty to enforce the laws incident to that state of the nation. The executive is charged with the execution of all laws, the law of nations, as well as the municipal law, by which the former are recognized and adopted. It is consequently bound, by executing faithfully the laws of neutrality, when the country is in a neutral position, to avoid giving cause of war to foreign powers....

The right of the executive to receive ambassadors and other public ministers, may serve to illustrate the relative duties of the executive and legislative departments. This right includes that of judging, in the case of a revolution of government in a foreign country, whether the new rulers are competent organs of the national will, and ought to be recognised, or not; which, where a treaty antecedently exists between the United States and such nation, involves the power of continuing or suspending its operation. For until the new government is *acknowledged,* the treaties between the nations, so far at least as regards *public* rights, are of course suspended.

This power of determining virtually upon the operation of national treaties, as a consequence of the power to receive public ministers, is an important instance of the right of the executive, to decide upon the obligations of the country with regard to foreign nations. To apply it to the case of France, if there had been a treaty of alliance, *offensive* and defensive between the United States and that country, the unqualified acknowledgement of the new government would have put the United States in a condition to become an associate in the war with France, and would have laid the legislature under an obligation, if required, and there was otherwise no valid excuse, of exercising its power of declaring war.

This serves as an example of the right of the executive, in certain cases, to determine the condition of the nation, though it may, in its consequences, affect the exercise of the power of the legislature to declare war. Nevertheless, the executive cannot thereby control the exercise of that power. The legislature is still free to perform its duties, according to its own sense of them; though the executive, in the exercise of its constitutional powers, may establish an antecedent state of things, which ought to weigh in the legislative decision.

The division of the executive power in the Constitution, creates a *concurrent* authority in the cases to which it relates.

Hence, in the instance stated, treaties can only be made by the president and senate jointly; but their activity may be continued or suspended by the President alone....

It deserves to be remarked, that as the participation of the senate in the making of treaties, and the power of the legislature to declare war, are exceptions out of the general "executive power" vested in the President, they are to be construed strictly, and ought to be extended no further than is essential to their execution.

While, therefore, the legislature can alone declare war, can alone actually transfer the nation from a state of peace to a state of hostility, it belongs to the "executive power" to do whatever else the law of nations, cooperating with the treaties of the country, enjoin in the intercourse of the United States with foreign powers.

In this distribution of authority, the wisdom of our Constitution is manifested. It is the province and duty of the executive to preserve to the nation the blessings of peace. The legislature alone can interrupt them by placing the nation in a state of war.

But though it has been thought advisable to vindicate the authority of the executive on this broad and comprehensive ground, it was not absolutely necessary to do so. That clause of the Constitution which makes it his duty to "take care that the laws be faithfully executed," might alone have been relied upon, and this simple process of argument pursued.

The President is the Constitutional EXECUTOR of the laws. Our treaties, and the laws of nations, form a part of the law of the land. He, who is to execute the laws, must first judge for himself of their meaning.... In reference to the present war in Europe, it was necessary for the President to judge for himself, whether there was anything in our treaties, incompatible with an adherence to neutrality. Having decided that there was not, he had a right, and if in his opinion the interest of the nation required it, it was his duty as executor of the laws, to proclaim the neutrality of the nation, to exhort all persons to observe it, and to warn them of the penalties which would attend its nonobservance.

The proclamation has been represented as enacting some new law. This is a view of it entirely erroneous. It only proclaims a *fact*, with regard to the *existing state* of the nation; informs the citizens of what the laws previously established require of them in that state, and notifies them that these laws will be put in execution against the infractors of them.

The Nature of the Foreign Relations Power

James Madison ("Helvidius")

NO. 1

Several pieces with the signature of PACIFI-CUS were lately published, which have been read with singular pleasure and applause, by the foreigners and degenerate citizens among us, who hate our republican government, and the French revolution; whilst the publication seems to have been too little regarded, or too much despised by the steady friends of both....

The substance of the first piece, sifted from its inconsistencies and its vague expressions, may be thrown into the following propositions:

That the powers of declaring war and making treaties are, in their nature, executive powers;

That being particularly vested by the constitution in other departments, they are to be considered as exceptions out of the general grant to the executive department;

That being, as exceptions, to be construed strictly, the powers not strictly within them, remain with the executive;

That the Executive consequently, as the organ of intercourse with foreign nations, is authorized to expound all articles of treaties, those involving questions of war and peace, as well as others;—to judge of the obligations of the United States to make war or not, under any *casus foederis* or even-

tual operation of the contract, relating to war; and to pronounce the state of things resulting from the obligations of the United States, as understood by the executive;

That in particular the executive had authority to judge, whether in the case of the mutual guaranty between the United States and France, the former were bound by it to engage in the war;

That the executive has, in pursuance of that authority, decided that the United States are not bound;—and,

That its proclamation of the 22nd of April last, is to be taken as the effect and expression of that decision....

If there be any countenance to these positions, it must be found...in the constitution of the United States....

Let us examine:

In the general distribution of powers, we find that of declaring war expressly vested in the congress, where every other legislative power is declared to be vested; and without any other qualifications than what is common to every other legislative act. The constitutional idea of this power would seem then clearly to be, that it is of a legislative and not an executive nature.

This conclusion becomes irresistible, when it is recollected, that the constitution cannot be supposed to have placed either any power legislative in its nature, entirely among executive powers, or any power executive in its nature, entirely among legislative powers, without charging the constitution, with that kind of intermixture and consolidation of different powers, which would violate a fundamental principle in the organization of free governments. If it were not unnecessary to enlarge on this topic here, it could be shown, that the constitution was originally vindicated, and has been constantly expounded, with a disavowal of any such intermixture.

The power of treaties is vested jointly in the

Excerpted from James Madison ("Helvidius"), in the *Gazette of the United States*, Sept. 18, 1793, Madison's italics.

president and in the senate, which is a branch of the legislature. From this arrangement merely, there can be no inference that would necessarily exclude the power from the executive class: since the senate is joined with the president in another power, that of appointing to offices, which, as far as relate to executive offices at least, is considered as of an executive nature. Yet on the other hand, there are sufficient indications that the power of treaties is regarded by the constitution as materially different from mere executive power, and as having more affinity to the legislative than to the executive character.

...That treaties, when formed according to the constitutional mode, are confessedly to have force and operation of *laws,* and are to be a rule for the courts in controversies between man and man, as much as any *other laws.*

They are even emphatically declared by the constitution to be "the supreme law of the land."

So far the argument from the constitution is precisely in opposition to the doctrine. As little will be gained in its favour from a comparison of the two powers, with those particularly vested in the president alone.

As there are but few, it will be most satisfactory to review them one by one.

> The president shall be commander in chief of the army and navy of the United States, and of the militia when called into the actual service of the United States.

There can be no relation worth examining between this power and the general power of making treaties. And instead of being analogous to the power of declaring war, it affords a striking illustration of the incompatibility of the two powers in the same hands. Those who are to *conduct a war* cannot in the nature of things, be proper or safe judges, whether a *war ought* to be *commenced, continued,* or *concluded.* They are barred from the latter functions by a great principle in free government,

analogous to that which separates the sword from the purse, or the power of executing from the power of enacting laws....

Thus it appears that by whatever standard we try this doctrine, it must be condemned as no less vicious in theory than it would be dangerous in practice. It is countenanced neither by the writers on law; nor by the nature of the powers themselves; nor by any general arrangements, or particular expressions, or plausible analogies, to be found in the constitution.

Whence then can the writer have borrowed it?

There is but one answer to this question.

The power of making treaties and the power of declaring war, are *royal prerogatives* in the *British government*, and are accordingly treated as *executive prerogatives* by British *commentators*....

NO. 2

Leaving however to the leisure of the reader deductions which the author, having omitted, might not choose to own, I proceed to the examination of one, with which that liberty cannot be taken.

> However true it may be, (says he,) that the right of the legislature to declare war *includes the right of judging,* whether the legislature be under obligations to make war or not, it will not follow that the executive is *in any case* excluded from a *similar right* of judging in the execution of its own functions....

A concurrent authority in two independent departments, to perform the same function with respect to the same thing, would be as awkward in practice, as it is unnatural in theory.

If the legislature and executive have both a right to judge of the obligations to make war or not, it must sometimes happen, though not at present, that they will judge differently. The executive may proceed to consider the question to-day; may determine that the United States are not bound to take part in a war, and, *in the execution of its functions*, proclaim that declaration to all the world. Tomorrow the legislature may follow in the consideration of the same subject; may determine that the obligations impose war on the United States, and, *in the execution of its functions*, enter into a *constitutional declaration*, expressly contradicting the *constitutional proclamation*.

In what light does this present the constitution to the people who established it? In what light would it present to the world a nation, thus speaking, through two different organs, equally constitutional and authentic, two opposite languages, on the same subject, and under the same existing circumstances?

But it is not with the legislative rights alone that this doctrine interferes. The rights of the judiciary may be equally invaded. For it is clear that if a right declared by the constitution to be legislative, leaves, notwithstanding, a similar right in the executive, whenever a case for exercising it occurs, *in the course of its functions;* a right declared to be judiciary and vested in that department may, on the same principle, be assumed and exercised by the executive *in the course of its functions;* and it is evident that occasions and pretexts for the latter interference may be as frequent as for the former. So again the judiciary department may find equal occasions in the execution of *its* functions, for usurping the authorities of the executive; and the legislature for stepping into the jurisdiction of both. And thus all the powers of government, of which a partition is so carefully made among the several branches, would be thrown into absolute hotchpot and exposed to a general scramble....

NO. 3

In order to give color to a right in the executive to exercise the legislative power of judging, whether there be a cause of war in a public

stipulation—two other arguments are subjoined by the writer to that last examined.

The first is simply this: "It is the right and duty of the executive to judge of and interpret those articles of our treaties which give to France particular privileges, *in order to the enforcement of those privileges"*; from which it is stated, as a necessary consequence, that the executive has certain other rights, among which is the right in question.

This argument is answered by a very obvious distinction. The first right is essential to the execution of the treaty, *as a law in operation,* and interferes with no right in question, is not essential to the execution of the treaty, or any other law: on the contrary, the article to which the right is applied cannot, as has been shown, from the very nature of it, be *in operation* as a law, without a previous declaration of the legislature; and all the laws to be *enforced* by the executive remain, in the mean time, precisely the same, whatever be the disposition or judgment of the executive. This second right would also interfere with a right acknowledged to be in the legislative department.

If nothing else could suggest this distinction to the writer, he ought to have been reminded of it by his own words, "in order to the enforcement of those privileges"—Was it in order to *the enforcement* of the article of guaranty, that the right is ascribed to the executive?

The other of the two arguments reduces itself into the following form: the executive has the right to receive public ministers; this right includes the right of deciding, in the case of a revolution, whether the new government, sending the minister, ought to be recognised, or not; and this, again, the right to give or refuse operation to preexisting treaties.

The power of the legislature to declare war, and judge of the causes for declaring it, is one of the most express and explicit parts of the constitution. To endeavour to abridge or *affect* it by strained inferences, and by hypothetical or singular occurrences, naturally warns the reader of some lurking fallacy.

The words of the constitution are, "He (the president) shall receive ambassadors, other public ministers, and consuls." I shall not undertake to examine, what would be the precise extent and effect of this function in various cases which fancy may suggest, or which time may produce. It will be more proper to observe, in general, and every candid reader will second the observation, that little, if anything, more was intended by the clause, than to provide for a particular mode of communication, *almost* grown into a right among modern nations; by pointing out the department of the government, most proper for the ceremony of admitting public ministers, of examining their credentials, and of authenticating their title to the privileges annexed to their character by the law of nations. This being the apparent design of the constitution, it would be highly improper to magnify the function into an important prerogative, even where no rights of other departments could be affected by it....

But how does it follow from the function to receive ambassadors and other public ministers, that so consequential a prerogative may be exercised by the executive? When a foreign minister presents himself, two questions immediately arise: Are his credentials from the existing and acting government of his country? Are they properly authenticated? These questions belong of necessity to the executive; but they involve no cognizance of the question, whether those exercising the government have the right along with the possession. This belongs to the nation, and to the nation alone, on whom the government operates. The questions before the executive are merely questions of fact; and the executive would have precisely the same right, or rather be under the same necessity of deciding them, if its function was simply to receive *without any discretion to reject* public ministers. It is evident, therefore, that if the executive has a right to reject a public minister, it must be

founded on some other consideration than a change in the government, or the newness of the government; and consequently a right to refuse to acknowledge a new government cannot be implied by the right to refuse a public minister....

That the authority of the executive does not extend to a question, whether an *existing* government ought to be recognised or not, will still more clearly appear from an examination of the next inference of the writer, to wit: that the executive has a right to give or refuse activity and operation to preexisting treaties....

As a change of government then makes no change in the obligations or rights of the party to a treaty, it is clear that the executive can have no more right to suspend or prevent the operation of a treaty, on account of the change, than to suspend or prevent the operation, where no such change has happened. Nor can it have any more right to suspend the operation of a treaty in force as a law, than to suspend the operation of any other law....

Yet allowing it to be, as contended, that a suspension of treaties might happen from a *consequential* operation of a right to receive public ministers, which is an *express right* vested by the constitution; it could be no proof, that the same or a *similar* effect could be produced by the *direct* operation of a *constructive power.*

Hence the embarrassments and gross contradictions of the writer in defining, and applying his ultimate inference from the operation of the executive power with regard to public ministers.

At first it exhibits an "important instance of the right of the executive to decide the obligation of the nation with regard to foreign nations."

Rising from that, it confers on the executive, a right "to put the United States in a condition to become an associate in war."

And at its full height, it authorizes the executive "to lay the legislature under *an obligation* of declaring war."

From this towering prerogative, it suddenly brings down the executive to the right of *"consequentially affecting* the proper or improper exercise of the power of the legislature to declare war."

And then, by a caprice as unexpected as it is sudden, it espouses the cause of the legislature; rescues it from the executive right "to lay it under an *obligation* of declaring war"; and asserts it to be "free to perform its *own* duties according to its *own* sense of them," without any other control than what it is liable to, in every other legislative act.

The point at which it finally seems to rest, is, that "the executive, in the exercise of its *constitutional powers*, may establish an antecedent state of things, which ought to *weigh* in the *legislative decisions*"; a prerogative which will import a great deal, or nothing, according to the handle by which you take it; and which at the same time, you can take by no handle that does not clash with some inference preceding....

If the meaning be as is implied by the force of the terms "constitutional powers," that the antecedent state of things produced by the executive, ought to have a *constitutional weight* with the legislature; or, in plainer words, imposes a *constitutional obligation;* the writer will not only have to combat the arguments by which such a prerogative has been disproved; but to reconcile it with his last concession, that "the legislature is *free* to perform its duties according to its *own* sense of them." He must show that the legislature is, at the same time *constitutionally free* to pursue its *own judgment,* and *constitutionally bound* by the *judgment of the executive.*

QUESTIONS FOR DISCUSSION

1. What are the constitutional powers of Congress in foreign affairs?
2. What role should the intent of the Framers of the Constitution play in determining the extent of congressional powers in foreign affairs today?
3. What powers in foreign affairs has the president assumed that are not mentioned in the Constitution?
4. What effect has Congress's power to declare war had on its power with respect to the president in military operations?
5. What impact would the granting of strong congressional powers in foreign affairs have on the policy of other nations toward the United States?

SUGGESTED READINGS

Barnhart, Michael, ed. *Congress and United States Foreign Policy: Controlling the Use of Force in the Nuclear Age.* Albany, N.Y.: State University of New York Press, 1987.

Carter, Ralph G. "Congressional Foreign Policy Behavior: Persistent Patterns of the Postwar Period." *Presidential Studies Quarterly,* 16 (Spring 1986), pp. 329–59.

Crabb, Cecil V., and Pat M. Holt. *Invitation to Struggle: Congress, the President, and Foreign Policy.* 3d ed. Washington, D.C.: CQ Press, 1988.

Drischler, Alvin Paul. "The Activist Congress and Foreign Policy." *SAIS Review,* 6 (Summer–Fall 1986), pp. 193–204.

Fisher, Louis. *Constitutional Conflicts between Congress and the President.* Princeton, N.J.: Princeton University Press, 1985.

Franck, Thomas M., and Edward Weisband. *Foreign Policy by Congress.* New York: Oxford University Press, 1979.

Johnson, Loch. *The Making of International Agreements: Congress Confronts the Executive.* New York: New York University Press, 1984.

Lindsay, James M. "Congress and Defense Policy: 1961 to 1986." *Armed Forces and Society,* 13 (Spring 1987), pp. 371–401.

Lofgren, Charles A. "On War-Making, Original Intent, and Ultra-Whiggery." 21 *Valparaiso University Law Review* 53 (Fall 1986).

Rodman, Peter W. "The Imperial Congress." *National Interest,* no. 1 (Fall 1985), pp. 26–35.

Szamuely, George. "The Imperial Congress." *Commentary,* 84 (Sept. 1987), pp. 27–32.

Wormuth, Francis D., and Edwin B. Firmage, with Francis P. Butler. *To Chain the Dog of War: The War Power of Congress in History and Law.* Dallas: Southern Methodist University Press, 1986.

See also Suggested Readings for Debates 1, 4, and 9.

3 Does the Supreme Court Have a Role in Foreign Policy?

YES

William J. Brennan, Jr.

Baker v. Carr, *Opinion of the Court*

NO

Felix Frankfurter

Baker v. Carr, *Dissenting Opinion*

Baker v. Carr, Opinion of the Court

William J. Brennan, Jr.

There are sweeping statements to the effect that all questions touching foreign relations are political questions. Not only does resolution of such issues frequently turn on standards that defy judicial application, or involve the exercise of a discretion demonstrably committed to the executive or legislature; but many such questions uniquely demand single-voiced statement of the Government's views. Yet it is error to suppose that every case or controversy which touches foreign relations lies beyond judicial cognizance. Our cases in this field seem invariably to show a discriminating analysis of the particular question posed, in terms of the history of its management by the political branches, of its susceptibility to judicial handling in the light of its nature and posture in the specific case, and of the possible consequences of judicial action. For example, though a court will not ordinarily inquire whether a treaty has been terminated, since on that question "governmental action... must be regarded as of controlling importance," if there has been no conclusive "governmental action" then a court can construe a treaty and may find it provides the answer....

While recognition of foreign governments so strongly defies judicial treatment that without executive recognition a foreign state has been called "a republic of whose existence we know nothing," and the judiciary ordinarily follows the executive as to which nation has sovereignty over disputed territory, once sovereignty over an area is politically determined and declared, courts may examine the resulting status and decide independently whether a statute applies to that area. Similarly, recognition of belligerency abroad is an executive responsibility, but if the executive proclamations fall short of an explicit answer, a court may construe them seeking, for example, to determine whether the situation is such that statutes designed to assure American neutrality have become operative....

Though it has been stated broadly that "the power which declared the necessity is the power to declare its cessation, and what the cessation requires," here too analysis reveals isolable reasons for the presence of political questions, underlying this Court's refusal to review the political departments' determination of when or whether a war has ended. Dominant is the need for finality in the political determination, for emergency's nature demands "A prompt and unhesitating obedience." Moreover, "the cessation of hostilities does not necessarily end the war power.... But deference rests on reason, not habit. The question in a particular case may not seriously implicate considerations of finality—*e.g.*, a public program of importance (rent control) yet not central to the emergency effort. Further, clearly definable criteria for decision may be available. In such case the political question barrier falls away: "[A] Court is not at liberty to shut its eyes to an obvious mistake, when the validity of the law depends upon the truth of what is declared.... [It can] inquire whether the exigency still existed upon which the continued operation of the law depended." On the other hand, even in private litigation which directly implicates no feature of separation of powers, lack of judicially discoverable standards and the drive for even-handed application may impel reference to the political departments' determination of dates of hostilities' beginning and ending....

This Court's deference to the political departments in determining whether Indians are

---

Excerpted from William J. Brennan, Jr., Opinion of the Court, *Baker v. Carr*, 369 U.S. 186 (1962). Footnotes have been omitted.

recognized as a tribe, while it reflects familiar attributes of political questions, also has a unique element in that "the relation of the Indians to the United States is marked by peculiar and cardinal distinctions which exist no where else....[The Indians are] domestic dependent nations...in a state of pupilage. Their relation to the United States resembles that of a ward to his guardian." Yet, here too, there is no blanket rule....

It is apparent that several formulations which vary slightly according to the settings in which the questions arise may describe a political question, although each has one or more elements which identify it as essentially a function of the separation of powers. Prominent on the surface of any case held to involve a political question is found a textually demonstrable constitutional commitment of the issue to a coordinate political department; or a lack of judicially discoverable and manageable standards for resolving it; or the impossibility of deciding without an initial policy determination of a kind clearly for nonju-

dicial discretion; or the impossibility of a court's undertaking independent resolution without expressing lack of the respect due coordinate branches of government; or an unusual need for unquestioning adherence to a political decision already made; or the potentiality of embarrassment from multifarious pronouncements by various departments on one question.

Unless one of these formulations is inextricable from the case at bar, there should be no dismissal for non-justiciability on the ground of a political question's presence. The doctrine of which we treat is one of "political questions," not one of "political cases." The courts cannot reject as "no law suit" a bona fide controversy as to whether some action denominated "political" exceeds constitutional authority. The cases we have reviewed show the necessity for discriminating inquiry into the precise facts and posture of the particular case, and the impossibility of resolution by any semantic cataloguing.

Baker v. Carr, Dissenting Opinion

Felix Frankfurter

The Court today reverses a uniform course of decision established by a dozen cases, including one by which the very claim now sustained was unanimously rejected only five years ago.... Such a massive repudiation of the experience of our whole past in asserting destructively novel judicial power demands a detailed analysis of the role of this Court in our constitutional scheme. Disregard of inherent limits in the effective exercise of the Court's "judicial Power" not only presages the futility of judicial intervention in the essentially political conflict of forces by which the relation between population and representation has time out of mind been and now is determined. It may well impair the Court's position as the ultimate organ of "the supreme Law of the Land" in that vast range of legal problems, often strongly entangled in popular feeling, on which this Court must pronounce. The Court's authority—possessed of neither the purse nor the sword—ultimately rests on sustained public confidence in its moral sanction. Such feeling must be nourished by the Court's complete detachment, in fact and in appearance, from political entanglements and by abstention from injecting itself into the clash of political forces in political settlements....

The cases concerning war or foreign affairs, for example, are usually explained by the necessity of the country's speaking with one voice in such matters. While this concern alone undoubtedly accounts for many of the decisions, others do not fit the pattern. It would hardly embarrass the conduct of war were this Court to determine, in connection with private transactions between litigants, the date upon which war is to be deemed terminated. But the Court has refused to do so. It does not suffice to explain such cases as *Ludecke v. Watkins*, 335 U.S. 160—deferring to political determination the question of the duration of war for purposes of the Presidential power to deport alien enemies—that judicial intrusion would seriously impede the President's power effectively to protect the country's interests in time of war. Of course, this is true; but the precise issue presented is the duration of the time of war which demands the power. And even for the purpose of determining the extent of congressional regulatory power over the tribes and dependent communities of Indians, it is ordinarily for Congress, not the Court, to determine whether or not a particular Indian group retains the characteristics constitutionally requisite to confer the power. A controlling factor in such cases is that, decision respecting these kinds of complex matters of policy being traditionally committed not to courts but to the political agencies of government for determination by criteria of political expediency, there exists no standard ascertainable by settled judicial experience or process by reference to which a political decision affecting the question at issue between the parties can be judged. Where the question arises in the course of a litigation involving primarily the adjudication of other issues between the litigants, the Court accepts as a basis for adjudication the political departments' decision of it. But where its determination is the sole function to be served by the exercise of the judicial power, the Court will not entertain the action.... The dominant consideration is "the lack of satisfactory criteria for a judicial determination...."

This may be, like so many questions of law, a matter of degree. Questions have arisen un-

Excerpted from Felix Frankfurter, Dissenting Opinion, *Baker v. Carr*, 369 U.S. 186 (1962). Footnotes have been omitted.

der the Constitution to which adjudication gives answer although the criteria for decision are less than unwavering bright lines. Often in these cases illumination was found in the federal structures established by, or the underlying presuppositions of, the Constitution. With respect to such questions, the Court has recognized that, concerning a particular power of Congress put in issue, "...effective restraints on its exercise must proceed from political rather than from judicial processes." It is also true that even regarding the duration of war and the status of Indian tribes, referred to above as subjects ordinarily committed exclusively to the non-judicial branches, the Court has suggested that some limitations exist upon the range within which the decisions of those branches will be permitted to go unreviewed. But this is merely to acknowledge that particular circumstances may differ so greatly in degree as to differ thereby in kind, and that, although within a certain range of cases on a continuum, no standard of distinction can be found to tell between them, other cases will fall above or below the range. The doctrine of political questions, like any other, is not to be applied beyond the limits of its own logic, with all the quiddities and abstract disharmonies it may manifest....

The Court has refused to exercise its jurisdiction to pass on "abstract questions of political power, of sovereignty, of government." The crux of the matter is that courts are not fit instruments of decision where what is essentially at stake is the composition of those large contests of policy traditionally fought out in non-judicial forums, by which governments and the actions of governments are made and unmade. Thus, where the Cherokee Nation sought by an original motion to restrain the State of Georgia from the enforcement of laws which assimilated Cherokee territory to the State's counties, abrogated Cherokee law, and abolished Cherokee government, the Court held that such a claim was not judicially cog-

nizable. And in *Georgia v. Stanton*, the Court dismissed for want of jurisdiction a bill by the State of Georgia seeking to enjoin enforcement of the Reconstruction Acts....

The influence of these converging considerations—the caution not to undertake decision where standards meet for judicial judgment are lacking, the reluctance to interfere with matters of state government in the absence of an unquestionable and effectively enforceable mandate, the unwillingness to make courts arbiters of the broad issues of political organization historically committed to other institutions and for whose adjustment the judicial process is ill-adapted—has been decisive of the settled line of cases, reaching back more than a century.

QUESTIONS FOR DISCUSSION

1. What role should the Supreme Court play in the conduct of foreign policy?
2. What is meant by the *doctrine of political questions?*
3. What effect has the doctrine of political questions had on the power of the president and Congress in foreign policy matters?
4. What kinds of foreign policy issues should be considered by the Supreme Court? Why?
5. What are the advantages and disadvantages of having the Supreme Court play a role in foreign affairs?

SUGGESTED READINGS

Bickel, Alexander. *The Least Dangerous Branch: The Supreme Court at the Bar of Politics.* 2d ed. New Haven: Yale University Press, 1986. Originally published Indianapolis: Bobbs-Merrill, 1962.

Champlin, Linda, and Alan Schwartz. "Political Question Doctrine and Allocation of the Foreign Affairs Power." 13 *Hofstra Law Review* 215 (1985).

Firmage, Edwin B. "The War Powers and the Political Questions Doctrine." 49 *University of Colorado Law Review* 65 (1977–78).

Henkin, Louis. "Is There a Doctrine of Political Questions?" 85 *Yale Law Journal* 597 (1976).

Newberry, Robert. "Constitutional Law: Political

Questions and the Conduct of Foreign Policy." 25 *Harvard International Law Journal* 433 (1984).

Reddish, Martin H. "Judicial Review and the 'Political Question.'" 79 *Northwestern University Law Review* 1031 (1984).

Scharpf, Fritz W. "Judicial Review and the Political Question: A Functional Analysis." 75 *Yale Law Journal* 517 (1966).

Smith, Jean Edward. *The Constitution and American Foreign Policy.* St. Paul, Minn.: West, 1988.

Tigar, Michael E. "Judicial Power, the Political Question Doctrine, and Foreign Relations." 17 *UCLA Law Review* 1135 (1970).

Timbers, Edwin. "The Supreme Court and the President as Commander in Chief." *Presidential Studies Quarterly,* 16 (Spring 1986), pp. 224–36.

4   Is the Separation of Powers an Impediment to Conducting Effective Foreign Policy?

YES

John Norton Moore

The Constitution, Foreign Policy, and Deterrence: The Separation of Powers in a Dangerous World

NO

Ted Galen Carpenter

Global Interventionism and a New Imperial Presidency

The Constitution, Foreign Policy, and Deterrence: The Separation of Powers in a Dangerous World

John Norton Moore

A central world order threat in the contemporary international system is the failure of deterrence against aggressive attack particularly, but not exclusively, secret warfare and subtle forms of mixed politico-military coercion. This threat is the synergistic product of, on the one hand, a growing network of radical regimes and movements that believe in the use of force to expand regime ideology and interests and, on the other hand, the democracies' historical difficulty in perceiving and deterring totalitarian aggression, as this difficulty is magnified in an era of sophisticated secret attack and accompanying political warfare.

A potential contributor (it will not necessarily always be so) to this difficulty is the principle of separation of powers—with its underlying rationale of checks on power. As with other potential contributors to the difficulty in democratic response, such as a vigorous and skeptical media and a population that strongly seeks peace and projects the same views to others, the separation of powers is a vital tenet of democracy itself. As important, in light of the contemporary threat to world order, those responsible for implementing the separation of powers must do so with an awareness of the effect on deterrence—and the challenge it poses for the democracies. In this connection,

John Norton Moore, "The Constitution, Foreign Policy, and Deterrence: The Separation of Powers in a Dangerous World," *Heritage Lectures*, 82 (Washington, D.C.: Heritage Foundation, 1986). Speech delivered at the Heritage Foundation, Oct. 31, 1986. Reprinted by permission of The Heritage Foundation.

sadly, the post-Vietnam congressional record is poor.

The precise parameters of congressional and presidential power have been debated throughout U.S. history, beginning with the famous debate between Alexander Hamilton writing as "Pacificus" and James Madison writing as "Helvidius." As Edward S. Corwin has written, the Constitution "is an invitation to struggle for the privilege of directing American foreign policy." Sometimes the ambiguity can be overstated. I believe that the scholars supporting a strong presidency, such as the late Quincy Wright or currently Robert F. Turner, are correct both on legal and policy grounds. Nevertheless, the degree of constitutional ambiguity has permitted periods of enhanced congressional activism in foreign policy, particularly when supported by popular myth. This would include the post-Vietnam period, one of the most active such periods in American history. Former Senator John Tower has pointed out that there have been more than 150 congressionally induced constraints placed on the exercise of presidential power within the last decade alone. The War Powers Act may be the most visible generic example.

It is important and appropriate that Members of Congress and the Executive Branch, as well as scholars and the public, appraise the effects of this congressional micromanagement of foreign policy, particularly its effect on deterrence. Analysis in this area should not focus solely on constitutional line drawing, it should also appraise the effects of particular forms of congressional action. In doing so today, I will focus on two sets of issues. First, an appraisal of the popular myths supporting heightened congressional activism in a post-Vietnam setting, and second, questions concerning the record of congressional micromanagement in enhancing or reducing deterrence.

No one questions that Congress has an important role to play in U.S. foreign policy. Congress appropriates funds for foreign as well as domestic matters, declares war and can terminate major hostilities, confirms senior foreign policy makers, and participates in approving the great bulk of international agreements. Yet we should also never forget that there is a vitally important, enduring rationale for why the Executive is better suited to leadership in foreign affairs. I can identify at least seven time-proved advantages of presidential foreign policy control.

First, the Executive can act with greater speed and decisiveness. Does anyone for a moment believe that Congress could have managed the Cuban missile crisis comparably with the speed it so urgently demanded?

Second, the Executive can act with greater secrecy when it is genuinely needed. Can anyone for a moment seriously believe that Congress could have handled a Grenadian rescue mission effectively?

Third, the Executive still has superior information flow. I say this with full awareness of the growth of a very large and able staff in Congress. Of course, there has been a massive increase in information flow on the Hill, but in my judgment it simply does not match having an embassy in every single country around the world sending in reporting cables, daily briefings from the Central Intelligence Agency, daily contact with the desk officers in the Department of State, and the many other sources of Executive Branch information flow. In short, I believe that the Executive is now and is always likely to be far ahead of Congress in terms of processing and acting on the overall information flow so critical to foreign policy decisions.

Fourth, congressional action is generally less flexible and tends to take a blanket approach. When you intervene by act of Congress, what do you do? Take, for example, the aid cutoff to Turkey. Legislation is basically a blunt instrument in dealing with foreign policy; it is quite difficult to fine tune legislation to meet all of the more complex realities.

Fifth, congressional action sometimes may be too responsive to popular opinion. It is true that we take living in a democracy very seriously. But we live in a representative democracy, in which the framers deliberately did not take opinion polls to resolve issues but rather sought to rely on the leadership of individual representatives. My own feeling is that, prior to conflict or during protracted conflict, the correct American actions to achieve deterrence are frequently quite unpopular. If the decision makers are more sensitive to the popularity of an action than to its correctness, they will ultimately undermine their policy objectives. And it should be remembered that they can err through popularly forced escalation as well as popularly forced withdrawal.

Sixth, it seems to me that the Executive can integrate negotiations and other options in ways that Congress cannot. And this, I suppose, leads to a related point: that Congress has difficulty in formulating an overall policy. In fact, a coherent policy is something that would be quite difficult for Congress to construct since by its nature it is more likely to react to the interests of its domestic political constituencies.

Finally—and I say this with some reluctance—there is a tendency toward greater partisanship in Congress. Moreover, Congress provides a forum for the multiplication of special interests, in terms of their ability to focus on particular issues.

Since those policies favoring Executive leadership in foreign policy are reasonably evident, why is the U.S. currently in this period of congressional micromanagement? I believe the answer largely rests in two popular myths, broadly accepted even if infrequently fully articulated following the national trauma over Vietnam. These are, first, the myth of superior congressional wisdom and its corollary, that of a flawed presidency; and second, a simplistic belief that it is American foreign policy entanglement that is the threat rather than the radical regime attack against which every American presidency has sought to respond. Both flow inexorably from the national trauma and widely believed myths of the Vietnam War.

The myth of superior congressional wisdom is just that—a myth. Many scholars have shown that Congress was a full partner in the Vietnam War up until the Tet Offensive. Congress then misperceived Tet as a military defeat, exactly as had the American public, and thereafter was single-mindedly bent on American disengagement. Its actions in passing the 1971 Cooper-Church Amendment and the 1973 Fulbright Amendments, as well as its reduction of military assistance to the South Vietnamese, resulted in reducing the potential of American deterrence in these areas to a virtual zero.

North Vietnam was so confident of American nonintervention as it tore up the just concluded 1973 Paris Accords that it committed 22 divisions to the attack against the South, leaving only its anti-coup division in the North. Predictably, South Vietnam was overwhelmed, even though a commitment of greater U.S. financial resources and airpower alone might well have stopped the regular Army invasion, as it did in the Easter offensive after Tet. Most important, whether or not further American resources should have been committed to Vietnam, could the North Vietnamese attack have been deterred or militarily reduced if there had been some uncertainty as to the American response? For the historical record, it should also be remembered that Congress did not embody great wisdom in rejecting the Versailles Treaty or in ritualistic neutralism before World War II, just to name several of the the more glaring examples.

As to the second myth, that American entanglement is the real threat and that Congress thus plays a vital role in checking such entanglements, this is a form of contemporary isolationism, again largely traceable to Vietnam. But America did not create the threat in

Vietnam; that came unequivocally from Hanoi. And it was not the fact of American engagement abroad that was at fault, but the form of that engagement. Vietnam is no more a reason for American disengagement from the world than choking is for withdrawal from eating. While it must be handled cautiously and realistically, to fail to engage in foreign affairs in the effort to deter the radical regime attack is to risk a subsequent and far worse global explosion and to accept destruction of the most important underpinning of modern world order. Moreover, and most important to the point of this discussion, congressional action contributed virtually nothing to remedying the defects in American engagement in Vietnam and, if anything, may have exacerbated them.

During the 1950s and 1960s, Congress played an affirmative role in deterrence. It passed the important Cuban, Middle Eastern, and Formosa Resolutions, contributing significantly to deterrence in those areas and demonstrating a joint executive-congressional resolve in deterring aggressive attack.

But in the post-Vietnam setting, Congress has pursued an opposite policy of focus on constraining, publicly and in advance, American foreign policy options. Obviously, such a policy whether or not embodying wise choices as to American engagements, severely undercuts deterrence. Let us look at a few examples in addition to those from the pre-World War II setting and the Vietnam settings already discussed.

In 1976, the Clark Amendment was passed, terminating United States involvement in Angola. The Clark Amendment and its parallel—the Tunney Amendment—were basically intended to cut off any United States covert assistance to any faction in the complex Angolan hostilities, in particular assistance to the anticommunist UNITA [National Union for the Total Independence of Angola] and FNLA [National Front for the Liberation of Angola].

Prior to the vote in Congress, President Ford had issued a stern warning to the Soviets, who had an airlift underway pouring in tons of supplies to the Marxist insurgents in Angola. Based on that warning, the airlift had at least been temporarily halted. As soon the Clark and Tunney Amendments were passed, however, the Soviet airlift to Angola was resumed with increased tonnage and ultimately large numbers of Cuban expeditionary forces moved in as well.

If we look to Lebanon in 1983, we see a variety of problems, such as whether one particular type of military deployment was more useful than another. It seems to me that the basic motivation for the Lebanon deployment was quite sound and that it was a reasonable policy option under the circumstances. In other words, it is in U.S. national interest to prevent Lebanon from being either dismembered or controlled by radical regimes. It also should be remembered that the U.S. went into Lebanon originally as part of a multinational effort with the important and laudable objective of protecting civilian populations from warlike massacres, as had recently occurred in Palestinian refugee camps. My judgment is that the effort to invoke the War Powers Resolution vis-à-vis the Lebanon situation, the debate on the Hill that attended the effort, and a second debate that took place after the attack on the American Marine barracks reduced deterrence in Lebanon and contributed to making the United States position there untenable. Again, whether or not we should have been engaged in Lebanon under the constraints imposed, congressional actions did little to alter that engagement under the accompanying constraints and may have contributed to the mix of engagement and constraints that ultimately proved untenable.

Finally, if we look to Central America today, we find a mixed, but not as monolithic, record of American disengagement, as in Vietnam. True, Congress has most recently pro-

vided, by a narrow margin, $100 million in *contra* assistance. But many of its early actions have certainly sent signals to Managua, Havana, and Moscow that a policy of secret warfare against Nicaragua's neighbor may be continued at acceptable risk. This includes the protracted twice yearly debates on human rights conditionality in military assistance to El Salvador without requiring an equivalent discussion of the level of Sandinista armed aggression against El Salvador, a rush to repudiate the low casualty strategy of mining Nicaraguan harbors against delivery of military supplies for the Sandinista armed attack, and the Boland Amendment (intended it is true to avoid more radical proposals). Such actions at least partially assured the Sandinistas that the U.S. would pull back from any ultimate sanction of seeking the overthrow of the Sandinista regime as in Nazi Germany following German aggression. Most important, while Congress has been preoccupied with constraints on U.S. action, it has passed nothing comparable to the Cuban or Middle Eastern Resolutions to add congressional voice to deterrence of Sandinista attacks against their neighbors.

The War Powers Act itself, clearly at least partly unconstitutional, may, as a generic measure, contribute to reduction in deterrence. As an Act of Congress, the War Powers Act has no authority to alter the constitutional structure of the separation of powers. Thus, the President may feel that he has a constitutional duty to oppose application of the War Powers Act in a time of national crisis when the nation can least afford the serious legal controversy that would ensue. That is, such a generically legislative, definitional approach to separation of powers initiated by Congress and passed over the veto of the President, would force him in a time of national crisis either to acquiesce in an assertion of congressional authority he may believe to be unconstitutional or to challenge the Act at a time when the nation can least afford confusion over the legal authority of the President. As in Lebanon, it also shifts national attention from the real issues of deterrence and limits of American effective action to a sterile legal confrontation between Congress and the President.

Now in addition to these examples, we should be aware that there are many proposals being seriously urged for additional constraints on the presidential authority in national security settings. For example, Dr. Jeremy Stone, a supporter of a nuclear "no-first-use" policy for NATO [North Atlantic Treaty Organization], has suggested one in a much publicized article in the Fall 1984 issue of *Foreign Policy* and held at least one substantial conference sponsored by the Federation of American Scientists (of which he is director) in November 1985 to discuss it. Stone proposes that, with certain possible exceptions, no nuclear weapons could be employed by the President in a NATO defense emergency absent prior approval by Congress or a specially created congressional committee. Dr. Stone has

also suggested in a nonlawyer statement of bad constitutional law that his proposal is constitutionally required. Needless to say, this proposal is not constitutionally required and could, if adopted, severely undercut deterrence—already strained in the NATO area.

The separation of powers is an important principle of the American democratic system. It is important, however, that, whatever the precise constitutional parameters of the foreign affairs powers, Congress should exercise its power with a realistic understanding of the rationale strongly favoring executive control of foreign policy. Too often we approach these issues solely as a matter of constitutional line drawing with the usual indeterminate answers at the edges. We also must begin to appraise congressional action—even if clearly within congressional competence—by a broad standard of contribution to an effective American foreign policy. In this connection, it is particularly important that we appraise the effect of congressional actions on deterrence. That, after all, is the key issue if we truly wish to avoid war.

Global Interventionism and a New Imperial Presidency

Ted Galen Carpenter

Recent debate about U.S. policy with respect to Lebanon, Central America, and South Africa suggests that the United States may be entering a new phase in the recurring conflict between Congress and the executive branch over the control of foreign affairs. This conflict does not merely involve constitutional or partisan political matters—as important as those might be—but reflects competing conceptions about substantive policy issues.

The current White House occupant [Ronald Reagan] is seeking to weaken or eliminate congressional restraints imposed on the executive during the 1970s, in order to regain the flexibility he believes is necessary to pursue America's cold war objectives. His congressional opponents are attempting to preserve those constraints not simply to enhance the power and prestige of the legislative branch, but because they fear that an unfettered president may pursue policies that would contravene fundamental American values or again plunge the United States into ill-advised military interventions. As before in our history, the conflict will likely determine the substance of American foreign policy, as well as which branch shall chart its course.

CONSTITUTIONAL INTENT

During the last decade and a half, Americans have grappled frequently and intensely with the question of legislative versus executive power over foreign affairs. The aftermath of the disastrous and divisive Vietnam War triggered a reassessment of the executive-supremacy doctrine that had held sway throughout the previous three decades. This change, however, was only the most recent occasion when the locus of authority in foreign policy has shifted. Debates on the question have flared periodically since the founding of the American republic. Indeed, a measure of tension is built into the structure of the Constitution itself. The shared powers and overlapping responsibilities of the legislative and executive branches create what renowned constitutional scholar Edward S. Corwin has aptly termed "an invitation to struggle" over foreign policy.[1]

The Framers of the Constitution invested the president with a number of powers in the arena of foreign affairs. He was authorized to receive the diplomatic representatives of other nations and to appoint, with the consent of the Senate, America's own diplomatic representatives. He was given the authority to negotiate treaties with foreign states, subject to Senate concurrence in the result. The president was also invested with the power and responsibility of commander in chief of the nation's armed forces.

But the Founding Fathers also granted significant foreign policy powers to the legislative branch. They gave Congress, not the president, the authority to declare war. In addition, they declared that Congress would be responsible for authorizing the raising of military forces and providing funds for their continued operation. Furthermore, foreign commerce was made subject to regulation by Congress, and the Senate was accorded the right to ratify or reject treaties negotiated by the president.

Ted Galen Carpenter, "Global Interventionism and a New Imperial Presidency," *Cato Institute Policy Analysis,* 71 (Washington, D.C.: Cato Institute, May 16, 1986). Reprinted by permission of the Cato Institute.

[1] Edward S. Corwin et al., *The President: Office and Powers 1787–1984,* 5th rev. ed. (New York: New York University Press, 1984), p. 201.

The delineation of power and responsibility between the two branches was less than precise. The delegates to the constitutional convention apparently envisioned a partnership between Congress and the president in foreign affairs, but they also applied the principle of checks and balances. What is clear is that the Founding Fathers did not invest the president with the vast array of unilateral foreign policy powers—particularly those involving U.S. armed forces—claimed by White House occupants during much of the 20th century, especially since World War II. One expert on constitutional history, W. Taylor Reveley III, muses, "If we could find a man in the state of nature and have him first scan the war-power provisions of the Constitution and then look at war-power practice since 1789, he would marvel at how much Presidents have spun out of so little."[2]

Ambitious presidents have relied upon allegedly "inherent" executive powers and the status of commander in chief to justify this vast expansion of presidential authority. However, the context in which the presidency was established fails to support claims to extensive executive power in foreign policy. Although the Founding Fathers did create several ambiguities regarding authority over foreign affairs (perhaps because foreign policy was not a priority concern at the time), where they did favor one branch, they favored Congress, not the president. This tilt was entirely consistent with their British Whig political bias, with its fear of excessive executive power.[3] While the president was to be the principal spokesman for the republic in foreign affairs and the focal point for diplomatic relations with other nations, the Framers had no desire to invest him with the foreign policy prerogatives of a monarch.

Even the president's powers as commander in chief are far less extensive than most recent presidents have alleged. The primary purpose of the constitutional provision was to assert civilian supremacy over the military, lest an aggressive general succumb to Cromwellian temptations during a wartime crisis. A subsidiary objective was to restrain legislative meddling in the day-to-day conduct of military strategy once hostilities were authorized—a concern stemming from congressional interference during the American Revolution. In addition, it implied that the president possessed the authority to repel attacks upon U.S. territory until Congress could act. But Congress alone was to declare war, and in the parlance of the times, "declare" essentially meant "authorize" or "begin."[4]

The Founders would likely be mystified at recent presidential contentions that although Congress "declares" wars, the president has the right to "wage" them with or without formal declarations. They would be astonished and probably appalled at the assertions of such chief executives as Harry Truman, Lyndon Johnson, and Richard Nixon that a president may conduct foreign policy and utilize the armed forces in any manner he deems necessary to foster his own conception of U.S. "interests." Executive supremacy in foreign affairs was not set forth in the Constitution.

---

[2] W. Taylor Reveley III, *War Powers of the President and Congress* (Charlottesville: University Press of Virginia, 1981), p. 29.

[3] An excellent discussion of the British Whig political doctrine and its influence on the American revolutionaries is found in Bernard Bailyn, *The Ideological Origins of the American Revolution* (Cambridge: Harvard University Press, 1967).

[4] Reveley, pp. 60–64. Further discussion of the views of the Founding Fathers on the division of foreign policy powers can be found in Corwin et al., pp. 200–201, 207–13; Arthur M. Schlesinger, Jr., *The Imperial Presidency* (Boston: Houghton Mifflin, 1973), pp. 1–34; Cecil V. Crabb and Pat M. Holt, *Invitation to Struggle: Congress, the President and Foreign Policy*, 2d ed. (Washington: Congressional Quarterly Press, 1984), passim; and Francis O. Wilcox, *Congress: The Executive and Foreign Policy* (New York: Harper & Row, 1974), passim.

That doctrine evolved from particular historical circumstances, and it is directly connected
to the rise of the United States as a global interventionist power.

DEVELOPMENTS BEFORE
WORLD WAR II

War is not only "the health of the state," as
social critic Randolph Bourne once observed; it
has especially promoted the health of the
American presidency.[5] It is no coincidence
that the greatest expansions of executive
power have taken place during wartime or
when a military crisis seemed imminent. On
those occasions, Congress has rarely shown
an inclination or ability to restrain presidential
power.

In the early stages of the Civil War, Abraham Lincoln called out state militias and
usurped other congressional prerogatives.
Later in the conflict, he even bypassed the
state and federal courts, ordering the trials of
civilians accused of certain wartime crimes to
be held before military tribunals—an action
the Supreme Court ultimately held to be unconstitutional.

America's flirtation with European-style imperialism in the late 1890s and early 1900s elic-
ited another wave of executive activism. Presidents Theodore Roosevelt and William
Howard Taft ordered American troops into action on several occasions without congressional approval to "restore order" in various
Caribbean and Central American nations.
Woodrow Wilson was equally brazen in that
regard, on two occasions even employing military coercion against Mexico. When World
War I erupted, Wilson resorted to unilateral
decision making in foreign affairs still more,
and at war's end he virtually ignored the

wishes of Congress in negotiating provisions
of the Treaty of Versailles.

From the founding of the republic until
World War II, two definite patterns emerged
with respect to executive power over foreign
policy. First, both the degree of authority and
the willingness to use it unilaterally expanded
dramatically in times of war and when the
United States has gone on interventionist
binges, as it did in Latin America in the early
1900s.

Second, following wartime executive aggrandizement, Congress invariably reasserted
itself and brought the presidency to heel. During the decade following James K. Polk's pursuit of aggressive Manifest Destiny, Congress
dominated the scene, virtually dictating the
substance and direction of U.S. foreign policy.
A similar congressional resurgence occurred
in the post–Civil War years following Lincoln's
unprecedented use of executive authority.
Woodrow Wilson's disregard of Congress during the peace negotiations ending World War I
resulted in the Senate's rejection of his cherished Treaty of Versailles. Congressional reas-
sertion continued thereafter, culminating in
the Neutrality Acts of the mid-1930s, which
(theoretically) prevented future presidents
from pursuing policies that might involve the
United States in unwanted and unnecessary
wars.[6]

Throughout the first century and a half of
the republic's existence, the foreign policy relationship between the president and Congress was like a pendulum. Sometimes it
swung in the direction of greater executive
power and sometimes it moved back toward
Congress, thus maintaining a relative balance.
Although the presidency did gradually acquire greater authority in foreign affairs during this period, the accretion was modest. By

---

[5] Quoted in William L. O'Neill, *The Progressive Years:
America Comes of Age* (New York: Dodd, Mead & Co.,
1975), p. 104.

[6] For a detailed, albeit hostile, account of the neutrality
legislation of the 1930s, see Robert A. Divine, *The Illusion
of Neutrality* (Chicago: University of Chicago Press, 1962).

the mid-1930s, Franklin Roosevelt was only slightly more powerful in foreign policy vis-à-vis Congress than were his 19th-century predecessors.[7] World War II and the subsequent cold war shattered that equilibrium, producing several ominous changes.

THE BIRTH OF THE IMPERIAL PRESIDENCY

The outbreak of fighting in Europe in the autumn of 1939 created an atmosphere of crisis in the United States. Openly sympathizing with the Allied cause and fearing that an Axis victory would imperil U.S. security, Franklin Roosevelt sought to weaken or evade the neutrality legislation that constrained his foreign policy options. On a few occasions, most notably in the passage of the Lend-Lease Act in early 1941, Roosevelt did respect congressional prerogatives—although he employed the disingenuous argument that indirect support for the Allies reduced rather than increased the ultimate risk of U.S. involvement in the fighting. More often, however, Roosevelt simply bypassed Congress while maneuvering the nation ever closer to a state of war. Trading U.S. destroyers to Great Britain for base rights in the Caribbean, proclaiming the western half of the North Atlantic an American defense zone and ordering U.S. naval vessels to sink German ships in that area on sight, convoying British ships, and imposing a draconian trade embargo on Japan all constituted steps in that process. All were ac-complished without congressional authorization or even participation.[8]

Following the Japanese attack on Pearl Harbor in December 1941, the executive's preeminence became even more pronounced. Congress's last significant act in the conflict was the formal declaration of war. Even more than previously, Congress deferred to presidential judgment and allowed the president great latitude. Roosevelt prosecuted the war largely as he and his military advisers saw fit, an approach that his successor Harry Truman continued. Major decisions reached with Great Britain and the Soviet Union on the conduct of the war, its objectives, and the nature of the postwar settlement were concluded by executive agreement rather than treaty. Congress was neither consulted about nor asked to approve the provisions of the Teheran, Yalta, or Potsdam agreements.

Roosevelt and Truman's example was followed well into the 1970s. Prior to World War II, virtually all important arrangements with foreign states were codified in treaties; executive agreements, which do not require Senate ratification, were reserved largely for minor and routine matters. Roosevelt and his successors turned this practice on its head: after 1940, presidents increasingly employed executive agreements on matters of vital import and invoked the treaty process primarily for routine and noncontroversial issues. By the mid-1970s, approximately 95 percent of all agreements between the United States and foreign

---

[7] One disturbing omen of future trends, however, was the 1936 Supreme Court decision in *United States* v. *Curtiss-Wright Export Corp.*, 299 U.S. 304, 57 S. Ct. 216; 81 L. Ed. 255 (1936). The Court adopted an extremely expansive view of presidential power in foreign affairs, contrasting it with the limited exercise of authority in domestic matters.

[8] Critical discussions of Roosevelt's mendacious maneuvering in 1940 and 1941 abound. Early accounts include Charles Callan Tansill, *Back Door to War* (Chicago: Regnery, 1952) and Charles A. Beard, *President Roosevelt and the Coming of the War, 1941* (New Haven: Yale University Press, 1948). A more recent analysis is found in Bruce Russett, *No Clear and Present Danger: A Skeptical View of the U.S. Entry into World War II* (New York: Harper & Row, 1972). Even a sympathetic study, William L. Langer and S. Everett Gleason, *The Undeclared War* (New York: Harper Brothers, 1953), contains an abundance of damning evidence.

governments during the previous three decades had been executive agreements.[9] It was indicative of how far this trend had progressed that the document ending U.S. involvement in the Vietnam War, signed in Paris in January 1973, was an executive agreement rather than a treaty. No development more graphically underscores the readiness of recent presidents to bypass Congress in the formulation of foreign policy.

THE COLD WAR AND THE IMPERIAL PRESIDENCY TRIUMPHANT

The historical ebb and flow of executive power in foreign affairs suggested the likelihood of a congressional resurgence following World War II. But that reaction was thwarted by cold war tensions and the failure of the United States to resume its prewar foreign policy of noninterventionism. For the first time, there existed a permanent state of crisis and an ever-present danger of war. Predictably, this situation strengthened the executive branch, perpetuating the artificially enhanced degree of presidential power that had evolved during the war. In time, the cold war environment enabled U.S. presidents to acquire foreign policy prerogatives exceeding even those exercised by their predecessors during wartime.

Initially, there were only faint signs that the cold war would further expand executive dominance over foreign policy. Although Truman outlined the so-called Truman Doctrine—wherein the United States pledged to aid "free peoples" resisting external aggression or internal "armed minorities"—as a unilateral declaration, the initial implementing measure, and aid package for Greece and Turkey, involved direct and substantial congressional participation. Likewise, Congress played an extensive role in the two subsequent major cold war

steps, the creation of the Marshall Plan in 1948 and NATO [North Atlantic Treaty Organization] the following year.

Nevertheless, the creation of the Central Intelligence Agency in 1947 was a disquieting sign, providing the executive branch with a potent new foreign policy tool. It also set in motion a cult of secrecy, a far more pervasive system of classifying information than had ever existed previously, and a growing executive determination to withhold sensitive information from the public and from Congress. Another indication of the nascent imperial presidency was the initial draft of Truman's proposed Mutual Defense Assistance Act in August 1949, which gave the chief executive virtually unlimited discretion in dispensing the military aid stipulated therein. Even Sen. Arthur Vandenberg, a vital supporter of Truman's earlier cold war initiatives, excoriated the administration's draft, asserting that it would make the president the "top warlord of the earth."[10]

It was the outbreak of the Korean War in 1950, however, that gave the budding doctrine of executive supremacy its greatest impetus. Although some of Truman's advisers urged him to request congressional authorization before sending U.S. military units to assist beleaguered South Korean forces, the president followed his own inclinations and the advice of Secretary of State Dean Acheson and declined to involve Congress. He stated that he would keep Congress "informed" of developments but emphasized that he would take that action solely out of courtesy, not from any constitutional or legal obligation.[11]

---

[9] Crabb and Holt, pp. 15–16.

[10] Arthur H. Vandenberg, Jr., and Joe Alex Morris, eds., *The Private Papers of Senator Vandenberg* (Boston: Houghton Mifflin, 1952), p. 507.

[11] *Public Papers of the Presidents of the United States: Harry S Truman, 1950* (Washington: Government Printing Office, 1965), p. 504. An excellent summary of the Truman administration's internal debate is contained in "Memorandum: Meeting at Blair House, July 3, 1950," Dean Acheson Papers, Box 65, Harry S Truman Library.

Truman and Acheson advanced the thesis that the president had the requisite authority to respond to a call from the United Nations to repel aggression against another member state without further congressional action because Congress had previously ratified the U.N. Charter. This thesis was extremely dubious—there was no evidence that Congress had intended to give the chief executive a blank check to use the entire American military establishment to further U.N. objectives.

The Korean War was a crucial event in the evolution of the imperial presidency—even more important than the Vietnam War. Although presidents had previously used military force without explicit congressional authorization, virtually every incident had been minor, involving little or no chance of serious warfare. Indeed, most of the episodes had involved action against small nongovernmental forces, such as brigands.[12] The Korean intervention was vastly different: for the first time in U.S. history, a president presumed to conduct extensive combat operations while bypassing Congress. It was a dangerous precedent. Even worse, it was a precedent that went largely unchallenged.

The opposition that did arise was confined largely to rightist political elements, centered mainly in the conservative wing of the Republican party. Sen. Robert Taft, for example, asserted with his customary bluntness that the Korean intervention was "a complete usurpation by the President of authority to use the Armed Forces of this country," and he insisted that Truman should at least request a joint resolution from Congress to legitimize his actions.[13] Several of Taft's conservative colleagues, including Senate minority leader

Kenneth Wherry, echoed those sentiments, but such critics constituted an ineffectual minority.

While some conservatives expressed grave misgivings about Truman's usurpation of congressional war powers, liberals vocally defended executive supremacy. It was a startling contrast to the ideological division that was to prevail two decades later. Congressional liberals vied with one another to insist that the legislative branch was too decentralized, parochial, and uninformed about the nuances of foreign affairs to play any significant role in the formulation or execution of foreign policy. Vigorous congressional participation may have been acceptable during the placid days of 19th-century isolationism, they argued, but in the atomic age, when the United States possessed "vital interests" around the globe and aggression could occur with dramatic swiftness, the United States must be able to respond with speed and decisiveness. Only the president, the argument went, possessed the requisite information and flexibility to act with dispatch.[14]

It was a distressing case of congressional abdication and self-flagellation. Too many congressmen were haunted by the memory of Pearl Harbor, believing that congressional "interference" in foreign policy through such measures as the Neutrality Acts, rather than Roosevelt's violation of those acts, had led to that disaster. Liberals were also the victims of their own enthusiasm for "strong" presidents in domestic affairs, as epitomized by Franklin Roosevelt and his New Deal. It was but a small step to the notion that a vigorous president was equally desirable and necessary in

---

[12] Schlesinger, pp. 89–91, 135.
[13] *Congressional Record*, 81st Cong., 2d sess., 1950, vol. 96, p. 9323.

[14] For samples of liberal views in 1950–51 on the proper scope of executive power in foreign affairs, see the speeches of senators Tom Connally, Henry Cabot Lodge, Paul Douglas, J. William Fulbright, and Herbert Lehman, in *Congressional Record*, 82d Cong., 1st sess., 1951, vol. 97, pp. 142, 148–49, 228–29, 520–51, 2542–43, 2738.

the conduct of foreign policy. In any event, Congress not only countenanced but contributed to the growth of the imperial presidency.

The Truman administration carried the assertion of alleged executive prerogatives in foreign policy to a new high. Truman himself could not have been more direct: "Under the President's constitutional powers as Commander in Chief of the Armed Forces, he has the authority to send troops anywhere in the world."[15] A short time later, a State Department position paper produced under the auspices of Dean Acheson expanded that thesis: "Not only has the president the authority to use the Armed Forces in carrying out the broad foreign policy of the United States and implementing treaties but it is equally clear that this authority may not be interfered with by the Congress in the exercise of powers which it has under the Constitution."[16] The paper was implying that Congress could not even utilize its constitutional power over appropriations, for example, to terminate the funding of a foreign military intervention it opposed. It would be difficult to envision a more forceful assertion of presidential supremacy.

Opponents of unrestrained executive power in foreign affairs did make a last attempt to stem the tide in late 1950 and early 1951. Emboldened by his expansion of presidential power in the Korean War, Truman attempted to enhance the scope of U.S. obligations to NATO by dispatching four U.S. Army divisions to Europe as part of a new multilateral army. His decision coincided with a disastrous reversal of U.S. military fortunes in Korea as mainland China intervened in the conflict. This reversal roused opponents of executive preeminence to dispute Truman's latest assertion of it, thus precipitating the so-called Great Debate.

Senate minority leader Kenneth Wherry expressed the opposition case most passionately:

> The wise, constitutional power of the President to order the armed services into action in defense of our country in the event of invasion...is being stretched into power for the President to order the armed services in peacetime anywhere in the world and into any situation....
>
> If Congress surrenders its powers to determine whether American troops shall join an international army in Europe, it will have set a dangerous precedent for the President to assign American troops to any other spot on the vast perimeter of Russia.
>
> Mr. Chairman, that is the road to encroachment on [other] prerogatives and responsibilities of Congress....That is the road to absolute dictatorship.
>
> It flies in the face of every precedent, every tradition and every principle upon which the United States has become the model for free men everywhere.[17]

Wherry's analysis was eloquent and prophetic, but he and his conservative allies lacked the political strength to derail the executive-supremacy juggernaut. The outcome of the Great Debate was an anemic, nonbinding Senate resolution admonishing Truman not to dispatch additional troops to Europe, beyond the four units he was already sending, without first consulting Congress. Thus ended the last serious congressional challenge to presidential preeminence in foreign policy until the 1970s.

The trend toward an imperial presidency gathered even greater momentum after the Great Debate. Truman's successor, Dwight

---

[15] *Public Papers of the Presidents of the United States: Harry S Truman, 1951* (Washington: Government Printing Office, 1966), p. 19.

[16] Reprinted in Senate Committee on Foreign Relations and Committee on Armed Services, *Assignment of Ground Forces of the United States to Duty in the European Area, Hearings*, 82d Cong., 1st sess., 1951, p. 92.

[17] Ibid., p. 670.

Eisenhower, avoided Korean-style military interventions but increasingly employed the CIA [Central Intelligence Agency] to conduct covert operations against hostile regimes. He did so successfully against Prime Minister Mohammed Mossadegh of Iran in 1953, President Jacobo Arbenz Guzman of Guatemala in 1954, and Premier Patrice Lumumba of the Congo (now Zaire) in 1960. The evidence indicates that Congress was largely unaware of these operations, and most members seemed to prefer it that way.[18]

Indeed, the magnitude of congressional deference to executive power was astonishing. In 1955, Congress passed a resolution giving Eisenhower virtually unlimited discretion to handle the Formosa Strait crisis. Two years later, it gave Eisenhower similar authorization to deal with alleged communist incursions in the Middle East.[19] These measures, allowing the president to use force as he deemed fit in some vague future contingency, constituted precisely the kind of action the Founding Fathers would have considered abhorrent. By 1960, it was becoming routine. Eisenhower's administration also repeatedly withheld vital information on foreign policy matters from the legislative branch under a dubious and broadly defined theory of "executive privilege."

Presidential disregard of Congress in the conduct of foreign affairs only increased after Eisenhower. Perhaps no event more graphically demonstrates how impotent the legislative branch had become in foreign affairs than the Cuban missile crisis in 1962. President John Kennedy did not consult Congress prior to taking action in the crisis; indeed, he informed congressional leaders only hours before going on national television to tell the American people. Consequently, Congress played no role in formulating policy on a matter that might easily have plunged the nation into nuclear war. Kennedy exhibited a similar disdain for congressional input when he intensified the American military presence in Vietnam, increasing the number of U.S. military personnel there from a few hundred to some 17,000 "advisers."

Kennedy's successor, Lyndon Johnson, showed only slightly greater willingness to involve Congress. He exploited an artificial crisis in August 1964 to maneuver Congress into passing the Gulf of Tonkin resolution, giving him the same type of blank check for Vietnam that Eisenhower had obtained for less serious situations in the Formosa Strait and the Middle East. The resolution stated that Congress approved and supported "the determination of the President, as Commander in Chief, to take all necessary measures to repel any armed attack against the forces of the United States and to prevent further aggression."[20] In asking for passage of the measure, Johnson underscored his belief that Congress might play a role in foreign policy, but only as a rubber stamp ratifying a strategy the president had already adopted. There was to be no meaningful consultation, much less a true sharing of responsibility. But the pursuit of docile congressional ratification through such means as the Gulf of Tonkin resolution was atypical of Johnson's foreign policy; he usually

---

[18] Sen. Leverett Saltonstall of Massachusetts epitomized the prevailing attitude about intelligence oversight when he expressed a "reluctance" to "seek information and knowledge on subjects which I personally, as a member of Congress and as a citizen, would rather not have." Quoted in Senate, *Final Report of the Select Committee to Study Governmental Operations with Respect to Intelligence Activities*, April 26, 1976, bk. 1, p. 149.

[19] For Eisenhower's view of those resolutions, see Dwight D. Eisenhower, *Mandate for Change, 1953–1956* (Garden City, N.Y.: Doubleday, 1963), pp. 459, 467–69, 608; and idem, *Waging Peace: 1956–1961* (Garden City, N.Y.: Doubleday, 1965), pp. 182–83. Eisenhower was quite candid on his seeing the resolutions as little more than moral support, contending that he had ample power as commander in chief to act on his own.

[20] Quoted in Schlesinger, p. 179.

ignored Congress entirely, as when he sent U.S. troops to "pacify" the Dominican Republic in 1965.

Along with the practice of disregarding Congress on foreign policy matters came even more grandiose executive-power claims. Johnson and his advisers openly asserted that the president did not require the Gulf of Tonkin measure to conduct his policy in Vietnam.[21] Most revealing was a passage contained in a 1966 State Department memorandum, which transformed the theory of defensive war and the president's power to repel sudden attack without explicit congressional authorization into a caricature. When the Founding Fathers invested the presidency with that authority, the document stated, "the world was a far larger place, and the framers probably [sic] had in mind attacks on the United States." But in the 20th century, "an attack on a country far removed from our shores can impinge directly on the nation's security." Therefore, the president has both the constitutional duty and power "to determine whether the circumstances of a particular armed attack are so urgent and the circumstances of a particular attack so threatening to the security of the United States that he should act without formally consulting the Congress."[22] This was a concise and breathtaking summary of the relationship between a global interventionist foreign policy and the theory of executive supremacy.

The Johnson administration represented the apogee of unrestrained presidential power. Executive authority had grown inexorably for nearly three decades in a perpetual crisis atmosphere. Historian Arthur Schles-

inger, Jr., summarizes the reasons for the evolution of presidential domination:

> The imperial Presidency was essentially the creation of foreign policy. A combination of doctrines and emotions—belief in permanent and universal crisis, fear of communism, faith in the duty and right of the United States to intervene swiftly in every part of the world—had brought about the unprecedented centralization of decisions over war and peace in the Presidency. With this came an unprecedented exclusion...of Congress, of the press and of public opinion in general from these decisions.[23]

The failure of U.S. policy in Vietnam halted that process, at least temporarily, stripping away the myth of an omniscient president pursuing wise and well-considered strategies to protect the nation's security. Lyndon Johnson and Richard Nixon chose to fight the Vietnam conflict as a presidential war, and the presidency bore full responsibility for the resulting debacle. Nixon attempted to imitate Johnson's expansive interpretation of the commander-in-chief clause, but Congress was through being deferential.[24] The long-delayed swing of the pendulum finally occurred, reestablishing a greater balance of power in foreign policy between the legislative and executive branches.

CONGRESSIONAL RESURGENCE

Reversing the foreign policy somnolence of the three previous decades, Congress exhibited a determination to rein in the imperial presidency even before the Watergate scandal. Congress repealed the Gulf of Tonkin resolution in 1971, thereby terminating the original authorization for U.S. military involvement in Vietnam. The following year, legislators en-

---

[21] See the comments of Undersecretary of State Nicholas Katzenbach in Senate Foreign Relations Committee, *U.S. Commitments to Foreign Powers, Hearings*, 90th Cong., 1st sess., 1967, pp. 82, 141.

[22] Leonard C. Meeker, "The Legality of United States Participation in the Defense of Vietnam," *Department of State Bulletin* (March 28, 1966): 484–85.

[23] Schlesinger, p. 208.

[24] Ibid., pp. 190–98; see also Thomas M. Franck and Edward Weisband, *Foreign Policy by Congress* (New York: Oxford University Press, 1979), pp. 13–23.

acted the Case amendment, which required that all executive agreements be reported to Congress. Then came Watergate, which presented congressional activists with an opportunity to impose reforms on an increasingly discredited and politically impotent chief executive. One crucial event in the drive to restore congressional prerogatives occurred in the summer of 1973, when Nixon was compelled to accept a cutoff of funding for remaining military operations in Southeast Asia. Most significant, however, was the passage of the war powers resolution, which took place in November of that year.[25]

Enacted over Nixon's veto, the resolution drastically curtailed the president's authority to employ the armed forces in pursuit of foreign policy objectives. The resolution specified that the president could introduce U.S. armed forces "into hostilities, or into situations where imminent involvement in hostilities is clearly indicated by the circumstances"—but only under three conditions: a declaration of war, specific statutory authorization, or a national emergency created by an attack upon the United States, its territories or possessions, or its armed forces. It is pertinent to note that the president could not respond unilaterally to an attack on a "friendly nation" or to a perceived threat (as he had, for example, in the Cuban missile crisis).

In addition to these limitations, the resolution required that the president "in every possible instance shall consult with Congress before introducing United States Armed Forces into hostilities" or situations in which hostilities were imminent. Moreover, he was to "consult regularly" until all combat operations ceased. In the absence of a declaration of war, the chief executive was to submit a written report within 48 hours specifying the reasons for using U.S. troops, his constitutional or legisla-

tive authority for doing so, and the estimated scope and duration of hostilities. Within 60 days (90 days in exceptional circumstances), any such operation would have to cease entirely unless Congress declared war or enacted a "specific authorization" for the continued use of U.S. troops, extended the 60-day limitation, or was physically unable to convene because of an armed attack upon the United States.[26] Although the war powers resolution contained some loopholes and ambiguities, placing strict time limits on the chief executive's deployment of troops in combat situations and establishing detailed reporting requirements to Congress theoretically prevented future presidents from unilaterally committing the United States to war as Truman had done in Korea and Johnson had done in Vietnam.

The resolution was a watershed event. According to two experts on the subject, Cecil Crabb and Pat Holt, "As much as any other step taken by Congress...this measure symbolized legislative disenchantment with the imperial presidency and a determination to become an equal partner with the executive in the foreign policy process."[27] As the Nixon presidency crumbled in 1974 and was succeeded by one that lacked any national mandate, Congress rediscovered its long-dormant foreign policy muscles. The legislative branch attached so-called human-rights and other restrictive provisos to aid and trade legislation, prohibited further U.S. interference in the Angolan civil war, restrained the operations of the CIA, and established committees to oversee the future activities of all intelligence agencies. By the late 1970s, the concept of an im-

---

[25] 50 U.S.C. 1541–48 (Supp. 1975).

[26] The law also contained a "legislative veto" provision, but legislative vetoes were declared unconstitutional by the Supreme Court in an unrelated case, *Immigration and Naturalization Service* v. *Chadha,* 462 U.S. 919, 103 S. Ct. 2764; 77 L. Ed. 2d 317 (1983).

[27] Crabb and Holt, p. 51.

perial presidency seemed little more than a distant and increasingly irrelevant memory. Indeed, some observers complained about a new congressional dominance and asserted that it created a distressing impotence, unpredictability, and unreliability in the conduct of American foreign policy.[28]

Although President Gerald Ford seethed under the restrictions imposed during the period of congressional resurgence, he lacked the political power to do anything about them. Ford's successor, Jimmy Carter, exhibited an ambivalent attitude. He initially supported a vigorous congressional role but later became disenchanted with what he perceived to be unwholesome interference with his foreign policy objectives, especially the Panama Canal treaties and the normalization of relations with the People's Republic of China.

THE REAGAN COUNTERREVOLUTION

In marked contrast to the political climate of the Ford and Carter years, political conditions in the 1980s suggest that many of the post-Vietnam reforms that limited untrammeled executive power in foreign policy could be overturned or at least weakened. Ronald Reagan, even more than Ford or Carter, views congressional actions in the field of foreign affairs with ill-disguised hostility. Many of his initiatives indicate that his ultimate objective is nothing less than a revival of unfettered presidential discretion.

Reagan has already made considerable progress toward restoring the imperial presi-

dency. He openly advocates a massive expansion of the CIA's covert operations, which had been sharply curtailed under Jimmy Carter. CIA director William Casey, apparently with Reagan's acquiescence if not blessing, has repeatedly undermined congressional oversight of U.S. intelligence operations. For example, the required disclosure to the Senate Intelligence Committee of CIA assistance in mining Nicaraguan harbors in 1984 consisted of a cryptic one-sentence statement in the middle of a lengthy report. The Reagan administration also assured Congress as late as 1984 that assistance given to the Nicaraguan *contra* forces was designed solely to interdict arms shipments to Marxist rebels in El Salvador, not to overthrow the Sandinista government. Yet mounting evidence, including statements by one-time prominent *contra* leader Edgar Chamorro, indicates that ousting the Sandinistas has been the explicit CIA objective since 1981.[29] Both episodes bear more than passing resemblance to the atmosphere of deception surrounding CIA covert operations at the zenith of the unrestrained presidency in the 1950s and 1960s.

In addition to evading congressional oversight and restrictions on CIA activities, the Reagan administration fights a running battle with its opponents on Capitol Hill concerning overall U.S. policy in Central America. The president has waged a concerted campaign for military-aid measures to the government of El Salvador and to the *contras* in Nicaragua. On more than a few occasions, he has exhibited extreme annoyance with congressional oppo-

---

[28] One rather surprising exponent of this view was former senator J. William Fulbright, an outspoken opponent of the imperial presidency in the late 1960s and early 1970s. Now he expressed "increasingly serious misgivings about the ability of Congress to play a constructive role in our foreign relations." J. William Fulbright, "The Legislator as Educator," *Foreign Affairs* (Spring 1979): 719. For a more positive reaction, see Douglas J. Bennet, Jr., "Congress in Foreign Policy: Who Needs It?" *Foreign Affairs* (Fall 1978): 40–50.

[29] A critical discussion of the Reagan administration's efforts to evade congressional oversight of CIA activities in Central America can be found in Stansfield Turner, *Secrecy and Democracy: The CIA in Transition* (Boston: Houghton Mifflin, 1985), pp. 163–70. On Chamorro's revelations and their aftermath, see "Nicaraguan Rebel Spokesman Expelled," *Dallas Morning News*, November 25, 1984; and Chris Hedges, "Ex-'Front Man' Talks of CIA's Secret War against Nicaragua," *Dallas Morning News*, July 14, 1985.

sition to such programs. But the ongoing attempt to diminish congressional restraints is not confined to Central American policy. The administration achieved a major victory in August 1985, when its political allies in Congress repealed the Clark amendment, which prohibited U.S. involvement in Angola's civil war. The path is now clear for the executive branch to provide military aid to the anticommunist UNITA rebels led by Jonas Savimbi, and the administration shows every intention of doing so.

Even more indicative of the president's attitude is his use of U.S. armed forces in contravention of the spirit, and perhaps even the letter, of the war powers resolution. Reagan committed American marines to Lebanon in mid-1982 as part of a multinational "peacekeeping" force and kept them there beyond the 60-day deadline provided for in the resolution. His rationale was that the troops were not involved in "hostilities" and that hostilities were not "imminent" as defined in that legislation—a highly dubious thesis, since the marines had already suffered casualties and were being subjected to a mounting barrage of artillery and sniper fire from Muslim militia units. Reagan stoutly resisted all congressional efforts to force a withdrawal of U.S. troops, eventually pressuring Congress to accept a "compromise" in September 1983 allowing him to keep the marines in Lebanon another 18 months.[30] Only the undeniable collapse of the administration's entire Lebanon policy, combined with the political considerations of an election year, impelled the president to withdraw the marines in early 1984. It is revealing that this decision was an executive-branch initiative; Congress was neither encouraged nor even allowed to play a role.

Reagan's cavalier treatment of the war powers resolution was apparent also with respect to the Grenada military operation. Despite the resolution's applicable provisions, the president did not consult Congress in advance; congressional leaders were given only a "briefing" the night before. Reagan insisted that U.S. troops were sent solely to rescue American citizens whose safety was threatened, a power any president clearly possesses in his capacity as commander in chief. Yet, it was evident that the Grenada invasion involved larger foreign policy objectives—specifically, the overthrow of Grenada's Marxist government. Reagan's unilateral decision to use military force thus undercut the purpose of the war powers resolution—that Congress should have a voice in decisions involving U.S. military action, not merely be presented with a fait accompli. Such conduct caused columnist Anthony Lewis to observe, "The Imperial Presidency is alive and well, more genial in appearance perhaps than in the 1960's, but just as menacing to our constitutional balance."[31]

Lewis's conclusion is verified by the administration's conduct during the recent military confrontation with Libya. In the days prior to the April 14 air strikes against Libyan military targets, administration officials consulted frequently with America's European allies. Yet Congress as an institution was not consulted; congressional leaders were "informed" barely four hours before the attacks took place. Once again, Congress has been excluded from any meaningful decision-making role, this time in a situation that has brought the United States to the brink of an undeclared war.

All of these actions strongly suggest that the Reagan administration is determined to minimize congressional participation in the conduct of foreign affairs. To achieve that objective, the administration has sought the re-

[30] Text in *Congressional Quarterly Weekly Report*, October 8, 1983, pp. 2101–2.

[31] Anthony Lewis, "The New Imperial Presidency," *First Principles: National Security and Civil Liberties* (July/August 1985): 2.

peal of restrictive legislation, and when that strategy has been impractical, it has eroded or evaded existing constraints. This policy is quite consistent with the president's personal views on the foreign policy powers of the executive branch. Indicative of his attitude is a statement he released upon signing the 1983 "compromise" resolution regarding the continued presence of American marines in Lebanon:

> I do not and cannot cede any of the authority vested in me under the Constitution as President and Commander-in-Chief of the United States Armed Forces. Nor should my signing be viewed as any acknowledgement that the President's constitutional authority can be impermissibly infringed by statute, that congressional authorization would be required if and when the period specified in...the War Powers Resolution might be deemed to have been triggered and the period had expired, or that...[the 18-month authorization] may be interpreted to revise the President's constitutional authority to deploy United States Armed Forces.[32]

The significance of the president's disclaimer should not be ignored. Reagan had already succeeded in obtaining legislation that seriously diluted the impact of the original war powers resolution, but he wanted more. In his previous utterances, he had studiously refrained from recognizing the validity of the resolution; this statement implied that he considered the measure unconstitutional, of no binding effect on any chief executive. It is an especially ominous development given the president's comments on another occasion: "We've got to get where we can run a foreign policy without a committee of 535 telling us what we can do."[33] Reagan clearly does not regard Congress as an equal, or even a junior, partner in the conduct of foreign policy. He

desires to regain the flexibility and virtually unlimited authority possessed by the occupants of the Oval Office early in the cold war. It should be no great surprise if in some future crisis Reagan goes on to repudiate the war powers resolution and the entire panoply of restrictive legislation.

THE INTERVENTIONIST RATIONALE

Reagan's efforts to revitalize presidential power to prosecute the cold war more vigorously reflect the assumptions of a sizable ideological community that embraces an interventionist foreign policy. Even during the earliest months of the Reagan administration, prominent spokesmen advocated a return to pre-Vietnam concepts of executive dominance. A 1981 article in *Foreign Affairs* by Sen. John Tower was typical.[34] According to Tower, the immediate post-World War II period was "marked by a reasonable balance between Congress and the President in the foreign policy decision-making process." That Tower would consider the years of unprecedented presidential supremacy an era of "reasonable balance" is most revealing, as is his subsequent assertion that "the balance has swung dangerously to the legislative side with unfavorable consequences for American foreign policy."[35]

Tower goes on to reiterate virtually every justification for executive supremacy that proponents have used since World War II. Congress, he argues, is too decentralized and represents too many "parochial" interests to "forge a unified foreign policy that reflects the interests of the United States as a whole." Conversely, the president has a "national mandate" and, unlike Congress, possesses

[32] *Congressional Quarterly Weekly Report,* October 15, 1983, p. 2142.
[33] Quoted in "Contra Aid Fight Irks Reagan," *Dallas Morning News,* May 22, 1985.
[34] John G. Tower, "Congress Versus the President: The Formulation and Implementation of American Foreign Policy," *Foreign Affairs* (Winter 1981–82): 229–46.
[35] Ibid., p. 230.

"the information, professional personnel," and other institutional tools to conduct a "consistent long-range policy." Congress as an institution is simply "ill-equipped to respond quickly and decisively to changes in the international scene." The latest attempt to restrain executive discretion prevents the United States from playing an active role in world affairs, just as in the 1930s "Congress tied the President's hands with disastrous consequences."[36]

It is remarkable that Tower's argument could easily have been penned by a liberal Democrat of the 1940s or 1950s. Tower's enthusiasm for presidential power reveals how far contemporary conservatives have strayed from the intellectual moorings of their ideological forebears. The contrast between his views and those expressed by earlier Republican luminaries, such as Robert Taft and Kenneth Wherry, could scarcely be greater.

Tower is quite candid about his ultimate objectives, contending, for example, that the war powers resolution "jeopardizes the President's ability to respond quickly, forcefully and if necessary in secret to protect American interests abroad." Furthermore, "If we are to meet the foreign policy challenges facing us in the 1980's, we must restore the traditional [sic] balance between Congress and the President in the formulation and implementation of foreign policy. To do so, much of the legislation of the past decade should be repealed or amended." Tower concedes that he is, in effect, "proposing a return to the situation that prevailed in the 1950's and 1960's."[37]

Richard Nixon's recent book *No More Vietnams* is equally blatant in emphasizing unrestricted presidential power as a prerequisite for an interventionist foreign policy. After blaming Congress for the fall of Southeast Asia to the communists, much as earlier interventionists invariably blamed congressional policy for the Pearl Harbor disaster, Nixon echoes Tower's desire to restore an unfettered presidency. He complains that the war powers resolution "makes it impossible for a President to act swiftly and secretly in a crisis," while the Foreign Assistance Act "limits aid to governments that do not have squeaky-clean human rights records." Such measures require a president to "wage war under Marquis of Queensbury rules in a world where good manners are potentially fatal hindrances."[38] Nixon asserts further that a president must be able to make expeditious use of the full range of U.S. military and intelligence forces, not "wait on the 535 members of Congress to make these quick, tough decisions for him."[39] It is imperative, the former president contends, to remove congressional constraints if the United States is to wage a successful campaign against the Soviet Union for control of the Third World. This assumption is chilling, given Nixon's views concerning the real "lesson" of the Vietnam conflict: "In Vietnam, we tried and failed in a just cause," Nixon insists. "No more Vietnams can mean that we will not *try* again. It should mean that we will not *fail* again."[40] A recipe for virtually unlimited intervention throughout the Third World,

---

[36] Ibid., pp. 230, 232–33.

[37] Ibid., pp. 239, 243. Appeals for a return to an unfettered presidency are often coupled with proposals to restore the other principal cold war shibboleth, "bipartisanship." Typical of the genre is Charles H. Percy, "The Partisan Gap," *Foreign Policy* (Winter 1981–82): 3–15; Ronald Reagan, "American Foreign Policy Challenges in the 1980's," *Department of State Bulletin* (May 1984): 1–6; and George Shultz, "Restoring Bipartisanship in Foreign Affairs," *Department of State Bulletin* (July 1985): 39–42. At its zenith, bipartisanship helped reduce the restraints on

and criticism of presidential cold war initiatives, which is precisely why interventionists want it restored.

[38] Richard M. Nixon, *No More Vietnams* (New York: Arbor House, 1985), p. 225. Sen. Barry Goldwater makes a similar point, asserting that the war powers resolution "attempts to deny flexibility to the president in defense of American citizens and their freedoms." See "Goldwater Urges Repeal of War Powers Resolution," *Dallas Morning News*, April 3, 1984.

[39] Nixon, p. 226.

[40] Ibid., p. 237. Nixon's emphasis.

Nixon's approach mandates executive supremacy as a key ingredient.

The Reagan administration is certainly not averse to such sentiments. The president has described America's Vietnam intervention as a "noble cause" and appears to have learned little from that debacle. Secretary of State Shultz has complained about the post-Vietnam legacy of congressional restrictions on "presidential flexibility." Those constraints, he contends, have "weakened our country" and have caused America to pull back from "global leadership."[41]

It is important to understand that an unfettered presidency is not, to cold warriors, an end in itself but only a powerful means to pursue a policy of global interventionism. This fact is amply demonstrated by what happens when cold warriors confront the occasional executive initiative to *reduce* U.S. involvement in Third World affairs. During the early years of the Carter administration, for example, some of the most outspoken congressional proponents of executive prerogatives suddenly became converts to the doctrine of congressional activism. Opponents of the Panama Canal treaties undertaken at Carter's initiative attempted not only to block their ratification but their execution, by refusing to appropriate the necessary funds. Carter encountered similar harassment when he attempted to normalize relations with the People's Republic of China and to abrogate America's mutual-defense treaty with Taiwan. Not only did congressmen who traditionally supported presidential foreign policy prerogatives seek to block that process through legislative action, they even filed a lawsuit in federal court.[42]

A more current example of the preeminence accorded interventionist foreign policy is a recent article by Rep. Jack Kemp that excoriates congressional interference in foreign policy, especially when the legislative branch limits the president's options.[43] Yet Kemp asserts that Congress should act as a "skeptic and critic" with respect to arms-control proposals and that it should press for retaliation whenever possible Soviet violations of existing accords emerge. In other words, congressional activism is warranted if it furthers hard-line cold war objectives but is undesirable if it achieves the opposite. Given the present administration's views of America's role in world affairs, however, today's cold warriors have much to gain from allowing the president the dominant foreign policy role that he seeks.

Indeed, the underlying rationale for the current campaign to restore executive dominance in foreign policy is that an unfettered presidency is an important precondition for an interventionist foreign policy. When John Tower and Richard Nixon advocate a return to the "traditional" relationship between Congress and the president, they are thinking of the halcyon days of the imperial presidency in the years following World War II, not the actual historical relationship. Likewise, their assertions that America has witnessed an era of "congressional dominance" in foreign affairs since the early 1970s are vastly overdrawn, for the country has something considerably more powerful than what political scientist Thomas Franck terms the "tethered presidency."[44] Although Congress has clearly recovered some of its foreign policy powers in the last decade, recent presidents still exercise a degree of uni-

[41] George Shultz, "The Meaning of Vietnam," *Department of State Bulletin* (June 1985): 14.

[42] Discussions of these and other incidents can be found in Franck and Weisband, pp. 275–86; I. M. Destler, "Congress as Boss?" *Foreign Policy* (Spring 1981): 170, 173–74; and Warren Christopher, "Ceasefire between the

Branches: A Compact in Foreign Affairs," *Foreign Affairs* (Summer 1982): 991–92.

[43] Jack F. Kemp, "Foreign Policy Agenda," *Washington Quarterly* (Spring 1985): 9–13.

[44] Thomas M. Franck, ed., *The Tethered Presidency: Congressional Restraints on Executive Power* (New York: New York University Press, 1981).

lateral discretion that would have astonished their pre-World War II predecessors.[45]

The argument that executive power must be increased to restore a balance between the executive and congressional branches is spurious. Greater balance existed in the mid- to late 1970s than at any other time in recent history. Those who make the argument object that an activist Congress prevents the president from conducting military and quasi-military initiatives similar to those of the 1950s and 1960s. Embracing an interventionist foreign policy leads them inexorably to advocate an unrestrained presidency as an essential device to implement that policy.

CONGRESS AS PARTNER AND WATCHDOG

Policy analysts who lack the extreme interventionist bias are nevertheless often ambivalent about the desirability of extensive congressional involvement in foreign policy. While noting that Congress may well have exercised a beneficial restraint on the executive in the post-Vietnam decade, they also point out that the decentralized nature of Congress creates overlapping areas of responsibility. At one time, for example, more than eight congressional committees, with a combined membership of 200, were involved in supervising U.S. intelligence agencies. Executive-branch officials have complained about having to testify before a multitude of committees, often simply to repeat the same information.[46]

Critics of congressional activism also make the valid point that Congress, being a lawmaking body, tends to view complex foreign policy issues as simply another arena for enacting statutes. The legislative process may create rigidity—repealing or amending a statute can prove both difficult and time-consuming—when changing conditions require dramatic and rapid shifts in policy. Although it may sometimes save the nation from a hasty and rash decision, Congress may also unnecessarily delay important actions.

An even more serious criticism of Congress is its occasional tendency to "grandstand" on emotionally charged foreign policy issues and even to sabotage important executive initiatives to court the favor of entrenched domestic pressure groups. A prime example is the Jackson-Vanik amendment, which makes U.S.-Soviet trade conditional upon Moscow giving public assurances regarding Jewish emigration. Other examples include current efforts to legislate economic sanctions against South Africa and to erect tariffs and other barriers against America's trading partners.[47] The cure for occasional congressional irresponsibility in foreign policy is not, of course, the restoration of an unrestrained presidency, but holding both Congress and the president accountable for foreign policy decisions. And this accountability requires that the public become more interested in and knowledgeable about foreign affairs.

The issues of congressional decentralization and the reduction of foreign policy issues to matters of mere lawmaking are more difficult to deal with. Several scholars who have grappled with these problems contend that Congress should play an important role in the formulation of foreign policy but should defer to the executive on the execution of that policy.[48]

---

[45] Reveley, p. 7; and Lee H. Hamilton and Michael H. Van Dusen, "Making the Separation of Powers Work," *Foreign Affairs* (Fall 1978): 21–22.

[46] Tower, p. 234; Franck and Weisband, pp. 210–21, 245–49; and Hamilton and Van Dusen, pp. 30–31.

[47] A concise discussion of ethnic "pressure group" influence on congressional foreign policy decisions can be found in John Rourke, *Congress and the Presidency: A Study of Interaction and Influence, 1945–1982* (Boulder, Colo.: Westview Press, 1983), pp. 261–66.

[48] Among those who employ this distinction are Christopher, pp. 999–1000; Hamilton and Van Dusen, pp. 28–29; Bennet, pp. 45–47; Crabb and Holt, p. 234; Fulbright,

This distinction is not entirely adequate. Clearly, such a large and diverse body as Congress ought not to attempt to micro-manage the execution of foreign policy. The legislative branch is structurally ill equipped to handle the day-to-day conduct of foreign affairs and the details and nuances of diplomacy. At the same time, it would be highly imprudent to allow the executive branch to implement policy without extensive ongoing supervision. An administration hostile to Congress can easily execute policy in such a way as to undermine or even obliterate congressional assumptions and objectives. In short, Congress must be both a vigilant watchdog and an equal partner in matters of foreign policy.

This dual role is difficult. In its role as partner, Congress must demand full and honest disclosure of all information pertinent to reaching a policy decision, and then it must accept its share of responsibility for that decision. Congress must also insist upon early and extensive consultation with the executive branch. Previous cold war presidents made a mockery of the consultative process, usually presenting a few congressional leaders with a fait accompli in the eleventh hour of an ongoing crisis. Congress cannot permit such presidential disdain and hope to preserve its newly regained foreign policy prerogatives.

In its role as watchdog, Congress must ensure that foreign policy is executed in accordance with established objectives. Here, willingness to assert congressional power is essential. It matters little if Congress attaches human-rights provisos to foreign aid legislation when it allows the president to issue bogus certifications of "adequate progress," as Reagan did for El Salvador in 1982 and 1983. Similarly, the war powers resolution has little impact when Congress is timid about enforce-

ment, as it was regarding U.S. military involvement in Lebanon in 1983. Just as Franklin Roosevelt made a farce of congressional neutrality legislation, Ronald Reagan or one of his successors may reduce the legislative restraints enacted during the 1970s to a heap of legal rubble. Ultimately, Congress itself must be the guarantor of its foreign policy prerogatives.

THE ROLE OF CONGRESS IN PRESERVING PEACE AND LIBERTY

Events have demonstrated that foreign policy initiatives—particularly long-term initiatives—cannot succeed without public support. Because members of Congress represent local constituencies, they tend to be more sensitive to undercurrents and shifts in public opinion.[49] Congress is thus a political early-warning system cautioning that contemplated or ongoing executive actions lack popular backing.

Proponents of unfettered presidential power contend that congressional sensitivity to public opinion is precisely why Congress should not become involved in foreign policy. They argue that the executive branch, possessing superior expertise and access to classified information, must sometimes pursue policies in conflict with the "whims" of public opinion. But this is arrogant elitism. Because the American people pay the price, both financially and not infrequently in lives, for foreign policy mistakes, they and their congressional representatives surely do have a role in determining policy. Moreover, such misadventures as the Bay of Pigs invasion and the Korean

---

p. 726; and Alvin P. Drischler, "Foreign Policy Making on the Hill," *Washington Quarterly* (Summer 1985): 165–75.

[49] Hamilton and Van Dusen, pp. 31–33. Long ago, Robert Taft concisely summarized the importance of congressional input, especially when a danger of armed conflict existed. "If the President has unlimited power to involve us in war," Taft warned, "war is more likely." *Congressional Record,* 82d Cong., 1st sess., 1951, vol. 97, p. 2988.

and Vietnam wars suggest that the much-touted wisdom and expertise of the executive branch are vastly overrated.

The overwhelming majority of foreign policy decisions are not made under emergency conditions. Whenever time permits, the president has both a legal and a moral obligation to include Congress in the decision-making process—even though it may be less "efficient," to do so. Congressional participation does not, of course, guarantee a prudent, non-interventionist foreign policy, but by adding another step to the decision-making process it significantly reduces the risk of acting rashly.

A vigorous congressional role in foreign policy is also crucial for maintaining domestic liberties. Policy analyst Bayless Manning contends that many "new" foreign policy issues—energy concerns, international trade, pollution control, and the like—are so intimately bound up with domestic concerns that Congress inevitably becomes involved in foreign policy anyway. According to Manning, the increasing prevalence of "intermestic" affairs precludes a return to congressional abdication in foreign policy.[50]

However, just because Congress has traditionally exercised great power in domestic affairs does not mean that it will continue to do so, much less be able to use that role to increase its authority over foreign policy. Congress once possessed extensive—indeed, dominant—powers in foreign affairs, only to lose them to executive encroachment. A resurgence of the imperial presidency in "traditional" foreign policy matters could readily lead to a drastic erosion of congressional authority throughout the entire range of "intermestic" and even predominantly domestic affairs.

The danger is not theoretical. The expansion of presidential power over foreign policy has often been accompanied by a similar aggrandizement in the domestic arena. In the final months of World War I and the immediate postwar period, the Wilson administration embarked on the "Red Scare," with massive violations of civil liberties. Franklin Roosevelt's administration arbitrarily interned more than 100,000 Japanese-Americans in concentration camps during World War II, asking congressional approval for it only as an afterthought. The early 1940s also witnessed an unprecedented regimentation of the U.S. economy, with executive-branch officials establishing production quotas, enforcing wage and price controls, and rationing "scarce" commodities. Dissent was not viewed with tolerance. When the management of Montgomery Ward balked at certain imperious administration demands, the company was seized and temporarily placed under direct government control.[51] What Roosevelt did to Montgomery Ward in the midst of a major war duly declared by Congress, Truman attempted to do to the steel industry during the Korean "police action," an undeclared, limited conflict. It was symptomatic of the times that the Supreme Court, not Congress, stifled this particular effort to expand executive power.[52]

Truman's defeat in the steel-industry episode did little to inhibit his successors. In August 1971, Richard Nixon imposed special import surcharges, suspended the convertibility of the dollar, and proclaimed a freeze on wages and prices. Although several statutory provisions arguably permitted the president to take such actions in the event of a national

---

[50] Bayless Manning, "The Congress, the Executive and Intermestic Affairs: Three Proposals," *Foreign Affairs* (January 1977): 306–24.

[51] A concise discussion of the Montgomery Ward episode can be found in Richard Polenberg, *War and Society: The United States, 1941–1945* (Philadelphia: J. B. Lippincott, 1972), pp. 171–75.

[52] *Youngstown Sheet and Tube Company, et al.* v. *Sawyer*, 343 U.S. 579; 72 S. Ct. 863; 96 L. Ed. 1153 (1952).

emergency, Nixon's contention that an emergency existed was questionable at best. He assumed that the "problems of ending a war"—his belief that the winding down of the Vietnam War was creating some economic dislocations—entitled him to make far-reaching domestic policy changes by executive fiat.[53] Of course, the most graphic illustration of the fact that an imperial presidency in foreign affairs inevitably corrodes domestic liberties was the Watergate scandal. Domestic surveillance and other efforts to intimidate and disrupt dissenting groups, conducted under the all-encompassing rubric of "national security," were hallmarks of the Johnson and Nixon administrations throughout the Vietnam War. Watergate was not, as many observers have simplistically concluded, an aberration—a manifestation of character defects peculiar to Nixon. Rather, Watergate was the symptom of a systemic disorder: it was the imperial presidency at its zenith, applied without restraint on the home front.

Even a post-Watergate president such as Jimmy Carter was not immune to the temptation to intervene in domestic affairs by executive fiat. His imposition of a grain embargo on the USSR, with its disastrous consequences for American farmers, following the Soviet invasion of Afghanistan in December 1979 was a prime example. At the very least, it represented an expansive interpretation of presidential authority under the Export Administration Act. Carter's application of pressure on the U.S. Olympic Committee to "persuade" it to honor the boycott he had already proclaimed of the 1980 Olympics—notwithstanding the desire of U.S. athletes to participate—is another case in point.[54]

An unfettered chief executive in foreign affairs does not merely heighten the danger of unwanted and unnecessary wars; it poses a potentially lethal threat to our entire system of checks and balances, thereby jeopardizing domestic liberties. To prevent the rebirth of the imperial presidency, it is vital that Congress preserve the statutory reforms enacted during the 1970s, especially the war powers resolution. It is equally important that the legislative branch enforce its newly regained prerogatives with sufficient determination. The "compromise" on U.S. military policy in Lebanon set an unhealthy precedent, and similar congressional retreats in the future would virtually guarantee the onset of a new imperial presidency. Finally, both Congress and the public must avoid excessive deference to supposed executive-branch expertise in foreign affairs. Especially in matters of war and peace, the views of the American people and their elected representatives should be paramount. The preservation of peace and liberty mandates a sustained and vigorous congressional role in directing the nation's foreign policy.

QUESTIONS FOR DISCUSSION

1. What criteria should be used in evaluating whether the American system of separation of powers has served U.S. national interests?
2. Which branch—the president or Congress—is better equipped to conduct foreign policy? What are the reasons for your answer?
3. How would you compare the conduct of foreign policy of the United States with its presidential system to the foreign policy of Great Britain with its parliamentary system?
4. What effect does a strong presidency have on U.S. global interventionism?

[53] Richard Nixon, "The Challenge of Peace," *Department of State Bulletin* (September 6, 1971): 253–57.

[54] Carter's own account of the grain-embargo and Olympic-boycott decisions can be found in his *Keeping Faith: Memoirs of a President* (New York: Bantam Books, 1982), pp. 474–78, 481–82. The text of his grain-embargo order is in *Public Papers of the Presidents of the United States: Jimmy Carter, 1980* (Washington: Government Printing Office, 1981), p. 32.

5. How has the separation of powers changed in foreign policy matters from 1789 to the present? How do you account for these changes?

SUGGESTED READINGS

Christopher, Warren. "Ceasefire between the Branches: A Compact in Foreign Affairs." *Foreign Affairs,* 60 (Summer 1982), pp. 989–1005.

Daly, John Charles, et al. *President vs. Congress: Does the Separation of Powers Still Work?* Washington, D.C.: American Enterprise Institute for Public Policy Research, 1981.

Henkin, Louis. "Foreign Affairs and the Constitution." *Foreign Affairs,* 66 (Winter 1987–88), pp. 284–310.

LaFeber, Walter. "The Constitution and United States Foreign Policy: An Interpretation." *Journal of American History,* 74 (Dec. 1987), pp. 695–717.

Rusk, Dean. "Foreign Policy and the Separation of Powers." In *Six Virginia Papers Presented at the Miller Center Forums, 1985,* ed. Kenneth W. Thompson. Lanham, Md.: University Press of America, 1986. Pp. 1–19.

Robinson, Donald L., ed. *Reforming American Government: The Bicentennial Papers of the Committee on the Constitutional System.* Boulder, Colo.: Westview Press, 1985.

Schlesinger, Arthur M., Jr. *The Imperial Presidency.* Boston: Houghton Mifflin, 1983.

Schultz, L. Peter. "The Separation of Powers and Foreign Affairs." In *Separation of Powers—Does It Still Work?* ed. Robert A. Goldwin and Art Kaufman. Washington, D.C.: American Enterprise Institute, 1986. Pp. 118–37.

Sundquist, James L. *Constitutional Reform and Effective Government.* Washington, D.C.: Brookings Institution, 1986.

U.S. Cong., Senate. *Taiwan Communique and Separation of Powers.* Hearings before the Subcommittee on Separation of Powers of the Committee on the Judiciary, 97th Cong., 2d Sess., 1982.

See also Suggested Readings for Debates 1, 2, 3, and 9.

5 Should Politics Stop at the Water's Edge?

YES

Charles H. Percy

The Partisan Gap

NO

Fred Charles Iklé

Beyond the Water's Edge: Responsible Partisanship in Foreign Policy

The Partisan Gap

Charles H. Percy

In recent years, some politicians have claimed that bipartisanship is dead. Yet the idea has not died. It cannot be allowed to wither away without dangerous consequences for U.S. diplomacy and the U.S. role in the world.

There is little disagreement about the challenge the United States faces. The Soviet Union has vastly increased its military strength and the scope of its diplomatic activity. It is increasingly in a position to exploit unstable areas of the world to the disadvantage of the United States. In Western Europe, U.S. alliance relationships have entered a period of new strains. Moreover, the developing countries are trapped in an economic maelstrom of huge debts and burgeoning populations at a time when international economic realities may well prevent the achievement of even their most modest aspirations.

How well the United States can meet these challenges will depend significantly on whether America is strong and unified. It will also depend on whether U.S. policies are supported by the American people and whether the United States is consistent to a point where both allies and adversaries fully understand where it stands and what its range of responses to international crises are likely to be.

Yet unity, support, or consistency is unlikely without a greater measure of bipartisanship. Without a joint approach to U.S. foreign policy, which both branches of government backed by substantial elements of both parties

must work to forge, the United States is likely to fall short of its foreign policy objectives.

The benefits of bipartisanship in the past have been substantial. Three crowning achievements of postwar U.S. foreign policy were the Marshall Plan, the North Atlantic Treaty Organization (NATO) treaty, and the United Nations Charter. None was possible without bipartisan support. Republican Senator Arthur Vandenberg, Democratic Senator Tom Connally, and President Harry Truman made history by joining forces to bring these major foreign policy initiatives to fruition. Their bipartisan approach was critical in putting Western Europe on the road to recovery, shoring up Western security, and laying the groundwork for an emerging postwar order compatible with American values.

Today, a bipartisan approach is more important than ever before. The heavy financial burdens that foreign policy decisions now place on the American people require that unity. In the years ahead, the American people must accept major sacrifices to restore both the fact and the perception of U.S. military, economic, and political strength. Continual backbiting and undermining of policies at home would only serve to weaken the country's ability to achieve this strength and with it to promote a more purposeful and constructive U.S. role in the world.

In times of crisis, the perception of strength resting on unity is crucial. Bipartisan support for the policies of President Kennedy in the Cuban missile crisis and President Carter in the Iran hostage crisis critically affected ultimate resolution of those two dangerous situations, which could have erupted in devastating war. In other instances, such as unwavering bipartisan support for the NATO alliance or for the new U.S. relationship with China—including the Taiwan Relations Act—bipartisanship has meant commitments could continue, changes in party control of Congress or the presidency notwithstanding. Con-

Charles H. Percy, "The Partisan Gap," *Foreign Policy*, no. 45 (Winter 1985–86), pp. 3–15. Reprinted by permission of *Foreign Policy*.

versely, when U.S. foreign policy has appeared on some key issues to vacillate in recent years, part of the blame frequently could be traced to the inability of recent administrations to maintain a bipartisan consensus on foreign policy issues.

THE NEED FOR CONSISTENCY

Those who now minimize the importance of bipartisanship in foreign policy overlook the nature of the U.S. system of government. Key foreign policy issues increasingly require formal congressional support before the administration can deliver on its commitments.

In particular, the drafters of the U.S. Constitution made the president the executive agent of the Senate in negotiating treaties, but also required a two-thirds majority of the Senate to ratify those treaties. Moreover, the rise of the so-called congressional veto, which allows Congress to block proposed executive branch action if one or both houses disapprove, has added a new dimension to the conduct of U.S. diplomacy. As a result, a president's success depends to a great extent on his ability to attract bipartisan support. Foreign countries will not consider the United States a credible negotiating partner in the absence of a bipartisan approach to foreign policy making.

In the 200 years of U.S. history, more than 100 treaties have been flatly rejected, failed to enter into force because changes made by the Senate were unacceptable to the president or others, or were withdrawn because of the strong opposition they engendered. The most significant examples have taken place in this century as the United States has assumed its new role as a world power. Senate rejection of the Treaty of Versailles was a major foreign policy embarrassment for President Wilson.

In more recent years Presidents Nixon, Ford, and Carter all suffered major foreign policy setbacks because of congressional opposition to what each regarded as a major foreign policy triumph. Congress did not act on the Threshold Test Ban Treaty negotiated by Nixon; it shelved the Treaty on Peaceful Nuclear Explosions negotiated by Ford; and it refused—after the Soviets invaded Afghanistan—to take up the SALT [Strategic Arms Limitation Talks] II treaty negotiated by Carter. This consistent record of legislative repudiation of executive branch arms control treaties causes deep concern among West European allies and suspicion within the Soviet Union.

Democracies—with frequent elections and accountability to the people, whose preferences may shift—necessarily confuse at times both allies and adversaries. Such confusion will usually crest when significant changes in party control of the Congress and presidency take place. New leaders will often find it necessary and desirable to make changes in foreign policy. But if changes reach the point of contradiction and contrast across the entire array of policy every four or eight years, the United States itself may become a major source of instability in the world. A new administration elected by popular mandate can and should put its stamp on U.S. foreign policy—as the Reagan administration is doing—without overturning abiding foreign policy goals.

What are these goals? Fundamentally, U.S. foreign policy seeks to achieve peace, freedom, extension of human rights, and economic progress, all in the framework of a stable international order. Each succeeding administration must stress and reinforce these essential policy goals.

The United States can no longer dominate events as it formerly could when it emerged from World War II greatly strengthened and had a monopoly of nuclear power. Consequently, in the 1980s each administration in pursuing America's overarching goals must demonstrate a degree of patience, perseverance, and constancy of purpose possible only through bipartisanship in formulating foreign policy. Secretary of State Alexander Haig, Jr. alluded to this vital point when he informed Congress in September 1981: "Change, even important and overdue change, must be balanced by the need for consistency."

The consistency Haig advocates will also affect U.S. public backing for American initiatives around the world. Clearly, no foreign policy that offends the basic political values or economic interests of the American people can gain or maintain support. To secure popular acceptance of policies, U.S. leaders must first respond to those values and interests. Yet an understanding of those interests and values does not constitute a foreign policy. If the relevant policy makers in the country fail to identify at least a few overriding foreign policy objectives that unite them, they will be unable to lead public opinion in any purposeful way. The public will hear a cacophony of voices. Popular attitudes will sour. Public opinion will devolve to a negative check on policy makers. Popular skepticism will prevent them from taking risks or making mistakes, but it will also prevent them from seizing opportunities or making gains.

Moreover, without a certain degree of unity within the U.S. body politic, foreigners will not develop the useful perception that the American president represents a purposeful nation, whose policies merit support from its friends as well as its people. Especially as the nation faces a growing number of stresses and crises in international affairs in the turbulent years to come, the president and secretary of state must be able to rely on the firm support of Congress and the public in their dealings with other nations. U.S. success in foreign relations will therefore depend to a significant extent on whether America's negotiating partners or adversaries believe that the president enjoys the bipartisan support of both parties in Congress. A president who is manifestly able to count on a high level of support in Congress is a more impressive negotiating partner than one who cannot.

FOREIGN POLICY PREDICTABILITY

Close cooperation between the White House and Congress can bring another strength to U.S. foreign policy: greater predictability. A country whose foreign policy is unpredictable not only unnerves its friends, but also unnecessarily threatens its adversaries. The former may be tempted to flee from and the latter to take advantage of what each sees as vacillating or confused policy. Conversely, bipartisanship helps friendly nations plan joint action of a constructive nature. By committing the United States to positions acceptable to majority opinion in both American political parties, the executive branch insures that changes in control of the houses of Congress and the executive branch will not seriously disrupt the fundamental thrust of U.S. policies.

Imagine the alternatives. A breakdown of traditional bipartisan support for NATO could eliminate the security benefits to the United States from the Western alliance. An outbreak of partisan wrangling over the details of the Middle East peace process could damage the bipartisan support for necessary military and economic assistance to Israel and Egypt and severely set back the search for peace and stability in the area. An erosion of the long-standing U.S. bipartisan support for the international development banks could threaten economic stability in the developing countries, which purchase 30 percent of U.S. exports.

Predictability in U.S. policy can also affect domestic politics in friendly states. America's West European allies, for example, warn that U.S.-Soviet arms control talks will have profound domestic implications for several of them. Yet unless the president can depend on support from a decisive majority in Congress, his options will be limited. An approach to arms control based primarily on partisan or domestic political considerations could well drive America's friends into the very estrangement all parties fear.

Adversaries must also know the limits they cannot exceed if unnecessary conflict is to be avoided. For them to understand the range of U.S. options, they must believe that U.S. actions in vital areas of national interest will not be second-guessed or debated to death.

Serious complications stand in the way of reaching a bipartisan consensus. The first is the role of Congress. In recent years, Congress has increased its power greatly. The sharpest increase in this power took place in the wake of the Vietnam war and the Watergate revelations. As a result, Congress has claimed much greater authority in foreign policy making than ever before.

Much of what has happened is positive. The Senate, for example, agreed to a definition of what constitutes a "national commitment." This definition may help preclude the kind of unilateral commitments made by the chief executive that have so disrupted the orderly process of U.S. foreign policy decision making in the past. The foreign affairs agencies—the State Department, the Agency for International Development, the Peace Corps, the U.S. International Communication Agency, the Arms Control and Disarmament Agency, and the Board for International Broadcasting—all now require an annual authorization of their funds. This requirement increases the degree of congressional influence and control. The Case Act requires the president to inform Congress of all executive agreements, and the War Powers Act stipulates the conditions under which the U.S. president can bring this country into a state of war. Finally, under the Arms Export Control Act, Congress is empowered to block major military equipment sales from the United States to other countries.

Although these steps were desirable, in other cases Congress sought more control over foreign policy than it could handle effectively. The congressional veto, for example, is an increasingly controversial tool. Yet some advocate extending the authority of the congressional veto to all executive agreements other than treaties. Such a step would delay the binding effect of every executive agreement and seriously cripple the day-to-day conduct of U.S. foreign affairs.

Congress already enjoys adequate instruments—oversight hearings, informal consultations, and especially the power of the purse—to modify or block a foreign policy proposal desired by the executive branch. Ultimately, the U.S. system must maintain a reasonable balance of power. Without question, Congress must remain equal to the executive branch as the framers of the Constitution intended. But the pendulum that has swung toward the legislative branch since 1970 ought now to swing back toward a middle ground that could contribute to greater efficiency in U.S. foreign policy making.

MUTUAL CONSULTATION

Several possibilities for reform exist. Congress now enjoys a provision to block even very small foreign defense equipment sales or sales of defense services. The president must report on these proposals to Congress. In the foreign assistance bill of 1982—the International Security and Development Cooperation Act—as reported out of the Senate Foreign Relations Committee in May, the affected dollar levels would be doubled, from $7 million to $14 million for sales of defense equipment and from $25 million to $50 million for sales of defense services. This step would help take Congress out of the oversight of the smaller military sales and restrict the option of oversight only to the more significant ones.

In addition, the Senate in October 1981 upheld the majority vote of the Senate Foreign

Relations Committee on several issues related to increasing executive branch flexibility. The Senate repealed prohibitions on aid to Angola, Chile, and Argentina, with certain conditions. Also, the president's authority to waive other provisions of the law in situations of national emergency or when such a waiver is determined to be in the vital national security interests was made more flexible. Indeed, the belief that Congress should involve itself so directly in the process of carrying out foreign policy by day-to-day oversight is a dangerous one.

The second major complication in the achievement of a bipartisan foreign policy is the composition of Congress. Both the structure of Congress and the role of the political parties within Congress complicate the achievement of bipartisan support for foreign policy decisions. Currently, more committees and subcommittees address issues related to foreign policy than ever before in history. The effect has been to splinter the traditional bases of power within Congress. The influence of the political parties has diminished, leading to more difficulties in developing cohesive coalitions on sensitive policy issues. Recent rapid turnover in Congress has also increased the obstacles to coalition building.

These trends suggest, however, an even greater need for an administration to work with congressional leaders of both parties to develop policies that can enjoy broad support. Any administration serves its own interests by promoting coherence in the congressional approach to foreign policy. Yet that task is impossible without regular and trusted exchanges of information on policy alternatives with the relevant congressional officials on both sides of the aisle.

Thorough discussion, which means frank exchanges of information and advice in an atmosphere of mutual respect, can accomplish many things. Consultation can give executive appointees and bureaucrats the benefit of congressional experience in judging whether the administration can win popular support for particular policies. Consultation gives members of Congress the benefit of sensitive information available to the administration and an opportunity to know the full rationale behind proposed policies. Consultation reduces mutual misunderstanding, helps moderate initial partisan reactions to new policies, and far better than briefings, helps reduce the chance that an unsatisfied member of either political party will vote simply along partisan lines. Therefore, both branches of government should look for ways to improve the frequency and quality of discussions.

The Office of Congressional Relations in the Department of State should take the lead in monitoring the frequency and quality of consultation between the department and Congress. The assistant secretary for congressional relations must seek to build a two-way bridge. He must identify and understand the priorities and concerns of members of Congress and report them early to the appropriate officials at the State Department, just as he serves in his role as a policy spokesman for the secretary of state on Capitol Hill.

Whenever possible, the Office of Congressional Relations should urge other State Department offices to consult with relevant congressional leaders in both parties early in the preparation of policy options. State Department liaison officers might profitably have permanent offices on Capitol Hill to expedite their work with the House and Senate.

Meetings of senators and congressmen at the department must increase in frequency at various levels. Working sessions, to exchange information and discuss ideas, help subcommittee chairmen and committee members from both parties with special interests and expertise in regional issues. In general, these meetings should be scheduled as needs arise. But the more regular they become, the more effective the executive-congressional relationship will be. It is important to Congress that the executive branch demonstrate that it welcomes congressional input and, where possible, incorporates that contribution into policy positions.

During times of foreign crisis, policy makers in the executive branch inevitably make the day-to-day decisions and responses to international developments required during a crisis. Because decisions made during crises can have far-reaching impact upon U.S. foreign policy in the long run, however, the executive branch should consult with Congress as the decisions are made.

The present structure of Congress deters useful consultation during crises. Executive officials justifiably complain about giving repetitious testimony to the House and Senate and often do not know whom they should consult. Thus, Congress should designate a more appropriate instrument to serve as a liaison—a first point of contact—with the administration as the need arises. Just as the executive branch creates ad hoc task forces to deal with crisis situations, so should Congress. Membership of such a committee should draw upon the leadership, including majority and minority leaders in both houses and the chairmen and ranking minority members of the Senate Foreign Relations and House Foreign Affairs committees.

As the crisis develops and its nature emerges, the leadership group should call on the expertise of the members of the foreign policy committees and then additional members of Congress with special interests and perspectives. The temporary committee would function during the crisis and immediately afterward, providing a rapid contact point for the executive branch. Then it would again fall to the standing foreign relations committees to assess the future implications of the crisis for broader American foreign policy goals.

The foreign travel plans of members of Congress provide an opportunity for enhanced and fruitful consultations if both branches of government will work to use that opportunity. Members of Congress understandably will resist any executive branch ef-

fort to program their travel so as to limit their contacts. Nevertheless, congressional leaders of both parties should urge their members to consult with key State Department officials prior to and after a trip abroad. Department officials should seek more aggressively to make contact with congressmen who have traveled. Currently, the executive branch does not adequately tap this valuable source of independent information.

THE SEARCH FOR CONSENSUS

Bipartisanship does not imply the stifling of debate or uncritical support for all White House proposals. No administration can effectively adopt and pursue policies without early and thorough consultation with Congress. But in many cases, the executive branch will not persuade Congress; even so, when the executive branch chooses to include members of Congress early and thoroughly in formation of major policy initiatives, the record shows that those initiatives more often than not succeed both in gaining wide support in Congress and in enduring over time.

In the case of the NATO treaty, the Senate Foreign Relations Committee held long executive sessions in February and March 1949, before the treaty was approved by Truman in April. Senators met with the secretary of state to discuss drafts and to work on the substance and style of the treaty. Both Republicans and Democrats on the committee examined every conceivable angle of the draft treaty in detail.

Compare this history with the Carter administration's handling of the SALT II treaty. The executive branch did invite a majority of the Senate to visit Geneva to observe the negotiators at work. But the administration failed to consult frequently with key senators about the substantive choices at crucial moments in the negotiation. Consultations could have lessened the subsequent opposition within the Senate that delayed ratification.

Naturally, any administration faces a dilemma. The Senate, to play its role, must be involved throughout the process; and involvement means that sensitive policy choices may become known to the general public. A review of the past decade, however, suggests that the United States benefits from continuous Senate involvement, even at the cost of some premature public disclosure. Such involvement can help prevent misunderstandings, distrust, and unnecessary problems in gaining Senate ratification of treaties negotiated by the president.

A good example of early and thorough executive-legislative cooperation occurred during negotiation of the 1963 Limited Test Ban Treaty. The Senate Committee on Foreign Relations was consulted on the draft articles as they were revised during the negotiating process. Subsequently, several committee members participated in the Moscow signing ceremony. The Republican leader of the Senate, Everett Dirksen, played a leading role in achieving a bipartisan consensus. In the negotiation of treaties, therefore, there is a useful place for the early, extensive, and continuing involvement of senators with the president's negotiating team. Also, in the setting of national commitments, that same thorough consultation is essential.

Do the circumstances that helped form a post–World War II consensus on foreign policy exist today? Certainly, the challenge is no less. In addition, as in the earlier period, there is a mandate in the country to revitalize the American economy and to meet Soviet challenges by strengthening U.S. military power and forging closer ties with allies. Strong majorities in both branches share these concerns, which can be the basis for the future bipartisan cooperation that is so essential to success in U.S. foreign policy.

For this cooperation to develop, more must be done than in the past. Executive branch officials must strive not to repeat past mistakes in which officials attempted merely to sell programs to Congress and not to include members in the shaping of those programs. Certainly, the administration will have an easier time persuading the current Congress, with little cost and with a gain in the coherence, breadth of support for, and quality of policy, if the members' views are sought early and an effort is made to accommodate their recommendations.

But the administration must take the initiative. Particularly after the impressive but difficult victory in avoiding Senate disapproval of the airborne warning and control system–F-15 aircraft enhancement sale to Saudi Arabia, it is necessary to reduce party differences and to search for consensus. The foreign policy bureaucracy must provide Congress with all the relevant information. In turn, members of Congress must assign sufficient staff and give enough of their personal time to the discussion. Above all, both the administration and the Congress must remain determined to reduce partisan differences and strive for consensus. Determination is necessary because a positive attitude toward bipartisanship was lost in the wake of the Vietnam war, with its divisiveness and trampling of congressional prerogatives and sensitivities by the executive branch.

No one should underestimate the benefits of bipartisanship. Nor should anyone underestimate the loss to the country if America's leaders fail to forge a bipartisan consensus. Today, a president may be forceful and his administration may be far sighted; yet without the necessary degree of comity with Congress, his foreign policy may fail on the great issues of the day—nuclear proliferation, arms control, the Middle East peace process, East-West relations, North-South differences, and international terrorism. The coherence sought by the executive branch will disappear, lost in a sea of partisan recriminations and congressional vetoes. Despite the obstacles to strengthening bipartisanship, it must be achieved if the United States is to maintain a leadership role in the world.

Beyond the Water's Edge: Responsible Partisanship in Foreign Policy

Fred Charles Iklé

In the United States, as soon as a party has become dominant, all public power passes under its control; its private supporters occupy all the positions and dispose of all administrative forces. Since most distinguished men of the opposing party are unable to surmount the obstacles which exclude them from power, it is essential that they can establish themselves separately.

Alexis de Tocqueville

A vexing feature of political discourse is the longevity of assertions contrary to fact. The allegation that foreign policy has little effect in American elections is a case in point. Why did Lyndon Johnson decide not to run in 1968, and why did his chosen successor, Hubert Humphrey, lose the presidential election? Was it because of the state of the economy and other domestic issues, or was it because of Johnson's setbacks in foreign affairs? Can we be sure which is the larger reason for George McGovern's landslide defeat—his positions on domestic affairs or his positions on foreign policy and national defense?

Clearly, foreign policy does play a role in elections, more visibly, of course, in presidential elections than in Congressional ones. The day-to-day moves in American diplomacy and the intricacies of armaments and military strategy are left for the specialists to fight over. But the votes of the general public are affected by

the broad thrust of foreign policy (*vide* George McGovern's defeat) and by the impact of foreign policy on life in the United States (*vide* Lyndon Johnson).

Since a presidential candidate can be undone by his current positions or his past decisions on foreign policy, and since presidential elections are clearly a partisan business, it stands to reason that there is a purely partisan interest in drawing foreign policy issues into election campaigns. That is to say, it is in the interest of each of the two major Parties to exploit foreign policy issues in a partisan context—except when one or the other Party believes that the record of its candidate cannot be effectively defended before the voters. The presidential candidate who disagrees with the foreign policy positions of his opponent and who feels that voters can be made to see he is right will not be muzzled by some "above-politics" plea for bipartisanship in foreign affairs.

Nor should he be. Partisanship in foreign affairs is not merely an instrument of electoral politics. It goes beyond that. Exercised with responsibility, it can serve the national interest. To say this may sound heretical, because the idea that foreign policy demands bipartisanship has become an article of faith. But if we exert some intellectual curiosity in examining this tenet, we can soon find that the exceptions are as weighty as the rule—an affliction of most propositions of political science. In many circumstances, a dose of partisanship is the best medicine with which to cure an ailing foreign policy.

Vigorous partisan airing of issues can be healthy. It permits the voters to get a better sense of what is at stake and brings home to them that they have a role and responsibility in shaping policy. Partisan debate complements and enlivens discussions among foreign affairs specialists and can help to induce in them a real world relevance and meaning for the public.

Fred Charles Iklé, "Beyond the Water's Edge: Responsible Partisanship in Foreign Policy," *Commonsense* 1 (Summer 1978), pp. 34–38. Copyright © 1978 by Republican National Committee, Washington, D.C. Reprinted by permission.

The partisan debate helps communication both ways. It forces both President and the opposition Party to present to the people their views and their vision of America's role in the world. And it induces the voters to convey what they expect of their country's foreign policy and what sacrifices they are willing to make for its success. This process will serve to articulate American objectives and values.

Opinion polls are no substitute. Without a live political debate, the polls tend to confront the voter with eviscerated choices—muted questions that raise neither hope nor fear. So it is not surprising that a quick telephone poll may show that most Americans have no views about Cubans in Zambia (where is Zambia, anyhow?), and that unemployment or inflation always wins out over SALT [Strategic Arms Limitation Talks] or the Panama Canal.

If the President fails to take the lead in articulating what the United States is willing to do for its national security and how it will shape its role in the world, he must not be allowed to escape blame because opinion polls mirror the same passivity. If some day in a poll fifty-one percent had said we should not send American troops to defend Alaska, we would not expect the President to start negotiations with Russia for the return of Alaska. There must be a better way to bring to official Washington what the nation really wants and needs.

This task cannot be left to opinion polls. It requires competing ideas, moderated so as to be broadly acceptable, but competitive, nonetheless. It requires the offer of new leadership. It requires the organizational backing and political follow-up that the Party is uniquely equipped to provide.

Responsible partisan opposition performs, among others, this useful function. It can help open up the foreign policy bureaucracy to ideas and criticism from the outside. It is no accident that members of the Foreign Service, no matter which Party is in power, are the most ardent advocates of a bipartisan foreign policy. The Foreign Service will rule as the priesthood of the orthodoxy as long as dissent seems a lonesome heresy. Bipartisanship protects the sanctioned view dispensed by the foreign policy establishment. Under this reign, debate is to be conducted in hushed voices at the Council on Foreign Relations or in seminars organized by foundations in New York and Washington. Without political partisanship, all these gatherings will be staffed by the same people, moving around in incestuous circles, while the occasionally invited dissenter serves merely as a garnish, like parsley at the edge of the plate.

We must beware of generalizations, however, about the relative merits of a partisan versus a bipartisan approach to foreign policy. This judgment depends greatly on whether or not Congress and the White House are controlled by the same party.

Bipartisanship, it is worth noting, got its halo when the Republicans in control of Congress supported President Truman's post-war foreign policy. Even before the Second World War ended, President Roosevelt was anxious to avoid, in the evolving plans for the United Nations, the fate that befell Woodrow Wilson's initiative for the League of Nations. President Truman and the Republican Chairman of the Senate Foreign Relations Committee, Arthur Vandenberg, managed a constructive collaboration on the American initiatives that helped shape the post-war world: the peace treaties, the Marshall Plan, and NATO [North Atlantic Treaty Organization].

Seen from the White House, the object of bipartisanship was to overcome the isolationist tendencies of Republicans in Congress. Even Secretary of State Dulles, during the first years of the Eisenhower Administration (one of those rare recent periods when Republicans controlled both the White House and Congress) felt he had to move carefully to avoid isolationist opposition from his fellow Republicans.

Since the 1960s, however, Republicans and Democrats have practically traded positions in terms of isolationist attitudes. Now it is the Republicans, in minority in Congress, who seek, with the assistance of independent-minded Democrats, to preserve our alliances and prevent our defenses from deteriorating further. It is a Democratic Administration that wants to withdraw U.S. ground forces from Korea, slash the Navy's ship-building program, give up or slow down several strategic weapons programs even before a new SALT agreement has been reached, indefinitely delay the production of the "neutron bomb" without any *quid pro quo* from the Russians, and watch passively as the Russians and Cubans extend their military intervention and police controls from one African country to another.

One is tempted to compare the isolationist movement after the First World War and the neo-isolationism of the 1970s—or perhaps we should call today's version "self-abasing withdrawal." The Senate's rejection of the League of Nations was brought about primarily by the isolationist stance of Republican Senators, but secondarily by Woodrow Wilson's stubbornness. The American rejection of the League has since been widely blamed for the unchecked rearmament of Nazi Germany and Nazi aggressions in the 1930s that led to World War II. There is no doubt that the United States went through an isolationist period after the First World War; but the sentiment against involvement abroad was rather bipartisan. After President Wilson's setback, the Democrats failed to make a *partisan* case for a constructive American role in world affairs. If one wants to put some of the blame for Hitler's unchecked rise in the 1930s on American party politics, one should perhaps look to *bipartisan* neglect of foreign affairs in the 1920s and 1930s, rather than to the Republican partisanship of Senator Henry Cabot Lodge and his colleagues.

Some of the isolationist sentiment in the United States in the 1920s and 1930s may well have been a reaction to the horrors of World War I and the unsavory image of European power politics. Similarly, the self-abasing withdrawal tendency of the last few years is clearly a reaction to the war in Vietnam. This new isolationism is particularly virulent among the Democrats who, holding second and third echelon positions in the Johnson Administration, struggled with the problems of the Vietnam war, and who have now become senior officials or advisors in the Carter Administration. Their troubled feeling about the war in Indochina drives them to hobble the American capability to intervene, under the slogan of "no more Vietnams"—the new battle cry that cheers on the retreat of American presence and influence abroad.

It should go without saying that partisanship on foreign affairs must not degenerate into opposition for its own sake. Heat and noise are inevitable in the political kitchen. But dishonesty and negativism stultify public debate and, if practiced by a powerful group in Congress, can destroy any foreign policy.

Foreign and defense policies have to cope with greater dangers than do domestic policies and they must protect the nation from powerful adversaries. Hence, a reasoned argument can be made that bipartisanship (or nonpartisanship) must play a larger role on foreign and defense issues than on domestic issues.

Moreover, certain policies for dealing with other countries require continuity over a long period of time. Our alliance commitments would become unworkable if they turned into an election issue every four years. Arms control negotiations and our military programs require planning for a decade ahead or longer. American influence throughout the world would suffer if nothing seemed settled in our principles for international affairs.

The design and planning of long-term policy initiatives might well benefit from partisan stimulation and criticism. But once a fundamental course of action has been clearly chosen, the nation cannot easily turn around. The claim that "politics should stop at the water's edge" has a certain validity if the American people have to make sacrifices in support of the chosen policy—in particular if American troops are involved in fighting. The force of this injunction, however, depends on the degree of consensus and clarity of purpose with which the national undertaking was started, and on the President's ability to maintain a sense of direction.

Without responsible partisanship in foreign affairs, the American people are denied the opportunity to express a choice and make a commitment. Without the nationwide resources of the Parties and the stimulation of the election process, the issues will remain remote and consensus superficial. And without the testing and tempering of partisanship, the nation cannot forge the genuine bipartisan support that will be needed in a period of severe trial.

QUESTIONS FOR DISCUSSION

1. What are the advantages of bipartisanship in foreign policy?
2. What are the disadvantages of bipartisanship in foreign policy?
3. How can bipartisanship in foreign policy be reconciled with the principles of democracy?
4. What are the strengths and weaknesses of strong presidential consultation with Congress in foreign policy matters?
5. What are the strengths and weaknesses of dictatorships as compared to a United States divided on foreign policy?

SUGGESTED READINGS

Burnham, Walter Dean. "Political Gridlock." *New Perspectives Quarterly*, 5 (Spring 1988), pp. 16–23.

Center for Strategic and International Studies. *Forging Bipartisanship*. Washington, D.C.: Center for Strategic and International Studies, Georgetown University, 1984.

Chace, James. "Is a Foreign Policy Consensus Possible?" *Foreign Affairs*, 57 (Fall 1978), pp. 1–16.

Edwards, George C., III. "The Two Presidencies: A Reevaluation." *American Politics Quarterly*, 14 (July 1986), pp. 247–63.

Falk, Richard. "Lifting the Curse of Bipartisanship." *World Policy Journal*, 1 (Fall 1983), pp. 127–57.

Gelb, Leslie H., and Richard K. Betts. *The Irony of Vietnam: The System Worked*. Washington, D.C.: Brookings Institution, 1979.

Kissinger, Henry A. "Continuity and Change in American Foreign Policy." *Society*, 15 (Nov.–Dec. 1977), pp. 97–103.

Reichard, Gary W. "Divisions and Dissent: Democrats and Foreign Policy, 1952–1956." *Political Science Quarterly*, 93 (Spring 1978), pp. 51–72.

Rourke, John T. "Congress and the Cold War." *World Affairs*, 139 (Spring 1977), pp. 259–77.

Schwenninger, Sherle R., and Jerry W. Sanders. "The Democrats and a New Grand Strategy." *World Policy Journal*, 3 (Summer 1986), pp. 369–418.

6 Is a System of Permanent Alliances in America's National Interest?

YES

John Foster Dulles

Challenge and Response in United States Policy

NO

George Washington

Farewell Address to the People of the United States

Challenge and Response in United States Policy

John Foster Dulles

The 35th anniversary of the founding of *Foreign Affairs* is a suitable occasion for comment on the evolution of United States foreign policy and the rôle we can play today in accord with our enduring national principles. During this third of a century, the American people have altered their conception as to the proper part which their Government should take in world affairs.

Since the founding of this nation, the American people have believed that it had a mission in the world. They have believed that "their conduct and example" ("The Federalist," No. 1) would influence events throughout the world and promote the spread of free institutions. But they have traditionally felt that it would be better for their Government to avoid involvement in international issues. So, with rare exceptions, the United States left the field of international politics to the governments of the "Great Powers" of the nineteenth century.

It took the First World War to bring us into major involvement in world crises and conflicts. Then in the decade of the thirties a series of critical events culminated in the greatest of all wars. By its end, a transformation had been effected. It had become obvious that the conduct and example of our people no longer, alone, sufficed to prevent recurrent challenges to our security and our way of life.

Excerpted from John Foster Dulles, "Challenge and Response in United States Policy," *Foreign Affairs,* 36 (Oct. 1957), pp. 25–30. Reprinted by permission of *Foreign Affairs.* Copyright (1957) by the Council of Foreign Relations, Inc.

It was also apparent that only in association with others could we repel such challenges. Furthermore, our national power had grown to be so impressive as to preclude its being merely a reserved, negative force.

Thus, since 1945, our Government has played a leading rôle in a coalition of free nations dedicated to the principles of international order to which our people have long subscribed.

There still remains a nostalgia for the "good old days." This is reinforced by recurrent demonstrations that, great as is our strength, we are not omnipotent. We cannot, by fiat, produce the kind of a world we want. Even nations which depend greatly upon us do not always follow what we believe to be the right course. For they are independent nations, and not our satellites. Our power and policy are but one significant factor in the world in which we live. In combination with other factors we are able to influence importantly the course of events. But we cannot deal in absolutes. This, to many Americans, is a source of worriment.

The American people may not yet have completely accepted the rôle that history has made inevitable. But at least a good beginning has been made. It is unlikely that there could now be a successful effort to withdraw the United States Government from official and active participation in international affairs. But in order that such participation should command popular support, our foreign policies should be more than politics. They must evidently reflect the traditional aspirations of our people.

II. COMMUNIST HOSTILITY

United States foreign policy since 1945 has been forced to concern itself primarily with one major threat to the peaceful and orderly development of the kind of international community the American people desire. This is the threat posed by those who direct the totalitarian system of International Communism. Because orthodox Communism represents a materialistic and atheistic creed, it inevitably is repugnant to those who believe in the supremacy of the spirit. Because it seeks world rule through the domination of all governments by the International Communist Party, it is repugnant to all who understand its purposes and, as patriots, cherish national independence. And because it employs fraud and violence to achieve its ends, it is repugnant to all who seek a world society of decency and order.

The United States, as the strongest nation of the non-Communist world, has had the major responsibility for meeting this challenge which, since 1950, has been able to exploit the resources of most of the Eurasian land mass and one-third of the world's population.

Since the death of Stalin in March 1953, there has been a Soviet disavowal of the ruthlessness of the Stalinist period. Internally, that disavowal has found some practical expression. Externally, Soviet policy has been marked by a more diversified range of political, diplomatic and economic tactics vis-à-vis the non-Communist world. This became especially pronounced in 1955. There were such gestures as the sudden consent to a long-overdue Austrian treaty and the overtures to Jugoslavia. At the "summit" conference at Geneva there were professions of peaceful intent and an agreement to reunify Germany by free elections. There were profuse offers of "assistance" to many nations and a plea for "cultural relations."

But nowhere, except perhaps in Austria, did the Soviets yield anything of substance or enter into genuine negotiations on basic issues. Economic and military "assistance" was a Trojan horse whereby influence could be gained to promote political subversion. There was no honest acceptance of Jugoslavia's right to have a national Communist government not dominated by International Communism. And in November 1955 at Geneva the Soviet Government flatly repudiated the July "summit" agreement for German reunification.

The year 1956 gave further evidence that the new rulers in Moscow were not essentially changed. Enticements were mingled with threats. When "de-Stalinization," proclaimed by the Twentieth Party Congress in February 1956, was interpreted in the satellites as justifying more freedom and independence, there were fierce reactions first at Poznan, Poland, and then in Hungary. Obviously, those who presently dictate the doctrines of International Communism are not in fact prepared to accept the consequences of their professed liberalization.

In all the 40 years of Bolshevik rule there is no episode more brutal than the Red Army suppression of the Hungarian people's 1956 uprising against intolerable oppression. And recent Soviet policies in the Near East are inexcusably mischievous.

That area, rich in cultural and religious tradition, yet stricken with historic dissensions and tragic poverty, was chosen in 1955 to be the scene of a new Communist hunt for power. Communist propaganda studiously sought to inflame animosities. The Soviet Government, drawing upon its semi-obsolete war equipment, stimulated an arms race. As a direct or indirect result, violence and bitterness were increased and abject poverty was riveted more firmly as some governments mortgaged the future economic productivity of the people in order to buy Soviet arms. It has indeed been a cynical performance by those who profess to love peace and to desire to uplift the masses.

More than a decade of cold war experience has confirmed our earlier judgments of International Communism. It, and the governments it controls, are deeply hostile to us and to all free and independent governments. Its basic doctrine precludes its changing of its own accord. Self-advertised changes must be considered as mere stratagems.

We need not, however, despair. International Communism is subject to change even against its will. It is not impervious to the erosion of time and circumstance. Khrushchev's speech of February 1956, the July 1957 shake-up in the ruling clique at Moscow, and Mao's speech of February 27, 1957, indicate that even in Russia and the China mainland Soviet and Chinese Communist régimes are confronted with grave internal pressures and dilemmas. The yeast of change is at work, despite all the efforts of "democratic centralism" to keep matters moving in a strictly Leninist pattern. The rulers in Russia do not find it possible to combine industrial and military modernization with the personal repressions of the Middle Ages; and the rulers in China will not find it possible to fit the richly diversified culture of the Chinese into a Communist mold of conformity.

The time may come, indeed we can be confident that it will come, when the nations now ruled by International Communism will have governments which, whatever their label, in fact serve their own nations and their own peoples rather than the insatiable world-wide ambitions of an international Party. There will be broadening participation in government. There will be increasing personal security under law. There will be a significant degree of freedom of thought and expression. And the workers will be permitted to have some choice of the work that they do and to enjoy more of the fruits of their labor. Under those conditions, the people, if not the masters of their government, will at least not be its abject slaves. Vast military power will no longer be completely at the disposal of those who accept no restraints either of a governmental or moral character and whose goal is world-wide rule. When that day comes, we can rejoice. Until that day comes, we shall need to remain on our guard.

III. COLLECTIVE SECURITY

During the last two decades, the United States has found it necessary to recast its ideas and policies regarding national security. The course of our thinking and planning has been in the direction of collective security. In our modern world no nation, however powerful, can find safety in isolation, and security for one is only to be achieved through coöperation with other like-minded nations.

The society of nations is undergoing the transformation that occurs whenever primitive societies develop. There is a gradual evolution from conditions where security is a matter of each for himself and the Devil take the hindmost, to a condition where security is a collective effort to which each contributes and from which each benefits. In that way there is greater security at less cost. The society of nations is gradually and painfully evolving from a primitive condition to one where security is a matter of collective effort and where defense is a common defense.

It is not easy to realize these principles in a world where people have long thought of sovereignty as a status unqualified by interdependence. Yet after a second generation of bitter experience, the United States, with many others, sees the indispensability of interdependence. Today we seek security through the strengthening of universal institutions, by regional arrangements, by maintaining military capabilities in conjunction with our allies, and by determined efforts to diminish the risk of surprise attack and to limit and control armaments.

In 1945 the United States took the lead in organizing the United Nations. We hoped that it would become an effective instrument of collective security. But it still falls short of being that. United Nations action in a divided world has often been paralyzed. For example, the U.S.S.R. has exercised the veto in the Security Council about 80 times. No joint U.N. military force has been set up as contemplated in the Charter, although Korea and Suez point to possible progress in this direction. Also, the Assembly, in the Suez and Hungarian crises of last fall, displayed surprising determination and virtual unanimity.

It is sometimes said by way of reproach that in these matters the United Nations applied a "double standard"—severity toward Israel, France and the United Kingdom, and leniency toward the Soviet Union. This charge has no basis in fact. The Assembly resolutions directed against the use of force in Egypt and in Hungary were equally peremptory.

The double standard was not in the United Nations, but in the nations. There was the moral sensitivity of the Western nations, and their decent respect for the opinions of mankind. There was the immorality of Soviet Communism, and its contempt for the opinions of mankind. We can rejoice that, among the nations, there are governments having standards higher than those of the Government of Soviet Russia. That is not a matter of reproach to them, or to the United Nations.

Despite hopeful indications of progress in the United Nations, the nations of the free world which felt endangered have, for the most part, felt it necessary to resort to collective, and usually regional, arrangements to safeguard their security. This has been in entire accord with the Charter. In this development the United States has assumed a major rôle and responsibility. Since 1945 we have entered into collective security treaties with 42 other nations and we have less formal arrangements with several more.

The first such treaty—the Rio Pact—was with our own neighbors of this hemisphere. We went on to broaden the base of collective security through a series of multilateral and bilateral pacts which now encompass much of the free world. The forces of NATO [North Atlantic Treaty Organization], now including the Federal Republic of Germany, stand guard over the treaty-defined North Atlantic region which includes the vital area of Western Europe. In the West Pacific and Far East, the SEATO [South East Asia Treaty Organization] and ANZUS [Australia–New Zealand–United States] pacts and four bilateral treaties establish the principle that a threat to one is the concern of all. In the Middle East, the Baghdad Pact and the Eisenhower Doctrine assure collective response to Communist aggression at points of special danger or weakness. This nearly world-wide system of regional collective security has served all the participants well. It has deterred aggression and given much-needed assurance to peoples who are especially exposed to attack.

We must, in candor, admit that all of the participants do not look upon these arrangements alike. Some consider them broad political alliances, binding the parties, at least morally, to support each other generally. But the net result has been to further the application of the principle of collective security within the society of nations.

Farewell Address to the People of the United States

George Washington

Observe good faith and justice towards all nations; cultivate peace and harmony with all. Religion and morality enjoin this conduct, and can it be that good policy does not equally enjoin it? It will be worthy of a free, enlightened, and, at no distant period, a great nation, to give to mankind the magnanimous and too novel example of a people always guided by an exalted justice and benevolence. Who can doubt but, in the course of time and things, the fruits of such a plan would richly repay any temporary advantages which might be lost by a steady adherence to it; can it be that Providence has not connected the permanent felicity of a nation with its virtue? The experiment, at least, is recommended by every sentiment which ennobles human nature. Alas! is it rendered impossible by its vices?

In the execution of such a plan, nothing is more essential than that permanent, inveterate antipathies against particular nations and passionate attachment for others, should be excluded; and that, in place of them, just and amicable feelings towards all should be cultivated. The nation which indulges towards another an habitual hatred, or an habitual fondness, is in some degree a slave. It is a slave to its animosity or to its affection, either of which is sufficient to lead it astray from its duty and its interest. Antipathy in one nation against another, disposes each more readily to offer insult and injury, to lay hold of slight causes of umbrage, and to be haughty and intractable when accidental or trifling occasions of dispute occur. Hence, frequent collisions, obstinate, envenomed, and bloody contests. The nation, prompted by ill will and resentment, sometimes impels to war the government, contrary to the best calculations of policy. The government sometimes participates in the national propensity, and adopts through passion what reason would reject; at other times, it makes the animosity of the nation subservient to projects of hostility, instigated by pride, ambition, and other sinister and pernicious motives. The peace often, sometimes perhaps the liberty of nations, has been the victim.

So likewise, a passionate attachment of one nation for another produces a variety of evils. Sympathy for the favorite nation, facilitating the illusion of an imaginary common interest, in cases where no real common interest exists, and infusing into one the enmities of the other, betrays the former into a participation in the quarrels and wars of the latter, without adequate inducements or justifications. It leads also to concessions, to the favorite nation, of privileges denied to others, which is apt doubly to injure the nation making the concessions, by unnecessarily parting with what ought to have been retained, and by exciting jealousy, ill will, and a disposition to retaliate in the parties from whom equal privileges are withheld; and it gives to ambitious, corrupted or deluded citizens who devote themselves to the favorite nation, facility to betray or sacrifice the interests of their own country, without odium, sometimes even with popularity; gilding with the appearances of a virtuous sense of obligation, a commendable deference for public opinion, or a laudable zeal for public good, the base or foolish compliances of ambition, corruption, or infatuation.

As avenues to foreign influence in innumerable ways, such attachments are particu-

Excerpted from George Washington, "Farewell Address to the People of the United States," House Document 504, U.S., 89th Cong., 2d Sess., 1966, pp. 20–28. First published in the *Daily American Advertiser* (Philadelphia), Sept. 19, 1796.

larly alarming to the truly enlightened and independent patriot. How many opportunities do they afford to tamper with domestic factions, to practice the arts of seduction, to mislead public opinion, to influence or awe the public councils!—Such an attachment of a small or weak, toward a great and powerful nation, dooms the former to be the satellite of the latter.

Against the insidious wiles of foreign influence, (I conjure you to believe me fellow citizens,) the jealousy of a free people ought to be *constantly* awake; since history and experience prove, that foreign influence is one of the most baneful foes of republican government. But that jealousy, to be useful, must be impartial, else it becomes the instrument of the very influence to be avoided, instead of a defense against it. Excessive partiality for one foreign nation and excessive dislike for another, cause those whom they actuate to see danger only on one side, and serve to veil and even second the arts of influence on the other. Real patriots, who may resist the intrigues of the favorite, are liable to become suspected and odious; while its tools and dupes usurp the applause and confidence of the people, to surrender their interests.

The great rule of conduct for us, in regard to foreign nations, is, in extending our commercial relations, to have with them as little *political* connection as possible. So far as we have already formed engagements, let them be fulfilled with perfect good faith:—Here let us stop.

Europe has a set of primary interests, which to us have none, or a very remote relation. Hence, she must be engaged in frequent controversies, the causes of which are essentially foreign to our concerns. Hence, therefore, it must be unwise in us to implicate ourselves, by artificial ties, in the ordinary vicissitudes of her politics, or the ordinary combinations and collisions of her friendships or enmities.

Our detached and distant situation invites and enables us to pursue a different course. If we remain one people, under an efficient government, the period is not far off when we may defy material injury from external annoyance; when we may take such an attitude as will cause the neutrality we may at any time resolve upon, to be scrupulously respected; when belligerent nations, under the impossibility of making acquisitions upon us, will not lightly hazard the giving us provocation, when we may choose peace or war, as our interest, guided by justice, shall counsel.

Why forego the advantages of so peculiar a situation? Why quit our own to stand upon foreign ground? Why, by interweaving our destiny with that of any part of Europe, entangle our peace and prosperity in the toils of European ambition, rivalship, interest, humor, or caprice?

It is our true policy to steer clear of permanent alliance with any portion of the foreign world; so far, I mean, as we are now at liberty to do it; for let me not be understood as capable of patronizing infidelity to existing engagements. I hold the maxim no less applicable to public than private affairs, that honesty is always the best policy. I repeat it, therefore, let those engagements be observed in their genuine sense. But in my opinion, it is unnecessary, and would be unwise to extend them.

Taking care always to keep ourselves by suitable establishments, on a respectable defensive posture, we may safely trust to temporary alliances for extraordinary emergencies.

Harmony, and a liberal intercourse with all nations, are recommended by policy, humanity, and interest. But even our commercial policy should hold an equal and impartial hand; neither seeking nor granting exclusive favors or preferences; consulting the natural course of things; diffusing and diversifying by gentle means the streams of commerce, but forcing nothing; establishing with powers so disposed, in order to give trade a stable course, to define the rights of our merchants, and to enable the government to support them, conventional rules of intercourse, the best that present circumstances and mutual opinion will permit, but temporary, and liable to be from time to time abandoned or varied as experience and circumstances shall dictate; constantly keeping in view, that it is folly in one nation to look for disinterested favors from another; that it must pay with a portion of its independence for whatever it may accept under that character; that by such acceptance, it may place itself in the condition of having given equivalents for nominal favors, and yet of being reproached with ingratitude for not giving more. There can be no greater error than to expect, or calculate upon real favors from nation to nation. It is an illusion which experience must cure, which a just pride ought to discard.

In offering to you, my countrymen, these counsels of an old and affectionate friend, I dare not hope they will make the strong and lasting impression I could wish; that they will control the usual current of the passions, or prevent our nation from running the course which has hitherto marked the destiny of nations, but if I may even flatter myself that they may be productive of some partial benefit, some occasional good; that they may now and then recur to moderate the fury of party spirit, to warn against the mischiefs of foreign intrigue, to guard against the impostures of pretended patriotism; this hope will be a full recompense for the solicitude for your welfare by which they have been dictated. . . .

The duty of holding a neutral conduct may be inferred, without any thing more, from the obligation which justice and humanity impose on every nation, in cases in which it is free to act, to maintain inviolate the relations of peace and amity towards other nations.

The inducements of interest for observing that conduct will best be referred to your own reflections and experience. With me, a predominant motive has been to endeavor to gain time to our country to settle and mature its yet recent institutions, and to progress, without interruption, to that degree of strength, and consistency which is necessary to give it, humanly speaking, the command of its own fortunes.

Though in reviewing the incidents of my administration, I am unconscious of intentional error, I am nevertheless too sensible of my defects not to think it probable that I may have committed many errors. Whatever they may be, I fervently beseech the Almighty to avert or mitigate the evils to which they may tend. I shall also carry with me the hope that my country will never cease to view them with indulgence; and that, after forty-five years of my life dedicated to its service, with an upright zeal, the faults of incompetent abilities will be consigned to oblivion, as myself must soon be to the mansions of rest.

QUESTIONS FOR DISCUSSION

1. What are the purposes of alliances?
2. What comments about foreign affairs from George Washington's Farewell Address are valid today?
3. What effect would the withdrawal by the United States from its alliances have on U.S. national security?
4. Had the United States not entered into any alliances in the post–World War II years, how would world politics have been affected?
5. Which U.S. alliances have been most effective? Why?
6. Which U.S. alliances have been least effective? Why?

SUGGESTED READINGS

Deibel, Terry L. "Hidden Commitments." *Foreign Policy*, no. 67 (Summer 1987), pp. 46–63.

Friedman, Julian R., Christopher Bladen, and Steven Rosen, eds. *Alliance in International Politics*. Boston: Allyn and Bacon, 1970.

Gilbert, Felix. *To the Farewell Address*. Princeton, N.J.: Princeton University Press, 1961.

Guhin, Michael A. *John Foster Dulles: A Statesman and His Times.* New York: Columbia University Press, 1972.

Holsti, Oley R., P. Terrence Hopmann, and John D. Sullivan. *Unity and Disintegration in International Alliances.* Lanham, Md.: University Press of America, 1985. Originally published New York: Wiley, 1973.

Hoopes, Townsend. *The Devil and John Foster Dulles.* Boston: Little, Brown, 1973.

O'Neill, Robert John. *Alliances and International Order: An Inaugural Lecture Delivered before the University of Oxford on 20 November 1987.* New York: Oxford University Press, 1988.

Osgood, Robert E. *Alliances and American Foreign Policy.* Baltimore: Johns Hopkins University Press, 1968.

Sabrosky, Alan Ned, ed. *Alliances in U.S. Foreign Policy: Issues in the Quest for Collective Defense.* Boulder, Colo.: Westview Press, 1988.

Walt, Stephen M. *The Origins of Alliances.* Ithaca, N.Y.: Cornell University Press, 1987.

Wolfers, Arnold, ed. *Alliance Policy in the Cold War.* Baltimore: Johns Hopkins University Press, 1959.

PART TWO

The Process of Foreign Policy

"The Constitution," said Justice Arthur Goldberg, "is not a suicide pact." Justice Goldberg was speaking of the absolute necessity to defend the nation against foreign aggression. But at the same time, Goldberg cautioned that those responsible for America's security were subject to the restraints imposed by the Constitution. "The imperative necessity for safeguarding rights and liberties under the gravest of emergencies," said Goldberg, "has existed throughout our constitutional history, for it is then, under the pressing exigencies of crisis, that there is the greatest temptation to dispense with fundamental constitutional guarantees which, it is feared, will inhibit governmental action."[1] Or as the Supreme Court said shortly after the Civil War: "The Constitution of the United States is a law for rulers and people, equally in war and in peace, and covers with the shield of its protection all classes of men, at all times, and under all circumstances."[2]

The problem of balancing American democracy and national security has been made much more difficult by the superpower responsibilities thrust on the United States at the close of World War II. Those responsibilities, borne now for almost fifty years, have led to an enormous growth in the size and authority of the federal government and a particular increase in the power of the executive branch. As one writer has suggested, "Imperial responsibility demands imperial government, which naturally encourages an imperial presidency."[3]

The current organization of the U.S. government for the conduct of for-

---

[1] *Kennedy v. Mendoza-Martinez*, 372 U.S. 144, 146 (1963).
[2] *Ex Parte Milligan*, 4 Wallace (71 U.S.) 2, 120 (1866).
[3] Charles Krauthammer, "The Price of Power," *New Republic*, 196 (Feb. 9, 1987), p. 23.

eign policy traces to the National Security Act of 1947. Although the United States (and its allies) emerged triumphant from World War II, it had become painfully apparent by 1945 that the American governmental structure was too disjointed and uncoordinated to provide effective foreign policy leadership. The Army and the Navy existed as separate cabinet departments; the Air Corps was a subordinate branch of the Army; intelligence gathering by the individual services went uncoordinated; and there was no institutional mechanism to bring the State Department, the Army, and the Navy together to fashion a common policy. Critics pointed to the debacle at Pearl Harbor and the failure to blend diplomacy and military power in arranging the boundaries of postwar Europe as prime examples of the need to provide better coordination for U.S. policy. In particular, the smooth functioning of the British war cabinet under Winston Churchill was cited as a useful example of how effective political leadership could bring together the diplomatic, military, and intelligence services and fashion an effective policy that was responsive to the government's desires.

The lessons of World War II, and to some extent the model of the British war cabinet, became the basis for the National Security Act of 1947. The military services were combined into a single cabinet-level Department of Defense; the Air Force was made an independent service; the military heads of the three services were given statutory recognition as the Joint Chiefs of Staff (JCS); a Central Intelligence Agency (CIA) was established to coordinate U.S. intelligence activities; and at the highest level, a National Security Council (NSC) was created. The NSC has four statutory members: the president, vice-president, secretary of state, and secretary of defense, plus such additional members (e.g., the director of Central Intelligence and the chairman of the JCS) as the president might designate. The purpose of the NSC, like that of the British war cabinet, is to ensure the coordination of U.S. diplomatic, military, and intelligence activities. But unlike Britain's war cabinet, the NSC—at President Harry S. Truman's firm insistence—is merely an advisory body.[4] Final constitutional authority rests with the president. The language of the National Security Act is explicit in that respect: "The function of the Council [NSC] *shall be to advise the President* with respect to the integration of domestic, foreign, and military policies relating to national security."[5]

Under President Truman, the NSC provided a forum for the discussion and integration of foreign policy. The staff was small, the secretaries of state (George Marshall and Dean Acheson) and the secretaries of defense (Louis Johnson and later Marshall) directed foreign and military policy, and President Truman made the final decisions. Under President Dwight D. Eisen-

---

[4] See esp. Demitrios Caraley, *The Politics of Military Unification* (New York: Columbia University Press, 1966), pp. 313–14.

[5] National Security Act, July 26, 1947, PL 253, 80th Cong., in *Documents of American History*, ed. Henry Steele Commager and Milton Cantor (Englewood Cliffs, N.J.: Prentice Hall, 1988), 2:541.

hower, the staff of the NSC was expanded to permit department coordination through an extensive committee system at the subcabinet level, but operational responsibility continued to remain in the departments. Unlike Truman, Eisenhower preferred consensus recommendations from the NSC, but he retained final authority and on more than one occasion—most notably on the subject of relief of the French garrison at Dien Bien Phu in Indochina—rejected that recommendation.

The emergence of the NSC staff as independent policy advocates commenced during the administration of John F. Kennedy. President Kennedy was not fully satisfied with the advice and responsiveness of the State and Defense departments and commissioned NSC staff director McGeorge Bundy to develop alternative policies on many national security issues. Under Bundy, the NSC staff played less of a coordinating role than a policy-making role. This practice continued into the administrations of Lyndon B. Johnson and Richard M. Nixon. The title of the NSC staff director was changed to national security adviser (NSA) to the president, and under Walt Whitman Rostow and Henry Kissinger the NSC staff began to assume an operational role as well. The president retained full constitutional authority, and the NSC provided him with the immediate means for conducting national security policy directly from the White House. The advantage was that the president could move swiftly to take important foreign policy initiatives, such as Nixon's opening to China in the early 1970s. The disadvantage was that the NSC became a rival to the established departments. U.S. policy sometimes was not only poorly integrated but badly executed as well. The operational control exercised by the White House over the ill-fated hostage rescue mission during the administration of Jimmy Carter and the Iran-Contra affair under President Ronald Reagan suggest that the NSC and its staff were something less than reliable as an effective tool of American policy.

THE DIPLOMATIC ESTABLISHMENT

The *U.S. Government Manual* provides that it is to the State Department that the president looks for his primary advice in the formulation and execution of foreign policy.[6] But in recent years the State Department has seen its authority steadily erode. As successive U.S. presidents have taken greater personal interest in foreign policy, the latitude for the State Department has diminished. The role of the White House staff has increased, while the role of State Department professionals has declined. Even the secretary of state no longer plays the dominant role in U.S. foreign policy that Acheson, Marshall, and John Foster Dulles exercised in the immediate postwar period.

The origins of the Department of State date to the Committee of Secret Correspondence established by the Continental Congress in 1775. Under the

---

[6] Office of Federal Register, National Archives and Records Administration, *The United States Government Manual, 1988–89* (Washington, D.C.: Government Printing Office, 1988), p. 422.

Articles of Confederation, a committee on foreign affairs chaired by John Jay handled American diplomacy. Following George Washington's inauguration as president, the First Congress created the Department of State, and Thomas Jefferson was appointed by Washington to be the first secretary of state. Under Jefferson, the United States had but two foreign missions—one in London, the other in Paris—and the entire department staff consisted of four clerks and a translator. Under President Reagan, the State Department's annual budget approached $2 billion; there were 144 embassies abroad, 4,000 professional foreign service officers (FSOs), and more than 23,000 employees.[7] Yet the political clout wielded by the State Department within the government today may well be less than that in Jefferson's time.

The State Department is the nation's diplomatic message center. Approximately ten thousand messages are processed daily. Several hundred of these deal with important policy matters, although the secretary of state is likely to see only a dozen or so and the president but one or two.[8] Critics contend that one of the reasons for the State Department's decline in policy making is that the career officers of the Foreign Service tend to be insensitive to presidential priorities. Regardless of the issue, advice from State (so it is charged) tends to stress minimizing risks, avoiding action, and adopting a long-term perspective.[9] In the words of I. M. Destler, the State Department "desk officer 'inherits' a policy toward country X, [and] he regards it as his function to keep that policy intact."[10]

President Franklin D. Roosevelt believed that the Foreign Service opposed the social and economic goals of the New Deal. As a result, he shut the State Department out of wartime diplomacy. President John F. Kennedy thought that the Department of State was incapable of providing the policy alternatives he sought or of effectively implementing the policies he adopted. The result, once again, was a concentration of diplomatic activity in the White House. President Richard M. Nixon also believed that State Department professionals were out of sympathy with his administration. Roosevelt had thought they were too conservative; Nixon considered them too liberal. But the result was the same. Increasingly, the most serious issues of foreign policy gravitated to the White House.

But the State Department remains America's repository of expertise pertaining to foreign affairs. It provides continuity from administration to administration as well as an understanding of distant societies that transcends American politics. This expertise has proved to be an advantage and a dis-

---

[7] Telephone interview with Ambassador Ronald Spiers, Deputy Assistant Secretary for Management, U.S. Department of State, May 17, 1989.

[8] Werner Feld, *American Foreign Policy: Aspirations and Reality* (New York: Wiley and Sons, 1984), p. 61. See also Gene Rainey, *Patterns of American Foreign Policy* (Boston: Allyn and Bacon, 1975).

[9] See esp. Robert Pringle, "Creeping Irrelevance in Foggy Bottom," *Foreign Policy*, no. 29 (Winter 1977–78), pp. 128–39.

[10] I. M. Destler, *President, Bureaucrats, and Foreign Policy: The Politics of Organizational Reform* (Princeton, N.J.: Princeton University Press, 1972), p. 158.

advantage. On the negative side, it means that State has no important domestic constituency in the United States. Unlike the Department of Defense
(or the Department of Agriculture, for that matter), there is no potential pool
of supporters ready to rally to its support. This lack of a domestic constituency inevitably diminishes the voice of the State Department in the councils
of government, particularly on Capitol Hill. On the positive side, the collective expertise of State Department professionals informs presidential decision
making and provides a much-needed stability to American foreign policy.
For example, it would be difficult to contemplate U.S.-Soviet relations without the pivotal role played by professional American diplomats since 1933.
But the State Department is there to be used as the president chooses. Under
the Constitution, only the president is responsible for the conduct of U.S.
foreign policy. And the secretary of state serves at the president's pleasure.

THE MILITARY ESTABLISHMENT

Since 1947, American military forces have been organized under a single
cabinet-level department: the Department of Defense (DOD). The Army,
Navy, and Air Force exist as separate military departments within DOD. The
secretary of defense is the president's ranking adviser on defense matters
and a statutory member of the NSC. The departments of the Army, Navy,
and Air Force each have a civilian secretary, but his or her functions are primarily administrative. Since 1949, the service secretaries have not been members of the cabinet or the NSC. The secretary of defense and the service secretaries provide tangible evidence of *civilian control* of the military. They serve
at the pleasure of the president and administer their departments in his
name.

Each military service is organized along strict *chain-of-command* principles.
The president, as the constitutional commander in chief, exercises the absolute right of command within the military.[11] The president is the highest
source of military authority. In this sense the president's role differs fundamentally from that of Britain's prime minister or West Germany's chancellor.
The U.S. president is the actual military commander of American armed
forces. His words are military commands. In Great Britain, it is the monarch
who heads the armed forces, and the prime minister, on behalf of the government, acts in the name of the crown. The prime minister's authority,
while real, is much more indirect.

The constitutional status of the president as commander in chief is a
source of immense foreign policy authority. It provides for an enormous concentration of power in the hands of a single individual. And except for the
political check exercised by the Congress and the electorate, that authority is
to be used by the president at his discretion in the national interest. As Justice Joseph Story said on behalf of the Supreme Court in the leading case of

---

[11] *Fleming v. Page*, 9 Howard (50 U.S.) 603 (1850).

Martin v. Mott, upholding President James Madison's use of the militia in the War of 1812, the president alone "is necessarily constituted the judge of the existence of the exigency, and is bound to act according to *his* belief of the facts."[12] This judgment and similar decisions by the Supreme Court give to the president extraordinary, singular authority. In foreign affairs, this authority is much more reminiscent of the royal prerogative exercised by the absolute monarchs of the seventeenth century than the head of a modern constitutional democracy. In positive terms, this permits the United States to respond immediately to threats from abroad. In a negative sense, it is a power that is exercised largely beyond the bounds of constitutional control.[13]

The senior military officer in each service is a chief of staff, not a commanding general. This arrangement reflects the reforms effected by Elihu Root, secretary of war during the administration of William Howard Taft, and is designed to emphasize the political control over the services exercised by the president. It is the president who is commander in chief; the ranking military officer is his chief of staff. The terminology in the Navy differs, but the effect is the same. (The ranking naval officer is the chief of naval operations, whose duty it is to "fight the fleet" under the president's direction.)

The uniformed chiefs meet to coordinate military policy as the Joint Chiefs of Staff. The JCS, like the NSC, is modeled after Britain's wartime example—in this instance, the Imperial General Staff. The purpose of the JCS is to ensure that the military activities of each service are fully integrated into U.S. defense policy. The JCS is presided over by a chairman appointed by the president, who is by statute the president's senior military adviser. The JCS is charged with the planning and conduct of military operations under the president's direction and is assisted by a Joint Staff composed of officers drawn from various services. The commandant of the Marine Corps is also a member of the JCS.

Like the State Department, the JCS system has come under heavy criticism. And like State, its strengths appear to be its weaknesses as well. The coordination and integration of military policy achieved by the JCS necessarily involves compromise. This situation has led critics (both inside and outside the military) to argue that the need to compromise divergent views reduces the ability of the JCS to provide clearly stated and incisive military advice and that its handling of operational matters has been marked by a similar indecisiveness.

THE INTELLIGENCE ESTABLISHMENT

No aspect of the conduct of foreign policy is more charged with danger for democratic processes than intelligence activity, and perhaps no aspect is

---

[12] *Martin v. Mott*, 12 Wheaton (25 U.S.) 19 (1827), italics added.
[13] *The Prize Cases*, 2 Black (67 U.S.) 635 (1862); *Ex Parte Quirin*, 317 U.S. 1 (1942). Compare *Youngstown Sheet and Tube v. Sawyer*, 343 U.S. 579 (1952).

more vital. Advance warning of the plans, intentions, and capabilities of foreign states is an essential ingredient of successful statecraft. But the requisite secrecy that surrounds such activity can itself spawn irresponsibility and abuse—as the Iran-Contra affair revealed. The Supreme Court has recognized the dilemma but for the most part has tilted in favor of the imperatives of national security. As Justice Robert H. Jackson stated in *Chicago and Southern Airlines v. Waterman:*

> The President, both as Commander in Chief and as the Nation's organ for foreign affairs, has available intelligence services whose reports are not and ought not to be published to the world. It would be intolerable that courts, without the relevant information, should review and perhaps nullify actions of the Executive taken or information properly held secret.[14]

Even the use of military intelligence agencies for domestic surveillance has been sustained by the Court.[15]

The Central Intelligence Agency was established in 1947 in an effort to consolidate U.S. intelligence activities. Under the terms of the National Security Act, the CIA is to:

1. advise the National Security Council on intelligence matters related to national security
2. make recommendations to the NSC for coordinating the intelligence activities of government agencies
3. correlate, evaluate, and disseminate intelligence within the government
4. perform additional services for existing intelligence agencies that the NSC believes can be done best by a central organization
5. perform other functions and duties relating to national security intelligence directed by the NSC.

The CIA succeeded the Office of Strategic Services (OSS), which had been created in World War II to collect and analyze strategic information for the JCS and to plan and operate such special services as might be directed. But the routine role of OSS was never clear, and the question of whether U.S. intelligence activities should be centralized under a single head or the nation was best served by a number of loosely coordinated but separate agencies was never resolved. And despite the label, the CIA is but one of several intelligence departments. The Bureau of Intelligence and Research (INR) in the State Department, the Defense Intelligence Agency (DIA), the National Security Agency (NSA), the Federal Bureau of Investigation (FBI), and the Department of the Treasury maintain distinct intelligence-gathering operations. The DIA and INR compete with the CIA in producing intelligence estimates of situations abroad, not infrequently with different results.

---

[14] *Chicago and Southern Airlines v. Waterman,* 333 U.S. 103, 106 (1948). See also *CIA v. Sims,* 417 U.S. 159 (1985).

[15] *Laird v. Tatum,* 408 U.S. 1 (1972).

The ultimate purpose of intelligence activity is to provide policy makers with advance warning. This is not easily done. Surprise is a fundamental reality of international politics, and no intelligence service can be clairvoyant. A related problem pertains to conflict between *intelligence* and *policy*. The conventional view holds that the analysis of intelligence information should be kept separate from policy formulation; this separation permits information to drive policy rather than allowing information to be distorted to support policy. But information analysis is not value free, and the distinction between policy and analysis is not as clear cut as it might appear. Finally, the issue of covert, clandestine operations has never been resolved. As the Tower Commission stated in its report, "Covert action places a great strain on the process of decision making in a free society."[16] The Iran-Contra affair is but the most recent example.

THE ROLES OF CONGRESS

Congress is the supreme legislative authority in the United States. Its control over public spending and the appropriations process is complete. Through its general oversight powers, it reviews the operation of government. In foreign policy, the Senate participates directly in the treaty process and must confirm senior executive and ambassadorial appointments. Most important, the war powers, other than the actual command of the armed forces, reside with Congress. As Alexander Hamilton noted in number 23 of *The Federalist Papers*, the war power of the United States is mainly an aggregate of the powers granted to Congress in Article I, section 8 of the Constitution.[17]

In the early case of *Talbot v. Seeman*, Chief Justice John Marshall noted, "The whole powers of war [were] by the Constitution...vested in Congress."[18] Marshall held to the view that Congress's power to declare war included the power to wage war, and in the leading case of *McCulloch v. Maryland* he listed the power "to declare *and conduct* war" as one of the enumerated powers from which he developed the doctrine of implied powers.[19] Chief Justice Salmon P. Chase in *Ex Parte Milligan* spoke of Congress's power to declare war as "necessarily" extending "to all legislation essential to the prosecution of war with vigor and success, except such as interferes with the

---

[16] John Tower, Edmund Muskie, and Brent Scowcroft, *The Tower Commission Report* (New York: Bantam Books, 1987), p. 15.

[17] Alexander Hamilton, James Madison, and John Jay, *The Federalist Papers*, ed. Clinton Rossiter (New York: New American Library, 1961), p. 153.

Article I, section 8 of the Constitution provides that "The Congress shall have power...To declare War, grant Letters of Marque and Reprisal, and make Rules concerning Captures on Land and Water; To raise and support Armies...; To provide and maintain a Navy; To make Rules for the Government and Regulation of the land and naval forces; To provide for calling forth the Militia...; To provide for organizing, arming, and disciplining, the Militia."

[18] *Talbot v. Seeman*, 1 Cranch (5 U.S.) 1 (1801). See also *Penhallow v. Doane*, 3 Dallas (3 U.S.) 54 (1795).

[19] *McCulloch v. Maryland*, 4 Wheaton (17 U.S.) 316, 407 (1819), italics added.

command of the forces and the conduct of campaigns."[20] In the aftermath of World War I, Chief Justice Edward D. White referred to the war power of Congress as "complete and undivided,"[21] while his successor, Chief Justice Charles Evans Hughes, described it as the "power to wage war successfully, [which] thus permits the harnessing of the entire energies of the people."[22]

The Supreme Court has recognized repeatedly that military action might occur without a formal declaration of war. As long ago as 1800 the Court distinguished between officially declared wars and partial, limited wars that were fought without a formal declaration. According to the Court: "Hostilities may subsist between two nations, more confined in nature and extent; being limited as to places, persons and things, and this is more properly termed imperfect war....Still, however, it is public war."[23]

As a general constitutional rule, the war powers entrusted to Congress include the exclusive authority to initiate offensive war. The president, as commander in chief, may respond to hostile attacks or threats of attack and enjoys total command of the armed forces. But the distinction is murky. Despite Congress's vast constitutional authority over the military, it is the president who usually makes the decision to deploy the armed forces.

Presidents from Thomas Jefferson to Ronald Reagan have used the military in combat when, in their judgment, the national interest required it. Occasionally presidential authority works in reverse. When a delegation from Congress called on President Grover Cleveland and told him, "We have decided to declare war against Spain over the Cuban question," Cleveland refused to fight. "There will be no war with Spain...while I am President," said Cleveland. As commander in chief, he said he would "not mobilize the army."[24]

Since World War II, U.S. use of forces abroad has increased significantly. Truman's decision to respond to communist aggression in Korea; the successive decisions of American presidents from Kennedy to Nixon to defend South Vietnam; and the use of force by Reagan in Grenada and Lebanon have raised important constitutional issues. Does Congress or the president have the final say? It is noteworthy that not all presidents have agreed on this question. Eisenhower, for example, declined to employ military forces abroad without explicit congressional approval. In 1955, when China threatened military action against the Pescadores and Formosa, and again in 1957 concerning Lebanon, Eisenhower asked Congress for specific authority to intervene.[25]

---

[20] *Ex Parte Milligan,* 4 Wallace (71 U.S.) 2, 131 (1866).

[21] *Northern Pacific Railway v. North Dakota,* 250 U.S. 135, 149 (1919).

[22] *Home Building and Loan Association v. Blaisdell,* 290 U.S. 398 (1934). See also *Lichter v. United States,* 334 U.S. 742 (1948).

[23] *Bas v. Tingy,* 4 Dallas (4 U.S.) 34 (1800).

[24] Robert McNutt McElroy, *Grover Cleveland, The Man and the Statesman: An Authorized Biography* (New York: Harper and Bros., 1923), 2:249–50.

[25] Formosa Resolution of 1955, 84th Cong., 1st Sess., H. J. Res. 159; Joint Resolution to Promote Peace and Stability in the Middle East, 85th Cong., 1st Sess., H. J. Res. 117.

Subsequent presidents have departed from Eisenhower's policy. When Kennedy intercepted Soviet ships carrying missiles bound for Cuba, he did so on his own authority as commander in chief without seeking official congressional approval. Similarly, the initial deployment of U.S. forces in Vietnam under Kennedy and Johnson was accomplished by presidential action alone. In 1964, when massive intervention appeared necessary, Johnson asked Congress for a resolution of support. But the Tonkin Gulf Resolution of 1964 differed fundamentally from the Formosa and Middle East resolutions passed under Eisenhower. Congress was no longer asked to *authorize* presidential action but to approve and support *"the determination of the president . . .* to take all necessary measures to repel any armed attack against the forces of the United States."[26] The change in wording was more than semantic; it marked a profound shift of the initiative from Congress to the president.

It was dissatisfaction with this shift, and the defeat in Vietnam, that led to repeal of the Tonkin Gulf Resolution in 1971 and passage of the War Powers Resolution (over Nixon's veto) in 1973. And while the constitutionality of the resolution is unclear,[27] it reveals the basic tension between the war powers of Congress and the commander in chief authority of the president.

The debates in this Part II explore the tension between the institutions of democratic government and the requirements of foreign policy. The first debate explores conflict between democracy and foreign policy. The second debate looks at the problem of covert operations. Are they appropriate in a democracy? The tension between Congress and the president over the War Powers Resolution is featured in the third debate. The fourth debate considers a different type of dispute between the president and Congress involving the treaty power. Are *executive agreements* (international agreements made by the United States and not submitted to the Senate) as binding as formal treaties, to which the Senate consents? The fifth debate studies the potential conflict between the White House and the State Department: Should the staff of the NSC (or should the State Department) provide the leadership for U.S. foreign policy? The final debate in Part II also focuses on the State Department. It asks whether more ambassadors should be drawn from the professional Foreign Service.

IS AN ACTIVE FOREIGN POLICY COMPATIBLE WITH DEMOCRACY?

The Iran-Contra affair has led to renewed questioning of the relationship between democracy and foreign policy. The rise of the United States to superpower status and the attendant obligations have admittedly placed strains on the fabric of domestic society. Indeed, from the time of Madison to the

---

[26] Tonkin Gulf Resolution, Aug. 10, 1964, Public Law 88-408, 78 Stat. 384.

[27] Tonkin Gulf Resolution repealed Jan. 1, 1971; War Powers Resolution, Nov. 7, 1973, Public Law 93–148, 87 Stat. 555 (codified as 50 U.S.C., secs. 1541–1548 (1976). See esp. *INS v. Chadha*, 462 U.S. 919 (1983), S. Ct. 2764.

present, critics of American internationalism have agreed that foreign responsibilities "will drain our economy, militarize our society, and corrupt our democracy," as Charles Krauthammer puts it.

The debate that follows addresses the question from a different perspective. Leon Wieseltier, writing in the *New Republic,* fears that the collapse of the Reagan policy in Latin America and Iran will lead to increased rather than decreased efforts to truncate democratic processes. "A conventional wisdom is aborning," says Wieseltier. It is "the proposition that there is a kind of zero-sum relationship between moral integrity and political efficiency, that the perfection of American democracy results in the imperfection of American foreign policy." This is the traditional Madisonian argument that foreign adventures will corrupt American democracy.

Wieseltier cites the views of neoconservative commentators, such as Norman Podhoretz of *Commentary;* the diplomat George Kennan (who "for half a century" has been "a tireless critic of the intrusion of democracy into diplomacy"); and Michael A. Ledeen, at one time a consultant on Iran to the NSC. Each, in a different fashion, argues that the problem with U.S. foreign policy is too much rather than too little political control. In Wieseltier's view, "You would have thought that Congress had just sold arms to the mullahs of Iran, traded weapons for hostages, smuggled illegal funds to the *contras.*" His conclusion is that although the U.S. system of government is cumbersome, it continues to offer the protection against despotism the Framers intended: "That is a system in which the thrilling sensation of rightness, the absolute conviction of certainty, counts for nothing against the decision of a majority."

Charles Krauthammer provides a spirited reply. He observes that while America may be less democratic than if it had no superpower responsibilities, "it is certainly true that overall we are far more democratic than we were 40 years ago" if one considers the extraordinary strides the United States has made in civil rights and civil liberties. But Krauthammer believes the sacrifices have been worthwhile for two reasons: (1) "for the long-run well-being of our own democracy"—which he doubts would survive in a hostile world; and (2) because promoting the democratic idea abroad "is an American vocation, for which we have long sacrificed blood and treasure." Nevertheless, he shares Wieseltier's concern for democratic process. If exceptions have to be made, they should be made by majority consent.

ARE COVERT OPERATIONS EVER APPROPRIATE IN A DEMOCRACY?

Covert operations seek to influence events abroad in such a way that a government's involvement is not apparent. Over the years covert operations have become one of the most controversial instruments of American foreign policy. And the record of their accomplishments has been spotty. The Iran-Contra affair has proved to be the most conspicuous failure, yet as McGeorge

Bundy, former national security adviser to Presidents Kennedy and Johnson, noted; "The dismal record of paramilitary operations over the past 25 years is entirely clear."[28]

Of course covert operations are not restricted to paramilitary undertakings. The clandestine support for individuals and organizations, the secret sponsorship of foreign media, false propaganda, concealed economic activity to disrupt the economy of a foreign state, and even assassination are tools sometimes used in covert activity. These methods raise important moral and ethical questions as well as questions pertaining to the desirability of interfering in the affairs of other countries. An additional problem concerns accountability. In 1974, Congress passed the Hughes-Ryan Amendment to the Foreign Assistance Act. This amendment requires that except *in extremis*, the president inform Congress "in a timely fashion" of the nature and scope of any CIA operation conducted for purposes other than obtaining information.[29] Various select and standing committees of the Congress have sought to monitor covert operations, but they have not always been successful. The resulting legislative dissatisfaction, which crested during the Iran-Contra hearings in 1987, has led to attempts to amend the Hughes-Ryan formula to require the president to notify Congress within forty-eight hours of approving any covert operation. And while this requirement would improve the quality of congressional oversight, it is not clear that it would enhance the efficacy of operations contemplated.

In the debate that follows, Angelo Codevilla and Roy Godson argue that covert action is an essential element of U.S. foreign policy. Codevilla served as a professional staff member of the Senate Intelligence Committee from 1977 to 1985 and is a senior research fellow at the Hoover Institution. Godson teaches government at Georgetown University and is coordinator of the Academic Consortium for the Study of Intelligence as well as a consultant to the NSC. They see the United States locked in a deadly struggle with the Soviet Union and define U.S. policy in bipolar terms. Their recommendations for improving covert action include the expansion of the American support network, better intelligence, and better security. "The efficient delivery of money and political support to friends, the efficient spread of rumors, and the mounting of serious paramilitary efforts require the participation of more people in more places and of more kinds of people than are or should probably be in the CIA," they conclude.

Lewis H. Lapham of *Harper's Magazine* provides a counter to the Codevilla-Godson view. He maintains that "consistently and without noteworthy exception, the use of covert military action in support of American foreign policy has ended in failure or catastrophe." He suggests that unless the United States is "willing to transform itself into a totalitarian state, even the theory

---

[28] Quoted in David B. Rivkin, Jr., "Covert Actions: Is It Justified?" *American Legion*, 124 (Mar. 1988), p. 24.
[29] Public Law 93–559, 84 Stat. 1804.

of secret war is absurd" and quotes President John Quincy Adams that America might thus "become the dictatress of the world [but]...no longer be the ruler of her own spirit."

THE WAR POWERS RESOLUTION: IS THE CURE WORSE THAN THE DISEASE?

The War Powers Resolution was passed over President Nixon's veto in 1973. The stated purpose of the resolution is to "ensure that the collective judgement of both the Congress and the president will apply to the introduction of United States Armed Forces into hostilities, or into situations where imminent involvement in hostilities is clearly indicated by the circumstances."[30] The resolution established an elaborate system of consultation between the president and Congress before the armed forces could be deployed and requires the president to submit periodic reports to Congress as the military situation evolved. It also requires the president to terminate U.S. military involvement after sixty days unless Congress declares war, approves an extension, or is unable to meet.

A serious question has been raised about the constitutionality of the War Powers Resolution. In particular, the requirement to withdraw U.S. forces in the absence of positive congressional approval may be of doubtful validity. Such provisions, known as *legislative vetoes*, have been held by the Supreme Court to be unconstitutional infringements of the separation of powers,[31] although the actual requirement of the War Powers Resolution has never been ruled on. More important, while some presidents have consulted informally with Congress before using military forces abroad, all have adhered to the position that the decision remains their prerogative as commander in chief.

The history of the War Powers Resolution since its passage in 1973 supports that view. President Gerald Ford used the military to evacuate American citizens from Danang, Saigon, and Phnom Penh in 1975 and to liberate the merchant ship *Mayaguez* from its Cambodian captors—all without congressional approval. Carter sent the Air Force to evacuate diplomatic personnel and American civilians from combat situations in Zaire and Cyprus and initiated the ill-fated hostage rescue mission in Iran without prior congressional authorization. Reagan's deployment of Marines in Lebanon was taken pursuant to his "constitutional authority...as Commander in Chief,"[32] as was the intervention in Grenada and the dispatch of military advisers to El Salvador. When Congress passed the 1983 Lebanon Resolution authorizing the president to keep U.S. forces there for eighteen months, Reagan made it clear that he might continue military operations beyond that time without seeking further congressional approval.[33]

---

[30] Public Law 93–148, 87 Stat. 555.
[31] *INS v. Chadha*, 462 U.S. 919 (1983).
[32] *Weekly Compilation of Presidential Documents*, 18 (Sept. 29, 1982), p. 1232.
[33] Ibid., 19 (Oct. 12, 1983), pp. 1422–23.

Regardless of its constitutionality, the War Powers Resolution reflects the basic tension between the Congress and the president in foreign affairs. While this tension is unavoidable (and may even be desirable) in a system of checks and balances, it occasionally makes the smooth functioning of U.S. foreign policy difficult. The ultimate check that Congress possesses is in the appropriations process. Whether it was the bombing of Cambodia in 1973 or military support for the Contras under Reagan, Congress's authority to provide or withdraw funds is final. This authority has led to efforts in the 100th Congress to tie the War Powers Resolution more closely to the appropriations process.[34]

In the debate that follows, Robert F. Turner, a deputy assistant secretary of state in the Reagan administration and now Associate Director of the Center for Law and National Security at the University of Virginia, maintains that the War Powers Resolution is not only unconstitutional but pernicious as well. He cites the sixty-day authorization requirement as affording encouragement to America's enemies to hold out in the hope that Congress would undercut the president. "The proper congressional role in national security matters," says Turner, "should be that of a full partner in the formulation of general principles and policies, rather than that of micro-manager or second-guesser of the President's execution of those policies."

An alternative view is presented by Professor Daniel P. Franklin of Colgate University, who argues that the War Powers Resolution has been effective, proving much more than a "parchment barrier" against unrestrained presidential power. "The fact that Congress often acquiesces in presidential initiatives in the use of force...does not necessarily mean that the resolution is a dead letter." In addition to the potential deterrent effect, Franklin believes that the War Powers Resolution strengthens the separation of powers by providing "an avenue...for a measured congressional response."

ARE TREATIES MORE BINDING THAN EXECUTIVE AGREEMENTS?

Article II of the Constitution provides that the president "shall have Power, by and with the Advice and Consent of the Senate, to make treaties, provided two-thirds of the Senators present concur." But treaties are not the only method by which the United States makes agreements with foreign countries. The Constitution recognizes that in addition to treaties, the United States may enter into "agreements" or "compacts" with foreign nations. But it does not indicate how treaties differ from agreements or compacts. Nevertheless, one thing is certain: A treaty requires the approval of two-thirds of the Senate before coming into force, an *executive agreement* does not.

From the time of George Washington, the United States has entered into executive agreements with other countries concerning such matters as postal rates, patents, trademark and copyright, and reciprocal trading arrange-

---

[34] Susan F. Rasky, "Senators Seeking to Overhaul War Powers Resolution," *New York Times,* May 20, 1988, p. A-3.

ments. But as the United States assumed a more active role in world affairs, more and more matters of political significance have come to be dealt with by executive agreements and not by treaties. The Rush-Bagot Agreement of 1817 limiting armaments on the Great Lakes was an early example of such "executive treaty making." But it was not until the administration of President William McKinley that major foreign policy issues came to be routinely handled by executive agreements—excluding the Senate from the process. The armistice with Spain in August 1898, which provided for the American occupation of Cuba and the Philippines; the Boxer Indemnity Protocol; the "Open Door" in China; and the 1908 Root-Takahira agreement between the United States and Japan to uphold the status quo in the Pacific were all consummated without reference to the Senate. So, too, was the Hull-Lothian agreement of 1940, by which the United States provided Great Britain with fifty American destroyers (in apparent violation of the Neutrality Acts). But it was the extensive use of executive agreements during World War II that has been the most controversial. The agreements at Tehran, Yalta, and Potsdam, which fixed the map of postwar Europe, were all concluded by executive agreement. The Senate's advice and consent were not asked. Nor was it asked to approve the quadripartite Berlin Accords of 1971, which represent a de facto peace treaty with East and West Germany. In fact, executive agreements rather than treaties have become the preferred presidential method for entering into understandings with other countries.[35]

This extensive use of executive agreements raises serious questions about the separation of powers, the role of the Senate in foreign policy, and the increasing aggregation of presidential power. Is it permissible for the president to bypass the Senate to conclude an agreement with a foreign state? What is the effect of that agreement? Can it be rejected or renounced by the Senate? Does the Senate (or Congress) have to be informed? From time to time the Senate has sought to reassert its authority, but generally without success. The proposed Bricker Amendment (named after the Republican senator from Ohio, John Bricker) to the Constitution in 1954, which among other things would have given Congress the power to annul executive agreements, was defeated in the Senate by one vote.[36] In 1972, Congress passed the Case-Zablocki Act, which requires that Congress at least be informed of all executive agreements. According to former Senator Clifford Case, there were more than four thousand executive agreements in effect at that time that Congress knew nothing about.[37] Some agreements, it would appear, still have not been revealed.[38]

---

[35] Between 1946 and 1977, the United States entered into 7,200 executive agreements compared to 451 treaties. See Loch Johnson and James M. McCormick, "Foreign Policy by Executive Fiat," *Foreign Policy*, no. 28 (Fall 1977), p. 117.

[36] S. J. Res. 1, 83d Cong., 2d Sess.

[37] James A. Nathan and Richard K. Oliver, *Foreign Policy Making and the American Political System* (Boston: Little, Brown, 1983), p. 115.

[38] Charles W. Kegley, Jr., and Eugene R. Wittkopf, *American Foreign Policy: Pattern and Process*, 2d ed. (New York: St. Martin's Press, 1982), p. 418.

Are executive agreements the same as treaties? Are they equally binding? In a classic debate, Professor Edwin Borchard, the Sterling Professor of International Law at Yale, and his successor, Professor Myres S. McDougal, address the issue. Borchard presents the historical view that executive agreements are inferior to treaties and are of less consequence. McDougal argues the contemporary position that the only real distinction is that a treaty requires the consent of two-thirds of the Senate, while an executive agreement can be concluded by the president alone. He maintains that they may cover the same subject matter and are equally binding.

SHOULD THE STATE DEPARTMENT (RATHER THAN THE NATIONAL SECURITY COUNCIL) LEAD IN FOREIGN POLICY?

Who makes foreign policy? There is no question that the president is constitutionally responsible for the conduct of U.S. foreign policy, under such broad directives as the Congress may legislate. But within the executive branch, where does the initiative lie? When the United States was on the periphery of world politics, foreign policy was routinely handled by a minuscule professional bureaucracy in the State Department. There was no serious problem of coordination, no vast military and intelligence apparatus, no foreign commitments, and few international responsibilities. Serious matters could not be brought to the personal attention of the president by the secretary of state, and there were no important bureaucratic rivals for power.

But World War II changed that. The superpower status thrust on the United States, and the accompanying responsibilities, have converted the problems of diplomacy to the problems of national security. The military component of international issues has expanded exponentially. Indeed, not infrequently, it is the military component that drives foreign policy. The Strategic Defense Initiative (or "Star Wars," as it is called), the Intermediate-range Nuclear Forces Treaty, strategic arms reduction, the Soviet army's withdrawal from Afghanistan, military aid to the Contras, the naval deployment in the Persian Gulf, the air strike on Tripoli, and the invasion of Grenada illustrate how central military considerations are to the conduct of U.S. foreign policy. In this context, it may appear natural that the role of the State Department in formulating U.S. policy has declined. Military and security considerations clearly have become more significant, and the power of the defense establishment has correspondingly increased. In addition, it would appear that the State Department has made little effort to acquire the technical skills in military and economic matters required to maintain foreign policy leadership.[39] What the conduct of American foreign policy requires is coherence, expertise, coordination, and responsiveness to the political leadership of the president and Congress. Whether this can best be provided by the Department of State is the subject of this debate.

I. M. Destler, a political scientist at the University of Maryland, argues

---

[39] Pringle, "Creeping Irrelevance," p. 135.

that U.S. foreign policy must be made less idiosyncratic and less dependent upon the personalities of White House advisers and that the stability of bureaucratic expertise provides an essential antidote to the tendency to lurch from crisis to crisis that recent administrations have exhibited. "If a president wants a more comprehensive, more effective foreign policy, he needs an institution with the depth and reach of the State Department."

The opposite tack is taken by Professor Duncan L. Clarke of American University. Clarke argues that the State Department is organizationally and temperamentally unsuited to direct American foreign policy. Aside from the lack of technical expertise, an inbred aversion to risk taking, and a relative unresponsiveness to presidential desires, Clarke maintains that the entire ethos of the Foreign Service conspires against a leadership role for the State Department. "FSO's [Foreign Service Officers] are thought of (and think of themselves) as diplomats whose principal duty is to execute, not make, policy."

> The FSO's "essence" is to represent their country overseas, send reports back to Washington, and negotiate with foreign governments. Successful performance of these functions requires a certain compromising, accommodating, and unabrasive style that does not lend itself to the combative, aggressive quality of Washington decision making.

While both Destler and Clarke wrote before the revelations of the Iran-Contra affair focused on the shortcomings of the NSC staff, both rejected an operational role for the NSC. For Destler, such a task detracts from the more important coordinating role the NSC should play. For Clarke it "inclines an administration toward a crisis or 'front-burner' orientation, since critical matters will claim much, if not all, of its time." Both agree that an operational role for the NSC imparts an unfortunate episodic quality to U.S. foreign policy.

SHOULD MORE U.S. AMBASSADORS BE DRAWN FROM THE FOREIGN SERVICE?

The principal U.S. representative in a foreign country is the ambassador. He or she is the American *chief of mission* and heads the *country team.* The country team is usually composed of representatives from a dozen or more government departments and agencies in addition to the State Department, and many of these representatives communicate directly with their individual Washington headquarters. The ambassador is responsible for the work of the embassy, but coordination among its various parts is an arduous task.

Even more important than the ambassador's administrative role as chief of mission is his representative function. He or she is the chief spokesperson and representative of the United States in the country to which he or she is *accredited.* In both a technical and an actual sense, the ambassador is the representative of the president in that country. According to Article II of the Constitution, the president, with the advice and consent of the Senate, "shall appoint Ambassadors, other public Ministers and Consuls." This arrangement reflects the diplomatic tradition that ambassadors are personal representatives sent by one head of state to another. In the eighteenth and nineteenth centuries, only the European great powers—Austria, Great Britain, France, Prussia, and Russia—exchanged ambassadors with one another. Lesser states, including the United States, were represented by ministers. But inflation hits everything, including diplomacy, and since World War I the senior representative of a state in a foreign country has been titled ambassador.

The dual functions of an ambassador as personal representative of the president and as chief of mission reflect an increasing tension. As embassies have grown larger, the administrative demands as chief of mission have increased. But the size of a legation is usually a function of the political importance of the post. Thus the political and representative functions of the ambassador grow apace. Few appointees excel at both responsibilities. Career FSOs appear to stress embassy management and political reporting; ambassadors appointed from outside the State Department tend to be linked more closely with the president and stress the representational aspect of their role. But there have been notable exceptions.

The United States is one of the few remaining countries to make a significant number of its ambassadorial appointments from outside the ranks of professional diplomats. To some extent this situation can be seen as a holdover from the days of widespread political patronage. But perhaps a more important reason is that the United States is also one of the few countries where responsibility for foreign policy remains concentrated in the hands of the head of state. In the United States, foreign policy is not a collective cabinet or politburo responsibility. And the personal authority of the president translates easily into the personal selection of ambassadors with whom he is familiar and in whom he has confidence. Franklin D. Roosevelt, for example, appointed about half of the U.S. ambassadors from the Foreign Service and the other half from outside. In the Carter administration, three-quarters of the ambassadors came from the Foreign Service. Under Reagan, the ratio was about 50:50, as in Roosevelt's time. There is no constitutional mandate for either pattern. It is the president's ultimate decision. And the record is unclear as to which course is preferable.

In 1982, Sen. Charles Mathias of Maryland introduced legislation to require the president to appoint at least 85 percent of the U.S. ambassadors from the foreign service.[40] While this proposal raises important constitutional issues pertaining to the separation of powers,[41] the focus of this debate pertains to the relative merits of the proposal. Charles S. Whitehouse, a former president of the American Foreign Service Association, argues that the pro-

---

[40] S. 1886, 97th Cong, 2d Sess. (1982).

[41] The appointing authority is "textually committed" to the president under Article II of the Constitution, and it is doubtful whether Congress can legislate on this subject.

posal would ensure a higher degree of professionalism among U.S. ambassadors and thus improve the quality of U.S. representation abroad. John Krizay, a former FSO, doubts that assertion. Krizay suggests that the fresh perspective that outside appointees bring to the State Department may outweigh their professional shortcomings. "No evidence has ever been developed that establishes that career ambassadors, as a group, are superior to non-career ambassadors," says Krizay. Both statements were given in testimony before the Senate Foreign Relations Committee considering Senator Mathias's proposal. The plan failed to win the necessary votes for approval in the Senate.

7 Is an Active Foreign Policy Compatible with Democracy?

YES

Leon Wieseltier

Democracy and Colonel North

NO

Charles Krauthammer

The Price of Power

Democracy and Colonel North

Leon Wieseltier

To live outside the law you must be honest.
—Bob Dylan

Welcome back *le mal américain*. Make room for the revival of "democratic overload." The breakdown of the Reagan administration over its clandestine commerce with Iran and the *contras* has fanned back into life the ancient anxiety that there is a contradiction between democracy and foreign policy. A mood of elegant pessimism is overwhelming Washington. Of course the policy toward Iran was wrong, of course those who broke the law should be punished—but still a higher extenuation is sought. With a fine Tocquevillian feeling, it is wondered whether the closed conduct of foreign policy is possible in an open society; whether the prestige of law in American society, or the participation of Congress in foreign affairs, or the Constitution itself, is responsible for the failures of American diplomacy; whether democracy suffers a permanent disadvantage against its enemies, whose very opposition to freedom, in a cruel irony of history, enables them to act freely in the pursuit of their interests. Oliver North is treated like a test that the American political system is failing to pass.

Item. In an essay written for *Partisan Review*, Washington foreign policy consultant Michael Ledeen complained that "foreign policy is so deeply enmeshed in our domestic stresses and strains that it is hard to determine where the 'domestic' ends and the 'foreign' begins." Ledeen attacked what he called "a pernicious pseudo-democratic theory according to which everyone is entitled to have a say in policy." The "would-be policy-makers" he assailed are Congress ("one cannot possibly conduct foreign policy with more than 500 secretaries of state"), the media ("in many ways the media have taken over the prerogatives of a secret intelligence agency"), and "the lawyers and the judges." Ledeen proposed a new elitism in foreign policy, citing Michel Crozier: "If society will no longer tolerate elites and political institutions do not provide the necessary safeguards for long-term planning...then democracy falls apart." The members of this elite should be "experts, not generalists," and "those few persons seeking to advance the national interests of the United States." (Presumably Ledeen counts himself in their number.)

When Michael Ledeen's involvement in the Iranian intrigue became known, *Partisan Review* wisely "postponed" his article. A pity, because the article is an excellent introduction to the mentality that delivered this debacle. Ledeen was loftily complaining of a lack of covert operations in the name of geopolitical visions even as he was a cog in one. And Ledeen's reliance upon Crozier provides a direct link between the Iranian intrigue and the neoconservative distrust of democracy. In the mid-1970s two works—Crozier's *The Trouble with America* and *The Crisis of Democracy*, a report for the Trilateral Commission with contributions by Crozier and Samuel Huntington—introduced the notions of "democratic overload" and "democratic distemper." Huntington, for example, took issue with Al Smith's famous dictum that "the only cure for the evils of democracy is more democracy." He argued instead that "some of the problems of governance in the United States today stem from an excess of democracy....The effective operation of a democratic system usually requires ·some measure of apathy and non-

Leon Wieseltier, "Democracy and Colonel North," *New Republic*, 196 (Jan. 26, 1987), pp. 22–25. Reprinted by permission of *The New Republic*. © 1987, The New Republic, Inc.

involvement on the part of some individuals and groups."

It was only a short distance from distrust of democracy to defeatism about democracy. That distance was traveled by the other authority of Ledeen's essay, the ultimate neoconservative crepe-hanger, Jean-François Revel, who wrote: "Democracy may, after all, turn out to have been a historical accident, a brief parenthesis that is closing before our eyes." *How Democracies Perish* (1983) was written to demonstrate that democracy "is not basically structured to defend itself against outside enemies seeking its annihilation." Thus did one of democracy's great defenders became one of democracy's great detractors.

Item. On the *New York Times* op-ed page December 23, Representative Jack Kemp correctly remarked that the pessimism of "Jean François Ravel" [sic] doesn't sit well with the optimism of Ronald Reagan. Still, Kemp wrote to sound a tocsin: "Many of the president's congressional opponents will attempt to use Iran as a means to lessen his power....Mr. Reagan must draw the line, and, if necessary, veto any reduction in his authority to conduct foreign policy." That same day Norman Podhoretz appeared in the *Washington Post* with "The Imperial Congress," which indicted Congress for "aggrandizing itself at the expense of the president," and more generally for treading illegitimately upon the foreign policy of the United States. Reading Kemp and Podhoretz, you would have thought that Congress had just sold arms to the mullahs of Iran, traded weapons for hostages, smuggled illegal funds to the *contras*.

Item. In these pages, my colleague Charles Krauthammer observed recently ("Divided Superpower," *New Republic*, December 22, 1986) that "the presidency finds itself in the permanent bind: to fulfill its obligations as leader of a superpower or to fulfill its obligations as leader of a democracy. Confronted with the choice, a president must choose the latter. But it is the choice itself—not the identity of the president or his management style—that is the source of our recurring crisis." And in *Time,* he wrote: "Americans may not like being a superpower, but they have no choice, there being no one else to carry the burden. So they have to face the responsibilities of power. And one of them is the necessity of secrecy."

Item. George Kennan, for a half century a tireless critic of the intrusion of democracy into diplomacy, wrote recently in the *New York Review of Books* urging a constitutional amendment to create "some sort of an advisory body...made up of persons remote from participation in partisan political activity...to look deeply into present trends and possible remedies and to tell both the legislative and executive branches of government of the things they *must* do, whether they like it or not, to head off some of the worst eventualities that seem now to be, almost unhindered, in the making." Such a body would find "a better use of the 'elder statesmen' who are to be found in such abundance in our society but whose experience, as things now stand, goes largely wasted." Call it government by Council of Foreign Relations. (Kennan's view was updated for the present crisis by Walter Isaacson, co-author of *The Wise Men,* a dense and worshipful account of Kennan and his colleagues in the postwar foreign policy establishment. In the *New York Times* in December, Isaacson suggested "the appointment of a panel of 'wise men,' an outside group of elder statesmen to give regular foreign policy advice to a foundering president.")

A conventional wisdom is aborning: the proposition that there is a kind of zero-sum relationship between moral integrity and political efficiency, that the perfection of American democracy results in the imperfection of American foreign policy. Or, to put it differently, that the perfection of American foreign policy may require the imperfection of American democracy. The adherents of this view cannot face the thought that the debacles in Iceland, in Iran, in Nicaragua, were simply poor policies, founded upon terrible judgment and clumsy action—that they tell more about a specific strain in American political culture than about American political culture itself, more about this president than about the presidency. Instead, like the man who concluded that God was dead because he had lost his faith, they conclude that the form of American government is flawed because it has failed to satisfy their desires.

The tension between the needs of a great power and the needs of a free society is a familiar feature of American history. The architects of the American system were reluctant to deprive the executive branch of the power to pursue American interests freely. In 1781, for example, the Department of Foreign Affairs (later the Department of State) was created, over the objections of radicals in Congress, precisely to diminish the disorderly influence of Congress upon American diplomacy. Robert R. Livingston, the first secretary of foreign affairs, counted among his achievements the establishment of his right to correspond with American representatives abroad without notifying Congress, expressly for the purpose of protecting the confidentiality of such communications. A decade later, during the controversy over Washington's Neutrality Proclamation, Alexander Hamilton became "Pacificus" to argue for the independence of the president in foreign affairs. The president, not the Congress, was "the organ of intercourse between the Nation and foreign Nations."

It was Tocqueville, naturally, who intuited the American tension most lucidly. In a famous passage of *Democracy in America*, Tocqueville declared:

> I have no hesitation in saying that in the control of society's foreign affairs democratic governments do appear decidedly inferior to others....

Foreign policy does not require any of the good qualities peculiar to democracy but does demand the cultivation of almost all those which it lacks.... [A] democracy finds it difficult to coordinate the details of a great undertaking and to fix on some plan and carry it through with determination in spite of obstacles. It has little capacity for combining measures in secret and waiting patiently for the result.... But these are just the qualities which, in the long run, make a nation, and a man too, prevail.

Tocqueville concluded with a peroration in praise of aristocracy. A democracy tends "to obey its feelings rather than its calculations." An aristocracy, on the other hand, "does not easily yield to the intoxication of thoughtless passions. An aristocratic body is a firm and enlightened man who never dies." Thus it was that "almost all the nations that have exercised a powerful influence on the world's destiny...were controlled by an aristocracy."

Let us call them neo-Tocquevillians, these reformers of democracy in the name of foreign policy who wish to adjust the system slightly to accommodate wild and wonderful intrigues. There are two matters that these neo-Tocquevillians must address, however, before they start tinkering with the time-honored methods of American statecraft. First, they must demonstrate that democracy's judgment about matters such as selling arms to Iran was inferior to the judgment of those who wanted to overlook democracy. Second, they must demonstrate more generally that the position of the United States in the world has been weakened by the vigorous exercise of American freedoms, particularly by the freedom of the press.

But all this, of course, they cannot demonstrate. Consider, for example, the question of secrecy. The neo-Tocques have decided that the United States may not survive as a great power without secrecy of the sort that would have protected Oliver North. North is the case that tells: if he falls, secrecy in government falls. But the CIA [Central Intelligence Agency] conducts many clandestine activities that are not in the style of Oliver North. They are successfully kept secret, and they are legal. (Of course, a war is rather hard to hide; but then a war is not an operation.) Judging from the "Casey accords," the protocols of confidentiality that William Casey and the Senate Intelligence Committee arrived at in 1984, the agency has not exactly chafed under congressional oversight. Oliver North's adventure, in short, caused a crisis precisely because it was *not* typical of clandestine American action. Those who wish to make it typical will simply make all clandestinity seem lawless, all concealment seem wrong. People are arguing against covert operations à la Oliver North; almost nobody is arguing against covert operations themselves. As usual, however, the Reaganites refuse to take yes for an answer. They will not let Frank Church rest in peace.

And secrecy from whom? In the case of Oliver North, it was not merely the American people, or the press, or the Congress, that was kept in the dark. It was...the government. North broke creative new ground in official deception. Hiding behind the recovered prestige of covert operations, he told *nobody.* Not (it appears) the president, not the secretary of state, not the secretary of defense. Empowered to engage some of the most strategically significant states in the world, inebriated by a feeling of direct access to the godhead, North freelanced. Are North's kinds of covert operations really needed to keep the barbarians at bay?

There was a period of American history when privateers were acceptable agents of American policy. The very sentence of the Constitution that grants Congress the power to declare war also grants it the power to grant "letters of marque," which were licenses granted to individuals by the government to make reprisals, generally at sea, against the forces of the enemy. (Naval consultants, we

might call them today.) But it is precisely because America became a great power that the institution of the marque was finally revoked. The foreign policy of a great power cannot be represented by adventurers.

Some of the neo-Tocques seem not quite offended by North's offenses because they approve of the policies he was advancing, especially aid to the *contras.* But there were other scams and stratagems that North might have pursued. Imagine, for example, that Oliver North, who was awarded a presidential medal for his help in providing AWACS [airborne warning and control system] to Saudi Arabia, concludes, as well he might, that the Arab-Israeli conflict is the most serious flash point in the Middle East after Iran; that it will not be resolved without the participation of Jordan; that Jordan's participation will require an American "gesture of goodwill"; that such a gesture must take the form of American arms. And so North orders missiles from the Pentagon. Naturally this must remain secret, because of the opposition of Congress.

Do I see some neo-Tocques squirming? Do they mutter that maybe American law cannot make itself scarce every time somebody in the Situation Room has a plan? After all, there is no country in the world whose interests in Washington are based more upon congressional activism in foreign policy than Israel. "The imperial Congress" is never more imperial than about the Middle East. Is Michael Ledeen offended by the influence of interest groups and "domestic political warriors" on behalf of Israel? Is Norman Podhoretz put out by Congress "aggrandizing itself at the expense of the president" when it blocks arms sales to Jordan?

It is not the open society's hobbling of foreign policy that worries the neo-Tocques. It is the open society's hobbling of a foreign policy that they support. Their argument, like Oliver North's, is with the political system of the United States. That is a system in which the thrilling sensation of rightness, the absolute conviction of certainty, counts for nothing against the decision of a majority. There is always a vote. Before the vote, zeal may convince. After the vote, zeal may corrupt. Of course the proudly procedural character of the American system has its special frustrations. But it offers protection against precisely that thrilling sensation of rightness, which over the centuries has caused more crimes and more abuses of power than parliamentarianism.

When the principle of congressional activism in foreign policy was renewed during the Vietnam War, and congressional oversight of intelligence was established in the wake of Watergate, the legislative branch harbored an intensely adversarial feeling toward the executive branch. And Congress may have trammeled the presidency too much. For example, it is hard to see how a successful policy against terrorism can be pursued with a law against assassination on the books. In the 1980s, however, the executive branch returned the compliment of the 1970s. Put simply, the White House detests the Congress. ("A tribe of pygmies up there on Capitol Hill," Patrick Buchanan called it a few weeks ago.) The Reagan administration perceives Congress only as an obstacle to be overcome, a mechanism to be manipulated. Oliver North deposited Iranian money in *contra* accounts *after* Congress had appropriated $100 million in military aid. Congress simply did not matter.

Might not the administration have been saved from its worst embarrassment if it had consulted with Congress? Picture the response of the Senate Intelligence Committee upon being informed, behind closed doors, that the National Security Council was about to ship arms to Iran. The senators who were not speechless would almost certainly have done their best to bring the White House to its senses, to challenge the freebooters at the NSC to defend their proposal against all the skepticism it warranted. Would it have been

partisan politics, or isolationist insecurity, to have tried to dissuade McFarlane and North from their trip to Tehran?

The neo-Tocques (or at least the *contra* supporters among them) want to change the rules in the middle of the game, because they are losing it. They refuse to face the fact that for six years, in a period of rising enthusiasm for America rampant, Ronald Reagan tried and failed to convince the country of the justness of the *contra* cause. There was nothing historically inevitable about the Boland amendment. Yes, there are isolationists in Congress. There will always be isolationism in America, for all the reasons that historians offer. There were isolationists in Congress, too, when Harry Truman and John F. Kennedy moved American foreign policy decisively toward diplomatic and military interventions. But it is hard to imagine Truman and Kennedy, often cited as inspirations by the current president, whining about the system, spinning little paranoid stories about the spectacular strength of political opponents, and so on.

In the end, Ronald Reagan failed to provide what the *contras* and the conservatives needed most: leadership. The democratic requirement that the president seek the approval of the people for his policies does not mean that the leader must be a follower. But in foreign policy, as in domestic policy, this president has proved to be the happy prisoner of the pollsters and the political consultants, who are the real shackles upon the political system of the United States.

Certainly the most repugnant of the extenuations of the government is the attack on the press. The administration is turning upon one of its own most cherished tools. No president since Kennedy has been treated so tenderly by the media as Reagan. More to the point, the White House has made fine and calculated use of the reporters swarming all around it. How dare an administration that has been planting stories for years wax righteous against leaks?

The leak has been a primary instrument of Reagan policy. But, once again, when the system fails to please the Reaganite, the Reaganite scorns the system.

The neo-Tocques call for a modification of the American democratic tradition. Its instructions and inhibitions, they believe, must be challenged. But they have already been challenged—by Oliver North. To be sure, the colonel did not develop a theory for modifying the American way. He merely modified it. Now Rambo, now Gomer Pyle, he insulted the principle of law that constitutes the distinction between democracy and the lesser forms of public life. Also, more than any other American, North doomed the *contras*. North's patriotism is plain, but it is hard to get too choked up about a man who would give his life for a country he cannot understand.

There may be a tension between being a great power and being a democracy. But there cannot be a contradiction. Such a contradiction would signify nothing less than the failure of the American experiment. The United States is a great power, and it shall remain a great power; but it shall never be a great power like Philip II's Spain or Frederick II's Prussia or Napoleon's France. It is the American idea, the American innovation, to be a great power with a difference, a great power with compunctions—a democratic great power. That is not easy; but it is not impossible. As a friend of mine who works for a liberal Democratic politician sagely remarked: What is the point of assassinating somebody in the name of totalitarianism? A loss of faith in the United States would be a high price to pay for Ronald Reagan's mistakes.

The Price of Power

Charles Krauthammer

I used to puzzle over the question of how American democracy could be adapted to the kind of role we have come to play in the world. I think I now know the answer: it cannot be done.

—William Fulbright

The Iran-*contra* affair has led to a renewal of the perennial debate about the relationship of democracy to foreign policy. Thus far the debate has focused primarily on one aspect of that relationship, namely: What does democracy do to foreign policy? Specifically, can a democracy, with all of its constraints on policy and procedure, carry out the responsibilities of a superpower? The converse to this question is equally important: What does foreign policy do to democracy? Specifically, are superpower responsibilities abroad an enemy of democratic forms at home?

The latter set of questions is crucial because they shed light on the debate about American intervention abroad. The debate generally revolves around moral and strategic issues: Is the United States a force for good abroad? By what right do we intervene in the affairs of others? Does it really matter to the security of the United States who rules in Managua or Kabul or N'Djamena? The North affair, however, highlights a different question, which has long and powerfully influenced the debate on interventionism: What will full engagement in the world do to the democratic experiment at home? In fighting terrorists and totalitarians, do we not become like them? And is

that worth a piece of territory in some godforsaken corner of the Third World?

The concern over domestic effects unites anti-interventionists of the left and right, since it does not inquire into American purpose or the nature of the Soviet threat. It does not matter which side of history one sympathizes with abroad. The point is that the costs of interventionism are too great for the domestic life of a democracy to bear.

The costs of superpower status are many. Economically, leading a vast alliance is a drain on American resources and energies. In social terms, superpower responsibilities inevitably encourage the centralization and militarization of authority. (Defense considerations, for example, drive everything from university education to space exploration to laser research.) And politically, imperial responsibility demands imperial government, which naturally encourages an imperial presidency, the executive being (in principle) a more coherent and decisive instrument than its legislative rival.

"Nearly four decades ago," writes Ted Galen Carpenter of the libertarian Cato Institute, "opponents of foreign entanglements cautioned that America could not operate as an empire abroad and remain a republic at home....Burdensome military taxation, the malignant growth of an imperial presidency, and the violations of civil liberties during the McCarthy era and the Vietnam War offered earlier testimony to the dangers arising from America's status as planetary gendarme."

This kind of critique of superpower status—that it will drain our economy, militarize our society, and corrupt our democracy—has strong echoes on the left as well. If there is a left-right difference, it is that liberals tend to emphasize more the economic costs of empire; conservatives, the cost to liberty. The American Catholic bishops' pastoral letter on the U.S. economy makes a strong point of criticizing military spending for taking away from human needs. Robert Nisbet, on the other

Charles Krauthammer, "The Price of Power," *New Republic,* 196 (Feb. 9, 1987), pp. 23–25. Reprinted by permission of *The New Republic.* © 1987, The New Republic, Inc.

hand, makes the classic argument that under-lay the original American aversion of standing armies: that the increasing militarization of American society, however necessary to meet external threats, is inimical to democratic institutions and individual liberties.

These complaints about the costs of empire are not new. Carpenter says the argument goes back 40 years, to the beginning of the postwar era. In fact, it goes back to the era of pre-war isolationism. "An extreme sensitivity to, and consequently an obsessive fear of, the domestic effects of foreign policy has been one of the hallmarks—perhaps *the* hallmark—of the isolationist outlook," writes Robert Tucker. Isolationists believed that "foreign involvement—and above all war—erodes constitutional processes and betrays the American promise. In the 1930s it was this belief that united such otherwise disparate figures as Norman Thomas and Senator Robert A. Taft."

Thomas opposed American intervention against fascism because he thought such adventures would prevent economic reconstruction at home. Taft's isolationism was rooted in the fear that interventionism and militarism would destroy free institutions at home, leading to socialist dictatorship.

The isolationist impulse today also owes much to the fear of domestic effects. That fear, like its interwar antecedent, is often "obsessive," but there is no denying its essential truth. Defending a worldwide alliance does encourage centralized authority, a military-industrial complex, the transfer of authority to the executive branch, and the imposition of secrecy on a wide range of government activities. To the extent that these tendencies limit public participation in and debate on public policy (e.g., the CIA carries out covert actions in the name of the American people but without their knowledge), they constitute a diminution of democracy. It is the price we pay, in the form of democratic practice—for what?

For two purposes. First, for the long-run well-being of our own democracy. The pre-war isolationists believed that American democracy could survive in a hostile, totalitarian world. That proposition—almost, but never, tested—remains dubious. There remains today a totalitarian threat. Both for reasons of safety and of nourishment, American democracy needs friends to survive. Our alliance commitments, our large military establishment are the product of many things, one of which is democratic self-interest.

And second, for an idea, the democratic idea. Promoting it abroad is an American vocation, for which we have long sacrificed blood and treasure. The constraints on our democracy required for the running of an alliance are another form of sacrifice, a kind of foreign aid program in which the transfer is made in the coin of democratic practice rather than cash. The most extreme example of this phenomenon (precisely what the pre-war isolationists had predicted and feared): to fight a world war that restored democracy to half a continent abroad required the vast centralization of power in the federal government at home.

The pre-war isolationists, like their present-day disciples, had a valuable insight into the tension between democracy and an interventionist foreign policy. And though it is certainly true that overall we are far more democratic than we were 40 years ago (consider only the extraordinary extension of civil rights and civil liberties), in some important ways we are less democratic than we would be had we no superpower responsibilities. And yet we have decided, as a democracy, that the trade is worthwhile.

This is not at all to say that we should be cavalier about the trade. Only that we should not deny it. We must do everything we can to minimize the injury that foreign policy does to democracy. If there must be secrecy, it should have the proper congressional oversight. If there must be covert action, it should be carried out by the CIA [Central Intelligence Agency], not covered up in the NSC [National Security Council]. And if there is to be war, even proxy war, Congress must approve.

How to manage the tension between being a superpower and being a democracy? I suggest an axiom, an exception, and a corollary.

The axiom: *No unilateral rule-breaking.* If the rules are no military aid to Nicaragua, no military aid to Nicaragua. If the rules are that we operate under the War Powers Act, then that power must be shared by the president and Congress until the Supreme Court rules otherwise. Lawbreaking by private citizens (civil disobedience) is fine, but only if they are willing to accept the legitimacy of the law in general and show it by going to jail. Lawbreaking by public officials is another thing altogether. There is no such thing as civil disobedience by a president. Presidential lawbreaking is either simple constitutional misconduct or, if the offenses are grave enough, high crimes and misdemeanors.

The exception occurs *in extremis.* The most obvious examples: In early 1861, Lincoln declared a blockade of the Confederate Coast, enlarged the army, and spent $2 million on the war effort without congressional approval. (Congress had not yet convened.) He suspended habeas corpus, which you don't ordinarily do even with congressional approval. During the Battle of Britain, FDR [Franklin D. Roosevelt] made the destroyers-bases deal with Churchill without congressional approval.

But there is a more general example. Theodore Draper ("The Reagan Junta," *New York Review of Books,* January 29) characterizes Reagan's running of foreign policy as government by junta. As a description of America today, it is a gross exaggeration. But government by junta is a fairly good approximation of government by War Cabinet, which is the way Britain was governed during World War II. And under which, as Martin Gilbert has

shown, the great decisions were taken by a tiny, civilian-military "Defence Committee" and were never debated in Parliament. They were never even communicated to Parliament, except in very rare secret session and, even then, only in outline. Even the most democratic polities have recognized the possible need to resort to semiauthoritarian government in extremis.

But only in extremis. However important Nicaragua may be, today is neither 1861 nor 1940. Wartime seems to me a fairly good definition of in extremis. Who is to judge? And doesn't allowing such a judgment put us on a slippery slope? The president judges, and of course that puts us on a slippery slope, but in real emergencies you can't help that. There were parchment barriers to FDR's sending destroyers to Churchill in violation of the Neutrality Act, but he did so anyway and it is a good thing he did.

The corollary: *Democracy may be adapted, even constricted, but only by consensual rule-making.* Paul Volcker has more power than any Cabinet officer. Yet elected officials cannot remove him from office for any of his policies. Is that not undemocratic? His answer might be: "It is democratic. Congress can always change the rules that govern my office." This answer highlights two distinct meanings of the word democratic: popular and constitutional. Congress has vested enormous power in the chairman of the Fed [Federal Reserve Board] and then made him unremovable, except for high crimes and misdemeanors. That certainly is a constriction of democracy defined as popular government. But because Congress established that relationship in the first place and can, in principle, change it, there is no violation of democracy defined as constitutional government.

It seems to me perfectly legitimate to constrict democracy in the populist sense, so long as such a constriction is necessary to meet some overriding national objective (like preserving the integrity of the currency by keeping it at some distance from popular control), and so long as that constriction is effected by democratic, i.e., constitutional, means. We have done so often. Over the last 200 years, we have made dramatic changes in the structure of American democracy, adapting it to our growing power and responsibilities in the world. We have decided to establish a secret service, a military-industrial complex, and a far more powerful executive than the Founders ever wanted.

Let me offer a further example of a "constricting" change. Some covert activities must now be reported to as many as eight congressional committees (intelligence, foreign affairs, armed services, and appropriations in both houses) with perhaps 400 staff members. Because these reporting arrangements multiply the possibilities of a leak that might endanger policy and people, both the Carter and Reagan administrations increasingly entrusted secret missions to the NSC, which has no oversight at all and which is not equipped to run these operations in any case.

To make covert operations more secure, and to return them to the CIA where they belong, we might limit the number of members of Congress and staff involved in oversight to a single Joint Intelligence Committee. And to stop leaks, we might levy extremely stiff penalties for those either in Congress or in the administration who are found to have breached confidentiality (for example, denial of security clearance for five years). I think that this would be a useful reform. I do not deny that it constitutes a diminution, albeit minor, of democratic practice (in the populist sense) since the scope of participation in the decision is reduced, as is the possibility of the operation ever being discussed publicly.

But this is tinkering. It will not ultimately be decisive in determining whether we meet our historic responsibilities as a superpower. One must not overestimate the importance of

procedural reform in this respect. As I tried to point out earlier ("Divided Superpower," *New Republic,* December 22, 1986), the heart of the American problem is not the structure of democracy, but the will of the demos itself. The problem is the frequent reluctance of democratic publics to face, in peacetime, foreign policy and defense needs. Americans remain deeply divided over how much to give up to meet the responsibilities thrust upon them after World War II. As any member of Congress running for re-election knows, and as any secretary of state trying to get a foreign aid bill passed knows, Americans prefer investment in domestic over foreign affairs.

As evidence that this problem is not one of structure, but of national will, consider France, also a democracy. Its public accepts its foreign burdens far more willingly than does the American public. France can dispatch 1,500 troops to Chad with not a tenth the protest aroused by 55 American advisers in El Salvador.

If the will of the demos is the problem, what to do? The only acceptable solution, it seems to me, is to try to change that popular will by persuasion. If President Reagan really wanted to aid the *contras* in 1984, he should have relentlessly taken his case on the stump and on the tube. Instead he chose to husband his popularity, lost the fight in Congress, and then let Ollie do it. If persuasion fails, as often happens, one must respect popular wishes, even if that means failing one's responsibilities as a superpower. This seems to me a fairly plain proposition. (It also seems to me plain that presidents and lieutenant colonels will feel constantly tempted to act otherwise. It is predictable that the North affair is not the last such we have seen.) For one who believes in the rule of law, then, the conflict between democracy and foreign policy may incline one toward melancholy and pessimism. It does not incline toward authoritarianism.

Some people are troubled when the dilemmas of democratic versus superpower responsibilities are raised. Theodore Draper writes: "The most far-reaching implication of this line of reasoning is that the president and those around him must substitute their will for the 'popular will,'" which is the road to Draper's "government by junta."

Must they? Suppose Draper presents an analysis of the relationship between welfare and dependency. Does that logic lead us to the far-reaching implication that government must cease aid to the poor? Draper could, with equal logic, favor restructuring the welfare system. Or he might even have no remedies to offer. He might, in fact, prefer the current system, it being the worst there is except for all the others. The purpose of his analysis might merely be explanatory: to understand why the system is so ineffective, and to counter those who attribute its defects to the venality of individuals or to the inherent laziness of the poorer classes.

There will always be those who take the logic of the democracy/superpower dilemma to the point of justifying presidential juntas. This is hardly proof, as Draper would have it, that "the Krauthammer dilemma is unreal." One does not reject the fact of a dilemma for fear that others might run the wrong way with it.

My colleague Leon Wieseltier ("Democracy and Colonel North," *New Republic,* January 26) rejects the democracy/superpower distinction for another reason: the consequences of facing it squarely are too disturbing; it cannot be because it must not be. He concedes that "there may be a tension between democracy and foreign policy"—which is precisely the point—then adds: "But there cannot be a contradiction. Such a contradiction would signify nothing less than the failure of the American experiment."

But a wish is not an argument. Could this democratic experiment really not fail? The most elementary test of a system is its ability to defend itself. The British experiment came perilously close to failure in 1940. (It was rescued largely by help from outside. For the United States today, there is no outside.) And in that same year, the French experiment in democracy failed utterly, the Third Republic ending in defeat, disarray, and occupation. The root of both the near-failure and the abject failure was precisely the democracies' refusal, in the '30s, to attend to their own defense. It is unpleasant to think that democracy might undermine itself, but that is insufficient reason to dismiss the possibility.

John Adams did not dismiss it. "There never was a democracy yet that did not commit suicide," he wrote to John Taylor. Pessimism about democracy is hardly an un-American trait. The isolationists were right that interventionism carries within it the possibility of subverting democracy. And their opponents were right when they argued that because of the public's natural preference for tending to domestic rather than foreign needs, a democracy can undermine its own foreign policy. There is indeed a conflict between democracy and foreign policy, a conflict that must be managed with great care. Step one is acknowledging its existence.

QUESTIONS FOR DISCUSSION

1. What are the weaknesses of democracy in the conduct of foreign policy?
2. What are the strengths of democracy in the conduct of foreign policy?
3. What would be the effect on foreign policy of a constitutional amendment creating an advisory body of experts to make recommendations on foreign policy?
4. How would you evaluate U.S. foreign policy since World War II in terms of de Tocqueville's observation about the weakness of democracy in conducting foreign policy?
5. Should the president have been given leeway to aid the Contras in Nicaragua in spite of congressional opposition? Why or why not?

SUGGESTED READINGS

Adelman, Kenneth L. "The Challenge of Negotiating by Democracies." *Presidential Studies Quarterly*, 16 (Spring 1986), pp. 206–12.

Clinton, David. "Tocqueville's Challenge." *Washington Quarterly*, 11 (Winter 1988), pp. 173–89.

Collier, Ellen C. "Foreign Policy by Reporting Requirement." *Washington Quarterly*, 11 (Winter 1988), pp. 75–84.

Joffe, Josef. "Tocqueville Revisited: Are Good Democracies Bad Players in the Game of Nations?" *Washington Quarterly*, 11 (Winter 1988), pp. 161–72.

Krauthammer, Charles. "Divided Superpower." *New Republic*, 195 (Dec. 22, 1986), pp. 14, 16–17.

Revel, Jean-François. *How Democracies Perish*. Garden City, N.Y: Doubleday, 1984.

Rubin, Barry. *Modern Dictators: Third World Coup Makers, Strongmen, and Populist Tyrants*. New York: McGraw-Hill, 1987.

Spanier, John, and Eric M. Uslaner. *American Foreign Policy Making and the Democratic Dilemmas*. 4th ed. New York: Holt, Rinehart and Winston, 1985.

Speer, Albert. *Inside the Third Reich*, trans. Richard and Clara Winston. New York: Macmillan, 1970.

Tulloch, Gordon. *Autocracy*. Dordrecht, The Netherlands: Kluwer Academic Publishers, 1987.

8 Are Covert Operations Ever Appropriate in a Democracy?

YES

Angelo Codevilla and Roy Godson

Covert Action

NO

Lewis H. Lapham

A Wish for Kings

Covert Action

Angelo Codevilla and Roy Godson

The use of the term as a strategic instrument of policy and the practice of "covert action" is peculiar to today's United States. Few governments have attempted to segregate to such a degree under one term and in one department of government (the CIA [Central Intelligence Agency]) all the things that governments can do quietly, swiftly, and unattributably to intervene in the affairs of other nations. Affecting what other nations do and the character of their governments is the very end of foreign policy, whether that end is pursued with a greater or lesser degree of openness.

Covert activities in the service of foreign policy fall into four categories: first, paramilitary, that is, the waging or promoting of war in a way that is covert or not fully attributable to the source or to third parties; second, secret political action, which involves encouraging forces friendly to one's own side or unfriendly to enemies; third, covert propaganda, which is spreading truths or falsehoods unattributably to alter the conditions in which governments act; and finally, secret intelligence support.

In the coming decade the United States will often find itself dealing with the Soviet Union, its satellites, and sympathizers, from a position of overall military inferiority. In practice that means that in a military clash with the Soviet Union in most parts of the old world, the

Excerpted from Angelo Codevilla and Roy Godson, "Intelligence (Covert Action and Counterintelligence) as an Instrument of Policy," in *Intelligence Requirements for the 1980s*, vol. 7: *Intelligence and Policy*, ed. Roy Godson (Lexington, Mass.: Lexington Books, D.C. Heath and Company, 1986), pp. 89–96. Reprinted by permission of the publisher. Copyright 1986, by the National Strategy Information Center, Inc.

United States may well lose. Elsewhere, policymakers would have to worry lest a military victory over local pro-Soviet forces become the cause of a wider war that would leave the United States worse off than the Soviet Union. The United States will thus be compelled to struggle primarily by nonmilitary means, which implies a much more purposeful approach to, for example, international trade and aid. But it also means that American foreign policy must take maximum advantage of every opportunity to create *faits accomplis*, to muster broad coalitions in opposition to Soviet clients and designs, and to keep the Soviets and their international coalition off balance, preferably quarreling internally. Lacking force, deception, coups d'état, upsetting the enemy's internal councils, and proxy warfare become less options than necessity.

This is not to argue that the United States can expect big gains "on the cheap" via covert action—quite the contrary. From the 1960s through the 1980s, the tendency to pursue covertly ends to which the U.S. government was not sufficiently committed led to a series of ill-conceived involvements ending in failure. In the late 1940s and early 1950s, the United States did make significant gains in such places as Iran and Guatemala despite the commitment of few resources and very little political capital. But in those years, the United States' prestige—that is, its reputation for success—stood high. No one had reason to believe that the United States would not overtly back up its covert victories, and pro-Soviet forces were not then in a position to contest them.

However, in the 1980s it is unlikely that pro-Soviet forces will allow to stand uncontested any gain that the United States makes covertly unless the United States has preparations to convince them it would not be worth their while to try, and unless the United States can actually defeat any such attempts. In any given situation in which the United States makes even a small commitment, it must expect its opponents to raise the stakes. Recent history has shown the Soviets that such tactics often succeed.

Recent history also teaches that a small investment of resources and political capital in covert activities can pay big dividends when such investment is part of a coherent, success-oriented plan pursued not only by the CIA, but by the government as a whole.

Undeniably the greatest postwar achievement of the United States was the restoration of Western European democracy in the face of the determined opposition of the Soviet Union and its numerous, well-organized followers. It was a major struggle for very high stakes. In key battles, covert action contributed to victory while keeping collateral damage to a minimum. For example, had the European Communist dockers, who were obstructing the arrival of American aid, not been defeated, the fragile consensus on which several European governments rested would have been shaken. They were defeated by forceful workers initially encouraged, financed, and organized by democratic U.S. and European trade unions and later supported by the U.S. government. In addition, the United States helped friendly parties to win key elections in 1948. Lesser victories might have prolonged painful struggles. But in these battles covert actions paled in significance beside the massive commitment to European democracy on the part of the American people. Americans entered the European political fray overtly by challenging Europeans to choose, by offering material help, and by lobbying friends and relatives. The presence of U.S. troops in the Continent did not hurt, either. The lesson should be plain: when the stakes are high, covert action can be useful as an adjunct to public efforts, and to the will to use military force, if need be.

In the 1960s "leftist" causes drew armed adherents all over the world, but in the 1980s efforts to fight the Soviet Union and its client states draw wide popular support in Latin America, Africa, and Asia. Today, the Soviet Union's major geopolitical conquests of the 1970s—Angola, Nicaragua, and Afghanistan, not to speak of Southeast Asia, are being challenged by guerrillas, most of whom, if victorious, would orient their countries toward the West.

No doubt we can supply these forces. Whether doing so can advance the cause of freedom in the world depends on our ability to formulate good policy. The American political system has openly debated whether, and to what extent, American covert aid should go to the anti-Communist forces in these wars. Yet there has been little discussion of what the alternative outcomes would mean to the United States and little contingency planning for measures designed to win. The debate over the extent of covert assistance to the anti-Soviet side, as well as even adherence to procedures, has preempted healthy discussions of ends and means.

Poland's upheavals in the 1980s also reminded many in the West that regardless of how fervently they may wish that the Soviet Union enjoy its empire undisturbed, religion and ethnicity, not to mention love of freedom, will continue to gnaw away at it. This means that Eastern European Communist leaders, facing hostile peoples and resting on parties tempted to identify with their own people rather than with Moscow, lead perilous political lives. The United States could prepare to make any given leader's career even more perilous just when he happens to be under the most intense pressure to do Moscow's work. Had the United States gathered information that would make impossible such a leader's position, it could release such information at the moment of maximum impact. In a crisis, the quality of the operation does not have to be high to achieve an effect.

Senior officials know that whatever they say and do in such crises is likely to have an effect. In 1980–81, Western intelligence services may unwittingly have lent themselves to the Soviet Union's war of nerves on Poland, and thus helped to strengthen Jaruzelski by speculating on a possible Soviet invasion with Jaruzelski caught as a "man in the middle." At the time, to dwell on the reasons why an invasion would be disastrous for Moscow and to highlight the differences that exist between the Polish people and the various Polish units especially tied to the Kremlin could have strengthened internal Polish forces. Had Jaruzelski been depicted as an agent of a foreign power, his then shaky hold on his job might have been loosened further. The means of covert political action might have included "black" propaganda and double-agent operations, perhaps backed by declarations by officials of international agencies that they would not deal with such a man. In addition, assets in the Polish government, had they existed, could have been withdrawn by public defection. This case is worthy of closer study because similar opportunities have already appeared half a dozen times in Eastern Europe, and, in some form, are likely to recur.

The nurturing of popular anti-Soviet movements in Eastern Europe is beyond the current state of the art of U.S. intelligence and is, more importantly, superfluous. Such movements arise naturally. But it is neither superfluous nor beyond our means to supply material assistance to the victims of Communist oppression in Eastern Europe and to their families. The covert networks to deliver this assistance can be built. Over the long run, a "safety net" for those who choose to stand up for their rights, combined with the well-timed subversion of the Soviet Union's most obsequious servants, might help to neutralize Eastern Europe, and perhaps even to turn it into a liability for the Soviet Union. The key word here is "help," for such covert activities would be useless unless they were a part of a coherent plan of political-economic measures and

military contingency plans aimed at reversing the "Sonnenfeldt doctrine."

Bolstering the "moderate faction" in the Kremlin has long been a dream of many U.S. makers of foreign policy. But the United States has never possessed either the intelligence to distinguish any of the Kremlin's factions from one another or the means to advance any one faction's fortunes. Concessions intended to strengthen one faction have tended to strengthen the regime as a whole.

There is reason to believe, however, that in the coming decade an across-the-board effort to impose defeats upon the Soviet leadership might well radically weaken the regime as a whole. Covert action could help by sowing dissension among the Soviet leaders for whom ideology is now less a source of motivation than the intellectual currency by which they conceive and transact the business of an oligarchy—in Mikhail Voslensky's words, a *Nomenklatura*. Because the *Nomenklatura*'s way of life is "feudal," there will probably be considerable room for providing some Soviet leaders with the opportunity to "do in" their bureaucratic opponents. A record of defeat certainly makes any bureaucrat easier prey for his fellows. Knowledge of one oligarch's embarrassing private activities (or of activities that might have an embarrassing interpretation) could be passed clandestinely to a second, or perhaps the fact that the second is conspiring against the first can be passed to a third.

The point of this strategy is not just to foster corridor games, but to weaken the fiber of the whole regime. Yet one cannot stress enough that such covert action by itself probably will not be effective. At best it would be but one contribution to a policy, the burden of which would have to be carried by economic warfare, diplomacy, and demonstrations that the era of Soviet military superiority is vanishing, never to return.

Coups d'état in dictatorships, as Moscow

well knows, have been efficient shortcuts to strengthening one's position in a given country, or to wiping out the gains the other side might have made by a long, laborious process. Many "Third World" nations today are ruled by dictators unfriendly to the free world who are supported by single parties and palace guards rather than by popular consensus. Most are vulnerable to extinction by the very means by which they arose. On the other hand, providing covert assistance to those who seek to establish more democratic rule can be a dangerous business and can cause more harm than good. Defending democratic or pro-Western forces against enemies both foreign and domestic can be expensive in political, economic, and military terms. If it is not feasible to deploy the necessary overt political, economic and military resources, it is probably better not to become involved at all. However, assisting those who wish to replace the ruling elite with a more democratically-oriented regime could be most useful in easing the path of a determined geopolitical offensive. Such a policy would help to fortify advanced bases quickly and would perhaps convince Moscow that the cost of attacking such prepared positions would be too high.

Using covert propaganda at a crucial time might convince Soviet leaders that foreign governments had made decisions that in fact they had not, say, in reprisal for a prospective invasion of Romania. This could throw off the timing of the Soviet decision long enough to permit the initiation of a diversionary military crisis. Perhaps the greatest usefulness of covert propaganda, however, is within the Soviet Union itself, on behalf of nationalist or religious causes dear to the Russian people but anathema to their leaders. Providing real information to the Soviet people about what is happening in their own country certainly fits into this category. Radio Liberty has helped to keep alive some hopes in the Soviet Union. But as the Hungarian revolution painfully

taught in 1956, the usefulness of such information depends largely on the existence of a policy that aims at liberation without bringing about World War III.

Finally, covert activities remain a key adjunct to regular military operations. For example, the rescue mission in Iran failed in its conventional components as well as in its command structure. The plan was flawed. But the work of the very special undercover forces that set up the rescue force's covert logistics in Iran was superb.

There is increasing evidence that Moscow places important emphasis on special operations. Indeed, the Soviet Union at present has forces available for special operations many times more numerous than those of the United States and in addition can draw on a vast pool of KGB, MVD, and GRU troops, and those of the regular military with a potential for special missions. Clearly, the Soviets encourage such thinking and preparations, while the United States rarely does, perhaps because in the U.S. system no one is responsible for the outcome of a conflict, or even of an operation. If and when the U.S. military system gives some individuals the authority to plan the difficult missions they might have to perform, those individuals might well decide to build the capability in special operations and languages that would facilitate such missions. Such capabilities are not built quickly, but when they are available, they save lives.

Since the late 1960s, covert actions have lacked support within the U.S. government and by the American public, in large part because they have not been elements of policies enforced within the government and fully espoused in the court of public opinion. The question is often asked how covert action can be made more acceptable. But covert action is not and should never be the primary issue. Policy is. If a policy is well understood and is accepted, chances are overwhelming that the major means necessary and proper to its success will not be opposed. In the context of a carefully formulated foreign policy, a variety of actions, overt and covert, will suggest themselves.

Just as important in a democracy are all those things that must be done if the general public is to bear the costs and risks of policy. That means much more public discussion by presidents about whom they are helping and whom they are fighting in the world, why they are doing it, and why their measures can be expected to succeed. Of course secrecy about some of the means by which the United States helps its friends and harms its enemies is essential. American support for the French resistance in World War II, for example, was proudly broadcast to the world, but the relationships between the individuals who received the actual aid and those who gave it were well-kept secrets.

Secrecy can also ease the participation of third parties, but this should not be overemphasized. The Soviet Union no more refrains from attacking Pakistan today out of innocence about the role of the two or three million Afghans on the east side of the Khyber Pass than it does out of modesty. It will refrain so long as it fears that the United States would resist and that the price would be too high. Pakistan should be under no illusion about that.

Further, if one follows the logic according to which covert action should not so inconvenience the Soviets as to raise the serious possibility of an overt Soviet riposte, one would rarely try to impose a defeat on the Soviet Union. Covert or overt political actions would be limited to inconveniencing the outposts of the expanding Soviet empire, causing it to achieve negligible successes or quiet failures. Acceptance of this logic, combined with the very covertness of covert action, would facilitate Soviet defeat by keeping the fundamental options, and their consequences, from public debate.

While the formulation and public articulation of policy would cure much of what ails U.S. covert action, several other changes are also necessary. The first concerns the organizational apparatus for covert action, currently seen as the exclusive province of the CIA. The efficient delivery of money and political support to friends, the efficient spread of rumors, and the mounting of serious paramilitary efforts require the participation of more people in more places and of more kinds of people than are or should probably be in the CIA. Traditionally what in the United States is now called covert action has been the job of diplomats and of private individuals, specially picked for an assignment because of their peculiar access and skills. Today's employees of the CIA, though they possess a variety of technical skills, suffer from insufficient diversity, particularly of cover. They are stereotyped and so is their access. If some of the tasks described earlier are to be accomplished, then many more kinds of people in a variety of U.S. government agencies, as well as some outside of government, will have to be recruited, trained, and employed in covert action. These people must possess skills in foreign languages and adaptability to foreign cultures, qualities that have become rare nowadays in the United States. This shortage of high-quality people can only be remedied by long-term programs.

Second, operations aimed at covert influence, as well as their success, are highly dependent on good intelligence. Concrete opportunities for exercising influence are not often apparent to casual observers. Responsible officials who are interested in such opportunities must be willing to focus collection, especially HUMINT [Human Intelligence] and SIGINT [Signal Intelligence] so as to find them. But focusing collection is not easy. Most people familiar with U.S. intelligence organization know that collectors in effect pick up what their current sources tell them and that existing sources have little latitude for responding to new tasks. To answer truly new questions, new sources are often required. To get different kinds of sources, a different kind of case officer may be needed.

These questions are not intended to underestimate the intellectual difficulty of tasking. The difficulty and the art of tasking is to describe what the collector should look for to trace the outlines of something, the very existence of which may be uncertain, and to describe hypothetically how to go about getting it. That is, where covert action is concerned, the policymaker who knows what effect he wants to achieve must work closely with the collector to define the collector's tasks. Detailed knowledge of an opportunity usually proceeds directly from the desire to take advantage of it.

Third, better covert action will require much better operational security. Getting better operational security will require a better understanding of the people through whom we deal. In some cases, in our eagerness to stay at arm's length from the operation, the United States has abdicated to third parties the judgments about who the key players are to be and how they are to be managed, and as a result, U.S. control over operational security has often been restricted to the least significant part of the operation. Although operations through third parties are sometimes inevitable, in fact they require more skilled personnel than others. They also require periodic unilateral checking of the third party's judgment.

Improving operational security also requires control of leaks at all levels. Investigations can help. But a demonstrated willingness to enforce policies on secrecy and disclosure, by firing, demoting, or exposing the guilty would probably be more effective.

A Wish for Kings

Lewis H. Lapham

Incompetent armies deify the commander.
　　　　　　　　　　　　—Prussian maxim

While watching last summer's hearings before the Iran-*contra* committees, and again in the late autumn while reading the text of the congressional report, I kept expecting to hear somebody say something—not loudly, of course, and maybe only through a handkerchief, but at least something—about our slave's faith in secret wars. Surely, I thought, here was a chance to renounce both the theory and practice of covert action. About the practice, the politicians were often critical, a few of them permitting themselves an occasionally acerbic remark about the blundering dishonesty of Attorney General Edwin Meese and Vice Adm. John Poindexter. But on the point of doctrine the committees remained as silent as a colony of Christmas mice. Not once during the entire three months of testimony, or throughout the whole 690 pages of the published narrative, did anybody—not a single congressman, lawyer, or witness—utter so much as a single word against the fatuous and cynical belief that the cause of liberty can be made to stand on the pedestal of criminal violence.

A few members of the committees worried about what they called "the paradox" or "the contradictions" implicit in the waging of clandestine warfare under the jurisdiction of "a free, open, and democratic society." A few

other members expressed the forlorn hope that covert actions might be limited in size and cost, or undertaken only with the written permission of the Congress. But in answer to any and all direct questions about the need to deal manfully with events not always to one's liking, all present bowed their heads and murmured in solemn unison, saying, in effect: "Yes, it is a very, very dangerous world, heavily populated with all sorts of dangerous enemies armed with all sorts of dangerous weapons, and in order to defend ourselves against threats of infinite number we have no choice but to resort—reluctantly, of course, and ever mindful of the temporary damage to our constitutional principles—to murder."

Nobody ever failed to reaffirm his faith in this doctrine despite its proven stupidity. Asked to swear fealty to what amounted to Clint Eastwood's theory of diplomacy, the committees knelt and prayed.

So did the chorus of attending journalists and the choir of once and future statesmen. The editorials in the larger papers regretted the loss of the nation's innocence, but they reminded their readers that it was no good pretending that the world is a big, blue sandbox. Two former secretaries of state—Henry Kissinger and Gen. Alexander Haig—appeared on all three television networks to assure their audiences that secret operations were not only wonderfully effective but also, if properly conducted (i.e., by gentlemen as accomplished as themselves), entirely in keeping with the principles of Thomas Jefferson.

And yet, if somebody were to draw up a balance sheet reflecting the consequences of the covert actions we have let loose in the world over the last forty years, I expect that even a Pentagon accountant might concede the bankruptcy of the enterprise. Consistently and without noteworthy exception, the use of covert military action in support of American foreign policy has ended in failure or catastrophe. Whenever the United States embarks on

Lewis H. Lapham, "A Wish for Kings," *Harper's,* 276 (Feb. 1988), pp. 13–15. Copyright © 1988 by Harper's Magazine. All rights reserved. Reprinted by special permission.

one of those splendid little adventures so dear to the hearts of the would-be Machiavels in the White House or on the National Security Council, the patrol boats sink and the wrong tyrant seizes the palace and the radio station.

Unless the country stands willing to transform itself into a totalitarian state, even the theory of secret war is absurd. When mounted on any sort of large scale or extended over a period of more than two weeks, covert actions hide nothing from anybody except the people paying the bills. The Iran-*contra* hearings made it plain enough that the arms-for-hostages deals were known to several foreign governments (Israel, Iran, Saudi Arabia, Brunei, and Countries 8–16) as well as to an impressive crowd of Swiss bankers, Washington clerks, and Lebanese arms merchants.

Nor do the American operatives have much talent for covert action. The historical record is embarrassingly clear on the point. In the immediate aftermath of the Second World War, the earliest prototype of the CIA [Central Intelligence Agency], under the direction of Allen Dulles (a.k.a. "The Great White Case Officer"), enjoyed a brief moment of triumph in a world still largely in ruins, at a time when the military and economic supremacy of the United States went unquestioned by German waiters, and when it was possible to hire native gun-bearers for the price of a bar of chocolate and a pair of nylon stockings. The American intelligence services placed a number of agents behind Communist lines in Europe; recruited émigré armies to recapture the lost kingdoms of Poland, Bulgaria, and the Ukraine; and assisted with the removal of governments thought to be subversive in Iran (1953), Guatemala (1954), and the Philippines (1953).

Within a very few years the victories proved to be illusory or, at best, ambiguous. Advance scouts for the émigré armies parachuted into the Slavic darkness and were never seen or heard from again. By over-throwing a popular but socialist regime in Iran (at the behest of the Anglo-Iranian Oil Company), the United States opened the way to the vanity and ignorance of the Shah of Shahs (who had trouble speaking Farsi), to the quadrupling of the Arab oil price, the revolutionary zeal of the Ayatollah Khomeini, and the current impasse in the Persian Gulf.

The forced departure of Jacobo Arbenz from Guatemala (because his form of democratic socialism offended the United Fruit Company) allowed for the arrival of a notably vicious military junta, and in the Philippines the outfitting of Ramón Magsaysay with anti-Communist propaganda served as prelude to the corrupt regime of Ferdinand Marcos.

By the end of the decade, the American variations on themes of subversion had acquired the character of grotesque farce. With the hope of eliminating Achmed Sukarno as the president of Indonesia (because he permitted Communists to take their elected posts in his government), the CIA in 1957 armed a cadre of restless Sumatran colonels and engaged a Hollywood film crew to produce a pornographic film. Entitled *Happy Days*, the film purportedly showed Sukarno (played by a Mexican actor wearing a mask) in bed with a Soviet agent (played by a California waitress wearing a wig). The coup d'état failed, and the film was understood as a joke.

In 1961 the bungled invasion at the Bay of Pigs (a.k.a. "the glorious march through Havana") ensured Fidel Castro's communist authority throughout Latin America. The subsequent attempts to assassinate him (at least five by the CIA's hired agents) quite possibly resulted in the assassination of John F. Kennedy.

By encouraging the assassination of Ngo Dinh Diem in Saigon in 1963, the United States allied itself with a policy of realpolitik no less cynical than the one against which it was supposedly defending the principles of justice. Four American presidents defined the expedition in Vietnam as a prolonged covert action and systematically lied to the American people as to the reason for our presence in a country with which we never declared ourselves at war. As a result of our effort to rid Indochina of Communism, Vietnam became a unified Communist state. As a result of our effort to teach the world the lessons of democracy, we taught a generation of American citizens to think of their own government as an oriental despotism.

The discovery of the CIA's mining of the Nicaraguan harbors in 1983 obliterated the precarious advantage that the *contras* (on whose behalf the mines were placed) so desperately needed in the American Congress. Similarly discordant effects have followed our interventions in Cambodia, Angola, and Laos.

So unequivocal a record of stupidity and failure begs the question as to why American officialdom persists in its idiot dream of invisible war. It isn't for lack of sound advice. The late Chip Bohlen, one of the wisest of American diplomats and once ambassador to Moscow, understood in the early 1950s that covert actions always take place at the not-very-important margins of not-very-important events. In 1961 President Dwight Eisenhower's Board of Consultants on Foreign Intelligence Activities reviewed the CIA's reputedly glorious record and was unable to conclude that "on balance, all of the covert action programs undertaken by the CIA up to this time have been worth the risk or the great expenditure of manpower, money, and other resources involved."

In the early years of the nineteenth century, John Quincy Adams took up the question of covert action and thought that America should send "her benedictions, and her prayers...wherever the standard of freedom and independence has been or shall be unfurled." But America doesn't send arms and munitions because "she goes not abroad in search of monsters to destroy."

Were America to embark on such a foolish adventure, Adams said, she would become entangled "beyond the power of extrication, in all the wars of interest and intrigue, of individual avarice, envy, and ambition, which assume the colors and usurp the standard of freedom. The fundamental maxim of [America's] policy would insensibly change from *liberty* to *force*.... She might become the dictatress of the world. She would no longer be the ruler of her own spirit."

Arthur Schlesinger Jr. quotes Adams in the winter issue of *Foreign Affairs* and then goes on to quote John le Carré to the effect that covert actions recommend themselves to "declining powers," to men and institutions feeling the loss of their strength and becoming fearful of shadows. In le Carré's observation it is the timid and servile mind that places "ever greater trust in the magic formulae and hocus-pocus of the spy world. When the king is dying, the charlatans rush in."

Enter, to music for military band, Henry Kissinger, General Haig, Admiral Poindexter, Colonel North, and the braided company of Washington mountebanks, sophists, and leaping acrobats that drags behind it the wagons of the national security state. In the American context, the king is the spirit of liberty, which frightened and cynical people no longer know how to rule, and which, gratefully, they exchange for what they imagine to be the shields of their enemies.

The theory and practice of covert military action inevitably subverts our own people as well as our institutions of government. The operatives in the employ of the White House or the intelligence agencies come to believe themselves surrounded by a host of evil spirits shrieking in a foreign wind. Paranoid and easily convinced of their virtue, they get in the habit of telling so many lies that they no longer know their friends from their enemies.

Hindsight, of course, is easier than foresight, but I wish that at least one member of the joint committees had taken the trouble to study the historical record and to raise his voice against the presiding superstition. I wish I wasn't so often reminded of a herd of docile cattle, lowing softly in a pasture, waiting for Clint Eastwood (or Admiral Poindexter or General Secord or Colonel North) to lead them safely to slaughter.

QUESTIONS FOR DISCUSSION

1. What effect do covert operations have on the maintenance of democratic institutions at home?
2. What effect does the existence of hostile dictatorships around the world have on the need for covert operations by the United States?
3. On the basis of what we now know about covert operations since the end of World War II, how would U.S. foreign policy have been different if the United States had not engaged in such operations?
4. What role should Congress play in executive decisions to use covert operations? Why?
5. What criteria should be used to evaluate the success or failure of covert operations?

SUGGESTED READINGS

Carver, George A., Jr. "Covert Action an Essential Form of Diplomacy." *Human Events,* 47 (Dec. 12, 1987), pp. 12–14.

Cimbala, Stephen J., ed. *Intelligence and Intelligence Policy in a Democratic Society.* Dobbs Ferry, N.Y.: Transaction Publishers, 1987.

Gates, Robert M. "The CIA and Foreign Policy." *Foreign Affairs,* 66 (Winter 1987–88), pp. 215–30.

Goodman, Allan E. "Reforming U.S. Intelligence." *Foreign Policy,* no. 67 (Summer 1987), pp. 121–36.

Marshall, Jonathan, Peter Dale Scott, and Jane Hunter. *The Iran-Contra Connection: Secret Teams and Covert Operations in the Reagan Era.* Boston: South End Press, 1987.

Prados, John. *Presidents' Secret Wars: CIA and Pentagon Covert Operations.* New York: Morrow, 1986.

Ranelagh, John. *The Agency: The Rise and Fall of the CIA.* New York: Simon and Schuster, 1986.

Ransom, Harry Howe. "The Intelligence Function and the Constitution." *Armed Forces and Society,* 14 (Fall 1987), pp. 43–63.

Report of the Congressional Committee Investigating the Iran-Contra Affair, With Supplemental, Minority, and Additional Views. Washington, D.C.: Government Printing Office, 1987.

Treverton, Gregory F. *Covert Action: The Limits of Intervention in the Postwar World.* New York: Basic Books, 1987.

Webster, William H. "The Central Intelligence Agency: Intelligence Gathering and Covert Operations." *Vital Speeches of the Day,* 53 (Oct. 1, 1987), pp. 738–40.

Woodward, Bob. *Veil: The Secret Wars of the CIA, 1981–1987.* New York: Simon and Schuster, 1987.

9 The War Powers Resolution: Is the Cure Worse Than the Disease?

YES

Robert F. Turner

The War Powers Resolution: Unconstitutional, Unnecessary, and Unhelpful

NO

Daniel P. Franklin

The War Powers Resolution: An Effective Mechanism of Congressional Control

The War Powers Resolution: Unconstitutional, Unnecessary, and Unhelpful

Robert F. Turner

Perhaps the most confident judgment one can make about the War Powers Resolution is that several of its most fundamental provisions are flagrantly unconstitutional. The Founding Fathers established a complex system of checks and balances based on co-equal, separate, and independent political branches. Even recognizing the existence of ambiguity concerning the precise limits of executive and legislative authority pertaining to the use of force abroad, it does not follow that either branch has the unilateral power to determine the limits of the other's authority. Attempts by Congress to modify its constitutional relationship with the executive branch by simple statute have been firmly rejected by the United States Supreme Court in the past.

Specifically with respect to the War Powers Resolution, there are at least four serious constitutional problems inherent in three provisions of the statute:

1. Although during the evacuation of Indochina and the Mayaguez rescue operation many members of Congress—including some key sponsors of the War Powers Resolution—acknowledged that the President had independent constitutional authority as Commander-in-Chief to rescue endangered United States citizens abroad, the specific language of sec-

tion 2(c) of the Resolution asserts that this power is limited to "a national emergency created by attack upon the United States, its territories or possessions, or its armed forces." Any attempt to give legal effect to this provision would be patently unconstitutional.

2. Section 5(b) of the Resolution would deprive the President of his constitutional authority as Commander-in-Chief during a period of hostilities after a period of sixty days if the Congress remained silent on the matter. (The President would be permitted to act as Commander-in-Chief for an extra thirty days in order to protect United States forces in the process of withdrawal from hostilities.) Hostilities by United States forces could be continued only if Congress affirmatively acted to authorize their use. The idea that Congress can by silence or inaction deprive the President of a fundamental expressed constitutional power—in a time of national emergency, no less—is incompatible with our system of separation of powers.

3. Section 5(c) of the Resolution would allow the Congress to deprive the President of his Commander-in-Chief powers at any time simply by passing a concurrent resolution. Such a resolution does not have the effect of law (and even a statute could not deprive the President of his independent constitutional powers), because it is not submitted to the President for his signature or veto as required by the Constitution's presentation clause. This constitutional difficulty was recognized by many congressional supporters of the resolution and by eminent constitutional scholars who testified in favor of war powers legislation during congressional hearings on the subject. Similarly, there is a danger that in practice the Congress would use the "silent veto" power to dictate the tactical conduct of military operations—an infringement of both the President's Commander-in-Chief power and his authority as Chief Executive of the nation.

Excerpted from Robert F. Turner, "The War Powers Resolution: Unconstitutional, Unnecessary, and Unhelpful," 17 *Loyola of Los Angeles Law Review* 683 (1984). Footnotes have been omitted. Reprinted by permission of the Foreign Policy Research Institute.

For the first reason, section 5(c) of the War Powers Resolution is unconstitutional on its face. For the second, it is incompatible with the spirit of the Constitution.

That these rather apparent constitutional difficulties were ignored by enough members of both the House and Senate to override a presidential veto may be explained in part, perhaps, by Senator Javits' expectation that the White House would agree to a "methodology" for involving the Congress in decisions to commit United States forces to combat and that the resulting document would thus "represent a *compact* between Congress and the President for making the Constitution work in what is generally admitted to be a gray area." Under this "compact" theory it might be contended that at least some of the constitutional difficulties would not be present, since one branch would not be imposing its interpretation on the other. While this might successfully have established a working methodology for the duration of the Nixon Administration, even under a "compact" theory it could not be held to bind succeeding Presidents (any more than Congress could by statute prohibit a subsequent Congress from enacting a new statute taking a contrary position). Article five of the Constitution sets forth various procedures for amending the Constitution, but nowhere is it provided that the acquiescence of one President can alter the constitutional authority of a successor in office. While a "Ninety-third Congress-President Nixon methodology" might have been useful and fully acceptable to a future Commander-in-Chief, it would not be legally binding.

Political considerations also helped to obscure some of the constitutional objections to the Resolution—particularly after it had been vetoed by President Nixon. The vote to override the veto was taken in the wake of the firing of Watergate special prosecutor Archibald Cox, and senators were quoted as saying, for example: "This is not the time to support Nixon"; "We simply have to slap Nixon down, and this is the vote to do it on"; and "I love the Constitution, but I hate Nixon more."

Even were there no constitutional difficulties with the War Powers Resolution, a review of its implementation during the past nine years demonstrates that it has been as ineffective in practice as it is unwise in theory. Congress lacks the expertise to deal hurriedly with complex foreign policy emergencies, and most members are too busy with other duties to remain up-to-date on even a prolonged crisis. During times of crisis, decisiveness is often essential. Failure will almost be guaranteed if there are 536 potential secretaries of state trying to make decisions by consensus. Congress is not structured to make rapid decisions, and the more controversial and important the decision, the more likely it is that at least some members will want to prolong the debate to avoid having to take a position that might later prove to have been politically unwise.

The experience during the Indochina evacuations provides a good example. President Ford asked the Congress on April 10, 1975, to quickly consider and clarify his authority to carry out a humanitarian evacuation. He requested action within nine days and was promised expeditious consideration, but nearly three weeks later Congress was still debating as communist troops overran the last areas of Indochina. As the last congressional staff member evacuated from Saigon during the final days of April 1975, I am particularly grateful that President Ford decided to proceed with the evacuation on his own authority. Another individual might have found it more politically expedient to continue beseeching Congress for authorization legislation, and then to point the finger of blame at the Democrat-controlled Congress for failing to act to prevent hundreds of Americans from being seized by Vietnamese communist forces.

There is no guarantee that in a future crisis

another United States President would act with the same degree of courage displayed in 1975 by President Ford. After the failure of President Carter's attempted Iranian rescue there were calls for his impeachment for violating the War Powers Resolution, and during hearings in the House Committee on International Relations following the Korean tree trimming incident in 1976 it was asserted that if in the future a President did not comply with the provisions of the resolution: "We will have to get a new President."

The requirement that the President must obtain congressional authorization or terminate hostilities after a sixty-day period may also prove to be mischievous in practice. It might encourage a President to escalate a conflict unnecessarily—with accompanying increased loss of life and property on all sides—in order to try to achieve a quick victory. President Nixon's fear that Congress would soon enact legislation terminating United States involvement in Indochina, for example, was a factor in the decision to bomb the Hanoi area in December 1972: "Faced with a perceived deadline in Congress and continued intransigence in both Saigon and Hanoi, the President's instincts were for a massive post-election escalation of the conflict to force North Vietnam to an agreement." While in the view of many (including myself) this was also a sound decision on military grounds, irrespective of possible congressional action, the fact remains that ideally such decisions should not be influenced by extrinsic domestic political considerations.

Alternatively, such a requirement might encourage an enemy to be more recalcitrant in the hope that by holding out a few weeks longer Congress would undercut the President's ability to prosecute the action. In such a situation, the President might conclude that it was necessary to make major concessions and sacrifice substantial United States interests in order to negotiate a quick truce and avoid the risk of having his commander-in-chief powers withdrawn and losing everything to the enemy.

Something of an analogy can be found in the experience of French Socialist Premier Pierre Mendès-France, who announced in June 1954 that he would resign if he did not succeed in arranging a cease-fire in Indochina by July 20 of that year. The communist delegations at the Geneva Conference realized that the longer they stalled the more concessions he would be willing to make to preserve his job. The serious negotiations took place during the final hours of July 20, and shortly before midnight the wall clock was unplugged to permit the French delegation to make a few more concessions within the artificial time deadline. Another, more recent, example of the harmful effects of an artificial negotiating deadline can be found in a review of the background to the Panama Canal treaties. Because President Carter refused to submit the nomination of his negotiator (Sol Linowitz) to the Senate for confirmation, by law the appointment could not extend beyond a period of six months. The treaties, which were filled with serious ambiguities, were agreed upon six months to the day after the appointment was made.

The War Powers Resolution might contribute to unnecessarily high United States casualties in other ways as well. Writing in the October 1980 issue of the Marine Corps Gazette, Major A. J. Ponnwitz argued: "An enemy who knows a withdrawal is imminent has most of the information necessary to prevent the success of the military mission, or at least, to inflict severe casualties on the retreating forces." In addition, the Resolution encourages the President to commit United States military personnel into potentially dangerous situations—where involvement in hostilities is possible but not so clearly indicated by the circumstances as to invoke section 4(a)(1) of the War Powers Resolution—either unarmed (as in the Zaire airlift and the 1976 evacuation of Lebanon), or inadequately armed for effective self-defense (as may be the case in El Salvador), so as to avoid the provisions of section 4(a)(2). Rules prohibiting United States military personnel from entering certain areas or accompanying host-nation troops on "offensive" operations may help to reduce the likelihood of their direct involvement in hostilities; but requiring that, if attacked, they defend themselves with rocks or other inadequate weapons makes little sense and should be unacceptable as a matter of national policy.

Even the formal reporting requirement, which was unchallenged by President Nixon or any of his successors—is not without risks. Senate Armed Services Committee Chairman John Tower has observed:

> Although the act does not specify whether the report to Congress must be unclassified, there remains the possibility that a confidential report would become public knowledge. In many cases the more urgent the requirement that a decision remain confidential, the greater the pressures for disclosure. Thus, by notifying Congress of the size, disposition and objectives of U.S. forces dispatched in a crisis, we run the risk that the report may get into the public domain. If this information becomes available to the enemy, he then knows exactly what he can expect from American forces and thus what risks he runs in countering American actions. This removes any element of surprise the U.S. forces might have enjoyed and eliminates any uncertainties the adversary might have as to American plans.

The War Powers Resolution has been heralded as the answer to future "Vietnams." Never again, it was said, would a President be able to commit United States soldiers to foreign wars without congressional participation in the decisionmaking process. While perhaps reassuring to the uninformed constituents of some congressmen, this rationale bore little resemblance to historical reality. Writing in the Virginia Law Review, Yale law professor (and

former Undersecretary of State for political affairs) Eugene Rostow observed:

> During the war in Vietnam...we experienced naked political irresponsibility. First, the President and Congress, acting together in a constitutional mode that goes back to the time of Washington, made a series of decisions involving us in the war....Later, when the war...became unpopular, many of the congressmen who had voted and voted and voted for [it] suddenly began to say that [it was] all the President's fault. They claimed that the President had involved the country in war through stealth and concealment....Then, having created the myth of presidential usurpation, Congress passed the War Powers Resolution to cure the imaginary disease.

Perhaps the greatest irony of the War Powers Resolution is that, despite its unconstitutional infringement upon the authority of the President, it would not have prevented the war in Vietnam had it been in effect in the early 1960's. In compliance with section 2(c)(2) of the Resolution, the use of United States Armed Forces in Indochina was clearly done pursuant to "specific statutory authorization." Further, there was sufficient consultation to satisfy the mandate of section 3, and the reporting requirements of section 4 would not even arguably have influenced the likely course of events. Finally, it was not until the 1970's—many years after the commitment had been made and the troops deployed—that a majority could be mustered in Congress to limit funding for the war, much less direct that the troops be withdrawn.

Many "lessons," of course, can be drawn from our Vietnam experience—but only a few are legitimate. Those legislators who reflexively cry "no more Vietnams" each time the president exercises the national muscle might benefit from a re-examination of Vietnam, and particularly the role Congress played. Perhaps the United States was doomed to failure in Indochina—we will never know. But the war was not lost militarily on the battlefield; it was lost in Washington when a frustrated Congress terminated funding. There are, no doubt, individuals who sincerely believe Congress acted wisely, but the consequences of the communist victory that followed in Indochina have been significant. To mention but a few:

(1) The fall of the United States–supported governments did not bring the much-heralded peace. On the contrary, there is evidence that more people may have died in the first three or four years of so-called peace in tiny Cambodia alone than were killed on all sides throughout Indochina during thirteen years of war.

(2) The "National Liberation Front" and "third-force" elements touted by congressional doves were promptly shoved aside by Hanoi's legions, who ruled Saigon as an occupational army following its "liberation."

(3) The people of Vietnam are in a far worse position today than they were a decade ago. Corruption and mismanagement have resulted in economic disaster, and human rights have deteriorated dramatically. There are more political prisoners, elections are far less free, there are fewer newspapers (none opposing the regime), and unapproved books have been publicly burned. Apparently to repay the Soviets for their extensive economic aid, thousands of Vietnamese workers have been shipped to the Soviet Union to work as laborers.

(4) Since "liberation," more than a million people have risked robbery, rape, and even death (some experts estimate that boat people have no more than a fifty-fifty chance of surviving the ordeal) to flee the new Gulag that Vietnam has become.

(5) United States interests in the region have suffered as well. Today Hanoi is closely allied with Moscow, and is providing the Soviet navy with access to extremely valuable port facilities along the southern coast of Vietnam. The new Vietnamese army is the third largest in the world (the United States Army ranks fifth).

If the War Powers Resolution does not resolve the conflict in legislative-executive relations regarding the use of force, what principles should govern the conduct of the two political branches in the national security policymaking process? Is there a solution, given the admitted ambiguities of the Constitution on this question? Probably so. At least there are steps that could be taken by both branches to substantially reduce the likelihood of disasters in legislative-executive relations such as were witnessed during the early and mid 1970's.

To begin with, each branch should recognize that the other has a fully legitimate role to play, and that no policy will succeed in the long run without the support of both branches. This is certainly true when the policy in question might involve a commitment of armed forces to hostilities. Taylor Reveley was certainly right when, in his recent book, *War Powers of the President and Congress,* he observed that "the Constitution does impose one iron demand on the President and Congress: that they cooperate if any sustained venture for war or peace is to succeed." . . .

Given the Vietnam experience, it should be even less necessary to emphasize the necessity of congressional cooperation in formulating policies involving the use of military force. In many instances, of course, a congressional role is mandated by the Constitution. But even were this not the case, in the long run congressional support is essential. First of all, even if the Commander-in-Chief already has a sufficient army and navy, for extended hostilities he will need congressional appropriations to purchase fuel and ammunition. More important, members who feel that Congress has been cut out of the decision-making process will be more likely to take their case to the people, and the resulting display of disunity will endanger public support and adversely affect the morale of our soldiers and the policies of our friends and foes alike. We need look back no further than Vietnam to realize the decisive role that these psychological factors can play.

Accepting the practical utility—indeed, the necessity—of effective cooperation between the political branches on policy questions involving the use of armed force, we must at the same time recognize the difficulty of trying to consult seriously during a period of crisis prior to making a decision. Certainly the President cannot be expected to talk individually with all 535 members of Congress, and at times events move so quickly that even the best-intentioned Commander-in-Chief can do little more than instruct his staff to keep congressional leaders informed. This is what consultation has come to mean in practice under the War Powers Resolution, but it is far less than Congress has a right to expect if the crisis is foreseeable. The solution may be for the two branches to maintain sufficiently close contacts on a regular basis so that, when an emergency requiring an immediate response does confront the President, he can take probable congressional attitudes into account from the start. When appropriate, of course, he would still need to seek formal congressional approval or authorization. But by maintaining continuous and close consultation with Congress, he would lessen the likelihood of being surprised by subsequent criticism and at the same time would be less likely to leave Congress with the feeling that it had been ignored.

It should be noted that consultation can take many forms. At least as important as formal hearings and sessions with congressional leaders in the White House are the more numerous informal exchanges that occur when administration officials encounter members of Congress at cocktail parties and in other off-the-record settings. Although there are risks involved—given the competing demands on a congressman's time and the instrumental role played by congressional staff members in the national security field, particularly when the subject matter is technical or the issues are highly complex—it is important for the executive branch to maintain regular contacts with key congressional staff members. This not only increases the likelihood that the administration will be aware of areas of special congressional concern, but also serves to better inform Congress about administration programs and policies.

The Constitution requires that the President, executive-branch officers, and all members of Congress take an oath of office to "support" or "defend" the Constitution of the United States. This should be kept in mind by both sides when issues of constitutional consequence are under consideration. During my years as a Senate staff member, on several occasions I heard other staff members, and even senators, assert that it was for the courts, not Congress, to worry about whether a statute was constitutional. This is not a responsible attitude. True, some issues are so complex that even constitutional scholars differ as to where fine lines should be drawn (or if they should be drawn at all). But ideally, in these gray areas, neither branch should seek to provoke a confrontation with the other.

In this regard, the executive branch could well be guided by the legacy of President Jefferson in his dealings with the Barbary powers. Although war had been declared by the Bey of Tripoli and the opinion was widespread that in such a circumstance the President needed no additional authority to initiate offensive hostilities, Jefferson nevertheless deferentially sought formal authorization from Congress to carry on the campaign. The guiding rule for the executive branch was expressed well by Alexander Hamilton, who wrote: "In so delicate a case, in one which involves so important a consequence as that of war—my opinion is that *no doubtful authority ought to be exercised by the President."*

If Jefferson should be the model for the executive branch, the Congress could learn from the late Senator Arthur H. Vandenberg, who served as President Pro Tempore of the Senate, chaired its Foreign Relations Committee, and worked closely with the Truman Administration to forge a bipartisan consensus on foreign policy. In a 1947 speech to the Cleveland Council of World Affairs, Senator Vandenberg said:

> This [bipartisanship] does not mean that we cannot have earnest, honest, even vehement domestic differences of opinion on foreign policy. It is no curb on free opinion or free speech. But it does mean that they should not root themselves in partisanship. We should ever strive to hammer out a permanent American foreign policy, in basic essentials, which serves all America.

On domestic issues, Senator Vandenberg was capable of being as partisan as most of his colleagues. No doubt he would have enjoyed watching the other party squirm on foreign policy matters as well, but he knew the extreme importance of national unity in facing a shrinking world. He once said: "In the face of any foreign problem, our unity is as important as our atomic bombs," and in one of his last public speeches—a Lincoln Day address in Detroit on February 10, 1949—he looked toward the future:

> It will be a sad hour for the Republic if we ever desert the fundamental concept that politics shall stop at the water's edge. It will be a triumphant day for those who would divide and conquer us if we abandon the quest for a united voice when America demands peace with honor in the world. In my view nothing has happened to absolve either Democrats or Republicans from continuing to put their country first. Those who don't will serve neither their party nor themselves.

In the sphere of foreign policy, where national unity is of such great importance, the President has a special status. As the Supreme Court noted in *United States v. Curtiss-Wright Export Corp.,* he is "the sole organ of the federal government in the field of international relations." He has an obligation to weigh the opinions of Congress and needs the affirmative approval of Congress to implement many policies; but no matter how hard he tries, if the issue is controversial, he cannot satisfy the wishes of all of the 535 members of the House and Senate. Not infrequently, the professional judgments of his advisers may lead him to pursue strategies that would not be chosen by a majority of the Congress. But so long as the President is pursuing policy goals shared by the Congress and the American people, he should be allowed substantial flexibility in his choice of tactics.

President Lincoln once observed: "In a storm at sea, no one on board can wish the ship to sink, and yet not infrequently all go down together because too many will direct and no single mind will be allowed to control." In a similar vein, two years after leaving office Thomas Jefferson wrote:

> Leave the President free to choose his own co-adjutors, to pursue his own measures, and support him and them, even if we think we are wiser than they, honester than they are, or possessing more enlarged information of the state of things. If we move in mass, be it ever so circuitously, we shall attain our object; but if we break into squads, every one pursuing the path he thinks most direct, we become an easy conquest to those who can now barely hold us in check. I repeat again, that we ought not to schismatize on either men or measures. Principles alone can justify that.

The proper congressional role in national security matters should be that of a full partner in the formulation of general principles and policies, rather than that of a micromanager or second-guesser of the President's execution of those policies. Certainly the initiation of significant offensive hostilities is such a policy decision, which under our constitutional system of government should not be made without the approval of Congress. But more detailed questions of how many and which forces to use, and how best to employ them, are beyond both the expertise and the constitutional jurisdiction of the legislative branch. Similarly, the recent practice of globetrotting congressmen traveling to international crisis spots to negotiate with foreign leaders—unless expressly authorized by the President—would have shocked the Founding Fathers and is a gross infringement on the constitutional authority of the President.

Clearly there are substantial benefits to be gained by presenting a united foreign policy to the world. It is difficult to prove conclusively, but a strong case can be made that the divisiveness in United States foreign policy during the 1970's was instrumental in Hanoi's decision to escalate the fighting in South Vietnam, and in Moscow's decision to deploy Cuban soldiers to seize control of the Angolan revolution. There may be some issues of principle on which agreement cannot be reached and regarding which bipartisan cooperation will prove impossible—but cooperation should always be the goal. This can only work, however, if both branches, and both political parties, make a full commitment to pursuing that goal in good faith.

While in practice the first step—legitimate consultation with the Congress—may belong to the President, in reality the controlling decision belongs to the congressional opposition. As Senator Vandenberg observed:

> Since the Constitution charges the President with primary responsibility in international relations, it is he who must start the process and set its boundaries. But in the final analysis the Congressional "opposition" decides whether there shall be cooperation. We cooperated. I express the belief that our patriotic Democratic friends

will follow this example when they are in the "opposition."

Unfortunately, those in opposition have the greatest incentives toward partisanship. Furthering the interests of their own candidates—or in many cases their own candidacy—is not accomplished by making the incumbent President look good; and, realistically, he is likely to get most of the public credit for successes. Even ignoring these considerations, there are substantial pressures on a congressman to undercut presidential foreign policy initiatives. For example, experience shows that the press gives more attention to the critics than to the supporters of national policy, and in politics press exposure can often be directly translated into votes. Furthermore, many foreign policy issues are of greater interest to a small but vocal ethnic, religious, or other special-interest group than to the population in general. Senator Tower has observed that "to the extent that Congress often represents competing regional and parochial interests, it is almost impossible for it to forge a unified national foreign policy strategy and to speak with one voice in negotiating with foreign powers."

The influence of ethnic pressures was very apparent during the Cyprus crisis in the mid 1970's. I heard several congressmen and senators say, in effect, "Don't talk to me about the strategic importance of Turkey—I don't have any Turkish restaurants in my district." Issues of war and peace are particularly susceptible to this sort of pressure—few intelligent legislators enjoy casting votes that may cost the lives of the sons and daughters of voting constituents. Thus the safest vote for an individual congressman often becomes the most dangerous for the nation—a vote of partisan dissension during a period of national crisis. There is a special irony here, in that while the congressman by his dissension is absolving himself from the consequences, the divisiveness he helps to create may be a central factor in encouraging the enemy to escalate the conflict—resulting in an even greater number of United States casualties.

In his 1975 Virginia Law Review article, Eugene Rostow wrote:

> When the Executive Branch deals with congressmen and senators who continue to vote for a war and then say, "there's no one here but us chickens" after the war becomes unpopular, a mode of suspicion develops which is rather hard to allay. I personally have dealt with congressmen and senators about Vietnam, often reminding them that the Administration had long been trying to achieve goals which they have recommended in political speeches—reconvening the Geneva Conference, for example. Typically, their response was, I know that, but you must remember that I have to be elected in my district. The President has to do what must be done. I must take care of my reelection. In short, a great many men slithered off the deck when the going got rough.

This attitude of political irresponsibility was a central factor in the creation of the War Powers Resolution—which was portrayed by many in Congress as a means of insuring that a future President would not bypass Congress as Johnson and Nixon had done in Vietnam. Congressional irresponsibility has also been apparent in the implementation of the War Powers Resolution. With the possible exceptions of the Indochina evacuations, providing a multinational force and observers for the Sinai, and the first Lebanon deployment in 1982, none of the instances examined in this study has been preceded by the kind of meaningful consultation envisioned in the Resolution. The stated purpose of the Resolution (and presumably the consultation requirement) is to "insure that the collective judgment of both the Congress and the President will apply to the introduction of United States Armed Forces into hostilities." The President can hardly consider the "judgment" of the Congress if his consultation amounts to having a staff member inform congressional leaders once a decision to act has been made and is in the process of implementation.

Except for the fact that his action was permissible under his independent constitutional authority (and thus, as applied, the War Powers Resolution was unconstitutional), President Ford's use of force in the Mayaguez affair appears to have been a violation of the consultation language of the resolution. During the same operation, the President violated the specific terms of the (unconstitutional) Cooper-Church Amendment and its progeny by using United States Armed Forces off the shores of Cambodia without specific congressional authorization. And yet his operation was viewed by the American people as a great success, and so liberals in the Congress generally praised his performance. The Senate Foreign Relations Committee even went so far as to unanimously adopt a resolution praising the rescue operation. As the New York Times (which also praised the operation) observed:

> In the *Mayaguez* case, Mr. Ford believed he was required to consult with Congressional leaders before acting. He seems instead to have informed them somewhat after the fact. Yet there was practically no criticism on legal grounds probably for several reasons: Criticism at a welcome moment of success would be politically risky at best.

In contrast, President Carter failed to consult before starting the first phase of his attempted rescue of United States citizens held hostage in Iran—when there was no Cooper-Church-type restriction on United States military activities in the region, and when complete secrecy was essential to any chance of success—and was sharply criticized in the Congress and the press. His rescue attempt failed. It does not seem unreasonable to expect the Congress to play by one set of rules. Further, if it insists upon prior consultation, Congress must be responsible enough not to leave the President swinging in the wind nearly three weeks later—as occurred before the Saigon evacuation—facing a crisis while Congress continues to debate. And if Congress really doubts that the President has constitutional authority to rescue endangered United States citizens in Indochina or Iran, it must apply this principle uniformly without respect to the ultimate success or popularity of the president's actions.

Finally, if Congress contends that the President cannot rescue endangered Americans without first securing formal authorization, it must be prepared to accept greater responsibility for the fate of those endangered citizens. Had President Ford accepted the argument of many in Congress that he lacked authority to rescue the last Americans from Phnom Penh because of the War Powers Resolution or other statutory constraints, and had those Americans suffered the fate of more than a million Cambodians under the subsequent rule of Pol Pot, we might wonder whether Congress would have willingly accepted any responsibility for their deaths.

For all of his faults and weaknesses—and I believe they were numerous—President Johnson recognized the importance of congressional participation in an effective foreign policy. He had, after all, served for many years as majority leader of the Senate. Reflecting on the failures of his Vietnam policy, he wrote in 1972: "I knew that if I wanted Congress with me at the crash landing, they had to be with me at the takeoff. But I forgot about the availability of parachutes."

One of the more perceptive analyses of the congressional role in foreign affairs was provided by Pat Holt, who spent thirty years on the staff of the Senate Committee on Foreign Relations and was its staff director at the time of the Indochina evacuations, the Mayaguez rescue, and some of the other operations discussed in this study. He writes:

> Senator Vandenberg said that Congress wanted to participate in the takeoffs as well as the crash

landings; actually it sometimes seems more interested in investigating crash landings than in participating in takeoffs. Despite the fact that it was clumsily executed, Mayaguez was a success, and there is little political mileage to be gained in a post mortem of the rescue of American citizens and the protection of freedom of the seas.

> After the failure of the Bay of Pigs invasion in 1961, the Senate Foreign Relations Committee held weeks of hearings rehashing all the bad advice Kennedy had received and trying to determine who had bungled what. After the success story of the missile crisis in 1962, Secretary of State Dean Rusk all but begged the Foreign Relations Committee to review—or investigate, if you will—the administration's handling of it, but no one was interested. The general principle seems to be that success has few autopsies; the corpse of a failure is picked to pieces.

The lessons of the congressional reaction to Vietnam and to various incidents after the War Powers Resolution was adopted are not encouraging. While the period may be historically atypical, during the 1970's Congress proved itself time and again to be a political creature with a conveniently selective institutional memory. More often than not, congressional attitudes toward specific situations appeared more attuned to public opinion polls than to the requirements of the law or the Constitution. Even after a commitment had been established by treaty, authorized by joint resolution of Congress, and reaffirmed for years by overwhelming congressional majorities through the appropriation of funds—as occurred in Vietnam—many members of Congress found no difficulty in pretending that the President was solely responsible and that Congress had unconstitutionally been excluded from the decision to commit troops. Yet, when the President did act essentially alone, without consulting Congress, if the operation was perceived by the public as a success, he was greeted with cheers.

If bipartisan cooperation in the formulation of national security policy is going to work,

Congress must commit itself in word and deed to playing a more responsible role. The practice of undercutting the President for partisan gain, or to placate a special-interest constituency, is a luxury we can no longer afford if we are to have a viable foreign policy.

The benefits to Congress of being a full partner in the formulation of foreign and national security policy are significant, and those to the American people are even greater; but they will not come cost free. Members of Congress must be willing to devote substantially greater time to keeping abreast of national security problems—time that will directly gain them few, if any, votes, because often they will not even be able to discuss the subject matter in public. Each hour spent in a classified briefing is an hour that cannot be spent with constituents or seeking newspaper headlines. Further, many of the briefings will be uninteresting and will pertain to matters that might—but usually will not—require formal congressional action or become issues of concern for most Americans.

In past years, few members of Congress have been willing to take time from their busy routines to attend such briefings. Former National Security Council staffer Dr. John F. Lehman has noted:

> Consultation as a process...requires as much active involvement on the part of Congress as on the part of the Executive. Failure to consult is a constant complaint from Congress, but the fault quite often lies with the members of Congress rather than the Executive. During the period 1969–73, for instance, the National Security Council had a standing offer to brief any member of Congress on whatever foreign policy issue he desired. The ground rules for such briefings were to provide the fullest and most highly classified information on the issue, but to allow no transcript and to provide no documents. According to the records of the NSC, this offer was taken up only three times in five years.

Lehman—who later served as deputy director of the Arms Control and Disarmament Agency and as secretary of the navy—also notes the "very sparse attendance at committee hearings" on national security issues, and says, "It is always difficult to round up an audience of any number on Capitol Hill to hear executive branch officials brief on a policy unless it is the crisis topic of the day."

A greater congressional role in this vital area will not only increase the demands on a member's time, it will also increase the likelihood that he will be held accountable by the American people for foreign policy failures. This is a serious risk, but it comes with the partnership role. Following failure of the Iran rescue attempt, an article in the *National Journal* noted:

> There is also the question of how much leaders of Congress really want to know about such risky ventures as the attempted rescue of the hostages. If they had been briefed fully and in advance in this case, they could have been held accountable, along with the President, for the mission's failure.

More recently, Stephen Chapman wrote:

> The crisis in Lebanon shows the limits of Congress' new role. Its idea of a partnership is to set policy when there is a political advantage to be gained, and to shirk responsibility when there are dangers....A true partnership requires that Congress not merely hold its veto over the President's head. Congress also has to help formulate answers to tough questions....Congress enjoys exploiting its newfound power on the easy issues—aid to El Salvador, CIA involvement in Angola. But on the more divisive ones, where there are political risks as well as benefits, it is happy to let the White House serve as point man....Once the President steps out, the dangers can be gauged. Then, and only then, will Congress make up its mind. That is how it thinks a partnership in foreign policy ought to operate—with maximum risk to the President,

and maximum opportunity for legislators. Some partnership. Some foreign policy.

Finally, full congressional participation in the making of national security policy will be impossible unless Congress finds a way to deal with the intentional or inadvertent disclosure of classified or sensitive national security information. To be successful, many operations are totally dependent upon secrecy. In effect, they are vulnerable to being "vetoed" by any individual who decides to go public with criticism. The Constitution does not require—and no workable set of rules could require—that sensitive national security operations have the approval of every single member of Congress. Indeed, there is evidence that the Founding Fathers expected that certain sensitive national security information would be denied to the Congress. Writing in *The Federalist,* for example, John Jay wrote in 1788:

> There are cases where the most useful intelligence may be obtained, if the persons possessing it can be relieved from apprehensions of discovery. Those apprehensions will operate on those persons whether they are actuated by mercenary or friendly motives, and there doubtless are many of both descriptions, who would rely on the secrecy of the president, but who would not confide in that of the senate, and still less in that of a larger popular assembly. The convention have [sic] done well therefore in so disposing of the power of making treaties, that although the president must in forming them act by the advice and consent of the senate, yet he will be able to manage the business of intelligence in such manner as prudence may suggest.

More recently, in *United States v. Curtiss-Wright Export Corp.,* the Supreme Court noted:

> [The President] has his confidential sources of information. He has his agents in the form of diplomatic, consular and other officials. Secrecy in respect of information gathered by them may be highly necessary, and the premature disclo-

sure of it productive of harmful results. Indeed, so clearly is this true that the first President refused to accede to a request to lay before the House of Representatives the instructions, correspondence and documents relating to the negotiation of the Jay Treaty—a refusal the wisdom of which was recognized by the House itself and has never since been doubted.

In recent years—particularly after the Watergate scandals and the accompanying investigation of intelligence abuses—Congress has been provided considerably greater access to sensitive national security information than was previously the case. Yet, unless Congress acts with a greater sense of responsibility, the executive branch must recognize that information provided on sensitive operations will be subject to "veto by leak" by any member. Following the Iranian rescue attempt Senator John Glenn, a former marine officer, said: "If I were on the raid, I wouldn't want it all over Capitol Hill." Although Senate Foreign Relations Committee chairman Frank Church was among the first to condemn President Carter for his failure to consult before the rescue attempt, the *National Journal* observed: "The White House surely recalls the last time Church was told a military secret—United States discovery of a Soviet brigade in Cuba—the first thing he did was call a press conference."

Clearly, if Congress expects to be provided the sort of sensitive national security information necessary to contribute to an intelligent policy decision, it must substantially improve its record of preserving secrets. As Barbara Hingston Craig notes in a recent issue of the *Journal of Policy Analysis and Management:*

> Presidential decisions such as the rescue attempt [in Iran] are made in light of data accumulated from highly classified intelligence files. Security concerns, however, preclude the president's sharing this information with members of Congress. Congress has yet to organize itself in such a manner that it can be trusted with sensitive

information.... In the House, for example, 17 of 22 committees deal with at least some aspects of foreign policy. In the Senate, 16 of 19 committees have some jurisdiction over foreign policy. To keep 535 persons informed who may feel free to disseminate what they learn thereby is clearly impossible. Nor is there any way at present for the president to deal with a smaller representative group. Changes in the last decade that have eroded the leadership's power and that have fractionalized and disaggregated the power of the body itself have worked to make it a collection of "loners."

Recently, former Director of Central Intelligence Stansfield Turner observed:

> To a greater extent than with executive branch oversight, the fear that information will leak may inhibit the agencies from taking risks. The danger of leaks is particularly high because the [congressional oversight] committees are larger than necessary; sensitive material cannot be restricted to only a few committee members. Moreover, *secrecy goes against the grain of most politicians.*

One of the most discouraging phenomena I witnessed during my years working with the Foreign Relations Committee was the disclosure to the press of information provided by the executive branch under injunction of secrecy. Indeed, on one occasion, in October 1975, the committee voted to "declassify" and make public the texts of classified agreements submitted to the committee by the Department of State. When Senator Robert Griffin—who had strongly opposed the decision—informed his colleagues the following day that the action violated both statutory law and Senate rules, the committee hastily called another meeting and voted to reclassify the documents it had already released to the press.

Fortunately, in at least one area—intelligence—there is some evidence that security measures have been improved. Congress has provided that the most sensitive operations are to be reported to only one committee of each

house, and impressive security measures have been taken to reduce the likelihood of sensitive information being compromised by those committees, but some problems still remain. It has been suggested many times over the years that Congress establish a joint committee on national security—comprised of key House and Senate leaders and representatives of each committee with major national security responsibilities—to represent the Congress in consultation with the executive branch on national security matters. This is certainly worth considering. Something needs to be done—the stakes are too high to permit the present arrangement to continue indefinitely.

One thing is clear. Nearly a decade of experience has demonstrated that the War Powers Resolution has not been a useful tool in facilitating improved executive-legislative cooperation in the formulation of national security policy. Not only are many of its provisions clearly unconstitutional, but it is fraught with practical difficulties as well. The limited consultation and the pro forma reports it has produced have done nothing to improve the relationship between the two political branches in the important business of defending the United States and promoting international peace and stability.

Barbara Craig noted that "there are no signs...that the resolution has been instrumental in bringing about a more cooperative partnership between the executive and Congress in regard to decisions about the use of armed forces." She added:

> The president has much to gain by developing a workable procedure for comity with Congress with regard to foreign policy. By involving that body, his own position could be strengthened. His ability to act decisively in the world community would be greatly enhanced if it were known to be based on the consent of Congress. And there's the rub. *The War Powers Resolution pits Congress and the president against each other.*

Not only does the Resolution pit the political branches against each other, but it does so resoundingly and before the entire world—with predictably damaging consequences. The proliferation of nuclear arms and other weapons of devastating destructiveness of necessity makes *deterring* a conflict a primary national security objective, and *winning* only a clear second choice. In reality, in modern warfare there may be no winners. Deterrence is a function of perceptions of capabilities and, equally if not more important, perceptions of the national will to employ those capabilities effectively.

The United States has made an inestimable contribution to international peace and security during the post–World War II era by convincing potential aggressors that the costs of aggression will greatly outweigh any perceived benefits. In part, this has been made possible by the creation of regional security and collective defense arrangements, perhaps the foremost of which is the North Atlantic Treaty Organization (NATO). Peace has also been furthered by occasional calculated saber-rattling by United States Presidents—from the Truman Doctrine in the Mediterranean, Eisenhower in the Middle East and Formosa, and Kennedy in Berlin and Cuba to Reagan in Central America. When appropriate, particularly serious threats have been met by both the President and the Congress through the enactment of joint resolutions—putting friend and foe alike on notice that the United States was united and fully committed to taking all necessary steps to help its friends resist aggression.

Over many years, and through many crises, this approach proved extremely effective in helping to keep the peace. But its success was predicated upon the existence of two critical perceptions in the minds of potential aggressors—that the United States was strong, and that it would use all of its strength, if necessary, to prevent the success of aggression.

Tragically, during the past fifteen years decisions made largely in the Congress have inadvertently led our adversaries to question both of these perceptions. Of course, Congress has not done this single-handedly. Numerous mistakes were also made in the executive branch. At the time of the 1962 Cuban missile crisis, the United States had an approximate twenty to one superiority over the Soviet Union in deliverable nuclear weapons. By 1965, Secretary of Defense McNamara concluded that the Soviets had given up on ever achieving nuclear parity with the United States, and on this premise requests to Congress to fund strategic programs during the late 1960s were quite modest. Most defense expenditures during the period were keyed to the growing conflict in Vietnam, and the strategic focus was on arms control agreements. The United States intelligence community was also not without blame, as it substantially underestimated the Soviet effort to close and even reverse the so-called missile gap. As a result, between late 1966 and the opening of the SALT [Strategic Arms Limitation Talks] I negotiations in November 1969, the total number of United States nuclear delivery vehicles decreased by forty-five, while those of the Soviet Union nearly doubled. At the same time, substantially adverse trends were also developing in the balance of conventional weapons.

However, the greatest harm, in this writer's view, was done by the Congress. When it became politically expedient to be a Vietnam "dove" (a transformation which not infrequently took on a strangely retroactive character, so that legislators who had voted for the Gulf of Tonkin Resolution and time and again to finance the war would suddenly proclaim with straight faces that they had opposed the war from the beginning), cutting the defense budget became something of a sport, and members of Congress virtually stood in line to get an opportunity to challenge commitments to other states as well. The Senate, for example, rather gratuitously passed the National Commitments Resolution, putting the world on notice that the United States had no national commitment to any country with which it did not have a formally ratified treaty or other congressionally approved defense relationship. In a similar vein, shortly thereafter the Congress announced to the world in section 8(a)(2) of the War Powers Resolution that in the event of an enemy attack on our closest NATO allies the President would not have legal authority to commit United States forces unless Congress decided to vote him that authority.

The Senate, in other words, essentially went full circle. It assured the world's potential aggressors that the United States had no obligation to assist any country with which it did not have a congressionally approved defense agreement, and it then joined the House in saying that for the President to have the power to execute our solemn treaty commitments he would need to seek the same type of formal congressional approval that would be required to assist a state with which the United States had no relations at all. This gave a new meaning to the concept of a commitment.

Senate passage of the National Commitments Resolution reminded some observers of a January 1950 speech by Secretary of State Dean Acheson outlining a United States defense perimeter that excluded South Korea. Pyongyang was apparently listening, because within a few months more than 60,000 North Korean soldiers invaded South Korea. At that point Acheson apparently decided that he had been mistaken and that South Korea was worth defending. Nearly 34,000 United States soldiers lost their lives in rectifying that mistake.

During the height of its anti-Vietnam irresponsibility, the Congress ignored this lesson. Not satisfied with having assured our adversaries that genuine United States defense commitments were few—and that those which existed were, legally speaking, essentially meaningless—the Congress began enacting other legislation limiting the President's flexibility in dealing with national security problems. According to Senator Tower, during the 1970's "over 150 separate prohibitions and restrictions were enacted on Executive Branch authority to formulate and implement foreign policy." Several of these laws virtually guaranteed our enemies that the United States would not effectively help to resist aggression in specific trouble spots like South Vietnam, Laos, Cambodia, and Angola. It may have been coincidental, but it is worth noting that upon enactment of those laws external communist forces substantially escalated their activities, and each of those states is today under Marxist rule.

Today, the War Powers Resolution continues to pit the Congress against the President. In El Salvador, where President Reagan is valiantly trying to dissuade Moscow and Havana from underwriting the overthrow of a popularly elected government, the prospects for meaningful peace are being jeopardized by the War Powers Resolution. Virtually every time the President speaks or acts firmly to deter the communists, his congressional critics cite the War Powers Resolution and tell the world— occasionally in language reminiscent of the old Ludlow Amendment—"He can't do that!"

Needless to say, this continuing display of divisiveness reduces the effectiveness of the President's efforts to deter Soviet and Cuban aggression. If the President's efforts at deterrence fail, America's long-term options would appear to be (1) watching feebly from the sidelines as Moscow and its well-armed clients subvert our neighbors to the south one by one or (2) eventually committing United States combat troops to a costly re-establishment of that national credibility which is the sine qua non for effective deterrence. If these are in fact our options, supporting the president at this time in an effort to deter aggression appears increasingly attractive.

Since its passage over a presidential veto in 1973, a number of members of Congress have expressed serious concerns about the constitutionality or practicality of the War Powers Resolution. Even Senator Frank Church, as Chairman of the Senate Foreign Relations Committee, expressed doubt about the ability of Congress to restrain the Commander-in-Chief by statute and concluded: "I wonder really whether we have done very much in furthering our purpose through the War Powers Resolution."

If Congress does not take the lead and repeal the resolution, the Reagan Administration would be wise to reassess its own public posture toward the statute. While the President's apparent effort to avoid a confrontation over the constitutionality of the Resolution is in many respects commendable, it may not be wise in the long run. The prominent constitutional scholar Charles Warren has written:

> Under our Constitution, each branch of the Government is designed to be a coordinate representative of the will of the people.... Defense by the Executive of his constitutional powers becomes in very truth, therefore, defense of popular rights—defense of power which the people granted him.
>
> It was in this sense that President Cleveland spoke of his duty to the people not to relinquish any of the powers of his great office. It was in

that sense that President Buchanan stated the people have rights and prerogatives in the execution of his office by the President which every President is under a duty to see "shall never be violated in his person" but "passed to his successors unimpaired by the adoption of a dangerous precedent." In maintaining his rights against a trespassing Congress, the President defends not himself, but popular government; he represents not himself, but the people.

If a future President concludes that it is necessary to ignore some of the Resolution's unconstitutional provisions, congressional critics can be expected to rely heavily upon any tradition of acquiescence by prior Commanders-in-Chief. The proper constitutional balance will therefore fare better if there is a well-established public record of presidential failure to recognize the validity of certain provisions of the statute.

The constitutional and practical difficulties posed by the Resolution also give Congress a strong incentive for readdressing this issue. The large majority of those who voted in 1973 to override the President's veto of the War Powers Resolution are no longer in the Congress. Now that its failure has been demonstrated and the acrimony resulting from Vietnam has receded, Congress could take a valuable first step in the direction of improved legislative-executive cooperation in this vital area—and in the process reaffirm its commitment to constitutional government—by repealing the War Powers Resolution.

The War Powers Resolution: An Effective Mechanism of Congressional Control

Daniel P. Franklin

In 1973 Congress overrode President Richard Nixon's veto and passed into law the War Powers Resolution. The resolution was designed to redefine and strengthen Congress's participation in making the decision to commit American troops to combat abroad. The sponsors of this new law hoped that by involving Congress more substantially in these types of decisions, a repetition of the unwise intervention in Vietnam and unauthorized executive conduct, such as the secret bombing of Cambodia, could be avoided. They intended fundamentally to redefine Congress's war power at a time when declared wars were improbable but the continued use of force was not unlikely.

A certain amount of euphoria and hyperbole accompanied the passage of the law. The override of President Nixon's veto represented a major symbolic defeat for a president beset by the Watergate scandal. Nevertheless, the statements and expectations of the bill's sponsors notwithstanding, over the last fifteen years the War Powers Resolution has produced, in reality, only a modest adjustment in the war powers relationship between the branches.

Even a modest adjustment, however, of something as important as congressional-presidential war powers constitutes a significant change. The War Powers Resolution has

Daniel P. Franklin, "The War Powers Resolution: An Effective Mechanism of Congressional Control," has been specially written for *The Conduct of American Foreign Policy Debated*.

been effective in curbing the presidential misuse of war powers. This is true despite the fact that recent court decisions have cast a shadow of doubt over the constitutionality of the law.

PROVISIONS OF THE RESOLUTION

An assessment of the effectiveness of the War Powers Resolution requires an analysis of the provisions and implementation of the law since 1973. The resolution has three basic provisions. First, the president "in every possible instance" is required to consult Congress before committing U.S. troops to hostilities. Second, the president is required to report to Congress within forty-eight hours after the commitment of troops as to the mission of those forces. Third, Congress can by concurrent resolution (a majority of both Houses of Congress with no presidential signature required) order the president to withdraw those forces from combat. In the absence of such a resolution or without an actual legislative endorsement (declaration of war or other authorization), the resolution requires that U.S. forces be withdrawn within ninety days (the time period beginning with the submission of the presidential report).

Despite the fact that these provisions seem rather far reaching in curbing presidential power, they are, in effect, relatively modest. For example, the requirement that the president consult with Congress prior to the commitment of forces is essentially optional. As a practical matter congressional leaders may not be available for consultation. Congress may not be in session, or there may not be time to call congressional leaders to the White House before an emergency decision must be made. Besides, it is not entirely clear what constitutes adequate consultation. According to the House Foreign Affairs Committee, four components determine the adequacy and effectiveness of presidential consultation with Congress:

(1) the "range" of members consulted should be broad enough to include the leadership, and ranking members of relevant committees

(2) the "timing" of consultation should be early in the policy-making process

(3) the executive branch should consult Congress on any "significant" foreign policy matter that would require some form of legislative endorsement

(4) consultation would be most effective if the president and Congress were to enter into consultations in a "cooperative spirit."

The committee concluded, however, that "the executive branch seldom consults effectively with Congress on foreign policy."[1]

The reporting requirement is also a rather mild restriction on presidential power. There are actually three types of situations in which the president is required to report to Congress pursuant to the resolution. If U.S. forces "equipped for combat" are dispatched to a foreign nation or if there is a "substantial" increase in the size of U.S. armed force contingents abroad, the president is required to report to Congress under the law. However, in those situations no time limit is imposed, nor does Congress have the option to terminate the commitment. Only when the president reports that hostilities are "imminent" are the congressional termination provisions of the War Powers Resolution in effect. Therefore, in only a very limited set of circumstances (albeit important ones) is the president potentially constrained by the resolution.

Finally, the termination provisions of the resolution, while seemingly substantial, are of dubious constitutionality. By authorizing Congress to terminate American interventions by concurrent resolution, the sponsors of the law included a *legislative veto*. A legislative veto provision in a law authorizes the president or some administrative agency to take a particular discretionary action that is then subject to the disapproval of one or both Houses of Congress. In the absence of a congressional vote of disapproval, the administrative action stands. It is thus said that Congress retains the right in these statutes to "veto" an executive action.[2] Congress has often relied on this device in the twentieth century as an after-the-fact procedure for controlling the executive. There are more than two hundred statutes in force, adopted by Congress since 1939, that contain some form of a legislative veto.

In 1983, the Supreme Court ruled, in the case of *INS* [Immigration and Naturalization Service] *v. Chadha*, at least one of these legislative vetoes (in the Immigration and Naturalization Act) unconstitutional.[3] While the court has not ruled directly on the constitutionality of the War Powers Resolution, the *Chadha* case does call into question the legality of all legislative vetoes.

In spite of the seeming weakness of its provisions, the War Powers Resolution is an effective mechanism of congressional control for two important reasons. First, the termination provisions apply in some form to the most critical situations in which the use of force is involved. More important, while the resolution is of dubious constitutionality, the law itself provides a formal, institutional arena in which the president and Congress can dispute

---

[1] War Powers Resolution, Nov. 7, 1973. Public Law 93–148, 87 Stat. 555. U.S. House of Representatives, Committee on Foreign Affairs, *Strengthening Executive-Legislative Consultation on Foreign Policy*, 98th Cong., 1st Sess., 1983, p. 1.

[2] The legislative veto should not, however, be confused with the president's veto, which is explicitly outlined in the Constitution. Legislative vetoes were originally devised by Congress to deal with the massive expansion of the executive branch authority in the aftermath of the passage of New Deal legislation in the 1930s. To the extent that Congress was required to delegate substantial authority to the executive branch (in order for the executive to implement new programs), the legislative veto was conceived of as a device for democratic control.

[3] *INS v. Chadha*, 462 U.S. 919 (1983).

matters of war and peace. Prior to the passage of the War Powers Resolution, Congress had substantially fewer and less flexible options for controlling the president's decision to use force.

THE WAR POWER IN THEORY AND PRACTICE

Under Article I, section 2 of the Constitution, the president is commander in chief and, as such, is the commander of all the military "when called into the actual Service of the United States." Under Article I, section 8 of the Constitution, Congress has the power to "declare War, grant Letters of Marque and Reprisal, and make Rules concerning Captures on Land and Water."[4] These seemingly overlapping constitutional provisions have created an ambiguous presidential-congressional relationship in war powers. In particular, it is not entirely clear what these provisions mean in the twentieth century.

The participants in the Constitutional Convention debated the wording of the clause establishing Congress's war power. They decided to substitute the phrase "declare war" for "make war" in this provision. This choice reflected a preference on the part of the Convention to confer on Congress a policy-making rather than administrative authority in supervising the armed forces. Presumably the commander-in-chief clause, then, fills the gap in administrative authority. It is an ambiguous authority, however, in the modern context. When the Constitution was written in 1787, the United States did not have a standing army.[5] Now, American forces are continu-

ously maintained and stationed all over the world. Certainly, the Founding Fathers did not mean to give the president unlimited discretion in the use of U.S. forces in the event that the country would require a standing army.

The genesis of the commander-in-chief clause is not entirely clear. This clause is unique in that it is the only section of the Constitution that confers a *title* rather than a *function*. This ambiguity probably reflects the lack of consensus in the Constitutional Convention concerning the distribution of war powers. Most members of the convention in 1787 preferred to have the United States defended by citizen militias recruited at the state level. To them, citizen militias represented the democratic ideal and also protected states' rights. The president, then, would act as commander in chief only when militias, with the cooperation of the states and Congress, were called to active duty. Others at the convention recognized the possibility that the federal government might have to maintain a standing army in times of emergency. A standing army, however, as an independent, undemocratic political actor, might become a threat to democratic society. Thus the commander-in-chief clause was left intentionally vague to allay the concerns of both sides of the controversy.[6] Obviously, this arrangement does not translate well in the twentieth century. It is clear, however, that the Founding Fathers intended the commander-in-chief role to be restricted to a military, not policy-making, function. About this section of the Constitution, Alexander Hamilton wrote in number 69 of *The Federalist Papers:*

The President is to be commander in chief of the Army and Navy of the United States. In this re-

---

[4] Letters of marque were eighteenth-century devices used by nations to license privateers to raid enemy shipping and installations.

[5] Actually, in 1784, the Continental Congress authorized the maintenance of an eighty-man standing "army" to guard military supplies. *Journals of the Continental Congress, 1774–1789,* XXVII (June 2, 1784), p. 518, cited in

---

Samuel Huntington, *The Soldier and the State* (Cambridge: Harvard University Press, 1957), p. 144.

[6] For a more complete discussion of this debate see Huntington, *Soldier and State,* chap. 7.

spect his authority would be nominally the same with that of the king of Great Britain, but in substance much inferior to it. It would amount to nothing more than the supreme command and direction of the military and naval forces, as first General and Admiral of the Confederacy, while that of the British king extends to the declaring of war, to the raising and regulating of fleets and armies, all of which, by the Constitution under consideration, would appertain to the legislature.[7]

As a practical matter, in the nuclear age, Congress may not be involved in advance in making emergency decisions concerning the use of force. There simply may not be enough time. Nevertheless, the Framers seem to have indicated that Congress has the authority not only to declare war but also to authorize the limited use of force. Particularly in the twentieth century, this tension between practical and constitutional considerations has tended to work to the advantage of the exercise of presidential power.

Since 1787, presidents have authorized the use of force at least two hundred times without the participation of Congress.[8] For example, when President Franklin D. Roosevelt, prior to World War II, ordered American destroyers to "shoot on sight" any German submarines spotted in the North Atlantic, the president never sought congressional consent for what was, in essence, an action that could have led to war with Adolf Hitler's Germany. In another instance, the actions taken by President Lyndon B. Johnson against the North

Vietnamese in 1964 were supported in advance by Congress under the Tonkin Gulf Resolution.[9] However, when in 1971 Congress repealed the Tonkin Gulf Resolution, President Richard M. Nixon claimed that his continued conduct of the war was authorized under the commander-in-chief clause and not pursuant to any congressional action.

Because President Nixon did not feel compelled at that point to withdraw U.S. forces from Vietnam, Congress's only remaining option was to cut off funds for the war. This option put Congress in a difficult position. The funding option is a blunt instrument. Congress has a number of other tools at its disposal to discourage a particularly objectionable policy, including nonbinding resolutions of disapproval or congressional committee investigations designed to create adverse publicity. However, none of these measures, short of a statutory cutoff of funds, is binding on the president. Yet, many members of Congress who opposed the war were reluctant to cut off funds to troops in the field. They could not justify putting American troops at risk for lack of funds. Besides, the appropriations process is subject to a presidential veto, which requires a two-thirds vote in both Houses of Congress to be overridden. This funding "route" puts Congress at a distinct disadvantage. Once a conflict begins, all the president needs is a vote of one-third plus one in either House of Congress in order to conduct a war. Thus, toward the end of the Vietnam War, members of Congress began to look for a more

---

[7] Alexander Hamilton, James Madison, and John Jay, *The Federalist Papers*, ed. Clinton Rossiter (New York: New American Library, 1961), pp. 417–18.

[8] This figure is debatable. According to Louis Fisher, the president has authorized a limited use of force without the consent of Congress about two hundred times in order to protect American lives and property abroad. This number would be much higher were the number of times the president has used the military as a "show of force" included. Louis Fisher, *The Constitution between Friends* (New York: St. Martin's Press, 1978), p. 226.

[9] The Tonkin Gulf Resolution supported the determination of the president "to take all necessary measures to repel any armed attack against the forces of the United States and prevent further aggression." Joint Resolution of Congress, H. J. Res. 1145, Aug. 7, 1964, in *Documents of American History*, ed. Henry Steele Commager and Milton Cantor (Englewood Cliffs, N.J.: Prentice Hall, 1988), 2:690. This resolution was passed in response to an alleged attack by North Vietnamese patrol boats against American destroyers operating in international waters in the South China Sea.

flexible approach to war termination, and the War Powers Resolution was the result.[10]

BEYOND THE PARCHMENT BARRIER: THE WAR POWERS RESOLUTION SINCE 1973

James Madison wrote in number 48 of *The Federalist Papers*:

Will it be sufficient to mark, with precision, the boundaries of these departments [the executive, legislative, and judicial branches] in the constitution of government and to trust to these parchment barriers against the encroaching spirit of power? This is the security which appears to have been principally relied on by the compilers of most of the American [state] constitutions. But experience assures us that the efficacy of the provision has been greatly overrated; and that some more adequate defense is indispensably necessary for the more feeble against the more powerful members of government.[11]

For Madison and the other Framers "parchment barriers" alone would not be sufficient to protect against the expansion of unrestrained political power. Therefore, besides the authorities of the branches of government outlined in the Constitution (where responsibilities are shared through a series of checks and balances), the Framers designed a political system based on the principle of the separation of powers. According to this principle, the political system would protect itself by pitting ambition against ambition as the coequal but *independent* branches of government competed for political power. The independence of the branches was to be guaranteed by requiring that no person serving in one branch could, at the same time, serve in another. It is this brilliant design contained in the Constitution that has helped to protect our liberty even as other provisions, such as the congressional authority to grant letters of marque and reprisal, have begun to lose their meaning.

The War Powers Resolution is more than a parchment barrier. The resolution reinforces the separation of powers. In the absence of the *will* in Congress to hold the president accountable to the law, the War Powers Resolution is an empty measure. But this fact, alone, does not distinguish the resolution from other laws. Any law, in the absence of enforcement, becomes a parchment barrier. However, more important, should a consensus form in Congress in opposition to the president's use of force, the War Powers Resolution enhances the ability of Congress to influence the course of an intervention.

It is rarely the case that the public opposes bold foreign policy initiatives (especially involving the use of force) in the short run. Even in the aftermath of foreign policy failures presidents tend to enjoy a brief period of enhanced popularity. President John F. Kennedy was the beneficiary of this kind of public support after the 1961 Bay of Pigs disaster, in which the United States sponsored a failed invasion of Cuba by Cuban exiles. Jimmy Carter experienced higher popular approval after the abortive Iranian hostage mission, in which eight U.S. servicemen were killed. In the long run, however, military interventions must be justified on their merits as the public and their political leaders consider the benefits of commitments versus the costs. It is at these times that a consensus may develop in opposition to a military engagement. At that point, when the will to resist develops, the War Powers Resolution becomes an important mechanism of control.

Since the passage of the resolution, the president has ordered the use of military force a number of times to achieve national policy

---

[10] Indeed, it is apparently the case that the Reagan administration continued funding the Contra rebels in Nicaragua despite the fact that Congress had explicitly cut off funding pursuant to an amendment sponsored by Rep. Edward P. Boland of Massachusetts.

[11] Hamilton, Madison, and Jay, *The Federalist Papers,* pp. 308–09.

objectives. Few of these interventions were very long in duration. Therefore, Congress was under very little pressure to challenge the president. However, on at least two occasions since 1973 in which the use of force has been both unpopular and long in duration (these two factors generally coincide), the War Powers Resolution has played an important and effective role in limiting the president's authority. Congress has used the resolution as a structure to allow its wishes to be known *and* to be incorporated into the president's strategy.

In general, presidents have ignored at least the spirit of the consultation requirement. Congressional leaders expect to be included, through consultation, in the actual policy-making process. However, there have been a number of impediments to consultation. Executive branch officials are often reluctant to include non-professional foreign policy decision makers such as members of Congress in the policy-making process.[12] Also, the institutional perspectives and needs of the presidency and Congress may be in conflict. Members of Congress are more likely to emphasize the public's right to know, while executive branch officials may tend to stress the importance of maintaining secrecy in diplomatic negotiations and military planning. For example, President Jimmy Carter did not consult with congressional leaders prior to the attempted rescue of American hostages in Iran for fear that details of the operation would then be leaked to the press. Time constraints also present an occasional impediment; the executive branch can act with greater speed than Congress. There are also structural problems

of consultation. It is not clear which members of Congress are to be consulted.[13]

In some cases in the last fifteen years, congressional leaders were not consulted for legitimate reasons. For example, when it became necessary for the United States to use force to cover the evacuation of American citizens from Saigon in 1975 (as the North Vietnamese Army advanced), President Gerald Ford was unable to consult congressional leaders, many of whom were visiting Beijing as members of an American diplomatic delegation at the time. In other cases, the president has simply ignored consultation requirements for no apparent reason. President Reagan, for example, failed to consult congressional leaders in advance of the invasion of Grenada in 1983. Finally, presidents have chosen to "consult" congressional leaders but only after the decision to intervene was made and set in motion, as was the case during the U.S. bombing of Libya in 1986.

In the absence of prior consultation, the president can simply confront members of Congress with a *fait accompli*. Once committed, the withdrawal of American forces becomes a much more politically and tactically formidable task. American allies look for signs of a lack of determination on the part of the United States. From the tactical standpoint, if the United States does not follow through on its commitments or if American troops are withdrawn before achieving their objectives, U.S. allies will begin to chart their own course in planning for national defense. Among other things, this could have a detrimental effect on the cohesion of North Atlantic Treaty Organization and U.S.-Japanese mutual defense arrangements. Therefore, once a military commitment is made, the case for or

---

[12] For a discussion of the justifications for not including members of Congress, see William Rogers, "Who's in Charge of Foreign Policy?" in *Conflict in American Foreign Policy: The Issues Debated*, ed. Don Mansfield and Gary Buckley (Englewood Cliffs, N.J.: Prentice Hall, 1985), pp. 162–67.

[13] For a more thorough discussion of these points, see U.S. House of Representatives, Committee on Foreign Affairs, *Strengthening Executive-Legislative Consultation on Foreign Policy*, pp. 40–48.

against withdrawal expands beyond the merits of the intervention itself. In addition, on the domestic political scene, once American forces are committed—and particularly when lives are lost—elected officials have a sense of great political risk if they support premature withdrawal of military forces. Studies of public opinion have shown that the public has strong emotional feelings about policies that have involved the loss of American lives.[14] Members of Congress do not want to be forced into supporting an intervention simply because the involvement is in progress and they were not consulted in advance.

The reporting requirement has presented a much greater obstacle to the president. There have been a number of instances in which the president has either ignored the law and failed to report or has reported without specifying under what section of the resolution the report was being made. In those instances, the responsibility for requiring the president to report that hostilities are imminent (and thereby trigger the termination provisions) then fell on Congress. In 1982, George W. Crockett and twenty-eight other members of Congress sued President Reagan on the grounds that the president had not reported, pursuant to the resolution, the presence of armed U.S. advisers in El Salvador. A Federal Court of Appeals dismissed the case but suggested in its decision that it was possible for Congress to declare unilaterally that hostilities were imminent.[15] At that point the president would have ninety days to withdraw (in the absence of congressional authorization). This procedure was almost put to the test in 1983.

In that year President Reagan dispatched a peace-keeping force of approximately two thousand Marines to Beirut, Lebanon. At the same time, an American naval task force was stationed off the coast to provide cover and support for the Marines. Initially, the president reported to Congress but did not specify under what section of the law the report was being made. In August of that year, Marines were regularly under fire and sustained casualties. By September, Marine commanders were given the authority to call in air strikes. Yet the president refused to report that hostilities were imminent because, according to the White House, "hostile fire was not directed at the Marines but was instead intended for the Lebanese Army."[16] At that point congressional leaders introduced a resolution designed to trigger the War Powers Resolution and require the president to withdraw the Marines. Rather than have the matter come to a vote, the White House and congressional representatives negotiated the Multilateral Force in Lebanon Resolution (H. J. Res. 364), which authorized the troop commitment for up to eighteen months. In the interim, between the time the Multilateral Force Resolution was approved and the eighteen-month time period expired, terrorist bombers killed 241 Marines in a raid on the Marine Barracks. The Marines were then withdrawn. The precedent, however, had been set: Congressional action intended to require the president to report under the War Powers Resolution had forced the president to negotiate a time limit for a troop commitment. The War Powers Resolution had worked.

The president's decision in 1987 to reflag Kuwaiti tankers and escort them in the Persian Gulf attracted the same sort of scrutiny. In September 1987, the Senate defeated (fifty to forty-one) an amendment to a defense authorization bill that would have forced President Reagan to invoke the War Powers Resolution. In April 1988, when U.S. naval forces

---

[14] See John E. Mueller, *War, Presidents, and Public Opinion* (New York: Wiley, 1973).

[15] *Crockett v. Reagan*, 720 F.2d 1355 (D.C. Cir. 1983).

[16] Congressional Quarterly Inc., *Congressional Quarterly Almanac, 1983,* (Washington D.C.: CQ Press, 1983), p. 114.

retaliated against Iranian oil installations in the Persian Gulf in response to a mining incident, congressional leaders were awakened in the middle of the night and consulted in such a way that House Majority Leader Tom Foley described as "meaningful."[17]

The termination provisions of the War Powers Resolution have not yet been brought to bear. It is not clear whether a court would order the president to withdraw U.S. forces from a combat situation should Congress vote a concurrent resolution of disapproval. The legislative veto has been, after all, declared unconstitutional. In the 1983 *INS v. Chadha* case, the Supreme Court decided that the legislative veto violated the presentment requirement of the Constitution. Pursuant to this requirement, Congress must present to the president for signature all acts of Congress that are to become law. Without the president's endorsement, actions such as concurrent resolutions cannot become law and cannot bind the executive to comply.[18] While the court's decision and others related to that decision have cast a shadow of doubt on the constitutionality of the War Powers Resolution, the courts have never directly ruled on the validity of the resolution itself.[19]

In fact, it could be argued that the *Chadha* case does not apply to the War Powers Resolution. Since the Constitution specifically authorizes Congress to declare war, Congress could, without the concurrence of the president, order war termination. The presentment requirement may not apply to policy functions that are, under the Constitution, exercised by Congress alone.

Nevertheless, even a hypothetical court challenge to a legislative veto of an armed intervention presents several problems for the president. First, a majority vote in both Houses in opposition to an intervention is a fairly clear symbolic, if not actual, repudiation of presidential policy. The president would be wise to consider the effect on the entire gamut of policy making of a decision to ignore Congress in this very important matter. Second, a court challenge to the legislative veto in the War Powers Resolution opens up a whole new "can of worms." The presidency gains flexibility from its largely undefined war powers relationship with Congress. In deciding on the legality of this particular legislative veto, the courts may also restrict the president. Allowing the president to intervene unilaterally for up to ninety days could be ruled an unconstitutional delegation of power by Congress to the president. In that event, the president would lose an important congressional endorsement of an unrestrained presidential war power. Finally, while the legislative veto provisions of the resolution may be unconstitutional, the *automatic* termination provisions still apply. If the president reports that hostilities are imminent (or Congress requires a report) and Congress does not act to authorize the use of force, the president is required to withdraw within ninety days. Even if Congress approves an intervention for a particular length of time, when that time period expires, would the president be required to withdraw? This is an unsettled matter. It is clear, however, that by ignoring the termination provisions of the War Powers Resolution the president faces the prospect of a constitutional confrontation with Congress.

It is difficult to argue whether and in what ways this implied threat affects presidential decision making. It is often argued that the presidential veto is more important as a threat to Congress than as a legislative tool. Congress must always be aware of the possibility of a veto and adjust its legislation accordingly.

---

[17] CBS Morning News Interview, Apr. 18, 1988.

[18] This requirement excepts cases in which a presidential veto is overridden.

[19] See also *City of New Haven, Conn. v. U.S.*, 809 F.2d. 900 (D.C. Cir. 1987) for a ruling on the constitutionality of the legislative veto in the Impoundment Control Act.

In the same way, the threat of a constitutional confrontation may deter or modify presidential plans. For example, the course of the Vietnam War could have been altered had the War Powers Resolution been in force. The war itself would not have been prevented, as the Tonkin Gulf Resolution passed in 1964 in both Houses by large majorities. However, several years later, members of Congress who were reluctant to vote to cut off funding for troops in the field may have been willing to vote for a resolution of disengagement (which would then be the responsibility of the president to implement). At the very least, the threat of a legislative veto could have improved cooperation between the White House and Congress during the war years.[20]

Whether or not the sharing of war powers contributes to a tactical improvement in policy making is another important question. There are certain potential costs for the president in consulting congressional leaders on these matters. There is a risk of leaks to the press or the possibility that congressional leaders may simply object to the president's plan. There are, of course, also benefits. Members of Congress have a unique, independent perspective, and they (especially the leadership) have a wealth of experience in both matters of policy and politics. Congressional leaders are not directly beholden to the president, unlike presidential staffers and political appointees, so they are free to express their reservations about a plan without fear of reprisal. It is likely that congressional leaders, even from the president's own party, would have objected to the Reagan administration's plan to trade arms for hostages with Iran had they been consulted (and the president would have benefited from that advice). Finally, meaningful consultation with congressional leaders creates bipartisan support. Nothing can guarantee the success of any policy. However, unanimity of support for a policy in a democracy, at least, is a guarantee of strength.

CONCLUSION

The War Powers Resolution is, indeed, more than a parchment barrier. The fact that Congress often acquiesces in presidential initiatives in the use of force or even in those situations in which the president chooses to ignore the letter of the law does not necessarily mean that the resolution is a dead letter. Congressional acquiescence reflects the fact that, in most cases, there is generally broad support for bold presidential foreign policy initiatives. However, in those cases in which there is significant opposition to presidential troop commitments, the War Powers Resolution provides an avenue (beyond the appropriations process) for a measured congressional response. Therefore, the War Powers Resolution facilitates congressional involvement of a type that is essential for the maintenance of the separation of powers.

QUESTIONS FOR DISCUSSION

1. What are the advantages and disadvantages of the president's involving Congress in the initial decision to use force?
2. What are Congress's war powers according to the Constitution?
3. What constitutes consultation in the meaning of the War Powers Resolution? Which congressional leaders should be informed and under what circumstances?
4. Had there been no War Powers Resolution, how would U.S. foreign policy have been the same or been different since 1973?

---

[20] This argument is made in more detail by Graham Allison in "Making War: The President and Congress," in *The Presidency Reappraised*, ed. Thomas Cronin and Rexford Tugwell (New York: Praeger Publishers, 1977), pp. 228–47. Allison also argues that the ninety-day time limit gives the president an incentive to order bold (even reckless) uses of force that are destined to be short in duration in order to preempt the interference of Congress.

5. Why have all U.S. presidents since 1973 refused to test the constitutionality of the War Powers Resolution?

SUGGESTED READINGS

Born, Gary B. "The President's War Powers." 23 *Texas International Law Journal* 153 (1988).

Glennon, Michael J. "The War Powers Resolution Ten Years Later: More Politics Than Law." 78 *American Journal of International Law* 571 (1984).

Himmelfarb, Sheldon. "War Powers Compromise: Euphemism for Shirking." *Los Angeles Times*, Nov. 1, 1987, pt. 5, p. 5.

Hyman, Harold M. *Quiet Past and Stormy Present? War Powers in American History.* Washington, D.C.: American Historical Association, 1986.

Noah, Timothy. "War Powers in Action." *New Republic*, 197 (July 6, 1987), pp. 11–12.

Roberts, Steven V. "War Powers? What War Powers?" *New York Times*, Oct. 6, 1987, p. A32.

Rostow, Eugene V. "'Once More Unto the Breach': The War Powers Resolution Revisited." 21 *Valparaiso University Law Review* 1 (1986).

TRB [Michael Kinsley]. "Ballots and Bloodshed." *New Republic*, 197 (Oct. 19, 1987), pp. 4, 49.

U.S. Cong., House of Representatives. *War Powers, Libya, and State-Sponsored Terrorism.* Hearings before the Subcommittee on Arms Control, International Security, and Science of the Committee on Foreign Affairs, 99th Cong., 2d Sess., 1986.

———. *The War Powers Resolution: Relevant Documents, Correspondence, Reports.* Subcommittee on Arms Control, International Security, and Science of the Committee on Foreign Affairs, 100th Cong., 2d Sess., 1988.

"The War Powers Act and the Persian Gulf: Pro and Con." *Congressional Digest*, 66 (Dec. 1987), entire issue.

Wicker, Tom. "A Law That Failed." *New York Times*, Jan. 7, 1988, p. A27.

10 Are Treaties More Binding Than Executive Agreements?

YES

Edwin Borchard

Treaties and Executive Agreements—A Reply

NO

Myres S. McDougal and Asher Lans

Treaties and Congressional-Executive or Presidential Agreements: Interchangeable Instruments of National Policy

Treaties and Executive Agreements—A Reply

Edwin Borchard

I

The authors of the articles under reply, Messrs. McDougal and Lans, have, like McClure, essayed to show that the treaty and the executive agreement are interchangeable, and, since executive agreements are simpler to conclude, they advocate disregarding as obsolete the treaty-making power, requiring, as it does, the consent of two-thirds of the Senate, and substituting for it the use of the executive agreement. In that demand they differ radically from the constitutional conclusions which the writer, as well as many other students of the subject, have reached.

To give their proposal a more "democratic" tinge, the authors propose what they call the Congressional-Executive agreement, which, as a Congressional approval of executive agreements *already made,* has no roots in history, but is deemed by the authors to stand on an equally good footing with the executive agreement concluded pursuant to an act of Congress, of which there are illustrations in the postal and tariff agreements concluded ever since early days in the case of postal agreements and since 1890 in the case of tariffs. The authors maintain that they are justified in advocating this step by reason of the alleged defects of the treaty-making power and by the fact that a "usage" has grown up not only in favor of the Congress-sponsored executive agreement but in favor of the agreement concluded by the President under his independent powers as Commander-in-Chief and diplomatic representative of the United States, from which they draw the inference that the executive agreement which is Congressionally *approved*—by simple majority—is a generous concession to the doubters of the consequences of a broad executive power.

The gentlemen begin their thesis with an analogy between the constitutional treaty and the executive agreement, by positing the supposed plenary power of Congress to deal with all aspects of foreign affairs, in spite of the fact that a constitutional amendment, discussed May 1, 2, 7, 8 and 9, 1945, was deemed by the Judiciary Committee of the House of Representatives to be necessary in order to give the House a voice in treaty-making. They then observe that the Congress has conferred on the President the power to make numerous executive agreements, notably in the field of tariffs, the mails (Postmaster General), copyright, trademarks, and on a variety of other subjects within the power of Congress. They also observe that the President may, by virtue of his own independent power as Commander-in-Chief and diplomatic officer, conclude numerous executive agreements, such as claims settlements, *modi vivendi,* provisional arrangements pending a treaty, protocols of agreement on particular diplomatic affairs, and even in late years a number of agreements with or without a time limit on subjects that cannot be considered unimportant.

They then maintain that since the Constitution leaves executive agreements unmentioned, it naturally draws no line between the subjects appropriate to treaties and to executive agreements; hence an arrangement or understanding on any subject can be called a "treaty" but, since it need not be submitted to the Senate, it may be included within the framework of an executive agreement. They

Excerpted from Edwin Borchard, "Treaties and Executives Agreements—A Reply," 54 *Yale Law Journal,* 616 (1945). Footnotes have been omitted. Reprinted by permission of The Yale Law Journal Company and Fred B. Rothman and Company.

then propose that since these things must be conceded to be valid, a conclusion by no means accepted, it is only a slight step to permit the President to make any executive agreement he desires and if Congress approves it, directly or indirectly, it becomes binding as law, national and international, so that the treaty-making power has become a needless encumbrance, a "vermiform appendix" which can be dispensed with as useless. . . .

Because "the powers of the Federal Government are ample to deal with any problem" of international relations, the conclusion is drawn that the President can make any treaty or agreement he likes, with Congress if necessary. An executive agreement is said to be "entirely upon a par with the treaty," on a "par in every respect." But the *Pink* case did not say this; the conclusion is a non-sequitur and rests solely on assertion.

"...throughout our history...international agreements" other than treaties are said to have been made "on all important subject matters" with identical consequences as in the case of treaties. This is an assertion, not a demonstration, and will be disproved presently. It could be said that some matters have uniformly been the subject of treaties.

> . . . the other relevant clauses of the Constitution [besides the "treaty-making" clause] granting powers to the Congress and the President . . . are meaningful only if they include the authorizing *or sanctioning* of international agreements.

In other words, Article I, Section 8, and Article II of the Constitution have no meaning, the gentlemen suggest, if they do not authorize or sanction international agreements. This is a non-sequitur.

> . . . hundreds of precedents confirmed by interpretations of Supreme Court Justices, Presidents, and Congressmen, and extending throughout the 150 years of our national history . . . sustain the use of Congressional-

Executive and Presidential agreements as alternatives to "treaties." . . .

One might suspect that this is slightly rhetorical; the Congressional-Executive agreement as a ratification of prior agreements is unknown in practice; the Presidential agreement is admittedly limited in scope, and hence could not be the alternative to a treaty.

Congressional-Executive agreements are not only those authorized by Congress within their authority, but "sanctioned by the Congress after the fact of negotiation." This is the authors' thesis. No evidence or practice supports the theory; if it is an agreement, not conclusive but subject to approval by Congress, it collides head-on with the function of the Senate. Moreover, would the authors include *all* agreements, or only those—necessarily limited—within the President's independent powers? If the latter are excluded, which do they include?

> [There is] an agreement-making procedure under the control, in some instances, of the Congress and the President, and, in other instances, of the President alone.

"...both constitutional practice and decision for 150 years and the words of the constitutional document itself," it is added, "completely confirm this view." There is no connection, it is submitted, between the powers conceded to vest in Congress and in the President and the authors' claim of Congressional power to *ratify* Presidential agreements. . . .

II

To prove that the authors' reasoning involves a fatal fallacy and that it is unwittingly unsound and impractical, the following pages have been written. On the practical side, apart from the fact that other opponents of the two-thirds rule, including *The New York Times*, Professor Colegrove, and some members of the

House of Representatives, regard the independent executive agreement, recently expanded beyond its normal, admitted functions, as not "honest," an "evasion of the Constitution," a "subterfuge," a "circumvention of the Constitution," it must be obvious that no great number of Senators will be found to vote for the proposed Congressional-Executive agreement, a device conceived to bring about the demise of the Senate's treaty-making power. Indeed, little in the recent history of politics justifies any belief in the theory that the Senate will or can voluntarily participate in the termination of its constitutional functions as the coequal partner in the making of treaties, or that it will silently acquiesce in the encroachment of an ambitious Executive upon its functions.

This is not to deny that Congress has a considerable and undefined power in the field of foreign relations under the "necessary and proper" clause. We have seen this power in operation in the Act of 1798 declaring limited hostilities with France, in the authorization or declaration of embargoes, in the annexation of foreign territory, in the Panama Tolls Act and its repeal, and in the so-called Neutrality Acts of 1794, 1818, 1935, 1937, 1939. But this is far from admitting the authors' thesis, as it is understood, that Congress can authorize the Executive to make any agreement in any department of foreign affairs, and that in the absence of advance authorization, it can approve, by joint resolution of Congress, what he has concluded definitively or tentatively.

Not only does an approved usage establish that a large number of subjects have been customarily dealt with by treaty, but it is submitted that the encroachments on the treaty-making power of recent years made by executive agreement cannot be blindly accepted as evidence of an established usage. Attorney General Jackson in the "destroyer deal" legal opinion of August 1940 indicated that a line of division could be found in the criterion whether the transaction could be immediately consummated or imposed future obligations upon the legislature, to which the Executive could not commit the country. The former, an executed act and requiring no legislative commitment, when performed in his function as Commander-in-Chief, he believed might be concluded by executive agreement; the latter, the imposition of future obligations, required a treaty. But wherever the line is drawn, in case of doubt, and in the event that there should be any substantial opinion in the Senate insisting that the arrangement should be made by treaty, no President should hesitate in adopting the method provided in the Constitution of seeking Senate approval instead of resolving the doubt in his own favor.

To make the Congressional-Executive agreement a reality and make the whole Congress rather than the Senate a partner in the treaty-making process assumes a radical change in the Constitution, the creation of machinery by which the Senate will voluntarily retire from the field and permit all agreements with foreign Powers to be made by the Executive or by the Executive with Congress, and the establishment of a method by which the agreement can be submitted to Congress for its examination and alteration, to be followed by Congressional adoption, rejection or change, and formal Presidential ratification. But since the President can, under the authors' suggested proposal, disregard any change made by Congress and make his own agreements, and since there seems to be an effort to portray his limited powers to conclude independent executive agreements as in reality unlimited, it is not apparent that he needs to submit any agreement to Congress. At least, he alone is ostensibly the judge as to what he will submit. Is this proposal supposed to impress Congress or the Senate? The House-proposed constitutional amendment reflected a realization of some of these difficulties with respect to treaties. But whereas the House failed to adopt on

May 9, 1945, the resolution of the Committee making majorities sufficient for consent to treaties, the authors propose to accomplish the same result without amendment. Can a more hopeless effort be envisaged? Needless to say, not a single member of the House in the debate of May 1, 2, 7, 8 and 9, 1945, supported the McClure theory, assiduously espoused by the authors. Much more practical would it be, as happened with the recent oil and aviation agreements and the Connally Resolution, for the Senate to use its influence to bring to a halt the gradual encroachment of the Executive on its prerogatives and to restore an adherence to the limited functions of the Executive in the making of independent executive agreements.

To exhibit graphically what has happened in recent years, John Bassett Moore has prepared the appended table which he has given me permission to use. It shows the recent treaties and executive agreements, tabulated according to year of publication:

Year of official printing	Treaties	Executive agreements
1930	25	11
1931	13	14
1932	11	16
1933	9	11
1934	14	16
1935	25	10
1936	8	16
1937	15	10
1938	12	24
1939	10	26
1940	12	20
1941	15	39
1942	6	52
1943	4	71
1944	1	74

While some of the recent executive agreements can be explained under the head of the war power, others, like the Wheat Agreement, the Silver Agreement, the Aviation and Air Transport Agreements, unemployment insurance benefits, the St. Lawrence Seaway project, agricultural experimental stations, health and sanitation, finances of foreign countries, to mention but a few, cannot be thus explained. To use this evidence of encroachment as evidence of a growing "usage" is to fail to distinguish the approved from the disapproved. It is like a writer on intervention who, writing on the "law of intervention," assembled all the interventions he could find, and, on the assumption that the law could be found in the practice of nations, induced the law from the practice, whether good or bad. This is not the first time that the violation of the limitations of law has been used to justify the doctrine of nullification. Fortunately, unlike some aspects of international law, the Constitution is a written document.

III

But what renders the gentlemen's thesis of the interchangeability of the treaty and the executive agreement unsustainable, in spite of the fact that McClure, Corwin, and Quincy Wright have lent their names to the thesis, is the fact that the treaty and the executive agreement exhibit fundamental differences, not explained away by such consoling expressions as "all but," "not very dissimilar," "most," "reasonably durable," or by such vague words as "functional," "instrumental," etc., etc. No light is thrown on the question by the statement of the authors that all forms of international engagement, whatever the name given them, are in effect "treaties," but the gentlemen imply, strangely, that they may all therefore be considered as executive agreements, constitutionally. "Treaties," in the constitutional and legal sense, have acquired a special significance, possessed by no other type of international document, because the Constitution mentions them alone and gives them a special constitutional protection. The "compact clause" shows that the Founders were not unaware of the distinction between treaties and lesser instruments.

The differences between treaties and executive agreements can best be shown by presenting an outline in parallel columns and then elaborating the outline in succeeding paragraphs. Both types of executive agreement are covered, those made pursuant to an act of Congress, about which there is little difficulty, and those not so made. They are not, however, confused. The outline follows:

Treaties	Executive agreements
1. A treaty, as is evident from *Missouri v. Holland,* is like a constitutional amendment. It can deal with any subject appropriate to international negotiation.	An executive agreement is strictly limited. It can deal only with subjects especially delegated by Congress or, if made independently by the President, can deal only with normal powers vested in the Commander-in-Chief and principal diplomatic officer.
2. A treaty can do what Congress cannot. It confers legislative power on Congress (*Missouri v. Holland*).	An executive agreement cannot do what Congress cannot. It cannot confer on Congress powers of legislation it did not have before.
3. A treaty must be ratified to be binding, according to American practice.	An executive agreement need not be ratified by the United States.
4. A treaty, as its name indicates, binds the United States for its duration. It cannot be repealed by act of Congress except for domestic purposes only. The international obligation remains binding.	An executive agreement, as its name indicates, "binds" only as long as it suits *both* sides. It morally "binds" only the signing Executive, not his successors. If they wish it to continue, it is by voluntary act. An executive agreement is subject to repeal by act of Congress domestically and internationally. Unilateral indication of desire to terminate suffices. Repeal of authorizing statute suffices.
5. A treaty has a special significance in constitutional law. It can repeal an act of Congress.	An executive agreement is unmentioned in the Constitution and has grown only through the necessity of making agreements of a character not to warrant submission to the Senate. It can be repealed by Congress at any time, but cannot repeal an act of Congress. It can of course be nullified or abrogated by treaty, prior or subsequent.
6. A treaty, by the Constitution, is the "supreme law of the land."	An executive agreement, with a few exceptions as to contrary state law or when made pursuant to act of Congress, is not supreme law of the land.
7. Only a new treaty can alter or modify an earlier treaty.	An executive agreement cannot alter or modify a treaty.
8. A treaty is submitted to the Senate for formal consideration and consent, rejection, amendment or reservations.	An executive agreement is not "submitted" to Congress for consideration or for approval, rejection, amendment or reservations. There is no procedure for subsequent approval, sanction or ratification by Congress.
9. A treaty lasts, with unimportant exceptions, as long as its terms provide.	An executive agreement is terminable at any time at the unilateral wish of one of the parties. This is true even if it purports to run for a given number of years. No successor to the President is bound by the latter's agreement, although he may consent to permit it to stand.
10. No secret treaty can be made by the United States. Treaties must be published.	An executive agreement invites secrecy since the President can make it without notifying anybody. Several secret agreements are now known.

No one would deny that the Constitution grows by gradual evolution, least of all a student of constitutional law. That is one reason it has continued to exist with only a few amendments. But to admit this is far from conceding the authors' thesis. Not only is there a difference in the substantive and procedural clauses of the Constitution, but the fact that some clauses have expanded, like the due process and interstate commerce clauses and others, is no reason why the treaty-making clause has become obsolete and a new device, the executive agreement, unmentioned in the Constitution, with or without Congress, has become the overpowering instrumentality represented.

The last-ditch argument of those who oppose a constitutional practice they would improve upon is that the constitutional provision is not "democratic." That is supposed to convince the doubter. If that had anything to do with the issue, I suppose the whole Constitution could be attacked as undemocratic, because the Founders did not too much favor control by the general mass of the people, only some of whom were voters in the separate states. But without using chameleonic terms, there is no reason why important questions should not be decided by more than a simple majority. Until lately this argument and the appeal to "democracy" in treaty-making, as in any other matter requiring a two-thirds vote, was rarely heard. As several of the House members suggested on May 1 and 2, 1945, if a voice for the House in treaty-making is desired, why not require that two-thirds of the House be added to the Senate two-thirds? Until then, the Constitution is not likely in this respect to be changed.

Charles Cheney Hyde, in discussing the recurrent proposals to strip the Senate of its treaty-making power by substituting majorities, has expressed himself as follows:

> The recourse to executive agreements revealed in the foregoing sections, however impressive in

scope and development, fails to show that the Government has in fact acted on the theory that the President, with or without the aid of Congress, may conclude in behalf of the United States any arrangement which could be concluded through the instrumentality of a treaty. There have been, moreover, instances where a Secretary of State has felt that for purposes of agreement the use of a treaty was obligatory.

> At the time of the adoption of the Constitution treaties, themselves distinguishable under the then existing practice from arrangements of lesser dignity, were the usual settings that were employed in the making of compacts of largest import and longest endurance. This circumstance strengthens the view that the exact provisions of the Constitution concerning the making of treaties did more than prescribe the manner in which they were to be concluded. The declaration that the President "shall have Power by and with the Advice and Consent of the Senate, to make Treaties, provided two thirds of the Senators present concur," sustains the conclusion that it was not to be rendered abortive by recourse to a different procedure for the use of which no provision was made, and that there were to be found tests of improper evasion in the character of what was sought to be achieved despite the absence of a specific textual prohibition. Otherwise, the scheme for the co-operative action of the President and the Senate would have been a relatively valueless injunction, and the solitary constitutional guide for contracting would have been of slight worth.

John Bassett Moore, the greatest authority in the field, authorized the writer to say in a review of McClure's book, where the gentlemen's thesis was first advocated, that Mr. Moore

> never intended by any of the passages quoted by Dr. McClure to convey the opinion that any part of the treaty-making power under the Constitution had been done away with or impaired by practice; and that, without imputing to Dr. McClure any purpose to misrepresent what he said, he thinks that the passages in question, when read in connection with the context, do not sus-

tain the theory of constitutional dilapidation in support of which they are cited.

We may conclude by another quotation from this wisest of statesmen. Speaking of the so-called *intelligentsia* of the country, which he holds largely responsible for foisting on the American people the theory of "peace by force," collective punishment of "aggressors," and Executive control or "leadership" in for-

eign affairs, John Bassett Moore says, referring to the popular faith in the Kellogg Pact:

> The Pact no doubt makes a strong appeal to our *intelligentsia,* easily the most emotional and most voluble and, as I often think, so far as concerns the realities of international life, the most uninformed, the most injudicious and the most susceptible to propaganda.

Treaties and Congressional-Executive or Presidential Agreements: Interchangeable Instruments of National Policy

Myres S. McDougal and Asher Lans

"It seems to me that an executive agreement ratified by joint resolution differs from a treaty largely in name only."

SENATOR FULBRIGHT

"It is now admitted that what was sought to be effected by the Treaty submitted to the Senate, may be secured by a joint resolution of the two houses of Congress incorporating all its provisions. This mode of effecting it will have the advantage of requiring only a majority of the two houses, instead of two-thirds of the Senate."

JOHN C. CALHOUN, in 1845, commenting on the procedure used for annexing Texas.

I

Above the holocaust of the present war has arisen a demand from the people of the United States for a foreign policy that will do everything humanly possible to prevent future wars and to secure their other interests in the contemporary world. The people have made up their minds as to the general kind of foreign policy they want. In elections and by-elections extending over a period of five years, in Congressional resolutions, and in the platforms and speeches of party candidates, a line of policy has been laid down as precisely as

the processes of voting and popular expression permit. Firmly, deliberately, and in large majority, the people have said that they want a foreign policy which continues our war-time alliances and which seeks to create upon that foundation both a new general security organization, with the United States as a leading member, and all the other supporting institutions necessary to secure the full advantages—such as economic well-being and the promotion of health, knowledge, and the maintenance of human dignity—that can flow from the free and peaceful cooperation of the peoples of the world.

This demand of the people of the United States is based upon an increasing consciousness that the world is shrinking ever more rapidly, irrevocably, and imperiously into what a late statesman aptly called "One World." It is now common knowledge that revolutionary developments in instruments of destruction, transportation, communication, and production; constant increases in population; increasing reliance upon natural resources of wide distribution; and consequent changes in the various institutions by which man carries on his activities have all combined to make the peace, prosperity, health, knowledge, respect for human dignity, and freedom of the contemporary world indivisible. The indivisibility of peace has seldom been stated with greater force than by Senator Henry Cabot Lodge, speaking in 1915:

> ...there is no escape from the proposition that the peace of the world can only be maintained as the peace and order of a single community are maintained, by the force which unified nations are willing to put behind the peace and order of the world. Nations must unite as men unite to preserve peace and order. The great nations must be so united as to be able to say to any single country, "You must not go to war"; and they can only say that effectively when the country desiring war knows that the force which the united nations place behind peace is irresistible.

Excerpted from Myres S. McDougal and Asher Lans, "Treaties and Congressional-Executive or Presidential Agreements: Interchangeable Instruments of National Policy: I," 54 *Yale Law Journal* 181 (1945). Footnotes have been omitted. Reprinted by permission of The Yale Law Journal Company and Fred B. Rothman and Company.

It needs no emphasis that contemporary developments in the technology of war increase the force of Senator Lodge's statement a thousandfold. Similarly, the indivisibility of economic prosperity has had recent confirmation in the catastrophic convulsions of a world-wide depression; and the great majority of people have come to see "the incontestable truth" that "there is a clear planetary indivisibility of production and employment." It is obvious that "most of us are now alive" and that "most of us are kept alive" by the "vast cooperative [work of a] world society." Even assuming that its security position may be impregnable, no nation today can seek refuge from technological imperatives by the erection of neo-mercantilistic trade barriers, without impoverishment of its standard of living. What is true of peace and prosperity is no less true of all our other democratic values. The judgment of the American people that their interests can no longer be protected by nineteenth-century neutrality, isolation, and inaction is based upon a realistic appraisal of the pervasive interdependence of all peoples. This basic condition of interdependence, the profound weakness of the world's present system of organization, and, conversely, the strong power position of the United States in the world society make it imperative that the United States not only participate, but take a leading part, in establishing a new order of political, economic, and cultural relationships and institutions, both in direct association with other nations, great and small, and through international organizations.

During the interregnum between the first World War and the present one, the United States vacillated uncertainly between a nostalgic isolationism and a growing realization of the need for international cooperation. Since 1941 it has, however, taken the initiative in promoting the organization of international agencies to deal with the multilateral tasks of preserving peace and coping with numerous economic problems, including the administration of post-war relief and reconstruction, the development of backward areas, the control of civil aviation and the stabilization of monetary exchanges. As the time approaches for the translation of tentative blueprints into appropriate working institutions, the great question in the minds of people, throughout the world, who remember the United States' withdrawal after the last war, is whether this government possesses constitutional procedures sufficiently democratic, flexible, and efficient to permit it to give effect to its majority will and, hence, to assume a position of responsibility and leadership in the world community upon which other governments can rely.

It should be clear that, if the United States is to secure its own interests and to assume a position of responsibility and leadership in the world community, its executive officers, who are charged with the task of conducting negotiations with other governments, must be able to treat the national body politic as a whole and must be able to canvass it promptly and efficiently as a whole for the majority will, without being subjected to delays, obstructions, and disintegrating efforts by minorities who conceive their interests to be different from the interests of the rest of the nation. One of the prime purposes for which this nation was established was to make it "one" with respect to the rest of the world; the causal factors which were urgent 150 years ago are obviously reinforced beyond all gainsaying today. The robot bomb and economic depression, like time, wait for no nation and can strike any part of the United States with equal ease. A leisurely diplomacy of inaction and of deference to dissident minority interests supposedly characteristic of past eras when economic and political change proceeded at a slower pace and the twin ocean barriers gave us an effortless security is no longer capable, if it ever was, of securing the interests of the United States.

The principal instrument by which the United States can, and must, cooperate with other governments in that total institutional process of reciprocities and counter-reciprocities which we call "foreign affairs" or "foreign relations" is, of course, the *agreement*, in all its many manifestations. It is in agreements between the member governments that all of the proposed new international organizations must find their legal bases, powers, responsibilities, and operating procedures. If the United States is to attain the goals of its foreign policy, it must, therefore, have efficient, flexible, and democratic procedures, responsible to the majority will, and to the whole nation, for the making, modification, and abrogation of international agreements. The executive officers of the United States must be able to act promptly and, hence, must be able to ascertain promptly that their action will be supported and implemented by the other branches of the government when that action corresponds with the majority will of the nation. Other governments must know, if they are to be willing to undertake indispensable joint commitments, that the United States can so act to implement integrated and responsible policy.

It is the thesis of this article, not at all novel, that the constitutional practice of the United States, hallowed by 150 years of tradition, does make available all the necessary procedures. The wise statesmen who drafted the Constitution of the United States not only gave the President a *permissive* power, "with the advice and consent of the Senate," "to make treaties, provided two-thirds of the Senators present concur," but they also gave both to the President and to the whole Congress broad powers of control over the external relations of the Government which are meaningless if they do not include the instrumental powers, first, to authorize the making of intergovernmental agreements and, secondly, to make these agreements the law of the land.

Throughout our national history, these broad grants to the President and the Congress have, furthermore, been in fact interpreted, by all branches of the Government, in hundreds of instances, to include such instrumental powers. The result is that our constitutional law today makes available two parallel and completely interchangeable procedures, wholly applicable to the same subject matters and of identical domestic and international legal consequences, for the consummation of intergovernmental agreements. In addition to the treaty-making procedure, which may—as the nation has found from bitter experience—be subjected to minority control, there is what may be called an "agreement-making procedure," which may operate either under the combined powers of the Congress and the President or in some instances under the powers of the President alone. The practices of successive administrations, supported by the Congress and by numerous court decisions, have for all practical purposes made the Congressional-Executive agreement authorized or sanctioned by both houses of Congress interchangeable with the agreements ratified under the treaty clause by two-thirds of the Senate. The same decisive authorities have likewise made agreements negotiated by the President, on his own responsibility and within the scope of his own constitutional powers, appropriate instruments for handling many important aspects of our foreign relations. Initial choice of the procedure to be followed for securing validation of any particular intergovernmental agreement lies with the President since it is constitutional practice unquestioned since Washington's day that the President alone has the power to propose or dispose in the actual conduct of negotiations with other governments. When a specific agreement is submitted to the Congress for approval or implementation, the Congress may of course question the procedure by which the President seeks validation of the agreement, but if the Congress is to act rationally—that is, appropriately to secure the best long-term interests of the whole nation—it should shape its action in terms of the policy issues involved in the specific agreement and not in terms of some misleading and unhistorical notion that the treaty-making procedure is the exclusive mode of making important international agreements under our Constitution.

This suggestion that the Constitution of the United States affords interchangeable procedures for effecting international agreements meets, it must be admitted, with a resistance that is difficult to understand in view of the historical record and of this nation's traditional preference for democracy. Some resistance comes from those who genuinely favor democratic, majority control of our foreign affairs but who, confused about a supposed exclusiveness of the treaty-making clause, think that a constitutional amendment is the only way out. The chief resistance comes, however, from those who explicitly favor minority control of foreign affairs because they fear what majority control may be able to achieve in an integrated, responsible foreign policy. Sometimes the dominant theme of resistance is mere defense of Senatorial prerogative, upon an assumption often none too unconscious that the safety of the nation and the sanctity of the Constitution would be imperiled if one-third of the Senate could not dictate the nation's foreign policy. At other times the theme is, more bluntly, that there are special minority interests in the country that must be given a delusive protection however much the interests of the whole nation, including the long-term interests of all its minorities, may suffer. The argument, whatever its theme in policy, is always bolstered by a legalistic attempt to find in the Constitution, because of a supposed latent intention of some of its Framers, unstated limitations upon the powers of the whole Congress and the President. The most complete statement of the case for retention of the

minority veto and the most complete revelations of the unpersuasiveness of the arguments by which it is sought to be sustained have come in a series of recent articles by Professor Edwin Borchard.

Writing in the September issue of the *Yale Law Journal* and the September-October issue of the *Lawyers Guild Review*, Professor Borchard has labored valiantly to demonstrate "the inherent unimportance and minor character" of the "executive agreement" and has sought to prove that important international obligations can be contracted only by utilization of the treaty-making power. Invoking a vague distinction from the writings of an eighteenth-century Swiss "natural-law jurist and positivist [sic], Emmerich de Vattel," he first attempts to construct a restrictive theory of Congressional and executive powers from the one brief and ambiguous phrase of the Constitution about the making of treaties and emphatically insists not only that the President has no independent powers to consummate important international agreements on his own but also that "there is no constitutional warrant whatever for the suggestion that the President has an option to submit [important compacts] either to the Senate as a treaty...or to the Congress for majority approval." He next compresses all executive agreements into one category to find that "the executive agreement" as "a general substitute for the treaty" is subject to "many objections": such agreements, he alleges, are "an evasion of the Constitution," "dishonest and dangerous to the entire Constitution and to law"; they contribute to the "recent unprecedented inflation of executive power" and "permit the President to involve the country in secret agreements"; they are of uncertain legal effect and duration and are terminable "unilaterally" "without incurring the charge of treaty violation"; they are "unsafe for the United States or any foreign country" "since, if congressionally approved, they can be congressionally disapproved at any time"; and, finally, not being expressly mentioned in the Constitution, they "do not have the constitutional dignity and force of a treaty." The suggestion that the two-thirds vote required for the Senate's approval of a treaty is undemocratic and hampers the integration of a responsible foreign policy for the whole nation Professor Borchard finds completely unpersuasive: "a treaty should be convincing enough to command a two-thirds vote," and "a unanimous vote of a jury" is required to "hang capital offenders." For a contrapuntal theme, in which the House of Representatives appears as the new villain in the piece, he suggests that reliance upon a majority vote of both houses of Congress for validating international agreements might remove debate and voting from their present allegedly nonpartisan level and plunge them into the turmoil of politics. Finally, Professor Borchard admonishes the defenders of executive agreements that the only "lawful" means of terminating minority control is through a formal amendment, changing the treaty-making provisions of the Constitution.

Writing in the November issue of the *American Bar Association Journal* Professor Borchard completes the circle of advocacy of minority control by arguing against amendment of the Constitution to permit treaties to be ratified by majority vote of both houses. His principal points are that "the desires of small states or states with special interests" deserve "protection" against agreements "concluded" by mere majority and that "the unprecedented inflation of the executive power is a strong reason for retaining the decisive requirement of the two-thirds rule." Reiterating his assertion that the participation of the House of Representatives might make more difficult the consummation of international compacts, Professor Borchard also, somewhat inconsistently, finds that "it is not possible to prove that the senatorial check has not on the whole

operated to the country's advantage." To quench the last possible hope of reform, he points out realistically that, regardless of its merits, the proposed amendments would never be approved by two-thirds of the Senate and that it is probably undesirable, in light of the complex problems now confronting Congress, to submit so important a proposal at this time.

It was some sixty years ago that Mr. Justice Holmes reaffirmed ancient wisdom in suggesting that the "secret root[s]" from which legal theories draw "all the juices of life" are "considerations of what is expedient for the community concerned," "moral and political theories," "institutions of public policy," "even...prejudices." Many commentators, including notably Professor James Bradley Thayer, have pointed out that these factors have a special importance in the field of constitutional law, where theories of jurisprudence are inextricably entwined with "statecraft, and with the political problems of our great and complex national life." Professor Borchard, commenting that "necessity knows no law," has sought summarily to dispose of a book by a "distinguished author" who "would have us believe that it is so important that the United States join an international organization to preserve the peace—he assumes this to be the goal of an international organization—that we must abandon the constitutional rule providing for consent of two-thirds of the Senate to ratify treaties." He has also urged that those who point out that our constitutional practice has created an effective alternative to the treaty-making procedure are motivated by the fear that a minority of the Senate may "prevent the association of the United States with a projected international organization, of a character still unknown." He has further characterized as "subversive propaganda" the "fashion to extol the executive agreement as an exemplification of democracy as opposed to the so-called undemocratic requirement of a two-thirds vote in the Senate."

The major policy premise from which Professor Borchard's own legal arguments stem is not difficult to ascertain. He makes it completely articulate. It is a strong conviction that the United States should abjure participation in international political organizations and retire beyond the Jericho-like walls of his own version of the nineteenth century juristic conception of neutrality. The opening and concluding paragraphs of his article in the September *Yale Law Journal*—characterizing the Treaty of Versailles as "a declaration of war," referring to the "projected international organization, of a character still unknown," and applauding Harry Elmer Barnes' encomium of "the Senate's treaty power" as "probably the last remaining bulwark of our national safety"—indicate that at least one reason for his opposition to the use of procedures other than the treaty procedure for consummating international agreements is the thought that retention of minority veto control may again produce a condition of stalemate, permitting once more a triumph of the statesmanship of withdrawal. This conclusion is further substantiated by his recent article on *Flaws in Post-War Peace Plans* in which he takes the position that "peace enforcement" among nations is a contradiction in terms, "at war with the fundamental facts of international life and with the theory of international law and relations," because "sovereign nations," "legally equal," "can not have, or be coerced by, any centralized superior."

For exploring in some detail the issues of law and policy thus joined, the subsequent Sections of this article will proceed in the following order:

First, an effort will be made to clarify the conventional taxonomy of the different agreements used in the United States' diplomatic practice and to indicate the one available criterion that the facts will sustain for distinguish-

ing between the different agreements permissible under our constitutional practice.

Second, the vague suggestions that the treaty-making clause is exclusive and that executive agreements must be confined to matters inherently unimportant will be refuted, and some indication will be made of the broad constitutional powers of the Congress and the President, no less effective or comprehensive than those of the President and the Senate, to authorize the making of international agreements and to make these agreements the law of the land.

Third, the full extent to which Congressional-Executive and Presidential agreements have become interchangeable with the treaty in the actual diplomatic practice of the United States will be described and it will be shown that there are no persuasive legal or policy reasons why interchangeability should not be extended to the few remaining problems upon which it has not yet been fully developed.

Fourth, some important examples of amendment of the Constitution of the United States by usage will be described for the purpose of showing that, if the practice of using Congressional-Executive and Presidential agreements interchangeably with the treaty is in fact a development by usage and not within the original contemplation of the Framers of the Constitution, it is a development not at all unique, but rather within the best traditions of our history.

Fifth, a comparison of the legal consequences which courts and other governmental officials attach to Congressional-Executive and Presidential agreements and to treaties will be made, and it will be shown that there are no important differences between these classes of agreements in binding effect or duration at either domestic or international law.

Sixth, the reasons that are alleged to have motivated the original adoption of the treaty-making procedure will be explored and their contemporary relevance appraised; the record of the Senate and the effect of the omnipresent threat of obstructionist tactics by its minority in thwarting the will of the majority and the national interest will be examined, and a brief description will be offered of the tactics that have been used, and are still available for use, by an intransigent minority. Finally, the suggestion that it is not undemocratic to require a two-thirds vote for the approval of important international agreements will be made the subject of at least mild wonder.

Seventh, and last, some indication will be made of how Congressional-Executive and Presidential agreements may be used, in thorough consonance with our best constitutional traditions, to meet certain of the more urgent problems of the post-war world, if the minority controlled treaty-making procedure should for any reason become inadequate to meet the responsibilities of that world.

QUESTIONS FOR DISCUSSION

1. What are the differences between a treaty and an executive agreement?
2. Why do presidents resort to executive agreements rather than treaties on some occasions and treaties rather than executive agreements on other occasions?
3. Who should decide whether a treaty is no longer valid? What are the reasons for your answer?
4. Should the role of the Senate in approving treaties be changed? Why? If so, how should it be changed?
5. What role does the changing power of the United States in the world from the late eighteenth century to the late twentieth century have on the question under debate?

SUGGESTED READINGS

Borchard, Edwin. "Should the Executive Agreement Replace the Treaty?" 53 *Yale Law Journal* 664 (1944).

DePol, Bruce F. "United States Military and Economic Assurances to Israel: Are Executive Agreements Legally Binding?" 13 *California Western International Law Journal* 273 (1983).

Hyman, Sharon G. "Executive Agreements: Beyond Constitutional Limits?" 11 *Hofstra Law Review* 805 (1983).

Johnson, Loch K. *The Making of International Agreements: Congress Confronts the Executive.* New York: New York University Press, 1984.

Levitan, David M. "The Foreign Relations Power: An Analysis of Mr. Justice Sutherland's Theory." 55 *Yale Law Journal* 467 (1946).

Margolis, Lawrence. *Executive Agreements and Presidential Power in Foreign Policy.* New York: Praeger, 1985.

Massaroni, Christopher. "The United States–Iran Hostage Agreement: A Study in Presidential Powers." 15 *Cornell International Law Journal* 149 (Winter 1982).

McDougal, Myres S., and Asher Lans. "Treaties and Congressional-Executive or Presidential Agreements: Interchangeable Instruments of National Policy: II." 54 *Yale Law Journal* 534 (1945).

Tananbaum, Duane. *The Bricker Amendment Controversy: A Test of Eisenhower's Political Leadership.* Ithaca, N.Y.: Cornell University Press, 1988.

U.S. Cong., Senate. *Treaties and Other International Agreements: The Role of the United States Senate.* A Study Prepared for the Committee on Foreign Relations, United States Senate, by the Congressional Research Service, Library of Congress, June 1984. S. Prt. 98–205, 98th Cong., 2d Sess.

U.S. Cong., Senate. *Treaty Ratification Process and Separation of Powers.* Hearing before the Subcommittee on Separation of Powers of the Committee on the Judiciary, 97th Cong., 2d Sess., 1982.

11 Should the State Department (Rather Than the National Security Council) Lead in Foreign Policy?

YES

I. M. Destler

State: A Department or "Something More"?

NO

Duncan L. Clarke

Why State Can't Lead

State: A Department or "Something More"?

I. M. Destler

Richard Neustadt asked the key question twenty-two years ago, on March 25, 1963. Summing up his wide-ranging, provocative testimony before Senator Henry Jackson's Subcommittee on National Security Staffing and Operations, he asked whether the U.S. Department of State could "be at once a department and then something more?"[1] In posing this question, he pinpointed a dilemma for officials of that department, and for other Americans concerned about the effective conduct of foreign policy.

One obvious answer would be no: the State Department is simply a department, and not a particularly large one at that. In its budget and in the number of employees, it is on the small side even if one includes the many foreign nationals on embassy payrolls. Its main task—that which preoccupies most of its employees—is very much the sort of operational work that departments typically perform: the management of our foreign relations, the mostly routine dealings with representatives of foreign countries. This includes, of course, the accumulation and analysis of information relative to these relations, and the conveying of advice to the president regarding them. But it

includes also, at the other end of the spectrum, such mundane tasks as managing overseas motor pools for officials of State, Defense, and other foreign affairs agencies.

Why then should anyone think of State as "something more" than a department? The main answer, of course, is that State's operational responsibilities are connected to a very major responsibility of the United States government—American foreign policy. This encompasses matters vital to the security of the United States: the negotiation of alliance arrangements and basing rights; the shaping of overall relations with key allies like Japan and key adversaries like the Soviet Union. More than any other issue area, foreign policy has preoccupied postwar presidents. Departments and agencies like Defense and the Central Intelligence Agency (CIA) are subordinate in concept, if not always in practice, to foreign policy purposes.

So *foreign policy* is something more than a typical departmental task. Indeed, the basic responsibility for United States foreign policy rests not in the secretary of state but in the president, by both constitutional doctrine and contemporary practice. The law creating the secretary's office underscores his dependence, calling on him to "perform and execute such duties as shall from time to time be enjoined or entrusted to him by the President of the United States...."[2]

But the job is far too large for the president, and is only one of several jobs that he must carry out. He therefore needs very substantial help. He could get this by building a large new presidential staff agency, a super National Security Council (NSC). But it is only natural to hope he can instead get the broad support he needs from the department with the most comprehensive operational role in

I. M. Destler, "State: A Department or 'Something More'?" in *Public Policy and Political Institutions: United States Defense and Foreign Policy—Policy Coordination and Integration,* ed. Duncan L. Clarke (Greenwich, Conn.: JAI Press, 1985), pp. 93–107. Reprinted by permission of JAI Press, Inc.

[1] U.S. Senate, Committee on Government Operations, Subcommittee on National Security Staffing and Operations, *Administration of National Security: Hearings,* 89th Cong., 1st sess., 1965, p. 103.

[2] Don K. Price, ed. *The Secretary of State* (Englewood Cliffs, N.J.: Prentice-Hall, 1960), p. 2.

foreign policy. This hope is encouraged by the tradition of the secretaryship as the senior U.S. cabinet position, and by a postwar history sprinkled with strong occupants like George Marshall, Dean Acheson, John Foster Dulles, and Henry A. Kissinger. It is encouraged also by the high quality of the United States Foreign Service.

So, can it be "a department and something more"? Can State combine the management of routine relations with the task of being the primary presidential agency for advising, directing, coordinating, and implementing U.S. foreign policy? Neustadt's tentative answer in 1963 was yes, *if* the Office of the Secretary, the staff supporting him, and his key deputies could "be rebuilt on a scale commensurate with the contemporary reach of foreign relations." Despite John F. Kennedy's formal assignment of the coordinating role, Neustadt judged that "the State Department has not yet found the means to take the proferred role and play it vigorously across the board." But the proposition was nonetheless worth one more try, because alternatives were less appealing.[3]

This was the standard answer of the 1960s, in prescription if not in practice. The State Department was not playing the larger role effectively, but this could and should be changed. John F. Kennedy and Lyndon B. Johnson developed an action staff in the White House, under the umbrella of the National Security Council. But they kept it small, and employed it to prod the State Department more than to supplant it. Hence the Heineman task force of 1967, dominated by Kennedy-Johnson luminaries such as Robert S. McNamara, McGeorge Bundy, Kermit Gordon, and Charles Schultze, urged that the secretary of state be made "preeminently the director and coordi-

nator, for and on behalf of the President, of all U.S. foreign and national security policy."[4] And, it urged that his department be restructured to support him in this role. Johnson spoke favorably of the report and put it in his desk drawer for priority action—it was said—in his next term!

But 1968 brought Johnson's withdrawal, and 1969 brought Richard M. Nixon in his stead. With Nixon's strong encouragement, national security assistant Henry A. Kissinger used his White House base to exclude not just the departmental rank and file, but Secretary of State William P. Rogers himself, from major foreign policy negotiations. And thereafter, aside from a partial recovery when Kissinger himself became secretary of state in 1973, the department remained in the shadows. In the Carter administration, national security assistant Zbigniew Brzezinski jousted with, and in the end prevailed over, Secretary of State Cyrus R. Vance. In the Reagan administration, Alexander Haig found it impossible to play the comprehensive leadership role that the Heineman report, and countless others, had urged for the secretary. His successor George Shultz has his frustrations also, particularly while Reagan intimate William Clark held the White House national security post.

With this mixed experience, the predominant thrust of expert prescriptions has begun to change. It comes as no shock to find Brzezinski, the most openly ambitious of national security aides, arguing in his memoirs that "the central role of the Assistant for National

[3] U.S. Senate, *Administration of National Security*, pp. 80, 81.

[4] "Organization for the Management and Coordination of Foreign Affairs," A Final Report of the President's Task Force on Government Organization, October 1, 1967, p. 8. This writer's full-blown prescription draws substantially on the experience and analyses of the sixties. See I. M. Destler, *Presidents, Bureaucrats, and Foreign Policy* (Princeton, N.J.: Princeton University Press, 1972), especially ch. IX. See also Destler, Leslie H. Gelb, and Anthony Lake, *Our Own Worst Enemy: The Unmaking of American Foreign Policy* (New York: Simon and Schuster, 1984).

Security Affairs should be openly acknowledged and even institutionalized."[5] But it is notable when Cyrus Vance's director of politico-military affairs, Leslie Gelb, writes that, in practice, "for a host of powerful reasons... Presidents soon turn away from the State Department as the crucible for making policy."[6] And before those men played those specific governmental roles, Graham Allison and Peter Szanton argued, in *Remaking Foreign Policy*, that "State should no longer be asked to play the role it has most cherished, been repeatedly assigned, and regularly failed to perform." Rather, they concluded, the role of State should be redefined as foreign advocacy: "The forceful argument, at every stage of the policy process, that the interests of the United States are most reliably advanced by policies and actions that meet the legitimate requirements of all nations."[7]

Again, why does all this matter? If the question were only the fate of Foggy Bottom or the United States Foreign Service, it would not make that much difference. If other people and institutions were really performing, comprehensively, the job of foreign policy leadership and coordination (supporting the president, orchestrating the foreign affairs agencies, assuring the quality, breadth, and representativeness of policy debates) there is no reason to make a national issue of the fate of one of the smaller executive departments.

Unfortunately, no one else has been performing this larger job at all effectively. The national security assistant can gain personal advantage over the secretary of state—and

usually does, to judge from the post-1960 record. But the result has been to make American foreign policymaking more idiosyncratic and personality dependent, not less. As Philip Odeen noted in his carefully worded inside assessment for Jimmy Carter, the "stress on the personal advisory role" of the NSC staff has led to neglect of its "institutional role," that of assuring that the broader process of policymaking was effectively managed.[8]

The preeminence of the national security advisor has meant concentration on a few issues to the neglect of others, as illustrated, page after page, in volume I of Henry Kissinger's memoirs.[9] It has inevitably exacerbated conflict, on issue after issue, between a State Department seeking to protect at least some of its policy role and its White House competitor. The Nixon administration on Bangladesh and the Carter administration on Iran offer two of the more egregious examples.

Finally, there is the danger that if the State Department cannot be "something more" than a department, it is likely to become something less. Its effectiveness in communications and negotiations is undercut if foreign governments begin to believe a rival person or institution "really" speaks for the president. And the lack of a solid domestic constituency—in contrast to every other department—makes State particularly dependent on White House confidence for its credibility. In fact, the role proposed by Allison and Szanton could actually end up weakening State further. There is no question that country advocacy is a crucial function, inadequately performed in Washington policy debates. But the reason, alas, is that

[5] Zbigniew Brzezinski, *Power and Principle* (New York: Farrar, Straus, Giroux, 1983), p. 536.

[6] Leslie H. Gelb, "Why Not the State Department?" in Charles W. Kegley, Jr., and Eugene R. Wittkoff, eds., *Perspectives on American Foreign Policy* (New York: St. Martin's, 1983), p. 287.

[7] Graham Allison and Peter Szanton, *Remaking Foreign Policy: The Organizational Connection* (New York: Basic Books, 1976), pp. 121–22, 125–26.

[8] Philip Odeen, *National Security Policy Integration*, Report to the President under the auspices of the President's Reorganization Project, September 1979; reprinted in U.S. Senate, Committee on Foreign Relations, *Hearing: "The National Security Adviser: Role and Accountability,"* 96th Cong., 2d sess., 1980, p. 109.

[9] Henry Kissinger, *White House Years* (Boston: Little, Brown, 1979).

it involves the regular transmission of bad news, news that most other policy participants do not want to hear. They feel, however naively, that such news can be disregarded or overridden.

What, more specifically, are the sources and limits of State Department influence on American foreign policy? How does this affect our broader foreign policy process? This essay will look first at power within the State Department, and then at State's interagency relations. It will conclude with an argument for a new look at the State-White House connection.

STATE FROM THE INSIDE

Organizationally, the Department of State is a complex entity with over twenty major subunits, seventeen with the status of "bureau." Some bureaus have broad subject responsibility (politico-military affairs, economic and business affairs); others are more narrowly focused, like those handling narcotics, and refugees. Some provide specialized support for the department as a whole: intelligence and research, for example, or administration, or personnel, or public affairs. Some carry out largely autonomous functions, like consular affairs. Others have a mandate to infuse the entire department with their perspective—human rights is an example. But the key bureaus, the core of the traditional department and still its most important, are the five which cover specific geographic regions: East Asia, Near East and South Asia, Europe, Latin America, and Africa.

In terms of State's *departmental* responsibilities, it is the regional bureaus that play the central role. They handle foreign relations, our dealings with the one hundred-plus countries with which we have diplomatic relations. This gives them the major ongoing leverage within the department. Any State official, of course, will gain influence if he is well connected to the senior officials on the "seventh floor," the part of the building housing the secretary, the deputy secretary, the four under secretaries, and the key staff offices. But otherwise, it is the regional bureaus which have intradepartmental primacy.

They manage communications with specific foreign capitals. They do not monopolize this function, but they have the predominant role within the department on most bilateral issues, most of the time. (The Bureau of International Organization Affairs, which resembles a regional bureau in some respects, has this role for dealings with multilateral organizations.)

Because their work constitutes the essence of the diplomatic profession as traditionally viewed, the regional bureaus have the primary allegiance of the foreign service officers (FSOs) in general and the political officers in particular. Regional bureaus offer the most valued, in general, of Washington assignments. These bureaus are further strengthened because of their influence on *overseas* assignments. Any FSO not willing to yield up his fate entirely to the functionings of a sometimes arbitrary personnel assignment system will want to reinsure his future career by developing his own sources of information, his own network of contacts and advocates who will alert him when attractive positions are opening up in particular embassies, and support his candidacy for those positions.

Finally, the regional bureaus tend to have "the action"—not always, but most of the time—on those issues where the State Department has primacy over other Washington departments. The economic and politico-military bureaus, the most important of those labelled "functional," tend to operate mainly in policy turf where other agencies, like Defense and Treasury, have primary responsibility.

Because the regional bureaus have these advantages within the department, they attract the best talent from the career foreign service. And while their country perspectives can create problems for their relationships with the secretary, they have the compensating advantage of being responsible for supporting him on those issues where he has the best chance at leading within the United States government: for example, on Middle East negotiations.

Many internal analyses of the department have recognized this imbalance and have proposed remedies. And there have been changes in the 1960s and 1970s. The Office of Politico-Military Affairs was created in 1962 and made a bureau less than a decade later. The economic bureau has been expanded and, at times, substantially strengthened. The involvement and expertise of the department in arms control negotiations has been expanded, especially in periods (such as the Carter administration) of mutually supportive relations with the semi-independent Arms Control and Disarmament Agency. And personnel training and assignment processes have increasingly given explicit recognition to the importance of these "functional" specialities. Still, they suffer relative neglect, at least in relation to what most nonforeign service analysts feel are the personnel competences the State Department needs.[10]

One striking evidence of departmental weakness on the functional issues has been the inability of the State Department to institutionalize an official, above the assistant secretary level, who can speak for the department in either of the crucial areas of economic policy or political-military affairs. For economics, an anomalous arrangement has persisted. The department has an undersecretary for economic affairs, and an assistant secretary for economic and business affairs who does not report to the economic undersecretary but around him to the secretary and the deputy secretary. The rationale is that the economic under secretary is a senior, seventh floor staff official who engages in interagency negotiations and arbitrates, within State, the claims of the regional and functional bureaus. But this arrangement makes his authority quite unclear; since he is separated from the department's major economic staff, it is frequently uncertain for whom he speaks, and with what substantive backing he speaks it. It should hardly be a surprise that effective undersecretaries for economic affairs have been the exception, not the rule.

In the political-military area, the situation is still more complicated, even bizarre. State has an undersecretary for political affairs, by protocol the department's number three official. But he is looked to not so much to coordinate the department's political-military work as to oversee the work of the regional bureaus and to serve as the representative of the career foreign service in the departmental leadership team. There is also an undersecretary for security assistance, science and technology. But as Barry M. Blechman and Janne E. Nolan have written, this office "has rarely functioned as was envisioned," but rather it has been "used largely as a sinecure to reward high ranking individuals for political favors."[11] Its incumbents have focused primarily on military aid and arms transfers. There is the director of politico-military affairs, a step below the two others in rank but possessing the only comprehensive staff for defense related issues. And there is, finally, the Arms Control and Disarmament Agency, housed in the State Department building, whose director reports both to the secretary and to the president.

All of this means that the Department of State is deeply divided, internally, on that

---

[10] See William I. Bacchus, *Staffing for Foreign Affairs Personnel Systems for 1980s and 1990s* (Princeton, N.J.: Princeton University Press, 1983).

[11] Barry M. Blechman and Janne E. Nolan, "Reorganizing for More Effective Arms Negotiations," *Foreign Affairs* 61 (Summer 1983), p. 1174.

broad range of issues for which the country perspective is not and cannot be predominant. It makes it harder for the department to provide the secretary with broad, cross-cutting analytic advice and analysis and operational support. This makes it harder, in turn, for the secretary to provide that support to the president.

The State Department has other weaknesses, looked at from the presidential perspective. Most important, it is weakly connected to politics in the presidential/electoral sense. On the other hand, its sensitivity to congressional currents and likely congressional action on foreign policy has improved substantially in recent years, and is often superior to that of the White House. On Reagan's politically costly 1981 decision to sell airborne warning and control system (AWACS) aircraft to Saudi Arabia, for example, it was Defense and the White House which pressed for action, while State warned accurately of the breadth of congressional opposition.[12]

But this moves us to the second perspective from which State can usefully be assessed—its relation with other agencies and the leverage it can assert over them.

STATE FROM THE OUTSIDE

As a department, State has leverage over other agencies because they depend on it operationally. They have interests in the communications and negotiations which the department coordinates or facilitates. They have people in embassies which the department manages and directs. But they are less interested in working with State on issues where they have, or seek to have, the main respon-

sibility. Treasury will not welcome the department's daily involvement in international monetary matters; Defense will seek to insure that State remains a very marginal participant in its already complex weapons planning and acquisition process, notwithstanding its crucial impact on U.S. allies and adversaries. All these tendencies, again, serve to reinforce the predominance of the regional and country perspective within the State Department, for it is the geographic bureaus which control most of the State resources which other agencies need.

However, there is a recognized role for the department as a senior participant, if not necessarily leader, in a wide range of "functional" foreign relations activities: trade agreements, arms sales, nuclear exports, international commodity arrangements, arms control negotiations, etc. Knowledgeable and bureaucratically effective State officials have or make opportunities to engage in these issues, thus creating openings for the exertion of influence.

But how much influence they can exert depends importantly on the influence of the secretary and, to a significant but much lesser degree, that of his principal seventh floor subordinates. It is the secretary's central role, or its lack, which is the primary subject of journalistic commentary about State, and not without reason. This factor fundamentally affects what the rest of the department does and can do.

On the positive side, the post of secretary of state remains not simply the senior cabinet post in a formal sense, but the most sought after. Presidents seem to care more about this appointment than any other cabinet position, and seem to expect that they will be dealing regularly and personally with the secretary of state, as they will not be, for example, with the secretary of agriculture or transportation.

The expectations surrounding the office offer its occupant opportunities as well as con-

---

[12] See I. M. Destler, "Reagan, Congress, and Foreign Policy in 1981," in Norman Ornstein, ed., *President and Congress: Assessing Reagan's First Year* (Washington, D.C.: American Enterprise Institute, 1982), pp. 71–77.

straints. He has a claim to engagement in major negotiations, and to the primary role, short of the president, as government foreign policy spokesman. But as Dean Acheson and countless others have observed, his effectiveness depends overwhelmingly on how he gets on—personally, politically, policy-wise—with his president.

Even when that connection is very strong, his department may get but a fraction of the benefit unless he shares engagement with, and delegates authority to, a wide range of departmental officials. And postwar history suggests how difficult it is for both relationships (the presidential-secretarial and the secretarial-departmental) to flourish simultaneously; they really have not, it seems, since the presidency of Harry S. Truman. In part, this reflects the personalities of particular secretaries: Dulles and Kissinger, for example, liked to work with a handful of trusted associates. But there is a larger problem. It is hard for the secretary to be responsive to the president and his perspective while responding to his department because the department's prime focus, relations with foreign countries, is only one of the president's major international concerns.

The secretary faces other types of dilemmas. Almost all who would reinforce his role argue that he must stay, primarily, in Washington. Certainly his involvement in specific overseas negotiations and conferences takes him away from "minding the store." It was when Cyrus Vance was off in the Middle East that Zbigniew Brzezinski got Jimmy Carter to move up the date for announcing normal relations with China, an action which disrupted the SALT [Strategic Arms Limitation Talks] II negotiations the secretary hoped to conclude a week later. But the secretary may feel he needs to travel and negotiate in person, to preempt a rival. Vance surely remembered how Kissinger's back-channel dealings on SALT and other issues had undercut Rogers. Similarly, the demands for public spokesman-

ship, congressional testimony, and appearances on the embassy circuit all offer the secretary specific advantages, but collectively they can capture and constrain him, reduce his flexibility. He can become the cabinet level version of Neustadt's "clerk," a label for a president whose name and office are used by others for *their* ends, but who is unable to move either the government or the nation in directions *he* wants to go.[13]

It may be that of all the senior U.S. government positions, that of secretary of state is most vulnerable to being so captured by the formal demands of countless claimants. And the secretary of state is more likely than not to face a formidable rival within the president's own house, the assistant for national security affairs. If this individual is a senior policy expert with a broad presidential mandate, and/or a close personal confidant of the president, the competition will be formidable. For, as Henry Kissinger noted in his memoirs, "the two positions are inherently competitive if both incumbents seek to play a major policy role."[14]

The disadvantages of the secretary vis-à-vis the national security assistant are less substantive than they are personal and institutional. It is often argued that the NSC advantage relates to a substantive breadth broader than State's, that only the NSC has the potential authority to integrate foreign, military, and economic policy. This may be true in form. But no national security assistant since 1960 has given priority to international economic policy in practice. And they have been engaged, as a group, very much less in military business than in diplomacy. Most important is the fact that presidential engagement in high diplomacy makes primary reliance on a White

[13] Richard E. Neustadt, *Presidential Power: The Politics of Leadership* (New York: John Wiley and Sons, 1960), especially ch. I.

[14] Kissinger, *White House Years*, p. 30.

House aide a tempting organizational short cut. The aide is more flexible, more immediately dependent on him and, therefore, more responsive to him.

The national security assistant's policy perspective is not necessarily broader. But it is usually more congruent, operationally, with that of the president. And the fact that presidents themselves are major foreign policy players in a personal sense tends to reinforce the role of the in-house aide who staffs this involvement. Interestingly, national security assistants have not tended to be particularly shrewd in U.S. national politics. Kissinger and Brzezinski had major domestic blind spots. William Clark seemed more inclined than most Reagan aides to fight for the purity of Reaganite policy principle, even at cost of a rise in the political temperature. But the operational pattern is fairly similar across administration—presidents and their assistant grab, willy-nilly, control over the hot issues, and manage them, while excluding most (sometimes all) of the State Department, most of the time. Meanwhile, nobody coordinates in the broader sense. The president gains flexibility and the appearance of movement in the short run; in the long run, problems pile up and may overwhelm him, as they did Jimmy Carter.

WHAT CAN BE DONE?

Present roles, traditions, perceptions, and institutional arrangements tend to define the problem as "State versus the White House." This is clearly a losing proposition for Foggy Bottom. If departmental leaders have to fight *against* White House aides for the president's personal confidence, it is not hard to guess who will win, most of the time. And without a strong presidential connection, the department's impact elsewhere will be limited. The "country advocate" role, which very much needs doing, may weaken State's influence

further; it is enormously hard to sustain, it makes more enemies than friends, and it makes State officials vulnerable to exclusion as purveyors of bad news just when such news is most needed.

More important, State versus the White House is a losing proposition for the country. For what has in practice replaced secretarial and departmental primacy has not been a superior, more organized, more comprehensive system of foreign policy management. Instead the result has been idiosyncratic ad hocery, more dependent than ever on the accidents of personality. If a president wants a more comprehensive, more effective foreign policy, he needs an institution with the depth and reach of the State Department.[15]

One option, in theory at least, would be for the president to build such an institution in his executive office. He might follow the path Neustadt suggested, but did not take, and create an international counterpart of the Office of Management and Budget (OMB). Brzezinski suggests steps in this direction: to "legitimate the assistant's central role in coordination and thus also in shaping national security policy," he might be made subject to Senate confirmation like the OMB director, and his job "might also be redesignated Director of National Security Affairs."[16] And his staff could be enlarged from the current norm of forty substantive professionals to over a hundred, making possible much more comprehensive coverage of country, regional, and functional issues.

---

[15] For a fuller discussion of how and why the growing White House foreign policy role has brought us a more *disorganized* foreign policy process, see my "National Security: The Rise of the Assistant," in Hugh Heclo and Lester M. Salamon, eds., *The Illusion of Presidential Government* (Boulder, Colorado: Westview Press, 1981), pp. 263–75. On the need for depth and reach in overall foreign policy coordination, see my *Presidents, Bureaucrats, and Foreign Policy.*

[16] Brzezinski, *Power and Principle*, pp. 536–37.

But the costs of such an organizational construction are substantial. It would bring many more issues to the White House than most presidents could handle, or would want to handle. It would duplicate and demoralize the State Department. It would add a new multi-level organization to the already cumbersome foreign policy process. And what the president got in formal scope and depth he would lose in flexibility, bringing him perhaps to create a new, smaller White House subunit to circumvent this one. Just such a thing has happened to OMB with the creation of the White House Domestic Council (now renamed Office of Policy Development). And it has happened *within* NSC staffs: Henry Kissinger, for example, maintained a small personal office which circumvented the senior NSC aides responsible for particular issues and regions.

The opposite course for a president, one which has found favor with this writer, would be a strategy aimed at transforming the State Department—or, at minimum, the secretary's extended office—into an effective lead agency for presidential policymaking. One element of such a strategy would be to cut State's prime competitor, the NSC staff, down to size. This would reflect the view that the secretary cannot operate credibly, on behalf of the president, if the president keeps a high-profile national security aide, and that the type of policy brokering and decision management and enforcement the chief executive does need from a close-in staff can best be done by a small, anonymous, highly professional "inside" group. The title of the head of this staff might therefore be *downgraded* to NSC executive secretary.[17] Without the disabling competitor, the secretary of state would be better able to lead, and the president might invest more energy in making their relationship work.

This remedy, too, has its drawbacks, prominent among them being those very State Department policy weaknesses set forth in the preceding pages. A president and secretary bent on this strategy *could* make it work, but they would have to do so quickly. For unless State leadership met presidential needs, the chief executive would turn elsewhere, whatever his original intent.

It may therefore be useful to think in terms of a middle course. One need not abandon his personal preference for one or the other of the above options, either a White House–centered or a State-centered foreign policymaking system. But it is very possible, indeed probable, that a president will opt for neither. He will not formalize and expand the White House national security operation, but neither will he slash it. In this very likely case, his administration's foreign policy coherence and effectiveness will depend, to an important degree, on whether he can get State and the NSC working together in *alliance*, together leading the government in developing and implementing *presidential* foreign policy.

Such an alliance could work. It requires, at minimum, two things: *a broadly shared policy perspective*, and, *compatible roles for the principal policy players*. What specific steps might be taken by the president and his senior advisers to establish these? How might they improve the odds that on most issues, most of the time, State and the NSC would reinforce and not undercut one another?

Working for the President

The shared policy perspective must begin with the fact that State and White House aides serve a common employer. Here the burden of proof is on State, and above all on the secretary to nurture *his* presidential connection. As Dean Acheson put it long ago, "It is highly desirable that from first to last both parties to the relationship understand which is the

---

[17] See I. M. Destler, "A Job That Doesn't Work," *Foreign Policy* (Spring 1980), pp. 80–88.

president."[18] But this imperative extends well beyond the secretary—to his key subordinates and their immediate staffs at the very least.

Of course, part of their duty to the president is to bring to his attention those oft-unwelcome foreign facts and foreign governmental interests which any sustainable policy must take into account and very often accommodate. But this must be done within a broader *American* policy framework. Indeed, the secretary and his entourage must see themselves above all as *presidential* advocates, within State as well as in the government-wide decision process. This will likely mean increased tension between State's seventh floor and the country-focused, operational perspective which is paramount in the regional bureaus. It will require that these bureaus be headed by strong assistant secretaries who carry the president's mantle also, even though they must be responsive to their subordinates' country-intensive focus and operational priorities. (And it would help if the seventh floor positions were restructured to establish under secretaries with clear authority over political-military and economic issues.)

Establishing Compatible Senior Roles

Even with a congruent policy perspective, senior presidential advisers can still become rivals if they seek to play the same sort of leadership role and become competitors for presidential and public recognition. So the next question, for those seeking to build a State–White House alliance, is whether both the secretary of state and the national security assistant can be strong without each threatening the other. The secretary is a statutory official—the person, short of the president, most visibly responsible for negotiations abroad and policy explanation at home. If the national

security assistant intrudes heavily on these roles, the secretary suffers severely. Critics ask who is "the real secretary of state." Rivalry becomes inevitable.

But a national security assistant who defers to the secretary in these spheres need not be relegated to insignificance. For he can still play a major role as the president's primary "inside" policy manager. He needs to work out this role *with* the secretary, not against him. But with presidential support and secretarial cooperation, he can oversee policy decisionmaking and implementation. He can orchestrate the process by which the administration sets and adjusts its basic policy lines. The president can insist that the secretary defer to him on this, and recognize that it will involve major substantive input by the assistant and other senior advisers, in directions the secretary will not always welcome. More specifically, the secretary would, in exchange for the assistant's restraint on grabbing headlines or negotiations, defer to the policy process rules that the assistant develops for the president. For example, he would need to take care not to use his one-on-one presidential relationship to resolve key matters without the assistant's participation or knowledge.

How might this work in practice? At policy-level meetings, the president might underscore the secretary's number two foreign policy status by directing that he preside at such meetings in the president's absence, and sometimes lead the discussion in his presence. The secretary might, in turn, call upon the national security assistant to set forth the main policy issues to be resolved, and later to summarize the balance of argument. On senior State appointments, the secretary would take the lead in recommending individuals to the president, and there would be a presumption in favor of his choices. But the assistant's mandate would certainly include reviewing these recommendations, and the performance of current incumbents, in terms of the broader

---

[18] Dean Acheson, "The President and the Secretary of State," in Price, ed., *The Secretary of State*, p. 33.

functioning of administration foreign policy-making. (In turn, the secretary could object if prospective senior NSC appointees looked unlikely to work constructively with State counterparts; indeed, the president ought to give the secretary a strong voice in the selection of the assistant himself.)

The assistant would thus be an active influence on the secretary and his department, but with the aim not of supplanting them but strengthening them and their capacity to do the president's work. Just as the secretary's staff would be working, in the larger sense, for the president, the NSC staff would be supporting the secretary and his presidential connection. Indeed, one of the assistant's most important jobs would be to nourish that relationship, to help see to it that those two heavily scheduled, multiply-pressured, out-front political executives kept in personal and policy touch.

If such an alliance were constructed, how would other departments react, above all DOD [Department of Defense]? If the effect were to render the Defense secretary and the Joint Chiefs marginal participants in issues like arms control or political-military strategy in Europe, they would bring their formidable resources to bear against it. But assuming that the White House and State followed the more sensible approach of engaging them regularly and dependably in this process—and the whole tradition of interagency decisionmaking would work toward such inclusion—Defense could live within such a system even though another might be its preference.

These principles do not, of course, represent the only way a president can run foreign policy, nor even the only good way. But it could prove a workable way. Unless presidents and secretaries of state can be encouraged to think systematically about alternative decisionmaking systems, they are likely to emulate their predecessors, intending one sort of arrangement and ending up with another and not knowing why. U.S. foreign policymaking will then remain chaotic, even as the relative American position declines to a point where chaos becomes less tolerable for our interests.

Why State Can't Lead

Duncan L. Clarke

Questions again have arisen about the management of U.S. foreign policy. In light of the real and feared roles of the National Security Council (NSC) in the arms-for-hostages arrangement with Iran, predictable calls for the State Department to assume overall direction of U.S. foreign policy are being made. The calls should go unheeded. The idea will not work.

Since 1947, with a few exceptions, the secretary of state has been a significant foreign-policy adviser to the president. Often he has been the leading adviser. Moreover, after the president, he usually has been the country's chief foreign-policy advocate and diplomat. These roles for the secretary receive broad endorsement.

But it also is often asserted that the secretary's own department should have the central, or at least leading, role in making and coordinating foreign policy. This view is wrong. In fact, there is a growing perception among informed observers that the State Department is ill-equipped to assume such a position of prominence. Contributors to a 1975 study by the Commission on the Organization of the Government for the Conduct of Foreign Policy (Murphy commission), for example, concluded that establishing the State Department as the centerpiece of foreign policymaking by constructing coordinating mechanisms around it simply would not work. Neither formal delegations of presidential authority nor powerful secretaries have enabled the department in

Duncan L. Clarke, "Why State Can't Lead," *Foreign Policy*, no. 66 (Spring 1987), pp. 128–42. Reprinted by permission of *Foreign Policy*.

the past to coordinate important activities of other departments and agencies.

There is a powerful bureaucratic reason for this persistent failure. The department encounters vehement resistance from other departments when the policy issues it tries to control affect their areas of jurisdictional responsibility and interest. Neither the Defense Department nor the Treasury Department will accept State's lead in their respective areas. Indeed, relatively few secretaries of state and defense have enjoyed close working partnerships. More often their relationships have been described as ranging from "peaceful coexistence" to "open warfare." Tensions in a State-centered system would burden the president with a disproportionate number of interagency disputes to resolve.

It is true that the NSC has not been notably successful in integrating defense and international economic policy into overall national security policy. But there is no indication that State can perform these functions more effectively. And the NSC has one key advantage over State: Only the NSC has the potential to integrate the various policy strands as a neutral broker. If the problem is ever to be mitigated, therefore, it is to the NSC and the White House, not to State, that an administration must look. If, by some miracle, State were offered the role of neutral broker, it probably should reject it. For State, like any other department, must be an advocate and representative within interagency councils to fulfill its essential missions. A stance of neutrality would ensure inadequate representation of State positions within interagency councils.

The two times that State has been assigned central coordinative responsibility it performed poorly. Presidents Dwight Eisenhower and Lyndon Johnson gave State central coordinative responsibility through the Operations Coordinating Board and the National Security Action Memorandum 341, respectively. Both systems failed partly because of the opposition of other departments and State's unwilling-ness or inability to play the role assigned. The historical record does not end there, however. Most modern presidents, either before or shortly after their inauguration, have indi-cated a desire for the secretary and the Depart-ment of State to play a leading role in formu-lating and directing foreign policy. Although some secretaries proceed to assume such a role, the department rarely does. A major rea-son for this is the gap between what presi-dents want and expect and what they come to believe State can or will give them. Among other things, they expect loyalty, responsive-ness to their needs and directives, an oppor-tunity to exercise foreign-policy leadership, and sensitivity to their domestic political re-quirements. No recent president has found the department able or willing to perform as expected.

Upon assuming office, President Richard Nixon reportedly told his staff that foreign policy was to be handled by the White House, "not by the striped-pants faggots in Foggy Bottom." The offensive language apart, such uneasiness about the State Department ap-pears to be the rule rather than the exception. Recent presidents seem quickly to have con-cluded that, except for the secretary and a handful of others, people in State are not to be trusted. Many New Deal, Kennedy, and Carter Democrats believed State to be hide-bound and resistant to progressive policies; many Eisenhower, Nixon, and Reagan Repub-licans were convinced it was infested with suspect left-wingers and liberals. Regardless of party, presidents often are disposed to blame State for unauthorized leaks of sensitive information.

Some of the more telling reasons for presi-dential suspicions relate to various traits and attitudes of the Foreign Service "subculture." I. M. Destler, an articulate advocate in favor of a strong role for State, has acknowledged that the department is "strikingly 'un-Presiden-tial,'" and that the Foreign Service subculture constitutes "a formidable problem for those who would make State *the* central foreign af-fairs agency."[1]

In any administration, the president's con-fidence is gained through demonstrated loy-alty and competence, which normally come only through daily interaction with the presi-dent. Usually only the president's White House advisers, including the national secu-rity assistant (NSA), and cabinet officials like the secretary of state can meet this condition. A sprawling bureaucracy cannot. Conse-quently, no postwar president has sought to build lines of confidence down through the State Department bureaucracy.

Every recent administration, therefore, has an inclination to center foreign policymaking in the White House, an inclination that is fur-ther strengthened by a sense that State is in-sufficiently responsive to presidential require-ments and directives. Secretaries themselves must be responsive to presidents if they are to retain the chief executive's confidence, but they confront a dilemma: They can either dis-tance themselves from their own department, thereby setting it adrift, or become State's ad-vocate at the risk of being suspect themselves. Either way, State suffers. Former Secretary of State Cyrus Vance was reasonably successful for a while in balancing these two roles, but as the struggle with former national security ad-viser Zbigniew Brzezinski for the president's ear intensified, he found the task more and more difficult. And former President Jimmy Carter finally was to conclude that "Cy Vance mirrored the character of the organization he led. He was...extremely loyal to his subordi-

---

[1] I. M. Destler, "A Job that Doesn't Work," *Foreign Pol-icy* 38 (Spring 1980): 80–88; Destler, "State: A Department or 'Something More'?" in *Public Policy and Political Institu-tions: United States Defense and Foreign Policy—Policy Coor-dination and Integration*, ed. Duncan L. Clarke (Greenwich, Conn.: JAI Press, 1985), 104.

nates, and protective of the State Department and its status."

The notion of responsiveness does not imply that State's advice is invariably wrong. But one element often mentioned by presidents and NSAs is State's reluctance to implement faithfully and promptly White House directives. Carter was disturbed by the apparent unwillingness in the State Department to carry out his directives fully and with enthusiasm; Brzezinski wrote in his book *Power and Principle* (1983) that he was "amazed at how skillful the State Department was in delaying the execution of decisions which it had not in the first place favored"; and former Secretary of State Henry Kissinger remarked in *White House Years* (1979) that Foreign Service officers (FSOs) "will carry out clear-cut instructions with great loyalty, but the typical Foreign Service officer is not easily persuaded that an instruction with which he disagrees is really clear-cut."

This perception that the secretary and, more often, the Department of State are insensitive to domestic politics also encourages presidents to favor the advice of NSAs. With some exceptions, State devotes little attention to framing its proposals in terms that will draw domestic political support. Presidents soon come to know that they and their staffs can frame decisions in a more politically acceptable manner. When the White House becomes convinced that State is irremediably out of touch with politics, the White House staff is well on its way to commanding policy.

Another factor inexorably pulls policymaking into the White House. Presidents searching for areas in which to demonstrate international leadership have always found foreign policy much easier to dominate than defense policy. When the White House decides to move boldly into a foreign-policy area, the State Department, and sometimes even the secretary, is often shunted aside. Reinforcing this tendency is the need to respond effectively to the growing global interdependence in international economic and security affairs during an era of instant worldwide communication. The requirements for policy integration and responsiveness to public opinion can best be met by the White House, not by State Department foreign-policy professionals.

Another shortcoming of the department is its lack of expertise. The Murphy commission and a 1970 State Department study informally known as the Macomber Report both agreed that State lacked the expertise to "manage and contain" officials from other departments in the international economic, defense, and intelligence areas. Nor has reform taken place. William Bacchus, special assistant to the undersecretary for management, wrote in 1983 that "State does not have the functional competence...to play anything resembling an integrative, policy development role....And there is little current indication that significant improvement is likely."[2]

Since the mid-1970s, some effort has been made to address this issue, particularly in the international economic and political-military fields. Yet the Foreign Service continues to be predominantly generalist in background and orientation and resists recruitment of specialists. This resistance has been rooted in a longstanding contempt for "lateral entry" specialists from outside government. They were thought incapable of comprehending the "real stuff" of foreign affairs. But the Foreign Service is also concerned that hiring more specialists may harm FSO assignment and promotion opportunities. Unless this pattern of resistance is broken, the Foreign Service's inconsequentiality to Washington-based policymaking will increase.

---

[2] William I. Bacchus, *Staffing for Foreign Affairs: Personnel Systems for the 1980's and 1990's* (Princeton: Princeton University Press, 1983), 52. See also Robert L. Rothstein, *Planning, Prediction, and Policymaking in Foreign Affairs: Theory and Practice* (Boston: Little, Brown, 1972), 39–41.

During the Carter and Reagan administrations, the State Department's Bureau of Politico-Military Affairs hired several excellent people from outside the department. Some FSOs in the bureau also acquired political-military skills on their own. But most of the bureau's FSOs had insufficient knowledge of the defense community and systems analysis.

Other areas where State has been recurrently faulted for its relative weakness are international economics, science and technology, and the department's Bureau of Oceans and International Environmental and Scientific Affairs. Perhaps most distressing, the Foreign Service exhibits deficiencies in what should be its core strengths—foreign area expertise and language facility. Despite considerable effort and expense, it appears that the competence of the FSO corps as a whole has not improved sufficiently in these two vital areas. Although there has been improvement in overall language competence, a 1986 State Department study concluded that State was "doing badly in developing real professional proficiency" in Arabic, Chinese, Japanese, and Russian.

A problem distinct from, but related to, inadequate expertise is the quality of State Department analysis and reporting. The analytic caliber of State's papers and reports has been criticized roundly by many inside and outside the building. Critics complain that State Department studies are long and too descriptive and often unsatisfactory. Based heavily on intuition, and almost never conceptual, many of the analyses are unaccompanied by reliable sources and information, or reflect the FSO's lack of adequate training and expertise; papers are so cautious and vague as to be of little use to policymakers who long ago concluded that such "waffling" constitutes the quintessential character of the "Fudge Factory at Foggy Bottom."

Another perception widely held outside the State Department is that the need to maintain "good relations" with a country or region predisposes FSOs to identify excessively with that country's interests at the expense of American interests. Many FSOs will confide privately that such clientism is a risk to be guarded against, though one that is starkly overdrawn by those whose norms, policy preferences, or bureaucratic interests put them in frequent conflict with the State Department. Others react heatedly—often in private, sometimes in public—to allegations of clientism, which they see as impugning their patriotism.

But whether there is truth to the charge matters much less than the fact that it is widely believed by officials in other departments, in Congress, and in the White House. FSOs may, with sound reason, argue that long-term U.S. interests are at times best advanced by accommodating legitimate concerns of other countries. Most foreign-policy decisions, and not a few domestic ones, are unlikely to be well informed if taken without an understanding of the thinking and concerns of foreign governments and peoples. Few officials have better insight into such matters than career diplomats who immerse themselves in the culture, politics, society, and language of another country. But presidents often view such "accommodationist" advice as soft and out of touch with more pressing American interests. Their inclination, once again, is to discount State's advice.

The notion that "the striped-pants" types are selling out to foreigners probably is held even more firmly in Congress. The department's usual relationship with Congress is at best uncomfortable, and State alone among executive departments lacks a significant public constituency. This is no help to the able FSO country specialist who, like the responsible intelligence analyst, often bears bad news that decision makers must hear. But there are few rewards for the messenger.

Other aspects and attitudes of the Foreign Service collectively diminish the prospect that the State Department will assume a central place in the direction and formulation of foreign policy.

Elitism

Except for many junior officers, FSOs see themselves as members of an elite corps of talented, nonpartisan, close-knit, and unjustly beleaguered professionals. Many Americans and their elected representatives also view the Foreign Service as an elite—one that is an ingrown, exclusive club enjoying undeserved perquisites. Although the public, or sectors of it, might admire or acknowledge certain elites—the Boston Celtics or the United States Marine Corps—most Americans seem to distrust self-perceived elites. And although the image of the Foreign Service probably has improved somewhat as terrorist incidents have taken their toll among the dedicated diplomats who serve the United States overseas, perceived FSO elitism remains a political liability for the department.

Elitism has other costs. It increases pressures for conformity within a system that already stifles individual initiative and creativity. It contributes to a certain "laager mentality," an "us-against-them" attitude frequently exhibited by FSOs toward many outside of State and even toward some political appointees and those with specialized expertise within the department. This can only distance the Foreign Service from the political leadership and larger governmental foreign affairs community with which it must interact.

Essence of the Foreign Service

The essence of Foreign Service work is another factor limiting the department's ability and disposition to play a leading policy role. FSOs are thought of (and think of themselves) as diplomats whose principal duty is to exe-cute, not make, policy. The FSOs' "essence" is to represent their country overseas, send reports back to Washington, and negotiate with foreign governments. Successful performance of these functions requires a certain compromising, accommodating, and unabrasive style that does not easily lend itself to the combative, aggressive quality of Washington decision making.

In short, the very qualities that serve FSOs well in their diplomatic capacity impede their performance in the Washington policymaking environment. Indeed, decision makers are often informed by analyses that are best prepared by a group that is only grudgingly tolerated by FSOs—experts with specialized knowledge and skills in, for instance, military, economic, or scientific affairs.

Lack of Innovation and Risk Avoidance

The historian Arthur Schlesinger, Jr., once observed that the Foreign Service officer has come to be known as a person for whom the risks always outweigh the opportunities. This may relate partly to the nature of the diplomatic profession. Diplomats are expected to reflect not their own, but their government's views. Great care must be taken not to exceed one's instructions. Every word must be carefully measured.

The Macomber Report found that the mores of the Foreign Service are not conducive to creative thinking and that conformity is prized above all other qualities. But there is more to it than this. Prevalent norms within the State Department inhibit direct confrontation of particularly sensitive issues and penalize risk takers. It can be hazardous to be creative, to go out on a limb. Initiative or premature insight may set back or destroy careers even when FSOs correctly read or predict evolving international events. An example is the fate of the department's old China hands, who were purged for submitting what are now regarded as perceptive reports on communist China. But there are others. Officers working on arms control issues or U.S.–Soviet relations have been especially vulnerable during the transition from one administration to another. The prudent course is the cautious course. "Fitting in" has a higher value than "standing out."

Management Is Merely Housekeeping

Internal State Department feuding and the department's lack of effective management practices also make a State-centered foreign policy seem implausible. Even casual observers have at least a general awareness of fights for turf between and among various regional and functional bureaus and other departmental units, and informed observers describe State as deeply divided and analogize its intradepartmental bickering to tribalism and clannishness.[3]

Of course, internal spats are common to other agencies as well. But what is less frequently encountered elsewhere in the executive branch are resistance to the very notion of management and a tradition that deemphasizes the standing and importance of managers. Among FSOs, management is equated with housekeeping or administration. Most FSOs, like most university professors, neither admire nor aspire to be administrators. Such attitudes mean that, despite several efforts, career development programs designed to augment State's managerial competencies have met with only limited success. Moreover,

only senior officials are positioned to be senior managers. If they take no personal interest in the subject and delegate this function entirely to subordinates, it will not have sufficient priority. This is true at the highest level: Few secretaries of state since George Marshall have paid adequate attention to managing their own department.

In summary, the State Department is so beset with problems and weaknesses that it cannot now or in the foreseeable future assume a central foreign-policy role. Therefore, it is time to put the illusion of a State-centered system to rest.

This does not mean that extreme centralization in the White House is an appealing alternative. Brzezinski's proposal to legitimate formally the NSA's policy primacy and occasional role as negotiator, to subject the NSA by law to Senate confirmation, and to enlarge substantially the NSC staff is more feasible than a patently unworkable State-centered system.[4] But like the highly centralized, closed White House–NSC system of the sort that characterized all but the first year of the Nixon term, his proposal has many faults.

First, such a system, with an NSA whose paramount role is that of a presidential policy adviser rather than a custodian-manager of the NSC system, undercuts the NSC's image as a neutral broker and undermines the important, legitimate policy advisory role of the secretary of state. This engenders friction between the secretary and the NSA that invariably becomes public knowledge— embarrassing the administration and confusing allies. The friction and confusion are further exacerbated when the NSA assumes the mantle of chief diplomat and public advocate of U.S. foreign policy. Moreover, an NSA who performs all these roles has little time to

---

[3] Destler, "State: A Department or 'Something More'?" 99; Destler, *Presidents, Bureaucrats and Foreign Policy: The Politics of Organizational Reform* (Princeton: Princeton University Press, 1972), 159; Bacchus, *Staffing for Foreign Affairs*, 69; Henry Kissinger, *White House Years* (Boston: Little, Brown, 1979), 27; Donald P. Warwick, *A Theory of Public Bureaucracy: Politics, Personality, and Organization in the State Department* (Cambridge: Harvard University Press, 1975), 33; Barry Rubin, *Secrets of State: The State Department and the Struggle over U.S. Foreign Policy* (New York: Oxford University Press, 1985), 245.

[4] Zbigniew Brzezinski, *Power and Principle: Memoirs of the National Security Adviser, 1977–81* (New York: Farrar, Straus and Giroux, 1983), 535–538.

manage the NSC system. Second, a tightly controlled, highly centralized system run from the White House can distance the president and the NSA from the greatest repository of expertise—the permanent government. Even an NSC staff of substantial size cannot substitute for the intelligence community, the Defense Department, the State Department, and other government agencies.

Third, when the White House runs the show so exclusively, it may not be able to build and sustain the kind of consensus with the bureaucracy, Congress, and the public that most successful long-term policies need.

The president and the NSA alone lack the time to handle all vital issues themselves, let alone secondary or tertiary ones. This inclines an administration toward a crisis or "front-burner" orientation, since critical matters will claim much, if not all, of its time. Long-term problems—nuclear proliferation, Middle East peace, NATO [North Atlantic Treaty Organization] cohesion, for example—invariably receive scant attention. Fortunately, there is virtually no support for a highly centralized system or for the Brzezinski alternative in Congress or among past or present senior government officials.

A preferred alternative to the Brzezinski option, the highly centralized Nixon-Kissinger system, or a State-centered system would be one roughly analogous to that in operation during much of the Ford administration, when Lieutenant General Brent Scowcroft served as NSA. The secretary of state, ideally, would here be a significant presidential foreign-policy adviser as well as the principal negotiator and policy advocate.

No system is acceptable, however, unless it meets the president's needs and style. Personal considerations will largely determine the NSC's role as well as the quality of advice the president receives. But whatever process a president decides upon, some structure is essential. Those who neglect the mechanisms

and procedures for formulating and implementing policy—as the Reagan administration did in 1981 and to a considerable degree thereafter—will encounter difficulties. Although there is no universally correct way to structure an NSC system, experience suggests certain guidelines:

- Although a president's subsequent behavior will speak much louder than formal directives, a written directive should be issued in the first week of the administration setting forth the NSC system and delineating the functions of the NSA, the secretary of state, and other key officials.
- There should be a formal method for preparing national security policy studies and issuing presidential decisions to facilitate White House policy direction.
- Senior interagency coordinating committees chaired by the NSC should have clear areas of responsibility and be supported by interagency working groups that develop option papers and oversee the policy analysis effort.

Most senior-level interagency management of the national security system must be delegated to the NSA and the NSC staff. As argued above, neither the State Department nor any other line department can perform this function effectively, and the president has neither the time nor the ability to manage the executive branch. However, presidents must take some interest in their policy processes and at times intervene personally. President Ronald Reagan has delegated authority excessively in what he calls "cabinet government," and no NSC since at least 1961 has been weaker than his. Only belatedly and under great pressure has Reagan intervened in his own overly decentralized system.[5] "Iranscam"

---

[5] Phil McCombs, "McFarlane and the Web of Rumor," *Washington Post*, 18 April 1986, D1; David Hoffman, "President's Aides Seek Harmony, *Washington Post*, 8 Septem-

may well turn out to be one of the many costs of presidential inattention to process.

The principal function of the NSA should be that of custodian-manager of the NSC process. In this capacity the NSA, it is hoped, would be seen more or less as a neutral arbiter who made sure that key officials were able to attend important meetings and communicate their views to the president. The NSA and a staff of at least 45 professionals would manage the NSC's crucial institutional and support functions. Other important NSC institutional functions would include assisting the president in delineating a policy framework, selecting issues for the president's attention and forcing decisions on pressing matters, managing the policy-analysis process, managing crises and crisis planning, and policing the implementation of presidential decisions. Apart from briefing the media on background information and perhaps dealing privately with individual legislators, the NSA should maintain a low profile, avoid delivering major policy speeches, and become involved in diplomacy only at the president's insistence and, then, in close consultation with the secretary of state. The CIA [Central Intelligence Agency], of course, not the NSC, should implement properly authorized covert operations.

The degree to which the NSA should also be a policy adviser to the president also must be resolved. A major concern is that the NSA cannot be both an influential policy adviser and a neutral arbiter. Moreover, an assumption of the former role would invite friction with the secretary of state. On the other hand, to be an effective manager and institution the

NSA must have an advisory role. This gives the NSA the stature and political clout to deal with powerful members of the cabinet. The problem, as is so often the case, is one of appropriate balance and personal style. Indeed, even if the NSA is principally a custodian-manager, which should be the case, many presidents will naturally solicit advice from NSAs with whom they are in daily contact. Yet the NSA must not usurp the rightful roles of the secretary of state.

The case of Reagan's second secretary of state, George Shultz, is probably illustrative of the maximum influence future secretaries can expect to have. Although Shultz has been influential in some security-related issues such as terrorism and U.S.-Israeli strategic cooperation, he has never come close to eclipsing the Pentagon and Secretary of Defense Caspar Weinberger in core defense policy and programmatic issues. Nor, despite his professional background in economics and prior government experience at the Office of Management and Budget and the Treasury Department, has he challenged Treasury's primacy in international economic policy. Although Shultz has become the president's leading foreign-policy adviser, there is little evidence that his department's stature has been elevated.

Shultz's prominence is due to an unusual combination of factors. Reagan has had no desire to act as his own secretary of state, no deep personal interest in international affairs, and little knowledge of the subject. Fortuitously, the secretary of state's frequent competitor, the NSA, has been strapped by presidential preference. Reagan's NSAs, except William Clark, have had their policy advisory roles restricted, and some NSAs were weak and ineffectual or unschooled and inexperienced in foreign policy. Despite this, by January 1982 the NSC, not State, had the primary interagency coordinative function. The NSC often performed its role inadequately—partly

ber 1985, A1; Joseph Kraft, "Star System," *Washington Post*, 8 December 1985, B7; Joseph G. Bock and Duncan L. Clarke, "The National Security Assistant and the White House Staff: National Security Policy Decisionmaking and Domestic Political Considerations, 1947–1984," *Presidential Studies Quarterly* 16 (Spring 1986): 271; See Laurence I. Barrett, *Gambling with History: Ronald Reagan in the White House* (New York: Doubleday, 1983).

because of excessive decentralization of authority and partly because the Reagan administration downgraded the NSA's policy advisory role.

Moreover, Shultz is a skilled, experienced, bureaucratic operator regarded highly by Congress and by many within the administration. His effectiveness was further enhanced, perhaps until his recent public statements on the Iran arms imbroglio, by his self-effacing, team-playing style. Beginning with former national security adviser Robert McFarlane, Shultz appeared to work out an informal alliance with the security assistant that acknowledged their respective roles, averted potentially harmful personal disputes, and served Shultz well in his dealings with Weinberger. Above all, Shultz has developed an unusually cordial personal rapport with the president. And personal compatibility with the president, as past secretaries attest, is always a crucial factor.

The secretary of state can still be important. However, recent history—certainly since 1961, and probably earlier—cautions against holding out great expectations for the secretary's own department.

Three categories of significant activities can reasonably be expected of State. Foremost among them are the implementation of foreign-policy decisions and the continued fulfillment of the traditional missions of the Foreign Service: representation, negotiation, and reporting. In this diplomatic arena the department and the Foreign Service possess unique experience and talent. Second, though less likely, an influential secretary who has the president's confidence might be able to draw some immediate staff and perhaps two or three senior departmental officers into a closer, more comfortable relationship with the White House. This is a far cry from a State-centered system, but it expands the scope of contact. Finally, State can and must continue to contribute to the whole range of substantive foreign-policy issues—in senior and lower interagency committees, in less formal contexts, and through the secretary and the seventh-floor staff. But in most instances the department will remain a contributor, not a leader, in the policy-formulation process. For it to aspire higher is only to court yet another blow to its prestige and reputation.

QUESTIONS FOR DISCUSSION

1. What should be the relationship between the national security adviser and the secretary of state? Why?
2. Why have some presidents relied more on their national security adviser than on their secretary of state for advice in foreign policy?
3. What are the strengths and weaknesses for the conduct of American foreign policy of a president's considering the State Department as "something more" than another department of government?
4. Does the nature of the organizational structure of the State Department strengthen the case for a dominant State Department? Why?
5. Who will play the greater role in foreign policy in the future: the national security adviser or the secretary of state? Why?

SUGGESTED READINGS

Barlow, Joel. "On Managing American Diplomacy." *Foreign Service Journal,* 58 (Feb. 1981), pp. 34–37, 43.

Bock, Joseph G., and Duncan L. Clarke, "The National Security Assistant and the White House Staff: National Security Policy Decisionmaking and Domestic Political Considerations, 1947–1984." *Presidential Studies Quarterly,* 16 (Spring 1986), pp. 258–79.

Brzezinski, Zbigniew. "The NSC's Midlife Crisis." *Foreign Policy,* no. 69 (Winter 1987–88), pp. 80–99.

Geyelin, Philip. "The Workings of the National Security System: Past, Present, and Future" [interview with Clark M. Clifford]. *SAIS Review,* 8 (Winter–Spring 1988), pp. 19–28.

Kondracke, Morton. "Out of the Basement: Cleaning up the NSC." *New Republic,* 196 (Jan. 5, 12, 1987), pp. 10, 12–13.

Lord, Carnes. "Executive Power and Our Security." *National Interest,* no. 7 (Spring 1987), pp. 3–13.

———. "Rethinking the NSC Role." *Comparative Strategy,* 6, no. 3 (1987), pp. 241–79.

Mulcahy, Kevin V. "The Secretary of State and the National Security Adviser: Foreign Policymaking in the Carter and Reagan Administrations." *Presidential Studies Quarterly,* 16 (Spring 1986), pp. 280–99.

Sorensen, Theodore C. "The President and the Secretary of State." *Foreign Affairs,* 66 (Winter 1987–88), pp. 231–48.

U.S. Cong., Senate. *The National Security Adviser: Political Accountability.* Hearing before the Committee on Foreign Relations, 96th Cong., 2d Sess., 1980.

———. *Organization, Structure, and Decisionmaking Procedures of the Department of Defense.* Hearings before the Committee on Armed Services, 98th Cong., 1st Sess., 1983, pt. 11.

12 Should More U.S. Ambassadors Be Drawn from the Foreign Service?

YES

Charles S. Whitehouse

The Case for Career Appointments

NO

John Krizay

The Case for Political Appointments

The Case for Career Appointments

Charles S. Whitehouse

The question of the appointment of ambassadors from outside the Foreign Service, which is addressed by your proposal, Mr. Chairman, is one which has been for years and continues to be of great interest to our association and its members. I feel personally well qualified to discuss this subject, having been twice an ambassador myself and having worked closely with career and noncareer ambassadors in the course of over 30 years in the Foreign Service.

Before addressing myself to the proposal, which the American Foreign Service Association wholeheartedly supports, that the number of political ambassadors be limited to 15 percent, may I say a few words about the general attitude of our members toward noncareer appointments.

First, we recognize that the appointment of ambassadors from outside the career is an American tradition. No other country assigns noncareer people to the extent that we do. But our membership realizes that, as a practical matter, every administration will want to appoint a certain number of ambassadors who are not Foreign Service officers.

Second, our association and its members believe that our country has been and can continue to be served by eminent and distinguished Americans from other professions, but with relevant skills and experience who are selected by the President to represent our country as ambassadors.

I served in Vietnam with Ambassador Bun-

ker and years ago in Belgium with Admiral Kirk. They were men of great experience and ability whose performances were superb. David Bruce, George Bush, Senator Mike Mansfield, Douglas Dillon, and many others have brought to diplomacy a lifetime of responsibility in foreign affairs and a degree of intimacy with certain foreign leaders which few, if any, career officers could have acquired.

The point I am making is that the association and the officers of the Foreign Service do not oppose a reasonable number of well-qualified political appointees. The issues with which our members have difficulty are, first, the selection of individuals who are not only lacking in direct experience involving foreign affairs, but whose careers in other fields are not particularly outstanding or even relevant to effective diplomacy. Second, the assignment of what appears to them to be an excessive number of such political appointees; and third, the increased assignment of political appointees to embassies in which personal ties to the President are not an important factor.

Members of the career Foreign Service can understand the desire of a President to have eminent Americans from outside the career service and who are close to him in a few of the more important posts. But it is hard for us to see the justification for 50 or 60 noncareer ambassadors, many to the more remote posts traditionally headed by Foreign Service officers.

We ask why? The answer we receive is that these men are loyal and have personal access to the President. But our response, in turn, is that the Foreign Service career officer is professionally committed to being loyal to the President and the country. For decades and decades this has been so. It is a strong tradition.

The commitment to a career of national service and the self-discipline which is required from the beginning permeates our professional ethic and infuses a spirit of loyalty to the Nation and to its leaders.

Charles S. Whitehouse, Statement, U.S. Cong., Senate, *To Amend the Foreign Service Act of 1980*, Hearing before the Committee on Foreign Relations, 97th Cong., 2d Sess., 1982, pp. 35–37.

Our further response is that personal access to the President is really not needed in most posts, and when it is, an able career officer can establish the necessary confidence. In fact, we wonder how long the machinery of Government and of foreign policy would stay in order if every ambassador felt free to call the President at any time. Yet we see political appointees in virtually all Western European capitals and spilling over into some of the most remote Third World posts as well.

I am making these points, Mr. Chairman, as our association believes that the issues I have cited are particularly significant today. We have done a study on the number of political appointments to ambassadorial appointments going back to the Roosevelt administration. This analysis clearly demonstrates that the proportion of political ambassadors approved by the current administration is higher today than it has been at least since Herbert Hoover's day.

Of the appointments made by President Reagan, 48 percent have been political and only 52 percent career. This has to be compared with a range of 55 percent by President Roosevelt to 73 percent career by President Carter. Until the past 15 months, the trend toward greater professionalism had seemed definitely established, despite some short-term variations, particularly at the start of most new administrations.

In an increasingly complex and dangerous world, this trend toward greater professionalism in the conduct of foreign affairs should be accelerated. In the past, spokesmen for the administration have emphasized that the ratio of ambassadors currently serving abroad remains within traditional limits. In order to reach this conclusion, the administration has to adjust its figures to include ambassadors to multilateral agencies.

A very fair and clear way of looking at this statistical question is to note that 23 posts previously filled by career officers are now occupied by political appointees, and conversely,

12 previously filled by political appointees are now filled by career officers. It has therefore been a net loss of 11 ambassadorships to the Foreign Service.

It is not my purpose to make ad hominem remarks about ambassadors now serving abroad. It is the view of our membership—and we have a unique opportunity to observe them first hand—that the President's appointees are, by and large, persons less distinguished and capable than many selected by earlier Presidents, and a surprising number are being sent to embassies from which the access to high administration officials, an attribute apparently given much weight by the White House staff, is in fact irrelevant.

There are those, Mr. Chairman, who will say that a 15-percent limit on political appointees is too rigid and that any administration should be given more latitude than your proposal permits.

We believe that its very rigidity gives this proposal special merit and will impose a discipline on future administrations that will assure the appointment of carefully selected individuals for a small number of posts as envisaged by the drafters of the Foreign Service Act of 1980 rather than the ever-increasing number of poorly qualified appointees we are seeing today.

There is one final point which I believe must be reaffirmed before this committee. And that is, the effect on the Foreign Service of what appears to be an increase in the number of appointees not only to ambassadorships but also to senior positions in the Department of State.

The Foreign Service is a small service and a proud service, with a proven record of loyalty to every administration it serves. Its personnel are stationed all over the world, often under conditions of considerable danger and discomfort, separations from families are frequent.

It is our view that a lifelong apprenticeship in a variety of positions abroad and in the foreign affairs agencies in Washington best prepares individuals for great responsibility in this field.

This view is clearly stated in the Foreign Service Act of 1980, but it undermines the Service when its capable, dedicated professionals are denied appointments at the top of their profession in order for an administration to meet some domestic political obligation.

We think our country deserves the best ambassadors it can get to represent it abroad. Approval of S. 1886 would be a most significant step in that direction, as it would provide for a very high degree of professionalism in our representation abroad, while still granting the President the authority to send carefully selected noncareer ambassadors to a significant number of foreign capitals.

The Case for Political Appointments

John Krizay

The bill, introduced by Senator Mathias to restrict the President's authority to appoint non-career ambassadors to 15 percent of the total number of ambassador positions, would appear to be based on two supporting arguments: (1) that it would create additional opportunities for advancement in the Foreign Service Officer Corps, thus enhancing morale and incentive; and, (2) that the quality of ambassadorial appointments would be improved if fewer "political" appointments were permitted.

As a former Foreign Service Officer with considerable experience outside government, I challenge these premises. Indeed, I would argue that any arbitrary limit on the number of non-career ambassadors would be detrimental both to the interests of national policy and to the well-being of the Foreign Service. The Foreign Service is already an overly in-bred organization, its outlook is already too narrow, and its views are too often thought to represent the interests of other governments over those of the United States. The appointment of non-careerists to key diplomatic positions strengthen—not weaken—the Foreign Service for they can bring to this tightly knit operation greater understanding of domestic political and economic interests that ultimately underly all our foreign affairs activities. The effort to improve the quality of diplomatic appointments should turn not toward limiting the number of non-careerists but toward setting standards and devising an appointments

mechanism that would apply to careerists and non-careerists alike.

It is no secret that, over the past 30 years, the State Department and the Foreign Service have steadily lost influence over the conduct of foreign relations. "Strong" Secretaries of State, typically, have kept this elite corps at arms length. And, in dealing with the myriad international problems, too technical or too obscure to warrant the Secretary's attention, State is frequently overshadowed or overruled by other Departments and Agencies who mistrust the State Department view.

This is a harsh judgment, and it gives me no joy to make this statement. But, one only has to read the memoirs of national leaders from the Truman Administration through Nixon and Kissinger to have this judgment corroborated.

Why has the State Department become such a minor cog in the foreign affairs machinery? The reasons are many and complex as I pointed out in an article in *Policy Review* in 1978. But, there is no question that the incestuous nature of the Foreign Service personnel system is central to any analysis of this phenomenon. This elite corps of talented—even brilliant—men and women operates with all the characteristics of an exclusive club, impervious to outside influence. Its system of selection, assignment, training, and promotion all revolve around the subjective judgments of those who are already club members, and even these judgments are closely monitored and scrutinized by those senior members under whose charge the club is managed. In service abroad, where relationships are often uncomfortably close, even one's social behavior and personal habits enter into the composite of impressions that are certain to influence recommendations regarding an officer's career direction and potential.

This is not an atmosphere where bold new ideas are readily accepted or where departures from a traditional mode of thinking can flour-

John Krizay, Prepared Statement, U.S. Cong., Senate, *To Amend the Foreign Service Act of 1980,* Hearing before the Committee on Foreign Relations, 97th Cong., 2d Sess., 1982, pp. 85–86.

ish. This overwhelming pressure to conform takes on an added significance when one considers that the entire operating structure of the Department of State and its posts abroad is geared entirely toward the observation and analysis of events occurring in other countries. Knowledge of even obscure happenings in obscure countries are valued highly; events of greater importance occurring in the United States are considered hardly at all. Members of this elite club may sneer at outsiders who cannot name the President of Zimbabwe while, they, themselves, are ignorant of the plight of International Harvester or of Firestone and the implications of these developments on our relations with important trading partners.

New ideas and, above all, reminders that Americans, too, have interests that extend beyond our borders can come to this organization, as now structured, only through new infusions of personnel. Presently, with few exceptions new entrants into the Foreign Service Officer Corps can occur at only two levels: at the very bottom and at the very top. Those coming in at the very bottom quickly learn the virtues of conformity. Only those entering at the very top can bring to the organization some sense of the opinions and concerns of the nation and some willingness to fashion the making and management of foreign policy to accommodate those opinions and concerns.

Non-career appointments in the Foreign Service thus, serve an important purpose and are needed. It is of particular significance to note that no evidence has ever been developed that establishes that career ambassadors, as a group, are superior to non-career ambassadors. Criteria on which such evaluations can be made are, to begin with, most difficult to construct. On the other hand, anecdotes are common, and they, typically, focus on the non-careerist who makes for better copy in the press and juicier gossip within the organization. Outsiders are seldom welcome in exclusive

clubs. The career service, too, has produced inept and even embarrassing ambassadors, but tales of their ineptitude rarely escape the confines of the Club. Additionally, criticisms of the non-careerist will almost inevitably be harsher if, for no other reason, because he may bring to the institution an approach to foreign affairs totally at variance with the traditional foreign service viewpoint. Innovations always run a greater risk of criticism and ridicule than safe, conventional ideas that deviate little from the established path.

There is, in other words, no objective basis for arguing that ambassadors drawn from the career service better serve our interests in dealing with other nations. Of course, ambassadorial appointments should be of the highest quality no matter whether from the career service or from sources outside. What is required is an accepted standard that may include background, language or language aptitude, managerial ability, and prior service in some capacity involving dealings with other nations. Restricting the numbers of outside appointments is a crude way to achieve a better quality of ambassadors, and it holds little prospect of success.

Nor will the professional Foreign Service Corps be better off as a result of such restrictions. The added 20 or 30 ambassadorial posts that might become available to the careerists over a given year would add little to the real opportunities of a Foreign Service career. Indeed it may be argued that passage of this bill would only contribute to an already unhealthy obsession with titles that diverts the energies of too many Foreign Service Officers away from the real purpose of their careers. For too long, the Department has pandered to this penchant for titles, creating a kind of phony aristocracy where no task is worth undertaking unless adorned with a title that exaggerates its substantive significance. Over the past 30 years, with no increase in total personnel, the number of Office Directors has increased from under 40 to over 150; the number holding the title of Deputy Assistant Secretary of State has increased from 7 to over 60; ambassadorships have been created where no ambassadorial function exists.

The Department of State does not need more titles to offer its professional staff. It needs, rather, a new sense of mission and a sense of greater and more effective participation in the foreign affairs process. Non-career appointments should be viewed as helpful in this regard, for they offer the professional Foreign Service a source of protection against the kind of pernicious in-breeding that, in decades past, has contributed so much to its decline.

QUESTIONS FOR DISCUSSION

1. What criteria should be used in determining how many appointees to ambassadorships should be political rather than career?
2. What effect do political appointees have on the conduct of foreign policy?
3. How essential is personal access to the U.S. president for an ambassador to be effective in diplomacy? What are the reasons for your answer?
4. What effect has the Foreign Service personnel system had on the power of the secretary of state (compared to the national security adviser) in the conduct of foreign policy?
5. What qualities of intellect and character are needed in a good ambassador? Are these qualities more likely to be found in a career or a political appointee? Why?

SUGGESTED READINGS

Davis, Nathaniel. "The Foreign Service and Presidential Control of Foreign Policy." *Foreign Service Journal,* 57 (Mar. 1980), pp. 8–14, 38, 40.

"Galbraith vs. Eagleburger: Loyalty and Guts." *Foreign Service Journal,* 63 (Jan. 1986), pp. 28–30.

Goshko, John N. "America's Fading Foreign Service." *Washington Post,* Apr. 26, 1987, pp. A1, A12; Apr. 27, 1987, pp. A1, A6; Apr. 29, 1987, pp. A1, A12.

Hackett, James T. "How the White House Can Regain Control of Foreign Policy." *Heritage Foundation Issue Bulletin,* 27. Washington, D.C.: Heritage Foundation, 1984.

Herz, Martin F., ed. *The Modern Ambassador.* Washington, D.C.: Institute for the Study of Diplomacy, Edmund A. Walsh School of Foreign Service, Georgetown University, 1983.

Lewis, Michael. "Why Political Interference Is Good for the State Department." *Orbis,* 32 (Spring 1988), pp. 167–85.

Maresca, John J. "Leaders and Experts." *Foreign Service Journal,* 63 (Feb. 1986), pp. 30–32.

Newsom, David D. "Leaders and Experts: Fitting into the Political Structure." *Foreign Service Journal,* 63 (June 1986), pp. 36–37.

Plischke, Elmer. "American Ambassadors—An Obsolete Species? Some Alternatives to Traditional Diplomatic Representation." *World Affairs,* 147 (Summer 1984), pp. 2–23.

Poullada, Leon B. "Leaders and Experts: The Professional Solution." *Foreign Service Journal,* 63 (Oct. 1986), pp. 24–25.

Silberman, Laurence H. "Toward Presidential Control of the State Department." *Foreign Affairs,* 57 (Spring 1979), pp. 872–93.

PART THREE

The Political Context of Foreign Policy

In the nineteenth century the United States, as a nation of immigrants bent on exploiting the opportunities of a new continent, avoided serious international involvement. This abstinence permitted the continent to be settled, the economy to be developed, and a diverse population to be assimilated. It also prevented the quarrels of Europe (and Asia) from becoming divisive domestic issues.

The freedom from serious involvement in international politics was new for Americans. In the early years of the Republic the wars between Great Britain and France divided Americans along political lines; the Federalists supported Britain, the more liberal Jeffersonians supported France. And the bitterness—which spilled over to other issues—almost pulled the nation apart. But after the War of 1812 these differences receded. Americans concentrated on nation building and turned their backs on international politics. The result was to fashion a uniquely American set of attitudes that have continued to play an important part in American foreign policy up to the present day.

First, the United States considered itself morally superior to the regimes of Europe. If the various monarchies were too reactionary, the French Republic was too radical. (This radicalism was as true of the Third Republic from 1875 onward as it had been of the First and Second Republics.) American democracy assumed a moral component. It was qualitatively better. And while the United States was on the periphery of international politics, this conceit could be indulged. If it imparted a curious moral tone to American pronouncements, so much the better.

Second, the American system of government—the elaborate system of checks and balances, the separation of powers, and the written Constitution—also came to be seen as uniquely superior. The protection of individual liberty was viewed as the true aim of government. These opinions dominated American politics at home and colored U.S. policy abroad.

Third, the protection afforded by America's geographic location allowed these ideas to flourish virtually without challenge. The result was that when the United States entered onto the world scene as a major participant, it came armed with a unique set of values and a certitude in their correctness.

Fourth, and perhaps most important, because the United States had not been seriously threatened by a foreign power for a century, it had little need to accommodate to the realities of international power. While European statesmen like Benjamin Disraeli and Otto von Bismarck subscribed to the doctrine of the primacy of foreign policy and the urgent necessity to protect the state from hostile neighbors, American leaders held to the view that domestic politics was the locomotive of foreign policy. The corollary was that democratic states were peaceful; nondemocratic states were not.

These ideas have dominated American thinking about foreign policy. They are proved or disproved depending on the perspective of the observer and the evidence selected. They are important because they set the tone and provide the attitudinal parameters within which U.S. policy is formulated.

The debates in Part III deal with the domestic context of foreign policy. Does America's role as a superpower threaten U.S. democracy? Specifically, does massive defense spending and the resultant relationship between the beneficiaries of that spending and the military pose a problem for U.S. political institutions? What role do the media play? Does television coverage of military operations undermine public support? British Prime Minister Margaret Thatcher barred on-the-site news coverage of the Falkland campaign in 1982, and the Reagan administration blocked journalists from accompanying American forces in Grenada in 1983. Do government restrictions of journalists during periods of U.S. military operations threaten First Amendment guarantees of a free press? And what about government secrecy? Does the public have a right to know? When, if ever, can that right be suspended? These questions deal with the impact of national security on domestic politics. They are important because they go the heart of the American system of government. And so long as the United States plays a major role in world politics, they are unlikely to abate.

A different set of questions pertains to the impact of domestic interests on foreign policy. For example, what role do ethnic and religious groups play in influencing U.S. policy? American reaction to *apartheid* in South Africa transcends ethical, racial, and political lines, but what about the dispute between Greece and Turkey over Cyprus? Does the large and articulate Greek population in the United States affect American policy? In World War I and to a lesser extent in World War II, German immigrants in the United States resisted American intervention. Japanese-Americans suffered in World War II because of fears (now proved groundless) that they might aid Japan during the conflict. Or consider Northern Ireland. To what extent do American Catholics of Irish ancestry influence U.S. policy? To what extent are they involved in the Irish struggle? These issues are inevitable in a nation of immigrants. One of the most important questions involves the state of Israel. Is the Israeli lobby too powerful? Does it have a marked effect on American policy in the Middle East? Do American political institutions such as the Electoral College enhance the influence of special interests in foreign affairs? Finally, we look at an important aspect of national power, the exclusive control of foreign relations by the federal government. Under the Constitution, the individual states have no role in foreign policy; foreign policy is a national monopoly. Is this monopoly necessary? Do the states sometimes have valid interests that should be protected and represented? Do individual localities? Or must the nation speak with one voice. As Justice Stephen J. Field said on behalf of the Supreme Court in the *Chinese Exclusion Case:* "For local interests the several States of the Union exist, but for international purposes...we are one people, one nation, one power."[1]

More so than in most countries, the interplay between domestic issues and foreign policy is a continuing process in the United States. A basic premise of American government is that *the people* influence policy through their representatives. The institutions of government are uniquely balanced to ensure that minority rights are protected. But do these same institutions afford an inordinate voice to special interests when it comes to foreign policy? An individual senator, a well-placed member of the House who may be a subcommittee or committee chairman, can often block important foreign policy legislation. Even the threat of doing so provides significant leverage. Seen in this context, the very strengths of the American representative system can also be its weaknesses. The power of special interests may overwhelm the larger national interest in foreign policy making. What is true in the House and Senate is true in the executive branch as well. The American Electoral College system of choosing a president gives the largest states extraordinary power. With 270 electoral votes required for election, and with the votes awarded by state on a winner-take-all basis, it is usually crucial for a successful candidate to carry such states as California (forty-seven electoral votes), New York (thirty-six electoral votes), and Florida (twenty-one electoral votes). Since each of these states is usually narrowly divided between Democrats and Republicans, a tightly organized, single-issue interest group can often determine the outcome. Quite obviously that affords such groups enormous leverage on presidential candidates—and on the foreign policy stands these candidates adopt.

So long as the United States was at the margin of international politics, these special characteristics of the American system mattered little. But as the challenges and opportunities of the international system have intruded upon the United States and as the risks from that system have not only become infinitely greater but sometimes threaten national survival, it is essential to inquire into the appropriate role of special interests in a free society. Public support for foreign policy is the touchstone of success. But achieving public

---

[1] *Che Chan Ping v. United States,* 130 U.S. 581, 606 (1889).

support is not easy, and many questions surround how the public voice should be injected into the policy process. In 1937, a proposed constitutional amendment (the Ludlow Amendment) that would have required a national referendum before Congress could declare war was narrowly defeated in the House of Representatives.[2] Few would argue that a referendum on war or peace would facilitate the conduct of U.S. foreign policy. But at the other extreme, should the people abdicate from all foreign policy decisions, trusting to those in office to protect the national interest? James H. Billington, the librarian of Congress, thinks not. Writing in a recent issue of *Foreign Affairs*, Billington argues: "International affairs cannot be a spectator sport any more than policymaking can be the preserve of a small group of elites. Many must be involved; many more persuaded.[3] The exigencies of the international situation provide the imperatives to which policy makers must respond. But the nature of that response, indeed, the overall nature and direction of U.S. foreign policy, flows from domestic dictates. The five debates that follow explore these questions.

The first debate in Part III looks at what is popularly known as the *military-industrial complex*. This complex may be defined as a system in which the armed forces, industries that cater to those forces, and elected public officials work cooperatively to increase military expenditures and in so doing benefit the members of the system. Have the effects of long-term defense spending been pernicious for American democracy? The second debate looks at the effect of television coverage on military operations. Does it promote or inhibit the development of a national consensus? The third debate examines the question of secrecy in government. Does governmental secrecy conflict with First Amendment constitutional rights, such as free speech and the free press? The role of special interests, in this case the Israeli lobby, is debated next. Do those who represent the interests of Israel have too much clout in the United States? Finally, we look at the federal government monopoly on foreign affairs. Should greater grass-roots participation in foreign policy be encouraged?

IS THE RELATIONSHIP BETWEEN THE MILITARY AND INDUSTRY IN THE UNITED STATES A THREAT TO THE DEMOCRATIC POLITICAL SYSTEM?

Is there a military-industrial complex? If so, does it pose a threat to American democracy? Or is the concept too glib, too facile, and too poorly defined? The defense industry provides the sinews of military victory. The Union's success in the Civil War owed as much to the proficiency of northern manufacturers as it did to the tenacity of U. S. Grant and William T. Sherman. In World War II the industrial strength of the United States again provided the margin of victory. America was the "arsenal of democracy," in Franklin D. Roosevelt's phrase.

---

[2] H. J. Res. 199, 75th Cong., 1st Sess.

[3] James H. Billington, "Realism and Vision in Foreign Policy," *Foreign Affairs,* 65, no. 3 (1987), p. 630.

Can the arsenal of democracy threaten democratic institutions? The answer is yes and no. Unless the nation's armed forces are provided with adequate equipment, democracy will be imperiled. But it is also true that the spending of large sums on defense procurement over a long period of time creates a special relationship between those who spend the money and those who receive it. Both share an interest that the spending continue. And as the size of the defense budget has increased, Congress has become progressively unable or unwilling to control expenditures. This situation results in part from Congress's lack of the information and expertise to make detailed judgments as to military requirements. But it also results from the fact that high defense expenditures provide money for every state and every congressional district: money for defense contractors, employees, and equipment; money for military bases and personnel. A more pernicious aspect of high defense spending involves political campaign contributions and other well-funded lobbying activities by military contractors. Do they erode Congress's ability to oversee defense spending? Can they corrupt the political process?

In the debate that follows, the editors of *New Times* (Moscow), a Soviet weekly of world affairs, stress the political consequences of the military-industrial complex. They see "militarism" as a "vital expression" of capitalism "at the monopoly stage of its development." They assert that the financial links between defense contractors and the military fuel defense spending, distort international relations, and increase the tension between East and West. According to the editors:

> The partnership between the arms business and generals goes beyond the bounds of common economic interests, of course. They pursue, separately and together, far-reaching political aims, seek to gear government policy to the interests of the military-industrial complex, and strive for power. The danger of the military-industrial complex lies in its political ambitions, in the role it plays in shaping the military and foreign policy of imperialist states.

Gen. James P. Mullins, who served as chief of logistics for the U.S. Air Force, argues that the military-industrial complex has been given unfair criticism. He traces the growth of the defense industry in the United States, its contribution to economic and scientific growth, and its essential role in national defense. "Taxpayers' dollars are not squandered when they are invested in the nation's defense," says General Mullins. Students will note that his argument stresses the military imperatives and economic benefits of defense spending.

DO THE MEDIA—PARTICULARLY TELEVISION—UNDERMINE AMERICAN SUPPORT FOR MILITARY OPERATIONS?

In 1918, when Imperial Germany asked for an armistice, the German army was entrenched less than fifty miles from Paris. Since the early days of 1914, not one battle had been fought on German soil. Not one foreign soldier had set foot in the Fatherland. As a result, it was exceedingly difficult for the German population to accept the fact that Germany was militarily defeated. The rumor quickly gained acceptance that the German army must have been "stabbed in the back."

The "stab in the back" myth dominated German thinking after World War I. It helped discredit the leaders of the Weimar Republic; it fueled German resentment against the terms of peace; and it greatly facilitated Adolf Hitler's rise to power. The Nazis made home-front treachery the centerpiece of their nationalist propaganda, directed at a population who still could not comprehend Germany's defeat.

Is a new "stab in the back" myth aborning in relation to the American defeat in Vietnam? Did the United States lose, or did the media, television especially, snatch defeat from the jaws of victory? In the debate that follows, Marine Maj. Cass D. Howell suggests that television cameras be barred from future battlefields. He traces the American withdrawal from Vietnam to the public revulsion that television spawned. Wallace B. Eberhard, a retired Army colonel, disputes the thesis that the media in general, or television in particular, had a pernicious influence on American efforts in Vietnam. "It is an article of faith that democracy functions best on a free flow of information," writes Eberhard, and television is a legitimate part of the process.

In 1985, a Task Force of the Twentieth Century Fund on the military and the media noted that "the presence of journalists in war zones is not a luxury, but a necessity." The task force pointed out that the media serve "as a vital link between the battlefield and the home front, reporting on the military's successes, failures and sacrifices." By so doing the media have "helped to foster citizen involvement and support, which [is] essential to military success."[4]

Col. Harry G. Summers, Jr., an American military analyst, reports that the Vietnam War marked a historic turning point in the military's relationship with the press—which until then had been extremely cordial. The antagonism between the military and the press since Vietnam, Summers contends, "has been built not on facts but on myths and stereotypes. This tendency is bad enough among Vietnam veterans, but it is even more extreme among younger officers whose attitudes are not tempered by first-hand experience."[5]

The fact is that whenever a war goes badly, the quest for scapegoats begins. And whenever military misadventures are reported, those who do the reporting inevitably share the blame. The Duke of Wellington complained about "the babbling of the English newspapers from whose columns the enemy constantly drew the most certain information on the strength and situation of the Army." During the Crimean War, Lord Clarendon, the British foreign secretary, lamented that "three pitched battles gained would not repair the mischief" done by the London *Times* war correspondent on the scene.[6] In our own Civil War it was the news media, and especially the photographs of Mathew Brady, that brought the fight-

---

[4] *Battle Lines: Report of the Twentieth Century Fund Task Force on the Military and the Media* (New York: Priority Press, 1985), p. 4.

[5] Harry G. Summers, Jr., "Western Media and Recent Wars," *Military Review,* 66 (May 1986), pp. 5–6.

[6] Duke of Wellington, quoted in Rupert Furneaux, *The First War Correspondent* (London: Cassels, 1944), p. 18; Lord Clarendon, quoted in Furneaux, p. 78.

ing home—and caused many a feckless Union general to be removed or replaced. Even General Grant despaired at having his plans revealed by the press.

Was the press performing a useful service? In addition to the vital role of informing the people from whom the army is drawn, critical reporting, one can argue, serves as an unofficial link between the field and higher military and civilian authority. It informs those in charge of military incompetence, poor judgment, and bungled opportunities. Was the press doing a disservice to the American war effort in 1943 when it reported that Gen. George Patton had slapped a shell-shocked soldier in an army field hospital? Gen. Dwight D. Eisenhower apparently did not think so. He relieved Patton immediately. Even Lord Clarendon recanted from his early criticism of the reporting from the Crimea. Without it, he said, "the deplorable state of the British army" would not have been brought to the attention of the ministers who were responsible.[7] Gen. Bruce Palmer, Jr., Army vice–chief of staff during the Vietnam War, reports that the military chain of command did not want to hear from subordinates in the field how badly the war against the Viet Cong was going. With official channels blocked, the media became the only means of communication.[8]

Can the erosion of U.S. domestic support for the Vietnam War be traced to television coverage? There are those who would argue that if TV cameras had recorded the carnage of Antietam, Gettysburg, or Cold Harbor, the American people in the North would have allowed the South to secede. But other observers contend that this assessment misses the point. In their view the Union persevered because Americans in the North believed the cause was just; in Vietnam, with infinitely fewer casualties, the public was never convinced. In this regard General Palmer captures the problem concisely:

> The very heart of the basic problem posed by the Vietnam [war] was the failure of our political leaders to grasp why it was necessary to go to war. In the absence of that understanding, it was difficult if not impossible for our government to explain the war to the American people and get them personally and directly involved.[9]

In Grenada, the military (perhaps with an eye on the successful Falklands campaign in which the British barred on-site media coverage) did not take journalists along on the assault. The resulting furor led to the appointment of a military review panel that concluded: "The American people must be informed about United States military operations. . . . Therefore, the panel believes it is essential that the U.S. media cover U.S. military operations to the maximum degree possible consistent with mission security and the safety of U.S. forces."[10]

---

[7] Ibid., p. 79.

[8] Bruce D. Palmer, Jr., *The 25-Year War: America's Military Role in Vietnam* (Lexington, Ky.: University of Kentucky Press, 1984), pp. 22–23. See also David Halberstam, "The Press in Vietnam and El Salvador," *Wall Street Journal*, Feb. 23, 1982, p. 34.

[9] Palmer, *25-Year War*, p. 17.

[10] *The Sidle Panel Report*, Office of the Chairman of the Joint Chiefs of Staff, June 6, 1984, pp. 3–4.

Students should note that in arguing the case against television coverage, Major Howell incorrectly states that the "public's right to know" enjoys no legal underpinning. The fact is, there is a clear line of constitutional precedent in which the right to information has been prominent in the rationale of the Supreme Court.[11]

DOES GOVERNMENTAL SECRECY CONFLICT WITH CONSTITUTIONAL RIGHTS?

In a famous civil liberties case, *Cox v. New Hampshire*, Chief Justice Charles Evans Hughes noted that the very liberties we hold most dear—the guarantees of the Bill of Rights—depend on the ability of the government to provide for the security of its people and to maintain order. He said: "Civil liberties, as guaranteed by the Constitution, imply the existence of an organized society maintaining public order without which liberty itself would be lost in the excesses of unrestrained abuses."[12]

The First Amendment guarantee of free speech and free press has been held to imply a right of the people to be informed.[13] As Chief Justice Harlan Fiske Stone observed in the famous *Caroline Products* case, this is one of the *fundamental* rights Americans enjoy, because the very essence of our constitutional system rests on an informed citizenry.[14] Accordingly, the Supreme Court has been especially vigilant in ensuring that the public's right to information is not infringed.

Are there circumstances in which the right to know must yield to the imperatives of national security? The answer unquestionably is yes. In *C & S Airlines v. Waterman*, a case dealing with the president's authority in foreign affairs, the Supreme Court, speaking through Justice Robert H. Jackson, noted that many national security decisions, of necessity, are taken on the basis of "information properly held secret."[15] In *United States v. Reynolds*, the Court explicitly recognized the right of the government not to "expose military matters which, in the interest of national security, should not be divulged."[16] In *United States v. Nixon*, the famous case on executive privilege in which the President was required to turn over tape recordings needed as evidence in a criminal case, Chief Justice Warren Burger suggested that had the information requested by the special Watergate prosecutor pertained to military or foreign affairs, the decision of the Supreme Court might be different. "In these areas...the courts have traditionally shown the utmost def-

[11] *Martin v. City of Struthers*, 319 U.S. 141 (1943); *Thomas v. Collins*, 323 U.S. 516 (1945); *Lamont v. Postmaster General*, 381 U.S. 301 (1965); *Stanley v. Georgia*, 394 U.S. 557 (1969).

[12] *Cox v. New Hampshire*, 312 U.S. 569 (1941).

[13] *Lamont v. Postmaster General*, 381 U.S. 301 (1965); *Stanley v. Georgia*, 394 U.S. 557 (1969), and the cases cited therein.

[14] *Caroline Products v. United States*, 323 U.S. 18 (1944).

[15] *C & S Airlines v. Waterman*, 333 U.S. 103 (1948).

[16] *United States v. Reynolds*, 397 U.S. 14 (1970).

erence to Presidential responsibility."[17] And most recently, in *Snepp v. United States*, the Court upheld the right of the government to prevent publication of sensitive material by a former Central Intelligence Agency employee.[18]

In effect, the question is not whether the government can keep matters secret because they are vital to national security, but how much should be withheld. What restrictions can justifiably be placed on the free flow of information? And most pointedly, did the Reagan administration go too far? The government's "Preliminary Joint Staff Study on the Protection of National Secrets" indicated that in 1984 the government classified 19,607,736 documents, which was a 9 percent increase over 1983 and a 60 percent increase over the last year of the Nixon administration.[19] Almost 250,000 federal government employees with access to classified material have been required to sign agreements allowing the government to examine and approve anything they wish to publish. The Federal Bureau of Investigation has asked some librarians to report library users who might be "hostile intelligence people" seeking information in public libraries. The Department of Defense has required academic societies to restrict the dissemination of *unclassified* scientific information. A National Security Council directive issued by Adm. John Poindexter in 1986 sought to restrict access not only to national security information, but to unclassified data affecting other government interests, including government or government-derived economic, human, financial, industrial, agricultural, technological, and law enforcement information. Under pressure from Congress, the administration withdrew the notice in March 1987, although the underlying policy, set out in NSDD 145, is still in place.

In the debate that follows, John Shattuck and Muriel Morisey Spence of Harvard University trace the dangers of information control. They point out that the government's attitude toward secrecy has ossilated. At times of stress, a restrictive policy has dominated; when tension relaxed, openness prevailed. Of course, the perception of threat is often in the eyes of the beholder. During the 1970s, for example, both the Ford and Carter administrations issued executive orders designed to curb the excessive secrecy of intelligence agencies. The Reagan administration in the 1980s has reversed that course. In the view of Shattuck and Spence:

> A decade of restrictive information policies has significantly affected important aspects of national life....Excessive secrecy—partly the result of an expanded classification system—has led to compartmentalized federal decision making, manifested in its extreme form in the Iran-contra affair. The public has been deprived of information it has paid for with tax dollars, and important values of free speech, academic inquiry, and democratic participation have been undermined.

---

[17] *United States v. Nixon*, 418 U.S. 683 (1974).
[18] *Snepp v. United States*, 444 U.S. 507 (1980).
[19] "Militarism in America," *Defense Monitor*, 15, no. 3 (1986), p. 4.

The opposite view is taken by Michael A. Ledeen, President of ISI Enterprises and a former consultant to the National Security Council. Ledeen stresses that "high-minded, abstract principles" about openness "are in conflict with a world where secrecy makes it own demands. If secrets...cannot be kept, good policy...is impossible." Ledeen examines historic American attitudes toward secrecy in government and concludes that the United States is unique. "There is no other nation in which the antipathy to secrecy is so strong, and the tension between secrecy and openness so intense." Ledeen makes the point that confidentiality and secrecy are sometimes essential to the free flow of ideas *within* government. Officials will not speak frankly to one another if confidences cannot be kept. He suggests the same is even more true in our dealings with foreign governments. In conclusion, Ledeen acknowledges that an accommodation between the conflicting requirements of secrecy and openness is essential. He suggests a distinction between "policy" and "operations." The public should be fully informed about U.S. policy preferences, but the operational details often must be kept secret.

IS THE ISRAELI LOBBY IN THE UNITED STATES TOO POWERFUL?

The American political system provides abundant opportunities for motivated citizens to make their influence felt. The right "to petition the government for a redress of grievances" is one of the fundamental political rights guaranteed by the Constitution. It enjoys a "preferred position" among the catalog of rights that we enjoy. And the diffuse nature of the federal structure, the divided sovereignty between state and national governments, the separation of powers, and various checks and balances provide numerous critical points at which pressure can be applied. The presidential election system in which votes are weighted state by state on a winner-take-all basis; the fractured legislative process in which 435 members of the House and 100 senators perform as individual legislators—responsible only to their conscience and constituency; our weak party system that exerts a minimum of centralized control; the high cost of electoral campaigns and the associated fundraising requirements; as well as the institutional structure of Congress itself permit a highly organized interest group to exert enormous influence on the American political process. There is nothing inherently sinister in this situation. The very essence of our constitutional structure insists that the majority will be tempered by minority rights and that every opportunity be provided for interested voices to be heard. The result is that special interests—whether those interests are the National Rifle Association, the Sierra Club, or the Moral Majority—have come to play an exceptional role in American politics.

Most interest groups deal with domestic political issues. Some interest groups, however, are concerned about foreign policy. Some commercial interests want Congress to enact legislation favorable or hostile to the exports of goods from foreign countries to the United States. U.S. labor unions seek to strengthen trade unions in other countries and also to challenge the power of multinational corporations.

Some groups have ethnic or ideological interests in foreign policy matters. A number of organizations have sought to influence U.S. policy in South Africa. Liberal organizations, such as Amnesty International, have directed their attention to getting the United States to support human rights in those countries where human rights are imperilled. One influential group, the American Israel Public Affairs Committee (AIPAC), deals with the nature of U.S. policy in the Middle East in general, and toward the state of Israel in particular.

Is the pro-Israeli lobby too powerful? Eric Alterman believes it is. Writing in *Regardie's*, a magazine published in Washington, D.C., he details the operations of AIPAC:

> All lobbies worth their salt...own some congressmen's votes on particular issues, but no lobby cuts as wide a swath in so many different circles; AIPAC's influence is felt not merely on the Hill, but in the White House, the Pentagon, the State Department, the Treasury, and in a host of buildings in between.

According to Alterman, that influence is manifested in congressional election campaigns (e.g., the defeat of Sen. Charles H. Percy of Illinois in 1984, the reelection of Sen. Alan Cranston of California in 1986); foreign aid and military assistance (Israel receives at least $3 billion annually); and general support for Israel's policy in the Middle East.

Mitchell Bard, a foreign policy analyst, provides a measured rebuttal. Bard notes that while

> Jews make up less than 3 percent of the U.S. population,...their geographic distribution forces candidates to pay disproportionate attention to their interests. Nearly 90 percent of the Jewish population is concentrated in 12 electoral college states, which alone hold enough votes to elect the President.

But Bard believes support for Israel is widespread in the United States and that the so-called Israeli lobby has proved that it is "unable to control U.S. policy in the Middle East." According to Bard, "The evidence indicates the lobby's influence is limited primarily to marginal issues that do not affect the general direction of U.S. policy. American foreign policy in relation to Israel...is, in the final analysis, determined by what both its leaders and the general public perceive as its best interests."

SHOULD GREATER GRASS-ROOTS PARTICIPATION IN FOREIGN POLICY BE ENCOURAGED?

According to Article I, section 10 of the Constitution, the states are expressly prohibited from conducting foreign relations.[20] In the words of Chief Justice-

---

[20] In the words of the Constitution: "No State shall enter into any Treaty, Alliance or Confederation....No State shall, without the Consent of Congress...enter into any Agreement or Compact with another State, or with a foreign Power."

John Marshall in the landmark case of *McCulloch v. Maryland*, "The sword and the purse, *all the external relations*, and no inconsiderable portion of the industry of the nation, are intrusted to its [national] government."[21] Or, as his distinguished successor, Chief Justice Roger Brooke Taney stated in *Holmes v. Jennison*, "One of the main objects of the Constitution [was] to make us, as far as regarded our foreign relations, one people, one nation; and to cut off all communications between foreign governments and the several state authorities."[22] The modern Supreme Court has been equally emphatic. In *United States v. Belmont*, Justice George Sutherland noted that "in respect of our foreign relations generally, state lines disappear. As to such purpose the state does not exist."[23]

The rationale that lies behind this consistent line of judicial authority is that the United States must speak with one voice in foreign affairs. During the period of the Continental Congress and the Articles of Confederation, Virginia and several other states declined to honor certain provisions of the peace treaty with Great Britain.[24] This situation embarrassed the United States to the point that other countries (Spain and France) declined to negotiate commercial agreements until it was clear who spoke for the United States—the national government or the thirteen individual states. The result was that the Constitution placed executive authority for foreign affairs in the hands of the national government. U.S. treaties were made the supreme law of the land, "any thing in the Constitution or Laws of any State to the Contrary notwithstanding" (Article VI).

Michael H. Shuman, president of the San Francisco–based Center for Innovative Diplomacy, recognizes the overall control of the national government in foreign affairs but asserts there is still sufficient latitude for states and municipalities to play an active role. He suggests four guidelines:

- Municipal measures designed to raise public consciousness about foreign policy issues should receive unqualified support.
- Other municipal initiatives should be tolerated "unless they pose more than a hypothetical danger to American foreign policy."
- The federal government should resort to legal sanctions only as a last alternative.
- In the specific areas where difficulties have arisen, the laws should be tightened.

Peter J. Spiro, a special assistant to the legal adviser in the State Department, urges prompt action to snuff out local initiatives. "Foreign policy must be made in Washington and not in the citizens' backyards," he contends. Spiro cautions that not only are the states and localities ill equipped to con-

---

[21] *McCulloch v. Maryland*, 4 Wheaton (17 U.S.) 316 (1819), italics added.
[22] *Holmes v. Jennison*, 14 Peters (39 U.S.) 540 (1840).
[23] *United States v. Belmont*, 301 U.S. 324 (1937).
[24] The leading case is *Ware v. Hylton*, 3 Dallas (3 U.S.) 199 (1796).

duct foreign policy, but that such action is unconstitutional as well. "Effective policy formulation at the federal level, requiring consensus among congressional, administrative, and bureaucratic players, is difficult enough. The infusion of other, less well-equipped actors in this process only can make matters worse." After tracing the development of federal supremacy in foreign affairs, Spiro notes that under existing constitutional doctrine, "local measures may be found inferior even in the absence of conflict with federal policy."

13 Is the Relationship between the Military and Industry in the United States a Threat to the Democratic Political System?

YES

New Times

Alliance of the Forces of Adventurism and Aggression

NO

James P. Mullins

What Is So Wrong with the Military-Industrial Complex?

Alliance of the Forces of Adventurism and Aggression

New Times

Much of what the military-industrial complex does is concealed from the public eye by the veil of military and business secrecy. On the whole, however, the formation of the military-industrial complex is no mystery if seen as a process and an outcome of the development of militarism under state-monopoly capitalism. It is from this angle that one can get a deep insight into the military-industrial complex as a social phenomenon. How do Western scholars assess this phenomenon? U.S. encyclopedias define militarism as "the predominance of the military class or prevalence of their ideals," "a spirit which exalts military virtues and ideals," "a policy of aggressive military preparedness." By such definitions capitalist scholars and propaganda seek to impress it on public opinion that militarism is a universal phenomenon characteristic of various countries irrespective of their socio-economic system. Such vague and empty definitions are used to back up the thesis, being spread in the West, about the U.S.S.R. and the U.S.A., NATO [North Atlantic Treaty Organization] and the Warsaw Treaty Organization being equally responsible for new arms spirals.

A scientific system of views on the problems of war and peace was worked out by Lenin, who stressed that militarism was the result and the "vital expression" of capital-

ism. The two world wars and the entire history of the present century have demonstrated the powerful activization of the militarist "vital expressions" of capitalism at the monopoly stage of its development. Militarism has become a truly monstrous product of imperialism.

NEW ASPECTS OF MILITARISM

It is important, however, to see not only the deep-seated causes of militarism but also the concrete specific features of its development in the second half of the 20th century. In the postwar period militarization of capitalist society has gained in scope, rate and intensity to an enormous degree. For instance, the average strength of the U.S. armed forces in any postwar decade was about ten times that in the 1930s. The number of those employed in the munitions industry was 3,275,000 in 1985 as against 314,000 in 1940. These figures speak for themselves.

It has become typical of the Western states to perpetuate the development of militarization processes, to keep million-strong armies and a big munitions industry in peace-time. The use of the latest advances in science and technology for the development and buildup of nuclear missiles and other weapons of mass destruction has assumed unprecedented proportions. More and more capitalist and developing countries are being drawn into war preparations with a view to creating and strengthening an aggregate military might of imperialism under the aegis of the U.S. and NATO.

The formation of military-industrial complexes, their activity and their increasing economic and political role in the West, the U.S. above all, over the past decades is a new phenomenon in the development of militarism brought about by its "permanence" and by a close interlacement in it of expansionist and counterrevolutionary traits in the conditions

---

"Alliance of the Forces of Adventurism and Aggression," *New Times: A Soviet Weekly of World Affairs* (Moscow), no. 52 (supp.), Dec. 30, 1986, pp. 2–7. Reprinted by permission of *New Times* (Moscow).

of major postwar changes in the alignment of world forces.

The military-industrial complex has no clear-cut organizational structure. It is an informal but very real alliance of certain organizations and individuals having common economic and political interests and maintaining steady partnership in the sphere of war preparations. It is a special faction of the ruling class of imperialist states which is identified with militarism and has all its interests in the arms race.

The military-industrial complex is an inalienable part of the process of the capitalist state merging with the monopolies into a single mechanism. In other words, it is a product of the development of state-monopoly capitalism, a new, specific feature capitalism has acquired in the second half of the 20th century.

Monopolies and the state are interconnected by thousands of links. In the postwar period they have developed a sharply pronounced trend towards interaction in the military sphere. In the structure of state-monopoly capitalism there has appeared, and consolidated its position, a military sector—the military-industrial complex especially interested in the acceleration of militaristic processes.

Of great importance, both politically and economically, is the private-property nature of the military-industrial complex. During World War II, for instance, the U.S. had 1,600 state-owned munitions factories which were later sold out to form the basis of a big private munitions industry. Today the U.S. has only 72 state-owned arms manufacturing plants. In the F.R.G. [Federal Republic of Germany] the private sector has also gained a firm foothold in the munitions industry, while in France and Britain state-owned and mixed arms companies constitute a much larger proportion of the total.

So the military-industrial complex as a social phenomenon of modern capitalism is intertwined with private-property interests, which unequivocally points to its capitalist origin and to its indissoluble connection with the capitalist system. This is as fundamental as the fact that the activity of the military-industrial complex amounts to a dangerous invasion by private-property interests of the public sphere—the sphere of the issues of war and peace pivotal to mankind's future. Naturally enough, arms corporations put their own selfish interests before the interests of the public which wants a lasting peace and security, and an end to the arms race.

Hence the futility of attempts by certain Western authors to present the military-industrial complex as a universal phenomenon characteristic of all the industrialized countries. These authors deliberately "divide" the responsibility for unrestrained militarism between the U.S.A. and the U.S.S.R. regardless of the fact that in socialist countries there is no nutritive medium for the military-industrial complex, i.e., no classes, social strata or professional groups economically and politically interested in war preparations.

"By dint of its social nature, imperialism ceaselessly generates aggressive, adventurist policy," the 27th Congress of the CPSU [Communist Party of the Soviet Union] pointed out. "Here we can speak of a whole complex of impelling motives: the predatory appetites of the arms manufacturers and the influential military-bureaucratic groups, the selfish interest of the monopolies in sources of raw materials and sales markets, the capitalists' fear of the ongoing changes and, lastly, the attempts to resolve their own, snow-balling problems at the expense of socialism."

ACCOMPLICES...

The conglomerate of institutions and individuals constituting the military-industrial complex pivots on the monopolies producing arms and combat equipment. As general contractors of the war ministries, these giant monopolies get the bulk of military orders from the government. With the present level of arms manufacturing concentration, a rather narrow and steady group of such monopolies is in control, although thousands of other companies are enlisted in the production of modern weapon systems as subcontractors and suppliers of materials and standard components.

Although the relationships between the large military-industrial corporations are not altogether free of rivalry, the emphasis is on considering each other's interests, cooperation, group profit-boosting strategy, coordinated action and other forms of monopoly practice. The munitions industry of the United States and of its chief NATO partners is among the economic sectors with the highest level of monopolization. The leading arms corporations of the imperialist states constitute the economic, material and technical basis of the military-industrial complex, its nucleus being the alliance between arms corporations and the top military echelons of the state machinery.

The partnership between arms business and the military establishment is a unique phenomenon in the system of relations between monopolies and the state. In the leading capitalist countries no monopoly engaged in civilian production has such multiple and steady links with any division of the state machinery.

The above-mentioned alliance comprises, on the one hand, the leading arms corporations which, with their high level of production and capital concentration, function as a stable monopolistic entity, and, on the other, war departments with their rigid centralized structure, which are superior to the other government bodies in their position, leverage and scope of activity. The military and arms manufacturers maintain active partnership in the production, scientific, technical, financial, economic, administrative, organizational and other spheres, i.e., in whatever has to do with the fulfilment of government arms orders by the corporations. These links keep strengthening in the process of personnel rotation and through the agency of various associations uniting representatives from arms business and military quarters.

...FOR THE SAKE OF PROFIT...

Numerous Western researchers show that government arms orders bring the monopolies fabulous profits. Arms manufacturers making higher profits than civilian producers is regular practice. The level of profit in civilian branches can be regarded as the munitions industry's bottom. It is superprofits that give arms corporations monopolistic domination.

This conclusion is borne out by the very logic of the munitions industry organization on the basis of capitalist property. It is precisely higher profit returned by arms manufacturing as compared with civilian production that provides the economic prerequisite for the emergence and development of capitalist enterprise in the munitions industry sphere. The military authorities of the NATO countries openly point to the stimulating effect of profits, to their importance in encouraging the private sector to intensify war preparations which siphon off resources from civilian production.

Profitability of the arms race is an important and politically significant aspect of the matter. It suggests that there are social strata which batten on war and war preparations and derive economic benefits from militaristic policies. Such strata are found in the U.S.A. and other capitalist states—but not in the U.S.S.R. or elsewhere in the socialist world.

The partners of arms corporations in the state machinery are also interested in preserving and increasing military spending.

This interest comes not merely from the high salaries, benefits and pensions the top officials of war departments get. There are ample indications that these officials also get a slice of the arms corporations' profits. Scandalous exposés of the last few years have shown the extent of corruption in the relationships between the partners in the military-industrial complex. Bribes (euphemistically called gifts and lecturers' fees) are offered, free pleasure jaunts and tourist trips arranged, and other services provided by arms manufacturers. Top war department officials are given lucrative posts in arms corporations upon retirement from office. What we have here is actually a system of intertwining economic interests of partners in the military-industrial complex—the interests of those whose incomes depend on the arms race and who derive profits and other direct and indirect benefits from the accelerated growth of militarism.

...AND POWER

The partnership between arms business and generals goes beyond the bounds of common economic interests, of course. They pursue, separately and together, far-reaching political aims, seek to gear government policy to the interests of the military-industrial complex, and strive for power. The danger of the military-industrial complex lies in its political ambitions, in the role it plays in shaping the military and foreign policy of imperialist states.

The links between arms corporations and the appropriate divisions of the state machinery are the strongest and the steadiest. But that is not all. Other divisions having to do with decision-making on military-economic and military-political matters are also involved in personnel rotation with the munitions industry. American surveys note the traditional contacts between arms manu-

facturers and the armed services and appropriations committees of U.S. Congress.

The military-industrial complex has strong propaganda backing in the West. In each NATO country there is a ramified network of links between the military-industrial elite, on the one hand, and the capitalist ideological apparatus, on the other, and its government and private divisions. This leads to the militarization of this apparatus and of the entire socio-political life in capitalist countries in general. The record of the military-industrial complex is not only that of carrying out programmes for the development of new weapon systems, but also that of invasion of the ideological sphere by militarism and using the mass media for the manipulation of public opinion. The 1980s have shown how effectively the military-industrial complexes can do that.

A characteristic feature of the military-industrial complex is that it broadly uses the latest in science and technology for military purposes, above all for the development of new-generation weapons and weapon systems. Science is being militarized in several ways. The arms corporations are expanding their research centres which work under contracts concluded with war departments. They enlist the cooperation of universities in military research and development. Besides, there are state research institutions specializing in weapon development. The military-industrial complex employs the best brains in science and technology. A continuous improvement of armaments and the need for high technology in their production have led to a sharp increase in government spending on military research and development and actually to a steady deformation of scientific and technological progress.

The military-industrial complexes of the U.S. and its NATO allies have the following features in common:

- a high degree of the concentration and monopolization of arms production, with relatively small groups of the biggest private, mixed and state-owned munitions companies predominating;

- partnership and multiple links (close personal relations and personnel rotation included) between the state, its military sectors above all, and the major producers of arms and combat equipment;
- a high degree of the militarization of science and an active use of the ideological apparatus, the mass media in particular, for militarist purposes;
- the existence of institutions, associations and other agencies ensuring permanent contacts and secret coordination of actions between the top men in arms corporations, the heads of war departments and other government bodies, scientists, functionaries of state and private ideological institutions.

DUAL ROLE

The activity of the military-industrial complex has two sides to it.

On the one hand, it carries out a service function as an instrument of the military-political course of imperialist countries.

On the other hand, the military-industrial complex has become a factor of the militarization of capitalist society in its own right. It is a special faction of the ruling class deriving substantial economic gains and advantages from the arms race and craving for political power.

The dual role of the military-industrial complex reflects the inner contradictions of this specific social phenomenon of modern capitalism. The role of the complex as an instrument of the entire ruling class manifests itself, above all, in the armed support of the exploitative order, in suppressing popular protest by force. But beyond this (which is a matter of cardinal importance) the activity of the military-industrial complex loses much of its distinctly class character and trans-

forms into the pursuance of narrow selfish interests. As a military force geared to external clashes, the complex serves the interests of the more aggressive quarters of monopoly capitalism rather than those of the entire ruling class.

The understanding of the internal contradictions of the military-industrial complex makes it possible, first, to assess more realistically the forces that stand behind the hypertrophied and excessive militarism of the U.S. and NATO (even as compared with the needs of the ruling class) and, second, the possibility of overcoming their resistance in the fight against the arms race.

It would be wrong, however, to overestimate the importance of the military-industrial complex and to ascribe to it alone the stepped-up adventurism of the policy pursued by Washington and its NATO partners. At the same time, it would be dangerous to go to the other extreme and to underestimate the pernicious role the complex plays today when it is vital to prevent new arms spirals and to go over to real disarmament. The military-industrial complex comes out as the main obstacle in this important effort—part of the overall struggle for peace and international security.

The record of the 1980s provides convincing evidence of the military-industrial complex having an ever greater influence on policy-making in the leading capitalist countries, the U.S. especially.

In the U.S.A. the development of links and partnership between arms corporations and the state authorities, the use of the ideological apparatus and science for military purposes proceeded more intensively after the war than in other capitalist countries. As a result, the influence of the military-industrial complex on the economy and politics is especially manifest there.

It is worth noting here the national traits characteristic of the military-industrial complex and closely connected with other national specifics of the development of state-monopoly capitalism. The components, scope and influence of the complex under concrete conditions are distinguished by certain specific features and reflect the policy of the given country and the interaction between domestic and international factors.

For all its peculiarities in this or that imperialist country the military-industrial complex has become an inalienable element of the state-monopoly structure in all of them. The functioning of a powerful permanent militaristic grouping of the ruling class certainly has its political consequences because the complex exists and operates in the system of interrelations with other groupings. These links bear direct relation to its political leverage.

It is not only a matter of the military-industrial complex's programme of stepping up militarism, aggravating the international situation and opposing arms limitation and reduction talks being ideologically attractive to the extreme right forces in the U.S. and its main NATO partners. The complex is becoming a centre of attraction for other reactionary forces and associations which increasingly rely on it politically and economically. Consequently, the military-industrial complex has come to be a serious factor of the strengthening of the ultra-right flank of the political front in the U.S.A. and other NATO countries.

In pursuance of its militaristic programmes the complex teams up with other factions of the ruling class, first of all with the transnational corporations the activity of which is the most striking manifestation of the expansionist ambitions of monopoly capitalism. This explains why the transnationals are interested in the militaristic policy. They need militarism as a state guarantee of economic expansion, as a means of keeping their multi-billion profits returned by their investments abroad. Washington officially admits the connection between militarism and expansion. The drafts of the federal budget submitted by the Administration to Congress in the 1980s list "protection of U.S. economic interests abroad" and "maintenance of access to critical resources" among the objectives of "national defence."

Besides, the major contractors of the war departments are transnational companies themselves. This is evidenced by their international operations in the civil sphere as part of a developed diversification of production, by their participation in arms export, in buying and selling licences for the manufacture of arms and combat equipment, in arms co-production schemes, in selling services involved in arms deliveries abroad. The fulfilment of government arms orders is becoming ever more closely intertwined with capitalist enterprise on the international scale.

Militarism is striking ever deeper root, so to say, in the Western business world. Arms contractors are among the biggest industrial companies, as a rule. Their bids for large arms orders are backed by all their assets, their overall influence in business and political quarters.

What's more, the possibility of launching campaigns in support of militaristic programmes is ensured by the very structure of arms business. This structure is characterized by a far-flung network of subcontract relations and of the appropriate economic interests. The general contractor firms engaged in the development and production of sophisticated and costly weapon systems are connected with thousands of subcontractors and suppliers enlisted in the fulfilment of government orders.

Drawn into war preparations, the businesses of the industrialized capitalist countries specializing in the production of components and materials find themselves dependent on the leading arms manufacturers for orders. This, of course, is a powerful lever in the hands of arms corporations. They use it to draw medium and small companies into the propaganda and lobbying activity for the state funding of new militaristic projects. The medium and small companies often become obedient tools of the military-industrial complex, especially at the local level, in constituencies, when it is necessary to obtain votes for the nominees of the complex or to organize "pressure from below" in support of certain military programmes.

A REALISTIC ALTERNATIVE

The record of the U.S.A. and other NATO countries shows that the influence of the military-industrial complex, especially in the political sphere, is by no means absolute. It has been proved on many occasions that this influence can be countered.

In the early 1970s the U.S. military-industrial complex came under heavy fire and had to take the defensive all along the line as a result of the activization of democratic forces caused by the dirty war in Vietnam and by the aggravation of the socio-economic problems of capitalism due to stepped-up militarization. The complex was forced to loosen its grip. This found its reflection not only in the stabilization but even in a relative reduction of the country's military spending. Fresh intensification of militarism in the U.S.A. in the 1980s shows that the military-industrial complex has taken the counteroffensive in an attempt to destroy the progress made towards détente and cooperation between countries with different social systems. "The U.S.A., its military-industrial machine remains the locomotive of militarism, for so far it has no intention of slowing down," the 27th Congress of the CPSU pointed out. "This has to be taken into consideration, of course. But we are well aware that the interests and aims of the military-industrial complex are not at all the same as the interest and aims of the American people, as the actual national interests of that great country." Facts show that an undivided sway of the military-industrial complex is not

a fatal inevitability. The extent of the real power gained by the complex depends on its own activity and on the strength of resistance to it, as also on the progress of socio-political struggle influenced, in turn, by the overall balance of forces in the modern world and by the intensity of anti-militaristic sentiment and action on national and international scale.

An analysis of various aspects of the activity of the military-industrial complexes in the U.S.A. and its NATO partners shows that, owing to the narrow class character of these groupings and to the ever more vigorous action by the socio-political forces opposed to them, capitalist society can be forced to reduce the sphere of militarization and the extent to which manpower, material and financial resources are used for military purposes. It is necessary to show that demilitarization of capitalist society on a wide scale is possible and feasible in principle.

Such demilitarization under pressure from anti-war forces and on the basis of international agreements in the sphere of disarmament cannot be regarded as a challenge to the capitalist system with its property relations and political institutions. Hypertrophied militarism is not a natural and eternal attribute of capitalism. A look at the capitalist world will show that the degree of militarization of national policy and of the national economy differs strikingly from country to country within it. Besides, in the capitalist countries there are groupings which have little or nothing to do with arms business, and, therefore, take a sober-minded view of the consequences of unrestrained militarism. The super-profits made by arms corporations often bring upon the military-industrial complex criticism on the part of capitalist leaders and groups demanding that war preparations be curtailed.

The struggle for the demilitarization of capitalist society is a challenge to super-militarism born of narrow class and group interests and aspirations which permeate the entire activity of the military-industrial complex and other extreme-right factions of the ruling class of imperialist states. This anti-militarism constitutes a truly democratic alternative to the imperialist policy of adventurism and aggression, an alternative which meets the interests not only of popular masses but also of the capitalist quarters alert to the danger of nuclear holocaust and taking a realistic stand on issues of war and peace. The fight against super-militarism, to end the arms race, for disarmament is a mass form of protest, a large-scale general democratic movement.

What Is So Wrong With The Military-Industrial Complex?

James P. Mullins

I don't know if you've ever noticed it or not, but we in American society are great ones for casting blame when things go wrong, even when things aren't really all that wrong, and even when the blame is substantially unjustified. When our favorite baseball team loses a game, we blame the "nearsighted" umpire, the lousy field conditions, or the poor lighting in the stadium. When our children don't do well in school, we blame the teachers, their books, or the local school board. The fact of the matter is we often fail to acknowledge the real causes: perhaps, our team isn't all that good, or our children aren't studying all that hard.

We also have the unfortunate tendency to attack the very foundations of the life and happiness we enjoy, often without rational or well-defined reasons in mind. For example, there are those who strike out blindly at all chemicals, feeling somehow that these substances are unnatural threats to physical well-being. Of course, what they don't realize is that we're all made up of chemicals, various hydrocarbons, amino acids, and enzymes, and that life itself is not only built around chemical reactions, in many ways, it's enhanced by them. Indeed, without the chemistry of modern medicine, the antibiotics, antihistamines, and steroids, our life expectancy might be half of what it is today.

In the same way, like life and organic chemistry, there are certain foundations on which American society is built—and from which it gains great sustenance. Yet there are those in this country who frequently attack these foundations, casting blame where it is not warranted, and undermining that which helps to secure the blessings of liberty. In fact, this is even true for the two most essential parts of American democracy: the military, and the free enterprise system. This is especially true when these two are combined into what is often disparagingly called the "military-industrial complex."

For some time now, I've been speaking out in support of America's free enterprise system of providing national defense, the special relationship between the armed forces and the private sector, that special relationship which has done so much for our nation and the free world. In recent weeks, I've been pleased to see others take on this issue and now I'm hopeful that many more will follow suit.

Because, frankly, I believe the military-defense industry complex needs more support and less criticism especially considering that it has kept us free for over 200 years and has protected and defended much of the free world from those dark forces which have always threatened it. That's why I think it's both appropriate and useful for me to summarize my view of the defense industry issue and look at some specifics I believe all of us need to address.

It's true that the words "military-industrial complex" are so laced with the pitfalls of unbridled emotionalism, that most people in either the military or private industry, will avoid using them at all cost. It's true that a degrading mythology of sorts has developed around our defense industry, a mythology which runs exactly counter to what it should be, given the reality of the situation. Because without the military and private industry working closely together in a free enterprise environment, much of the technological excellence we rely

James P. Mullins, "What Is So Wrong with the Military-Industrial Complex?" *National Defense*, 68 (Feb. 1984), pp. 61–63. Reprinted by permission of the American Defense Preparedness Association.

on for our survival simply would not exist, and without much doubt, neither would we.

ARSENAL OF DEMOCRACY

In 1939, when the great threat of Axis tyranny grew relentlessly around us, Franklin Roosevelt recognized the tremendous advantage this nation had in its free enterprise system. He knew what could be achieved if only private industry were properly incentivized. In fact, that's why he dubbed American industry the "Arsenal of Democracy" and that's why he provided the necessary incentives.

As early as 1938, at the time of the Munich crisis, FDR quietly ordered the armed forces to modernize their wartime production plan. A full 18 months before Pearl Harbor, the government actually began incentivizing industry. In fact, on May 14, 1940, just five weeks before the fall of France, Congress authorized a buildup of 4,500 military planes. Then, on the next day, as an afterthought, it raised the total to 10,000 aircraft. As we all know, industry began responding with the best equipment, in the greatest numbers, and at competitive prices.

That's why all those popular myths about a sleepy defense establishment caught off guard by the Japanese attack are so much hogwash. Indeed, by August 1940, shipyards had already hired 80,000 new workers, while aircraft plants employed an additional 50,000. As huge industrial plants started mushrooming overnight, the free enterprise system shook off the last vestiges of the great depression, and began to show the world just what it was capable of doing.

Two years before we entered World War II, American factories delivered about 3,600 military airplanes. But during 1941, by exploiting the strengths of free enterprise, we increased production over 500 per cent to over 18,000 military airplanes delivered. That was nothing compared to what we did once Pearl Harbor

was attacked, and our private industry was really given the "green light" to defend democracy.

During 1942, we increased production to 47,000 airplanes then substantially raised this figure the following year, putting another 85,000 warplanes into Allied hands. And in 1944 alone, American free enterprise cranked out another 100,000 airplanes, effectively crushing the forces of tyranny with the massive power of American industrial might. In fact, it was the millions of weapons and spare parts we produced during a 44-month period which allowed us to win that great conflict, and which prevented the enslavement of the free world. Indeed, without our defense industry, we would have lost World War II.

Perhaps we owe an even greater debt to our free enterprise system for its achievements during the post-war period—because that's when we in this country faced an even greater menace. One which, unlike that of World War II, could threaten the towns and cities in America's heartland, towns and cities which, until then, had been invulnerable.

As modern military technology evolved, and our potential adversaries, especially the Soviets, developed the strategic systems against which there was no defense, we were faced with building a strong and unquestioned deterrent, one which could prevent an attack against our country, and ensure the survival of democracy. Considering the speed at which technology was evolving, and the continuing pressure of an ever-growing threat from the Soviet Union, this was truly an undertaking of immense proportions.

In fact, just consider what it required over a few short years in terms of strategic bomber production alone. After the war, in 1945, we relied primarily on the B-29, but within two years, we were already producing the new B-36 because we needed a bomber which could fly almost three times as far, 25 per cent higher, and carry four times the payload.

Even as we began taking deliveries on the B-36, we were already testing a pure jet bomber. Because with rapidly advancing technology, we could not risk relying on a deterrent force which couldn't effectively penetrate to the target. That's why, by 1951, we would start receiving some 2,000 B-47's which could cruise two and a half times faster than the B-36. That's why, within a year, the first of over 800 B-52's appeared on the scene because, already, we foresaw the need for a plane which could fly 10,000 feet higher than the B-47 and carry four times as many bombs.

That really was a remarkable period for the military, our private defense industry, and this country. Because it saw the foundation laid for what has proven to be the most effective deterrent ever known to man. Indeed, it showed again, to friend and foe alike, what American free enterprise is capable of doing and above all else, it has prevented another world war.

In fact, without the deterrent provided by those 400 B-36's, those 2,000 B-47's, and those 800 B-52's, all systems designed and built by the "Arsenal of Democracy," we almost certainly would have been involved in another great conflict. We, along with the rest of the free world, would almost certainly have paid a grievous price in terms of lives lost, property destroyed, and humanity degraded. That's why life, liberty, and the pursuit of happiness is, quite literally, the real heritage of our military-industrial complex.

WHY THE POOR IMAGE?

Considering all the good it has done, considering the contributions it has made, the question arises as to why our defense industry suffers in so many quarters from such a poor image? Why is it so frequently maligned, often by the very people it has benefited the most? In general, of course, it shares in the ridicule most big business has been held up to in recent years, especially in the media. More specifically, it also suffers because the public does not have a good understanding of defense spending, particularly in terms of the size of military budgets, the impact of this spending on society in general, and the credibility gap created by celebrated cases of defense industry fraud or abuse.

Clearly, many Americans do not view big business as a positive influence in their society. That's often because they've been taken in by the fictional villainy of, say, a "J. R. Ewing" on TV's "Dallas," frequently not recognizing it for the melodramatic mythology it really is. Indeed, as pointed out by the Non-Profit Media Institute, "Two out of three businessmen on television are portrayed as foolish, greedy or criminal; almost half of all work activities performed by businessmen involve illegal acts, and television almost never portrays business as a socially useful or economically productive activity."

Now this isn't to say that there aren't those business activities which are not productive, and which we all could do better without; quite frankly, that can be said of any activity in any society just about anywhere, and at any time. The fact of the matter is that, in our society today, it is American business which pays the bills and it is American business which serves as the pump to keep our economy going. Since the economy is really the environment in which we all exist, it is American business which really determines how well we eat, how comfortably we live, and how much good we can do for our fellow human beings.

One way or another, business pays the salaries most Americans live on. Business supplies the fuel which our government runs on, and business provides the essential goods and services that all of us depend on. Indeed, as American business goes, so goes the United States, and frankly, so goes the entire free world.

I believe the defense industry has suffered from the same undeserved image that American business in general has, only perhaps the image is even worse. The substantial size of our defense industry and the large numbers of dollars involved attract a great deal of attention. There's certainly no doubt in anyone's mind these days that defense is big business in this country. That doesn't mean defense spending is the wasteful and unproductive drain on our economy which many believe it to be.

Most importantly, of course, Americans have received the greatest benefit of all from the investment in defense they've made. After all, we haven't been attacked and we're still a free and democratic society. A strong American defense also lends a great deal of credibility to our country and the free world. It creates a stable environment, one in which more business investment may occur, and it gives great underlying strength to the American economy.

It's also important for Americans to understand that defense represents only 17 per cent of our total public spending, which is down from a post-war high of 36 per cent in 1955. In fact, today it represents only about 6 per cent of our total gross national product, less than half of what the Soviets now spend, and about 17 per cent of what we spent during the height of World War II. By the way, if we fail to maintain an adequate deterrent, and are drawn into, say, another large-scale conventional war, the cost would be astronomical.

For example, have you ever considered what the price would be to fight World War II again? That conflict cost us about $542 billion, including $54 billion for veterans' benefits which we're still paying today, and $200 billion for interest on war loans. Remember that wasn't a totally conventional war. Nuclear weapons were used at Hiroshima and Nagasaki effectively bringing a rapid conclusion to the conflict, and without doubt, saving a great many lives on both sides.

In terms of dollars alone, if we took the total price of fighting World War II and assumed just a 5 per cent annual inflation rate since 1945, we'd find that the cost of fighting that war again would exceed $4 trillion which, I might point out, is considerably more than our entire gross national product.

Now if we took out a 30-year, $4-trillion-loan at the going rate today, our payments would amount to about $46 billion per month. Thus, assuming we even survived the war, we'd be forced to pay around $552 billion annually on our war debt, in addition to whatever the cost of national defense would be by then.

PREVENTION MOST IMPORTANT

That, I contend, could "break the bank," destroying our economy and with it, our society. So one can safely say that a conventional war is not an acceptable alternative, as some contend, to maintaining an adequate nuclear and conventional deterrent. Because the name of the game is not winning a war, rather it is preventing one in the first place.

Americans also need to be aware that defense dollars are not just investments in defense. Money in the military budget is not poured into some dark abyss, never to be seen again. In fact, 41 per cent of the 1983 defense budget goes directly to paying salaries: to putting money into the pockets of over 5 million employees in our nation's defense program. What they do with it, of course, is spend it in stores, and save it in banks, credit unions, or savings and loans. They use it to buy cars and homes, they use it to send their kids to school, they use it to pay their taxes, and they give it to charity. Indeed, a large part of every defense dollar directly supports hundreds of local communities. Many of these are in economically-austere environments which otherwise would have limited sources of reliable financial support.

A large portion of defense spending also goes directly into the taypayer's pocket by creating other jobs, and paying other salaries in the private sector. A government defense contract does not just represent money allocated to hardware. It represents good, productive employment for hundreds of thousands of Americans, employment that otherwise would not exist. How about the money put solely into military hardware? Much of it buys the same products the average American consumer buys: from clothes and food, to cars and typewriters.

Just think about the extent to which American industry, across the board, directly benefits from military purchases. Or think about the share of manufacturing and marketing overhead which the military pays, a burden which otherwise would be passed along to the American consumer in the form of higher prices.

Military spending also provides this nation with another major benefit. That's to encourage technical innovation and stimulate scientific discovery. Military applications do require a great deal of advanced research and development in fields ranging from aerodynamics to human factors. Because they serve to push the state-of-the-art across the board, they do generate many spin-off technologies from high-speed micro-processors to satellite-based communication systems, all of which, in one way or another, benefit the American public.

How about education? What role has the military and industry partnership played in educating Americans? How many colleges and universities underwrite their rising costs with defense contracts, industry grants, or ROTC [Reserve Officer Training Corps] programs and how many bright students owe their educational opportunities to the defense dollars we've spent? Think about the skills base our modern military

provides American society. Virtually everyone entering the armed forces receives some type of specialty training from truck or aircraft mechanics, to computer programmers, to medical technicians. Just how much does their training contribute, over the years, to the well-being of this country?

Clearly, taypayers' dollars are not squandered when they are invested in the nation's defense. For our defense industry is not that dark abyss into which everything good is given, and from which nothing good is returned. Tragically and dangerously, there are many in this country who think it is and that's really where we come in. I believe it is our job, as members of the military and the defense industry, to tell it like it is. In many cases, we need to come out of the shadows and put the facts on the table where they can be legitimately and objectively evaluated. For timidity in this regard has served, and will continue to serve, no cause but the wrong cause.

In addition, we must also live up to our real heritage and never ever give even the appearance of impropriety. That means we must ensure the taxpayers of this nation that they're receiving every ounce of national defense possible from every dollar spent. Frankly, as you all know, we haven't done very well in this regard lately, not with the parts pricing "horror stories" we've seen circulating. Those reports of $1,000 plastic stool caps may not seem significant to a statistician viewing the entire defense budget, or the country's GNP [gross national product] but they are very significant to the average American citizen and rightly so. They can quickly undermine the credibility of our entire defense program and further erode the image of our "Arsenal of Democracy."

ALLOW COMPETITION

This alone, I believe, represents a serious danger to our country's security, and the security of the free world, and this alone, I believe, we must do something about right now. What that means, of course, is getting in sync with the basic laws of supply and demand. That means again taking advantage of the strengths of free enterprise and that means incentivizing competition across the board.

Because virtually all the defense acquisition problems we've encountered recently, the aging plants, disappearing contractors, vanishing skills, long lead times, and high prices, virtually all of these came about as a result of our meddling with the free enterprise system, by our limiting competition, or allowing it to wither away.

Fortunately, working closely with private industry, the Air Force has already come a long way in remedying this situation. We're effectively using the system now to provide more visibility to cost increase anomalies first by giving our people the means to challenge any price which they believe is out of line and by establishing validated prices so that we can better judge what increases we do find.

We're also improving, throughout the system, the procurement procedures we use, and we're taking better advantage of new management technologies which have recently become available. In fact, we're already seeing substantial results and in many cases, we're getting our money back.

In conclusion, let me just say that there's no reason Americans should not be proud of their military-industrial complex because it has worked well in the past, and it can continue to work well in the future. We must press hard for an open, competitive environment. We must improve the way we do business and we must take better advantage of the inherent strengths of the free enterprise system.

We do indeed face a grave threat today: a threat to our free way of life and a threat to our very survival. That vital partnership of the mili-

tary and private industry does give us the "trump card" we need. It can generate that "Yankee ingenuity" we've relied on successfully now for over 200 years. In fact, with the proper incentives, American free enterprise can produce the best material, at the lowest price, and in the least amount of time. I'm confident that, as has always been the case in the past, the American military will continue working hand-in-hand with the private sector. Together, ultimately, we'll get the job done. Together, we'll continue to protect and defend the many blessings provided by our free and democratic way of life.

QUESTIONS FOR DISCUSSION

1. What should be the legitimate relationship between the military and industry in the United States?
2. What is the impact of the military-industrial complex on the foreign policy of the United States?
3. What criteria should be used in measuring the impact of the military-industrial complex on defense spending and on foreign policy?
4. How do military-industrial relationships compare with relationships between other government agencies and their clients (e.g, education, environment, and housing)?
5. What role do the president and Congress play in controlling the military-industrial complex?

SUGGESTED READINGS

Adams, Gordon, and David Gold. "Recasting the Military Spending Debate." *Bulletin of the Atomic Scientists,* 42 (Oct. 1986), pp. 26–32.

Anderson, Joan B., and Dwight R. Lee, "The Political Economy of Military Waste." *USA Today Magazine,* 115 (May 1987), pp. 30–33.

Dumas, Lloyd. "The Military Burden on the Economy." *Bulletin of the Atomic Scientists,* 42 (Oct. 1986), pp. 22–26.

Fuqua, Don. "Defense Industry and Government: Partners or Antagonists?" *Aviation Week and Space Technology,* 127 (Sept. 7, 1987), pp. 133, 135.

Koistinen, Paul A. C. *The Military-Industrial Complex: A Historical Perspective.* New York: Praeger, 1980.

Mills, C. Wright. *The Power Elite.* New York: Oxford University Press, 1956.

Morrison, David C. "Defense and Industry." *Government Executive,* 19 (Sept. 1987), pp. 38–40, 42, 44.

Randolph, Bernard P. "Defense Programs: Folklore and Facts." *Vital Speeches of the Day,* 54 (Jan. 1, 1988), pp. 162–64.

Sapolsky, Harvey M. "Equipping the Armed Forces." *Armed Forces and Society,* 14 (Fall 1987), pp. 113–28.

"Two Trillion Dollars in Seven Years." *Defense Monitor,* 16, no. 7 (1987), entire issue.

14 Do the Media—Particularly Television—Undermine American Support for Military Operations?

YES

Cass D. Howell

War, Television, and Public Opinion

NO

Wallace B. Eberhard

A Familiar Refrain But Slightly out of Tune

War, Television, and Public Opinion

Cass D. Howell

"You know you never defeated us on the battlefield," said the American colonel.
The North Vietnamese colonel pondered this remark a moment. "That may be so," he replied, *"but it is also irrelevant."*

Conversation in Hanoi, April 1975[1]

How could a country win all of the battles and yet lose the war? How could a country as rich and powerful as our own, superior in every measurable category of military strength, emerge as the loser with one of the world's smallest and poorest countries? Why are our greatest victories remembered as defeats? Why would a Congress that approved the Gulf of Tonkin Resolution in 1964 with only two dissenting votes turn its back on its South Vietnamese ally when the North Vietnamese launched a full-scale conventional invasion only eight years later?

In seeking answers to these questions, it becomes readily apparent that the U.S. defense of South Vietnam was brought to its unhappy conclusion by a failure of U.S. will and not by a failure of U.S. arms. There are surveys alleging a shift of national sentiment from strong support of the war effort to 65 percent of the American public believing that U.S. involvement in Vietnam was not just a mistake but was also

"immoral."[2] If this reported shift of support is accurate, and I believe it is, the question then arises, "What accounts for this change of beliefs?" And, equally important, why did U.S. resolve evaporate during Vietnam in contrast to all of our other foreign wars? In short, what was unique about the Vietnam War?

In virtually every aspect, Vietnam had far more similarities than differences to previous U.S. conflicts. It was a foreign war fought by a citizen army against a dedicated and capable foe. It was not the longest (U.S. Marines conducted an antiguerrilla war in Nicaragua for more than 20 years), bloodiest, toughest nor even the most savage. And, for all the exotic weapons that were used, it was still primarily the foot soldier's war.

The great difference between the Vietnam War and its predecessors lay not in its conduct but in its image, an image shaped by a powerful new influence—television. It was this medium, more than any other factor, which was instrumental in the shift of American public and congressional opinion from a position strongly supporting to one strongly condemning the U.S. defense of South Vietnam.

To assess the impact of television on the Vietnam War, it is important to remember that the chief victim was not the U.S. soldier or warfighting capability but the morale and will power of the American public. Elected public officials, from the president on down, were almost uniformly optimistic about the prosecution of the war, so a change in public attitude would not seem to be attributable to them. Military officers and spokesmen were positive about our efforts, especially during the war's first years, and this attitude was prevalent throughout the ranks as well.

According to a 1980 Veterans Administration study, 71 percent of those Vietnam veterans sur-

Cass D. Howell, "War, Television and Public Opinion," *Military Review*, 67 (Feb. 1987), pp. 71–79. Reprinted by permission of *Military Review*.
[1] Harry G. Summers Jr., *On Strategy: A Critical Analysis of the Vietnam War*, Presidio Press, Novato, Calif., 1981, p. 1.

[2] Joseph A. Amter, *Vietnam Verdict: A Citizen's History*, Continuum Publishing Co., N.Y., 1982, p. 349.

veyed said they were glad to have gone to Vietnam, 74 percent claimed to have enjoyed their tour there and 66 percent expressed a willingness to go back.[3] Many did volunteer for two or more tours, and the percentage of volunteers serving was higher than in World War II. The war did not pose any great hardships on the home front. Indeed, under President Lyndon B. Johnson's Great Society initiatives, conditions for many Americans actually improved. And, as wars go, casualties were exceptionally light—annual fatalities were short of the deaths caused by automobile accidents.

The public's information about the war was obtained, to a great degree, from the news media, a media buttressed, for the first time, by a new and powerful force—television. The power and impact of television was *the* deciding factor in turning American public opinion from one of supporting the U.S. defense of South Vietnam to one of opposing it. How? In an article entitled, "Dangerous to Your Health," columnist Michael Novak conveyed his interpretation of the grist of television news:

Television does not tell you anything you could not learn more fully and in context from the papers, and the best magazines. What then does television add? In a word, *impact*. To watch television news is to submit to wallops in the solar plexus. The moving pictures on the news are not pruned from reels of tape for the sake of calmness and objectivity. They are chosen for power.[4]

Without doubt, war was made to order for television. It has all the elements of visual drama: life-and-death struggles in vivid color, raw emotions readily visible, triumphs and tragedy. The Vietnam War's two most famous filmed sequences were the point-blank execution by pistol shot to the head of a Vietcong prisoner during the Battle of Hué in 1968 and that of the little Vietnamese girl running naked down the road, her body burned by napalm from an attacking South Vietnamese plane during the 1972 communist offensive. Ironically, neither of these incidents involved U.S. participation, and their impact *in Vietnam* was minimal. In the United States, however, the impact of these scenes was tremendous and uniformly negative. Practically everyone old enough to have viewed the newscasts during those years remembers those scenes.

This is the essence of television—*impact*. Those same scenes described in print would evoke only a fraction of the emotion produced by the vivid footage. The response of the American public ran along the lines of, "We are over there mixed up in all of this, and it is horrible and we have got to get out."

The 1968 Tet offensive fostered much the same reaction. If this event had been reported as the great allied victory it was, it could have significantly bolstered U.S. confidence and undermined Hanoi's will power. Instead, exactly the *opposite* happened. It was reported by the news media as an allied defeat, particularly by hysterical television coverage, undermining U.S. confidence and bolstering the North Vietnamese's morale. The Communists lost almost as many men in one month as we did in 10 years, yet that was not the impression conveyed to the public. General Bruce C. Clarke said the enemy:

...took the battle down around the Caravelle Hotel (press billeting) and so, from the standpoint of the average reporter over there, it was like the acorn that fell on the chicken's head and it said "The sky is falling!"[5]

---

[3] Stanley Karnow, *Vietnam: A History*, Viking Press, N.Y., 1983, p. 466.

[4] *Television and American Culture*, edited by Carl Lowe, H. W. Wilson, N. Y., 1981, p. 99.

[5] Lieutenant Colonel Chandler Goodnow, Lieutenant Colonel Louis G. Michael, Colonel Edward A. Partain and Lieutenant Colonel Sidney R. Steele, *News Coverage of the TET Offensive*, Research Paper, US Army War College, Carlisle Barracks, Pa., 1969, p. 90.

General Harold K. Johnson, then chief of staff of the Army, summed up the situation:

> ...loss of confidence after the recent TET offensive was just about the reverse of what it should have been. After the dust of battle had settled down, it was very easy to see that we and our South Vietnamese ally fared very well indeed. The young South Vietnamese government held fast—in fact, more erect than even the South Vietnamese expected of a three month old infant. Its army fought generally well, and, in many cases, extremely well. Few defections from the man on the street and none identified from the army or the government. The enemy's losses were staggering and he did not attain a single objective. But what happened here in the United States? We suffered a smashing, catastrophic psychological defeat—a defeat which we imposed on ourselves.[6]

Tet 1968, or at least the televised perception of it, proved to be the watershed event of the Vietnam War. It had immediate political implications in the 1968 presidential campaign and provided the catalyst for discarding what little remained of the impartiality of the reporters and anchormen covering the war. They were, by the end of Tet, cynical and dovish, and they conveyed their feelings to the American public. Walter Cronkite was regarded as the one person in the entire country who most of the public could "trust wholeheartedly" (73 percent, compared to Richard M. Nixon and Hubert H. Humphrey at 57 percent each.)[7] You cannot underestimate the impression made when Cronkite, after returning from a first-hand assessment of the Tet offensive, said:

> I think that it is time for us to face the facts in Vietnam—that we are in a no-win situation and it is time for us to get out. . . . We came here with the best of intentions—and we failed.[8]

From here on there would be no talk of "winning" in Vietnam, only arguments over the best way of getting out. General William C. Westmoreland, surveying the war in retrospect, wrote in disgust: "Press and television created an aura not of victory but of defeat, which, coupled with vocal anti-war elements, profoundly influenced timid officials in Washington."[9]

Unique among U.S. conflicts, the Vietnam War was widely perceived as an "immoral" war. This was due, in large part, to any number of questionable activities that went on there. But was it immoral? Evaluate these vignettes:

> The American advisor was with his unit on a long-range patrol deep into guerrilla controlled territory. They halted on the banks of a river to make preparations to cross. As the American advisor and his provincial counterpart stood and conferred, a local peasant astride a handsome white horse appeared on the opposite shore. The American captain remarked aloud, "A wonderful horse. I'd surely like to have him." The advisor's counterpart spoke a few words in the local dialect and a shot rang out. The peasant toppled from the horse and splashed into the river in a pool of blood. The stunned advisor turned and said, "Did you order that man shot?" The reply: "Hell, sir. You said you wanted the horse. Anything the captain says is our command. We have discipline here, sir."[10]

[6] *Ibid.*, p. 192.

[7] George Arthur Bailey, *The Vietnam War According to Chet, David, Walter, Harry, Peter, Bob, Howard and Frank*, Thesis, University of Wisconsin, University Microfilms International, Ann Arbor, Mich., 1973, p. 77.

[8] Cleveland Amory, "What Walter Cronkite Misses Most," *Parade*, 11 March 1984, p. 4.

[9] Douglas Kinnard, *The War Managers*, University Press of New England, Hanover, N.H., 1976, p. 166.

[10] Burke Davis, *Marine! The Life of Lt. Gen. Lewis B. Puller, USMC (Ret.)*. Little Brown & Co., Boston, Mass., 1962, pp. 35–36.

This scene was with U.S. Marines on a search-and-destroy mission:

> It was only twenty miles by air but it seemed like hundreds on the rough trail. The C.O. [commanding officer] kept the pace fast and the men were constantly wet from rain or sweat. The few enemy they found were diseased and crippled wretches who were too weak to pull themselves off the trail. The Marines bayoneted them all, not wasting any bullets. The C.O. wrote later in his after action report: "The pig-sticking was fine."[11]

It can scarcely be argued that these incidents reflect any great concern for morality. However, these incidents did not occur in Vietnam but during U.S. Marine campaigns in Haiti in the late 1910s and on Cape Gloucester, New Guinea, during World War II. The U.S. leader, in both cases, was Lewis B. ("Chesty") Puller, winner of five Navy Crosses and a future lieutenant general.

During the Battle of the Coral Sea in 1942, the survivors of sunken Japanese transports were strafed in their lifeboats until the sea ran red with their blood. Commander "Mush" Morton routinely surfaced his submarine to machine-gun Japanese civilians on their fishing boats. Other wars were no different. The point is that nothing happened in the Vietnam War that had not occurred, either in degree or frequency, in any other war in which Americans had fought. What, then, accounts for this perception of the Vietnam War being immoral?

> To many civilians it is axiomatic that the Vietnam War was the cruelest ever waged. To those of us who experienced war first-hand, this is hard to understand. To the evidence of Vietnam cruelty portrayed by the horrible picture of the little girl running down the road seared with napalm, one asks about the tens of thousands of little girls incinerated in the fire bomb raids on

Dresden and Tokyo in World War II only to be told, "But that was different." To the terrible picture of the Saigon police chief shooting the Viet Cong terrorist, one asks about the summary justice of the French Maquis or the Italian partisans and their photographs of [Benito] Mussolini and his mistress strung up by their heels, only again to be told, "That was different." To those condemning the remarks of the Army captain in the Delta that "We had to destroy the town to save it," one quotes the Continental Congress's orders: "If General Washington and his council of war should be of the opinion that a successful attack may be made on the (British) troops in Boston, he (may) do it in any manner he may think expedient, notwithstanding the town and the property in it may thereby be destroyed." Yet again the answer, "That was different." And the critics were right. It was different....

We had concealed from the American people the true nature of war at precisely the time that television brought its realities into their living rooms in living color. As a result, to many Americans, Vietnam became the most destructive, the most horrible, the most terrible war ever waged in the history of the world. This viewpoint had persisted in the face of all historical evidence to the contrary.[12]

Television had changed the *perception* of war, not the nature of it. More than any other factor, it was the television camera that brought home the reality of war that shocked the nation and broke its will. A war had not been fought on U.S. soil since 1865. Its population, save the 5 percent or so that actually saw combat, had never experienced the tragedy and unspeakable cruelties of war unlike many citizens of other nations.

When the true face of war unfolded before them, the American public watched with growing revulsion and horror. In their living rooms and in vivid color, they saw what napalm *really* does when it hits someone, what happens to a man when he steps on a land

---

[11] *Ibid.*, p. 200.

[12] Summers, *op. cit.*, p. 23.

mine and what dead children look like when collected and stacked after a rocket attack. This was what war was all about, and the American public was sickened and repulsed. War had not changed, but now everyone could see it for what it was. In Humphrey's words:

> ...this is the first war in this nation's history that has been fought on television where the actors are real. Where, in the quiet of your living room of your home, or your dormitory, or wherever you may be, these cruel, ugly, dirty facts of life and death in war and pain and suffering come right to you; and it isn't Hollywood acting. I've had letters from mothers that have seen their boys shot down in battle....[13]

It would be of some benefit to speculate what the outcome of the American Civil War might have been had there been a color television in every home in the land, especially in the North. What would have been the impact of seeing panicking Union forces running from the enemy at the Battle of Bull Run—a full-fledged rout! What would have been the effect on war support if the draft riots of New York City had reached into every home, showing almost 300 people being killed?

Would full visualization of General William T. Sherman's scorched-earth march through Georgia, including the "zippo raid" on Atlanta, make him remembered as a hero or as a war criminal? What would have been the effect of televising even a relatively minor battle such as the one at Cold Harbor, Virginia, where 6,000 Union soldiers were cut down in 20 minutes—an entire year's casualties in Vietnam! How much enthusiasm for the war effort would have been left after watching Army surgeons saw the mangled arms and legs off screaming soldiers without the benefit of anesthesia? These scenes—even if they are fairly

and objectively done—would, nonetheless, have a terrific negative impact. And we cannot be guaranteed a fair and unbiased portrayal.

The impact that television can convey poses some crucial problems that will inevitably have to be faced at some unknown but foreseeable date. Have we hamstrung ourselves to the enemy's advantage? What if Puller had had a television crew along recording the scenes described earlier? Would he have gone on to be the U.S. Marine Corps' greatest hero, legendary leader and scourge of the enemy? Most likely, he would have been cashiered or court-martialed—to the enemy's infinite advantage. This is not to excuse wrongdoing. It is to serve notice that the advent of massive television coverage on the battlefield will affect not only the lives and careers of our men but also the public's perception of our forces and, ultimately, the prosecution of war itself.

Where does all of this leave us? Are we going to have to hire some Madison Avenue public relations experts as part of each commander's special staff? ("Sorry, colonel, we can't shoot that fire support mission, camera crews are observing nearby.") Or is it enough just to recognize the leanings of the media and their power and try to live with them? In retrospect, it is easy to see that the unlimited and often biased reporting of the Vietnam War severely limited the military's prosecution of it by undermining public support for the cause. It is not a possibility but a probability that this will occur again should the United States go to the defense of another ally.

Television is too powerful—it has too much impact. It is clear that, if we accept this erosion of public will power, our cause, however just and necessary, is doomed. The enemy knows he does not have to win many battles to win the war as long as he keeps the war on television and drags it out interminably. What an enviable position!

It is not necessary, however, that we inflict an arbitrary defeat on ourselves. What we

---

[13] Goodnow, Michael, Partain and Steele, *op. cit.*, p. 141.

need, contrary to the wide-open and unrestricted policies of Vietnam, is not freedom of press but freedom *from* the press—more specifically, freedom from the television camera and its interference. This proposal sounds radical, inconceivable and *un-American*, but it is not. Censorship during U.S. conflicts is an established, tried and true method of preventing the enemy from gaining advantage. It is essential to remember that the Vietnam War was an aberration. In every other U.S. war, varying degrees of news censorship, ranging from total exclusion from certain operations to prior screening of material to be broadcast or published, were imposed. This policy of limiting and restricting media coverage, sometimes at the request of the media itself, was the norm for almost two centuries.

It was not until the Vietnam War that the policy of unfiltered and unsupervised news coverage was instituted. Harkening back to our previous experiences, we naively assumed extensive press coverage was necessary to build support for our cause. That theory may have been valid in the distant past, but Vietnam and subsequent events have proved that television had a different effect—with greater amounts of television coverage, *less* public support results. Grenada proved the opposite side of the coin. With less television coverage, more public support resulted.

Much is made of the "public's right to know." This is not a legal right but is a concept invented by the news media to ensure *their* access, not the public's, to newsworthy events. One should never forget that the networks and publishers are corporations, just like General Motors or Exxon, in that they have to make a profit to stay in business. They have a product to sell, and limiting access to news interferes with their ability to generate sales. Broadcasters, in particular, could considerably enhance their credibility by forgoing the announcement of

"exclusive" scoops and donate the evening news, commercial free, as a public service.

Certainly, it is legitimate to ask, "The public's right to know—*what?*" Everything? Is it not enough to inform everyone that U.S. forces are in combat with the troops of "X" country after an amphibious assault and that casualties are moderate at this time? What purpose is served by the current practice of filming the sweating backs of soldiers trudging through the jungle, lying dead or being bandaged when wounded? The public—broadcasters' and publishers' cries to the contrary—has no *right* to these scenes although we would surely be curious about them. Remember the lawsuits that followed the news media's exclusion from Grenada? You do not because there were none. No legal basis exists for challenging that policy of exclusion.

We do not need censorship in its most drastic form—the total exclusion of all news media from a war zone—but an adaptation to fit the times. *In our next war, the television cameras must stay home!* Television reporters can accompany their print brethren to the battlefield, but they must not be allowed to take cameras with them. They can file written dispatches or depart the country to file a videotape report sans battlefield footage.

On the face of it, this might seem discriminatory, unfairly restricting one branch of the media while allowing others to operate on a business-as-usual basis. That impression is basically correct. However, the exclusion of television does not entail any new laws or court decisions. Television has always had more stringent restrictions than print journalism.

Every television station has to have government permission in the form of a license to operate. No newspaper needs a government license to publish. Moreover, television has rules such as the Federal Communications Commission's Fairness Doctrine which prevents it from presenting totally one-sided issues. Newspapers and maga- zines may have any format they choose and can be openly conservative, liberal, commu- nist, and so forth. It is noteworthy that our federal court system prohibits television (but not print journalism) coverage of its court- room proceedings. If we can afford that safe- guard to accused criminals, can we not pro- vide that same benefit to our fighting men?

One thing is certain. If we fail to act, if we continue unlimited television coverage in a war zone, something that no other nation per- mits, we will inevitably suffer. We must not fail to learn the *real* lesson of the Vietnam War.

A Familiar Refrain But Slightly out of Tune

Wallace B. Eberhard

Media bashing is one of America's favorite sports. It ranks right up there with fussing at Uncle Sam for spending too much money on toilet seats for airplane privies, lamenting the quality of public education and picking apart the every move of your favorite football team the morning after the big game. It may also be one of the nation's oldest pastimes. Presidents were among the earliest to hone this skill. The Thomas Jefferson who told us, "Were it left to me to decide whether we should have government without newspapers or newspapers without government, I should not hesitate for a moment to prefer the latter," also is the one reputed to have written, "I read but only one newspaper and that more for its advertisements than its news." And so, media bashing by military folks is only a subspecies of a larger critter.

There are many views on how to straighten out some of the military-media equation in the next war. In particular, there is one grand stroke presented that can take care of the one variable which, according to some people, kept the United States from waging the Vietnam conflict to a successful conclusion. "It was the television camera that brought home the reality of war that shocked the nation and broke its will." Therefore, "In our next war, the television cameras must stay home!"

Unfortunately, this passionate plea is a hollow one based on a series of inaccurate perceptions of both the Vietnam conflict and the media, including their role and rights in our democratic society. And many who wear the uniform are short on historical insight on the relationships between the military and the media.

First, consider the dwindling public support for the Vietnam conflict. The literature on Vietnam grows almost daily. Writers with military and scholarly backgrounds are feeding their words to the bookstores with remarkable regularity. Certainly, it is a healthy endeavor. We are both fascinated and horrified by our wars. We are proud and amazed at the individual skill and courage of U.S. service members and at our collective ability to wage wars. We are also horrified at the human cost and outraged at the sheer stupidity exhibited on occasion by both military and civilian leaders.

Despite our many national flaws, we are able to dissect our past in a creative and thoughtful (if not always instructive) way. Vietnam literature is useful and predictable in its growing magnitude and variety. But support in all of this for the television as the ultimate culprit in the loss of the conflict is scant. For instance, in a recent review of a book about the People's Army of Vietnam, Colonel Harry G. Summers Jr. wrote:

> It wasn't the North Vietnamese propaganda or even the antiwar movement that turned the American people against the war. It was their all-too-correct perception by fall 1967 that the government didn't know what it was doing.[1]

As a reservist and citizen who watched, read and waited, this squares well with the way it was viewed by many back home. No single factor drained the reservoir of national will as time went by. The casualties mounted, and the butcher's bill was paid in flag-draped coffins that came home to small towns and

---

Wallace B. Eberhard, "A Familiar Refrain But Slightly out of Tune," *Military Review*, 67 (Feb. 1987), pp. 71, 80–84. Reprinted by permission of Wallace B. Eberhard.

[1] Colonel Harry G. Summers Jr., "Vietnam: Asia's Mighty Military Machine," *Washington Post Book World*, 1 June 1986, p. 5.

large. There was always light at the end of the tunnel, but the tunnel's end was never within reach. The war indeed was on the news nightly, but that was only an additional reminder of a muddy, bloody, winding road to nowhere in Southeast Asia.

In his book, *On Strategy: A Critical Analysis of the Vietnam War*, Summers pays close attention to the relationship of the media to the failing support of public opinion. Still, he does not assign blame for the loss in Vietnam to either print or broadcast media.[2]

Summers is not the only Army officer who finds fault enough to go around in analyzing the conflict. General Bruce Palmer Jr. gives a viewpoint of one close to the top of the leadership pyramid in *The Twenty-Five-Year War: America's Military Role in Vietnam*. He, too, is critical of both strategy and tactics but without venom for the media. Nor does he advance any proposals to ban cameras from future battlefields.[3]

Major General Dave R. Palmer has written a lively and critical account of military involvement that also finds a host of reasons outside the media's performance for the ultimate failure of U.S. policy in Vietnam.[4] His assessment of journalistic performance is realistic although open to challenge:

> ...the news media must...bear some responsibility for having muddied issues in the war. Never before had a combat zone been so saturated with newsmen. At any given time they numbered in the hundreds, blanketing that small corner of the globe. One might think then, that reporting would have been better than ever.

But, it now appears that press coverage remained generally below the standards set in previous wars.[5]

There is little doubt about some of this assessment. The war was broadly covered by battalions of newsmen (and women). They came from the centers of media power—New York and Washington—but they also came from Toledo and Atlanta and smaller communities. Just as the Vietnam battlefield was the place to be for the professional warrior (and not once but twice or three times), so it was for the professional journalist with pen and camera. Open to debate are the issues of whether the media muddied the Vietnam picture and whether the coverage was "below the standards set in previous wars." Is it fair to assign the responsibility to clarify matters to the media when they were not always perfectly clear in Saigon and Washington? And just what *were* the standards of reporting for previous wars?

But Palmer sticks with his conclusion that "the American press failed to clarify the war in Vietnam and, not unfairly, can be accused of adding to the public bewilderment."[6] One can at least respect this kind of tempered, if critical and unsubstantiated, appraisal of news media performance, but it belongs on the back burner while we deal with the current thesis.

Too much reliance is placed on the impact of television in particular and mass media in general. The formation of public opinion is a complex process, and the adage that Rome was not built in a day fits here. We are conditioned over time by genes, upbringing, education, peers, significant others, critical life experiences and culture, to name a few factors in opinion formation. We are much more a print-oriented society than is generally believed (especially if you listen only to some of the pro-

[2] See, for example, Harry G. Summers Jr., *On Strategy: A Critical Analysis of the Vietnam War*, U.S. Army War College, Carlisle Barracks, Pa., 1982, pp. 23–25, 96–99, 106 and 120.

[3] Bruce Palmer Jr., *The Twenty-Five-Year War: America's Military Role in Vietnam*, University Press of Kentucky, Lexington, Ky., 1984.

[4] Dave R. Palmer, *Summons of the Trumpet: U.S.–Vietnam in Perspective*, Presidio Press, Novato, Calif., 1978.

[5] *Ibid.*, p. xx.

[6] *Ibid.*

broadcasting propaganda). The data suggest that "TV is far from a dominant source of news," according to Lawrence W. Lichty of the University of Maryland.[7]

Although the television news audience is large—50 million or so on any given evening—it is also uncertain. Whether CBS' Dan Rather or any other anchorman dominates the American consciousness is also debatable. Lichty cites a Simmons survey showing Rather named as a regular source by only 9 percent of those polled in a national survey of adults and their media habits. Sixty-eight percent were regular newspaper readers, while 25 percent read *Reader's Digest* and 13 percent read *Time* magazine.[8] Sources for news abound, and we get much more news from print than most of us realize, particularly local news. Lichty's conclusion was that there is little support for the assumption that television news turned us against the Vietnam War. "There is no empirical evidence that TV news 'shapes' mass public opinion—or that any news medium does."[9] All in all, the stated assumption of the overwhelming impact of television on the course of the war seems quivery at best. Important? Influential? Yes, but how?

A second major premise is that the public's "right to know" is a filament floating about, woven into whole cloth by the news media. On the contrary, there is a large body of democratic philosophy and current law that brushes this contention aside. It is an article of faith that democracy functions best on a free flow of information and opinion between and among the people, the media and the government, meaning those who exercise power in the people's name, from the local courthouse to the Capitol in Washington, D.C.

It is the governed who are ultimately supreme and the officeholders who (ostensibly) handle affairs in the name of the people. If there is no "right" and "need" to know about government and its actions, we have turned 180 degrees, in the direction of the divine right of kings who, of course, can do no wrong. This was discontinued in Mother England 300 years or so ago. That the news media act as a surrogate for the people has become an accepted fact of life. The American people seem reluctant to get their own information about government firsthand except on rare occasions. Most citizens either cannot or will not get out of an evening to see their local governmental bodies at work.[10]

We are forced to turn to the media for accounts of such things, especially in trying to keep up with national affairs. The coverage we get from print and broadcast media is imperfect, at best, but it is the best way anyone has found so far to keep the public informed about their government. And the interest in reporting on government helps to keep it honest, if not perfectly so. Turning off the news flow, as some suggest, only breeds skepticism and suspicion, no matter for what reason. A South African government may use repression of the media in tandem with the oppressive system of apartheid and make it seem to work, but only briefly. Ultimately, something of the truth of the matter will come out in one way or another.

The right of access to events is nothing new or manufactured solely by the media in this country. Its legal context was imported from

---

[7] Lawrence W. Lichty, "Video versus Print," *Wilson Quarterly*, Special Issue, Volume 6, 1982, p. 55.

[8] *Ibid.*, p. 54.

[9] *Ibid.*, pp. 55–56.

[10] As a weekly editor in a small town in Michigan, I frequently was the only reporter covering local government and the only soul present when the village council or school board met. Who wants to give up a seat by the fireside to monitor the government in action when the snow is blowing and the wind chill is minus 10 degrees?

England where journalists won the right to cover Parliament. By statute, common law or custom, the citizens and the news media have access to most governmental bodies and activities on most occasions. The "Sunshine Laws" at state and federal levels are designed to let the light in on government at work. And another body of state and federal laws lets people find out what is on the endless miles of public records, from the local level to the federal bureaucracy. It is not the media that use the federal Freedom of Information Act the most but lawyers, citizens and various interest groups.[11]

Although that right of access to actions and records may be occasionally curtailed in the interest of national security, custom has put the press corps on battlefields since the war correspondent emerged during the Crimean War. They followed Union and Confederate forces, went into action with troops in the Philippine Insurrection, slogged through trenches with World War I doughboys, landed on Omaha and Utah Beaches in Normandy, went in with troops at Inchon Harbor and spread out all over Vietnam during that lengthy conflict.

It is not an unnatural thing that a new medium—television—should participate in this dangerous activity so Americans might be offered yet another viewpoint—instant and visual—of their Armed Forces at work. Broadcast journalists are admitted virtually everyplace that print reporters go. Television and still cameras are not permitted to work in federal courtrooms, but a majority of state courts *do* permit televising the judiciary system in session. The U.S. Supreme Court ruled some years ago that televised trials do not abrogate the rights of the accused.[12] With the departure of Chief Justice Warren E. Burger—an adamant foe of broadcasting from federal courts—the climate may change at that level.

It is evident that some of the professional warrior class have not done their homework about the Vietnam War or the media. A survey dealing with media relations conducted at the U.S. Army War College shows that more than 50 percent of the senior officers surveyed had spent less than one day with members of the news media during their time in service.[13] Soldiers, sailors, airmen and Marines are about the business of preserving peace by being able to wage war if called upon. Too seldom are they taught much about the kinds of rights and values they may be required to defend, including the First Amendment trilogy of free speech, free press and freedom to practice (or ignore) religion. The curriculum at the mid- and senior-level service institutions gives little more than a lick and a promise to all of this.

I would offer the opinion that the professional journalist has more understanding of and respect for the profession of arms than vice versa. There is a continuous attempt to impose the military view of how the media ought to do their job rather than beginning with an attempt to understand what the media are, how they operate and why they are as critical to the functioning of our society as a potent military establishment. The analysis of the media-military relationship in military publications is often aimed at perpetuating the tension between the news media and the military establishment.[14] Strangely enough, the Si-

---

[11] For a full discussion of access to governmental meetings and records, see Harold L. Nelson Jr. and Dwight L. Teeter Jr., *Law of Mass Communications: Freedom and Control of Print and Broadcast Media*, 5th Edition, Foundation Press, St. Paul, Minn., 1986, pp. 457–88.

[12] See *Chandler v. Florida*, 449 U.S. 560 (1981).

[13] Lieutenant Colonel Gerald W. Sharpe, *Army/Media Conflict: Origins, Development and Recommendations*, Study Project, U.S. Army War College, Carlisle Barracks, Pa., 30 May 1986.

[14] See Colonel Harry G. Summers Jr., "Western Media and Recent Wars," *Military Review*, May 1986, pp. 4–17, for a thoughtful appraisal of the role and responsibility of

dle Commission that met in the wake of the Grenada operation seems to have led to the establishment of a workable method for taking a press pool along if a similar expedition has to be mounted.

One January night in 1965, I heard an articulate speech by a woman photographer for *National Geographic* at the Michigan Press Association in East Lansing. She was all of 5 feet tall, maybe 100 pounds at the end of a full meal. She spoke of Vietnam, from which she had just returned, and what was going on in the fields, rice paddies and government as best as she could perceive it. Her straightforward account left the audience with sober faces. Later, we chatted briefly in a crowded hospitality room about the Vietcong and artillery, about soldiers and what might happen next over there. By the end of the year, Dickey Chapelle, 47, was back in Vietnam, but her foot found a land mine and she died soon after.

It does little honor to those 58,000 who died fighting the war or the 45 who died reporting it to carry on a pointless feud. We can, however, advance the cause of freedom a mite by reflection and dialogue while we are yet at peace. To quote Summers, it is time for the military and media to "put aside their common antagonisms in favor of their common interests."[15] Well said if only we can make those first steps toward finding out what those common interests *are.*

QUESTIONS FOR DISCUSSION

1. How should the press cover U.S. military operations?
2. How would you compare television to other forms of media in the coverage of U.S. military operations?
3. What effect would the banning of U.S. television journalists have had on the antiwar movement during the Vietnam War?
4. What effect does press coverage have on the conduct of U.S. armed forces?
5. How do dictatorships deal with press coverage of military operations? Do dictatorships, consequently, have an advantage over democracies in conducting military operations?

SUGGESTED READINGS

Baker, Brent. "Wanted: A Professional Press." *U.S. Naval Institute Proceedings,* 110 (July 1984), pp. 74–76.

Casey, William T. "Our National Secrets: The Intelligence Community and the Press." *Vital Speeches of the Day,* 53 (Dec. 1, 1986), pp. 98–100.

Harris, Brayton. "Focusing the Debate." *U.S. Naval Institute Proceedings,* 112 (Dec. 1986), pp. 51–54.

Hughes, Wayne P. "Guarding the First Amendment—for and from the Press." *Naval War College Review,* 37 (May–June 1984), pp. 28–35.

Mandelbaum, Michael. "Vietnam: The Television War." *Parameters,* 13 (Mar. 1983), pp. 89–97.

Mitchell, Michael C. "Television War." *U.S. Naval Institute Proceedings,* 112 (Apr. 1986), pp. 52–56.

Nimmo, Dan. "Televised Coverage of International Crises." *National Forum,* 68 (Fall 1987), pp. 7–11.

Summers, Harry G., Jr. "Western Media and Recent Wars." *Military Review,* 66 (May 1986), pp. 4–17.

Upchurch, Richard L. "Wanted: A Fair Press." *U.S. Naval Institute Proceedings,* 110 (July 1984), pp. 68–74.

Venanzi, Gerald S. "Democracy and Protracted War: The Impact of Television." *Air University Review,* 34 (Jan.–Feb. 1983), pp. 58–72.

Zoll, Donald Atwell. "The Press and the Military: Some Thoughts after Grenada." *Parameters,* 14 (Spring 1984), pp. 26–34.

---

the media in covering conflict. While not entirely realistic in its conclusions or clear in its understanding of what the media "ought" to be doing, it is written from a standpoint of understanding and hopeful of what might be done to open dialogue.

[15] *Ibid.,* p. 16.

15 Does Governmental Secrecy Conflict With Constitutional Rights?

YES

John Shattuck and Muriel Morisey Spence

The Dangers of Information Control

NO

Michael A. Ledeen

Secrets

The Dangers of Information Control

John Shattuck and Muriel Morisey Spence

For the past decade, the federal government has established a network of policies that restrict the availability, shape the content, and limit the communication of information. This net includes an expanded classification system, limits on the exchange of unclassified information, the use of export controls to restrict technical data, and restraints on contacts between U.S. and foreign citizens. The architects of the new policy have also curtailed the role of government in both collecting and publishing many categories of scientific and statistical information.

The cumulative impact has been to restrain academic freedom, hamper technological progress, and undermine democratic decision making. Consider the following examples:

- In 1983 the White House issued a directive requiring more than 120,000 government employees with access to classified materials to sign a lifetime agreement: they would submit for prior clearance any material they wished to publish.
- In 1985, the Department of Defense (DOD) required the Society of Photo-Optical Instrumentation Engineers (SPIE) to restrict attendance at a conference where unclassified papers would be presented to U.S. and Canadian citizens and permanent U.S. residents. Scientists allowed to attend had to sign an "Export Controlled DOD Tech-

nical Data Agreement," promising that they would obtain an export license before sharing information from the conference with foreign citizens.
- The Federal Communications Commission (FCC) decided in 1986 to publish its proposed actions in the Federal Register only in summary form, making public comment more difficult.
- The FBI [Federal Bureau of Investigation] has asked some librarians to report library users who might be "hostile intelligence people."
- In 1984, the Department of Housing and Urban Development (HUD) drafted a research contract with a Harvard scholar that would have required him to submit results of HUD-sponsored research for review 6 months before publication. The scholar would also have had to submit results on related work not funded by HUD. The contract would have given the agency the right to demand that the scholar make "corrections" in data, methodology, and analyses. After months of negotiation, Harvard decided to refuse the contract.

The trend toward greater control of information is predictable in some respects: information is an important national resource that the government understandably seeks to manage. Nevertheless, the government's efforts in these areas should be fundamentally different from its management of other public resources: it should be guided by a heavy presumption, based on the Constitution and our national history, that open communication and the free flow of information have great social utility. This presumption should be overcome only in particular cases where the government can show a substantial public necessity, such as a concrete risk to national security.

Advocates of extensive government control of information have relied on two justifica-

John Shattuck and Muriel Morisey Spence, "The Dangers of Information Control," *Technology Review*, 91 (Apr. 1988), pp. 63–73. Reprinted with permission from *Technology Review*. Copyright 1988.

tions. The first is the need to protect national security—a concept that under the current administration has become nearly limitless. The idea that broad categories of information must be kept from hostile ears and eyes has shaped a growing array of government decisions. This philosophy has supplanted the long and widely held view expressed by Vannevar Bush, President Truman's science advisor, that "a sounder foundation for our national security rests in a broad dissemination of scientific knowledge upon which further advances can more readily be made than in a policy of restrictions which would impede our further advances in the hope that our potential enemies will not catch up with us."

The second asserted justification for restrictive information controls is that the federal government must curtail its deficit spending and excessive regulation. The policies that result, however—including the FCC decision not to publish the complete text of its proposed rules—limit access to much information about government decision making.

The negative effects of these policies could be substantial. As a 1982 report by the National Academy of Sciences (NAS) concluded, the continued health of U.S. science requires open exchanges among researchers worldwide. The Soviet Union's experience illustrates the danger of a restrictive information policy. The American Physical Society cites official controls on scientific communication as the cause of the well-known Soviet lags in solid-state electronics and biology.

Restraints on the flow of scientific information can also hurt the U.S. economy. An April 1987 NAS report indicates that controls on the export of manufactured goods and information cost the U.S. economy 188,000 jobs and $9 billion a year. Exporters report sales losses to Japan and other nations because of these controls. And limits on the participation of foreign citizens in the U.S. economy deprive the nation of needed foreign expertise. For exam-

ple, 40 percent of all doctoral engineers entering the work force every year are foreign citizens.

A further victim of controls, ironically, is likely to be U.S. security itself, as the long-term technological progress on which it depends is impeded. Finally, if these trends persist, they will erode a long national tradition of free speech and public access to information.

THE U.S. TRADITION OF OPENNESS

The pattern of government information controls is one of historical shifts between openness and secrecy. The U.S. tradition of open communication stems from the Constitution, which guarantees freedom of speech, thought, religion, and the press. It also obliges the federal government to publish regularly information on its spending and taxing activities and their effects on the citizenry.

The late nineteenth century saw the beginnings of a long period of growth in the amount of economic and social data collected and circulated by government. During the first half of the twentieth century Congress repeatedly resisted efforts by the executive branch to impose official secrecy on the expanding number of federal agencies.

World War II ushered in an era of increased consciousness of national security and more restrictive information policies. President Roosevelt instituted procedures for classifying information in 1940, relying on a 1938 statute restricting public access to military installations, equipment, and "information relative thereto." World War II also prompted the founding of a large intelligence bureaucracy. After the war Congress gave agencies such as the Atomic Energy Commission and the Central Intelligence Agency [CIA] authority to bar communication of some information to protect national security.

A countertrend toward more open government began with enactment of the Freedom of

Information Act (FOIA) in 1966. Congress strengthened the FOIA in 1974, and two years later passed the Government in the Sunshine Act requiring federal agencies to open more of their meetings to the public. During the 1970s the Ford and Carter administrations both issued executive orders designed to curb the excessive secrecy of intelligence agencies over the previous decade.

Presidents Nixon and Carter also narrowed the classification system. In a far-reaching 1978 executive order, President Carter stipulated that even if information fell into one of seven restricted categories, it was not to be classified unless its unauthorized disclosure reasonably could be expected to cause "identifiable damage" to the national security. The order also called for documents to be automatically declassified after six years and prevented them from being reclassified. Significantly, information could not be restricted for the first time after an agency received a request for it under the Freedom of Information Act.

Meanwhile, demand for government information mushroomed with the expanding federal role in areas such as civil rights, environmental and consumer protection, public health and safety, and employment relations. This demand was spurred by a technological revolution that enabled both public and private sectors to store and disseminate growing amounts of information. But in the early 1980s, as demand for government-collected information continued to climb, the principles of public access again began to erode—this time to an unprecedented degree.

EXPANDING THE CLASSIFICATION SYSTEM

The Reagan administration has used a panoramic definition of national security to justify an extensive network of restrictions on many categories of government information. Rich-ard V. Allen, former national security advisor to President Reagan, asserted in 1983 that national security "must include virtually every facet of international activity, including (but not limited to) foreign affairs, defense, intelligence, research and development policy, outer space, international economic and trade policy, and reaching deeply into the domains of the Departments of Commerce and Agriculture."

Supplementing this concept is the theory of an "information mosaic": the idea that hostile elements can use sophisticated search techniques to assemble bits of seemingly harmless information into insights that threaten national security. An often-cited example of how this could be done is the blueprint for manufacturing an H-bomb published by *Progressive* magazine in 1979. The authors of the article amassed their information from unclassified data scattered through scientific journals.

Proponents of the mosaic theory have used it to fashion a broad expansion of the classification system. President Reagan issued a 1982 executive order giving federal officials authority to classify more information than ever before. Instead of having to demonstrate "identifiable damage" to national security, today officials need only point out that "disclosure reasonably could be expected to cause damage to the national security." The order created a new presumption in favor of classification when officials are in doubt about whether secrecy is necessary. It also eliminated the requirement that information be declassified within a prescribed length of time, and gave officials new authority to classify documents already in the public domain.

The Reagan system appears to allow classification to occur at any stage of a project and to be maintained indefinitely. The net effect could be to inhibit researchers from making long-term intellectual investments in fields that are likely to be classified at a later date, such as cryptography and laser science.

Language from a research contract with the Department of Energy reflects this new policy: "If the grantee believes any information developed or acquired may be classifiable, the grantee shall...protect such information as if it were classified." This provision places the burden on researchers to determine what data to withhold, and does not specify how long they must comply. Such policies have prompted fears, in the words of one scholar, that "academic research not born classified may die classified." There is recent evidence that fears of retroactive classification are justified. In 1987 a federal appeals court upheld the National Security Agency's right to remove 33 documents from a library at the Virginia Military Institute.

NEW USE FOR EXPORT CONTROLS

The current administration has used the export-control laws to extend its sweeping view of national security. These laws—particularly the 1979 Export Administration Act—were enacted primarily to regulate the flow of goods and machinery. Yet they are increasingly being used to restrict the flow of intangible items such as unclassified technical information, both domestically and abroad. The asserted justification is that technical data are different from other information protected by the First Amendment because they can be used to create dangerous items such as weapons. And since technical information has immediate economic use, it resembles commodities more than ideas, according to this philosophy.

Such an outlook is new because there have traditionally been only two ways to restrict information. One is the classification system, for information controlled by government. The other is the doctrine of prior restraint, used for information not controlled by government in extraordinary circumstances involving a clear and present danger to national security. The government's burden of proof in such situations is very

heavy, as illustrated by its unsuccessful effort to enjoin the *New York Times* from publishing the Pentagon Papers.

The Department of Defense has cited the export-control laws in pressuring scientific societies to limit foreign access to DOD-sponsored research results—as evidenced by the restrictions on the 1985 meeting of the Photo-Optical Society. When the presidents of 12 leading scientific organizations—including the American Association for the Advancement of Science and the American Chemical Society—protested these restrictions, the administration attempted to clarify the situation. The White House issued National Security Decision Directive (NSDD) 189, which exempts unclassified basic research from control—"except as provided in applicable U.S. statutes." But this did not assuage fears. One such statute, of course, is the Export Administration Act. DOD also issued a rule early in 1986 requiring scientists to submit all DOD-funded research for prior review "for consideration of national security at conferences and meetings."

Events at a June 1986 Linear Accelerator Conference, a biennial international gathering of nuclear physicists, revealed that not much had changed. The authors of 13 DOD-sponsored papers submitted them for clearance six weeks before the conference, as required. On the morning of the conference the Defense Department informed the authors for the first time that they could not present their papers—on the grounds that doing so would violate the export-control laws. Conference organizers appealed the decision, and after a hastily called meeting DOD officials cleared 10 of the papers—approving 1 only five minutes before it was delivered. One of the papers not approved had already been published.

To avoid such problems, some societies have informally barred foreign researchers from conferences. These include the Society of Manufacturing Engineers, the American

Ceramics Society, and the society for the Advancement of Material and Process Engineering. Nevertheless, restricted meetings are still more the exception than the rule. According to a 1986 survey by the American Association for the Advancement of Science, two-thirds of scientific societies with policies on foreign participation prohibit restricted meetings.

The Reagan administration's interpretation of the export-control laws has also forced scientists to be wary in their contacts with foreign citizens in classrooms, libraries, and research laboratories. The FBI's notice to librarians that they must report on "hostile intelligence people" is one such example. Another occurred in 1984, when DOD initially told UCLA's Extension Division that it could enroll only U.S. citizens in a course entitled "Metal Matrix Composites" because it involved unclassified technical data appearing on an export-control list. In 1981 the State Department attempted to require universities to report campus contacts between U.S. citizens and Chinese exchange students. Strong objections from universities led the department to abandon the policy.

The administration has also tried to restrict foreign nationals' use of U.S. scientific instruments. Supercomputers are a prominent example. The National Science Foundation (NSF) is the major funder of supercomputers at five universities, which will act as consortia for unclassified basic research. The Defense Department wants the universities to limit foreign scholars' access to these machines. Scientists have reacted with dismay, fearing that such restraints on unclassified work will undermine the quality of their research. Universities object to the prospect of policing researchers on campus.

The NSF has proposed guidelines designed to balance these concerns. Under the proposal, students from all countries could use supercomputers for regular course

work. Soviet-bloc scientists could also use the machines for research in fields with no direct links to defense or intelligence functions. Officials from the departments of Defense and State as well as the White House have been reviewing the NSF proposals for more than two years without resolution.

The National Security Agency has designated some scientific fields as inherently sensitive and therefore subject to scrutiny under the export laws. A prominent example is cryptography, which has been so designated since 1981. Many cryptologists now submit their work to NSA for review before it is published to forestall even more stringent controls. The field of nuclear energy is also becoming increasingly secret. In 1981, at the request of the Reagan administration, Congress authorized the secretary of energy to regulate "the unauthorized dissemination of unclassified nuclear information."

By far the broadest category of information targeted for control is that maintained in electronic databases throughout academia, industry, and government. A National Security Council directive issued in October 1986 by John Poindexter, former national security advisor, laid out the policy. The directive sought to restrict unclassified information affecting not only national security but also "other government interests," including "government or government-derived economic, human, financial, industrial, agricultural, technological, and law enforcement information."

Poindexter's directive prompted fears that U.S. intelligence agencies would monitor virtually all computerized databases and information exchanges in the United States. The White House withdrew the notice in March 1987 under pressure from Congress, but the underlying policy—as set out in NSDD 145—is still in place. This calls for "a comprehensive and coordinated approach" to restricting foreign access to all telecommunications and automated information systems. The justification is again the mosaic theory—that "information, even if unclassified in isolation, often can reveal sensitive information when taken in the aggregate."

In December 1987, partially in response to the database controversy, Congress passed the Computer Security Act. This legislation transfers responsibility for developing a government-wide computer-security system from the National Security Agency to the National Bureau of Standards. But the act is silent on whether new categories of restricted information can be introduced as part of the security program.

PREPUBLICATION REVIEWS AS CENSORSHIP

The federal government's funding of many information-producing activities puts it in a unique position to influence the content of research or restrict its publication. Recent developments show that such restraints can undermine the objectivity of research, and sometimes constitute official censorship.

A 1980 Supreme Court decision set the stage for allowing the government to examine a wide range of documents before they are published. In *Snepp v. United States* the Court accepted the government's argument that a former CIA agent's book violated his agreement to give the CIA a chance to determine whether the material "would compromise classified information or sources." This ruling led to CIA review of all proposed publications by current and former employees, not only those necessary to "protect intelligence sources and methods from unauthorized disclosure."

Three years after the Snepp decision, the White House issued NSDD 84 requiring 120,000 federal employees and contractors to agree to lifetime reviews of anything they wished to publish. This directive also allowed the government to give employees polygraph tests while investigating unauthorized disclosures of classified information. The new policy further required agencies to set up regulations governing "contracts between media representatives and agency personnel, so as to reduce the opportunity for negligent or deliberate disclosures."

Testifying before Congress on NSDD 84, Thomas Ehrlich, then provost of the University of Pennsylvania, noted that prepublication review would discourage academics from serving in government, depriving the country of their expertise and insight. Ehrlich noted that the policy would also thwart criticism of government, since those "in the best position to provide that criticism"—academics who have served in Washington—would be enjoined from discussing their experience.

Under pressure from Congress, the administration suspended the prepublication-review provision in September 1984. However, it left in place a similar 1981 requirement that government employees with high-level security clearances sign a lifetime agreement—Form 4193—to submit all writings, including fiction, for prepublication review.

A 1986 General Accounting Office report concluded that suspension of the supposedly broader requirement has had little effect. The GAO found that the government had examined 21,718 books, articles, speeches, and other materials as part of the review process in 1984. In 1985, after the policy supposedly changed, the number grew to 22,820. By the end of 1985, at least 240,776 individuals had signed Form 4193. From 1984 through 1985, current or former government employees made only 15 unauthorized disclosures in their books, articles, and speeches.

Restrictions on publication can also be a source of conflict between the CIA and its civilian researchers, many of whom are academic scholars. Until recently, most CIA contracts required consultants and researchers to submit all their writings for prepublication review. Many universities chose to forgo such contracts rather than agree to the restrictions.

In 1986 the CIA narrowed prepublication review to "the specific subject area in which a scholar had access to classified information." But the new rule continues to pose problems for scholars because they are likely to concentrate their research in their fields of specialization. Any later writing they do in those fields will apparently still be subject to CIA review.

Tension between funding agencies' interest in obtaining a certain research product and scholars' desire to avoid constraints are not uncommon, but this tension has risen to new levels. The conflict between Harvard and the Department of Housing and Urban Development, which wanted to review a scholar's research results for six months before publication, is one example. Harvard also objected to a NASA [National Aeronautics and Space Administration] policy requiring grantees to obtain the agency's permission before copyrighting, publishing, or otherwise releasing computer software produced under contract. Harvard obtained an exception to this rule for one contract, but the underlying policy remains in place.

CIA contracts are a source of tension for scholars because the agency has traditionally required that the scholars not reveal that it funds their research. In 1986 the CIA recognized that a blanket rule would create "misunderstandings and suspicion," so contractors now can name their sponsor unless "public association of the CIA with a specific topic or subject would prove damaging to the United States." But this exception seems to apply to a broad range of circumstances, including where "acknowledged CIA interest in its affairs" would "create difficulty with a foreign government," or where "CIA interest in a specific subject...could affect the situation itself."

Such secrecy undermines the credibility of academic work.

REDUCING PAPERWORK—AND INFLUENCING POLICY

A pivotal point in the evolution of government information policy occurred in 1980 when Congress enacted the Paperwork Reduction Act (PRA). The current administration has used the act to cut back to a troubling degree the amount of information agencies collect and publish.

The Paperwork Reduction Act was a response to growing public concern about the burden of complying with federal requests for information, including tax and health-care forms and a wide variety of other required reports. The Commission on Federal Paperwork estimated in 1974 that these requirements cost citizens and government a total of $100 billion a year. Yet as the Senate Committee on Governmental Affairs noted when approving the PRA, the government must collect information to fulfill important national goals, including promoting research, protecting civil rights, ensuring safe working conditions, and—above all—informing the public about the workings of government itself.

To streamline the process of collecting data, the PRA established an Office of Information and Regulatory Affairs (OIRA) within the Office of Management and Budget (OMB). The OIRA director is charged with determining whether the information a federal agency collects is "necessary for the proper performance of its functions," including "whether the information will have practical utility."

Concerned about potential abuse of these provisions, Congress explicitly stated that they do not authorize interference with "the substantive policies and programs of departments, agencies and offices." Such interference, however, has become increasingly common.

An early example was a 1981 OMB directive requiring departments to cut the costs of producing both written and audiovisual materials. In response, the Department of Education created the Publications and Audiovisual Advisory Council (PAVAC), which rejected numerous requests from grantees to publish research results and information for the public. Yet as one research director pointed out, many contracts require grantees to publish the results of their work.

After examining the pattern of refusals, the House Committee on Government Operations concluded that the PAVAC review process was based on vague and content-related criteria—including whether the publication was "essential" or "timely"—that amounted to censorship. Moreover, the committee found that the review process had had no "cost-effective" results.

Since 1981 the administration has taken further steps to transform OIRA—and thus OMB—into a policymaking agency. The administration greatly expanded OIRA's authority with a January 1985 executive order requiring agencies to submit their regulatory plans to OIRA before making them public. OMB then reviews them for "consistency with the administration's policies and priorities." The agency has used this authority to interfere with efforts by the Department of Health and Human Services to require aspirin manufacturers to include warnings about the dangers of Reye syndrome on their labels. OMB has also hampered efforts by the Environmental Protection Agency to ban some uses of asbestos.

OMB has used the criteria of "necessity" and "public utility" in the Paperwork Reduction Act to decide which projects other agencies can fund. A prominent example has been research sponsored by the Centers for Disease Control (CDC)—which OMB must approve, under the PRA provision that it review plans by federal agencies to collect information from 10 or more people.

A congressional committee asked researchers at the Harvard School of Public Health and New York's Mount Sinai School of Medicine to examine this process. After reviewing 51 projects CDC had submitted between 1984 and 1986, the study authors concluded that OMB was more likely to reject projects focusing on environmental or occupational health than those concerned with infectious diseases or other conventional illnesses. Research on reproductive topics, such as birth defects and venereal disease, was also more likely to be rejected. The authors noted that the proposed research had withstood the scrutiny of the peer-review process, and that OMB lacked the expertise to evaluate its practical utility. The authors concluded that the agency showed a "demonstrable bias" in thwarting efforts "to answer public demands for information on serious public health questions."

The administration has also tried to shift the burden of collecting and publishing information to the private sector. According to a 1985 OMB directive—Circular A-130—agencies must see that information is disseminated with "maximum feasible reliance on the private sector" and the use of charges to recover costs. This policy led in 1986 to efforts to scale down the National Technical Information Service (NTIS)—a clearinghouse for a wide range of scientific and technical data. The Commerce Department originally proposed discontinuing the NTIS entirely, selling it to the private sector, or contracting with a private entity for some or all of its functions.

This proposal prompted extensive criticism by legislators, libraries, universities, and industries that rely on the service, as well as by officials in the Public Health Service and the departments of Energy, Agriculture, and Defense. The Commerce Department's own staff concluded that "extensive privatization presents substantial costs and risks for the government, for NTIS customers and for the information industry as a whole." Critics worry that information without commercial appeal might go unpublished, and that private companies might be unwilling to maintain information over a long period of time. Changing the structure of NTIS could also hamper the influx of foreign technical information, which occurs through government-to-government agreements involving the NTIS.

The administration has responded by announcing—in a brief paragraph in the proposed 1988 budget—its decision to offer the private sector "the opportunity to operate NTIS on contract, with the government retaining overall policy direction." This has convinced neither the House nor the Senate. Both have voted in separate legislation to prohibit further privatization of NTIS without express congressional authorization. This prohibition has not yet received final approval.

Congressional dismay over OMB's attempts to manage information has also sparked efforts to cut OIRA's funding. This prompted OIRA director Wendy Gramm to set up a policy of disclosing OMB exchanges with other agencies regarding draft and final regulations. When Congress reauthorized the Paperwork Reduction Act in October 1986, it made this disclosure policy law and included a separate budget line for OIRA to allow close congressional oversight.

UNDERMINING THE FREEDOM OF INFORMATION ACT

The Freedom of Information Act (FOIA) has become an increasingly important tool for gaining public access to government information, but recent actions by the administration have made it harder to use.

In amending the act in 1986, Congress stipulated that fees for searching and reproducing documents could be waived or re-

duced when "disclosure of the information is in the public interest." The legislators recognized that exhorbitant fees can be a substantial impediment to academic researchers and non-profit groups that apply for information. The legislation's sponsors further specified that "a request from a public interest group, non-profit organization, labor union, library or...individual may not be presumed to be for commercial use" unless the information is being sought solely for a profit-making purpose.

Despite these indications of congressional intent, the fee guidelines issued by OMB in March 1987 could significantly raise the cost of requesting information under the act. The new guidelines allow "educational institution(s)" to obtain documents for the cost of reproduction alone, excluding the first 100 pages. However, OMB defines educational institutions as entities that "operate a program or programs of scholarly research." This excludes public libraries, vocational schools, and a wide variety of other educational groups that may not be associated with research. The new OMB guidelines also expressly reject the presumption that a request "on the letterhead of a non-profit organization [is] for a noncommercial request."

The nonprofit National Security Archive has challenged these restrictions in federal district court. The case was argued in late January; a decision is still pending.

REVERSING THE TREND

A decade of restrictive information policies has significantly affected important aspects of national life. The United States has lost some of its ability to innovate in a world increasingly driven by technology. Excessive secrecy—partly the result of an expanded classification system—has led to compartmentalized federal decision making, manifested in its extreme form in the Iran-contra affair. The public has been deprived of information it has paid for with tax dollars, and important values of free speech, academic inquiry, and democratic participation have been undermined.

The recent race to develop a high-temperature superconductor, in contrast, provides dramatic evidence of the advantages of open communication, especially in science. The two scientists who first succeeded in creating a relatively high-temperature superconductor were German and Swiss nationals working for IBM, an American company, in Zurich. Their research, funded by the U.S. Defense Department, set off a race around the world to develop practical ways of putting the discoveries to use. If federal policies had prevented these scientists from sharing their results, their work might still be unknown.

In mid-March 1987 thousands of physicists from around the world gathered in New York at a meeting of the American Physical Society to discuss the latest developments in this field. Such a meeting would not have been possible if DOD had prevented foreign nationals from attending.

Only one segment of the industrialized world has been left out in the cold during this extraordinarily fertile period of discovery and exchange. The Warsaw Pact nations have played no part in the superconductor frenzy. No one has sought to exclude them, but they are weighted down with bureaucratic restraints on travel, contacts with foreigners, and the use of telephones and copying machines.

Reversing the trend toward more government control of information should be a top priority of the next president. Within the first 100 days, the new administration should issue an executive order on information policy liberalizing the classification and export-control systems, and curtailing OMB's authority over the collection and dissemination of information. The president should also work with Congress to amend the export-control laws, the Paperwork Reduction Act, and the Freedom of Information Act.

The new executive order should establish a presumption that information generated both inside and outside the government will be freely available—except where it can demonstrate a substantial public need, such as a clearly defined threat to national security. The government should not restrict any information based on its speculative relationship with other data: the mosaic theory leaves no chance for practical limits on information controls.

In a democracy, the management of information and ideas must be guided by a heavy presumption that open communication is essential to society's well-being. Experience shows that the free flow of ideas is vital to the fabric of national life, powering the engines of innovation, guaranteeing national security, and protecting personal freedom.

Secrets

Michael A. Ledeen

We Americans are intensely ambivalent about secrecy. We know that any country, even the most "open," must be able to keep secrets from its enemies in order to survive, yet we fear that secrecy may undermine democratic society: if we do not know the full truth, how can we be expected to make informed and intelligent decisions about our future? Our antipathy to secrecy is embodied in Woodrow Wilson's call for "open compacts, openly arrived at." This bit of conventional wisdom remains strong, even though many of the most successful foreign policy actions in the recent past—from the Nixon-Kissinger opening to China to the Camp David talks—would have been impossible without secret contacts and discussions.

The most recent appeal to "openness" in foreign policy came from Rep. Lee Hamilton of Indiana, the Chairman of the House Foreign Affairs Committee, and co-Chairman of the Iran-*contra* Investigation, who declared that policies made in secret are inevitably inferior to policies that emerge from full, open debate. It is all wonderfully high-minded and unexceptionable; it is also unworkable. These high-minded abstract principles are in conflict with a world where secrecy makes its own demands. If secrets—of various sorts—cannot be kept, good policy and good relations are impossible.

The American distrust of secrecy is unique even among societies that share our commitments to democracy and freedom. The great

Michael A. Ledeen, "Secrets," *National Interest,* no. 10 (Winter 1987–88), pp. 48–55. Reprinted by permission of *The National Interest.*

chasm between the United States and other democratic countries is nicely illustrated by an exchange between Alexandre de Marenches, former head of French Intelligence and Christine Ockrent, in their recent best-seller *Dans le secret des princes:*

> *(de Marenches)*...the sensation-seeking press cannot resist scoops...because it has found through more or less honest methods (who knows where?), let us say documents alleged to have come from the Pentagon. The press then prints things that only help the enemy and damage the United States. I find that totally irresponsible.
>
> *(Ockrent)* In other words, the American press, which one tends to elevate to the status of a model, would be, in your opinion, an irresponsible press?
>
> *(de Marenches)* No. I am much more nuanced. But certain elements in the American press are dangerous because they work against the interests of the United States....

What makes Americans' attitudes toward secrecy so different? First of all, there is our unique notion of popular sovereignty: Americans believe that authority flows directly from the people to elected officials, and that the elected officials should be continuously accountable to the public. There is very little room in this political universe for the notion of "reason of state": the idea that the state itself has interests that may, on occasion, supersede those of the citizenry. For most Americans, the very notion of "state" is a virtually meaningless abstraction. For even our closest democratic allies, *raison d'etat* is a thoroughly acceptable justification for action.

Our elected officials do not swear an oath to defend the national interest; they swear to uphold the Constitution, which in turn defines the rights of individual citizens. Elsewhere, leaders swear to defend the interests of the nation. We believe that all citizens are politically equal, and therefore entitled to the same information; in most other countries it is taken for granted that the political elite is entitled to know far more than the public at large.

This is not to say that there is not a demand for greater openness in other countries (there often is, and the United States is often held up as a positive example by those fighting against restrictions on the flow of information), nor that there are not Americans concerned about excesses of information-sharing in the United States. But there is no other nation in which the antipathy to secrecy is so strong, and the tension between secrecy and openness so intense. Even Great Britain, in so many ways the model for our own political culture, has an Official Secrets Act—and libel legislation—that makes the British Government—and media— far more close-mouthed than ours. The willingness of the British Government to wage an extensive legal battle against the publication of—and quotation from—*Spycatcher*, a recent memoir by a former British intelligence official, would be unimaginable here.

THE REQUIREMENTS FOR SECRECY

Good policy depends upon both good information and good judgment, and good judgment is best achieved through candid discussion within the policy-making community. If our policy makers cannot openly speak their minds to one another, their errors in judgment are less likely to be discovered and corrected. And they are not going to speak openly if they fear that their remarks— complete with undeleted expletives—are going to be revealed to the world at large.

The requirement for candor in the policy-making community is often mischaracterized, as if secrecy were inevitably the enemy of open discussion. While that may be true if the insistence upon secrecy is carried to such an extreme that our top policy makers no longer listen to the full range of opinion on the issues, or withhold information to which the public is entitled, it is important not to confuse the two sorts of "openness": one refers to candor, the other to the number of participants. We need candor, but we do not need large meetings or a large number of participants, or full public debate *at every stage* of the policy process, or even of every aspect of policy.

The matter is clearer still with regard to relations with foreign leaders. In most cultures, it is taken for granted that it is sometimes necessary for leaders to do things which they would not wish to admit in public. Yet it is urgent for the government of the United States to know these leaders' real desires and intentions—as opposed to their public posturing. These real intentions can be discovered only through private conversations—if they are really private. For if the contents of private conversations leak out to the public, foreign leaders will cease to be candid with American officials, to the great detriment of the American national interest.

Some years ago, when the debate over SALT [Strategic Arms Limitation Talks] II was raging in Congress, I was present at a discussion between a top European leader and two extremely influential former American officials. The European—who had publicly called for the ratification of the SALT II Treaty—was imploring the two Americans to do everything possible to defeat the Treaty. One of the Americans wryly said to the European, "and if we succeed, will you not denounce the United States for failing to support the negotiating position of our President, and for being unreliable allies?" "Quite so," replied the European, "but you must try to block the treaty nonetheless."

Americans are often shocked by this sort of hypocrisy, and our instinct is to demand it be exposed. Yet this would only make matters worse, for exposure has the sole effect of depriving us of the honest thoughts of foreign leaders, and their knowledge as well. In the 1970s, following the exposures involving the

CIA [Central Intelligence Agency] and White House, foreign leaders concluded that the American Government could no longer keep secrets, and thus a considerable volume of knowledge was withheld. Foreign governments shared their knowledge of sensitive subjects like terrorism with a handful of trusted American friends, some in government, some outside. But the American bureaucracy never acquired the information, and thus when people like Secretary of State Alexander Haig—who had learned a lot from the Europeans during his stint as Commander of NATO [North Atlantic Treaty Organization]—asked that information on the Soviet role in international terrorism be brought to the attention of Congress and the public in the early 1980s, he discovered that the information was not available inside the American Government. This made the quest for a rational counterterrorist policy all the more difficult.

Our own elected officials have reached similar conclusions about the discretion of the bureaucracy, and this has led to the use of outsiders as "back-channels" between top American officials and their foreign counterparts. The most famous of these cases is ABC newsman John Scali, who was the secret intermediary between President Kennedy and Soviet Communist Party leader Khrushchev during the Cuban Missile Crisis. In such cases, it is convenient to use a single intermediary, without having to go through the usual bureaucracy. In addition to the convenience (decisions can be made by a handful of persons rather than innumerable officials), it is easier to keep the entire affair secret as well. Finally, if our interlocutors attempt to exploit the contacts for their own purposes, an outsider can very easily be denied. It is far more difficult to wash the government's hands of a full-time official. Interestingly enough, in almost all cases these channels function well, with maximum security.

The pattern, then, is the opposite of that claimed by the conventional wisdom: secrecy actually encourages the free flow of information and candid expression, while exposure limits the flow of knowledge and forces top officials to speak guardedly, if at all.

If secrecy is important in the free flow of ideas both within and among governments, it is absolutely vital in the area of intelligence. For there is far more than embarrassment at stake: we are dealing with human lives. In many countries in the world, we badly need people to commit treason in the name of *our* interests, and much of the information we need to defend ourselves can only come from individuals who risk their careers or even their lives to tell us the truth. They are most unlikely to do so if they fear they will be exposed by us; a handful of such cases will deter a far larger number of other people from cooperating with us, both now and in the future. This is precisely the position in which we find ourselves today, for the torrent of revelations that has emerged from the various investigations into the Iran-*contra* affair has reinforced the fears of the mid-seventies. As the *New York Times* reported in August, once again our allies have restricted the flow of sensitive information to the American Government.

The need for secrecy applies to all clandestinely-gathered information, whether it involves human sources or more mechanical means of gathering data. Some years ago, the intelligence community was shocked to discover that a low-level CIA employee named William Kampiles had sold to the Soviet KGB (for the paltry sum of $4,000) data about the capabilities of the most secret American spy satellite, the KH-11. The loss of secret information about the KH-11 threw into question the accuracy of the "information" gathered by such satellites, for once the Soviets knew what the KH-11 could "see," they could take steps to deceive it, or to conceal things from its field of vision. And it is not even necessary for information to be given directly into the hands of a hostile intelligence organization for such damage to be done to the national interest: every time a journalist reveals the "discovery" of some kind of clandestine information-gathering program, whether it be a surveillance satellite, electronically-equipped aircraft or seafaring vessels, or a working relationship with a foreign government, we pay a heavy price. And, paradoxically, the risk is run whether the journalistic "revelation" is true or false, for it invariably puts the targets of information-gathering operations on greater guard, thus making it more difficult to learn things about them.

THE SEARCH FOR A WORKABLE POLICY

Is there some way to balance the demands of a democratic society—above all, the requirement that the public know what leaders are doing—against the imperative of secrecy?

The "solutions" that we have adopted are embodied in two acts of legislation: the Freedom of Information Act, and "oversight." This curious term—which technically means something quite different from the process it is meant to describe—refers to the use of small groups, whether in Congress or in the courts, to monitor the ongoing behavior of the executive branch, in order to ensure that no violations of due process or the intent of Congress occurs. There used to be no less than eight such "oversight committees" in Congress, but in recent years the number has been thankfully reduced to two: the Select Committees on Intelligence in both the House of Representatives and the United States Senate. The "oversight process" is hailed by its defenders as an advance for "openness," but in reality it is simply a method for Congress to expand its territory. The legislators are expected to keep the secrets secret, just as if they were members of the intelligence community. The public only comes to know about the secrets if someone violates his vow to maintain secrecy. Thus, "oversight" merely expands the number of people who are in the know; it does not enhance the public's ability to evaluate the performance of the government.

On the other hand, "oversight" has a limiting effect on the Executive Branch, for in practice there are certain kinds of secret actions that invariably leak when they are shared with Congress. Some years ago, I heard Admiral Bobby Inman—then Deputy Director of Central Intelligence—argue against a proposed covert action on the grounds that "this sort of thing always leaks from the oversight committees." The proposal was scrapped, just as others were when Senator Joseph Biden threatened to "leak" them if, against his recommendations, they were put into effect. So, by bringing Congress into the act, some secret actions are blocked, and others are sabotaged by leaks from hostile legislators.

In a more serious effort to ensure that the public is reasonably informed, Congress a few years back passed the Freedom of Information Act (FOIA), which makes it possible for interested persons (they need not be citizens of the United States) to demand that the Executive Branch release previously-classified information.

The FOIA is on balance a good thing, although not nearly so good as it ought to be. To the extent that information can be declassified and released to scholars, journalists, and even businessmen, we the people are better off for it. However, the shortcomings of the Act are considerable:

• The decisions on declassification are sometimes made by people who are not in a position to be able to evaluate the sensitivity of the information. Thus, information damaging to American national security has been released.

• The Act applies only to the Executive

Branch, not to the judiciary or to the Congress (probably because Congressmen wrote the Act in the first place). Thus, it is hard to view matters in full context, since in many policy matters the documents from a single branch of government may be incomplete and even badly misleading. If we are concerned about "the public's right to know," we should ensure that the public obtains the fullest possible picture of events. FOIA should apply to Congress as well as to the Executive Branch.

- The declassification procedures are often exasperatingly slow, and reflect the basic principle that it is far more difficult to correct an original error than to avoid the mistake in the first place.
- The most devastating consequence of the FOIA is that officials of the Executive Branch, fearful that anything they write may be dragged into public view at some later date, take care to craft their written documents in such a way that they cannot cause future embarrassment. This means that many of the most crucial decisions cannot be documented—officials either do not write it down, or write it down in a way to place themselves in the most favorable possible light. Thus the historians of the post-FOIA world are going to have an extremely difficult time reconstructing contemporary events. No less a personage than Dr. Henry Kissinger has said that, henceforth, the crucial exchanges between government officials will be spoken—either face-to-face or on the telephone—rather than written.

So once again, efforts to make government more open to public scrutiny end by producing the opposite effect.

THE MEDIA

Many violations of secrecy occur through the media, which are used by those who hold the secrets to convey secret information to the public. Since the media play such a central role in the conflict between openness and secrecy, they are invariably at the center of the debate. This is sometimes unfair, for the major burden for keeping secrets should fall upon those who hold them: officials of the American Government. And in cases where abuses of power are occurring, there may be no other way to call the practitioners to account, other than "leaking" the facts to the media. But this does not mean that the media should be exempt from accountability, even though some American media spokesmen have made claims that verge on such a position.

In extreme cases, the media have claimed for themselves the rights and privileges of a secret intelligence agency: total protection of sources and methods, a unilateral right to decide whether to pay for information and when or whether to release it, and a refusal to subject their analyses or even claims as to matters of fact to outside authority for evaluation. In essence, such a position amounts to a total right of secrecy for the media, with all the attendant risks of abuse that exist in other institutions. Democracy needs a free press, but it also needs a responsible press. If, as media spokesmen constantly argue, government can only be made accountable if it is open, why should the media—unique among all major American institutions—avoid accountability by being granted the right of total secrecy?

The media respond by stressing the importance of protecting their sources, arguing that if journalists were routinely required to identify them, there would undoubtedly be a shortage of "inside" sources. There is something to this; people are more likely to provide explosive information behind the shield of anonymity than to go "on the record." And an open society needs to encourage people to tell the truth to the public, even when the truth is terribly embarrassing. Thus it is essential that sources be protected whenever possible. But should this protection extend to cases where journalists hold information essential to the identification of criminals? Should it apply to cases where information clearly damaging to national security has been supplied to the media, and through them to our enemies? If, as Justice Holmes put it, a man has no right to cry "fire" in a crowded theater, do the media have the right to jeopardize the national security because sensitive information has been placed in their hands?

If it were agreed that the media do not have an absolute right to reveal secrets, and formalized into law, some of the information currently reaching the public would remain secret. Contrary to the claims of the advocates of ever-greater openness, this might actually help the policy process. For one thing, members of Congress would not be able to blackmail the Executive Branch by threatening to "leak" information about actions of which they disapprove. If legislators disagreed with proposed actions, they—like others charged with responsibility for foreign policy—would have to make a convincing case within the policy-making fora. Furthermore, without the constant threat of secret information finding its way into the media, candor would increase, thus making it more likely that good policy will emerge. And finally, as foreign governments come to realize that secrets can be kept in the United States, they will share a greater quantity of sensitive information with us, to the great benefit of our policies.

Veil, by Bob Woodward, shows all the flaws of the current state of affairs. Woodward presents dozens of stories about alleged CIA operations, some true, some false, some half-true, as is inevitable with a person writing under pressure of a deadline about highly complex matters. There is little concern for national security (indeed, if he is telling the truth, he has almost certainly doomed several foreign citizens who made the mistake of cooperating with the government of the United States), and in one major respect the damage exists whether or not the book is accurate. For anyone contemplating bringing sensitive information to an American government official, a book like *Veil* will freeze the blood, since it shows both that American officials talk about subjects that are properly secret, and that American journalists will write about anything, whatever the potential cost of life, limb or the national interest. In my view, such a book ought not to be published.

It will be objected that this is a call for censorship, no matter how limited it may be. This is quite true, but other democracies' experience with the censorship of sensitive national security information should encourage skeptics to conclude that the gains will outweigh the undeniable losses.

Americans are usually surprised to learn that even in countries where the national interest is explicitly held to be superior to the requirements for free speech, journalists often find the arrangements quite satisfactory. I attended a seminar three years ago in Israel on the role of military censorship; the participants, to a man, were highly critical of the Begin government in office at the time, and could have been expected to attack the practice of military censorship. I was amazed to hear that all of them—including the editors of the leading newspapers in the country—agreed that they had never been prevented from publishing a story which they felt urgently needed to be told. In fact, several of them said that they wished the censor had been more active in certain cases, because they had published stories which, in retrospect, they wished they had not.

Israeli journalism is every bit as aggressive and rough-and-tumble as the American variety, and the reaction of the Israelis should give us all pause. On the other hand, there are clearly dangers of excess in the practice of censorship, as I believe has occurred in the British efforts to suppress *Spycatcher,* a book which provides very little new information (most of it had appeared in books published in Great Britain), and reveals nothing of any sensitive activities in the past fifteen years. We need to find a reasonable middle ground between those who think that secrecy is solely the responsibility of the government (and hence the media alone should decide whether to publish or broadcast anything that comes into their possession), and those who believe that anything "classified" should remain out of public sight.

TOWARDS A FAIR BALANCE

The demands of secrecy versus openness bring into conflict two legitimate, but opposed interests. Good policy, good relations, and successful operations all require at least a certain degree of secrecy, and it will not do for the advocates of openness to demand that all or even most classified information become public knowledge. On the other hand, the public is entitled to reasonably complete information.

The ideal solution is for the Executive Branch to explain its policies, and the thinking that went into their formulation, as fully as it possibly can, so that the public can at least follow the analytical process. No one can reasonably demand that the government share its secrets with the world at large, but it is certainly reasonable to expect our leaders to explain to us what they are doing, and (to the extent possible) why. Thus, while the public is not entitled to know what foreign leaders said to our officials in private conversations, our top policy-makers should be able to give the American public the "lessons learned" from such conversations. The same principle applies to other areas where secret information plays a role in policy: the secrets should remain secret, but the consequences of the secrets should be shared.

To be sure, this ideal is far more easily stated than practiced, for even with the best will in the world, governments must sometimes withhold information from the public. But this almost always attaches to operations, and not to overall policy. The exception to this rule is the case of a secret operation, which, if successful, would lead to a substantive shift in overall policy, as in the case of the secret diplomacy that led to Nixon's *demarche* to the People's Republic of China. Since most Americans approve of the results of the secret diplomacy, there has been little criticism of the way in which it was conducted. But many of the stinging attacks that have been directed at Reagan's handling of the Iran-*contra* initiatives can just as easily be aimed at Nixon and Kissinger for the China policy, or, for that matter, at F.D.R. [Franklin D. Roosevelt] for his covert assistance to Great Britain in 1939–41. Both were in conflict with the publicly-stated objectives of American foreign policy; both were carried out behind the backs of Congress. The difference between these initiatives and the Reagan debacle is that they achieved their objectives before they were discovered. Here there is no formula for salvation: successes are applauded, and failures condemned, and that is that. But in both the Nixon and Roosevelt cases, had the policy been made public at the time it was being conducted, the national outcry would have been deafening, and the policy would have been wrecked. Would Messrs. Inouye and Hamilton retroactively approve a full investigation into both affairs, complete with public exposure of the role of foreign agents (like Intrepid) and private American citizens in the operations? Would Mr. Hamilton lecture F.D.R. about the superiority of publicly-debated policy over secret operations, when it is quite likely Great Britain would have foundered without the secret American support?

Whatever the evaluation of a given policy, there is nothing to be said for the shocking disclosure of secrets that has accompanied the debate and investigations. Much has been made about the conflict between Congress and the Executive Branch during the Iran-*contra* hearings, but in fairness to the legislators it must be said that by far the greater leakage of secrets has come from the Executive Branch. From the very beginning, the White House, the State Department and the CIA have shown a remarkable insensitivity to the requirements for secrecy. The names of sensitive foreign contacts have been revealed, the formats of secret American documents (such as presidential "findings") have been made public (thereby enabling the KGB to make better forgeries), methods and names of secret communications have been published, and the inner workings of the intelligence community have been held up for public examination. In short, those who wish to obtain our secrets have been provided with many of them, and given a road map to those they may wish to acquire in the future. While much of this information has emerged from the testimony, depositions, and documentation released by the various investigatory committees of Congress, the bulk of it was unilaterally made available by the White House, and much was published by the Tower Commission, which was appointed by the President.

Some feeble case might be made for the astonishing refusal of the White House to assert any degree of "executive privilege" in this matter (although those foreigners who cooperated with us in the belief we would never reveal their identities would no doubt disagree), there is even less to be said for the wholesale delivery of secret documents to the "independent counsel," Judge Walsh. The members of his staff obtained instant clearances, and could not have received the sort of exhaustive background investigations to which the authors of the secret documents were subjected. Unlike the officials of the government itself, the Walsh people were not required to demonstrate a valid "need to know" the contents of, for example, *all* of the NSC documents concerning international terrorism and the steps taken by this country to combat it. There are many foreign governments who would love to know the contents of those documents; have steps been taken to ensure the full security of the Walsh operation? One can only say, on the basis of a few trips to their offices, that there is little sign of thoroughgoing physical security. But that is not the central issue here; the point is that the Executive Branch quite quickly abandoned the fight to keep its secrets secret; thereafter, many national secrets were in the hands of a variety of people, many of whom were reading their first secret document. Thus did the Reagan Administration demonstrate its lack of seriousness in the defense of its own secrets.

If there is to be any hope for a reasonable approach to the question of secrecy, the Executive Branch will have to do far better. It must fight for the right to retain secrets, at the same time that it shows greater sensitivity to the public's right to be informed about the basic elements in our foreign policy. It must initiate the national debate on the need to protect secrets, including some measures to call the media to greater accountability. And it must engage the Congress, the courts and the media in such a way as to produce a workable compromise between the two legitimate demands—for secrecy and openness—that are today so violently in conflict in our society. Since this administration clearly lacks the vision and the will to embark on such a challenging enterprise, we can only hope that the next president will be capable of doing so.

QUESTIONS FOR DISCUSSION

1. What criteria should be used in determining which former government employees (if any) should be required to submit for prior clearance any material they intend to publish?
2. What constraints (if any) should the U.S. government impose on U.S. scientists to restrict their ability to share information with scientists from other nations?
3. What criteria should be used in deciding whether domestic surveillance should be used against domestic opponents of U.S. foreign policy?
4. What criteria should be used in providing information on national security matters to the American people?

5. What should be the relationship between academic scholars and the CIA? What are the reasons for your answer?

SUGGESTED READINGS

Edgar, Harold, and Benno C. Schmidt, Jr. "Curtiss-Wright Comes Home: Executive Power and National Security Secrecy." 21 *Harvard Civil Rights–Civil Liberties Law Review* 349 (Summer 1986).

Feldman, Martin L. C. "Why the First Amendment Is Not Incompatible with National Security Interests." *Vital Speeches of the Day*, 53 (Apr. 15, 1987), pp. 394–98.

Greenberg, Daniel S. "A Hidden Cost of Military Research: Less National Security." *Discover*, 8 (Jan. 1987), pp. 94, 96, 98, 101.

Halperin, Morton. *National Security and Civil Liberties: A Benchmark Report*. Washington, D.C.: Center for National Security, 1981.

Kotz, Nick. "The Government's Need for Secrecy vs. the People's Right to Know." *Naval War College Review*, 37 (May–June 1984), pp. 35–41.

Menges, Constantine C. "How Democracies Keep Secrets." *Public Opinion*, 10 (Jan.–Feb. 1988), pp. 10–13.

Ramirez, M. Christina. "The Balance of Interests between National Security Controls and First Amendment Interests in Academic Freedom." 13 *Journal of College and University Law* 179 (Fall 1986).

Science Technology and the First Amendment: Special Report. Washington, D.C.: Office of Technology Assessment, 1988.

"Symposium: Toward a Government Information Policy—FOIA [Freedom of Information Act] at 20." *Public Administration Review*, 46 (Nov.–Dec. 1986), pp. 603–39.

U.S. Cong., House of Representatives. *1984: Civil Liberties and the National Security State*. Hearings before the Subcommittee on Courts, Civil Liberties, and the Administration of Justice of the Committee on the Judiciary, 98th Cong., 1st and 2d Sess., 1983–84.

16 Is the Israeli Lobby in the United States Too Powerful?

YES

Eric Alterman

Pumping Irony

NO

Mitchell Bard

Israeli Lobby Power

Pumping Irony

Eric Alterman

Fatima Said, a congressional reporter for the National Association of Arab Americans, was in a bad mood that was getting worse. She was supposed to cover a House Foreign Affairs Committee hearing that would address the amount of aid that Israel would receive from the United States, and she had arrived at the hearing room at 8:30 A.M., an hour early. She had been the first person in line.

But Said wasn't allowed into the room for the beginning of the hearing. There were no seats available for the general public, a guard told her; they had all been claimed by congressional staffers. Then, as she was digesting this information, the chairman of the Foreign Affairs Committee, Dante Fascell, ambled into the room. Alongside him, talking animatedly, was the primary nemesis of the National Association of Arab Americans: Douglas Bloomfield, the chief lobbyist for the most influential lobby in Washington, the American Israel Public Affairs Committee [AIPAC].

Bloomfield sauntered in with Chairman Fascell just seconds before the hearing began. When Said was finally allowed into the room, just before 10 o'clock, she noticed that Bloomfield and another AIPAC lobbyist were seated in the section normally reserved for guests of the White House. The second lobbyist had apparently entered from an anteroom that's reserved for congressmen and their staffs.

It surprised no one that AIPAC got everything it wanted for Israel.

Here's another measure of AIPAC's formi-

dable reputation: Said, who's planning to apply for U.S. citizenship, asked that her real name be disguised lest her association with an AIPAC adversary prejudice her application. Her request may be slightly paranoid, but the acronym *AIPAC* tends to evoke such feelings in many people, particularly those with whom it disagrees.

AIPAC's success in building a bulletproof consensus on Israel's behalf on Capitol Hill is almost without precedent. If power in Washington can be measured by the degree to which one appears to be powerful, AIPAC is a veritable nuclear reactor. The White House and the State Department rarely make a move in Israel's direction without first consulting it. Democratic presidential candidates ask for its reaction before they hire foreign policy advisers. An adviser to Walter Mondale once compared its clout to organized labor's. Some say that there are congressmen who won't tie their shoes without AIPAC's approval.

Without a doubt, AIPAC is the most powerful ethnic lobby to emerge in recent American history. A case can be made that it is, in fact, the most powerful Washington lobby of any kind. All lobbies worth their salt, from the NRA [National Rifle Association] to the Friends of the Earth, own some congressmen's votes on particular issues, but no lobby cuts as wide a swath in so many different circles; AIPAC's influence is felt not merely on the Hill but in the White House, the Pentagon, the State Department, the Treasury, and in a host of buildings in between. And its influence doesn't depend on the assistance of a friendly administration; more often than not, it's the other way around.

But success breeds resentment, and AIPAC's seems to have bred more than most. The growth of what AIPAC likes to call "Jewish political muscle" raises a number of troubling questions, not only for the nation but for the American Jewish community. AIPAC has aligned itself with the most hard-

Eric Alterman, "Pumping Irony," *Regardie's*, 8 (Mar. 1988), pp. 107–8, 111, 113, 146, 148–49. Reprinted by permission of the author.

line aspects of Israel's foreign policy agenda: Israel's invasion of Lebanon, support for its neofascist allies in Latin America and elsewhere, and support for its "iron-fist" treatment of the Palestinians in the occupied territories. The lobby has also made it impossible for both the legislative and the executive branches to deal with the problem of the Palestinian people and their representation by the PLO [Palestine Liberation Organization] in anything but the grossest, most demagogic fashion.

Resentment against AIPAC's strong-arm tactics appears to be growing in nearly all of the circles in which the lobby operates and even in its own backyard: the American Jewish community. Many Jewish doves have been alienated by AIPAC's support of Israel's most militant elements and its dismissal of the traditional idealistic Jewish agenda in favor of hard-nosed, Cold War–tinged realpolitik. This split is epitomized by the actions of Nahum Goldmann, a lifelong Zionist and a founder of the Jewish lobby that became AIPAC; Goldmann asked President Jimmy Carter to try to destroy it. Rabbi Arthur Hertzberg, the former president of the American Jewish Congress, has publicly called for AIPAC to be disbanded. "You can only push so far," says Hertzberg.

Congressmen can be pushed around, but they can't be made to like it. A former Pentagon official quoted in *The Lobby*, Edward Tivnan's study of AIPAC, noted, "It's not that AIPAC is too powerful. The problem is that it is out of control. It is a self-stimulating machine with no corrective device. If you don't agree, you get savaged. . . . They want 100 percent cooperation, or else, they claim, there will be another holocaust."

The man behind the rise of AIPAC is the seemingly mild-mannered Thomas Dine, who has been the lobby's executive director since October 1980. Dine's first order of business, in early 1981, was to try to bring about the con-

gressional defeat of the Reagan administration's plan to sell advanced surveillance airplanes to Saudi Arabia. AIPAC lost the battle but won the war. Since then Dine has increased the lobby's membership by 500 percent (to 55,000), tripled the size of its Washington staff, and opened branch offices in New York, Los Angeles, San Francisco, and Austin. The lobby's current budget is over $6 million. Most significant, more than 100 Israel-oriented political action committees have sprung up around the country, many of them run by individuals who have close connections to AIPAC (which, despite its name, is itself not a PAC [political action committee]). These PACs contributed nearly $7 million to congressional candidates in the 1986 election. As a result, the Palestinians have precious few friends on Capitol Hill.

A sort of fear and trembling is induced in people when they're asked to talk about AIPAC—a visceral response that the group's executive director has done his best to encourage. Dine, who refused a half dozen requests for an interview for this article, has been quoted as saying, "We think it's better to be strong and criticized than weak, ignored, and not respected."

On Capitol Hill there's more than respect for AIPAC; there's fascination, even awe. Paul Findley, an 11-term congressman who was defeated in an election in which, in Dine's words, "Jewish money made the difference," says that "the mere mention of the word *AIPAC* brings a sober, furtive look. AIPAC means power."

Findley should know. After he lost his seat to an AIPAC-backed opponent in 1982, he wrote *They Dare to Speak Out*, an attack on AIPAC's alleged censorship and intimidation tactics. After the book was rejected by nearly every established publisher in the business, it was finally printed by a tiny Connecticut house—thereby, in Findley's eyes, proving its point.

AIPAC's goal is to ensure that no more Paul Findleys arrive in Congress to replace the one it helped to defeat. A quick look at the numbers indicates that AIPAC is doing a pretty fair job. Israel, a country with slightly more than three million people, will receive roughly $3 billion in U.S. aid this year, under terms more favorable than most parents tender their kids' allowances. Meanwhile, 45 African countries will receive a total of one-third that amount. Israel's peace partner, Egypt, is the only nation that even remotely competes with Israel's level of aid. The nations receive approximately 40 percent of U.S. foreign assistance funds, but the Egyptians are being given a per capita sum of about $50 while the Israelis are being given $1,000.

The numbers tell only a small part of AIPAC's success story. There are, it seems, 101 ways in which the organization's victories over the National Association of Arab Americans, the Arab-American Institute, and the Arab-American Anti-Discrimination Committee can be measured. The Arab groups, which are smaller and less firmly entrenched than AIPAC, have nevertheless tried to cool U.S. favoritism toward Israel by emulating some of AIPAC's tactics. But so far their efforts have been to little avail.

When AIPAC held its annual policy convention at the Washington Hilton last May, the mood was one of self-congratulation bordering on outright euphoria. Despite the bad press that Israel had received as a result of its role in the Iran-contra scandal and the Pollard spy case—in which it was learned that Israel had hired an American Jew to spy on the U.S. government at its highest levels—Dine stood before the 1,000 pro-Israel activists and said, "We may have just had the worst 12 months on record in terms of publicity, but we had one of the best years on record in terms of concrete legislation." The lobby's victories included sweetheart deals for Israeli products coming into the United States, joint military production efforts between the Israel Defense Forces and the Pentagon, and

vastly increased foreign aid in a year marked by Gramm-Rudman budget cuts. The 1986 edition of AIPAC's legislative report, a review of the lobby's accomplishments, is more than 60 pages long.

AIPAC's banquet had the air of a giant bar mitzvah, but with a difference: more than 100 senators and congressmen and about a half dozen presidential candidates attended it. The usually staid George Shultz lost all sense of decorum when he led the crowd in a chant of "PLO. Hell, no." The group, which had once feared that Shultz's business ties to the Arab world would color his view of Israel, responded with near pandemonium every time he opened his mouth. When someone from the audience asked him to run for president, the crowd erupted into a standing ovation. (One might argue, however, that they were applauding their own ability to transform Shultz into a mouthpiece for the pro-Israel line.)

Compared to the AIPAC event, the National Association of Arab Americans' convention at the Vista International Hotel in June was a rather understated affair. Only a few hundred people attended, and only a handful of congressmen showed up. None of the administration officials on hand made the slightest attempt to pander to the audience, as Shultz had done at AIPAC's banquet. And when the visitors went to Capitol Hill to lobby, just as AIPAC's activists had done, they were met not by smiling congressmen but by uninterested staffers who repeatedly checked their watches. If AIPAC is the Arnold Schwarzenegger of lobbies, then the Arab-American lobby is the Rodney Dangerfield.

"AIPAC is beyond lobbying," explains a congressional aide. "They don't even need to call my boss anymore. If we see the words 'Saudi arms sale' somewhere in the newspaper, we call them and say, 'Put us on the list.'"

That's exactly what happened in May and again in September, when the administration again tried to sell Saudi Arabia missiles and planes. Within a nanosecond of congressional notification, hundreds of congressmen and senators lit up AIPAC's switchboard and offered to sign a letter to protest.

Faris Bouhafa, a media specialist for the Arab-American Anti-Discrimination Committee, accuses U.S. congressmen of acting like "automatons" when it comes to AIPAC's desires. When foreign aid issues arise, a surprising number of the congressmen who sit on key committees rely on staffers who have been trained by, and presumably for, AIPAC. A congressman who had an opening on an important committee received more than 80 applications for the job from people who had been interns and staffers at AIPAC or who had attended its training sessions. Two of the three finalists for the job had AIPAC connections.

One of the consequences of the ubiquitousness of AIPAC's staffers can be gleaned from the small print of a 1987 draft report by the House Subcommittee on Europe and the Middle East. The report notes that because Israel's grants were to be made on an "expedited basis"—in other words, Israel was to receive its money during the first 30 days of the fiscal year instead of in quarterly disbursements—the U.S. government would forfeit $35 million in lost interest. Congress had not appropriated the extra money as part of the Israeli aid program.

Another ramification is that these congressional staffers can act as moles for AIPAC, increasing its access to Hill intelligence and classified data. Thus, if a congressman is planning to do something that AIPAC doesn't approve of, he may very well receive a number of calls from his Jewish constituents—all of whom are in AIPAC's legendary data base and who were major contributors to his campaign. He may also receive a call from the Israeli ambassador.

A careful reader may have noted that few people who aren't publicly associated with the Arab cause are willing to be quoted on the

record as being against AIPAC. The research for this article included fruitless attempts to induce former AIPAC staffers to break the organization's shroud of secrecy. One congressional staffer who had reportedly left his job over differences with Dine spent a couple of days mulling over whether to talk, but in the end decided to keep quiet.

Whether or not AIPAC deliberately intimidates people, the fact remains that many people are intimidated. According to James Zogby, the executive director of the Arab-American Institute, AIPAC is "intolerant of debate and employs McCarthyite tactics to taint, smear, discredit, and otherwise destroy the credibility" of its opponents. Zogby, who has been attacked by AIPAC in a controversial publication called *The Campaign to Discredit Israel* (which many people consider to be a thinly disguised enemies list), thinks that AIPAC's campaign against Arabs and Palestinians "smacks of the kind of anti-Semitism that has traditionally been practiced against Jews."

AIPAC is both admired and detested by the political community in which it operates. Michael Hudson, the head of Georgetown University's Center for Arab Studies and another anointed AIPAC enemy, believes that "the bottom line on AIPAC is that they like to hit below the belt. Their influence is not conducive to a rational Mideast policy."

David Sadd, the director of the National Association of Arab Americans, admits that he's sometimes disgusted by the lobby's arrogance and intolerance but that he can't help but admire its effectiveness. A congressional staffer notes that no office on Capitol Hill can match AIPAC's efficiency: "If I call them up at three o'clock and say I need talking points on a particular bill, they will have them over here by five o'clock. Whole speeches can take a little longer."

Much of the credit for the transformation of AIPAC from the David to the Goliath of lobbies belongs to Dine, a self-confessed "Brooks Brothers Jew," according to Tivnan's study. When Dine took over AIPAC from the irascible and undiplomatic Morris Amitay, few people in the Jewish political community had heard of him. Certainly no one expected him to emerge as the community's most powerful leader.

Dine was raised in Cincinnati and attended a Reform temple there. He received degrees from Colgate and UCLA, and after stints with the Peace Corps, the U.S. Foreign Service, and the Brookings Institution, he worked as an aide to senators Frank Church, Edmund Muskie, and Edward Kennedy. When AIPAC's search committee announced its choice, a number of people who knew him were surprised to learn that he was Jewish.

Dine is what he calls "a new Jew." In America this often means—as it does with Dine—a Jew who has little or no cultural or religious background but does have an overwhelming commitment to the state of Israel and is willing to exert himself financially or politically on its behalf. His ascent to the top of America's most influential Jewish organization reflects a generational transition in the Jewish political community. Previously the leaders of the community, including those who had helped to found AIPAC, were either rabbis or learned Jews; many of them were European refugees who had been steeped in the classic Jewish traditions, where Talmudic disputes are routine and intellectual and moral introspection is endless. But to many American Jews, particularly those who came of age after the Holocaust, relentless self-questioning and adherence to absolute codes of moral behavior are unaffordable luxuries in a world that harbors enemies such as Hitler. Many Jews with the latter mind-set have transferred their hatred of Hitler and European fascists to anti-Israel Arabs and their allies in the Soviet Union. Thus, they believe, compromises with one's enemies—based on either moral or ide-

alistic grounds—would only sow the seeds of Israel's (and ultimately the Jewish people's) destruction. To this generation, politics is, to borrow from Karl von Clausewitz, the continuation of war—a war that the Jews' enemies have been fighting as long as there have been Jews.

Dine's mettle was first tested during the bitter dispute over the proposed sale of AWACS [airborne warning and control systems] to Saudi Arabia in 1981. In a secret meeting Dine presented AIPAC's directors with a memo of his strategy to defeat the proposed sale and then asked each of them to destroy the document in his presence.

When AIPAC's opponents tried to convince Americans to view the controversy over whether to sell the airplanes as a contest between President Reagan and Israel's unpopular prime minister, Menachem Begin, the specter of political anti-Semitism in the United States was raised as visibly as it had ever been. The Reagan or Begin formula may have achieved its ugliest manifestation when, according to Tivnan, a wavering Republican senator received a pro-AWACS call from Gerald Ford in which the former president reportedly asked, "Are we going to let the fucking Jews run American foreign policy?" (Ford denies having said this.)

AIPAC leaned on every legislator with everything it had. Upon hearing that the late senator Edward Zorinsky of Nebraska was planning to vote in favor of the sale, Dine called, Vito Corleone–style, to say, "I can't stop you, but I wish you wouldn't, because I want you to have a good relationship with the pro-Israel community, and they are not going to forget this one." In what may be a record for shameless lobbying (no mean achievement), AIPAC mailed a copy of the pulp novel *Holocaust* to each senator three days before the vote.

Dine slaughtered Reagan in the House, but the administration squeaked out the four-vote victory it needed in the Senate. It was, in Dine's words, "the benchmark. We lost the vote but we won the issue." In the following days Secretary of State Alexander Haig asked for Dine's help in getting a foreign aid bill passed. And after the lobby's performance on the AWACS issue, whenever arms sales were proposed to Arab governments other than Egypt, the State Department usually consulted Dine first. In addition, AIPAC's membership rolls grew and its financial picture brightened, making it an even more formidable adversary for an administration that wanted to display any sympathy whatsoever for the plight of the Palestinians.

The dramatic improvement in AIPAC's ability to persuade didn't come about simply because everyone felt sorry for it after it lost the AWACS fight. It was rather the result of the lobby's willingness to make veiled threats and to back them up with political assassinations. Only a few casualties were necessary before most congressmen got the point.

AIPAC's most celebrated victim, Charles Percy of Illinois, was viewed by all but the most secure pols as a sort of horse's head to anyone who considered stepping out of line. After the defeat of the well-connected and well-liked Republican senator in 1984, "the Percy factor" became an important addition to Washington's political lexicon.

Percy had committed two unforgivable offenses. First, as the chairman of the Senate Foreign Relations Committee he had played a major role in shepherding the AWACS bill through the Senate. Second, shortly after taking over the committee, he had commented that Yasser Arafat, the chairman of the PLO, was "more moderate" than some of the organization's radical elements. When Percy came up for reelection, AIPAC declared war against him on two fronts. Tom Corcoran, a right-wing Republican who challenged him in the primary, received $285,000 from 55 pro-Israel PACs. With Percy weakened but not yet fin-

ished off, Paul Simon was abetted to the tune of $3.1 million.

In case anyone failed to understand the point, Dine spelled it out for them. "All the Jews in America, coast to coast, gathered to oust Percy," he said. "And the American politicians—those who hold public positions now and those who aspire—got the message."

More than $1 million of Simon's out-of-state help reportedly came from Michael Goland, an AIPAC member in Los Angeles. In a less than subtle attempt to exploit this success, in 1986 Senator Rudy Boschwitz of Minnesota invited Goland to speak with two colleagues who were wavering on a Saudi arms package. At the meeting Goland speculated on what it would be like for the two members if they were the targets of negative advertisements similar to those that had brought Percy down. The tactic backfired when the two senators walked out. Alan Simpson of Wyoming noted, "You cannot build friendship on threats of intimidation or talk of political retribution or the ancient game of keeping score." Nevertheless, the package, which had already been emasculated in an attempt to placate AIPAC, was roundly defeated.

The exact connection between AIPAC and the pro-Israel PACs—almost all of which have nondescript names such as Roundtable PAC, National PAC, and Hudson Valley PAC—is a matter of considerable controversy. AIPAC would have it that it wouldn't know a pro-Israel PAC if it fell and broke its nose on it; the PACs, including the one directed by Dine's predecessor, Amitay, deny any direct connection to the lobby. The law dictates that it be this way; any connection would be a violation of federal election laws. In 1986, according to the *Wall Street Journal,* 51 of these pro-Israel PACs were operated by AIPAC officials or by people who held seats on one of AIPAC's two governing bodies.

There's also a remarkable degree of consistency in their donation patterns. For instance, in 1986 Senator Robert Kasten of Wisconsin received $117,000 from 31 pro-Israel PACs, none of which was located in Wisconsin; 19 of the PACs had officers who were also members of AIPAC's executive committee or national council. A half dozen of these AIPAC-affiliated officers vehemently deny receiving anything but the most general information from AIPAC. Still, the coincidence is rather amazing. When one AIPAC-connected PAC officer was asked why his group donated to Kasten rather than to his opponent, Ed Garvey, the officer reportedly replied that as the president of the NFL Players Association Garvey hadn't taken a strong enough position against the 1981 AWACs sale.

Dine refuses to discuss the issue with reporters. However, he authorized an AIPAC spokesman to read a statement to the *Wall Street Journal* in which AIPAC denied "most forcefully that any such coordination occurs," and insisted that the consistency of outlook is "a function of the nature of political activism and in no way connotes affiliation or connection."

One of AIPAC's greatest strengths is its obsessiveness. Dine apparently believes that if any dissenting legislator goes unpunished, his colleagues will perceive it as a signal to steal the cookies from the cookie jar.

In 1982 James Thompson, the governor of Illinois, received sustained support from the Chicago Jewish community, presumably because his opponent, Adlai Stevenson, had made a number of anti-AIPAC votes in the Senate. The fact that Thompson's job had nothing to do with the Middle East wasn't seen as relevant by either Dine or AIPAC's supporters. Again, Dine spelled out the message for the politically hard-of-hearing: "The memory of Adlai Stevenson's hostility toward Israel during his Senate tenure lost him the Jewish vote in Illinois—and that cost him the election."

In 1986 AIPAC worried that Senator Alan Cranston of California, a staunch AIPAC ally, was in danger of defeat by Republican congressman Ed Zschau. Zschau, who has had a troubled relationship with AIPAC, was reportedly approached by Goland at a reception. Zschau was told, "I'm going to get you like I got Percy." Goland's employees then approached a far-right, anti-Zionist candidate, Edward Vallens, with offers of $120,000 in campaign funds—allegedly from "very conservative Republicans who don't want Zschau in there"—to run a third-party campaign in order to split the anti-Cranston vote. Vallens received 109,856 votes. Zschau lost by 116,000.

Campaigns such as Cranston's, in which AIPAC and the Jewish PACs go all out on behalf of liberal Democrats (who are traditionally favored by Jews) are becoming increasingly rare. When Dine took over the organization, he apparently decided to redirect its sails into the winds of Reaganism. AIPAC's literature began to pay almost Reaganite attention to the Soviet threat. An AIPAC insider quoted by Tivnan put it this way: "We want to broaden Israel's support within the Right—with the people who don't care what's happening on the West Bank but care a lot about the Soviet Union."

To this end, AIPAC began to support New Right candidates over progressive candidates simply because they had voted for aid to Israel. Congressman Barney Frank of Massachusetts, one of the few legislators who's willing to criticize AIPAC on the record, says that he shares the organization's general philosophy when it comes to the Middle East but is bothered that the group lets "right-wing Republicans get off much too easy." Frank thinks that AIPAC forces liberals to work harder than New Right candidates to win its support because AIPAC fears to tread on the toes of its newfound allies.

Indeed, in the immediate aftermath of the AWACs loss Dine pinpointed the location of the lobby's weakness as "a lack of personal relationships" with the New Right senators who had been elected in the Reagan landslide of 1980. To address the problem, AIPAC launched a campaign designed to ingratiate itself with the Christian Right. It sponsored prayer breakfasts on Capitol Hill with televangelists Jimmy Swaggart and Pat Robertson. It embraced the views of Jerry Falwell and other leaders of the movement even though one of them insisted that "God does not hear the prayers of a Jew." In perhaps the most bizarre example of its toadying, AIPAC failed to criticize the Far Right's hatchet man, Congressman Robert Dornan, when he called a Soviet spokesman a "disloyal, betraying, dirty little Jew."

The saying "If money talks, early money shouts" has become a cliché in the political world. The money provided by wealthy Jews to PACs that are directed by AIPAC members can ensure that a candidate gets a full hearing and prevent his opponents from getting the opportunity to speak out against him. In 1986 right-wing senators in New York and Pennsylvania were boosted so powerfully by early pro-Israel money that their opponents were never given a chance to defeat them.

Dine's denials to the contrary, almost no one in Washington believes that AIPAC doesn't act as a guide, both for candidates and for PACs, when it comes to doling out pro-Israel money. Young candidates are often approached by local AIPAC members when they're still in their state legislatures. The candidates are tutored on the Middle East and then financed when they decide to run for Congress.

This aspect of AIPAC's work doesn't particularly annoy politicians; it is, after all, the kind of old-time machine politics that everyone understands. What ticks off many congressmen is how little running room AIPAC gives even to its friends—particularly to liberals.

"AIPAC refuses to grant that, just as we have to vote for at least one big weapon system each year, we've also got to be able to go against the Israel lobby once in a while to prove our independence," explains an aide. "They demand 100 percent every time, even when it hurts, even when they don't need you."

One occasion that definitely raised the level of congressional resentment against the lobby was Dine's decision to help the administration press for a foreign aid bill in 1984. The bill included a number of Central American provisions that most liberals couldn't stomach. AIPAC made it clear that the vote would be considered a test of loyalty, even though congressmen had assured Dine that Israel's portion of the aid would be retained even if the bill failed. The bill passed, according to many observers, largely because of AIPAC's lobbying.

AIPAC's adversaries are convinced, perhaps out of wishful thinking, that the resentment that has been building in Congress against the lobby's strong-arm tactics will soon manifest itself in an angry backlash. Indeed, signs that AIPAC might be heading for trouble are easy to see. The Pollard case, the Iran-contra connection, and recent television coverage of Israel's harsh military occupation of the West Bank and Gaza present a considerably less rosy picture of the Jewish state to Americans than the one that AIPAC presents to Congress. A recent *Los Angeles Times* poll indicates that Americans, including Jewish Americans, are far more sympathetic to a Palestinian state and far more open to negotiations with the PLO than AIPAC will allow any congressman to be. Moreover, AIPAC's relentless campaign to shut down the PLO's information office in Washington and its United Nations mission—seen by many to be a violation of First Amendment rights and international law—has been criticized across-the-board in the media and has even left a number of Israel's staunchest supporters noticeably uncomfortable.

But will the Arab lobby be able to exploit the undercurrent of resentment? When push comes to shove, as it inevitably does with AIPAC, Americans still like and admire the Israelis and not the Arabs. Phenomena such as terrorism and oil shortages, which AIPAC's literature highlights, ensure that in the near future the Arabs will remain as unpopular with Americans as they are today. Indeed, when Arab leaders such as Jim Zogby and former senator James Abourezk offer their help to political candidates, they are told, according to Zogby, "that the best thing your people can do for me is to leave me alone."

Of course, many American Jews object to the militantly right-wing definition that AIPAC has given to the term "pro-Israel," but these Jews remain underorganized and unfunded. The few times that major Jewish leaders questioned the policy of unquestioning support for the Israeli hard line, they quickly ceased to be major Jewish leaders.

At the opening session of AIPAC's convention, Robert Asher, the group's president, told the audience, "AIPAC is not—I repeat, not—the most powerful lobby in Congress.... All we have ever asked is that members hear our story and vote their conscience."

Seated next to Asher on the dais was Dine. I bet he was trying hard not to laugh.

Israeli Lobby Power

Mitchell Bard

A recent headline in the *Sacramento Bee* read: "Has Israel become our 51st state?" The article, reprinted from the *Washington Post*, argued that U.S. policy is one-sidedly pro-Israel because of the influence of the Israeli lobby. This is just one example of the mythology that has grown around the Israeli lobby and its purported power. If we examine the record of the lobby's efforts to influence American Middle East policy, it becomes clear the lobby is not the omnipotent pressure group its critics assert.

First, we need to be clear about what the Israeli lobby is composed of. It is not the "Jewish" lobby because a large proportion of the lobby's members are not Jewish. It is also not restricted to the registered lobbyists who work on Capitol Hill. The Israeli lobby is comprised of those individuals and organizations that directly and indirectly influence American policy to support the State of Israel.

The role the Israeli lobby plays in American politics is exemplified by the blatant pandering for Jewish votes in the last Presidential election. Jews make up less than 3 percent of the U.S. population, but their geographic distribution forces candidates to pay disproportionate attention to their interests. Nearly 90 percent of the Jewish population is concentrated in 12 electoral college states, which alone hold enough votes to elect the President.

Fundraising is obviously of vital interest to political candidates, and Jews have historically been major contributors to political campaigns. This support is now being channeled through Israel-related political action committees [PACs]. Much has been made of these committees by Israel's detractors, who claim the lobby is trying to "buy" votes. You cannot buy Congressmen, but you can buy access, and that is what the lobby is interested in. Jews have been careful to try to keep these PAC activities quiet because of the fear of an anti-Semitic backlash, but there is an increasing feeling among Jewish leaders that the pursuit of "Jewish interests" is no less valid than similar efforts made by unions, business, and other minorities. It is true that some incumbents who have bad records on Israel-related issues have been targeted for defeat by the PACs, but it is usually difficult to know if a candidate is pro-Israel because of receiving a contribution or receives a donation as a result of taking a position in support of Israel.

Controversial legislative proposals have turned the spotlight onto the Israeli lobby. The annual foreign aid bill is the main focus of lobby attention. Foreign aid is one of the least popular programs in Congress because there is no constituency for it. The persistence of the Israeli lobby is generally credited with insuring passage of the foreign aid bill each year.

Foreign aid is usually cited by the organization that is registered to lobby for Israel, the American Israel Public Affairs Committee (AIPAC), as an example of the lobby's effectiveness in Washington. If one looks at the last 10 years, the record is indeed impressive: Israel has received over $20 billion in aid, with over $15 billion in military aid. The lobby has also succeeded in persuading Congress to increase aid levels above administration requests several times, such as in 1982 when Congress voted to increase aid despite the U.S. recession, unhappiness over the Israeli invasion of Lebanon, and the opposition of the Reagan administration. It has not always been this way.

Mitchell Bard, "Israeli Lobby Power," *Midstream*, 33 (Jan. 1987), pp. 6–8. Reprinted by permission of *Midstream*.

Prior to the Yom Kippur War, U.S. aid to Israel was trivial, totaling $1.5 billion from 1946 to 1971. Even recent figures are less impressive when examined closely. Though AIPAC trumpets its influence when soliciting members, the reality is that the level of aid negotiated by the lobby has been declining in real terms. Executive Director Tom Dine admitted as much in a rebuttal to the *Post* article cited above: "Discounting debt service, aid has declined by 27 percent since 1976; adjusted for inflation, it has declined by 65 percent."

Arms sales to the Arabs have also focused attention on the influence of the Israeli lobby. The argument against the sales is that they pose a threat to Israel. On several occasions the Israeli lobby has successfully pressured the U.S. government to modify sales to Arab states, but when the lobby attempted to stop the sale of F-16s and AWACS [airborne warning and control systems] to Saudi Arabia the lobby failed. In both cases a unique convergence of the interests of "big business" and key leaders in the Senate enabled the administration to overcome the Israeli lobby's opposition.

When the intention of the Reagan administration to sell Stinger missiles to Jordan and Saudi Arabia became known in 1984, AIPAC used its now familiar strategy of enlisting co-sponsors for a resolution opposing the sales. When it became clear that a majority of Senators opposed the sale, the resolution was withdrawn. A majority had been opposed to the AWACS sale also, but President Reagan was willing to fight a long and bitter battle to insure that the sale went forward. Why was he unwilling to do the same in 1984? There are two likely reasons: the Stingers were not seen by the Arabs as a test of the U.S. commitment as the AWACS had been, and it was an election year. The Arabs have, in fact, become realistic enough to know that pressing for the sales would be futile. Reagan did, however, demonstrate great resourcefulness in circum-venting Congressional opposition by using his emergency powers to ship 400 Stingers to Saudi Arabia.

In May, 1986 the President decided to try once more to obtain congressional approval for an arms sale to Saudi Arabia, but the Saudis' consistent opposition to Middle East peace negotiations, support for the PLO [Palestine Liberation Organization], and generally anti-American foreign policy, led Congress to veto, for the first time, the proposed sale.

An even more divisive issue in 1984 was the bill introduced by Senator Daniel Patrick Moynihan to move the U.S. Embassy to Jerusalem. Despite all its alleged power, the Israeli lobby's most glaring failure has been its inability to convince any President to recognize Jerusalem as the capital of Israel. Ironically, Moynihan's initiative caught the lobby by surprise. There was no great desire to bring the issue up, but the lobby did mobilize its resources to try to get the bill passed. Again, a large number of co-sponsors were recruited to support the bill, but it was opposed by the administration, and, even more embarrassing, privately by the Israeli government, which saw the move as necessary in principle, but inadvisable at the time.

A major schism in AIPAC developed between those who saw the opportunity for success finally at hand and hoped to take advantage of election-year pressure to get the Jerusalem bill adopted and those who agreed with the Israelis that it was not worth fighting with a President who is considered a friend of Israel over an issue that has lingered for years and can afford to linger a few more. After the administration threatened to veto the bill, Congressional support waned and most efforts were redirected toward passing a non-binding resolution calling on the President to move the Embassy.

The Israeli lobby is effective in putting items on the political agenda. When it comes to setting policy the lobby's influence is far more limited than many of its critics contend. In fact, major diplomatic and military decisions remain largely outside the reach of lobby influence. Thus, the Sinai disengagement agreements, the Syrian-Israel agreement, the American commitment to veto Security Council condemnations of Israel's retaliatory raids, and the Camp David Peace Treaty were decisions made with little or no input from the Israeli lobby.

In general, support for Israel varies with individual pieces of legislation. Issues that are less central to overall U.S. Middle East policy are more sensitive to lobby pressure. Examples include the anti-boycott legislation; a resolution to re-examine U.S. membership in the U.N. if Israel were expelled; and the prohibition of payments to UNESCO [United Nations Educational, Scientific, and Cultural Organization] because of Arab-sponsored resolutions condemning Israel. None of these bills would have been introduced in the absence of lobby pressures.

As noted at the outset, the Israeli lobby is not composed entirely of Jews; it has formed coalitions composed of unions, clergymen, black leaders, and scholars. Opinion polls show that 20 percent of non-Jews are as pro-Israel as Jews, thus Israel enjoys the backing of one of the largest veto groups in the country. This support rests on several foundations. Americans, for example, share a socio-cultural heritage with Israelis and respect the fact that Israel is a bastion of democracy in a region dominated by autocratic regimes. Until recently, Israel was supported as the underdog in a David and Goliath struggle for survival against the Arab world. Since the display of military might Israel employed in Lebanon, it is more common for people, particularly conservatives, to support Israel for the opposite reason, that is, as a strategic asset powerful enough to counter radical Arab governments and deter Soviet expansionism.

Support for Israel on the basis of strategic reasons has grown while there appears to

have been an erosion of support on the basis of moral considerations. This may be partly due to Israel's occupation policies which have drawn criticism from not only Israel's detractors but also many of its defenders, but it is also attributable to the change in the composition of Congress. As the years pass, the Holocaust becomes a more distant event and the legislators who had lived through that period and supported Israel because of a personal attachment to the Zionist cause have been replaced by people who see Israel as just another country. In order to maintain support in this political climate, the lobby must rely more heavily on the tools of political influence.

The most visible element of the Israeli lobby is AIPAC, an organization that has grown considerably in the last few years and now has a staff of 80 with a budget of about $5 million. AIPAC is not the first domestic lobby to concern itself with foreign affairs, but it is generally regarded as the most powerful. The lobby strives to remain non-partisan and thereby keep friends in both parties. It also addresses issues in terms of the national interest of the United States so as to attract broad support. This does not mean AIPAC does not have a close relationship with Israeli officials; it does, albeit unofficially. Even so, there are times when the lobby comes into conflict with the Israeli government. For example, when Reagan announced his peace plan in 1982, AIPAC's Director Tom Dine was quoted in *The New York Times* as saying the plan had some good points (and many bad ones) after the Israelis had rejected the plan *in toto*.

While AIPAC's success on Capitol Hill has been limited there is no doubt that the lobby makes its presence felt. According to Senator Charles Mathias:

> When an issue of importance comes before Congress AIPAC promptly and unfailingly provides all members with data and documentation, supplemented, as circumstances dictate, with tele-

phone calls and personal visits. Beyond that, signs of hesitation or opposition on the part of a Senator or a Representative can usually be relied on to call forth large numbers of letters or telegrams, or visits and phone calls from influential constituents.

The Senator's last point reveals an important element in the lobby's success—constituent involvement.

No matter how skillful lobbyists are, they cannot provide a legislator with what the politician considers most important, the votes to insure reelection. Through its network of at least 75 different organizations that in one way or another support Israel, the Israeli lobby is able to mobilize voters and potential voters for political action. Since Jews normally vote in greater numbers than any other ethnic group, in excess of 90 percent, politicians have a strong incentive to pay attention to the lobby's interests.

Most of the organizations that comprise AIPAC's network cannot legally devote a major portion of their time to lobbying, but the majority of their leaders have input into the lobby's decision-making process as members of AIPAC's Board of Directors. Perhaps more important is the bureaucratic machinery of these organizations that enables them to disseminate information to their members and facilitate a rapid response to legislative activity.

A second coordinating body for the lobby is the New York–based Conference of Presidents of Major American Jewish Organizations. It is composed of the leaders of over 30 different organizations and is responsible for articulating and formulating the "Jewish position" on most foreign policy issues. The Conference allows the American Jewish community to present a united front when pressing its case on decision-makers, something its opponents are unable to do.

A less visible means of influence employed by the Israeli lobby on Capitol Hill is a network of pro-Israel Congressional aides. Both the current and former directors of AIPAC were ac-

tively involved with Israel-related legislation as Congressional aides. Tom Dine was a legislative aide to Senators Frank Church and Edmund Muskie, and Dine's predecessor, Morris Amitay, was an aide to Senator Abraham Ribicoff. Amitay explained the behind-the-scenes activity of the aides:

> There are a lot of guys at the working level up here...who happen to be Jewish, who are willing to make a little bit of extra effort and to look at certain issues in terms of their Jewishness, and this is what made things go in the last couple of years. These are all guys who are in a position to make the decisions in these areas for those senators. You don't need that many to get something done in the Senate. All you need is a certain commitment to get something done and, if guys are willing to put time into that instead of a million other things they have to do, if they're willing to make a couple of calls, if they're willing to become involved, you can get an awful lot done just at the staff level....The senators have a million things to do and they'll take the recommendation [of their aides] most times.

After he became director of AIPAC, Amitay tried to discount the influence of the network, but it remains an important component of the Israeli lobby.

The Israeli lobby is unable to control U.S. policy in the Middle East as its detractors claim. The evidence indicates the lobby's influence is limited primarily to marginal issues that do not affect the general direction of U.S. policy. American foreign policy, in relation to Israel and other countries is, in the final analysis, determined by what both its leaders and the general public perceive as its best interests.

QUESTIONS FOR DISCUSSION

1. What criteria should be used in evaluating the strengths or weaknesses of the pro-Israeli lobby?
2. What other ethnic or nationality groups with links to foreign countries play a role in U.S. foreign policy? Is their influence stronger or weaker

than that of the pro-Israeli lobby? What are the reasons for your answer?

3. Is Israel a strategic asset for the United States? What are the reasons for your answer?

4. What are the sources of strength and sources of weakness of the pro-Israeli lobby?

5. How would you compare the political behavior of a foreign policy lobby with the political behavior of a domestic policy lobby?

6. What role should interest groups play in the conduct of U.S. foreign policy? What are the reasons for your answer?

SUGGESTED READINGS

Felton, John. "Administration, Hill Put Peace Pressure on Israel." *CQ Weekly Report,* 46 (Mar. 5, 1988), pp. 631–34.

Fialka, John W. "Linked Donations: Political Contributions from Pro-Israel PACs Suggest Coordination." *Wall Street Journal,* June 24, 1987, pp. 1, 21.

Karny, Yo'av. "Byzantine Bedfellows." *New Republic,* 196 (Jan. 14, 1987), pp. 23–25.

Khoury, Nabeel. "The Arab Lobby: Problems and Prospects." *Middle East Journal,* 41 (Summer 1987), pp. 379–96.

Pear, Robert, with Richard L. Berke. "Pro-Israel Group Exerts Quiet Might As It Rallies Supporters in Congress." *New York Times,* July 7, 1987, p. A8.

Samhan, Helen Hatab. "Politics and Exclusion: The Arab American Experience." *Journal of Palestinian Studies,* 16 (Winter 1987), pp. 11–28.

Shipler, David K. "On Middle East Policy, a Major Influence." *New York Times,* July 6, 1987, pp. 1, 4.

Spiegel, Steven L. "Toward an American-Israeli Strategic Partnership." *Global Affairs,* 1 (Fall 1986), pp. 8–17.

Tivnan, Edward. *The Lobby: Jewish Political Power and American Foreign Policy.* New York: Simon and Schuster, 1987.

Uslaner, Eric M. "One Nation, Many Voices: Interest Groups in Foreign Policy Making." In *Interest Group Politics,* ed. Allan J. Cigler and Burdett A. Loomis. 2d ed. Washington, D.C.: CQ Press, 1986. Pp. 236–57.

17 Should Greater Grass-Roots Participation in Foreign Policy be Encouraged?

YES

Michael H. Shuman

Dateline Main Street: Local Foreign Policies

NO

Peter J. Spiro

Taking Foreign Policy away from the Feds

Dateline Main Street: Local Foreign Policies

Michael H. Shuman

Ever since serving as the birthplace of the United Nations, San Francisco has been actively involved in international affairs. In nonbinding referendums, its voters have urged U.S. military withdrawals from Vietnam and El Salvador. Its current mayor, Dianne Feinstein, has traveled around the world, negotiating trade pacts with both Shanghai, China, and Haifa, Israel. To protest apartheid, the city's Retirement Board has divested $337 million in pension funds from businesses operating in South Africa. To challenge the federal policy of sending Salvadoran and Guatemalan refugees back to the war zones from which they fled, the city has instructed its police not to cooperate with the U.S. Immigration and Naturalization Service (INS). And after the downing of the South Korean airliner in 1983, its supervisors condemned the act and voted to kick the Soviet consulate out of the city.

To many in the professional foreign-policy community, San Francisco's activism is just more sourdough and beatniks, and municipal foreign policies in general seem to be purely symbolic acts by a handful of radical localities. Yet more than 1,000 U.S. state and local governments of all political stripes are participating in foreign affairs, and their numbers are expanding daily. Most of these policies involve concrete acts of education, research, lobbying, policing, zoning, contracting, and investing. Collectively, their influence on U.S. foreign policy is growing. More than 900 local

governments, for example, passed a nuclear freeze resolution and helped pressure President Ronald Reagan to launch the Strategic Arms Reduction Talks in Geneva. By refusing to cooperate with the Federal Emergency Management Agency's "crisis relocation planning," more than 120 cities helped derail its civil defense program. And by divesting billions of dollars in assets out of firms doing business in South Africa, more than 70 cities, 13 counties, and 19 states helped persuade the administration to replace "constructive engagement" with limited economic sanctions.

How far America's municipal foreign policies will go is unclear, but they can no longer be dismissed as simply aberrant, trivial, or unconstitutional. Further, their analogues are springing up throughout the world, even in some authoritarian countries. This trend of "thinking globally and acting locally" may both weaken national governments' traditional autonomy over foreign affairs and open new conduits for citizens to shape global politics directly, through the governments to which they are closest.

If the history of the 1799 Logan Act is any indication, official U.S. sympathy for popular participation in foreign affairs has existed since the earliest days of the Republic. Despite the act's ban on efforts by individual Americans to change foreign officials' positions on controversies involving the United States, it has never been enforced, suggesting broad government tolerance—if not tacit approval—of citizen participation in foreign affairs.

And this participation is likely to continue to grow. Today, the once-prohibitive real economic costs of such private diplomacy are plummeting. A typical overseas airline flight, for example, now costs one-sixth what it did in 1940. A telephone call to Tokyo is less than one-sixtieth as expensive as 50 years ago. Over the next few years, foreseeable transportation and communications breakthroughs may usher in an era in which millions of

Michael H. Shuman, "Dateline Main Street: Local Foreign Policies," *Foreign Policy,* no. 65 (Winter 1986–87), pp. 154–74. Reprinted by permission of *Foreign Policy.*

Americans could, at least in theory, practice some types of diplomacy.

The still declining confidence of Americans in their government's foreign-policy institutions, and their evident dissatisfaction with many specific U.S. policies on arms control, Central America, and elsewhere, have already stimulated impressive citizen efforts. To improve superpower relations and to refute Reagan's characterization of the Soviet Union as "the focus of evil in the modern world," a record number of American peace, youth, and educational groups have journeyed to the Soviet Union.[1] Tens of thousands of private American citizens are now working with Soviets on joint cultural, scientific, and economic projects and are communicating regularly through telex messages, slow-scan video machines, satellite "space bridges," and computer networks. "Citizen diplomacy" has flourished even in such areas as arms control. In May 1986, for example, the Natural Resources Defense Council and the Soviet Academy of Sciences agreed to set up advanced seismic detection devices near the nuclear test sites of each other's countries.

Conservatives have fostered their own brand of citizen diplomacy. According to *Newsweek*'s August 26, 1985, issue, private assistance to the Nicaraguan *contras* to that point had reached $25 million, one-third of which was being spent on ammunition and weapons. New Right fund raiser Richard Viguerie told the magazine that "conservatives have decided to do for the freedom fighters what the American left of the '30s did for the communists in Spain."

Nor are these voices likely to fall silent with a more popular, moderate, and nuanced foreign policy. If Americans continue to embrace participatory over representative democracy,

bipartisanship in foreign policy may become an anachronism. Whatever foreign policies Washington pursues, some groups will feel left out, and even tiny minorities will increasingly have the power to weaken or circumvent federal initiatives.

Americans seeking more foreign-policy clout are increasingly finding tools in their own back yards—the half-million local officials who are rarely more than a telephone call or a public meeting away. These Americans have discovered that, unlike nongovernmental organizations (NGOs), the traditional channels of subnational diplomacy, local governments can confer on their foreign affairs activism both money and legitimacy. Mayors, for example, may lack the influence of national ambassadors, but they are usually taken more seriously than most individual citizens or NGOs. Thus in late 1985 Feinstein and seven other mayors succeeded where other private initiatives failed and convinced the Soviet Union to allow 36 people to emigrate.

Local officials on the whole have been surprisingly receptive to citizen requests for municipal foreign policies. In the early 1980s, grassroots pressure for the nuclear freeze motivated an estimated 700–800 local officials to join two organizations committed to reversing the arms race: Local Elected Officials of America (LEO-USA) and Local Elected Officials for Social Responsibility. During the December 1985 convention of the National League of Cities (NLC), Mayor Tom Bradley of Los Angeles made municipal foreign policies the centerpiece of his keynote address.

> The right of cities to be heard on these crucial issues derives from two fundamental principles.
>
> First, local government is closest to the people.... [Second,] many of our national policies are felt first—and in the end most profoundly—in America's cities.... Democracy works best when the widest possible spectrum of interests participate fully.... [C]ities can enfranchise many who might otherwise never be

---

[1] See the Friends Committee on National Legislation and the Institute for Soviet-American Relations, "Visa Update," *Surviving Together*, February 1984: 2, 13.

heard. There can be no better reason for cities to participate with all the vigor and imagination we can muster.

Although some local officials have resisted municipal foreign policies, regarding them as unnecessary meddling, a growing number are implementing them to protect local interests directly affected by world events and U.S. policies. The clearest examples are cities that manage borders with other countries. As the political scientist Raymond Rodgers observed in the October 1967 issue of the *American Journal of International Law,* for more than a century, American border states and communities have entered into agreements with Canada and Mexico (and, sometimes, their local subdivisions) on such issues as road and bridge oversight, electric power, water management, motor vehicle registration, civil defense, fire prevention, and border patrols. Without local management, the movement of people and goods across borders would be slower and more expensive and problems such as illegal immigration and drug traffic would be even worse than they are today.

Municipalities have also launched foreign policies to protect their citizens from costly global problems, especially warfare. "Cities of the world unite," the political scientist Kenneth Boulding once wrote, "you have nothing to lose but your slums, your poverty, and your military expendability."[2] Internationally, it is no accident that cities like East and West Berlin; Coventry, England; Dresden, East Germany; Guernica, Spain; Hiroshima, Japan; and Verdun, France, all of which were destroyed in wartime, also have some of the most active foreign policies.

Perhaps the biggest reminder for American cities of their connection to global problems is the $286 billion U.S. military budget. Many

city governments believe that, dollar for dollar, money cut from programs such as General Revenue Sharing and Community Development Block Grants is being siphoned off into MX missiles and "Star Wars" research. Even the minority of communities benefiting in the short term from military contracting—like Los Angeles, San José, California, and Boston, which traditionally have sought more military contracts—are beginning to worry about the long-term consequences of increasing dependence on military spending. As indicated by the Jobs with Peace resolutions that these localities and nearly 80 others have passed, some local officials fear that the boom-and-bust swings of military spending may ultimately leave them economic ghost towns.

In addition, foreign policy can bring money and jobs into the community. U.S. states began heavily promoting foreign trade in the late 1970s. By 1980, they were spending $18.8 million on promoting exports, roughly the same level as the Department of Commerce, and $8.5 million on attracting foreign investment. Forty states have 66 offices all told in 17 countries—up from three states in 1970. Moreover, with the active encouragement of the NLC and the U.S. Conference of Mayors, more than 180 cities, port authorities, and development and trade agencies have been promoting trade and investment abroad.

Some of the benefits local governments are seeking in foreign affairs are cultural, not economic (though cultural ties often beget economic ties). No less than 759 U.S. communities have 1,120 "sister" relationships with cities abroad. Six of these are with Soviet cities—with 12 more to follow.

Finally, many local officials and citizens have embraced the logic of the Nuremberg trials and believe that they have a duty to fulfill international norms and laws. The 22 American cities and two states providing sanctuary for refugees from El Salvador and Guatemala have acted not out of self-interest—most antic-

---

[2] Kenneth E. Boulding, "The City as an Element in the International System," *Daedalus* 97, no. 4 (Fall 1968): 1123.

ipate that the newcomers will soak municipal resources and compete for scarce jobs—but because they are appalled at INS policies. Similarly, cities have divested from firms doing business in South Africa despite concerns about lower rates of return. Moral dimensions like these frequently have been raised by local racial, ethnic, and religious groups with close ties to oppressed groups abroad. Given America's social mélange, the number of global issues that might ultimately surface in municipal forums seems practically limitless.

MUNICIPAL ACTIVISM

Municipal foreign policies fall into three rough categories: consciousness-raising measures, unilateral measures, and bilateral measures. Most local governments, whether they realize it or not, are involved in raising public consciousness on foreign affairs through education, research, and lobbying. Virtually every municipality has international affairs–related curricula in its public schools, its adult education courses, and its museums and cultural centers. A smaller number of cities have sponsored public education of a more partisan variety. New York and Milwaukee high schools teach "peace studies" courses. San Francisco, Cambridge, Massachusetts, and Boulder, Colorado, have produced and disseminated pamphlets describing the effects of nuclear war and arguing for a nuclear freeze. Alabama requires its teachers to contrast the U.S. and Soviet governments and to "lay particular emphasis upon the dangers of communism [and] the ways to fight communism." In the field of research, California and New Jersey have established their own peace research programs. And Los Angeles, Pittsburgh, and Baltimore now require annual reports on the economic impact of military spending.

Lobbying is another form of consciousness-raising, albeit highly directed and politicized. In August 1984, Mayor Raymond Flynn of Boston urged 100 other mayors to join Boston in divesting their municipal funds from firms doing business in South Africa. Nonbinding statements on foreign-policy issues are also forms of lobbying. Using these measures, San Francisco and Seattle have protested U.S. policy in Central America, Los Angeles has registered its concern on Soviet human rights policies, and Berkeley, California, has condemned the U.S. invasion of Grenada and urged a halt to U.S. support for aerial bombing in El Salvador.

Local foreign policies are also conducted through unilateral use of policing, zoning, contracting, and investing powers. New York State and New Jersey, in cooperation with the cities of New York and Newark, protested the Soviet shooting down of the South Korean airliner by denying Soviet United Nations representatives access to local airports. More than one dozen state liquor commissions responded to the incident by banning sales of Soviet-produced vodka.

Not only have 120 cities refused to cooperate with federal civil defense plans, but also 118 communities and counties have passed zoning ordinances banning nuclear weapons production within their city limits. The organization Nuclear Free America estimates that nearly 13.8 million Americans now live in "nuclear free zones." Although most are still merely consciousness-raising measures, some of these ordinances are already beginning to affect defense contractors.

With more than $300 billion in investments and $500 billion in annual expenditures, state and local governments are beginning to recognize their enormous economic power. In addition to divesting assets, cities such as Oakland, California, are also assessing penalties against contract bids coming from firms doing business in South Africa. Pittsburgh has banned all city purchases from corporations that either do business in South Africa or supply goods and services to other corporations doing business there. And Hoboken, New Jersey, Amherst, Massachusetts, and Takoma Park, Maryland, have prohibited any municipal contracts with firms producing nuclear weapons.

Further, U.S. cities have negotiated thousands of bilateral foreign agreements. Many of these agreements are tantamount to political treaties. Boulder, for example, has an agreement with Jalapa, Nicaragua, to help build a preschool—a pact clearly designed to challenge U.S. policies in Central America. Similar motives can be found in Portland, Oregon's and Seattle, Washington's sister-city relationships with Nicaraguan cities or Berkeley's ties with rebel-controlled San Antonio Los Ranchos in El Salvador. Burlington, Vermont, went even further, arranging for a ship to carry 560 tons of humanitarian goods, including 30 tons of medical supplies, to its sister city in Puerto Cabezas, Nicaragua.

A few cities have established permanent foreign-policy bodies—bodies that can be viewed as miniature state departments. In late 1985, Seattle commissioned a feasibility study for establishing a $225,000 per year office of international affairs to coordinate its programs involving trade, tourism, and 13 sister cities. Between 1981 and 1982, Washington, D.C., Cambridge, and Boulder established peace commissions with modest budgets and staffs. Many of these programs are attracting bipartisan support.

In *Foreign Affairs and the Constitution*, the Columbia University law professor Louis Henkin expressed this element of conventional wisdom: "The language, the spirit and the history of the Constitution deny the States [and local governments] authority to participate in foreign affairs, and its construction by the courts has steadily reduced the ways in which the states can affect American foreign relations." Why, then, have so few municipal foreign policies been judicially invalidated?

The discrepancy between constitutional theory and practice reflects different definitions of state and local government participation in foreign affairs. Legal scholars have pointed out that the Constitution forbids local governments from assembling their own armies or navies, declaring war, entering into treaties, violating national treaty commitments, and levying duties on imports or exports. Since these scholars could not imagine how else local governments might influence foreign affairs, the legal case against municipal foreign policies has always seemed obvious. But very little of today's municipal activism falls into any of these forbidden categories. And attorneys and courts have found that countervailing constitutional principles render the general legal wisdom almost meaningless.

The most impressive feature of U.S. law on municipal foreign policies is the paucity of cases. The few relevant court pronouncements have been so ambiguous and contradictory that few city attorneys have been convinced that their municipal foreign policies were clearly illegal and not worth trying. Examining the three categories of local foreign policies helps explain this surprising conclusion.

Consciousness-raising measures pose one basic legal question: Can a local government undertake education, research, and lobbying that challenge the foreign policies of the federal government? Thus far, the Supreme Court has given local governments a broad license to express themselves as they please, provided they do not impair the speech rights of those with opposing views. Some legal scholars have argued for greater restrictions, particularly when public officials are restricting access to public forums or speaking on behalf of their own re-election, but others have disagreed. If municipally sponsored speakers intended to change the views of foreign officials concerning disputes with the United States, the Logan Act could be invoked. The prevailing legal view, however, is that the act unconstitutionally infringes free speech.[3] The bottom line appears to be that local governments are free to launch educational, research, and lobbying programs on any foreign-policy issue they wish.

The federal government could clamp down on consciousness-raising measures by exercising its powers to prohibit individuals from traveling abroad. Over the years, the Supreme Court has decided that the Fifth Amendment accords Americans only a privilege to travel internationally—a privilege that the president has received more and more discretion to withhold or revoke whenever he has compelling "foreign policy justifications," according to the Court's 1984 ruling in *Regan v. Wald.* In practice, however, executive interference with Americans traveling abroad has been rare. Current regulations ban Americans only from traveling to Cambodia, Cuba, Iran, Laos, North Korea, and Vietnam, and even in these cases the ambitious traveler can usually get exceptional permission. Future presidential bans on the travel of local officials are possible but unlikely. Not only could these bans easily be circumvented by using the telephone or mail, but they also would be unlikely to withstand political outrage from Congress, the states, and the public.

Unilateral measures pose more difficult legal questions, but again, impediments seem minimal. Policy needs to be examined in light of three constitutional doctrines: the Supremacy Clause, the Commerce Clause, and the 1968 Supreme Court ruling in *Zschernig v. Miller.*

The Supremacy Clause states that whenever the federal government has an explicit law, whether in foreign or domestic policy, any inconsistent state or local law is to be pre-empted. In recent years, however, the Supreme Court has shown increasing sympathy toward state initiatives. It has underscored that "federal supremacy is not lightly to be presumed"—as the 1952 ruling in *Schwartz v. Texas* put it. And thus, stipulated the Court in *Silver v. New York Stock Exchange* (1963), "the proper approach...is an analysis which reconciles the operation of both statutory schemes with one another rather than holding one completely ousted." The Court has shown particular reluctance to pre-empt states when they use their "police powers" to legislate the protection of public health and safety.[4]

Applying these principles, the Massachusetts Supreme Court recently upheld a Cambridge ordinance that prohibited a local Pentagon contractor from testing, storing, transporting, and disposing of five highly toxic chemical warfare agents. Rejecting the Arthur D. Little Company's challenge to this law, the court concluded that despite the "explicit constitutional commitment of the national defense to the Federal government...not every regulation which has some incidental effect on a defense program is invalid."

Of course, resistance to pre-emption does not mean total abstinence. Courts can still invalidate municipal foreign policies that are clearly at odds with a federal law. Thus the New York–New Jersey effort to ban airport landings by Soviet U.N. personnel was arguably unconstitutional since it violated the 1947 U.S. treaty establishing U.N. headquarters in New York City. Similarly, in the 1986 case of *Radiation Technology, Inc. v. the County of Union*, a New Jersey federal district court declared that a local nuclear-free-zone ordinance was pre-empted by the Atomic Energy Act. Yet most federal laws and policies dealing with foreign affairs are highly ambiguous.

---

[3] See, for example, Detlev V. Vagts, "The Logan Act: Paper Tiger or Sleeping Giant?" *American Journal of International Law* 60, no. 6 (April 1966): 296–298.

[4] See *Metropolitan Life Ins. Co. v. Mass.*, 105 S.Ct. 2380, 2398 (1985); and *Silkwood v. Kerr-McGee Corp.*, 104 S.Ct. 615, 621 (1984).

What, for example, is U.S. policy in Nicaragua? Washington maintains formal peacetime diplomatic relations with Nicaragua, but is also aiding efforts to overthrow the government. Thus it seems unclear how readily a court would pre-empt, say, Boulder from building its child care facility in Jalapa.

Local governments are also beginning to argue that some of their municipal foreign policies cannot be pre-empted because they are upholding international law, which they believe the Constitution makes binding on all officials, local and national. Some sanctuary cities, such as Takoma Park, contend that they are upholding U.S. treaty obligations under the Geneva Conventions of 1949 to protect fleeing refugees more faithfully than are INS deportation policies. Takoma Park and other "nuclear-free zones" also cite America's international obligations under such treaties as the Hague Convention of 1907, which bans weapons of indiscriminate destruction. Twenty years ago, these arguments might have been summarily dismissed, but today some courts are taking them seriously. In April 1985, an Illinois state judge instructed a jury deliberating over seven demonstrators who had resisted arrest at the Waukegan Great Lakes Naval Training Center to consider that "[t]he use or threat of use of nuclear weapons is a war crime or an attempted war crime"; the defendants were acquitted. And in July 1985, an INS judge in Texas held that the standards of international humanitarian law are binding on all Salvadoran deportations.[5]

A second legal issue in regard to unilateral activities is posed by the Commerce Clause, which forbids state or local governments from infringing on interstate or international commerce. The Commerce Clause is concerned first with preventing a state from favoring its own goods over those from other states or countries; by this logic, measures like the 1983 state bans on the sale of Soviet-produced vodka are probably illegal. The Commerce Clause is also designed to prevent local regulations from interfering with the free flow of national commerce. For example, a court could strike down nuclear-free zones by determining that they were unduly hampering the "interstate market" for nuclear weapons components. The city attorney for Portland, however, has argued that such national concerns are greatly outweighed by the city's interest in protecting public health and safety.

Commerce Clause questions have also been posed with respect to selective contracting and investing. But the Supreme Court may have put these concerns to rest in its ruling on the 1983 case of *White v. Mass. Council of Construction Employers.* There it pronounced, "[W]hen a state or local government enters the market as a participant it is not subject to the restraints of the Commerce Clause." Whether the courts extend the logic of *White* to foreign commerce remains to be seen. Already, however, this logic has led several city legal counsels in Oakland and elsewhere to conclude that selective investment and contracting would withstand judicial scrutiny.

The most significant legal obstacle to unilateral municipal foreign policies remains the case of *Zschernig v. Miller.* Before this case, states and localities had assumed that they were free to act in foreign affairs, provided they did not violate any explicit federal law or the Commerce Clause. The argument that courts could interfere with municipal foreign policies where the federal government had not acted was dismissed by the Supreme Court as "farfetched" in the 1947 case of *Clark v. Allen.* In both the *Zschernig* and the *Clark* cases, state laws in Oregon and California, respectively,

---

[5] *People v. Jarka,* No. 002170, Circuit Court of Lake County, Waukegan, Illinois, 15 April 1985. It should be noted that, in the Texas case, even though the INS judge, Michael C. Horn, accepted that the INS was bound by humanitarian law, he held that the refugee had not met his burden of proof that grave human rights breaches were taking place in El Salvador.

refused to let a resident alien inherit property because the alien's home country barred U.S. residents from inheriting property. Both state laws were protesting the confiscatory nature of inheritance laws in communist countries. Yet in *Clark*, the Court upheld California's statute because it had only an "incidental or indirect effect" on U.S. foreign relations, whereas in *Zschernig*, it struck down Oregon's statute because of "its great potential for disruption or embarrassment."

Courts and legal scholars have struggled for nearly two decades to reconcile these cases, the facts of which were virtually identical. Some have argued that *Clark* was eclipsed by *Zschernig*'s broad language prohibiting all municipal foreign policies with "a direct impact upon foreign relations [that] may well adversely affect that power of the central government to deal with those [foreign relations] problems." Others have read *Zschernig* more narrowly, pointing out that the Court's continuing refusal to overrule *Clark* shows its tolerance to some municipal foreign policies. This interpretation seems to be supported by the Supreme Court's post-*Zschernig* decisions upholding New York's and Montana's inheritance statutes, both of which were arguably more intrusive than the Oregon statute struck down in *Zschernig*.[6]

Still, just what *Zschernig* now means remains unclear. In the nearly two decades since the *Zschernig* doctrine was first articulated, the Supreme Court has not sought once to expand or clarify it. Lower courts have developed a wide array of formulas for its interpretation, including whether the local foreign policy has more than an "incidental or indirect effect" on the country's foreign policy; whether the policy involves "sitting in judgment" of another country's ideology, politics, or legal system; or

how the municipality's interests balance against the policy's impact on foreign affairs. These criteria are so vague and depend so heavily on each case's peculiar facts and circumstances that it is hardly surprising that few cities have been deterred by the highly uncertain prospect of a *Zschernig* violation.

Whenever the Supreme Court returns to *Zschernig*, it should consider eschewing unnecessary activism and abandoning the doctrine entirely. Is it really sensible for courts to halt municipal foreign policies tolerated by the executive and legislative branches? Henkin suggested in *Foreign Affairs and the Constitution* that

> Article I indeed forbids the States to make treaties and do other specified acts in foreign relations, but these, singly or together, do not support the general exclusion announced in *Zschernig;* and the prohibition to the States of some things might even imply that others are permitted....Nor is there support for *Zschernig* in the history of the Constitution in practice.

Bilateral measures raise all these questions plus one more: Does the agreement constitute an unconstitutional treaty or compact?

The Constitution prohibits state and local governments from entering into "treaties" with jurisdictions abroad, but allows "compacts" so long as they receive congressional approval. The distinction has never been clear, but since no state or local government has been so ill-advised as to call its agreement with another country a treaty, "the different constitutional treatment," according to Henkin, "has lost all practical significance." The requirement that compacts obtain congressional assent stands as a theoretical obstacle to bilateral agreements, but the Supreme Court has invalidated such an international agreement only once—in an 1840 extradition case. Since then, state and local governments have signed hundreds, perhaps thousands, of bilateral agreements without congressional con-

---

[6] In both cases, the Supreme Court affirmed lower courts. *Ioannou v. New York*, 391 U.S. 604 (1968); and *Gorun v. Fall*, 393 U.S. 398 (1968), 399 U.S. 901 (1970).

sent and without one syllable of concern from the Supreme Court.

Thus localities can only guess what the law is now. Since the Constitution speaks of interstate and international compacts in the same clause, the legal principles governing interstate agreements may well someday also govern international agreements. Back in 1892, the Supreme Court announced in *Virginia v. Tennessee* that the only interstate agreements requiring congressional consent were those "which may encroach upon or interfere with the just supremacy of the United States." In 1977, these principles were restated in *U.S. Steel Corp. v. Multistate Tax Comm'n*, when the Court upheld an agreement by 21 states to provide for uniform state tax treatment of multinational corporations. As Justice Byron White's dissenting opinion argued, if the Court found that compact acceptable without congressional consent—especially considering that it created a commission that attempted to block Senate ratification of a tax treaty signed with Great Britain—"there is very little life remaining in that section of our Constitution." For now, the historical acquiescence of Congress to bilateral agreements suggests that only explicit legislative disapproval will lead the courts to invalidate them.

RATIONALES FOR TOLERANCE

Yet the question remains whether municipalities today should continue to have such freedom to launch their own foreign policies. Certainly the conventional wisdom has long argued for preserving a federal monopoly on foreign policy. The Supreme Court has consistently resisted applying federalist principles to international affairs. In the 1941 case of *Hines v. Davidowitz*, the Court wrote, "Our system of government is such that the interest of the cities, counties and states, no less than the interest of the whole nation, imperatively requires the federal power in the field affecting foreign relations be left entirely free from local interference." Similar views have sometimes been expressed by the executive and legislative branches. "We cannot have individual states and cities establishing their own foreign policies," said Senator Richard Lugar (R.-Indiana), chairman of the Senate Foreign Relations Committee, in an August 15 speech concerning local South Africa–related divestment.

But like the courts, the executive and legislative branches often denounce municipal activism and yet effectively sanction it through incoherence. In the last 2 years, the Department of Defense has criticized the seven governors who refused to allow or who attached conditions to their National Guard units' participation in military exercises in Honduras; the INS has pleaded with cities not to create sanctuaries; and the Department of Commerce has expressed concern that state export-financing programs might violate the General Agreement on Tariffs and Trade. Yet in none of these cases did Washington launch legal action to stop activities that it denounced (though despite the unanimous condemnation by the National Governors' Association of this administration's stance, the Pentagon is trying to rewrite national laws concerning gubernatorial discretion over their National Guard units). Congress has also refused several specific requests to halt municipal foreign policies. In 1984, for example, it turned down a resolution by Representative Philip Crane (R.-Illinois) to prohibit Washington, D.C., from divesting its public funds from firms making loans to or doing business in South Africa, a measure that might have implied congressional dissatisfaction with other divestment initiatives. Last September, Lugar asserted that the sanctions Congress was about to pass against South Africa would pre-empt all state and local efforts in the field. The House reacted by passing a resolution expressly denying any intent to pre-empt municipal efforts and implicitly bolstering other municipal foreign policies.

Although this tolerance for municipal foreign policies might merely reflect federal inefficiency, timidity, or ineptitude, it also probably reveals three important underlying rationales. First, Washington may be recognizing that international affairs, like many domestic issues, have become too complicated to run effectively as a monopoly. In trade, for example, the Department of State has actually briefed activist governors, assisted state and local trade representatives through its embassies and consulates, and lent Foreign Service officers to states. The Departments of Commerce and Agriculture have been similarly cooperative. The last thing an overworked, underfunded executive branch needs is direct micromanagement of thousands of local investment, cultural exchange, and border coordination activities.

The federal government may also believe that ultimately these policies are unstoppable. When the city attorney of Oakland informed the city council that federal regulations preempted its proposed initiative to ban its port from handling South African cargo, for example, he recommended instead selective investment and contracting. Even if the federal government cut off every unilateral and bilateral initiative, cities would still have the constitutionally protected consciousness-raising powers.

Perhaps the most important reason for federal tolerance may be the unwillingness of most presidents, members of Congress, and judges to subordinate America's core political values to the exigencies of foreign policy. Cutting off consciousness-raising measures ultimately means suppressing basic freedoms of speech, assembly, and travel. Restricting unilateral measures means trampling on traditional local autonomy in zoning, policing, contracting, and investing—an outcome that states-rights conservatives would oppose as

vigorously as internationalist liberals. And restricting cities' ability to enter into foreign economic agreements means dismantling the principles of free trade. America's politicians may be starting to view municipal foreign policies as an inevitable, indeed laudable, step in the maturation of a democracy.

Yet it is not difficult to envision future municipal foreign initiatives that could threaten national security and welfare. The traditional concerns—that one municipality's affront to another country could trigger a backlash against the entire country or that a disunited U.S. foreign policy could weaken the country against foreign challenges—certainly have merit. But Congress and the president have always had the power to stop these errant initiatives through specific legislation. If the country cannot await legislation, the president can always stop a municipal action with an executive order. Washington's record strongly indicates a belief that both creative local initiatives and a coherent national policy are desirable—a choice courts should respect.

Unless America becomes a police state, municipal foreign policies are here to stay. The challenge for the federal government is not, as one *Wall Street Journal* commentator recently wrote, how "Congress and the courts should move against [municipal foreign activism] while it remains largely restricted," but instead how these branches should encourage those policies that benefit U.S. foreign policy and carefully discourage those that do not.[7] Four guidelines might be particularly useful.

The first entails unqualified support for all consciousness-raising measures. For the sake of the principles underlying the First and Fifth amendments, America should be

---

[7] Peter Spiro, "Get States and Cities off Foreign-Policy Stage," *Wall Street Journal,* 24 September 1986, 28.

willing to embrace the freest possible exchange of ideas, people, books, and audiovisual materials. Adhering to this guideline, Congress might begin by narrowing presidential discretion in banning travel abroad and scrapping the Logan Act. The government might also help support more citizen and municipal initiatives. Reagan's creation of a special U.S.-Soviet Exchange Initiative Office is a step in the right direction, though the effort could be vastly improved were it to provide real funding instead of merely diplomatic assistance.

With respect to unilateral and bilateral measures, the government should adhere to a second, more qualified guideline: Tolerate municipal initiatives unless they pose more than a hypothetical danger to American foreign policy. As discussed earlier, cities are passing these initiatives not just to meddle in other people's affairs but also out of legitimate local concerns. Federal attempts to quash them with legal maneuvers instead of a carefully reasoned policy that enjoys public support will simply anger affected populaces and prompt new, equally irksome initiatives accomplishing the same goals. For example, bans on local South Africa–related divestiture—which cities would view as tantamount to federal instructions on investing their own money—could be skirted by turning pension funds over to municipal employees' unions that could then selectively invest. The only realistic federal approach is one that proscribes those few municipal activities that pose real dangers and leaves the rest alone. Unilateral and bilateral activities, in other words, should be presumed acceptable.

With regard to dangerous initiatives, it would be wise to stick to a third guideline: Try working with the offending municipality rather than immediately resorting to legal attacks. In the same way that federal officials have worked closely with municipal and state officials to harmonize their various trade policies, federal officials should try to involve mayors and other citizen representatives in the formulation of U.S. policies concerning national security, immigration, Third World development, and human rights. Tapping local wisdom not only could mollify much local activism, but also could help prevent foreign-policy disasters.

A final recommendation: Tighten the laws governing those very few nonfederal initiatives that have already caused serious international mischief. The most obvious initiatives that come to mind—thus far undertaken by citizens and not cities—are exports of weapons, ammunition, and military support equipment. One possible remedy would be to strengthen the Neutrality Act by enforcing it through an independent prosecutor rather than relying on the political whims of the Justice Department.[8]

Together, these guidelines suggest a fundamental new direction for U.S. federalism—one that would have seemed strange to the framers of the Constitution. But the Founding Fathers knew that the Constitution, as well as the international norms, customs, and rules it absorbed, would be an organic, evolving body of law. In the Supreme Court's seminal 1936 opinion on how the Constitution should relate to international law, *United States v. Curtiss-Wright Export Corp.*, Justice George Sutherland recognized that ultimately the federal government's foreign affairs powers would have to be understood "not in the provisions of the Constitution, but in the law of nations"—by which he meant primarily the dynamics and realities of the international system. This "law of nations" was once thought of as unchanging. But now it is regarded as being in a state

---

[8] Jules Lobel, "The Rise and Decline of the Neutrality Act: Sovereignty and Congressional War Powers in United States Foreign Policy," *Harvard International Law Journal* 24 (1983): 1–17, esp. 67–71.

of rapid evolution. One of the most important changes involves the principle that individuals as well as states have rights and duties under international law, as enunciated by the Nuremberg trials, the Universal Declaration of Human Rights, and the Genocide Convention. Certainly it is plausible to begin nudging America's 18th-century constitution into the 21st century by according individuals and their municipal representatives power to participate in the international decisions increasingly affecting their daily lives.

Taking Foreign Policy away from the Feds

Peter J. Spiro

Deep through the American character runs an antipathy to political over-centralization and the extended authority of the national apparatus. One symptom of this aversion has been a historical reluctance to cede state and local control to the federal government; another is a basic conviction that many policies and programs are formulated and implemented more effectively at the nonfederal levels of administration. Although Washington's power now knows few bounds, the principles of federalism are more vital today than they have been at any time since World War II, and it is at least an arguable proposition that in many areas the federal government has become an increasingly cumbersome forum in which to manage the needs of the nation.

The renewed importance of nonfederal authorities to the general governance is by and large to be welcomed in the traditional realms of state and local concern—those relating, for instance, to the varying health, welfare, and educational needs of the subnational units. In recent years, however, states and localities have turned their attention to a sphere they previously had dared not to invade—foreign policy and national defense. On issues as diverse as apartheid and arms policy, the country is witnessing an unprec-

edented wave of state and local actions intended to affect various U.S. positions in world affairs. In at least one case (U.S. relations with South Africa), this purpose has been realized.

Such state and local interference in foreign policy is not and has never been appropriate to the U.S. system of federalism. In its posture toward other nations, both in peace and in war, the United States must stand as exactly that—a federation, where one policy binds all. This is not to say that the sovereignty of the people, to use Tocqueville's phrase, should be impaired in any way by virtue of the unique nature of these decisions; the electorate always may, and always does, make its wishes known and effected through congressional and presidential elections, the former of which allows the representation of differing state and local viewpoints on foreign-policy issues. But there can be no bypassing of the federal structure once Washington has cast its dye in such matters. Unlike the administration of schools, sewers, and the like, there is little advantage to, and much potential for disaster in, the local management of foreign policy.

For a start, most states and cities are ill-suited to the task. Not commanding the sorts of resources commanded by policymakers at the federal level, they are more liable than their federal counterparts to arrive at misguided or uninformed results. Nor are local authorities apt to take account of the consequences of their acts in other jurisdictions. Local foreign policies tend to give citizens of urban areas and academic communities (those that have shown the greatest tendency to act in the area) a power beyond what they would command with their equal vote within the federal system. Finally and most important, the potency of widespread local action on world issues gives rise to the possibility of a corresponding powerlessness at the federal level where the two conflict. At best, such local measures serve to dilute

Peter J. Spiro, "Taking Foreign Policy away from the Feds," *Washington Quarterly,* 11 (Winter 1988), pp. 191–203. Reprinted by permission of the MIT Press, Cambridge, Mass.

This article was completed before [Peter J. Spiro] assumed his current position as special assistant to the legal adviser, U.S. Department of State, and does not necessarily represent the views of the U.S. government.

federally formulated policies. At worst, they can render federal action ineffectual.

State and local foreign-policy measures are not only unsound for policy reasons, they are unconstitutional as well. Indeed, it was in part if not primarily because of disunity on foreign-policy matters that the Founding Fathers abandoned loose confederation and moved toward a stronger central government. Since then the Supreme Court decisively has struck down local laws where they are directly inconsistent with federal policies. But it also has invalidated local action where, even in the absence of a national posture, it has or is intended to affect foreign commercial or diplomatic relations. If the courts are to stay true to these well-established constitutional standards, much of the recent nonfederal activity must be cast aside. The matter is one of process. That local foreign policies largely have been characterized to date by leftist positions is immaterial, for once the cities and states grow accustomed to their new-found role they will surely take other positions as well. As the leading advocate of increased state and municipal activism himself admitted, "even tiny minorities will increasingly have the power to weaken or circumvent federal initiatives."[1] Surely this is not a desirable result, for it will inevitably enfeeble foreign-policy decision making across the board. Effective policy formulation at the federal level, requiring consensus among congressional, administrative, and bureaucratic players, is difficult enough. The infusion of other, less well-equipped actors into this process only can make matters worse.

CITIES AND STATES JOIN THE FRAY

More than 1,000 city, county, and state governments have involved themselves in some way in foreign policy issues. Not all of these activities are intolerable; indeed, some are not only benign but also beneficial. The key to distinguishing acceptable from unacceptable local measures lies in highlighting not so much their isolated characteristics as their relationship and interplay with the federal foreign-policy process. Three basic categories of local foreign-policy action emerge from this perspective. First, there are those forms of participation that are too insignificant to influence the course of national issues, in either practice or potential. Second, for many years state and local entities have pursued initiatives in trade and transborder cooperation that are not intended in any way to undermine federal policies and that at bottom implicate matters of largely local concern. Third, a growing number of states and localities have enacted foreign-policy and defense-related measures that interfere, both in terms of their intent and their impact, with unfettered federal decision making in the area. It is these activities around which the controversy revolves and in which one finds local activism both constitutionally and politically offensive.

This last category must be set apart from forms of local participation that pose no such problem, lest one give credence to activist imputations of a Politburo mentality to those who oppose their efforts.[2] There have emerged, most notably, certain activities that may be characterized as de minimis in nature—that is, failing to rise to a level of practical concern even where they may not coincide with the objectives of federal foreign policy.

Examples include nonbinding resolutions passed by state or local legislative bodies or by

[1] Michael H. Shuman, "Dateline Main Street: Local Foreign Policies," *Foreign Policy,* no. 65 (Winter 1986–87), p. 156.

[2] "A Message From the Editor," *Bulletin of Municipal Foreign Policy* 1:2 (Spring 1987), p. 1.

referendum; other statements by nonfederal officials on world affairs, however controversial; the renaming of streets for foreign-policy reasons; and local public education programs relating to the arms race along with similar public awareness initiatives. The Soviet Union may have taken offense when Washington, D.C., changed the address of its embassy to "One Andrei Sakharov Plaza," likewise with South Africa when New Haven renamed one of its avenues after Bishop Desmond Tutu. But neither nation was likely to react with concrete retaliation. In the early 1980s more than 800 U.S. localities passed nuclear freeze resolutions, calling upon the superpowers to end the production of atomic weapons. Yet these purely hortatory measures posed no threat to the continued production and deployment of nuclear armaments as the federal government saw fit. Similarly, "peace" curricula in such localities as San Francisco and Cambridge are not liable to constrain national security policy formulation. If nothing else, they should invite the presentation of opposing viewpoints, whether from federal or other sources.

ERRANT MAYORS AND SORORIAL PROVOCATION

Local officials, no doubt, sometimes too freely can pass judgment on foreign-policy matters. In one three-month period during the winter of 1986–1987, for example, Mayor Edward Koch of New York managed to provoke the ire of the Soviets by calling their government "the pits," of the Greeks by accusing Prime Minister Andreas Papandreou of anti-Semitism, and of American Poles by praising Polish leader Wojciech Jaruzelski during a visit to that country. Such statements hardly are to be encouraged, especially when made in a public capacity. But Mayor Koch and other local figures prone to this sort of editorializing do share First Amendment freedoms with the private citizenry, and may speak as they please. Once

again, because these excursions are a matter of words and not of action, they cannot be expected to be met more than in kind.

Perhaps more disturbing is a recent wave of politically oriented "sister-city" arrangements between U.S. and foreign localities. According to the private foundation Sister Cities International, U.S. cities have created such ties with 1,153 of their foreign counterparts. Usually intended to facilitate trade, tourism, or cultural exchanges, these affiliations are often innocuous enough, as is clearly the case between Los Angeles and Mexico City, New York City and Tokyo, and Vail and St. Moritz. Of late, however, the motivating force behind many sister-city relationships has been more to send a foreign policy message to Washington than merely to cement subnational ties. Thus, one pro-Sandinista organization has sponsored more than 70 sister-city agreements between Nicaraguan and U.S. towns that have channeled more than $20 million in humanitarian aid to the Nicaraguan participants—all this despite decidedly unfamilial relations between the two countries at the national level.[3]

This brand of local foreign policy marks the edge of the de minimis exception. In theory, the sister-city phenomenon could cross that line, as might be the case were links established with countries with which the United States does not maintain diplomatic relations. (Seattle should not seek ties with Tripoli or Pyongyang.) But such steps remain largely symbolic, with little potential for significant interference in the conduct of U.S. foreign relations.

SOME FOREIGN POLICY SHOULD BE LOCAL

In contrast to measures taken in protest of federal postures stand those of a more practical

---

[3] See Jeffrey Pasley, "Twisted Sisters," *The New Republic,* June 22, 1987, pp. 14–18.

bent. This second category of state and local foreign policy–related actions encompasses two types of state and local initiatives: programs designed to encourage foreign investment and commerce with the acting jurisdiction and transborder agreements negotiated with localities in Canada and Mexico.

Foreigners have come to command increasing billions of dollars in U.S. investments, and it is now almost de rigueur that governors and big city mayors work to attract these commitments to their constituents' benefit. Nonfederal officials routinely conduct international trade missions, and almost all of the U.S. states have established permanent commercial representation in one or more foreign nations. These efforts have intensified as foreign corporations seek manufacturing outposts in the United States in the form of large, location-specific projects—automobile plants, most notably—that promise significant employment and other economic gains.

Also on the rise are agreements between border communities and their Canadian and Mexican counterparts. These arrangements relate to the management of such mutual concerns as highways and bridges, energy and water supplies, border crossings, and fire prevention. Although many date to the advent of modern transportation and technology in the early decades of this century, population growth along the borders, particularly to the South, has heightened the utility of such nonfederal programs. San Diego, for one, has consolidated all aspects of its relationship with neighboring Tijuana in a single (and unprecedented) department of "binational affairs." One commentator has gone so far as to suggest a Mexican–Gulf South Association, to include Mexico and six adjoining U.S. states, to look after matters of regional concern.[4]

---

[4] [Raymond S.] Rodgers, "The Capacity of the States of the Union to Conclude International Agreements," *American Journal of International Law,* vol. 61 (1967), p. 1021.

Activities in trade and transborder administration pose no danger to the effective maintenance of federal foreign policy. Unlike other local forays into world affairs, they are nonideological and are not intended to undermine federal measures; their purpose, rather, is only to achieve concrete benefit for the acting jurisdiction. (As with sister-city relationships, an exception would seem appropriate where trade with an unrecognized nation is at issue. Arizona's contemplated opening of a trade office in Taiwan is one such an example.) Commercial initiatives have been facilitated by the departments of state and commerce; and Congress ordinarily has blessed border compacts where consent has been requested, as the Constitution at least technically requires it. Even in the face of plausible legal theories to forbid these programs, it is improbable that anyone would find reason to challenge them. And for good reason: in these spheres nonfederal entities simply do a better job. Nonfederal action, in this respect, is not only tolerable but also desirable, sometimes necessary.

CROSSING THE LINE

The same cannot be said of local measures that pose a potentially serious threat to federal oversight of truly national foreign-policy and defense matters. To some great extent, many of the activities discussed above have only become more prevalent as a matter of degree. Local executive officials and legislative bodies, for instance, often have seen fit to criticize federal foreign-policy platforms, as was evident during the Vietnam War. Similarly, they have been known to seek out official contacts with their foreign counterparts. But the 1980s also have witnessed the advent of new mechanisms for local foreign-policy involvement, qualitative innovations of far greater potency. Chief among these, in terms of prevalence and impact, are measures that limit a locality's holdings and purchases of investments and of goods and services according to foreign-affairs criteria, so-called divestment and procurement activities. This last category of local participation in foreign policy—better characterized as local interference in foreign policy—also includes laws enacted in outright defiance of and directly mandating noncompliance with federal programs relating to foreign affairs and national security. The list of issues subjected to such local action is now a long one. Several jurisdictions have gone as far as to create their own official departments of foreign affairs— mini state departments, in effect—to coordinate these initiatives; and a lobbying and information network, the Local Elected Officials Project, has been established to promote local foreign policies nationwide.

CITIES AND STATES AGAINST APARTHEID

Of all local foreign-policy activities, the divestment movement has been the most successful in affecting the course of a single controversy—what stance the United States should take toward the apartheid regime in South Africa. In response to the 1976 riot in Soweto, a handful of small communities in the United States, along with the state of Wisconsin, passed measures to divest pension and educational portfolios of securities in corporations with operations in South Africa. The campaign gained full steam in the wake of subsequent and more enduring disturbances sparked in 1984. Since then, more than 100 states and localities have taken some form of concrete anti–South Africa action. Increasingly, these measures call not only for the sale of South Africa–related investments but also for prohibitions on all governmental contracting with the same roll of black-listed companies. Michigan recently became the first state to adopt a selective-purchasing policy, joining such municipalities as New York, Los Angeles, and San Francisco. Divestment statutes and ordinances have required the sale of almost $20 billion in stocks and bonds.

The success of the anti-apartheid movement has emboldened some local jurisdictions to take similar action in other contexts. State governments have divested the securities of companies doing business in the Soviet Union and Iran. Massachusetts has moved to withdraw its pension funds from financial institutions that lend to those who sell armaments to Great Britain for use in Northern Ireland, and similar moves have been made in several other states. Divestment measures have been contemplated against Libya, Poland, and Sri Lanka, and countries that do not pay "fair" wages to industrial labor. Localities also are taking this route in the area of national security affairs. At least nine cities and counties have implemented divestment or procurement policies directed against U.S. concerns involved in the manufacture of nuclear weapons.

Where they create calculated incentives to discourage targeted areas of commercial activity, divestment and selective purchasing measures do not prohibit any private conduct outright, nor do they expressly challenge federal policy. Other local action, however, has moved into the realm of direct regulation and confrontation. In various combinations, more than 50 localities, including the city of Chicago, have banned nuclear weapons research, manufacture, transshipment, or deployment within their jurisdictions. At least two states and several localities have refused to cooperate with the Federal Emergency Management Administration, the agency charged with coordinating nuclear evacuation planning and procedures. Although rebuffed in court, a dozen governors recently challenged federal authority to conduct National Guard training exercises in Central America over their objection. Finally, to protest the Reagan administration's immigration policies, at least 30 cities have enacted "sanctuary" ordinances that prohibit municipal assistance in deportation procedures and enforcement.

THE MODEL OF INTERFERENCE

The distinguishing characteristics of these local activities are that they are intended to affect foreign policy and defense issues of truly national concern (as opposed to trade initiatives and transborder agreements) and that they have the actual potential to do so (as opposed to those distinguished by de minimis qualities). Such issues as relations with South Africa and other countries, nuclear weapons capabilities, and the readiness of military reserve forces are, first of all, of primarily national concern insofar as they do not, or should not, turn on questions of peculiarly local interest, in either formulation or consequences. That the localities have acted with the purpose of influencing the course of these controversies is evident by the very nature of the measures they have taken. Some, apparently under the direction of counsel aware of possible legal infirmities, have attempted to cloak their intentions in the guise of traditionally respected local concerns. Divestment measures, for example, often are defended on the grounds of sound portfolio management; corporations with South Africa operations, so the argument goes, make for risky securities because of political volatility in that country. Were this the case, divestment action might be justifiable. But for virtually all U.S. companies with a presence there, South Africa revenues account for a tiny percentage of total profits; these investments would not be compromised even if South Africa were to fall cleanly into the Indian Ocean. In fact, divestment legislation promises no tangible benefit to the acting community. Behind the pretext lies the real motivation of these measures: to help bring about the fall of apartheid by forcing a U.S. corporate withdrawal.

But so might Mayor Koch like to bring about the fall of the Soviet Communist party by insulting its hegemony. The last critical factor is one of impact, actual or potential. If every state had the constitutional capacity to declare itself a nuclear free zone, the federal government might find itself in a position in which it was powerless to deploy such weapons. Less obviously, if a significant number of jurisdictions decided to break all commercial ties with firms involved in the nuclear weapons industry, the Pentagon could find difficulty in placing its contracts most efficiently. State and local governments collectively command hundreds of billions of dollars in their investment portfolios (some $300–500 billion) and budgetary expenditures (estimated as high as 15–20 percent of total U.S. gross national product).

The best demonstration of how this financial weight can be thrown around once again relates to nonfederal anti–South Africa action. Since 1984 direct U.S. corporate investment in South Africa has been reduced by more than half. This withdrawal has occurred despite the general continued profitability of operations in South Africa and despite continued federal encouragement of most forms of this investment. The bottom line is that companies understandably are not willing to sacrifice a lucrative slice of the U.S. domestic market for the 1 or 2 percent of total business that South Africa provides. When, for example, Phibro-Salamon Corporation faced a choice between holding on to its small South Africa subsidiary and a $200 million contract with the city of Los Angeles, it was understandably for the latter.

These local interferences in foreign affairs may be rooted in a basic frustration with the difficulties of prompting federal action. More likely, they have resulted from a feeling among certain vocal and significant minorities that their particular foreign-policy views have no chance of winning majorities on the Hill or of receiving any welcome at the White House; with no prospects at the federal level, these activists have lowered their sights to more receptive audiences in state capitals and city halls. The strategy has proved successful. The force of concentrated and coordinated action at the nonfederal level has won the practical implementation of their policies even in the absence of federal approval.

But the dangers of allowing these activities to flourish are many. Voters in states and localities that have shown a tendency to take foreign-policy initiatives should not have more influence on these national issues than their brethren in communities that have not so acted. Yet that has been the result in the South African example, and the same could transpire in the other areas that promise to be the target of future local activism. More important is the way in which local action may lead to the wrong policies. Cities and states do not share with the federal government the advantage that comes with having thousands of representatives overseas. Nor are nonfederal entities in a position to consider the consequences of their activities in other localities and for the nation as a whole. To take one ludicrous yet instructive hypothetical, were Michigan to declare war on Canada, it would not consider necessarily the repercussions of its aggression for residents of Wisconsin. At a more plausible level, if Michigan launched a divestment and selective purchasing campaign against trade with Japan, and Japan retaliated by restricting imports from the entire United States, the interests of the regions that profit from such commerce would be swallowed without the sorts of opportunity for reasoned and negotiated policymaking that one finds in Washington. And in a case that is already a reality, local proponents of anti–South Africa legislation have shown no inclination to contemplate the significance of South Africa's strategic importance to the nation as a whole despite the

moral abhorrence justly associated with the apartheid regime.

WHERE CONGRESS HAS FAILED, THE COURTS SHOULD MOVE IN

It is well within congressional powers to put a halt to nonfederal intrusions into the realm of foreign-policy and national security matters. But there are inherent problems to this method of clipping local foreign policies before they get seriously out of hand. Congress probably would find it necessary to enact disabling legislation on each specific issue that has been subject to local action; simply invalidating all nonfederal foreign-policy measures would suffer from problems of vagueness and overbreadth. Congress apparently also has assumed a crippling tendency to approach the general question of local action as one not of process but rather of politics. Thus, during the South Africa controversy legislators have been reluctant to condemn divestment measures for fear of appearing to support the apartheid government, even though most of these local laws are plainly inconsistent with the federal stance toward South Africa. The long-term consequences of permitting cities and states to establish themselves in the foreign-policy arena have not been sufficient to overcome this fear.

The judiciary provides a better forum in which to reestablish federal primacy in the area. For the most part, judges are not subject to the pressures that plague their legislative colleagues. They would be obligated to consider the broad issues of federalism presented by local foreign policies without regard to the political merits of each case— e.g., whether continued economic ties with South Africa are desirable, or whether nuclear weapons are necessary to the national defense. Once the basic principle of exclusive federal control was reasserted through one or two test cases in the federal courts, moreover, it would apply across the board to all local measures found to interfere with U.S. foreign relations or national security.

It is only a matter of reasserting, as opposed to creating, this principle as the law. As a general proposition, the federal government has enjoyed nearly exclusive powers over foreign policy and defense since the dawn of the Republic. Such was the intent of the framers of the Constitution. Subsequent case law has been sparse, if only because federal superiority has faced so rarely significant challenge. But those instances in which the courts have ruled on the question, including several relevant Supreme Court decisions, demonstrate that local interference in foreign policy is not only ill-advised but also unconstitutional.

THE LEGAL CASE AGAINST LOCAL INTERFERENCE IN FOREIGN AFFAIRS

The abandonment of the Articles of Confederation and the call to a constitutional convention were motivated, at least, in part by the weaknesses of the new Union on the international scene. The Articles provided only for the loose cooperation of 13 otherwise independent republics; standing alone, they were highly vulnerable to encroachments both from Europe and among themselves. The Constitution sought to rectify the drawbacks of confederation by granting increased powers to the central government and by proscribing certain activities by the states in the areas of foreign relations and defense. Although the document itself did not speak broadly in terms of a foreign affairs power, its supporters defended it in such general terms. "If we are to be one nation in any respect," wrote James Madison in *Federalist 42*, "it clearly ought to be in respect to other nations." Constitutional law since has developed to present three possi-

ble objections to the sort of activities that have characterized recent state and local intrusions into foreign policy.[5]

Under the Supremacy Clause and what is known as the doctrine of preemption, nonfederal entities may not take action inconsistent with federal policy. Such conflict is apparent when compliance with both local and federal measures is impossible, as where a state court struck down a Staten Island referendum initiative that would have banned the docking of nuclear-equipped vessels despite the U.S. navy's stated intention to do so.[6] It need only be shown that the nonfederal measure is inconsistent with any federal action, from treaties and statutes on down to a federally sponsored contract. One state restriction on the enrollment of Iranian students in public universities, for instance, was invalidated in the wake of a contrary administrative regulation.[7] Combined with other conceded powers over foreign affairs, it is on this ground that Congress might disable most local intrusions in foreign affairs, on an issue-by-issue basis, by formally stating that they are inconsistent with federal policy.

But Congress has not been willing to make such statements for the same reason that it has not passed legislation proscribing local interference in foreign affairs. This problem already has reared its head in the South African example. In the fall of 1986 Congress passed the Comprehensive Anti-

[5] For more detailed analysis of local foreign-policy activities, with a focus on divestment legislation, see Peter J. Spiro, "State and Local Anti-South Africa Action as an Intrusion Upon the Federal Power in Foreign Affairs," *Virginia Law Review* 72:4 (May 1986), pp. 813–850, and K. Lewis, "Dealing with South Africa: The Constitutionality of State and Local Divestment Legislation," *Tulane Law Review*, vol. 61 (February 1987), pp. 469–517.

[6] *Fosella v. Dinkins*, 66 N.Y. 2d 603 (N.Y. Appellate Division, 1985).

[7] *Tayyari v. New Mexico State Univ.*, 495 F. Supp. 1365 (New Mexico U.S. District Court, 1980).

Apartheid Act that, while affirming the advantages of a benevolent corporate presence in South Africa, did place some constraints on bilateral commercial ties. The measure was not clearly preemptive insofar as corporations could comply both with it and with more restrictive local laws simply by cutting their South Africa ties. (The federal act did not go so far as to require continued operations there.) Nor did the wording of the legislation expressly address the question of how the local and federal measures might interact. What remained were contradictory statements on the preemption issue, with House members generally indicating an intent to let local anti–South Africa laws stand, the Senate demonstrating an intent to have them be stricken. Judicial determination of preemptive effect would be correspondingly problematic.

The second legal attack hinges on the constitutional prohibition on nonfederal obstruction of foreign and interstate commerce. Here it need only be shown that the local action in some way burdens trade or other commercial relations—even in the absence of conflicting federal policy—and that the imposition of this burden is not justified by any legitimate local interest, ordinarily characterized by health, safety, or other welfare-related concerns. Where no such interest exists, any action that tends to impede the free flow of goods and services across state and national borders must fall.

Cities and states that have pursued intrusive foreign policies cannot tender the necessary justification under this analysis. Many purport to have a moral interest in these activities, yet no court, state or federal, has ever recognized this sort of intangible as a defense to commerce clause attack. Other rationalizations are likewise infirm. In barring the deployment of nuclear weapons, for instance, several localities have made it evident that the reason they would not care to host these arms is that they are not interested in being the target of Soviet missiles. But the obvious analogy here, of course, is that we do not allow individuals to avoid the draft for fear of death.

Some have argued that divestment and selective purchasing laws come under the so-called market-participant exception to the commerce clause. Under this exception, nonfederal governments are not subjected to commerce clause restraints when they behave as would private parties in a market context—in other words, when they act as buyers and sellers and not as regulators. This defense would seem to save local divestment and procurement measures, since these laws involve activities common to all marketplace participants and not peculiar to government institutions. The exception, however, has emerged only where the acting jurisdiction stood to benefit from the challenged measure by way of economic gain. Actions motivated by foreign-policy or moral considerations result in no such benefit. The market-participant rule, moreover, has never been applied in a situation involving foreign commerce, and the Supreme Court has reserved expressly opinion on the question.

THE ZSCHERNIG DOCTRINE

The final possibility for invalidating local foreign-policy interferences would be under the rule of *Zschernig v. Miller*, which confirmed a sweeping and exclusive foreign affairs power in the federal government. In that 1968 case, the Supreme Court struck down an Oregon probate law that in practice discriminated against citizens of East Bloc nations in inheritance matters. Condemning state judicial decisions in which "foreign policy attitudes...are the real desiderata," Justice William O. Douglas held that state and local actions that have more than "some incidental or indirect effect" on foreign relations could not be tolerated. The decision essentially set an intent-plus-impact standard by which to measure the constitutionality of local foreign policies.

Zschernig was not a judicial shot out of the blue. On the contrary, it was built atop a long line of Supreme Court observations on federalism and its role in the making of foreign relations, or lack thereof. Among other such decisions stands *Holmes v. Jennison*, which in invalidating an early nineteenth-century extradition arrangement between Vermont and Canada, noted, "It was one of the main objects of the Constitution to make us, so far as regarded our foreign relations, one people, and one nation." Striking down a state law going beyond federal alien registration statutes before World War II, *Hines v. Davidowitz* declared "the interest of the cities, counties and states...imperatively requires that federal power in the field affecting foreign relations be left entirely free from local interference." Perhaps most eloquent was Justice Sutherland in a 1937 holding that confirmed the validity of the Litvinov Assignment in the face of contrary state property law. "In respect of all international negotiations and compacts, and in respect of our foreign relations generally, state lines disappear. As to such purposes, the State of New York does not exist."

What distinguishes the *Zschernig* ruling is that, as with the commerce clause analysis, local measures may be found infirm even in the absence of conflict with federal policy. In its breadth, however, *Zschernig* expands the proscription of local interference in foreign policy to cover those activities that do not admit to economic consequence. The doctrine presents, moreover, a more constitutionally honest argument than does the commerce clause in this context. In most instances, after all, the cities and states are using economic measures only as a means to foreign-policy ends, and it is the ends themselves, not the mechanisms by which they are achieved, that are constitutionally offensive. Finally, *Zschernig* logically

might be extended to combat local activities in the realm of defense matters, in which national unity of action would seem even more imperative than in foreign-policy matters.

It is true, as proponents of local foreign affairs activity are quick to point out, that *Zschernig* has lain largely dormant, at least at the level of the Supreme Court since it was handed down in 1968. The simple explanation is that there has been little opportunity to put the rule to use in the absence, until recently, of significant local interference in foreign affairs. Moreover, several state court cases have reaffirmed its principles. A 1969 California Supreme Court ruling invalidated a state "Buy America" law that restricted official purchases from foreign suppliers on such grounds.[8] And in a 1977 decision directly apropos of the divestment movement, the New York Court of Appeals overturned a municipal agency's ban on employment advertising for South Africa–based companies insofar as it "might have been considered offensive by the Republic of South Africa and...been an embarrassment to those charged with the conduct of our Nation's foreign policy."[9]

Although upholding the theory of federal exclusivity in foreign relations, two more recent cases have upheld actions typical of emerging local foreign policies on the grounds that they did not cross the impact threshold of "indirect or incidental." The Supreme Court of Massachusetts refused to strike down a Cambridge ordinance banning the storage, testing, and disposal of chemical warfare agents within its limits on the basis that by itself the measure was unlikely to have a signif-

---

[8] *Bethlehem Steel Corp. v. Board of Commissioners*, 276 Cal. App. 2d 221 (California Supreme Court, 1969).

[9] *New York Times Co. v. City of New York Commission on Human Rights*, 41 N.Y. 2d 345 (N.Y. Court of Appeals, 1977).

icant effect on federal defense programs.[10] A Maryland state trial court, meanwhile, blessed Baltimore's divestment ordinance after concluding that the divestment movement as a whole has not contributed directly to the growing corporate withdrawal from South Africa.[11] The latter decision may have resulted from the failure of the party challenging the law (the board of the pension fund required to divest) to present adequate evidence of divestment's effect on U.S. ties with South Africa. The analysis pursued by the Massachusetts court is less defensible: taken in isolation, the foreign-policy activities of any one jurisdiction almost always will appear insubstantial. It is, rather, the collective weight of such activities that poses the threat to properly unfettered foreign relations decision making. In any event, these two cases hardly close the book on the question. Only in the last few months has the debate begun in earnest.

THE NEED FOR ACTION

The national interest demands that local interference in foreign and defense policy be curtailed before the federal government finds itself hamstrung by hundreds of would-be secretaries of state touting their own parochial agendas. Liberals who might tend to support much of the recent wave of local measures on substantive grounds should remember that the tables could turn should they gain power at the federal level. Conservatives who might defend these activities as valid assertions of states rights should remember that foreign and domestic affairs are fundamentally different under the lens of federalism. The goal of a

coherent and unified foreign policy is one that should be shared by all.

The federal government necessarily must take the lead in efforts to contain local action because its institutional prerogatives are those challenged. In practical terms, only the White House and the executive departments can command the unity of design that such efforts would demand. An educational, nonconfrontational approach should characterize the first steps in what would amount to a lobbying campaign by the federal government on its state and local counterparts. The State Department could be charged with monitoring the nonfederal activities. Where significant local measures face possible enactment, it might dispatch representatives to explain in nonpolitical terms the deeper repercussions of such activities. Mayors, governors, and other nonfederal officials should be urged privately to exercise restraint and to act responsibly where they confront foreign-policy matters in their public capacities. The federal government can impress with greater intensity upon both the electorate and local lawmakers that certain decisions may be made only on a national basis and that only through federal channels should active dissent be expressed. In the meantime, of course, local authorities should be encouraged in those activities that do not constitute interferences—the trade initiatives and transborder agreements that are entirely consistent with the federal direction of foreign policy.

Granted, this sort of venture probably would fail in stopping continued local action in the area. Local leaders now find foreign-policy issues useful in distracting attention from problems in their own backyards. Such issues also have begun to figure prominently in local election contests, in which special interest groups successfully air sometimes extreme positions unopposed by competing constituencies. Foreign policy is fast becoming as ordinary an element in local politics as sewers and schools.

---

[10] *Arthur D. Little v. Commissioner of Health and Hospitals of Cambridge*, 395 Mass. 535 (Supreme Judicial Court of Massachussets, 1985).

[11] *Board of Trustees of the Employees' Retirement System of Baltimore v. Mayor and City Council of Baltimore*, no. 86365065, Circuit Court of Baltimore City (unpublished, 1987).

And so the case would have to be put before the courts. The judiciary, of course, cannot decide controversies with which it is not presented. Private parties have proved unwilling to challenge local foreign-policy action even where it results in commercial injury; as has been the case with Congress, corporations fear identification with unpopular positions on the underlying substantive issues. While privately deploring divestment legislation, for instance, they have concluded that an attack on these laws would leave them looking pro-apartheid, which in turn would create larger dollar losses than the restrictions themselves.

Given such private sector reluctance, federal policymakers must proceed on their own. The Reagan administration is well positioned to launch the legal campaign against local foreign policies. At this late point in its tenure, it need not be overly concerned with political appearances. It could single out less controversial measures, such as Boston's divestment of companies selling arms to Great Britain, as test cases. The government need pursue only one or two such attacks in each of the major areas of local interference, preferably until a victory in the Supreme Court. Once one law fell, the rest would follow, and those cities and states that have acted will come to understand that they have acted illegitimately, or at least that they will not succeed in further efforts. However much the cities and states might protest, foreign relations is one of those spheres in which the majority view must govern. Were dissenting elements able to act on their platforms in every instance, serious fragmentation would fast undermine the national coherence critical to U.S. dealings with other nations. Foreign policy must be made in Washington and not in the citizens' backyards.

QUESTIONS FOR DISCUSSION

1. What does the Constitution say about the power of the federal government vis-à-vis the states in the conduct of foreign policy?
2. What kinds of foreign policy issues are states and localities likely to get involved in?
3. Have the states and localities been effective in any foreign policy matters? If so, why? If not, why not?
4. What should the federal government do in response to state and local activism in foreign policy matters?
5. What effect would the strengthening of the role of state and local governments in the conduct of foreign policy have on U.S. foreign policy?

SUGGESTED READINGS

Brock, David. "Municipal Hue and Cry Makes Foreign Policy Waves." *Insight* (*Washington Times*), 3 (Apr. 6, 1987), pp. 18–20.

Cox, Hank. "Down and Out in the People's Republic of Takoma Park." *Regardie's*, 8 (Sept. 1987), pp. 58–63, 180, 182, 184, 186, 188, 190.

Fish, Peter A. "The Constitution and the Training of National Guardsmen: Can State Governors Prevent Uncle Sam from Sending the Guard to Central America?" *Journal of International Law*, 4 (Winter 1988), pp. 597–637.

"Foreign Policy in Federal States." *International Journal*, 41 (Summer 1986), entire issue.

Foster, Nancy. "Citizens Jam Nuclear Radio Network." *Bulletin of the Atomic Scientists*, 44 (Nov. 1988), pp. 21–26.

Lewis, Kevin P. "Dealing with South Africa: The Constitutionality of State and Local Divestment Legislation." *Tulane Law Review*, 61 (Feb. 1987), pp. 469–517.

Spiro, Peter J. "State and Local Anti-South Africa Action As an Intrusion upon the Federal Power in Foreign Affairs." 72 *Virginia Law Review*, 813–50 (1986).

PART FOUR

The Consequences of Foreign Policy

In Part IV we turn to six policy issues confronting the United States. Three deal with America's superpower status and hinge on relations with the Soviet Union. Those debates involve the utility of the policy of containment, the effectiveness of arms control in serving U.S. security interest, and the general question of U.S. military presence in Western Europe: To what extent should the United States devolve its frontline defense role to its NATO allies? The fourth and fifth debates deal with more general policy issues. The fourth looks at free trade and inquires about its benefits. Does the United States gain or lose? This question may be especially relevant given the 1988 agreement with Canada that in ten years will make North America above the Rio Grande a free trade, duty-free area. The fifth debate looks at a particularly sensitive area of foreign policy—relations with nondemocratic, dictatorial regimes, many of which are strategically located. Should the United States take active measures against all dictatorships? The final debate considers whether the United States is in such relative decline that it must reign in excessive defense spending and devote more resources to domestic economic and technological development.

These six policy issues are set in the institutional and political context examined in Parts I, II, and III. Does Madison's admonition to Jefferson that foreign relations appears to be that aspect of government "most susceptible to abuse" appear relevant? Is there an increasing danger of a "loss of liberty at home"? Would free trade, for example, threaten the uniqueness of the United States? Will it sap American jobs? And what about dictators abroad? Has *national security* assumed such overriding and immediate importance that the ideas of democracy occasionally must take second place to strategic considerations?

U.S. relations with the Soviet Union are the centerpiece of superpower status. In seeking to contain communist expansion, have we surrendered too much liberty and individual freedom? John Locke maintained that there could be no liberty at home unless the nation was defended from its enemies abroad. Has our forty-year policy of containment worked effectively? Have we indeed secured the liberty we cherish? Has the price been too high?

Recall Harold Lasswell's observation about the "garrison state"—a product of international tension and technological development. Does the Intermediate-range Nuclear Forces Treaty suggest that East and West are learning to live with these problems? Does it offer a pragmatic accommodation? Or does it threaten the very essence of American security?

Finally, students should consider President Dwight D. Eisenhower's admonition in this context. What he referred to as the "military-industrial complex" is sustained by America's global responsibilities. The relation is recognized. One can scarcely be reduced or increased without affecting the other. Is the economic decline of the United States inevitable because of high defense expenditures?

SHOULD CONTAINMENT CONTINUE TO BE U.S. POLICY TOWARD THE SOVIET UNION?

When the wartime alliance between the United States and the Soviet Union fell apart after Germany's defeat, the United States initiated a policy to contain Soviet expansion. That policy, which came to be known as *containment*, was publicly described by the diplomat George F. Kennan in a famous 1947 *Foreign Affairs* article, "The Sources of Soviet Conduct."[1] The article did not initiate a new policy toward the U.S.S.R.; it restated what was existing American policy at that time and reflected the long-held views of the leading figures in the Foreign Service that future U.S.-Soviet cooperation was unlikely.[2] Kennan argued that for historical and ideological reasons the Soviet Union would seek to expand its political control beyond its postwar boundaries. He saw Soviet expansionism as a threat to the United States and urged that America respond with a policy of "long-term, patient but firm and vigilant containment." Kennan recommended "the adroit and vigilant application of counter-force at a series of constantly shifting geographical and political points, corresponding to the shifts and maneuvers of Soviet policy." While political observers as disparate as columnist Walter Lippmann, Sen. Robert Taft, and Gen. Lucius Clay disputed Kennan's assessment,[3] it fell on receptive ears in Washington and became the hallmark of American foreign policy.

---

[1] "X" [George F. Kennan], "The Sources of Soviet Conduct," *Foreign Affairs*, 25 (July 1947), pp. 566–82.
[2] See especially Daniel Yergin, *Shattered Peace: The Origins of the Cold War and the National Security State* (New York: Penguin, 1977), pp. 168–71.
[3] Walter Lippmann and Lucius Clay (who was U.S. military governor of Germany after World War II) believed the Soviets were militarily and economically incapable of attacking the West. Taft concurred in that assessment and feared that a subsequent U.S. military buildup would lead inevitably to a stronger central government—which he opposed. See Walter Lippmann, "A Year of Peacemaking," *Atlantic Monthly*, 178 (Dec. 1946), pp. 36–38; Jean Edward Smith, "General Clay and the Russians," *Virginia Quarterly Review*, 64 (Winter 1988), pp. 20–36.

Supporters of containment can point with some justification to its success; the map of Europe has not changed since 1948. On the other hand, containment's initial critics, such as Lippmann and Clay, could argue that the policy was a self-fulfilling prophecy: since the U.S.S.R. was incapable of military expansion in Europe in the immediate postwar period, a policy based on preventing expansion was bound to succeed. More to the point, it could be argued that in adopting a policy aimed at the Soviet Union, whatever possibility there was in 1947 for cooperation with the U.S.S.R. was jettisoned. The Marshall Plan, the Berlin Blockade, and the creation of the North Atlantic Treaty Organization (NATO) were the inevitable results. It is also important to recognize that containment, as initially conceived, was oriented toward the situation in Europe. Its applicability to situations elsewhere—the Middle East, Central America, Africa, and Asia—is much more problematic, and the results to date far less satisfactory.

In the debate that follows, Francis P. Sempa, who is Assistant District Attorney of Lackawanna County, Pennsylvania, argues for the continued vitality of the containment thesis. Sempa traces the doctrine to the geopolitical theories of Sir Halford J. Mackinder, the great British geographer at the turn of the century, who argued that the Eurasian heartland was the "pivot area of world politics."[4] As Sempa demonstrates, Mackinder's argument was updated and applied to America's postwar situation by scholars such as James Burnham,[5] Hans Morgenthau,[6] and Nicholas Spykman.[7] Sempa maintains that the geopolitical imperatives which impelled the United States to seek an advantageous balance of power in postwar Europe remain as true today as they were in Mackinder's (or Kennan's) time.

The contrasting view is presented by Earl C. Ravenal of Georgetown University and the Cato Institute. Ravenal argues that acceptance of the containment thesis has saddled the United States with "continuing high costs associated with the requisite military preparations and the occasional egregious costs of heightened crises and regional wars." But even worse, he suggests, has been "the risk, under certain circumstances, of being plunged into nuclear war." Ravenal cautions against accepting the containment doctrine on faith alone: "The question of the perpetuation of containment will not be determined by its abstract desirability, or even by its 'necessity,' but rather by whether containment is viable strategically and consonant with domestic values."

In particular, Ravenal takes issue with the idea that containment can be selectively applied. If the threat of communism is universal, then containment must be universal. He maintains that those who advocate selectivity

---

[4] Halford Mackinder, *Democratic Ideals and Reality* (New York: W. W. Norton, 1962). Originally London: Constable and Co., 1919.

[5] James Burnham, *The Struggle for the World* (New York: John Day, 1947).

[6] Hans Morgenthau, *Politics among Nations* (New York: Alfred A. Knopf, 1949).

[7] Nicholas Spykman, *America's Strategy in World Politics* (New York: Harcourt, Brace, and Co., 1942).

seek to escape from the burdens containment implies. As an alternative, Ravenal suggests a policy of strategic disengagement and nonintervention. In such a program the United States would seek to avoid military confrontation and entangling alliances. It would rely upon strategic deterrence to protect American interests, which would be much more narrowly defined.

This debate is not about the nuts and bolts of force structure or the nitty-gritty of reciprocal defense postures. It addresses the fundamental theoretical questions and concepts that underline U.S. foreign policy in the contemporary context.

DO ARMS CONTROL AGREEMENTS SERVE U.S. SECURITY INTERESTS?

Arms control seeks to place restraints on the numbers and possible uses of particular weapons systems. Disarmament, by contrast, seeks to eliminate all weaponry. Nuclear disarmament aims at the elimination of nuclear weapons. Since World War II and the explosion of nuclear devices at Hiroshima and Nagasaki, American military strategy has emphasized the destructive effect of nuclear weapons. They provide the cornerstone of U.S. defense policy and the principal deterrent to global war. But nuclear weapons are a mixed blessing. While their very destructiveness helps ensure that they will not be used, the dangers of their possible employment have led to extensive efforts to control their use and reduce their numbers. These efforts have been sporadic, uneven, and often greeted with considerable skepticism. The results are uncertain. Many question not only the efficacy of arms control, but whether (even if successful) it enhances American national security. Others believe it is too little and too late. Still others point to arms control as the most reliable path to curtail defense expenditures, avoid nuclear accidents, and reduce the risk of nuclear war.

The history of nuclear arms control and disarmament divides into three periods. During the first, from 1946 to 1957, proposals for nuclear disarmament dominated the negotiating agenda. These were put forward during a period of intense cold war hostility and extreme asymmetry in nuclear force levels. They were designed primarily for their propaganda effect rather than to reach substantive agreement. In 1946, the United States proposed to place all aspects of nuclear development under the control of the U.N. General Assembly. Known as the Baruch Plan after the U.S. negotiator Bernard Baruch, the proposal included a promise that once the General Assembly's control of nuclear development was in place and functioning, the United States would destroy its atomic arsenal, provided all other states pledged not to pursue atomic weapons. The Soviet Union rejected the Baruch Plan and proposed that the United States disarm first and that an international organization then be established, subject to a system of great power vetoes. The differences between the two proposals could not be bridged, and it is doubtful that the Congress would have been willing to implement the Baruch Plan in any case, as it called for the sharing of U.S. atomic secrets. In 1953, the Eisenhower administration proposed an Atoms for Peace Plan that called for international cooperation in the peaceful uses of atomic energy. This proposal led to the creation of the International Atomic Energy Agency but had no impact on nuclear weapons. In 1957, Eisenhower offered the Soviet Union the Open Skies Proposal, which aimed to reduce the danger of surprise attack by permitting aerial surveillance of one another's territory. The Soviet Union rejected the plan, believing it a device to legitimize U.S. espionage.

The second phase of nuclear diplomacy began in 1958 with attempts to negotiate an East-West agreement to prevent surprise attacks. This phase marked the transition from disarmament to arms control and led to the Limited Test Ban Treaty in 1963, the Nuclear Nonproliferation Treaty in 1968, and the Anti-Ballistic Missile (ABM) Treaty and the Strategic Arms Limitation Treaty (SALT I) in 1972. The Limited Test Ban Treaty prohibits nuclear weapons tests or any other nuclear explosions in the atmosphere, in outer space, and under water. The Nuclear Nonproliferation Treaty seeks to limit nuclear weapons of the superpowers as well as to prevent the number of nuclear weapons states from increasing. The United States and the Soviet Union have joined with many other countries in ratifying the test ban and nonproliferation treaties.

The SALT agreements, however, involve only the United States and the Soviet Union. SALT I, a five-year agreement that entered into force in 1972, provides for a mutual limitation on intercontinental ballistic missiles and submarine-launched ballistic missiles that can reach targets several thousand miles away. SALT II, which was never accepted by the U.S. Senate but whose terms were adhered to informally by the Soviet Union and by the Carter administration and for several years by the Reagan administration, was an extension and expansion of SALT I.

The second phase of nuclear diplomacy reflected a recognition that both sides could benefit by particular arms control measures and that negotiations were not necessarily a "zero-sum game" in which the winnings of one side came at the expense of the other.

Thomas Schelling, a leading theorist of arms control, suggests that the third and present phase of nuclear diplomacy commenced in 1973. Unlike the second phase, in which the benefits were mutual, the third phase has been characterized by the lack of "any coherent theory of what arms control is supposed to accomplish." According to Schelling, rather than restraining the arms race, arms control has become the principal tactic by which it is being fought. In particular, Schelling criticizes the fixation on numbers and quantitative measures of weapons systems rather than the qualitative nature of those systems and whether they have a stabilizing or destabilizing effect.[8]

A good example of the fixation with numbers is the negotiations over SALT II. As it finally emerged, SALT II was a complicated document setting

---

[8] Thomas C. Schelling, "What Went Wrong with Arms Control?" *Foreign Affairs,* 64, no. 2 (Winter 1985–86), pp. 219–33.

intricate numerical ceilings on nuclear forces. The Reagan administration attacked the treaty for allegedly giving the Soviets a military advantage, and it was never submitted to the Senate for approval.

On the other hand, the 1988 Intermediate-range Nuclear Forces (INF) Treaty between the United States and the Soviet Union focuses on weapons systems. Under the terms of the treaty, the Soviet Union will eliminate its SS-20 and other intermediate-range missiles in Europe and the United States will remove its Pershing II intermediate-range missiles and ground-launched cruise missiles. Such missiles have a capability of hitting targets between 1000 and 5000 kilometers. An important feature of the agreement is the extent of on-site verification permitted to both sides. Does the INF Treaty suggest that a fourth phase of the nuclear debate has begun? Does it indicate that both the United States and the Soviet Union recognize once again that mutual advantages can accrue from arms reduction? The current proposals of the Soviet Union and President Bush for slashing forces in Europe suggest that this might be the case.

The debate that follows focuses on the strategic implications of arms control. Do agreements with the Soviet Union serve America's long-term security interests? The *Defense Monitor*, a publication of the Washington-based Center for Defense Information, traces the recent history of arms control agreements and argues that U.S. policy under President Reagan has undercut them. The *Defense Monitor* points to the accelerated military buildup of the Reagan years, the unilateral U.S. decision in 1986 to exceed the voluntary limits of SALT II, and the reinterpretation of the ABM Treaty to facilitate development of the Strategic Defense Initiative ("Star Wars") as examples of American actions that undermine arms control. The *Defense Monitor* contends that such actions by the United States will make future arms control agreements more difficult to negotiate and that they will limit American ability to monitor the size and composition of Soviet nuclear forces. One of the most useful aspects of the *Defense Monitor* article is the recapitulation of existing nuclear agreements and the discussion of how they have been affected by recent developments. The *Defense Monitor* maintains that arms control agreements make nuclear war less likely; that the absence of arms limitation agreements reduces the opportunity for the United States to monitor the size and composition of Soviet nuclear forces; that arms control agreements reduce the burden of military spending; and that effective compliance facilitates the ability of the United States and the Soviet Union to resolve their differences in other areas.

Syndicated columnist Charles Krauthammer challenges each of these assertions. He argues that while arms control may give the illusion of reducing the threat of war, "the real potential cause of war is decidedly non-nuclear: it is the conflict of interests and ideology that plays itself out in geopolitical competition and regional conflicts around the world."

Krauthammer disputes the thesis that arms control saves money. Instead, he argues that it actually requires larger expenditures because existing nuclear arsenals have to be redesigned and reconfigured. Even more important, as the military burden shifts from nuclear to conventional weaponry, the costs rise enormously. "Conventional deterrence may or may not be as effective as nuclear deterrence in preventing war," he concludes, "but one thing is certain: it is far more expensive."

Krauthammer questions whether arms control prevents accidents. Above all, he doubts that it reduces the risk of nuclear war. To the contrary, he believes stability derives from nuclear redundancy. The more nuclear weapons a country possesses and the more varied the weapons systems, the less likely an opponent will be to attempt a preemptory attack. In Krauthammer's words, "Large numbers [of nuclear weapons] promote stability because they provide each side with a cushion in case it miscalculates the size of the other side's threat." He believes that the principal danger of nuclear war arises not from the United States or the Soviet Union, but from "tiny arsenals in the hands of unstable powers."

SHOULD THE UNITED STATES DEVOLVE ITS FRONTLINE DEFENSIVE ROLE IN EUROPE TO ITS NATO ALLIES?

U.S. forces have been deployed in Western Europe continuously since World War II. From 1945 to 1948, they garrisoned the quadripartite occupation of Germany, along with Britain, France, and the Soviet Union. Since the Berlin Blockade of 1948, they have been literally in the front line of Western Europe's defense against communist aggression. In 1948, and for at least a decade thereafter, Europe struggled to recover from the most devastating war since the sixteenth century. Its economy was in shambles, unemployment was rampant, and food and housing were in short supply. In a very real sense Western Europe was incapable of defending itself, and America stepped into the void.

The North Atlantic Treaty Organization (NATO), founded in 1949, was conceived primarily as a military alliance among the democracies of Western Europe, the United States, and Canada to deter Soviet aggression. But the situation today differs fundamentally from the situation forty years ago. The nations of Western Europe, including a revived and prosperous West Germany, have recovered completely from World War II. Their affluence rivals and sometimes surpasses that of the United States. Their scientific, technical, and educational achievements often exceed those of the United States. But their defense commitment—in terms of frontline military forces—lags far behind. Is it appropriate for the United States to continue to bear the principal burden in the defense of Western Europe? Should the Europeans do more? Does it make sense for young men and women from Des Moines to be deployed in defense of Darmstadt? From the larger perspective, is the U.S. frontline defense of Western Europe merely one of the ancillary responsibilities of superpower status? More pointedly, can it be argued that American troops on the Elbe and the Danube are not there simply to defend Germany but to defend the United States? That the defense of Boston and Baltimore is best conducted four thousand miles to the east? Alternatively, is NATO unduly occupied with the Soviet threat? How can unity be advanced and the European pillar of NATO strengthened? Are NATO's capabilities matched to its missions? Is corrective action required? As NATO approached its fortieth anniversary, David P. Calleo of the Johns Hopkins School of Advanced International Studies observed, "The real issue is not whether NATO should change but how."

One of the most persistent questions pertains to the role of the United States, which currently maintains 300,000 troops in Europe and spends about $150 billion annually—or 45 percent of the U.S. defense budget—to maintain them there. Can the American contribution be reduced? Are the nations of Western Europe doing their share? Should the United States transfer (or devolve) greater responsibility to its allies?

A substantial shift of relative resources from the United States to Europe has occurred since 1949. But at the same time, it is generally conceded that the U.S. interest in Western Europe's independence and prosperity remains as great as ever. The idea that the United States is selflessly defending the territory of others is untenable. Nevertheless, a legitimate question arises as to how the alliance can equalize the burdens of defense. This discussion, frequently referred to as *burden sharing*, takes various forms. Data relating to relative defense contributions among the NATO countries are easy to come by.[9] The interpretation of that data is more difficult, however. Depending on how the statistics are juggled, the United States is doing more than twice as much, about the same as, or somewhat less than its European allies.

It is true that the United States paid about 69 percent of alliance defense costs in 1986. What is often overlooked is that the nations of Western Europe provide 53 percent of NATO's tanks, 54 percent of combat aircraft, 83 percent of combat naval ships, 58 percent of active duty military personnel, and 80 percent of NATO's reserve strength.

The most serious distortion comes from measuring those efforts mainly as the percentage of gross national product (GNP) spent on defense. Compared with America's 6.5 percent, the large NATO allies average 3.7 percent. But the American figure is deceptively high, for it includes expenditures in the Pacific, Korea, for strategic nuclear forces, and for the larger U.S. military infrastructure. In addition, the European figures tend to be understated because of much lower manpower costs. Each NATO nation (except Great Britain and Canada) employs military conscription, and draftees are paid far less than volunteer members of the U.S. armed forces. Belgian recruits, for ex-

---

[9] See, for example, the annual issues of *Military Balance,* published by the International Institute for Strategic Studies in London.

ample, receive the equivalent of $4 a day; the figure in the West German Bundeswehr is comparable.

In the debate that follows, Calleo argues that the devolution of some U.S. responsibilities would strengthen the NATO alliance and restore its deterrent credibility. Calleo is less concerned with burden sharing than with what he perceives as the erosion of the American nuclear guarantee. He recommends an expanded European nuclear capacity as a means of replacing "a devalued American promise to sacrifice itself for Western Europe." Twenty years of deterioration in NATO, says Calleo, ought to be sufficient to prompt a new direction for American policy. He believes that mutually reinforcing U.S. and European nuclear deterrents will "firmly restore the balance of terror" and that the added risk of nuclear war will be negligible.

Colin S. Gray, president of the National Institute for Public Policy in Fairfax, Virginia, disputes Calleo's findings. Gray argues that while the arguments for devolution "are not without merit, they are still fatally flawed." He maintains that NATO's present structure is more or less adequate and that it is in America's national interest to retain its leadership role in the alliance. "It is a geopolitical fallacy to believe that the United States can enhance its security either by washing its hands of its current Eurasian security responsibilities, or by altering dramatically the military terms of many of those responsibilities," he contends.

Gray and Calleo share a fear of a denuclearized Europe. Gray would continue to rely on the American deterrent, Calleo on a joint European nuclear effort. Both agree that disengagement would be contrary to America's national interest.

IS FREE TRADE GOOD FOR THE UNITED STATES?

Since the election of Franklin D. Roosevelt in 1932, the United States has been the world's most vigorous supporter of free trade and a staunch opponent of protectionist trade barriers. But with the U.S. trade deficit at $170 billion in 1987 and $137 billion in 1988, calls for protectionist legislation have increased dramatically. These calls have been fueled by the shrinking U.S. manufacturing sector, hard-core unemployment in industries hit the hardest by foreign imports, and a growing American tendency to spend more rapidly than America produces, thus exacerbating the trade deficit. Charges that U.S. jobs are being exported to foreign countries, that research and development are suffering, that the U.S. industrial infrastructure is threatened, and that the United States will become a permanent debtor nation have forced the United States to take a hard look at its traditional support of free trade.

Advocates of free trade point to Britain's tariff reductions in the early nineteenth century, culminating with the repeal of the Corn Laws (laws that severely restricted imports of grain in order to support Britain's farmers), which ushered in a century of unparalleled economic growth. Those who supported the Corn Laws argued that British wages would fall if trade was not restricted; in fact, wages rose rapidly with more open trade. As a consequence, Britain became the engine of economic growth for the world in the nineteenth century.

In a similar manner, advocates of free trade point to the negative impact of restrictive tariff policies in the early 1930s. They suggest that the length and severity of the Great Depression was directly related to the unprecedented tariffs imposed by the United States in the Smoot-Hawley Act of 1930 and to similar actions taken by other countries in retaliation.

Free-trade advocates find more recent support for their theories in the newly independent countries of the Third World that pursued autarchic economic policies and sought to restrict trade. Most evidence indicates that their efforts to be economically independent stunted economic growth. By contrast, those less-developed areas that pursued more open economic policies, notably Hong Kong, Singapore, and Taiwan, have experienced remarkable economic growth. For example, in the twenty years between 1960 and 1980, per capita income in the Philippines (restrictive trade policies) increased fourfold; per capita income in Taiwan (nonrestrictive trade policies) increased sixteenfold.

The advocates of protection rest their perhaps equally formidable case mainly on two premises. The first suggests that high-wage countries like the United States cannot compete with countries where wages are low. If all countries have more-or-less equal access to world markets for capital and technology, those countries with low wage scales will always underprice the products from high-wage countries.

The second major argument of those who would protect U.S. industry is the *unlevel playing field*. According to this view, the world is dominated by nationalist (protectionist) economic policies. The competitive, open environment postulated by free-trade advocates simply does not exist. While the United States plays by the rules of the free market, foreign governments support particular industries with subsidies, tariffs, and other forms of trade protection. The result is an unlevel playing field in which U.S. producers face an uphill battle.

In the debate that follows, Steven E. Daskal, a defense analyst based in northern Virginia, argues that free trade contributes directly to global (and American) prosperity. He suggests that the true price of protectionism is the subsidization of inefficient industry. The consumer "gets less and pays more." In Daskal's opinion, "Free trade allows consumers around the world to buy more for less, which in turn creates more revenue for businesses." Free trade means that governments have less need to provide tax-supported benefits, "thus relieving the need to continue increasing taxes, inflation, or deficits."

The counterargument is presented by John M. Culbertson, an economics professor at the University of Wisconsin at Madison. Writing in the *Harvard Business Review,* Culbertson maintains that "our blind allegiance to free trade threatens our national standard of living and our economic future." He urges that the United States immediately impose import quotas on certain goods in order to retain market share for American producers and that provisional targets be set specifying how much of the U.S. market would be available to foreign-made products. Failure to do so, he contends, will erode U.S. industry to the point that a lower standard of living will become inevitable.

SHOULD THE UNITED STATES TAKE ACTIVE MEASURES AGAINST ALL DICTATORSHIPS?

Democracies are still in the minority among the nations of the world. In its political sense, modern democracy is a system that allows for free elections; majority rule; and freedom of speech, press, and assembly. Dictatorships lack these features. Some dictatorships are characterized as authoritarian in which the leaders are for the most part content in ruling, thus limiting the government's involvement in the day-to-day life of citizens. Other dictatorships are often described as totalitarian in which a regimentation of the citizenry is far more extensive. Both authoritarian and totalitarian regimes may be brutal in dealing with opposition parties and the population they are supposed to serve although they differ in the goals they wish to achieve.

As a democracy, the United States must deal with a world in which many countries do not share its political values. In the period since World War II, it has supported some dictatorships and opposed others. How should the United States deal with dictatorships?

In the debate that follows, Professor Roy Lechtreck, a political scientist at the University of Montevallo in Montevallo, Alabama, argues that the United States maintains a double standard toward foreign dictators. Right-wing *authoritarian* regimes such as Chile are embraced; left-wing *totalitarian* regimes such as Cuba are castigated. He suggests that American policy reflects U.S. business interests (which often receive favorable treatment from rightist dictators). Lechtreck points out that *multinational corporations* sometimes shamefully exploit the labor force and natural resources of less-developed countries and that the bargain U.S. business makes with the dictators in charge (who may be skimming profits) is a bad one. He rejects the thesis that communist regimes pose a much greater danger to peace than right-wing dictatorships; the facts, he contends, simply do not support that premise. Perhaps the most telling aspect of Professor Lechtreck's argument is his contention that the double standard toward dictators is counterproductive. "Our support of authoritarian dictators inevitably leads the oppressed [within that country] to seek the support of totalitarian dictators, and, if the oppressed win their freedom, they naturally join the totalitarian bloc." He urges that the United States not only cut off aid and support to foreign dictatorships (he puts the grain sale to Russia in this category), but that it invoke stern economic measures to bring down or modify these regimes.

Ted Galen Carpenter of the Cato Institute agrees with Lechtreck that it makes little sense for the United States to favor right-wing dictators while opposing those of the Left. He sees this inconsistency as an unfortunate relic of the cold war mentality that has driven U.S. foreign policy since the Truman Doctrine in 1947. But he disputes Lechtreck's solution. While Lechtreck would engage U.S. economic muscle to modify dictatorial regimes, Carpenter argues for a policy of "benign detachment." He believes that U.S. ideological hostility toward left-wing regimes has involved the United States needlessly in "futile or mutually destructive confrontations" and that the "cosy relationship" with right-wing dictatorships "has undermined America's credibility as a spokesman for democracy, caused Third World peoples to equate both capitalism and democracy with U.S. hegemony, and established a milieu for rabidly anti-American revolutions." Carpenter rejects categorically the right of the United States to intervene in the internal affairs of other countries, even in the name of democracy. Such "meddlesome paternalism" reflects the "siege mentality" that besets U.S. policy when dealing with less-developed countries, he believes.

Carpenter's prescription of benign detachment from *all* Third World dictatorships, regardless of their ideological orientation, provides an objectivity to American foreign policy that he believes in the long run will aid democracy. "The United States has no holy writ to destabilize the governments of Cuba or Nicaragua because it finds them repugnant, nor to preserve autocratic systems in South Korea or Zaire because it considers them congenial."

IS THE UNITED STATES IN RELATIVE DECLINE?

The economic realities upon which a successful foreign policy must be based are sometimes overlooked, but they have recently come to the forefront in a debate over America's superpower status. The United States emerged from World War II as the dominant world power. Its manufacturing output approached half of the world's total production, and American technology and economic leadership set the pace for postwar recovery. In that context, the United States was the unquestioned leader of the noncommunist world, and the defense burdens it undertook appeared to be a natural corollary.

But in the more than four decades since the war, U.S. military commitments have remained more or less constant, while the U.S. share of world manufactured output and global gross national product (GNP) has declined significantly. In absolute terms, America has never been wealthier. Living standards and per capita income have never been higher; unemployment has never been lower. But since the beginning of rearmament activities in 1948, the United States has devoted huge sums to the military in an effort to maintain its position of leadership. While U.S. allies in Europe have also made considerable contributions, they have not made the financial investment in defense that the United States has made. In Asia, Japan's contribution to its own defense has been minimal. Some analysts believe that the U.S. relative economic decline is attributed in part to the large expenditures the United States makes to defense.

One of the leading critics of American failure to reorient economic priorities is Professor Paul Kennedy of Yale University. The author of a major bestseller, *The Rise and Fall of the Great Powers* (1987), Kennedy argues that the United States, like Spain in the seventeenth century, France in the eighteenth, and Britain more recently, is the victim of *imperial overstretch*. Its global commitments have outdistanced its domestic capacity.

> A small investment in armaments may leave a globally overstretched power like the United States feeling vulnerable everywhere, but a very heavy investment in them, while bringing greater security in the short term, may so erode the commercial competitiveness of the American economy that the nation will be less secure in the long term.

A counterargument is presented by Professor Joseph S. Nye, Jr., director of the Center for Science and International Affairs at Harvard University. Nye suggests that what appears to be a relative American decline in the 1980s is largely attributable to using the extraordinary postwar period of the 1950s as the base from which to measure American economic power. The 1950s were an anomaly, and American productiveness was overstated because of the relative absence of economic activity elsewhere.

Nye acknowledges that profound changes have occurred since World War II. But he suggests that these changes—such as the diffusion of economic growth—have resulted from U.S. policy and are not contrary to America's long-term goals. Professor Nye stresses that what appears to be a relative change in the U.S. position is in reality a reflection of the increased complexity and interdependence of the international system. It is simply less feasible today for *any* country to exercise a decisive influence over the whole system.

Nye disputes the thesis that defense expenditures adversely affect rates of economic growth: "The myriad effects of defense spending are very complex, and the net effect is difficult to sort out." He points to South Korea and China, both of which spend much more on the military than Japan, but both of which have significantly higher rates of economic growth than Japan. He also points out that even after the military buildup of the Reagan years, the United States is spending a smaller proportion of GNP on defense than it did in the 1950s and early 1960s (before the Vietnam War). If anything, he suggests that it is the Soviet Union that suffers today from *imperial overstretch*, not the United States.

Nye concedes that the United States faces serious problems. The country spends too much and invests too little. The United States will have to spend more, he argues, on education, technologies, infrastructure, and the development of human resources. Above all, the United States must resist the protectionist impulse that would cut it off from the open flow of goods, talents, and information. "The openness of American society, as manifested in the success of new immigrants, is a great source of strength not shared by the Soviet Union or Japan." According to Nye:

> Seen in this perspective, the appropriate U.S. strategy is not to withdraw from international commitments in the illusory hope of...arresting the change in its relative power position. On the contrary, such measures would contribute to, rather than arrest, the relative decline of American power because the sources of that change are mainly outside the United States.

Nye urges that resources be transferred from consumption to investment and that, abroad, the United States continue to invest in those institutions and defense arrangements that afford leverage on the many issues in which the United States is heavily dependent.

18 Should Containment Continue To Be U.S. Policy toward the Soviet Union?

YES

Francis P. Sempa

Geopolitics and American Strategy: A Reassessment

NO

Earl C. Ravenal

An Alternative to Containment

Geopolitics and American Strategy: A Reassessment

Francis P. Sempa

Ever since the late 1940s, the dominant goal of U.S. foreign policy has been to contain Soviet power within the geographical boundaries established at the end of World War II. In an absolute sense, the Policy of Containment has failed. Soviet power has extended into Southeast Asia and Southwest Asia, Africa, the Middle East, the Caribbean Sea and Central America. Soviet naval power girds the major bodies of water on the globe. In a more limited sense, however, containment has succeeded: the map of Europe has not been altered in nearly forty years, nor has, in geopolitical terms, the map of Central Asia.

Containing Soviet power was the subject of George F. Kennan's famous 1947 article in *Foreign Affairs*, "The Sources of Soviet Conduct." Kennan argued that, for historical and ideological reasons, the Soviet Union would seek to expand its political control beyond the immediate postwar geographical boundaries. He urged the United States to respond with a policy of "long-term, patient but firm and vigilant containment." He called for "the adroit and vigilant application of counter-force at a series of constantly shifting geographical and political points, corresponding to the shifts and maneuvers of Soviet policy...."[1] This policy was not a magnanimous offer to protect the peoples of Europe and Asia from Soviet tyranny:

it was based on the central assumption, heightened by two wars, that the security of the United States was ultimately at stake in the balance of power on the Eurasian landmass.

Kennan is rightly regarded as the theoretical "father" of containment. Yet, the roots of his concept go back to 1904, when a British geographer delivered a paper to the Royal Geographical Society. Halford J. Mackinder is known as the founder of modern geopolitics; he might also be called the "grandfather" of the Policy of Containment.

HALFORD MACKINDER'S ANALYSIS OF HISTORY

Mackinder entitled his paper "The Geographical Pivot of History." In it, he drew a geopolitical sketch of the globe, identifying the inner core area of Eurasia as the "pivot area" of world politics. The key characteristics of this "pivot area" were its extensive, continuous flatlands and its inaccessibility to seapower. Reviewing the history of the nomadic invasions of Huns, Avars, Magyars, Khazars, Cumans, Kalmuks and Mongols, Mackinder wrote: "For a thousand years a series of horse-riding peoples emerged from Asia through the broad interval between the Ural Mountains and the Caspian Sea, rode through the open spaces of southern Russia, and struck home into Hungary in the very heart of the European peninsula...."[2]

Particularly revealing were the Mongol invasions, in which "all the settled margins of the Old World sooner or later felt the expansive force of mobile power originating in the steppe. Russia, Persia, India and China were

---

Francis P. Sempa, "Geopolitics and American Strategy: A Reassessment," *Strategic Review*, 15 (Spring 1987), pp. 27–38. Reprinted by permission of the U.S. Strategic Institute.

[1] George F. Kennan, *American Diplomacy* (Chicago: University of Chicago Press, 1951), p. 99.

[2] Halford J. Mackinder, *Democratic Ideals and Reality* (New York: W. W. Norton & Co., 1962), p. 250. This 1962 edition contains the original 1919 work, as well as "The Geographical Pivot of History" and "The Round World and the Winning of the Peace." All references to Mackinder's writings are from the 1962 edition.

either made tributary, or received Mongol dynasties."[3] Updating history to 1904, Mackinder wrote:

> Russia replaces the Mongol Empire. Her pressure on Finland, on Scandinavia, on Poland, on Turkey, on Persia, on India, and on China replaces the centrifugal raids of the steppe-men. In the world at large she occupies the central strategical position held by Germany in Europe. She can strike on all sides and be struck from all sides, save the north.[4]

Mackinder completed his global sketch by placing the rest of Eurasia outside the pivot area in "a great inner crescent," and putting Britain, southern Africa, Japan and North and South America in the "outer crescent." Toward the end of his paper Mackinder issued the following warning: "The oversetting of the balance of power in favor of the pivot state, resulting in its expansion over the marginal lands of Euro-Asia, would permit the use of vast continental resources for fleet-building, and the empire of the world would then be in sight."[5] He suggested three possible contenders for world empire: Germany, Russia and China. Geography offered them this opportunity, but Mackinder pointed out that the power balance was determined by many factors, including "the relative number, virility, equipment and organization of the competing peoples."[6]

Thus, 43 years before Kennan's article, Mackinder foresaw the rise of a powerful state occupying the "pivot area" and aspiring to global hegemony. After Germany's failed bid for continental domination in World War I, Mackinder greatly expanded on his 1904 ideas. The result, in 1919, was a 200-page *tour de force* entitled *Democratic Ide-*

als and Reality, a book that remains the classic work on modern geopolitics. Drawing on his vast knowledge of geography and history, Mackinder analyzed the struggles of ancient Egypt, Greece and Macedonia, the Roman Empire, Europe and the eastern barbarians, and the British Empire. History, according to Mackinder, consisted ultimately of the struggles for power among states and empires. And the key to those struggles could be found in geography.

The uncomfortable reality of the geographical conditions of our planet, according to Mackinder, was that "the grouping of lands and seas, and of fertility and natural pathways, is such as to lend itself to the growth of empires and in the end of a single world empire."[7] The world consisted of the following geographical elements: one ocean covering nine-twelfths of the globe; one continent covering two-twelfths of the globe; and many smaller islands making up the remaining one-twelfth. The one great continent encompassed Europe, Asia and Africa; he called this the "World Island." The central strategic position on the World Island was the inner area of Eurasia, previously referred to as the "pivot area," but which Mackinder now called the "Heartland." He described the Heartland as "a great continuous patch in the north and center of the continent. That whole patch, extending right across from the icy, flat shore of Siberia to the torrid, steep coasts of Baluchistan and Persia, has been inaccessible to navigation from the ocean. The opening of it by railways...and by aeroplane routes in the near future, constitutes a revolution in the relations of men to the larger geographical realities of the world."[8] He concluded that it

---

[3] Ibid., p. 254.
[4] Ibid., p. 262.
[5] Ibid.
[6] Ibid., p. 263.

[7] Ibid., p. 2.
[8] Ibid., pp. 73–74.

was from this great region that the threat to the rest of the world would emerge.

THE BASIC MACKINDER CONCEPT

To grasp more fully Mackinder's grand conception, we must address it in a piecemeal fashion. The first key concept concerns the struggle for power between insular and peninsular powers. Mackinder takes us back to the ancient struggle between peninsular Greece and insular Crete, and describes how a unified Greece (under the Dorians) was able to use the greater resources of the peninsular mainland to conquer Crete; later, however, the Athens-Sparta rivalry "prevented a full exploitation of the peninsula as a sea-base."[9] This same geographical relationship was highlighted in the conquest of (insular) Britain by a united Latin peninsular power, the Roman Empire. Still later, and on a greater scale, a fragmented European peninsula was unable to challenge successfully the seapower base of Britain: France (under Napoleon) and Germany (under Wilhelm II) both failed in this quest.

With this historical-geographical background, Mackinder asks the reader to picture the vast Eurasian-African landmass (the World Island) and North America in a peninsular-insular perspective. "But," he writes, "there is this vital difference, that the world-promontory, when united by modern overland communications, is in fact the World Island, possessed potentially of the advantage both of insularity and of incomparably great resources."[10] Then he poses the ominous questions:

What if the Great Continent, the whole World Island or a large part of it, were at some future time to become a single and united base of seapower? Would not the other insular bases be outbuilt as regards ships and outmanned as regards seamen? Their fleets would no doubt fight with all the heroism begotten of their histories, but the end would be fated.[11]

The second of Mackinder's key concepts, closely related to the first, relates to the relative advantage of landpower over seapower. Seapower, according to Mackinder, is ultimately dependent upon an adequate landbase. It was its magnificent landbase (in resources and skilled manpower) that made Great Britain a great seapower. But a greater peninsular landbase, once united under a single power and free from challenges from another landpower, will achieve naval supremacy to defeat the less strongly based insular power. Thus, in Mackinder's strategic conception, a landpower that gains control over a large part of the Eurasian-African landmass could harness the vast resources of its landbase to constructing the world's most powerful navy and overwhelming all remaining insular powers.

Mackinder's third and most important concept was that of the Heartland. This great, largely unbroken plain of inner Eurasia, inaccessible to seapower, provided its occupant the opportunities to expand in all directions except northward. In 1919 Mackinder included within the Heartland the Black and Baltic Seas, the middle and lower Danube, Asia Minor (Turkey), Armenia, Persia, Tibet and Mongolia (these were additions to his original concept). He foresaw a "fundamental opposition between East and West Europe"[12]—between the Heartland and the Coastland. Remarkably, in light of ensuing history, he placed the frontier of the East-West

---

[9] Ibid., p. 53.
[10] Ibid., p. 65.

[11] Ibid., p. 70.
[12] Ibid., p. 125.

struggle in the center of Germany. He explained that the nations of Western Europe

> must necessarily be opposed to whatever Power attempts to organize the resources of East Europe and the Heartland.... We [Britain and France] were opposed to the half-German Russian Czardom because Russia was the dominating, threatening force both in East Europe and the Heartland for a century. We were opposed to the wholly German Kaiserdom, because Germany took the lead in East Europe from the Czardom, and would then have crushed the revolting slavs, and dominated East Europe and the Heartland.[13]

Mackinder also recognized that the nations of Western Europe, by themselves, could not counterbalance a single power controlling Eastern Europe and the Heartland: in World War I "West Europe had to call in the help of America, for West Europe alone would not have been able to reverse the decision in the East."[14] It was toward the end of *Democratic Ideals and Reality* that Mackinder issued his famous dictum: "Who rules East Europe commands the Heartland: Who rules the Heartland commands the World Island: Who rules the World Island commands the World."[15] In yet another prophetic comment, he warned the idealists of his time: "No mere scraps of paper, even though they be the written constitution of a League of Nations, are, under the conditions of today, a sufficient guarantee that the Heartland will not again become the center of a world war."[16]

THE GEOPOLITICS OF WORLD WAR II AND ITS WAKE

Twenty-two years after the publication of *Democratic Ideals and Reality*, the Heartland and

Eastern Europe did indeed become the center of a world war. American memories and perceptions of that conflict tend to focus, quite naturally, on the battles in Western Europe and the Pacific. Yet, the greatest land war in history raged for four years on Germany's eastern front. Hitler's racist notions of Germany's destiny to dominate the Slavic peoples blended well with German geopolitical theories. The German school of *Geopolitik,* headed by Dr. Karl Haushofer, studied and debated the geopolitical theories of Mackinder, Friedrich Ratzel and Rudolf Kjellen, and adapted Mackinder's conceptions into a blueprint for Eurasian hegemony. Interestingly, Dr. Haushofer advised not only Hitler but also Stalin prior to the German invasion of the Soviet Union.

The war challenged one part of Mackinder's famous dictum: Germany, having conquered Eastern Europe, failed to take command of the Heartland. But the war's outcome brought about Mackinder's geopolitical nightmare: a single power now ruled Eastern Europe and the Heartland.

Was Soviet world hegemony now inevitable? Not necessarily, according to Mackinder's last published work on this topic: a 1943 article in *Foreign Affairs* entitled "The Round World and the Winning of the Peace." In it he contended that his concept of the Heartland "is more valid and useful today than it was either twenty or forty years ago."[17] Further revising the boundaries of the Heartland, he described it roughly in terms of the territory of the Soviet Union. He then warned:

> All things considered, the conclusion is unavoidable that if the Soviet Union emerges from this war as conquerer of Germany, she must rank as the greatest land power on the globe. Moreover, she will be the Power in the strategically strongest defensive position. The Heartland is the

---

[13] Ibid., p. 139.
[14] Ibid., p. 149.
[15] Ibid., p. 150.
[16] Ibid., p. 114.

---

[17] Ibid., p. 276.

greatest natural fortress on earth. For the first time in history it is manned by a garrison sufficient both in number and quality.[18]

Yet, Mackinder now added a feature to his grand conception: the "Midland Ocean." It consisted of three elements: "a bridgehead in France, a moated aerodrome in Britain, and a reserve of trained manpower, agriculture and industries in the eastern United States and Canada."[19] He rated the Midland Ocean as being of "almost equal significance" to the Heartland. He thus foresaw, or prescribed, the North Atlantic Alliance.

Mackinder's ideas were influential in the United States in the immediate postwar years. *Democratic Ideals and Reality* was reprinted in 1942, a year before Mackinder's final article in *Foreign Affairs,* and his conceptions were analyzed and debated. His influence is discernible in some of the foreign policy writings of Walter Lippmann. In *The Century of Total War,* Raymond Aron noted, ominously, that "Russia has in fact nearly achieved the 'world island' which Mackinder considered the necessary and almost sufficient condition for universal empire."[20]

Nicholas Spykman, then Professor of International Relations at Yale University, essentially accepted Mackinder's geographical view of the world, but argued that coastal Eurasia (Mackinder's inner crescent, which Spykman renamed the "Eurasian Rimlands"), not the Heartland, was the key to world power. Spykman went so far as to issue a counterdictum to Mackinder's: "Who controls the rimland rules Eurasia; who rules Eurasia controls the destinies of the world."[21] More will be said about Spyk-

man's ideas below. But Mackinder's influence also was prominent in the writings of Professor Robert Strausz-Hupé and of the Foreign Policy Research Institute he founded at the University of Pennsylvania in the 1950s.

JAMES BURNHAM'S ADDITIONS TO GEOPOLITICS

Not all those who were influenced by Mackinder's works saw containment as the most effective strategy for dealing with the Soviet geopolitical threat. In 1944 James Burnham, then working for the Office of Strategic Services, wrote an analysis of the Soviet threat to the West which he later expanded into a book entitled *The Struggle for the World.*[22] In two subsequent volumes, Burnham extended his analysis and advocated policies designed to win what he called the "Third World War."

Burnham adopted Mackinder's geopolitical conception, adding to it the revolutionary dimension of Soviet communism. After the communist conquest of China, he urged American policymakers to turn from containment to a policy of "liberation." Viewing China as an appendage of Soviet power (which it essentially was at the time), he argued that the Soviet Union now effectively controlled the bulk of the World Island.

Containment, Burnham contended, was a defeatist policy for two main reasons. First, as a revolutionary ideology, Soviet communism could not be contained behind traditional geographical borders, because the Soviets would expand through political warfare waged by surrogate forces in other countries. Second, Soviet conquests (including China) already gave it command of so much of Eurasia that "if [they] succeed in consolidating what they have already conquered, then their complete

---

[18] Ibid., pp. 272–273.
[19] Ibid., p. 277.
[20] Raymond Aron, *The Century of Total War* (Boston: The Beacon Press, 1955), p. 111.
[21] Nicholas Spykman, *The Geography of the Peace* (New York: Harcourt, Brace & Co., 1944), p. 43.

[22] James Burnham, *The Struggle for the World* (New York: John Day Co., 1947).

world victory is certain....That is why the policy of containment, even if 100 per cent successful, is a formula for Soviet victory."[23]

This is not the place to analyze and critique James Burnham's proposed policy of "liberation" as an alternative to containment. Suffice it to say that his chief contribution to the geopolitical debate was to combine Mackinder's geographical insights with an analysis of the political implications of the Soviet's revolutionary ideology.

Burnham noted: "For the first time in world history, the inner Heartland possessed a mass population, a high level of political organization, and a considerable industrialization."[24] He drew a circular map of the world, placing the Soviet Union in the inner circle, coastal Eurasia and northern Africa in the middle circle, and the rest of the world in the outer circle. From its central strategic location, the Soviet Union would, he predicted, exert political pressure on the surrounding areas. Echoing Mackinder, Burnham, in *The Coming Defeat of Communism*, described the Heartland as "the most favorable strategic position of the world."[25] And in *Containment or Liberation?*, he echoed Spykman in describing the geopolitical position of the United States: "Geographically, America, as an off-shore island, has much the same relation to Eurasia as Britain to Europe."[26] He then warned:

A balance of power does not now exist on the Eurasian continent. On the contrary, there is domination or potential domination by the single Soviet system. That this is true becomes obvious if we assume the power influence of the United States to be withdrawn from Eurasia. At once, probably without fighting, all of the Eur-

asian nations still outside of the Soviet Empire would have to submit to Soviet control.[27]

To these geopolitical concepts Burnham added his analysis of what he called the "communist conduct of contemporary war." He believed that Soviet offensive moves would most often take the form of proxy warfare: "The Soviet power has the advantage of fighting in such a way through auxiliary forces during what the rest of the world regards as peacetime, a time therefore when the opponent feels inhibited from taking adequate countermeasures."[28] Furthermore, the Soviets divide the world into the "zone of peace" and the "zone of war."[29] Burnham concisely explained this concept in his 1964 classic, *Suicide of the West*:

"The zone of peace" means the region that is already subject to communist rule; and the label signifies that within their region the communists will not permit any political tendency, violent or non-violent, whether purely internal or assisted from without, to challenge their rule. "The zone of war" is the region where communist rule is not yet, but in due course will be, established; and within the zone of war the communists promote, assist and where possible lead political tendencies, violent or non-violent, democratic or revolutionary, that operate against non-communist rule.[30]

Thus, according to Burnham, the major threat to the West was not a direct Soviet attack on Western Europe, but the gradual expansion of Soviet power via surrogate forces combined with, and assisted by, the gradual collapse of Western resolve. Burnham thus ac-

[23] James Burnham, *Containment or Liberation?* (New York: John Day Co., 1953), p. 251.

[24] Burnham, *The Struggle for the World*, p. 96.

[25] James Burnham, *The Coming Defeat of Communism* (New York: John Day Co., 1950), p. 14.

[26] Burnham, *Containment or Liberation?* pp. 113–114.

[27] Ibid., p. 114.

[28] Burnham, *The Coming Defeat of Communism*, p. 83.

[29] These terms were first used by Robert Strausz-Hupé, James Dougherty, William Kintner, and Alvin Cottrell in their 1959 work, *Protracted Conflict*, but the concept was implicit in Burnham's earlier works.

[30] James Burnham, *Suicide of the West* (Chicago: Regnery Books, 1985), pp. 227–228. This book was originally published in 1964.

curately forecast not only the "Brezhnev Doctrine," which gave explicit expression to the "peace zone/war zone" dichotomy, but also the principal salients of Soviet conflict strategy in the "Third World" that unfolded more fully in the 1970s.

SPYKMAN'S PRESCRIPTIONS FOR U.S. POLICY

The creation of the North Atlantic Treaty Organization in 1949 marked an historic departure in U.S. foreign policy. Mackinder's theory offered the geopolitical foundations for this departure, but it was Nicholas Spykman who turned this theory into central prescriptions for U.S. policy.

During the war, Spykman had written an elaborate geopolitical critique of American isolationism in *America's Strategy in World Politics* (1942). The book's two central themes were that the United States: (1) must adopt a policy of *Realpolitik* in the recognition that "power" was the real governing force in international relations, and (2) must recognize that the Eurasian power balance directly impacts on American security.

The American scholar most frequently identified as the founder of the "power politics" school of thought is Hans Morganthau. His book, *Politics among Nations,* written in 1948, became a standard text for the (new) study of international relations in American universities.[31] Yet, six years before the publication of Morganthau's book, Nicholas Spykman had anticipated many of its ideas.

"The struggle for power," wrote Spykman, "is identified with the struggle for survival, and the improvement of the relative power position becomes the primary objective of the internal and external policy of states. All else

is secondary, because in the last instance only power can achieve the objectives of foreign policy."[32] Spykman was well aware of the tendency among American policymakers to inject moralism into foreign policy. He counselled:

> The statesman who conducts foreign policy can concern himself with values of justice, fairness, and tolerance only to the extent that they contribute to or do not interfere with the power objective. They can be used instrumentally as moral justification for the power quest, but they must be discarded the moment their application brings weakness. The search for power is not made for the achievement of moral values; moral values are used to facilitate the attainment of power.[33]

Spykman believed that each nation's quest for security inevitably led to conflict, because "the margin of security for one is the margin of danger for the other, and alliance must, therefore, be met by counter-alliance and armament by counter-armament in an eternal competitive struggle for power. Thus it has been in all periods of history."[34]

But it was the second theme of *America's Strategy in World Politics* that earned Spykman a lasting place in the field of geopolitics. This theme was that "the first line of defense of the United States lies in the preservation of a balance of power in Europe and Asia."[35] Spykman explained that throughout the Nineteenth Century the United States enjoyed the *de facto* protection of the British fleet for its hemispheric security, leaving America free to pursue her "manifest destiny." The tides of the Twentieth Century had changed all this.

Echoing Mackinder's concept, Spykman posited that "the position of the United States in regard to Europe as a whole is...identical

---

[31] Hans J. Morganthau, *Politics among Nations* (New York: Alfred A. Knopf, 1949). Morganthau first discussed this topic in *Scientific Man vs. Power Politics* (1946).

[32] Nicholas Spykman, *America's Strategy in World Politics* (New York: Harcourt, Brace & Co., 1942), p. 18.
[33] Ibid., p. 18.
[34] Ibid., p. 24.
[35] Ibid., p. 4.

to the position of Great Britain in regard to the European Continent....We have an interest in the European balance as the British have an interest in the continental balance."[36] Writing when the war's outcome was still in doubt, Spykman warned of the consequences of a victory for the Axis powers: "If the German-Japanese Alliance should be victorious on the Eurasian landmass and become free to turn its whole strength against the New World, the United States could not defend the hemisphere."[37]

Thus, the immediate imperative was the defeat of the Axis powers. But this was not enough, according to Spykman, because "the end of a war is not the end of the power struggle."[38] He argued: "Because of the distribution of landmasses and military potentials, a balance of power in the transatlantic and transpacific zones is an absolute prerequisite for the independence of the New World and the preservation of the power position of the United States. There is no safe defensive position on this side of the oceans. Hemisphere defense is no defense at all."[39] Isolationism will not guarantee us peace or security. On the contrary, "it will be cheaper in the long run to remain a working member of the European power zone than to withdraw for short intermissions to our insular domain only to be forced to apply later the whole of our national strength to redress a balance that might have needed but a slight weight at the beginning."[40]

In *The Geography of the Peace*, Spykman's last work (published posthumously in 1944), he expressed relief at the imminent defeat of the Axis powers, but urged American policymakers not to forget the peril which had faced them earlier in the war:

> The most significant fact...about the situation which confronted us when, at the beginning of 1942, Germany and Japan had achieved a good part of their objectives was the existence of a political alliance between them. We were then confronted with the possibility of complete encirclement, in which case we might have had to face the unified power of the whole Eurasian landmass. The strength of the power centers of the Eastern Hemisphere would then have been overpowering. It would have been impossible for us to preserve our independence and security. If we are to avoid the conclusion of such an encirclement in the future, our constant concern in peacetime must be to see that no nation or alliance of nations is allowed to emerge as a dominating power in either of the two regions of the Old World from which our security could be threatened.[41]

Hence, he argued, "the safety and independence of this country can be preserved only by a foreign policy that will make it impossible for the Eurasian landmass to harbor overwhelming dominant power in Europe and the Far East."[42]

GEOPOLITICAL FOUNDATIONS OF U.S. POSTWAR POLICY

Since the late 1940s, U.S. policy has been based essentially on the three geopolitical factors discussed above: (1) America's security would be gravely imperiled if all or most of Eurasia should become politically dominated by a hostile power (Spykman and Mackinder); (2) the power that controls the heartland of Eurasia—the Soviet Union—poses the greatest threat of Eurasian domination (Mackinder); and (3) the Soviet Union, guided by its revo-

---

[36] Ibid., p. 124.
[37] Ibid., p. 444.
[38] Ibid., p. 457.
[39] Ibid.
[40] Ibid., pp. 467–468.

[41] Spykman, *The Geography of the Peace*, (New York: Harcourt, Brace & Co., 1944), p. 34.
[42] Ibid., p. 60.

lutionary ideology, will seek to expand its global power through surrogate forces (Burnham and others).

Viewed in this light, American foreign policy, notwithstanding inevitable discontinuities of policy in a democratic nation, has generally (perhaps even "instinctively") been based on those geopolitical precepts. The postwar alliances forged by the United States—most prominently NATO [North Atlantic Treaty Organization], CENTO [Central Treaty Organization] and SEATO [South East Asia Treaty Organization]—were designed to counter direct Soviet pressures on the rimlands of Eurasia, as has been the more recent U.S. entente with Communist China. Direct U.S. military interventions in the Korean and Vietnam Wars, as well as in Guatemala, the Dominican Republic and Grenada, were designed to counter the expansion of Soviet power through surrogate forces, as are the current U.S. policies of assistance to anti-communist forces in Nicaragua, Angola and Kampuchea. American support for such countries as Israel, Egypt, Saudi Arabia, Iran (before the fall of the Shah), Pakistan and Oman has been designed to block the expansion of Soviet power into the Middle East/Persian Gulf region. Our specific policies have not always been wise or effective, but they have hewed to fairly consistent geopolitical considerations.

COLIN GRAY AND GEOPOLITICS IN THE NUCLEAR AGE

If the principal bond of American foreign policies since World War II has thus been geopolitical, that bond has come under increasing challenge. The extent of that challenge is reflected, intellectually, in the virtual eclipse of geopolitics in the American academic realm beginning in the late 1960s. It is reflected, politically, in the deepening cracks in the postwar bipartisan consensus during the past two decades.

The phenomenon's causes are complex. They seem to center on America's painful experience in Vietnam. Yet, the intellectual challenge to geopolitics antedates Vietnam. It came apace with the advent of nuclear weapons of mass destruction and the long-range means of their delivery—and the notion that this "military revolution" had transfigured the globe, rendering obsolete such "traditional" theories of power as geopolitics.

The most cogent discussion of the application of geopolitical thought to the nuclear age is provided by the U.S. strategic analyst, Colin Gray, in his book, *The Geopolitics of the Nuclear Era*.[43] In 67 pages, Gray presents a geopolitical framework for understanding current international relations.

Relying heavily on the concepts of Mackinder and Spykman, Gray uses classic geopolitical terminology: the Soviet Union is the "Heartland superpower," Western Europe and non-Soviet Asia are the Eurasian "Rimlands," and the United States is the "insular maritime superpower." Moreover, he dispenses with such standard cliches concerning the East-West relationship as "mistrust," "misunderstanding," "managing the relationship," "causing tensions," etc. The governing force in international relations, according to Gray, is power. The United States and the Soviet Union are engaged in a permanent struggle, the immediate objects of which are the Rimlands of Eurasia. Control of all or most of the Rimlands by the Soviet Union would give the Kremlin overwhelming political dominance on the Eurasian-African "World Island." Therefore, the overriding geopolitical goal of American foreign policy has been since 1945, and must continue to be, to prevent that contingency.

Nuclear weapons, Gray explains, must be viewed *within* this geopolitical framework.

---

[43] Colin Gray, *The Geopolitics of the Nuclear Era: Heartland, Rimlands, and the Technological Revolution* (New York: Crane, Russak & Co., Inc., 1977).

They are a part of and therefore subordinate to balance-of-power considerations. He warns:

> In geopolitical perspective, the American defense community has yet to come to terms with the likely consequences of parity, let alone inferiority. Strategic parity means that the United States has no margin of strategic nuclear strength which could be invoked on behalf of endangered friends and allies in Eurasia.[44]

For forty years the Soviet Union has enjoyed a geographical and conventional military power advantage with respect to the Eurasian Rimlands. Throughout this period, the United States has sought to offset this imbalance with nuclear weapons. In the 1970s, however, in the face of a massive Soviet buildup, U.S. strategic nuclear superiority receded into a position of at best "parity," if not inferiority. This dramatic shift in the nuclear balance affected both Soviet and European attitudes: it emboldened a more aggressive Soviet foreign policy, expressed in the invasion of Afghanistan, and it convinced Europeans of the declining credibility of the American "extended deterrent" over Western Europe—the basis of the U.S. postwar "guaranty" to Europe in the Atlantic Pact.

According to Gray, arms control efforts that seek to confirm nuclear "parity" ignore fundamental geopolitical realities. In the long run, "parity" cannot adequately counter the enormous conventional military advantage of the Soviets and their permanent geographical advantages. This leaves the Western Alliance with two options: "either the maritime alliance [NATO] must sustain a very robust local denial capability, or the United States must invest in a significant margin of strategic nuclear superiority."[45] The first option has proven thus far politically infeasible; the second option is an arms control heresy. Yet, what answer is there to Gray's ominous questions:

> How are the Eurasian-African Rimlands to be defended against the Heartland power, if strategic parity (or, more likely, parity-plus) is conceded to that power? If superiority in the European theater is conceded? And if anyone, worldwide, who can read a newspaper or listen to a radio can learn that the Soviet Union is on the ascendant in gaining influence in potential (and actual) base areas in Africa and South Asia?[46]

Gray also rejects the "neo-Mahanian" view in the United States that naval superiority can substitute for inadequate ground forces in Europe. "The Soviet Navy," he writes,

> may, and should, be blown out of the water, its forward facilities on African and South Asian littorals also demolished; but time would not be on the side of the maritime alliance. By compelling the maritime alliance to fight hard for unhindered access to Eurasia, the Soviet Navy would be buying time for Soviet conquest of critical portions of the Rimlands (should Blitzkrieg campaigning overrun its time-table). In the world of the 1980s and 1990s, an eventual *total* naval victory for the United States would be of little value if, in the meantime, the peninsular European bridgehead were lost.[47]

GEOPOLITICAL IMPLICATIONS FOR NATO

The combination of geographical position, conventional military superiority and a standoff at the strategic-nuclear level gives the Soviet Union an overall military and, therefore, political advantage over the United States in the struggle for Europe. This implication has not escaped the notice of statesmen and strategists on both sides of the Atlantic. In 1982, Franz Josef

---

[44] Ibid., p. 62.
[45] Ibid., p. 53.

[46] Ibid.
[47] Ibid., p. 59.

Strauss, former Defense Minister of the Federal Republic of Germany, warned: "The principal danger to the West...is not a war in the sense of a large-scale military conflict, but rather the Soviet Union's harnessing of its mounting military capabilities to a process of political intimidation, with the long-term objective of achieving first the neutralization of Western Europe and then the Sovietization of all Europe."[48] A year later, General Bernard Rogers, Supreme Allied Commander in Europe, asked: "How long can we permit the gap between NATO and Warsaw Pact force capabilities to widen before the military situation is so adverse that NATO nations find themselves politically intimidated, economically coerced and subject to blackmail?"[49]

As was noted above, Colin Gray proposes two basic alternatives for escape from NATO's present predicament: (1) establishing a "robust local denial capability," or (2) reattaining clearcut nuclear superiority. In the light of current trends—and of the politically feasible, both in the United States and the Alliance—Gray's two alternatives might be compromised into a single prescription: (1) an improved NATO conventional denial capability in Europe, and (2) a more credible U.S. nuclear strategy and force structure.[50]

The first element of the prescription requires a concerted harnessing of technological advances in the West relevant to conventional defenses: particularly precision-guided munitions and "deep-strike" capabilities designed to disrupt and deny any potential Warsaw Pact conventional attack. This includes the wherewithal for an "extended air-defense" (i.e., antimissile defense) proposed by West German Defense Minister Manfred Woerner.[51] The second element in the prescription entails the urgent modernization of the U.S. strategic arsenal in survivable, counterforce capabilities (e.g., MX missiles) which, combined with emergent strategic defenses under the Strategic Defense Initiative, can reinvigorate the U.S. "nuclear guaranty" to the Alliance.

More important than any specific measures, however, is the recognition that the size and structure of Western forces, and the strategies for their use, should be determined by geopolitical realities, rather than by abstract principles of "balance," particularly in the arms control context. Weapons "freezes," "equal" reductions, "zero solutions," and other ostensibly equitable or balanced proposals ignore the geopolitical advantages enjoyed by the Soviet Union by virtue of its control of Eastern Europe and the Heartland. Arms control, like all other facets of our foreign and defense policies, should be viewed and pursued within a global geopolitical context.[52]

---

[48] Franz Josef Strauss, "Manifesto of a German Atlanticist," *Strategic Review*, Summer 1982, p. 13.

[49] Bernard Rogers, "Greater Flexibility for NATO's Flexible Response," *Strategic Review*, Spring 1983, p. 14.

[50] In Gray's most recent writing on this topic, he does not specifically advocate nuclear superiority. He advises NATO to focus on "denying the prompt acquisition of important territorial 'prizes'; supporting, threatening, reviving, or creating continental distractions; gaining leverage through seizure of important assets; shifting the balance of forces progressively in one's favor; flexibility and surprise in application of force from the sea; and eroding the enemy's confidence in the likelihood of victory." See "Keeping the Soviets Landlocked," *The National Interest*, Summer 1986, pp. 35–36.

[51] Manfred Woerner, "A Missile Defense for NATO Europe," *Strategic Review*, Winter 1986, p. 19.

[52] This is especially true of the ongoing Mutual and Balanced Force Reductions in Europe (MBFR) negotiations. As Carnes Lord recently explained: "...any mutual withdrawal of U.S. and Soviet forces from Europe would have grossly asymmetrical consequences. Any U.S. units removed from Central Europe would have to be withdrawn thousands of miles across the Atlantic to the United States, while Soviet troops withdrawn to their homeland could remain less than 500 miles from the inner-German border. This asymmetry has grown increasingly severe during the lifetime of MBFR, as steady improvements in the quality and quantity of Soviet forces in Europe have increased Soviet chances of a quick victory and made more problematic the resupply and reinforcement of NATO's central front by the United States." Carnes Lord, "The MBFR Mystery," *The American Spectator*, June 1986, p. 14.

THE SOVIET CONCEPT OF "CORRELATION OF FORCES"

The Soviet view of the world is based on what they term the "correlation of forces." This is a comprehensive measurement of power that includes such objective factors as military forces and economic, social, political and geographical considerations, as well as subjective factors such as a given nation's—or alliance's—unity, "morale," intentions and resolve. The "correlation of forces" thus serves as an explicit guide to Soviet global strategy, which is geared—just as explicitly—to changing the "correlation" in the Soviets' favor.

The "correlation of forces" is essentially a geopolitical concept. We may recall that Mackinder, too, introduced into his theory such subjective elements as the "virility" and "organization" of competing peoples. The Soviet concept is comprehensively global and cast in a "zero-sum" mold, holding that the loss of American or Western influence and power in a given locality or region reduces the relative global power position of the "imperialist bloc," thereby commensurately enhancing the relative power position of the Soviet Union and the "fraternal socialist states." This is so even when lost Western influence in a particular locality or region is not directly supplanted by Soviet power and influence—Iran being a perfect recent example. Those who chide the present U.S. Administration for viewing developments in Central America, for example, in an "East-West" rather than a "regional" context should be aware of the fact that this is precisely how those developments are viewed from Moscow.

GEOPOLITICS AND MORAL IDEALS

Geopolitical concepts do not provide statesmen with specific policy prescriptions, setting forth when it is appropriate to use such tools as military force, economic and military assistance, or covert operations, let alone determining the means and content of diplomacy with allies and adversaries. Rather, geopolitical concepts offer a global framework within which both grand strategy and specific policies can be formulated and implemented.

Unfortunately, as Halford Mackinder so keenly recognized over sixty years ago, democracies often succumb to the temptation of basing their foreign policy on ideals rather than geopolitical realities. Woodrow Wilson succumbed to this temptation at the end of World War I, as did Franklin Roosevelt near the end of World War II. Both leaders placed their sincere hope for peace in a world organization which would represent "mankind."

Similarly today, American idealists place their hopes for peace and a better world in disarmament treaties and "democratic" revolutions. Such idealism may be an expression of American societal values, but it can be projected outward onto a values-diverse world only at the risk of exposing the wellspring of those values— our society itself—to enormous dangers. We have witnessed the consequences for U.S. policy when the "corrupt Thieu regime" in Saigon came to overshadow the implications of a communist takeover of Indochina, and when the "crimes of the Shah" obscured the imperative of Western access to the Persian Gulf. And we confront the danger today of permitting alleged "human rights violations" by the Contras in Nicaragua to distort our view of U.S. strategic stakes in Central America under attack by surrogate forces of the Soviet Union.

Such idealism is not limited to the liberal sectors of the American political spectrum. Some U.S. conservatives are still reluctant to recognize the "opening" to Communist China staged by President Richard Nixon during his first term. The Sino-Soviet rift—between the two most powerful communist nations and, more important, the two largest countries on the Eurasian landmass—is one of the crucial geopolitical developments of the second half of the Twentieth Century. Pleas on behalf of the position and claims of the Republic of China (Taiwan), however morally valid, do not alter the global geopolitical realities. An independent and antagonistic China compels the Soviet Union to sustain significant military forces on its long border with the PRC—forces that could otherwise be added to the already prohibitive weight of the Soviet military posture in Europe.

Other conservatives have voiced doubt about the wisdom of maintaining a large U.S. ground presence in Europe. They correctly argue that our European allies are quite capable of doing more in their own conventional defense, permitting the United States to concentrate on its capabilities to meet contingencies in other important areas of the world, such as the Persian Gulf region, and to buttress its strategic deterrent. This would make for a more logical division of resources among Alliance members. But the logical is not always the politically feasible. Perhaps the decision to substantially reduce American forces on the continent would, as commentators like Irving Kristol and Senator Sam Nunn have suggested, "shock" the Europeans into spending more for their security. Yet, can we afford to take such a risk? Are we prepared to live with the consequences if Europeans are, instead, "shocked" into political accommodation with the Soviet Union?

In geopolitical terms, China and Western Europe are two large weights on the peripheries of the Eurasian landmass adjacent to the Soviet Heartland. The effective control of either territory by the Soviet Union—through direct conquest or political hegemony—would drastically shift the "correlation of world forces" in Moscow's favor. Mackinder's ominous vision of a Heartland-based world empire would come precariously close to realization.

THE IMPERATIVES OF U.S. STRATEGY

Thus, in geopolitical terms, the alignments of Western Europe and China cannot be viewed separately. Both are crucial players in denying the Soviets hegemony over Eurasia and overwhelming political predominance on the World Island. The loss or neutralization of either power center would set in motion an inexorable series of global power trends leading to a relentless retreat by the United States into a "Fortress America," increasingly isolated economically, politically and spiritually from the world-at-large, and with the psychological incubus of beleaguerment bearing down on its free institutions and values.

If this prospect is to be averted, U.S. foreign policy must deal with the world as it is, not as we wish it to be. We must formulate— or reformulate—a grand strategy based on fundamental geopolitical realities. Containment of Soviet Heartland power must remain the cornerstone of this strategy— meaning our continued ability to project adequate power along the periphery of the Soviet empire in an arc extending from Norway, across Central Europe, through the Balkans, the Middle East and Southwest Asia, curving from south-central Asia to Korea and Japan. This translates into maintaining and strengthening NATO, helping to stabilize the Middle East–Persian Gulf region, strengthening our relationship with China, and maintaining the U.S. forward positions in Australia, the Philippines, Korea and Japan. But to direct containment of Soviet power must also be added an effective strategy for countering indirect Soviet thrusts spearheaded by surrogate forces in Africa, Asia and our own hemisphere. The first step in developing such a strategy is a clearer understanding of the geopolitical implications of ostensibly "local" or "regional" conflicts.

Most Americans might be startled to discover that current American foreign policy has its intellectual roots in concepts first formulated over 80 years ago by a British geographer. Events since then fully justify Colin Gray's assessment of Mackinder as "the most influential and perceptive geopolitical thinker." As Robert Nisbet has commented: "Every geopolitical apprehension that Sir Halford Mackinder expressed some six decades ago in his *Democratic Ideals and Reality* has been fulfilled."[53]

Mackinder, and later thinkers such as Spykman and Burnham, were able to look beneath and beyond the immediate political events, grasping the essential and enduring aspects of international relations. They recognized and emphasized the two most permanent and therefore most significant factors in world affairs: geography and power. They observed and analyzed events with cold objectivity, but did so in order to help preserve and protect the small portion of the world where liberty and freedom exist. It is up to a new generation to ensure that their counsels were not in vain.

---

[53] Robert Nisbet, *History of the Idea of Progress* (New York: Basic Books, Inc., 1980), p. 331.

An Alternative to Containment

Earl C. Ravenal

It has often been said that "containment has stood the test of time." Yet, "compared to what?" asks the hoary joke. Containment must be arrayed against its costs, the expectations held of it, and the projected costs and expectations of alternative doctrines of national strategy. Indeed, containment has been subjected to critiques from both sides: that its accomplishments have been meager, and a more ambitious strategy is in order; or that its costs and risks are excessive, well beyond the necessary and beneficial.

For almost four decades, since the beginning of the cold war in the late 1940s, America's national strategy has been devoted to the containment of the Soviet Union and Soviet-inspired communism. In that time, the paradigm of America's national strategy has consisted of two basic elements: deterrence, and forward defense or alliance—both devoted to containing communist power and influence. Deterrence is roughly equated with our strategic nuclear forces; we seek to maintain at least a balance of strategic nuclear arms with the U.S.S.R. and to provide a nuclear umbrella over our allies and various other countries. Forward defense or alliance involves our protection, mostly by means of general purpose forces, of allies and other countries that oc-

Earl C. Ravenal, "An Alternative to Containment," *Cato Institute Policy Analysis,* 94 (Washington, D.C.: Cato Institute, Nov. 25, 1987). Reprinted by permission of Pergamon Press. This study appears in different version as "Containment, Non-Intervention, and Strategic Disengagement," in Terry L. Deibel and John Lewis Gaddis, eds., *Containing the Soviet Union* (Oxford: Pergamon, 1987).

cupy strategic positions or have sympathetic social and political values.

COST AND RISKS OF CONTAINMENT

The problem with the strategy of containment has not only been the continuing high costs associated with the requisite military preparations and the occasional egregious costs of heightened crises and regional wars; it has also been the risk, under certain circumstances, of being plunged into nuclear war. The costs can be attributed mostly to the generation of conventional forces, primarily for the defense of Europe; the risks can be attributed to reliance on the earlier use of nuclear weapons, also particularly in a confrontation arising from a conventional war in Europe. To some extent, cost can be transmuted into additional risk, and risk can be transformed into mere cost—that is what is meant by "lowering" or "raising" the nuclear threshold. But the choice itself arises from the policy of containment.

Imbalance of Commitments and Resources

Perhaps the high cost of our present national strategy could be tolerated, if it could be demonstrated that the cost was already more than strictly necessary to implement the strategy, and if the nation found itself in comfortable fiscal circumstances. Neither is the case. Powerful critics assert, with considerable empirical support in the quantification of global and regional power balances, that even the $314 billion that the Reagan administration requested for defense for FY [fiscal year] 1986, let alone the $289 billion that Congress finally granted, is grossly insufficient to execute the task of containing Soviet communism around the world. William Van Cleave proposed a 1986 defense budget $50 billion higher than Reagan's request.[1] And Leonard Sullivan Jr.'s estimate for projecting a confident conventional defense against Soviet arms envisions defense authorizations reaching 10 percent of GNP—a budget of about $446 billion for 1987.[2]

So, if anything, we are spending too little, not too much, to implement our present policy of containment.[3] Another indication of this fact is the continuing shift of strategic concern to the Persian Gulf at the relative expense of Europe. This process, begun in the last two years of the Carter administration, can be measured in terms of the number of American land divisions, tactical air wings, and naval carrier battle groups primarily allocated to the Gulf (for 1987, 5⅔ land divisions and an equivalent portion of tactical air and surface navy, out of a total of 21 land divisions, army and marine). Our explicit acquisition of this "new" area of strategic responsibility would

not be unduly troublesome, were it not for the administration's additional assumption of multiple simultaneous deployments. In his FY 1986 posture statement, for example, Secretary of Defense Weinberger states:

> Our forward-defense strategy dictates that we be able to conduct concurrent deployments to widely separated areas of the globe. Our present goal is to achieve the capability to deploy forces to a remote theater such as Southwest Asia, while maintaining an acceptable capability to reinforce NATO and key areas of Northeast Asia.[4]

The intention to deploy forces simultaneously raises the issue of double counting. A close reading of the force allocation embodied in Secretary Weinberger's statement indicates that, to some extent, the Pentagon intends a double assignment of certain units—characteristically for the Persian Gulf and also for Europe or East Asia and the Western Pacific. This not only violates the first law of thermodynamics, but also raises the question of the strategic overextension of general purpose forces. In more general terms, it suggests an imbalance of commitments and resources.

The Avoidance of Hard Choices

This problem did not originate with the Reagan administration. It has characterized U.S. force planning since the two-and-a-half war doctrine of the Kennedy administration and even the one-and-a-half war doctrine of the Nixon administration—and before either of those, the Eisenhower administration. But the Reagan administration has exacerbated the contradiction, with its implication of a wider strategic scope of simultaneous responses to Soviet aggressions, and with its more tangible implementation of the commitment to defend the Persian Gulf and Southwest Asia without

---

[1] "Defense Strategy: A Debate," in George E. Hudson and Joseph Kruzel, eds., *American Defense Annual, 1985–1986* (Lexington, MA: Lexington Books, 1985).

[2] "The FY 84 Defense Debate: Defeat by Default," *Armed Forces Journal International*, May 1983.

[3] This is an entirely different argument from that of the critics of containment who ridicule its passive stance and its failure to bring about the originally advertised downfall or evolution of the Soviet government. The latter point of view is sometimes labeled "containment-plus." It is the program of, for example, most of the authors gathered in Aaron Wildavsky, ed., *Beyond Containment: Alternative American Policies toward the Soviet Union* (San Francisco, CA: ICS Press, 1983). Wildavsky himself denigrates existing American policy as "minimal containment," "piecemeal resistance," and "defensive." He proposes to bring about nothing less than "political pluralization" within the Soviet Union, indeed as a necessary condition for avoiding the eventual Soviet move to "subjugate" the United States. Yet, as is typical of such advocates, Wildavsky purports to eschew "physical force," instead begging the essential question by postulating the sufficiency of mere "political warfare," a sort of Radio Free Europe writ large, a lot of noise at ramparts more substantial than the walls of Jericho. The most that can be said for this sophisticated troublemaking is that it is cheap—except that Wildavsky and other such militant hawks would add it to, not substitute it for, everything we are doing in the tangible defensive dimension.

[4] *Annual Report*, FY 1986, p. 39.

significantly increasing the force structure or overall military manpower. Of course, there is no law against creating such gaps and contradictions, and they can often be maintained for some time, since these states of affairs are not always tested sharply or conclusively by events. But ultimately, events, or the foreshadowing of events by analysis, will challenge these relationships. And something will have to give.

The urgent question, then, is whether the United States can afford even its present scope of containment, let alone the more rigorous, demanding, and consistent version of the Reagan administration's strategy proposed by its still more hawkish critics. How can we pay for it and in what ways? What the United States faces, toward the end of the Reagan administration, is a crisis of solvency, in several pertinent senses of the word: not merely fiscal solvency, but also a gross misalignment between the country's strategic objectives in the world and its manifest willingness to pay for them.

It will not do for proponents of vigorous containment to impugn the patriotism of those who see our situation as arguing for significant retrenchment, or to dismiss the fiscal problem by reciting the abstract proposition that our economy could support even higher defense spending, for example, by sharply raising taxes. The fact that there are options does not make them more desirable than current policy, or more politically feasible. All of the fiscal options (taxes, inflation, more government borrowing) are not simply unpalatable, but destructive. Resources (and support) are not automatic; to be available to the state, they must be mobilized from society. Even if the government could balance its books by exacting more resources in the form of taxes (and possibly also conscription at low military wages) to support a large defense establishment and extensive foreign commitments, that would be just the end of one problem and the beginning of another.

Solvency means that the external and internal stances of this country comport with each other. An extensive, engaged foreign policy and a large, active military posture require big, intrusive, demanding government. If, as we were promised, the Reagan administration favors a more reserved, less extensive government, then we must have a more detached, disengaged foreign policy. The dilemma is especially cruel for this conservative president [Ronald Reagan], who said in his first inaugural address that "government is the problem."

THE PROBLEM OF ANALYSIS

The broad challenge to contemporary American foreign policy is how to perpetuate containment of the Soviet Union in an era of multiple constraints, both international and domestic. Some of these constraints are limits, and thus are more or less unalterable. Others are trade-offs—that is, the price we have to pay, in terms of the larger objectives of our state and society, to contain the Soviet Union. We must consider whether our society is really committed to pay that price, not just rhetorically, but objectively; that is, not just in the verbalizations of a crust of elites, but in the supportive actions of all of society, taken as a policy-making system. For the question of the perpetuation of containment will not be determined by its abstract desirability, or even by its "necessity," but rather by whether containment is viable strategically and consonant with domestic values. Among those values are economic solvency and the quality of society, including our accustomed freedoms and the unique political system that we undertake to defend in the first place.

Gimmicks and Wishful Thinking

The question of perpetuating containment is therefore profound and complex. Yet, in typical critiques of containment, the goal of containing the U.S.S.R. is assumed; it is taken as indispensable, not challengeable in itself. True, various constraints (e.g., budgetary, demographic, resource, popular support) are often enumerated. But such exercises generally move abruptly, negligently, and optimistically to a proposed series of mild correctives. Questions relating to the sufficiency of the proposed moves are begged, simply in the way the moves are described. Often, as a centerpiece of these proposals, certain "force-multipliers" or other gimmicks are suggested, such as "dual-missioning" of our forces—that is, treating the units the United States keeps in Europe and Northeast Asia as expeditionary forces, available for broader regional assignments. Such superficial analyses and wishful prescriptions usually ignore the obvious dilemma: that global "flexibility" can be achieved only by robbing the primary areas of some measure of our protection. There are several problems, for example, with the proposal made by Col. John Endicott.[5] First, the forces he would generate or liberate from their overall units and contingently deploy to other regional situations are not sustainable. They are rump units, or rather, detached arms and legs without their torso, which has been left behind. They are dependent on a few days of transportable supplies, then on pre-positioned logistics that will be vulnerable, because they will be known and high-value targets for a determined enemy.

Second, even the flexibly deployed forces are costly. Their pre-positioned supplies are, after all, redundant. The lines of communication to their assigned outposts must be protected by our anti-submarine systems and our carrier battle groups against determined attempts at interdiction. The locations to be

reached are, by definition, the farthest off, and therefore require the greatest amounts of airlift and sealift. Moreover, the equipment to be lifted is not as light as proponents of these forces indicate: Airmobile units, with their helicopters, are notoriously bulky, and the high rates of fire that must be sustained entail heavy logistics, even if the units are classified as "light." There will be a need for a thick base structure along the way to the far-off theaters, and this, in turn, will entail subsidies and defensive obligations to local countries.

Third, above all, proponents of dual-missioning have to cope with the prospect of simultaneous conflicts, for example, in Europe and in Southwest Asia. Our adversaries will not be so obliging as to play to American convenience. Serious trouble in a peripheral area is bound to be accompanied by tension at the center. In any case, nervous allies will not cheerfully part with the cutting edge of American forces primarily detailed to their defense. That, among other things, is already the trouble with the Rapid Deployment Force under Central Command—at least with Secretary of Defense Weinberger's concept of such forces: They are to be double-hatted or even triple-hatted units. But we are not fooling anyone but ourselves; certainly not our allies, and even less our adversaries. (One is reminded of Kurt Vonnegut's description, in his novel, *Galapagos,* of the Ecuadorian navy: It consists of four submarines, which choose to remain submerged and incommunicado and have not been heard from for 15 years.)

The proponents of this dual-missioning scheme assure us that "political costs should be minimal," since "U.S. commitment to the defense of Western Europe and South Korea would be evident and continuing." But I would not be so sure of this proposition. Long before such units were actually shifted out of their primary region of deployment, in some crisis, the designation of these units as swing forces would have illustrated the inconstancy

---

[5] "Forward Deployed Expeditionary Forces," in Terry L. Deibel and John Lewis Gaddis, eds., *Containment: Concept and Policy* (Washington, D.C.: NDU Press, 1986).

of our commitment. In any case, if such forces were more needed in the outlying theaters, we would have, or should have, permanently deployed them there in the first place. (Indeed, in the case of Asia, the scheme of force flexibility rests on the ability of South Korea and Japan to handle their own conventional defense.) Why, then, shift American forces merely temporarily? (And, ironically, the worst time to move them would be in a crisis.) Why not withdraw them in any case, and entirely?

The Nature of Foreign Policy

Proposals for limited change fail because of their underlying methodology, a way of thinking that characterizes much of the current debate on containment itself. Simply put, containment may be a nice idea, but foreign policy is not made of attractive ideas peddled with competitive virtuosity and zeal. Certainly a policy such as containment is not self-executing; there are the essential questions of what may be needed to implement the policy, whether those things will be forthcoming, and at what price. Only in the context of these questions can we understand the scope of our choices, or even understand what it means to "choose." Most policy writing, whether official or critical, consists of lists of things that "must" be done. Rarely is it based on an assessment of costs, limits, and feasibility, or a comparison of alternatives. Rarely does it invoke numbers, or even imply quantities of things that must be exacted or expended. Gaps are bridged, if at all, by pure verbalisms, exhortations of "will," or the mere advocacy of shifts in our orientation.

But policy, particularly foreign policy, is not a set of items that must be obtained, preserved, or remedied in the world, without reference to situation or contingent cost. It is certainly not the official expression of objectives of state. Rather, policy is an entire system's probable responses to future contingent challenges over a range of issues and geographical areas. Many of the elements that form these responses will not be determined by national authorities. Some policy determinants consist of institutional, military, and resource dispositions that make it more likely that we will respond in a certain way. Other determinants include situations at the time of future decisions or actions, also to varying degrees beyond our control, though not totally beyond our prediction. That is why the description of a proposed foreign policy must begin by tracing the constraints of the international and domestic systems. These are the starting points in the partially predictive process that indicates what our foreign policy orientation "ought" to be.

This kind of real-world analysis must be applied to containment as the emblematic American foreign policy of the past four decades. An old expression inquires whether the game is worth the candle. Any critique of containment should ask: (a) What is the game? (b) What is the requisite candle? (c) Can we afford the candle? (d) Is there another game in town?

UNIVERSALITY AND THE MIRAGE OF SELECTIVE CONTAINMENT

We start with the name of the game—the concept of containment. At the outset, we encounter an essential dispute: Was containment originally intended to be universal in its application? More interestingly, is containment by its very nature, or rather by the nature of the threat it is designed to meet, universal?

Kennan's Original Formulation

A literal reading of George Kennan's original "text" indicates that containment was to be universal. Indeed, Kennan made containment's universality the centerpiece of his published analysis of Soviet conduct in 1947, in his celebrated image of the Soviet threat:

> Its political action is a fluid stream which moves constantly, wherever it is permitted to move, toward a given goal. Its main concern is to make sure that it has filled every nook and cranny available to it in the basin of world power.

Further, Kennan prescribed:

> a long-term, patient but firm and vigilant containment...[through] the adroit and vigilant application of counterforce at a series of constantly shifting geographical and political points, corresponding to the shifts and maneuvers of Soviet policy...a policy of firm containment, designed to confront the Russians with unalterable counterforce at every point where they show signs of encroaching upon the interests of a peaceful and stable world.[6]

Kennan now claims that he has been grossly misinterpreted; that he always intended to emphasize geographical selectivity (that is, Europe and its approaches from the east, the south, and the sea), and to confine our response primarily to economic means[7]— a retrospective exegesis, or prosthesis, for which there is some support in his unpublished and State Department work at the time.[8] Nevertheless, given Kennan's characterization of the Soviet threat, one wonders how a geographically and functionally limited American response could have been sufficient. That is particularly so if the purpose of containment was not to make a token defense, but to present Soviet leaders with such a prospect of frustration that the motives and dynamic of their society would be profoundly al-

tered. Hydraulic metaphors, no less than their subject, should flow in all directions. If the threat is of such a character that there is a case for containing it at all, then containment must be universal. Selectively containing that kind of threat is like trying to hold water in a two-dimensional vessel.

The Illusion of Selectivity

Nevertheless, selectivity is the most prevalent kind of argument purporting to mitigate the need for extensive armament and deployments in the implementation of containment. It can take two forms: selectivity of commitment, that is, of the objectives of our policy and strategy; and selectivity of means, of the military forces and weapons which support it.

Selectivity of commitment is proposed as a way of bringing obligations and costs into line (and also as a way of minimizing the occasions for war). The argument for selectivity fixes on places and defensive objects that "matter," that make a difference according to some criterion. Virtually all proponents of selectivity would still contain our adversaries in some sense; but they are selective in that they strive for some principle of limitation and impute to their more extreme opponents the scheme of "universality."

Most proposals of selective intervention— as diverse as those of Kennan, Robert W. Tucker, Stanley Hoffmann, and Ernst B. Haas[9]—are subject to the same problems. In the last analysis, all lead back to, or are operationally indistinguishable from, the more

---

[6] "X" [George F. Kennan], "The Sources of Soviet Conduct," *Foreign Affairs* 25 (July 1947): 566–582.

[7] See "'X' Plus 25: Interview with George Kennan," *Foreign Policy* (Summer 1972): 14ff., referring to Kennan, *Memoirs: 1925–1950* (Boston: Little, Brown/Atlantic Monthly Press, 1967), passim.

[8] See, for example, John Lewis Gaddis, *Strategies of Containment* (New York: Oxford University Press, 1982).

[9] George F. Kennan, *The Cloud of Danger* (Boston: Little, Brown/Atlantic Monthly Press, 1977); Robert W. Tucker, "The Purpose of American Power," *Foreign Affairs* (Winter 1980–1981): 241–274; Stanley Hoffmann, "The New Orthodoxy," *The New York Review of Books*, April 16, 1981, and "Foreign Policy: What's to Be Done?" *The New York Review of Books*, April 30, 1981; Ernst B. Haas, "On Hedging Our Bets: Selective Engagement with the Soviet Union," in Wildavsky, *Beyond Containment*.

comprehensive versions of containment. This is true in several respects: (a) They support virtually all the same objects of our defense; objects, as it turns out, that comprise the major portion of our present and projected defense expenditures.[10] (b) They would implicitly support, in addition to the supposedly necessary prime objects, a host of minor, intrinsically dispensable objects "for the sake of" the major objectives. (c) When and if these proposals are costed out, they may turn out to be even more expensive than the supposedly universal schemes they would supplant. This is because, in emphasizing certain situations as "vital," they tend to add these to all the others, which they are wary of discontinuing. (d) Finally, the logic of threat and response, coupled with the diagnosis of the nature or "source" of the threat, leads these supposedly limitationist arguments back to an espousal of any act or response that would constitute effective containment. Selectivity becomes universality, though the authors of these proposals sometimes disown or disfigure their intellectual offspring.

An able statement of selectivity is that of Robert W. Tucker. Tucker argues for "moderate containment," or "a limited policy of containment," and he would "concentrate" American strategic attention on the Persian Gulf.[11] His requirement for intensified defense of the Gulf seems at least halfway toward the ability to stand off a Soviet incursion, as well as to discourage an indigenous disruption or refusal of oil on assured and reasonable terms. Though he does not demonstrate how our military force would accomplish this result, it is clear that it would require a larger, more ready and sustainable rapid deployment force.

We already spend some $49 billion a year to prepare to defend the Persian Gulf (out of about $65 billion that can be considered to be attributable to regions other than Europe and East Asia). Tucker's scheme for a more comprehensive defense of the Gulf might add another $10 or $12 billion a year to the cost of defending this region. And since Tucker would not give up the defense of Western Europe, which costs $133 billion a year, there is no category of arms that he would cut appreciably, except such minimal forces as we keep for intervention in Central America. Even there he asserts the propriety of American force if Soviet or Cuban support is discovered.

George Kennan, too, starts by seeking a principle that limits American political and military intervention and ends by asserting and implying a scope of instances that is tantamount to virtually universal involvement. In his book, *The Cloud of Danger*, Kennan advocates "the reduction of external commitments to the indispensable minimum...the preservation of the political independence and military security of Europe, of Japan, and—with the single reservation that it should not involve the dispatch and commitment of American armed forces of Israel."[12] True, Kennan

---

[10] The three main theaters, which virtually all proponents of supposed selectivity of American commitment, intervention, and deployment would retain (Europe/NATO, the Middle East including the Eastern Mediterranean and the Persian Gulf/Southwest Asia, and East Asia/Western Pacific), take $224 billion of the $240 billion for general purpose forces, out of the $312 billion initially requested defense budget authority for FY 1987. Thus, the peripheral regions, some part of which most proponents of selectivity might dispense with, take only about 5 percent of the defense budget. There may be good and even sufficient reasons for not intervening in such peripheral areas, but they are not budgetary. In this respect, at least, selective containment is hardly less demanding than supposed global containment.

[11] Tucker, "The Purpose of American Power," p. 256.

[12] *The Cloud of Danger*, p. 229. No doubt Kennan would now also include the Persian Gulf/Southwest Asia. Evidence for this surmise is in Kennan's article on the Op-Ed page of the *New York Times* in the immediate aftermath of the Soviet invasion of Afghanistan in late December 1979, in which, after calling for "mature statesmanship," he hastened to reassure: "These words are not meant to express opposition to a prompt and effective strengthening of our military capabilities relevant to the Middle

would like to abandon "several obsolescent and nonessential positions: notably those at Panama, in the Philippines, and in Korea."[13] But he cannot deny the extent to which the primary commitments depend, physically and psychologically, on those "nonessential" positions.

In fact, one should not be unduly impressed by modifying and mollifying adjectives such as "limited," "selective," or "moderate"; for when one becomes concrete, the imperative of containment usually overrides the qualifications. The problem is generic to selective versions of containment. Containment, of its essence, must remain contingently open-ended. The circumstances of Soviet aggressive or expansive behavior are not subject to American definition and limitation; implicit in the definition of "the Soviet threat" is that the Soviets exercise the initiative. Therefore, once committed to containment, how can we keep it limited?

Stanley Hoffmann also proposes a "selective policy." He criticizes the "new orthodoxy" and its "fundamentalist response": "projection of a bipolar grid" on the world, "neo-nationalism," "emphasis on military power," "too militant [a] view of Soviet expansionism," and a "world-wide crusade." But he would defend essentially the same places and objects as his more extreme opponents, and in much the same ways, especially in Europe, where the conventional force balance trends are "disturbing" and where we "need...middle-range nuclear weapons capable of hitting the Soviet Union."

Throughout Hoffmann's critique there is an avoidance of choice. In the Persian Gulf, for instance, "the U.S. would be in a tragic position if it had to choose between economic disaster and a military intervention that could be economically futile and would be politically catastrophic." (Yes, but which way would his argument fall if we had to choose?) Again, "the aim of foreign policy ought to be to make it possible for each of the two powers to play its own game, in such a way as not to violate the vital interests of the other." (A good rule. But should we adopt it unilaterally, asymmetrically, if "their" game *does* violate our vital interests?) In another place, Hoffmann proposes "to provide extended deterrence by means other than American military and nuclear might alone." (What is the function of "alone"? If we have the nuclear might, what else do we need? If we do not have it, what good are the other means?)[14]

The problems of selectivity are seen even more clearly in the essay of Ernst B. Haas. Haas's plan "scales down and redefines some American world order values, recognizing that we cannot, without risking our own ruin, continue the attempt to mold the world in our image." It also aims at a "delinking of issues." Haas even permits himself to be skeptical of the existence of "a Soviet threat," or, for that matter, a "free world." Confronted with the question, "where should we be ready to fight?" Haas recites the familiar litany: "Western Europe, Japan, South Korea, and the Pacific." To this he adds "regimes so close to the United States as to afford the adversary an opportunity for offensive action...Canada and Mexico...." To this already substantial list Haas appends two nonstrategic criteria: "the military defense of all democratic countries against Soviet threats, provided these countries wish to be defended...[and] threats by allies of the Soviet Union against Third World countries with a democratic tradition."

East....[As for the] big stick...who could object?" George F. Kennan, "On Washington's Reaction to the Afghan Crisis: 'Was This Really Mature Statesmanship?'" *New York Times*, February 1, 1980.
[13] *The Cloud of Danger*, p. 230.

[14] Hoffmann, "The New Orthodoxy" and "Foreign Policy."

There is yet another, economic, objective: "key commodities that are essential for the economic welfare of the democratic countries."[15]

These proposed objects of American protection are not in themselves absurd. The point is that, in the name of "selectivity," they add up to a good part of the world—all we are now committed to defend, and perhaps more. My calculation is that the areas and objectives that Haas mentions are already costing the United States about $237 billion out of the $240 billion we plan to spend for general purpose forces in the 1987 defense budget. Verbal criteria, such as "selective engagement," do not save Americans much or absolve us from the risk of confrontation and escalation.

The Real Alternatives

In the end, "selective" containment is not the only alternative to universal containment. Rather, it is just a middle position between universal intervention and consistent nonintervention (the uninvited guest at this contentious banquet). Limitationists think their middle positions must be more realistic, simply because the extreme positions are unacceptable or unmentionable. But because of its contradictions and its operational correspondence with more extensive containment, this middle position is instead almost fictional. It is an artifact of the debate, not a real policy. The extremes of universal containment and consistent disengagement may be unpalatable, but that is just the point. The choice of extreme positions approximates the present predicament of the United States. In the face of this real and poignant choice, the formula of "selective" intervention or "moderate" containment is more an incantation than a proposal.

---

[15] Haas, "On Hedging Our Bets."

DEFINING THE CONTAINMENT PROBLEM AWAY

But selectivity in its various forms is not the only false approach invented to avoid the burdens and risks of containment. Several positions of the liberal center and liberal left either deny the need to contain or attempt to subsume the containment paradigm in a new and presumably more acceptable framework.

Some of these arguments deny the empirical premise—the "threat"—and attempt to explain away a succession of Soviet moves, both regional intrusions and arms buildups. There are three variants: (a) "we are still ahead"; (b) "their moves are not what you think they are"; and (c) "their moves are somehow our fault, reactions to our own provocations." All are the familiar stuff of the former revisionists of the cold war. They may have once been useful correctives, but over the past decade they have had to become more imaginative, even fanciful. For some reason, whether compensatory or aggressive, the Soviets have mounted a major political and military challenge to the West; at least they have done a collection of things that equate to such a challenge, and done so in the knowledge that they would be so interpreted. Rather than deny the problem in order to justify doing less, a realistic analysis would admit the seriousness of U.S. inaction in order to measure its consequences against those of confronting the problem directly.

Searching for a New Yalta

Another escape (generally a liberal one) from the responsibility of dealing frontally with "the threat" is the positing of "deals," a new round of global negotiations with the Soviet Union. Though proponents of this course of action would be uncomfortable with the parallel, this would be tantamount to another Yalta—in three respects. First, the concept is grandiose; a new deal would not be a series of ad hoc technical agreements, but a comprehensive renegotiation of the boundaries of "East" and "West" and the rules of conduct in and between those spheres. Second, "deals" do not represent one nation's adjustment to situations; they are not unilateral, consisting of measures entirely within our own competence to devise and execute. Indeed, they toy casually with the fate of other nations, whose abandonment or preservation are the agenda of the two superpowers. Third, above all, if there are to be deals at all instead of unilateral counter-threats, they must codify the farthest reaches of Soviet penetration and influence, and leave the rest, as in Lenin's dictum, "negotiable." Thus, deals simply define away the problem of our inability to act by making it part of the settlement.

The Pursuit of an Elusive World Order

Still another attempt to solve the problem of America's situation in the world is to find a surrogate goal that is more congenial or putatively more amenable to solution than the unilateral pursuit of security. The classic solution is to posit "world order norms," conditions of the international system that should be sought instead of the narrower and presumably more contentious security interests of the United States. An elaborate expression of this thesis is Stanley Hoffmann's book, which embodies in its title the choice he sees as meaningful and critical: *Primacy or World Order*.[16]

But the kind of world order we would recognize as congenial or livable would include a vast component of American primacy. World order is not self-enforcing, and no one can hope for overarching impartial mechanisms or wish for the dominance of another great power. So in the critical cases it would even be

hard to distinguish world order from effective American primacy. More important, it would be hard to distinguish the amount of American power needed for the more direct and comprehensible tasks of self-protection from the amount (presumably, Hoffmann would say, the lesser amount) sufficient to establish world order. Indeed, it might take a concentration and persistence of American power far in excess of the more modest requirements of our own security to enforce world order. That effort would often be misspent, and might also be frustrated. Our simple will to move the international system toward a more cooperative, "managed" basis would likely meet the residual suspicion of our major antagonists in the world, or the competition of ambitious, rising regional contestants, or the hostility of a myriad of other less powerful but dissatisfied nations who do not relish our intrusive distribution of the things of the world, however constructive we may think it is.

THE QUESTION OF MEANS

If the objects of containment cannot be selectively limited, and the containment problem itself cannot be defined or subsumed out of existence, perhaps some relief from the burdens of extensive containment can be found in the means through which the policy would be executed. One approach is to assert that military means are interchangeable with "non-military means," and that the substitution is a matter of choice or preference. But this proposition is not much more than a placebo. Everyone hopes that in a crisis of conflicting interests, diplomacy, economic inducements, and sympathetic ties will help resolve the problem. But it is fair to ask, what if those non-military instruments do not work? Or what if they work only because military instruments lurk in the background—that is, if they depend for their efficacy, in the last analysis, on the threat of force? Simply to ignore

---

[16] Stanley Hoffmann, *Primacy or World Order: American Foreign Policy since the Cold War* (New York: McGraw Hill, 1978).

this problem is to be thrown back on a non-policy: hoping that nothing happens.

The argument of "non-military means" amounts to a displacement, actually a transcendence, of the security problem. Again, one version is represented in the current writings of George F. Kennan. Kennan's attitude toward the Soviet challenge and America's predicament is expressed poignantly in an article in the *Atlantic* called "Cease This Madness,"[17] which is an impassioned appeal directed to the leadership of both the United States and the Soviet Union. Laying about him evenhandedly with imputations of blame—equating, for example, the Soviets' depriving their youth of liberty with our society's granting them too much liberty—he proceeds to impugn the "madness" that underlies the "dreadful militarization of the entire East-West relationship." He avers: "For the maintenance of armed forces on a scale that envisages the total destruction of an entire people there is no rational justification."

There is no question that Kennan is describing a real peril to humanity; but his remarks only underscore the tragic predicament of both nations, the perverse but still recognizable rationality of arms competition. What one would call, ruefully, strategic interdependence is not "madness" in the ordinary sense of the word. Kennan's frequent charge of "militarization" and his rather vague advice, "...thrust [these] destructive powers...from you," in the end simply reflect his longstanding impatience in the presence of military factors, an impatience born of the disdain of the diplomatist to do his homework in the military stuff of the strategic nuclear age. What remedy follows from this dual ascription of cause: madness and militarization? Simply, that "the decisionmakers of the two super-powers...should...take their military establishments in hand and insist that these become the servants, not the masters and determinants, of political action"—as if the military created the foreign policies of either state.

The Role of Military Force

A variant of the argument for "non-military means" is the well-worn thesis of the disutility of military force. This is another attempt to avoid the price, and even the calculus, of our national objectives. The argument plays upon an equivocation: first, that U.S. military power, in relation to that of others, is in decline; second, that military power in general is less usable, less translatable into political advantages.

It is probably true that pure application of military force is declining in its effect on situations, that it is increasingly cost-ineffective, and that its means are becoming more widely diffused among multiple centers of political and strategic initiative. But military force is still integral to the structure of international relations.[18] And, of course, military power can be decisive if asymmetrically possessed in a particular situation.

As for non-military means, one can cite a variety of instruments to influence other parties, through incentives as well as threats.[19] Everyone favors non-military instruments,

---

[17] George F. Kennan, "Cease This Madness," *The Atlantic*, January, 1981.

[18] Indeed, the debate about the efficacy of military force is over the extent to which the structure of the international system is determined by strategic or nonstrategic factors, resting, in turn, on the distribution and exploitation of military or non-military resources and advantages. This is a debate conducted by, among others, Seyom Brown, "The Changing Essence of Power," *Foreign Affairs*, January 1973, and *New Forces in World Politics* (Washington, D.C.: Brookings, 1974); and by Robert W. Tucker, "A New International Order?" *Commentary*, February 1975, and *The Inequality of Nations* (New York: Basic Books, 1977).

[19] A striking inventory of such non-forcible (or at least non-violent) means is presented in Richard W. Fogg, "Creative, Peaceful Approaches for Dealing with Conflict," *Journal of Conflict Resolution*, June 1985.

where they are appropriate. But one needs force, or at least residual force, to defend a nation's security decisively and confidently. If the object is to minimize the use of military force, then the task is to devise a system and a foreign policy that do not occasion violent intervention. Non-military means might have to be taken into the calculus, but they do not excuse us from the calculation.

The Concept of National Will

An associated confusion arises when we ask whether our political leaders could enhance American power in the world by mobilizing national "will." It had become a fashion to deplore the supposed absence of "presidential leadership," at least until the Reagan restoration of 1981, in which America was dealt the semblance of presidential leadership in spades. Now various pundit-journalists, professorial strategists, and even many national security bureaucrats talk almost obsessively about will. Foreign challenges and problems are seen as tests of our resolve; Vietnam was a "trauma" that impaired our capability to respond to threats; we are paralyzed by a "failure of nerve."

But this terminology itself is a tissue of anthropomorphisms and misleading abstractions. We are not talking about "will" in some primal personal sense; we are talking about the operation of a complex political and social system, not even an organism except in a mostly misleading metaphor.

The politics of "will" stems from a profound misconception of the nature and function of foreign policy, embodying a curious mixture of necessity and choice. The necessary, proper, and exclusive referent of foreign policy is held to be external, having to do with the state of the outside world, not the impact of it on our own political or social or economic system; and rather abstract, such as global and regional power balances and assessments of

relative credibility. "Interests" are held to reside objectively, and almost implicitly, in objects of our foreign policy or in situations themselves, when in fact they are more the result of our own perceptions of relevance and immediacy, and of our tangible commitments, which forge the linkages between events elsewhere in the world and our own indicated responses.[20] And yet, in apparent contradiction, our responses are seen as a matter of choice, an exercise of will. Indeed, policy itself is most often defined as a set of authoritative declarations of intent, when, operationally, policy is more a set of contingent predictions about our own probable future response—in short, what we will be able to do as much as what we would like to do.

The Issue of Constraints

Thus, our interests, far from being unarguable external impositions on us, evolve more from the abstract sense we insist on making of the world and the way we intellectualize foreign objects and situations. And policy, far from being a matter of pure choice or will, is more determined by constraints, both external and internal. If there was a trauma occasioned by the Vietnam War, it has to be analyzed in terms of what the war revealed about the con-

---

[20] A further word about "threats": No pile of facts (for example, about the military capabilities or the intentions of the Soviet Union), no matter how high or deep, leads by itself to any conclusion, particularly a policy conclusion. What is essential in disposing a nation's response to some challenge or state of affairs is the "major premise," which is always an "if-then" proposition; in other words, a general policy statement. Indeed, a nation's "policy" can be considered a summation of the important major premises relating to possible events or occurrences across geographical areas or in functional areas of national activity. Thus, it is well to take seriously the facts of, say, the Soviet state and leadership. But such sobriety in itself neither disposes the factual determination nor dictates the policy conclusion. Odd as it may seem, there is no necessary connection between taking threats seriously and doing something about them.

strained operation of our own system and about our constrained ability to coerce the conduct of others in the international system. What is not appreciated, even by those who consider themselves foreign policy "makers," is that you don't "make" foreign policy as you make boats or houses or gadgets or soup. The question is not even *who* makes policy, but *what* makes policy.

To determine the responses of our system, then, we cannot look to factors of will, predilection, or even intention. Rather, we are thrown back on the analysis of (a) the strategic orientation that is conditioned by our preparations and built into our institutions, and (b) our capabilities and constraints. Those factors constitute, respectively, the logic and the logistics of national action. They are what make certain responses both "necessary" and yet at times impossible.

Thus, a proper theory of national conduct would have to include:

1. the probable limits of Soviet expansion and other challenging activity, without our deterrence or counterintervention
2. the ability of the United States to live with these situations
3. what it could cost to counter Soviet or other actions at various stages, and the comparison of these costs with the costs of other things our system could do
4. the alternatives we have, and the effects that would occur in the international system if we were to exercise some large-scale alternative choices.

AN ALTERNATIVE DOCTRINE

The entailments and disabilities of containment suggest the consideration of a major, coherent alternative. Such a policy would be one of strategic disengagement and non-intervention. In such a program, both of the cardinal elements of the present U.S. strategic paradigm would change. Instead of deterrence and alliance, we would pursue war avoidance and self-reliance. Our security would depend more on our abstention from regional conflicts and, in the strategic nuclear dimension, on finite essential deterrence.

America's Core Values

In a program of non-intervention, the United States would defend primarily against an umbra of direct threats to those values that are so basic that they are part of the definition of state and society: our political integrity and the safety of our citizens and their domestic property. Because those values are inalienable, their defense would ipso facto be credible. We would also defend against a penumbra of challenges that are only indirectly threatening but are relevant because of their weight, momentum, direction, and ineluctability. We would be looking for a new set of criteria, decision rules, if you will, that condition and bound our responses to future events that could be considered challenges. This definition is intensive, rather than extensive, in nature.

Nor are these rhetorical terms. As I have discussed at greater length elsewhere,[21] our military program would be designed to defend the most restricted perimeter required to protect those core values, a much smaller perimeter than the one the United States is now committed to defend. We would defend against military threats directed against our homeland. That is not, in the first instance, an overtly geographical criterion, and deliberately not. We should not be fixated on drawing lines in the sand; rather, we should be concerned to characterize correctly the

---

[21] See Earl C. Ravenal, *Defining Defense: The 1985 Military Budget* (Washington, D.C.: Cato Institute, 1984).

nature and import of other countries' actions, and appreciate the characteristics of foreign events that cause us to consider them "threats." Functional criteria may be less definitive than geographical ones, but they are more important.

The concomitant of this restricted definition of American interests and of the threats to them is that the United States would encourage other nations to become self-reliant, to hedge. In fact, many foresighted countries already discount American protection in a wide range of possible cases, despite our formal obligations to come to their assistance. This does not imply that all these countries face imminent threats; simply that some are impressed more by the reality of our circumstances than by our reassurances and have drawn the appropriate conclusions.

War avoidance invokes primarily, though not exclusively, the strategic nuclear component of this counterparadigm. We will always need a strategy that discourages direct nuclear attacks on our homeland or intolerable coercion of our national political choices by nuclear threats. But today, given the parity between the nuclear arsenals of the two superpowers, our safety depends on maintaining a condition that is called crisis stability, wherein both sides have a strong incentive to avoid striking first with their nuclear weapons.

Toward Nuclear Stability

A design for nuclear stability would look like this: Since an enemy's first strike must logically be a damage-limiting attack against our nuclear forces, we should eliminate systems as they become even theoretically vulnerable to a Soviet pre-emptive strike. Land-based systems are inevitably vulnerable, despite the efforts of a succession of administrations to put them in multiple or closely spaced

shelters (as with the MX), or to acquire a redundant and dispersed force (as with the prospective Midgetman single-warhead missiles). Instead, we should move to a dyad of strategic nuclear forces: ballistic missile submarines and bombers armed with medium-range air-launched cruise missiles. Then, to discourage further a Soviet first strike, we should not target Soviet missiles (nor does it make any strategic or moral sense to aim at Soviet cities). Rather, we should develop a list of some 3,000 military targets such as naval and air bases, concentrations of conventional forces, military logistical complexes, and arms industries that are relatively far from large civilian population centers. Finally, since nuclear war is most likely to occur through *our* escalation in the midst of conventional war, probably in Europe, or possibly in the Middle East, we must confront our attitude toward the first use of nuclear weapons. I believe we should impose upon ourselves an unconditional doctrine of no first use.

Assessing the Soviet Threat

The two elements of war avoidance and self-reliance constitute a new paradigm, a principled policy of non-intervention that should be a major alternative. We would no longer consider peace to be seamless and indivisible. There might well be continuing troubles in the world, including cases where a Soviet-sponsored faction perpetrates a forcible revision of the local military balance. If we were to intervene, we might win a few rounds, as in Grenada in November 1983. But the list of feasible interventions is far shorter than the list of desirable ones, and even shorter than the list of "necessary" ones.

But what of the expected, and frequent, charge that a non-interventionist foreign policy would lay the world open to Soviet expansion or revolutionary violence? In the last analysis, a true non-interventionist position does not depend on trust in Soviet intentions: It takes Soviet power seriously. It simply accepts the possibility of suffering some foreign losses in order to preserve the integrity of our own economy, society, and political system. Yet there are reasons, also, to doubt the unvarnished projection of a Soviet political-military windfall. These reasons depend on a more sophisticated calculus of the motives (the propensity to intervene) of a potential aggressor; on an unavoidably complex analysis of the course and future of the international system; and on a somewhat speculative projection of the status of Western Europe without America.

First, it is difficult to determine just how the Soviet Union would react to a non-interventionist American foreign policy. However, a potential aggressor will consider not simply the odds of victory or defeat; he must weigh whether his potential gains, minus the predicted costs of achieving them, exceed what he could achieve without attacking. That is a very different, and a much more discouraging, calculus.

Beyond that, a serious proposal of non-intervention must make some assumptions about the world—that is, the global political-military balance, specifically between the United States and the Soviet Union, and the situation in strategic regions of the world. The international system is not just an inert environment for the making of foreign policy, or so much malleable clay or putty for the designers of an active and manipulative foreign policy. The structure or design of the international system is also in important ways a determinant of foreign policy, a framework within which each nation must choose. Its characteristics are to some extent alterable by individual nations, more or less according to their power, and the United States will continue to have preeminent ability to set and modify those parameters

through its own choices and actions. But to do so requires a further expense or effort and is arguably less efficient than a policy of operating within the parameters.

A New International System

The evolving international system will offer increasing challenges and temptations, but it also will impose greater costs and risks for less ample and less secure gains, all within the social, economic, and political constraints of the domestic system, which are themselves becoming tighter and more troublesome. The world that we will confront as we move beyond the turn of the millennium will evolve further from the world that we have experienced during the past four decades, in six critical dimensions.

The first is the high probability of troubles, such as embargoes, expropriations, coups, revolutions, externally supported subversions, thrusts by impatient irredentist states, and calculated probes of defense perimeters; these will be neither resolved nor constructively equilibrated by some benign balance of power mechanism.

The second tendency is increasing interdependence. But this has a different implication from the one that proponents would recognize. Interdependence is a set of functional linkages of nations: resources, access routes, economic activities and organizations, populations, and the physical environment. These areas harbor problems that could be aggravated to the point where they became threats to the security of nations, demanding but not suggesting solutions.

The third element of the future international system is the probable absence of an ultimate adjustment mechanism, in the form of a supranational institution that can authoritatively police the system, dispensing justice and granting relief, especially in those extreme cases that threaten to unhinge the system.

The fourth factor is an interim conclusion of the first three: Stabilization, the long-range action of states to bring about conditions in the external system that enhance their security, will take the form of unilateral interventions rather than collaborative world order.

The fifth future condition—perhaps the most important one—is the unmanageable diffusion of power, beyond some ideal geometry of powerful but "responsible" states. Instead, this process is likely to proceed to a kaleidoscopic interaction of multiple political entities. By all measures of power—military (nuclear or conventional, actual or potential), economic (total wealth or commercial weight), or political (the thrust to autonomy and achievement)—there may be 15 or 20 salient states, not necessarily equal, and not necessarily armed with nuclear weapons, but potent to the point of enjoying the possibility of independent action. This diffusion of power will have several aspects. One is that limits will become evident in existing polities, and cracks will appear in existing military alliances. Another aspect of diffusion is the impracticality of military power, whether nuclear, conventional, or subconventional—quite a different matter from the absolute or relative disutility of military force.

The sixth condition that will complicate the enforcement of international order is the incoherence of domestic support, not just in our country but to a certain extent in all, and not just when political systems are free from external pressure, but precisely when they most need steady support. The lack of public support might not prevent intervention, but it might critically inhibit its prosecution. (This, in my view, is the enduring lesson of Vietnam.)

The net result of these tendencies is that general unalignment, as a pattern or type of international system, is likely to succeed the

present multipolar balance of power, just as the balance of power succeeded the earlier regime of bipolar confrontation. This would be a world of circumscribed regional powers. Though absolute technological and military disparities might increase, there might be more equality of usable power among the present superpowers, great powers, and middle powers, including some accomplished or would-be regional hegemonic states.

Implications for the United States

In the face of such a world, the policy choice for the United States is whether to attempt to control its environment, or simply to adjust. Although challenges and opportunities will arise, it will be increasingly unnecessary and undesirable for the United States to intervene in regional situations. It will be unnecessary because the very presence of either a regional hegemonic state or a situation of perpetual conflict will be an obstruction to the other superpower, or to any other external power. There would be less potential profit for any intervenor, making our own abstention less risky. It will be increasingly undesirable for the United States to intervene in regional situations because these situations will be messy and interminable. They will tend to be profitless, because intervention will be expensive, and results, even if achieved, will be transient.

Of course, for the United States the most important region is Europe. What would be the probable status of Europe without American protection? I would envisage a Europe that is independent politically and diplomatically and autonomous strategically, and that acts in greater military concert, though not political unity. Actually, Europe could go quite far toward defending itself without American help. It need not be "Finlandized," either in whole or in part. If the United States were to withdraw, the principal European countries would probably increase their defense spending gradually, perhaps to 5 percent or 6 percent of their gross national product. The countries of Western Europe, even if not formally united in a new military alliance, have the economic, demographic, and military resources, and the advantage of natural and man-made barriers, to defeat or crucially penalize a Soviet attack.[22]

The United States can make large cuts in its defense budget if and only if a policy of strategic disengagement and nonintervention is adopted. We could defend our essential security and our central values with a much smaller force structure than we have now. Such a force structure would provide the following general purpose forces: 8 land divisions (6 army and 2 Marine Corps), 20 tactical airwing equivalents (11 air force, 4 Marine Corps, and 5 navy), and 6 carrier battle groups. With the addition of a dyad of nuclear forces (submarines and cruise-missile–armed bombers), this would mean manpower of 1,185,000 (370,000 army, 315,000 air force, 365,000 navy, and 135,000 Marine Corps). The total defense budget at the end of a decade of adjustment would be about $158 billion in 1987 dollars. In contrast, the Reagan administration originally requested, for 1987, 21 land divisions and 46 tactical airwing equivalents, with 14 carrier battle groups; this force requires 2,181,000 men and a budget authorization of $312 billion.

These differences will multiply greatly unless we change our course. The way we are headed, the defense budget will be about $530 billion by 1996, and cumulative defense spending during that decade will be over $4.1 trillion. Under a noninterventionist policy, the 1996 defense budget would be 58 percent less, and the cumulative cost over a decade would be under $2.6 trillion.[23]

ADVANCING THE DEBATE

The case for non-intervention is not a pure prescription of a state of affairs that is inherently and universally attractive. It is prescription mingled with prediction. Non-intervention is proposed as an adjustment to the world as it is shaping up and to the constraints of our polity, society, and economy. Our national orientation should not depend entirely on whether some objective, such as containment, is worthy of our commitment. Worthy causes are not free. As in all things, there is a price to be paid, and that price has been growing higher. The multidimensional costs of containment (the specific acts and the general stance of perpetual preparedness) should be weighed against the consequences of not containing and not preparing to contain. Part of the prediction is that our country, taken as a decisionmaking system, will not pay those costs.

The consistent pursuit of non-intervention by this nation will entail a fundamental change in its foreign policy and national strategy. We would have to test our foreign and military policies against the harder questions about national security. In the first instance, this means distinguishing sharply between the interests of our allies and dependents and the interests of our own country. We would also have to learn to differentiate even our own interests from our security. This is not to deny that our other interests (defined in terms of the objective goals of actual individuals and orga-

---

[22] See the more ample treatment of this point in Earl C. Ravenal, *NATO: The Tides of Discontent* (Berkeley, CA: University of California, Institute of International Studies, 1985).

[23] These figures, based on official Pentagon estimates for the first five years, assume, for the five-year period 1992–1996, 4 percent inflation plus 2 percent real annual increases. My alternative assumes, for the entire period 1987–1996, 4 percent inflation only, with my prescribed cuts taken over a 10-year period.

nizations) are real, and mostly legitimate. It is rather to challenge the automatic notion that we must prepare to defend our panoply of interests by the use or threat of force, overt or covert, wholesale or piecemeal, through proxies or by ourselves.[24] And it is to challenge the notion that "milieu goals"—the shape and character of the international system, "balance" in general or with a particular antagonist, and even the more abstract concept of order in the system—should be assimilated into the schedule of objects that we must pursue and, by implication, defend. Sometimes, in the typical inflated and debased political rhetoric of our time, these more abstract and generic milieu goals are disguised as more immediate, even vital, security interests. But "vital" should be reserved for those truly supreme interests that derive so strictly from our identity as a nation that they could not credibly be alienated, even by an official expression.

When put up against these more stringent criteria, most interests are alienable, in the sense that we can choose not to defend them against all kinds of threats. We can draw back to a line that has two interacting and mutually reinforcing characteristics: credibility and feasibility—a line that we must hold, as part of the definition of our sovereignty, and that we can hold, as a defensive perimeter and a strategic force concept that can be maintained with advantage and within constraints over the long haul.

Such a national strategy would not, admittedly, maximize gross American "interests" in the world. But it would be de-signed to optimize the net interests of American society in the world, in terms of the value of these interests measured against the costs (and costs disguised as risks) of defending them. Ultimately, we may have to settle for less than we would like—even for less than we think we need.

QUESTIONS FOR DISCUSSION

1. What role does geographical location play in international politics?
2. Is a Eurasian balance of power still worth fighting for? What are the reasons for your answer?
3. What relevance do nuclear weapons have on the validity of geopolitics?
4. What is containment?
5. Has containment been successful? What are the reasons for your answer?
6. Have the changes in the Soviet Union in the realm of *glasnost* (openness) and *perestroika* (restructuring) changed the validity of the containment policy? What are the reasons for your answer?
7. What are the alternatives to containment? What are the strengths and weaknesses of the alternatives?

SUGGESTED READINGS

Beres, Louis Rene. *America outside the World: The Collapse of U.S. Foreign Policy.* Lexington, Mass.: Lexington Books, 1987.

Bialer, Seweryn. "Gorbachev's Move." *Foreign Policy,* no. 68 (Fall 1987), pp. 59–87.

Deibel, Terry L., and John Lewis Gaddis, eds. *Containment: Concept and Policy.* Washington, D.C.: National Defense University Press, 1986.

Gaddis, John Lewis. *The Long Peace: Inquiries into the History of the Cold War.* New York: Oxford University Press, 1987.

Hixson, Walter L. "Containment on the Perimeter: George F. Kennan and Vietnam." *Diplomatic History,* 12 (Spring 1988), pp. 149–63.

Hough, Jerry F. "The End of Russia's Khomeini Period." *World Policy Journal,* 4 (Fall 1987), pp. 583–604.

---

[24] As in the case of the Persian Gulf, some national interests cost more to defend than they are worth. See the analysis in Earl C. Ravenal, "Defending Persian Gulf Oil," *Intervention,* Fall 1984, and "The Strategic Cost of Oil," testimony before the Subcommittee on the Panama Canal and the Outer Continental Shelf, Committee on Merchant Marine and Fisheries, U.S. House of Representatives, 27 June 1984.

Isaacson, Walter. "Will the Cold War Fade Away?" *Time*, 130 (July 27, 1987), pp. 40–42, 44–45.

Krauthammer, Charles. "When To Call off the Cold War." *New Republic*, 197 (Nov. 16, 1987), pp. 18–21.

Layne, Christopher. "Requiem for the Reagan Doctrine." *SAIS Review*, 8 (Winter–Spring 1988), pp. 1–17.

Leonhard, Wolfgang. "The Bolshevik Revolution Turns 70." *Foreign Affairs*, 66 (Winter 1987–88), pp. 388–409.

Lynch, Allen. "The Restructuring of Soviet Foreign Policy." *Bulletin of the Atomic Scientists*, 44 (Mar. 1988), pp. 40–43.

Maynes, Charles William. "America's Chance." *Foreign Policy*, no. 68 (Fall 1987), pp. 88–99.

Yanov, Alexander. *The Russian Challenge and the Year 2000*. New York: Basil Blackwell, 1987.

19 Do Arms Control Agreements Serve U.S. Security Interests?

YES

Defense Monitor

The Unravelling of Nuclear Arms Treaties: Another Step toward Nuclear War

NO

Charles Krauthammer

The End of Arms Control

The Unravelling of Nuclear Arms Treaties: Another Step toward Nuclear War

Defense Monitor

Recent events demonstrated a sharp contradiction between the Reagan Administration's rhetoric on negotiating nuclear arms reductions and its actions. President Reagan has said many times that he is committed to negotiating an arms limitation agreement with the Soviet Union, yet his actions have undermined both the prospects for new agreements and the effectiveness of existing agreements.

President Reagan announced in May 1986 that the U.S. would no longer be bound by the SALT [Strategic Arms Limitation Talks] II Treaty limits. At the October 1986 summit meeting in Reykjavik, Iceland with Soviet leader Mikhail Gorbachev, the President reaffirmed his intention either to abrogate the Anti-Ballistic Missile (ABM) Treaty or to modify it in a way that would render it meaningless. These actions have accelerated a trend that may unravel the fabric of all existing U.S.-Soviet arms limitation agreements. Although existing agreements are far from perfect, their loss opens the door to an unrestrained arms buildup, makes both nations less secure, and moves us another step closer to nuclear war.

THE DEMISE OF SALT II

SALT II, signed by President Jimmy Carter and General Secretary Leonid Brezhnev in 1979, established numerical limits on strategic nuclear

"The Unravelling of Nuclear Arms Treaties: Another Step toward Nuclear War," *Defense Monitor* 16, no. 1 (1987), pp. 1–8. Reprinted by permission of the Center for Defense Information.

delivery vehicles—land-based intercontinental ballistic missiles (ICBMs), submarine-launched ballistic missiles (SLBMs), and long-range bombers. Although Mr. Reagan never submitted it to the Senate for ratification, he repeatedly promised not to "undercut" the Treaty so long as the U.S.S.R. showed equal restraint.

On 28 November 1986 the U.S. exceeded one of the SALT II limits by equipping the 131st B-52 bomber with cruise missiles. This action pushed the U.S. over the 1,320 limit on the total number of multiple warhead ICBM and SLBM launchers and bombers carrying cruise missiles. Shortly afterwards, the Soviet government announced that, "The U.S.S.R. refrains for the time being from abandoning the limitations under SALT I and SALT II." The Soviets, however, cannot be expected to continue to adhere to the SALT agreements if the U.S. persists in its present plans to continue the expansion of its nuclear forces with additional bombers and missile-firing submarines.

END OF ANTI-BALLISTIC MISSILE (ABM) TREATY

President Reagan has abandoned SALT II and has placed the ABM Treaty in jeopardy. The ABM Treaty, signed in 1972 by President Nixon and General Secretary Brezhnev, prohibits the development and deployment of nationwide anti-ballistic missile systems. Such systems are designed to shoot down missiles as they approach their targets.

The Treaty permitted the U.S. and the Soviet Union to have two ABM sites, one around the national capital and one around an ICBM field. The subsequent 1974 protocol limits each country to one site. (The U.S. deployed an ABM system at Grand Forks Air Force Base, North Dakota but deactivated it in 1976. The Soviets still have their one authorized site around Moscow.)

The Treaty also limits the U.S. and the Soviet Union to "no more than one hundred

ABM launchers and no more than one hundred ABM interceptor missiles" and restricts radars which could be used as part of a territorial ABM system. It limits qualitative improvements of ABM technology as both countries agreed "not to develop, test, or deploy ABM systems or components which are sea-based, air-based, space-based or mobile land-based." The Treaty allows limited development, testing, and deployment of only one kind of ABM system: *fixed land-based.*

Continued adherence to the ABM Treaty is incompatible with the development, testing and deployment of Star Wars systems. This is because Star Wars will consist of space-based ABM systems, exactly the types of systems that the ABM treaty prohibits.

Treaty Language

In October 1985 the Administration announced that it had reinterpreted the ABM Treaty to permit the development and testing of space-based ABM systems based on new technologies that did not exist when the treaty was signed, such as the laser and particle beam systems envisioned in the Star Wars program. The new U.S. interpretation is primarily based on Agreed Statement (D) which accompanied the Treaty. It says "the parties agree that in the event ABM systems based on other physical principles...are created in the future, specific limitations on such systems and their components would be subject to discussion."

The Agreed Statement actually makes the Treaty more strict. While allowing for the limited development and testing of *fixed land-based* ABM systems, "based on other physical principles," this treaty clause prohibited the deployment of such systems without amending the Treaty first. The Administration twisted this statement in a way that conflicts directly with the purpose of the Treaty—to prohibit the development of nationwide ABM

systems. Further, at the time the treaty was signed, the Nixon Administration, the U.S. Senate and the Soviet Union understood and accepted the interpretation that prohibited the development and testing of all space-based ABM systems and components.

Gerard Smith, the chief U.S. negotiator of the ABM Treaty, rejected the new interpretation and stated that it would make the Treaty a "dead letter." John Rhinelander, the legal adviser to the U.S. ABM Treaty negotiators, told the House Foreign Affairs Committee, "This rationale is absurd as a matter of policy, intent and interpretation. If the Administration sticks with it as the best legal interpretation of the Treaty, then the Administration has effectively repudiated the ABM Treaty as a legal instrument."

The Soviet Union rejected the Administration's attempt to change the accepted interpretation of the Treaty. At the Iceland summit, it proposed linking deep reductions in offensive nuclear weapons to a commitment not to withdraw from the ABM Treaty for 10 years. This proposal included the understanding that both sides would adhere to a traditional interpretation. President Reagan agreed to the 10-year time frame, but refused to make a commitment to continue to observe the interpretation that both sides have followed since the Treaty was signed.

The Administration says that it wants to "extend" the ABM Treaty. In reality it is telling the Soviet Union that it plans to terminate the Treaty, which is of unlimited duration, after 10 years. It is also demanding that the Soviet Union agree to full-scale testing of space-based and mobile ABM systems which the Treaty prohibits. The Administration has cautioned the Soviets that if they refuse to accept the new interpretation, it will reserve the right to withdraw from the Treaty unilaterally after six months notice. If the Administration has its way, either the ABM Treaty will lose all significance or the U.S. will abandon it.

WHAT HAPPENS WITHOUT SALT II

Accelerated Buildup

In 1986 the Congressional Research Service (CRS) published a report on the potential growth of U.S. and Soviet nuclear forces over the next 15 years without SALT II. The study estimated that without SALT II constraints the number of strategic warheads (warheads with intercontinental-range delivery systems) could grow up to 213 percent for the U.S. and 393 percent for the Soviet Union.

In June 1985 Lawrence Gershwin, a CIA [Central Intelligence Agency] official, testified before two Senate subcommittees that, "While the Soviets would not necessarily expand their intercontinental attack forces beyond some 12,000 to 13,000 warheads...in the absence of arms control constraints, they clearly have the capability for significant further expansion, to between 16,000 and 21,000 deployed warheads by the mid-1990s....It is certainly evident that without any SALT II constraints whatsoever, the Soviet potential to have a substantially higher number is clearly there."

Without SALT II restrictions both sides will likely accelerate their pace of building and deploying additional nuclear weapons to gain an advantage or to avoid being put at a disadvantage. Such a development would result in further waste of resources while increasing the risk of nuclear war. It would also jeopardize future efforts to limit the types and reduce the number of nuclear arms.

No Limits on Multiple Warhead Missiles

SALT II not only limits the overall number of U.S. and Soviet long-range ballistic missile launchers and bombers, it also contains specific limits on MIRVed [multiple independently targetable reentry vehicle] systems (systems that can deliver multiple warheads). It constrains these MIRVed delivery systems with three interlocking sublimits: 1) 1,320 MIRVed land and sea-based ballistic missile launchers plus heavy bombers with long-range cruise missiles; 2) 1,200 MIRVed land and sea-based ballistic missile launchers; and 3) 820 MIRVed land-based ballistic missile launchers. SALT II also freezes the number of "heavy" ICBMs and limits the maximum number of warheads on ICBMs to 10 and on submarine-launched ballistic missiles (SLBMs) to 14. The Soviets have complied with all of these provisions.

The removal of SALT II ceilings on MIRVed systems would leave no restrictions on extremely accurate new weapons such as the U.S. MX ICBM or the Soviet SS-24 ICBM. In the short term both sides could add these new systems without making any compensating reductions to stay within the Treaty's limits. In the long term both countries could exceed the limits with the new weapons alone, not counting the older weapons that otherwise would have been dismantled.

Highly accurate, multiple-warhead ballistic missiles can hit their targets in under 30 minutes and destroy land-based missiles in their hardened silos. Thus they jeopardize each nation's capability to retaliate, increasing the likelihood of nuclear war by raising incentives to launch a first strike during a crisis. Either country might strike first if it thinks it must do so in order to avoid losing its own missiles in an attack by the other side.

Abandoning the SALT II limit on the maximum number of warheads permitted on ICBMs would put the U.S. at a disadvantage. The Soviets could rapidly increase the number of their ICBM warheads by simply adding them to their existing land-based missiles. The Soviets have almost 400 more land-based ICBMs than the U.S., most of which are better suited than U.S. ICBMs to carry and deliver numerous MIRVs because of their greater size and payload capabilities.

No Rules of the Road

The United States and the Soviet Union have emphasized different types of systems to deliver nuclear weapons. The U.S. has concentrated on submarine-launched ballistic missiles (SLBMs) and bombers, while the U.S.S.R. has stressed land-based intercontinental ballistic missiles (ICBMs). The SALT II Treaty and its agreed statements and common understandings help compare the different types of delivery systems. Accounting rules help to alleviate fears that either nation has any exploitable advantage under the terms of the treaty. For example, the U.S. and the U.S.S.R. agreed to make minor structural alterations to bombers carrying cruise missiles to distinguish them from other bombers. SALT II also established counting rules to help circumvent the problem of determining the number of warheads on a missile. A missile is counted as having the maximum number of warheads with which it has been tested, even though many may actually be deployed with fewer warheads.

Without such "rules of the road" it would be nearly impossible to verify numerical limits imposed by future agreements. It could take years to reestablish the yardsticks necessary to measure the quantity and quality of each other's nuclear weapons in a mutually acceptable way.

Increased Costs

A 1986 Congressional Budget Office (CBO) study asserted that the President's decision to abandon SALT II could cost the U.S. over $100 billion in the next ten years. ($100 billion is more than five times the total federal outlays for education in fiscal year 1986.) A private group, the Center on Budget and Policy Priorities, published a report in June 1986 estimating that as a result of a U.S. and Soviet breakout from SALT II the United States might have to spend an additional $128.5 billion by the end of 1996. Such expenditures, especially in a time of huge federal budget deficits, would be a heavy burden on the national economy.

Unpredictability

SALT II adds an important degree of predictability to the nuclear arms competition. By providing data on the number of strategic offensive arms that are subject to the treaty's limitations and imposing limits on the numbers and types of those that can be deployed, the agreement gives U.S. and Soviet military planners an idea of the forces they will confront in the future. Without the treaty, the loss of predictability could accentuate force planning based on "worst case" assumptions. The infamous bomber and missile "gaps" of the 1950s were the direct consequences of "worst case" planning and resulted in gross overreaction by the U.S. which led to an expensive, dangerous acceleration of the nuclear buildup in both nations.

Less Information

Without SALT II, the U.S. would have more difficulty acquiring information about Soviet nuclear forces. There would no longer be a commitment not to interfere with national technical means (NTM) of verification such as photo-reconnaissance satellites. Neither country would be prohibited from deliberate concealment measures such as camouflaging nuclear weapon sites. Neither would be required to notify the other in advance of certain ICBM flight tests. The U.S. would stand to lose more than the Soviet Union if these provisions were abandoned. While the U.S. depends heavily on NTM for its information on Soviet nuclear forces, the Soviet Union has more access to similar information about U.S. forces through open sources.

WHAT HAPPENS WITHOUT ABM TREATY

Increased Danger

The deployment of extensive ABM systems would make both the U.S. and the Soviet Union less secure. Defensive systems which can prevent missiles from reaching their targets threaten the other nation's ability to retaliate effectively after an attack. Each side sees the development and deployment of extensive ABM systems as evidence that its adversary is preparing to fight and win a nuclear war. Specifically, defensive systems are interpreted as part of a first strike strategy in which one side plans to eliminate a high percentage of its adversary's nuclear forces by initiating an attack with its offensive weapons and then repelling the remainder of the depleted forces with its defensive weapons. In his 1983 "Star Wars" speech President Reagan said, "If paired with offensive systems, [defenses] can be viewed as fostering aggressive policy, and no one wants that," but this is exactly what present U.S. plans will do.

Leaders suspicious in a time of crisis that an attack was imminent might believe that if they waited too long to "press the button" they would lose many of their nuclear weapons to an enemy first strike and their remaining forces would not be able to penetrate their adversary's ABM systems. In the absence of elaborate defenses, however, both sides can be confident that the number of warheads that would survive an attack would be sufficient to devastate their adversary, thus removing all rational incentives to strike first.

A 1985 Congressional Research Service (CRS) study concluded that the Soviet Union could destroy no more than 40 percent of U.S. strategic warheads by attacking first and the U.S. could destroy only 52 percent of Soviet strategic warheads. In the present situation, in which defense is severely limited, effective retaliation is not threatened. Thus neither country could be rationally tempted or provoked to launch a nuclear attack first. The extensive deployment of ABM systems, however, would challenge the effectiveness of retaliatory forces and increase the likelihood of a nuclear attack.

Offensive Buildup

The past military response to increased defense has been increased offense. In the 1960s when the Soviets began developing ABM systems to defend against U.S. ICBMs, the U.S. reacted by developing multiple-warhead (MIRVed) missiles to maintain its ability to penetrate Soviet defenses. In a 1985 memorandum to President Reagan, Secretary Weinberger wrote, "Even a probable [Soviet] territorial defense would require us to increase the number of our offensive forces and their ability to penetrate Soviet defenses to assure that our operational plans could be executed." If the Reagan Administration officially alters or abrogates the ABM Treaty, then the Soviets will likely react by building more numerous and more sophisticated offensive nuclear weapons. General Secretary Gorbachev has often stated that the Soviet Union will do exactly this if President Reagan proceeds with SDI. Secretary Weinberger told the Senate Armed Services Committee in 1985, "I think [the Soviets] will try to overwhelm or otherwise defeat a strategic defense."

Reinterpretation or abrogation of the ABM Treaty will permit the development of extensive defensive systems, precluding future reductions in strategic offensive nuclear weapons and accelerating the buildup of both offensive and defensive arms.

Increased Costs

Without the ABM Treaty, the United States and the Soviet Union would no longer have a legal commitment not to deploy territorial defenses. Star Wars, which most of the U.S. scientific community believes would not work effectively, would cost hundreds of billions of dollars. Official Administration figures project research and development costs for SDI approaching $40 billion through 1991. Another $30 billion is likely to be spent through 1993. Production and deployment costs will dwarf even these figures. A Johns Hopkins University study estimated that a "comprehensive defense" deployed by the year 2005 could cost up to $770 billion. Former Secretaries of Defense James Schlesinger and Harold Brown have estimated that the program potentially could cost $1 trillion.

Loss of the SCC

Scrapping the ABM Treaty will also result in the loss of the Standing Consultative Commission (SCC), a forum comprised of American and Soviet representatives. Established in 1972 by the ABM Treaty to resolve questions concerning compliance, the SCC has been used successfully in the past. In 1982 the Arms Control and Disarmament Agency (ACDA) reported, "Both the United States and the Soviet Union have raised a number of questions in the Commission relating to each side's compliance with the SALT I agreements. In each case raised by the United States the Soviet activity in question has either ceased or additional information has allayed U.S. concerns."

Instead of seeking clarification of Soviet actions in this forum, the Reagan Administration has publicly trumpeted charges of Soviet noncompliance. The high profile nature of these allegations gives the Soviet

Union no politically acceptable alternative but to deny them across the board. The U.S. representative to the SCC, General Richard Ellis, has reportedly not been authorized to resolve SALT II compliance disputes, but only to resurrect old accusations. As a result, no effective use has been made of the SCC during the Reagan Administration. The Administration announced that it will no longer discuss SALT II compliance issues in the SCC. Clearly the Administration is more interested in using the alleged Soviet violations as a pretext for dumping SALT II than in resolving the differences.

UNRAVELLING OF OTHER AGREEMENTS

U.S. security would be weakened not only by the loss of SALT II and the ABM Treaty, but also by the resulting potential loss of other important agreements. An enormous amount of time and effort has been put into building a fragile structure which the Administration is now systematically tearing down. As the U.S. political and legal commitment to controlling nuclear weapons dwindles, the effectiveness of all of these agreements will erode. If SALT II can be so capriciously abandoned and ABM Treaty provisions unilaterally reinterpreted, then the foundation of U.S.-Soviet arms limitation agreements may begin to crumble and other accords, described below, may become pieces of paper with no significance.

Agreements That Limit Where Nuclear Weapons Can Be Deployed

- The 1959 Antarctic Treaty prohibits the United States and the Soviet Union from establishing military bases, carrying out military maneuvers, or testing weapons in Antarctica.
- The 1967 Outer Space Treaty prohibits the United States and the Soviet Union from

deploying nuclear weapons or other weapons of mass destruction in outer space.

- The 1967 Latin American Nuclear Free Zone Treaty commits the United States and the Soviet Union to respect the denuclearized status of the Latin American zone where receipt, storage, installation, deployment and possession of nuclear weapons are prohibited.
- The 1968 Non-Proliferation Treaty prohibits the United States and the Soviet Union from transferring nuclear weapons to non-nuclear weapon states and from assisting those states in any way to acquire nuclear weapons or devices.
- The 1971 Seabed Treaty prohibits the United States and the Soviet Union from deploying nuclear weapons on the ocean floor.

The loss of these agreements could result in the spread of nuclear weapons into more areas, enabling more people to start a nuclear war.

Agreements Aimed at Lowering the Risk of Accidental Nuclear War

- The 1963 Hot Line Agreement commits the United States and the Soviet Union to maintain a direct communications link between the two governments for use in a time of crisis.
- The 1971 Accidents Measures Agreement commits the United States and the Soviet Union to notify each other of the detection by missile warning systems of unidentified objects and of any planned missile launches which will extend beyond national territory in the direction of the other country.
- The 1973 Prevention of Nuclear War Agreement commits the United States and the Soviet Union to enter into urgent consultations with each other when relations

between the two countries appear to involve the risk of a nuclear conflict.

The loss of these agreements would increase the risk of accidental nuclear war.

Agreements Restricting Nuclear Explosions

- The 1963 Limited Test Ban Treaty prohibits the United States and the Soviet Union from conducting nuclear tests in the atmosphere, in outer space and underwater.
- The 1974 Threshold Test Ban Treaty (unratified) prohibits the United States and the Soviet Union from conducting underground nuclear weapon tests with yields exceeding 150 kilotons.
- The 1976 Peaceful Nuclear Explosions Treaty (unratified) prohibits the United States and the Soviet Union from conducting individual underground nuclear explosions for peaceful purposes with a yield exceeding 150 kilotons or any group explosion with a total yield exceeding 1,500 kilotons.

The loss of these agreements would complicate the negotiation of a Comprehensive Test Ban (CTB) Treaty which is the first essential step towards halting and reversing the nuclear arms buildup.

INADEQUATE CONTROL

Although arms limitation agreements have been useful, there is room for improvement. SALT II and the ABM treaty have not slowed down dangerous technological developments, nor have they prevented rapid growth in the number of nuclear warheads deployed by the United States and the Soviet Union in long-range delivery systems.

Technological advancements have not been effectively slowed because arms limitation agreements have not included a comprehensive ban on testing nuclear weapons. Continued testing has given both countries the information required to proceed with designs for new weapons.

New Weapons

MIRVs Multiple Independently-targetable Reentry Vehicles (MIRVs), first deployed in the 1970s, are extremely dangerous weapons which were not constrained by the SALT I Interim Agreement and were restricted only in part by SALT II. A MIRVed missile carries numerous warheads that can be individually programmed to strike separate targets. Therefore one missile can destroy many targets. For example, a U.S. MX or Soviet SS-18 ICBM equipped with 10 warheads could destroy up to 10 land-based missiles containing as many as 100 warheads. Because they could be used to nullify a large amount of the opposition's retaliatory forces, such weapons increase the plausibility of a preemptive attack.

Cruise missiles Long-range cruise missiles, first deployed in the 1980s, are another dangerous technological development. These pilotless, jet-propelled drones—launched from the air, land, and sea—have not been adequately constrained by arms limitation agreements. Cruise missiles can be easily concealed because of their relatively small size and mobility. It is also extremely difficult to distinguish cruise missiles with nuclear warheads from those with nonnuclear warheads. These complications pose a serious problem in assessing each side's nuclear strength and for negotiating numerical limits on weapons. In addition, cruise missiles are potentially threatening to retaliatory forces. They are extremely accurate and difficult to detect on early warning radar because they fly at low altitudes. An advanced version of the U.S. cruise missile which incorporates new radar-evading "stealth" technology is under development to

increase its potential for surprise attack even further.

New Versions of Old Weapons

Arms limitation agreements have not prevented either side from developing more sophisticated, more effective, and more dangerous forms of old weapon systems. Both countries continue to upgrade all three legs of their nuclear triads. These constant "improvements" in weapon systems are part of the preparation to prevail in a nuclear war which both sides agree is unwinnable.

Massive Growth in Warhead Numbers

Arms limitation agreements have not prevented massive growth in the number of U.S. and Soviet nuclear weapons. The number of U.S. strategic warheads has more than tripled since 1970 from 3,742 to 11,766. The number of Soviet strategic warheads has increased more than five-fold since 1970 from 1,861 to 9,442. It is difficult to conclude that either side is safer today after 16 years of the buildup made possible through continued nuclear testing.

NUCLEAR WAR-FIGHTING

During the 1970s and 1980s as more accurate multiple-warhead missiles were developed, U.S. nuclear weapons doctrine evolved in a direction that led to unlimited requirements and the creation of first-strike capabilities.

In July 1980 Jimmy Carter signed Presidential Directive (PD) 59 codifying the U.S. nuclear weapons doctrine known as "countervailing strategy." This document called for expansion of U.S. nuclear weapons capabilities to give the President a wider range of options during a nuclear war.

The Reagan Administration appears to be carrying the countervailing strategy one step further with its own ill-conceived notion of nuclear superiority. The Administration's policy was stated in the FY 1984–1988 Defense Guidance, "U.S. nuclear capabilities must prevail even under the conditions of a prolonged war." After being challenged over these plans to "prevail" in a nuclear war, Secretary of Defense Weinberger responded, "You show me a Secretary of Defense who is not planning to prevail and I'll show you a Secretary of Defense who should be impeached." The FY 1983 U.S. Budget states, "U.S. defense policies ensure our preparedness to respond to and if necessary, successfully fight, either conventional or nuclear war."

The Administration has pushed for the development and deployment of accurate, potent, multiple-warhead missiles like the MX and the Trident II SLBM, as well as strategic defense forces, which could give the United States a first strike capability.

There is only one legitimate military purpose for U.S. nuclear weapons today: to convince Soviet leaders that they can gain no advantage by attacking the United States. More first strike weapons will not achieve this objective—they will only increase the risk of nuclear war.

NEW AGREEMENTS

As the Iceland summit revealed, there is tremendous opportunity to negotiate mutually beneficial agreements with the Soviet Union given the political will. Such agreements could help both countries to reduce the risk of nuclear war, ease the economic burden of nuclear arms competition, and improve U.S.-Soviet relations.

The primary obstacle to progress appears to be President Reagan's insistence on developing and testing Star Wars. The President fails to realize that an unfettered SDI is incompatible with offensive arms reductions. As former Secretary of Defense Harold Brown said, "To the extent that the U.S. is committed to SDI, I think arms control is not going to be feasible. Indeed I think existing agreements will either erode or be abandoned."

Offense/Defense Tradeoff

If the U.S. is willing to compromise on Star Wars development and testing, significant arms limitation agreements could be achieved. Star Wars is geared to defend against the same weapons that the United States would most like to reduce: MIRVed ballistic missiles. Instead of spending hundreds of billions of dollars to defend against the threat posed by these weapons, it would make more sense to alleviate that danger through negotiations.

Contingent upon 10-year adherence to a strict interpretation of the ABM Treaty, the Soviets agreed at Iceland to a 6,000 limit on the number of ballistic missile warheads and air-launched cruise missiles (ALCMs). Because the Soviets have more than 6,000 warheads on their ICBMs alone, this agreement would require the U.S.S.R. to make deep reductions in its strategic nuclear forces. While these reductions may not be deep enough, they would be a step in the right direction and could lay the groundwork for greater reductions in the future.

Ending Nuclear Explosions

There is also great potential for an end to all nuclear explosions. A ban on all nuclear testing would stop further dangerous new developments in nuclear weapons technology and reduce the risk of nuclear war. General Secretary Gorbachev has repeatedly urged President Reagan to negotiate an end to nuclear tests and has backed up his words with actions. The U.S.S.R. started a nuclear testing moratorium on 6 August 1985 and has extended it until 1987. In July 1986 the Soviets allowed U.S. scientists to place seismic monitors in the U.S.S.R. near the main Soviet test site and stated their willingness to accept more extensive on-site verification measures. The Reagan Administration continues to call the Soviet initiatives only "propaganda."

One of the main reasons that the Administration wants to continue testing is that the development of the X-ray laser—an important part of the Star Wars program—requires more testing.

COOPERATION AND UNDERSTANDING

Clearly, there is no panacea. Just decreasing the levels of nuclear weapons will not eliminate the possibility of nuclear war. The problem that confronts the United States and the Soviet Union is a problem that is inherently political, not military. Progress must be made ultimately in people's minds. Hostile attitudes and perceptions must be changed if we are to reduce the risk of nuclear war. Simply put, the United States and the Soviet Union must learn to live together peacefully despite the great differences in their respective political and economic systems.

The United States has dramatically improved its relations with the People's Republic of China despite ideological differences. With enough effort, U.S.-Soviet relations could evolve positively in a similar way. In order to achieve this vital goal, we must embark on a dynamic program to generate cooperation and understanding between our countries. The United States and the Soviet Union could begin by creating blueprints for mutually beneficial joint ventures covering the entire spectrum of human activity. Practical programs for working together in science, space exploration, education, trade, health, environmental protection, and other nonmilitary areas could help shift our focus away from ideological and political differences toward cooperative solutions to problems of common concern. This basic shift from confrontation to cooperation can start with improved and expanded arms limitation measures to reduce mutual fears in both nations.

The End of Arms Control

Charles Krauthammer

In the 1970s, the conservative opposition to arms control was based as much on psychology as on strategy. Whatever the strategic effects, argued opponents, arms control had disastrous psychological effects. It lulled the West into a false sense of security about Soviet intentions, encouraged passivity to the Soviet threat, and led to a weakening of Western resolve and defenses.

There is some truth to this argument, but not much. Arms control alone should not bear the full weight of blame for the silly euphoria about the Soviets that swept the West in the '70s. The euphoria was part of the general atmosphere of détente that was created by frequent and chummy summitry, by increased trade and other cooperative ventures (like the absurd Soyuz-Apollo lovefest), and by the (Western) assumption that all geopolitical competition and conflicts would be newly subjected to mutual restraint. Arms control was but a small part of the story.

Moreover, even if arms control does lull, some lulls are worse than others. The 1970s lull turned out to be rather unilateral. While the West rested, the Soviets vigorously expanded both their overseas empire and their nuclear advantage. (Hence Harold Brown's immortal definition of the arms race: "When we build, they build. When we cut, they build.") The coming decade, however, will be quite the reverse. Having bitten off too much, the Soviets are in a period of at least tempo-

rary consolidation. Even if the worst of the charges laid at arms control are true, some Western relaxation in a period of Soviet relaxation is not a mortal danger. The costs might well be worth bearing, assuming there are other benefits to arms control.

Finally, before rejecting arms control for its negative psychological effects, consider its positive psychological effects. Any agreement, no matter how bad, shores up at least temporarily Western belief in deterrence. "The more compelling arguments for reducing nuclear weapons tend to be political," writes Joseph Nye. "The marginal effects such cuts may have on strategic stability are far less important than ensuring a broad base of public support for nuclear deterrence." Recent history has borne this out dramatically. The early '80s saw a vast mobilization against nuclear weapons and deterrence. With the resumption of arms talks, the agreement on INF [intermediate-range nuclear forces], and the prospect of a START [Strategic Arms Reduction Talks] treaty, the movement fizzled. If arms control helps keep the West committed to deterrence, at the cost of some lulling, then perhaps it is worth the bargain.

But what if these "political," i.e., psychological, effects are based on illusion? Arms control is reassuring because Western publics believe that nuclear treaties reduce the chances of nuclear war and thus make the world safer. What if this belief is false? If nuclear reductions, such as the 50 percent reduction contemplated in the coming START treaty, actually leave us less safe, should we be signing treaties merely to satisfy irrational, if popular, beliefs?

Thomas Schelling, one of the first and most acute of this country's thinkers about nuclear weapons, several years ago asked the emperor's new clothes question about arms control: "Who needs arms control if economical and reliable retaliatory weapons are available that are neither susceptible to pre-emption nor ca-

Charles Krauthammer, "The End of Arms Control," *New Republic*, 199, no. 9 (Aug. 29, 1988), pp. 26, 28–31. Reprinted by permission of *The New Republic*. © 1988, The New Republic, Inc.

pable of pre-emption?" It is the kind of question only a child, a neophyte, or a sage with the benefit of 30 years of nuclear jesuitics behind him could ask. "On the 'arms control' interest in reducing numbers [of nuclear weapons]," writes Schelling, "nobody ever offers a convincing reason for preferring smaller numbers." No one does, and yet the enthusiasm for the 50 percent reductions envisioned in the START treaty (if the bugs, such as verification, can be worked out) is nearly universal. As we begin the ostentatious dismantling of INF missiles and anticipate the dawning of the START era, it is time to pause and return to Schelling's question: Why exactly are we embarked on this enterprise?

The popular faith in arms control—the belief that cutting numbers is in itself a good thing—rests on three assumptions.

1. Arms Control Saves Money If arms control saves money, the sums are negligible. Generally speaking, however, it may increase defense expenditures. This is because treaties like START decrease stability (the survivability of one's deterrent force) by eliminating redundancy. In order to regain the *pre-existing* level of nuclear stability, the United States will be forced under START to overhaul, reconfigure, and redesign drastically its strategic nuclear arsenal in order to make it a survivable and reliable retaliatory force. START will create such pressure to cut the number of America's best retaliatory weapons—ICBMs [intercontinental ballistic missiles], SLBMs (submarine-launched ballistic missiles), and ALCMs (air-launched cruise missiles)—that a myriad of proposals are already on the table for redesigning the U.S. strategic deterrent to maintain its survivability. At sea, this may mean a new fleet of smaller submarines, so our reduced SLBM force is spread over more boats. In the air, it may mean a heavy reliance on manned bombers, which are extremely expensive but practically unregulated under START

"counting rules." On land, it may mean redesigning old or inventing new systems that are mobile, super-hardened, or otherwise protected (by some version of SDI [Strategic Defense Initiative], for example) to compensate for the loss of safety in numbers. All that costs money.

But even if START led to no increase in nuclear expenditures, it would certainly lead to an overall increase in defense expenditures. That is because nuclear arms control puts more of a burden for deterrence on conventional defense. The most ardent arms control advocates not only recognize this fact, they celebrate it. Michael Dukakis, for example, opposes almost all nuclear modernization but wants still to appear tough on defense. He therefore goes to extraordinary lengths to advocate bolstering conventional defenses. In a speech to the Atlantic Council in June, Dukakis went so far as to declare the goal of developing the ability "of fighting—and winning—a conventional war" in Europe, something the Europeans, who have experienced two conventional wars this century on their soil, are no doubt delighted to hear. Conventional deterrence may or may not be as effective as nuclear deterrence in preventing war (again: the history of this century is hardly an argument for conventional deterrence), but one thing is certain: it is far more expensive. The same bang will require many more bucks.

2. Arms Control Prevents Accidents Another illusion. As Nye points out, "The sheer number of weapons is not the major factor governing the odds of accidental war." The crucial factor is the technical sophistication of the nuclear weapons and their trigger mechanism. And this improves as new systems are introduced. If your life depended on its reliability and accuracy, would you rather trust in a vacuum-tubed Univac computer circa 1958 or in five hand-held Sharp calculators circa 1988? The key to reducing the chances of accidental war is nuclear modernization, not numbers reduction.

3. *Arms Control Reduces the Risk of Nuclear War*
Our intuition tells us that the fewer nuclear weapons in this world, the less our chance of getting killed by one. That intuition does not stand up to the most elementary analysis. Schelling dispatches it quite succinctly: "For the most part, people simply think that smaller numbers are better than bigger ones. Those who believe we already have ten times what we need never explain why having merely five times as many should look better." The nuclear hysteria of the early '80s was generated by the repeated reminder that we had constructed for ourselves a world in which Armageddon could occur at any minute. But what can arms control do to prevent that? You either reduce the number of weapons below the level that can bring Armageddon, or you don't. If you do, then you have abolished deterrence and ushered in a period of nuclear insecurity and instability unknown since the earliest days of the nuclear age (when bomb shelter drills were not the silly exercises they appear to us today). And if you don't reduce nuclear arsenals below the point at which you can destroy the other side once over, then what's the point of arms control? The balance of terror persists. The nuclear nightmare is in no way abolished.

There is only one circumstance under which reducing numbers, say a 50 percent cut, makes sense: as a way station to zero. But except for President Reagan and a few other nuclear naïfs, no one thinks that zero nuclear weapons is either achievable or desirable. In a world of total disarmament, the premium on cheating, hiding, and secret rearmament would be extraordinary. Lacking a retaliatory threat, every country would be at risk from nuclear breakout and blackmail by every other country. In a world of Qaddafis and Khomeinis and Saddam Husseins, ignoring for the

moment the Soviets, there could not be a more unstable nuclear regime. Not even Hobbes could have imagined a world of such perpetual danger and universal insecurity.

In the absence of world government (a nightmare of a different sort), we will have to rely on deterrence for safety against nuclear (and chemical and biological) attack for generations. Safety depends on deterrence, and, all things being equal, there is safety in numbers. The more nuclear weapons you have, scattered in more places, delivered in more ways (to complicate defenses), using a greater variety of physical principles (ballistic missiles, cruise missiles, gravity bombs), the less the chance that any adversary would ever consider a pre-emptive nuclear attack on you— i.e., the less the chance of nuclear war. There is safety in redundancy. Arms control, if taken seriously, aims to reduce that redundancy.

Now, all things are not always equal. Some kinds of nuclear weapons are more destabilizing to the nuclear balance than others. Arms control that specifically reduced or eliminated these destabilizing weapons might be worthwhile. The House Armed Services Committee report on START sets out clearly the criterion for evaluating any arms control regime. The chief purpose of arms control, it argues, is "to improve what is called crisis stability and thereby reduce the possibility of nuclear war. Stability is achieved when it is unlikely that either side will strike pre-emptively in a time of international crisis. Reductions and limits may or may not promote crisis stability. Those that do are worthwhile." And those that don't are not. The arms control that we are engaged in now—quantitative arms control, number reduction—does not.

Why not?

Nuclear weapons don't launch themselves. People launch them. But there is a sense in which nuclear weapons—or more precisely, their force structure, meaning the way in which they are arranged and protected—can, during a crisis, incline the leaders of one side or the other to launch. If a leader thinks that his military power is in danger of being pre-emptively destroyed, he may, if he reaches a point where he thinks war is inevitable, be tempted to launch his own weapons pre-emptively. If his weapons had not been structured so that his choice in a crisis was only "use 'em or lose 'em," he would have no such temptation.

If arms control is to have any point, other than to salve consciousness or appease public opinion, it must increase nuclear stability. One has to ask, therefore, what any agreement does to force structure. How will the nature of the nuclear arsenals on the two sides be changed by an arms control agreement? And will that change make pre-emption (a first strike) more or less likely in a crisis?

Absolute numbers tell you very little about crisis stability (except for the rule that the more launchers you have and the more dispersed they are, the better). What counts for crisis stability is a ratio: the ratio of A's accurate warheads to B's targets, such as missile silos. If A has many more warheads than B has targets, then A could in a crisis launch (or better: threaten to launch) a fraction of its arsenal in a pre-emptive attack, wipe out B's retaliatory force, and still have enough warheads left over to force B to capitulate. If, on the other hand, the ratio of warheads to targets is 1, then there is no incentive for and thus no threat of pre-emptive attack. War may one day come, but the configuration of the superpowers' arsenals will in no way have contributed to it.

What does the 50 percent reduction of START do to the crucial warhead/target ratio? "All experts agree," writes Henry Kissinger, "that if existing U.S. strategic forces are cut by 50 percent, the vulnerability of the land-based and submarine-based strategic forces will increase immediately and mount progressively as the accuracy of Soviet missiles and the ef-

fectiveness of Soviet anti-submarine forces grow." Kissinger does the calculation for you: "Today the Soviet Union has 3,080 SS-18 warheads aimed at 1,000 U.S. silos. After START, assuming the United States retains its most effective weapons, the Soviets would have 1,540 warheads aimed at 364 silos, thereby raising the ratio of warheads to silos from 3.08:1 to 4.2:1. It is hard to argue that such a result would be a contribution to 'stability.'"

James Woolsey, former undersecretary of the Navy under President Carter, points to another source of increasing vulnerability of the U.S. nuclear arsenal. The 1983 Scowcroft Commission Report, which Woolsey helped write, argued that the ICBM leg of the triad was not yet in danger of pre-emption because of the difficulty the Soviets would have in launching a simultaneous attack on both American bomber bases and ICBM silos. "That was a position that was described by some of media at the time"—the *New Republic* included—"as doing away with the window of vulnerability," argues Woolsey. "It was no such thing—it was saying that we had more time to shut the window of vulnerability than some people had been suggesting." Now, argues Woolsey, that time is running out. The Soviets are about to open the window wide with their new fleet of quiet Delta 4 and Typhoon submarines, whose new SSN-20 and SSN-23 missiles could be drawn up close to American shores and simultaneously attack the land and air-based leg of the American nuclear arsenal in the 1990s.

"Arms control is not creating these problems," writes Woolsey. "What is creating the problem is not having a survivable ICBM force. But this type of pressure, under a deep reductions regime for arms control, can, at the margin, make the problem harder." What makes it harder is that under a 50 percent cut, it makes sense to cut the oldest, least reliable, least accurate weapons, such as the silo-based, single-warhead Minuteman II, of which the

United States has 450. That would leave the United States its most accurate, most modern weapons. But they are highly MIRVed [multiple independently targetable reentry vehicle], i.e., they carry many warheads per missile. That means fewer targets for the Soviets to think of pre-empting in a crisis. And that means more, not less, nuclear instability.

Now, to avoid this obvious consequence of START, there are schemes for creating more baskets for our nuclear eggs. But they are costly and complicated. Minuteman II, for example, could be redesigned to make it more safe and accurate. There are schemes for building a new fleet of smaller subs so as to disperse our submarine deterrent. Or for plugging up some of the missile tubes on existing Trident subs and thus enabling us to deploy more subs without breaking START limits on SLBMs. It is possible that after chopping up subs and sealing missile tubes, after restricting or destroying some of our most modern nuclear weapons, after rebuilding and redesigning our ICBM and bomber forces and perhaps building a whole new submarine fleet, we might return to the level of nuclear stability that we enjoy right now. The question is: What's the purpose of this enormous, expensive, uncertain Rube Goldberg exercise?

The only point is to reduce absolute numbers. But the goal of any defense policy should be nuclear stability. Absolute numbers, in themselves, are irrelevant.

Indeed, reduced numbers can easily become the enemy of stability. How? One essential requirement for arms control is verifiability. If you can't verify and confirm what weapons the other side has, the whole arms control enterprise collapses. Which leads to the paradox. Small, concealable weapons are bad for arms control because they are hard to verify. But they are good for stability, because they are hard to target. Both effects stem from the same cause: these weapons are hard to find. And if you can't find a weapon, that means that you can't count it for arms control purposes, but it also means that you can't target it for first-strike purposes. Which means it is always there for retaliation.

Because of the verification problem, the United States took the position at the START talks that mobile missiles should be banned or severely restricted. And the Soviets took the same position vis-à-vis sea-launched cruise missiles. (The argument over SLCMs and the mobiles shows how the arms control is less a search for nuclear stability than it is a struggle for unilateral advantage. Both SLCMs and mobiles pose severe verification problems. But the United States wants to cripple only mobiles and the U.S.S.R. wants to do the same only to SLCMs. Why? Because the Soviets have a big lead in mobiles and the United States has a big lead in SLCMs.) If arms control is your objective, then it makes sense to ban these weapons. But if strategic stability is your objective, then you would want as many of these running around as possible since they are virtually invulnerable.

"Almost all experts agree," writes Kissinger, "that mobile missiles are to all practical purposes unverifiable in the vast expanse of the Soviet Union." Senator Al Gore disputes this and has come up with an elaborate scheme for corralling missiles in various locations and in effect chaining them to fixed missile silos during peacetime. That way they can be counted. But, of course, that way they can be targeted. And suddenly unchaining and dispersing them in a time of crisis would be a disastrous impetus toward nuclear war, comparable to the European mobilizations of August 1914 that set in train World War I. The Air Force has a similar idea of chaining the small mobile ICBM to existing Minuteman silos in the northern states. Brent Scowcroft, John Deutch, and Woolsey point out that this would leave the missiles vulnerable to "rather straightforward Soviet efforts to put them at risk—e.g., depressing the trajectory of Soviet submarine-launched missiles, thus enabling them to catch the northern-deployed mobile ICBMs before they could get far enough from their known parking spots."

Gore recognizes these difficulties and argues for a very elaborate scheme whereby a certain percentage of mobile missiles would be allowed to roam free and exercise in peace-time. But the problem recurs: the fewer mobiles that are allowed to roam around, the more vulnerable the ICBM force becomes to pre-emptive attack. And the more mobiles that are allowed to roam around, the more unverifiable becomes any treaty.

But who cares about verifiability? What's the point of restricting mobiles with arms control? Single warhead mobiles, such as the Soviet SS-25 and the U.S. Midgetman, are so stabilizing that the more deployed on both sides the better. "If the United States had a survivable mobile ICBM," write Scowcroft, Deutch, and Woolsey, "the Soviets would need so much throwweight to attack it (it would require a massive barrage attack) that any cheating they could do by covertly deploying mobile ICBMs themselves would be strategically insignificant."

The verification problem is even worse with another very stabilizing nuclear system, the SLCM, easy to hide and too slow for use as a pre-emptive weapon. It is the perfect retaliatory weapon. But there is no known way to verify SLCMs, which is why the United States wants them left out of any START treaty. If that happens, it might be the best thing to be said about START.

There is another way in which verifiability becomes an enemy of stability. It involves what are called "counting rules." There is no way to know how many warheads one side actually puts on a missile. In the past, therefore, each side had to count the maximum number of warheads that *could* be put on a missile against its arms control ceiling, regardless of how many it *actually* put on the missile.

For example, if the American D-5 SLBM was tested with ten warheads, each missile would count as ten regardless of how many the United States actually put on the D-5. This approach is a service to verifiability, since no verification of warhead numbers is required. But this approach is destabilizing because it pushes each side to pack as many warheads onto a missile as possible. It thus increases the ratio of warheads to targets. If you are being counted for the maximum number of warheads, you might as well pack them on. But packing multiple warheads onto missiles is one of the chief sources of nuclear instability today.

The Washington summit came up with a solution for START. Henceforth counting rules would be negotiated. The D-5 missile is now agreed, arbitrarily, to be carrying eight warheads even though it can carry ten. Similarly, the Soviet SSN-23 will be counted as carrying four missiles, even though it has been tested to carry eight to ten. What these artificially low counting rules do is allow each side to spread its deterrent force over more missiles, which makes for more redundancy, which makes for more stability. Fine. But what happened to verifiability? Under arbitrary counting rules, the number of warheads each side thinks the other has becomes utterly unverifiable and thus can be significantly underestimated. There is no way to know whether the Soviets have four or ten warheads on the SSN-23. This antagonism between verifiability and stability is insoluble. The best that can be said for the new counting rules is that, given the choice, they sacrifice the requirements of arms control to the requirements of stability. That's more than can be said for the proposals to ban or limit mobiles and SLCMs.

Dramatic quantitative arms control is a threat to stability for yet another reason. Large numbers promote stability because they provide each side with a cushion in case it miscalculates the size of the other side's threat or in case the other side suddenly increases its threat by means of a technological breakthrough or cheating. If one side makes a technological breakthrough, say in anti-submarine or in anti-ballistic missile warfare, that could put the other side's deterrent in jeopardy. The more redundancy that side has both in that threatened system and in others, the less such a technological breakthrough matters—and the more stable the nuclear balance.

Numerical arms control works the other way. The more the number of weapons is reduced, the more the premium on technological breakthrough or cheating. Suppose both sides have 10,000 warheads and one side conceals 1,000. In strategic terms, that means nothing. But suppose both sides, thanks to arms control, have only 500 warheads and one side is hiding 1,000. It has achieved clear nuclear superiority and the capacity—and the incentive—for preemptive attack in a crisis. The more deeply nuclear arsenals are cut, the more cheating matters, the more the safety of the world comes to depend on airtight verification. But why depend on inherently imperfect verification regimes? Schelling's question returns: "Who needs arms control if economical and reliable retaliatory weapons are available?"

At the beginning of the 1980s, agitation over the nuclear issue reached its peak, when it became an axiom that nuclear arms control was the most important issue of the day. In fact, the lessons of 40 years show that arms control between the great powers may be the least important issue of the day. Great powers do not use nuclear weapons. Both superpowers have now lost very costly and painful wars against very weak Third World adversaries that have no nuclear weapons. Neither superpower came close to exercising its unilateral nuclear advantage. In the very early years of the nuclear era, it was still possible to think of a great power using nuclear weapons. Hiroshima did, after all, occur. But Hiroshima drew its model from World War II strategic bombing. "Little Boy" was conceived by the United States as a way to concentrate a whole bomber fleet's weapons into one package. But thanks to the vast numbers of nuclear devices on both sides and the dazzling variety of systems for delivering them, the great powers have come to recognize that their nuclear arsenals are useless as actual instruments of war.

Not all countries have come to that recognition, however. The real threat for the future will come from tiny arsenals in the hands of unstable powers. There the Hiroshima model still applies. Iraq used poison gas against Iran and might very well have used nuclear weapons had it not been stymied by Israel's uniquely energetic non-proliferation policy. All the more reason for the great powers to retain overwhelming arsenals as a deterrent against attack by unstable and demonstrably barbaric states.

Superpower arms control has concerned itself almost exclusively with capping or reducing numbers. This exercise has always been a bit of a charade. The one exception is the ABM Treaty, a rare example of qualitative arms control that banned not only a class of weapons (so did INF, to little effect) but an entire concept of nuclear warfare, namely nuclear defense. Apart from ABM, most arms control has accomplished very little. The offensive weapons caps of SALT [Strategic Arms Limitation Talks] I and SALT II did little to change the likelihood of war. To the extent that force structure can promote or undermine crisis stability, they might have marginally increased the likelihood of war because they created incentives for MIRVing. But in the end, the real determinant of war is the degree to which the interest and values of the superpowers conflict and the degree to which either side is prepared to risk war to advance those interests and values. Nuclear force structure has a marginal effect. The absolute number of nuclear weapons has none.

The great gestures and ostentatious treaties capping these numbers are public events conducted largely for political reasons, i.e., to satisfy the popular faith that numerical cuts make a real difference in reducing the risk of nuclear war. In fact, these weapons make convenient bargaining counters precisely because they are so unusable. They are like poker chips with no bank behind them. That is why they served as the subject of choice for superpower negotiations during the first 40 years of the cold war, when the superpowers were so antagonistic that there was nothing else to talk about. Nuclear arms control created the illusion of agreement and provided a choreography of conciliation without really changing anything on the ground. The main purposes of arms control was to symbolize the lessening of tension between the superpowers. It could do that well because the agreements concerned something abstract and airless. Arms control worked best when—and because—it was useless.

Arms control is thus a legacy of the infancy of the cold war. It gave the illusion of reducing the threat of war. But the real issue, the real potential cause of war is decidedly non-nuclear: it is the conflict of interests and ideology that plays itself out in geopolitical competition and regional conflicts around the world. If, as many are saying, the Soviet Union is preparing to enter a new era of relations with the West, then it is time for us both to turn to the real war and peace issues of this world and give up our comfortable, distracting arms control obsession.

QUESTIONS FOR DISCUSSION

1. Why do countries enter into arms control agreements?
2. Do democracies have disadvantages over dictatorships when entering into arms control agreements? What are the reasons for your answer?

3. What is the relationship between arms control agreements and the preservation of national security?
4. Which arms control agreements have been the most successful and which have been the least successful? What are the reasons for your answer?
5. What would have been the consequences to U.S.-Soviet relations had the two superpowers not entered into any arms control agreements?

SUGGESTED READINGS

Barash, David P. *The Arms Race and Nuclear War.* Belmont, Calif.: Wadsworth Publishing Co., 1987.

Berkowitz, Bruce D. *Calculated Risks: A Century of Arms Control: Why It Has Failed and How It Can Be Made To Work.* New York: Simon and Schuster, 1987.

Bethell, Tom. "Arms Control: The Untold Story." *National Review,* 40 (Feb. 19, 1988), pp. 32, 34, 36–37.

Carnesale, Albert, and Richard N. Haass. *Superpower Arms Control: Setting the Record Straight.* Cambridge, Mass.: Ballinger, 1987.

Fairbanks, Charles H., Jr., and Abram N. Shulsky. "From 'Arms Control' to Arms Reductions: The Historical Experience." *Washington Quarterly,* 10 (Summer 1987), pp. 59–73.

Lamb, Christopher J. *How To Think about Arms Control, Disarmament and Defense.* Englewood Cliffs, N.J.: Prentice Hall, 1988.

McGwire, Michael. "Why the Soviets Are Serious about Arms Control." *Brookings Review,* 5 (Spring 1987), pp. 10–19.

Talbott, Strobe. *The Master of the Game: Paul Nitze and the Nuclear Peace.* New York: Knopf, 1988.

Turner, John. *The Arms Race.* 2d ed. New York: Cambridge University Press, 1988.

Wallop, Malcolm, and Angelo Codevilla. *The Arms Control Delusion.* San Francisco, Calif: ICS Press, 1987.

20 Should the United States Devolve Its Frontline Defensive Role in Europe to Its NATO Allies?

YES

David P. Calleo

NATO's Middle Course

NO

Colin S. Gray

NATO: Time To Call It a Day?

Nato's Middle Course

David P. Calleo

Unless the gods surprise us, NATO [North Atlantic Treaty Organization] will reach its 40th anniversary in 1989. Celebration seems very much in order. More than anything else, NATO embodies the geopolitical coalition between the United States and Western Europe that has contained the Soviet Union on its home ground and given America a wide margin of power to shape the world's political and economic structures. Thanks to NATO, the 20th century became the "American Century," and much of the world has enjoyed a liberal and prosperous Pax Americana.

Now, however, there exists on both sides of the Atlantic Ocean a strong sense that NATO's structure has grown obsolete. Radical NATO reform seems particularly appealing to retired statesmen, including former Secretary of State Henry Kissinger, former national security adviser Zbigniew Brzezinski, and former West German Chancellor Helmut Schmidt. The real issue is not whether NATO should change but how. Logically, proposals for reform fall into three broad categories: burden sharing, devolution, and disengagement. The differences among them are critical for NATO and for U.S. foreign policy in general.

Since the 1950s American administrations have urged greater burden sharing—that is, West Europeans should contribute more to their own defense while primary leadership still should remain with the United States.

Over the years the real situation has evolved in the opposite direction. While the Americans have continued to command, a substantial part of Western Europe's military forces—especially all those of France—has been withheld from NATO. Proposals for devolution would aim to reverse this trend by giving primary responsibility for leading the alliance to the West Europeans while continuing significant American participation. Proposals for disengagement, however, urge that the United States leave NATO altogether.

Individual proposals often appear to fall into one category but actually fall into another. Kissinger, and Schmidt, among others, called for the Supreme Allied Commander Europe (SACEUR) of NATO to be West European rather than American. But there remains the thorny question of how this European SACEUR would have access to American nuclear weapons. This proposal seems more an elaborate form of burden sharing than devolution because it would leave the American deputy in control of the weapons critical for West European defense. To take another example, the writer Christopher Layne has proposed the gradual end of American engagement in NATO.[1] Although he calls his proposal devolution, it seems more accurate to call it disengagement.

Proposals for disengagement do not necessarily imply political as well as military estrangement. Layne, for one, is not indifferent to Western Europe's welfare or hostile to close transatlantic ties, but he believes that NATO as currently constituted is doomed to dissolution and sees no salvation so long as the United States remains within it. Meanwhile, some neoconservative critics of NATO, like the economist Melvyn Krauss

David P. Calleo, "NATO'S Middle Course," *Foreign Policy*, no. 69 (Winter 1987–88), pp. 135–47. Reprinted by permission of *Foreign Policy*.

[1] See Christopher Layne, "Atlanticism without NATO," *Foreign Policy* 67 (Summer 1987): 22–45.

and the publisher of the quarterly *National Interest,* Irving Kristol, reflect considerable animosity toward the West Europeans, along with deep skepticism about whether U.S. and West European interests can be reconciled.

Critics of NATO's present arrangements have a powerful case. Clearly, the substantial shift of relative resources from America to Europe since the 1950s suggests a parallel shift in the central responsibility for West European defense. At the same time, the U.S. national interest in West European independence and prosperity is as great as ever. NATO thus needs reform that goes beyond burden sharing but stops short of disengagement.

The debate over NATO reform needs to be seen in the context of what might be called the "American Problem." Since the debacle of U.S. involvement in the Vietnam War, events and trends have evidenced a continuing decline in America's ability to dominate global affairs. How to perceive that decline and what to do about it have become the fundamental issues in the American foreign-policy debate. The decline is relative rather than absolute and results not from the failure of postwar U.S. policy but from its success. The recovery of Western Europe and Japan, the development of the Third World, and the peaceful containment of the Soviet Union all have been basic aims of American policy. But the net result has been an inexorable diminishing of the American political, economic, and military preponderance enjoyed at the end of World War II. Under a benign Pax Americana, the distribution of global wealth and power inevitably has grown more plural.

The trend is not toward a new hegemon. The Soviets are not the principal beneficiaries of America's decline. Militarily, they are threatened more by the rising new powers than by the United States, and it is not their moribund economy that challenges America's pre-eminence. Instead, the world is no longer susceptible to anyone's hegemony. The danger is not a Pax Sovietica but global anarchy. The postwar institutions have so depended upon American predominance that the whole system seems likely to collapse without it.

The statecraft of recent administrations has not enjoyed much success in coping with this relative loss of U.S. power. Washington still attempts to play the same global geopolitical role it did in the 1950s. Throughout most of the 1970s, American policy restlessly searched for expedients to keep up appearances while reducing costs or transferring them to others. In the 1980s, the Reagan administration has scorned such "hegemony on the cheap," but its effort to reaffirm American dominance has yielded uncertain military benefits and an astonishing growth of debt. The financial and commercial consequences of America's attempt to shore up its eroding world position now weigh heavily on the U.S. and world economies. The U.S. economy has fallen from being the liberal world's principal support to becoming its principal liability. The American Century has produced the American Problem.

Since neither hegemony on the cheap nor the reaffirmation of American leadership has proved to be successful, some formula is urgently needed to preserve the postwar system's benign interdependence while devolving the burdens of global management to fit the new balance of global resources.

So far, the American political imagination has been very slow to rise to the occasion. Across the political spectrum, a hegemony-or-nothing mentality drives American thinking. Unfortunately, this mentality condemns the United States to either exhaustion or isolation.

The most practical escape lies in the reform of NATO. Still the critical link in the postwar global system, the Atlantic alliance is also its microcosm. NATO reveals how American hegemony has become unworkable, but it also presents the most promising prospect for creating a more suitable pattern of relationships.

Obviously, reforming NATO has risks. But at this point, the risks of change seem a good deal less certain than the accelerating deterioration of present arrangements.

HEGEMONY ON THE CHEAP

NATO's particular problems have changed little during the past 40 years, but trends in the global environment have made them far less manageable. Militarily, NATO always has been an American nuclear protectorate. Rather than trying to match Soviet conventional power in Europe, the United States chose to remain the Continent's hegemonic protector by threatening to initiate the first use of nuclear weapons to stop a Soviet invasion. This policy, known as "extended deterrence," was an early instance of hegemony on the cheap. Ideal when the United States was more or less invulnerable, the arrangement grew increasingly unsatisfactory as Soviet strategic capabilities increased dramatically to rough parity with American forces. With the United States directly at risk, NATO has become an "entangling alliance" to a degree unimagined by the Founding Fathers.

American strategy attempted to adjust to the new strategic environment by shifting from a doctrine of "massive retaliation" on Soviet cities to one of "flexible response"—a full continuum of graduated responses designed to limit nuclear destruction to the minimum needed for stopping an attack. In addition, "counterforce" doctrine sought to limit intercontinental nuclear warfare to strikes against the enemy's military targets.

These changes have transformed hegemony on the cheap into an expensive arms race. Flexible response has required a large standing ground force in Western Europe that commits 10 of the army's 18 divisions. Five units are stationed in Europe, while an additional 5 units are kept on reserve in the United States to be moved to Europe on short notice.

All the forces needed for the NATO commitment have been reckoned officially to absorb roughly 45 per cent of recent American military budgets.[2] While some sort of U.S.-Soviet arms race was inevitable, maintaining the credibility of the American threat to commence a nuclear war has required a frantic technological scramble for an offensive "superiority." The American arsenal progressed from missiles to multiple independently targetable re-entry vehicles to mobile missiles, and now to strategic defense.

To reassure Western Europe and convince the Soviet Union that American deterrence will not falter, the United States also has deployed several hundred nuclear missiles on West European soil. In some cases they are located so close to the front lines that their use upon Soviet conventional attack would have to be virtually automatic. And because some of these weapons would strike the Soviet Union, instantaneous intercontinental retaliation could be expected. The West Europeans, meanwhile, have tended to resist building up NATO's conventional forces on the ground that doing so would suggest a lack of will to use the nuclear deterrent and hence actually increase the risk of war.

Americans cannot help but notice that West Europeans feel quite comfortable behind the U.S. nuclear shield. West European defense expenditures as a proportion of gross domestic product, 3.7 per cent, fell well short of America's 6.7 per cent as of 1985. Nor do the Americans feel adequately recompensed. Western Europe always has resisted serving as a forward base of American power, available automatically for diplomatic and economic pressure on the Soviet Union or for military

---

[2] See Earl C. Ravenal, "Europe without America: The Erosion of NATO," *Foreign Affairs* 63, no. 5 (Summer 1985): 1026. For other, higher, estimates, see Melvyn Krauss, *How NATO Weakens the West* (New York: Simon and Schuster, 1986), 25.

expeditions beyond the NATO region. Instead, Western Europe, for the most part, is busily extending economic ties to the U.S.S.R. and making its own arrangements with Middle Eastern countries. To some American critics the U.S. protectorate merely subsidizes West European tendencies toward neutralism, disunity, and weakness.

The "free-riding" West Europeans, however, have themselves grown increasingly dissatisfied. Extended deterrence has grown less plausible, and Western Europe's military security has grown more uncertain. As a form of diplomatic deterrence, the West Europeans have adopted a long-range strategy of trying to coax the Soviet Union and the rest of Eastern Europe into an interdependent relationship of benefits and restraints that would make war unprofitable and promote internal evolution of the Eastern regimes. The contrast between America's cyclical Soviet diplomacy and Western Europe's finely tuned accommodation becomes ever more difficult to reconcile.

A parallel divergence has been taking place with respect to Third World relations. Western Europe depends much more on the Third World for trade and raw materials than does the United States. As major events like the Vietnam War and the oil shocks have revealed America's declining ability to guarantee their interests, West Europeans have developed independent economic and political relationships with the Third World, often in competition with American interests. West Europeans find that American demands for NATO's support in Third World regions have become a growing embarrassment, as seen in such episodes as the 1982 stationing of peace-keeping forces in Lebanon and their abrupt withdrawal in 1984, the U.S. air raid against Libya in April 1986, and the U.S. policy of sending naval escorts to the Persian Gulf in 1987.

Since the mid-1960s, West Europeans and Americans have also had strong differences over general economic policy. The U.S. economy's recurring instability—with its financial shocks, giant swings in trade and capital balances, and corresponding bursts of protectionist sentiment—has greatly complicated European economic management. Europeans tend to blame an undisciplined American domestic economic policy and to resent the way America's global position is used to export the consequences.

But West Europeans cannot ignore easily the link between the massive U.S. domestic budget and trade deficits and the costs of America's military protectorate in Western Europe. Thus a kind of systemic justice permits the United States to manipulate the world monetary system so that the rich allies pay, at least indirectly, the costs of their own defense. Unfortunately, America's comparative disadvantage in sending forces to Europe means that the whole arrangement is neither militarily efficient nor economically cost-effective. The ensuing monetary instability imposes heavy burdens on the global economy. In short, the NATO relationship, central to the whole postwar structure, has gradually become a critical mechanism for its disintegration.

In theory, devolution seems a sure way to resolve NATO's difficulties. The increasingly intractable problems of American extended nuclear deterrence, for example, can be assuaged logically by endowing NATO with a stronger conventional defense or a European-directed nuclear defense. In practice, one goes with the other. In either case, only the West Europeans actually can provide the resources. By definition, only they can manage an indigenous deterrent. But if the West Europeans are to provide these things for NATO, and, in particular, if France is to play the critical role, as it must, then American hegemony becomes unneeded. Meanwhile, it is an obstacle: As long as West Europeans can assume that Americans will sustain Europe's military balance indefinitely, their own military cooperation seems redundant and unwelcome.

Diplomatically, devolution also would sensibly ease transatlantic tensions over Soviet relations. No amount of American importuning will force the West Europeans to abandon their long-range, pan-European strategy. The danger for the United States is not that Eastern and Western Europe gradually will develop more intimate relations but that Soviet military power will come to dominate those relations.

Of course, devolution of command would make it even more difficult to count Europe as a forward base for projecting U.S. power. But this pretention already is unreal. Devolution, if anything, should make the West Europeans more receptive to American concerns. A Western Europe in charge of its own defense certainly would not be any less eager to cooperate with the United States in Africa and the Middle East, or less reluctant to pass militarily sensitive technology to the Soviet Union.

For years analysts have thought devolution desirable but infeasible because West European states are considered too weak and disunited to take control of their own defense.[3] The key to West European military cooperation is the Franco-German relationship. France's partial disengagement from NATO is, in fact, the alliance's greatest military weakness. Yet for 30 years France and West Germany have steered the European Economic Community, by far the most successful experiment in intergovernmental cooperation in modern times, and one that penetrates deeply into the domestic politics of 12 West European countries. Compared with the complexities of managing the European Economic Community, a military coalition with as concrete and obvious a goal as balancing the Soviet Union

hardly seems an unrealistic challenge. But Western Europe never will develop a complementary military coalition so long as American military hegemony makes it superfluous.

Finally, devolution would help relieve the fiscal burden that weighs so heavily on the U.S. and world economies. Realistically, the American budget deficit can be brought under control only if there are major cuts in the defense budget, which in turn requires a basic rethinking of America's military role, commitments, and force structure. West European defense is one area where enormous American budgetary savings might be made without diminishing either U.S. or European security.

A DIFFERENT GLOBAL BALANCE

Devolution needs to be differentiated from disengagement. If the United States no longer supplied 10 standing divisions for NATO, it could still provide 3 or 4. If an American general no longer commanded all of NATO, an American commander in Europe still could serve under a European SACEUR—as General John Pershing served under Marshal Ferdinand Foch in World War I. And if the West Europeans developed their own nuclear deterrent, the United States still could continue its own nuclear guarantees to Europe.

The United States would stay on in NATO because it has a vital interest in Europe's independence and well-being. Aside from the United States itself, Western Europe contains the world's greatest assemblage of economic and financial power. As in the United States, political and economic liberty is deeply implanted and reliably practiced. Militarily, Western Europe has two nuclear powers and three of the world's half-dozen largest modern armies. The Soviet Union allied with Western Europe would constitute quite a different global balance.

Many American analysts hold an instinctive resistance to devolution. Most defend the

---

[3] See, for instance, Josef Joffe, "Europe's American Pacifier," *Foreign Policy* 54 (Spring 1984): 64–82.

present hegemony. Of those who do not, most seem to believe that the United States should, quickly or slowly, disengage completely. These views in effect are two sides of the same unilateralist coin: If the United States cannot determine what a coalition does, it should not mix with it. This hegemony-or-nothing bias disables American policy.

Neoconservative writers like Krauss are, at the moment, the most conspicuous advocates of unilateral disengagement. They are often acute critics of NATO's current weaknesses. They nurse strong grievances over how Western Europe enjoys American protection but refuses to support American policies toward the Soviet bloc or the Third World. Neoconservative critics, therefore, urge withdrawal. Their reasoning reflects a fundamental misunderstanding of the realities of power in a plural world.

As any votary of the free market should understand, independent and powerful states are inclined to act in their own self-interest. From the perspective of America's geopolitical interest, it is rash to pull out of NATO in anger because the West Europeans cannot be cured of an interest in détente.

As a practical matter, the neoconservative argument for disengagement would do little to advance anti-Soviet policies. Without allied cooperation, an American policy of sanctions or technology denial would merely hurt the United States, since the Soviet Union could buy whatever it needed elsewhere. By the same token, it is difficult to conceive how breaking with the European allies would improve American prospects in the Middle East, Asia, Africa, or Latin America.

The real grievance of NATO's right-wing critics is that NATO entangles, whereas the driving force behind their world policy is a heroic denial of American dependence on any other country. In this view, the European connection is a source of weakness, not strength. The NATO allies most certainly do not encourage the sort of anti-Soviet and interventionist foreign policy that a writer like Krauss apparently prefers. But the real obstacle to unilateral liberty is not that the United States still has allies, but that it needs them more than ever. The United States no longer has the resources to impose its will alone. NATO's function is no longer to organize the dominion over others, nor to replace their strength with American strength, but to mobilize their forces for shared purposes.

The Atlantic alliance is no longer a cover for American hegemony, as traditional American Atlanticists wish, nor is it an impediment to an illusory American self-sufficiency, as the unilateralists fear. The NATO alliance does not trammel America's liberty to act as it pleases. On the contrary, it is the channel through which a relatively weakened United States can continue to exert effective influence throughout the world. NATO, moreover, serves as a training ground for life in a pluralistic world. It implants within America's own increasingly undisciplined political system a mechanism for reminding Washington that even the greatest countries are subject to a balance of power and that national self-interest has to be defined and pursued in a cooperative framework.

The hegemony-or-nothing syndrome, with its underlying aversion to entanglement, by no means is limited to neoconservatives. It also flourishes among American strategic and arms control specialists, on the left as well as on the right. Their deep fear of entrapment in a European nuclear war has traditionally led them to insist on American hegemony in NATO and to oppose independent European nuclear deterrents. In the 1960s their fear led them to join with the Soviets in trying to freeze the bipolar nuclear regime through the 1968 Treaty on the Nonproliferation of Nuclear Weapons, which West Germany finally was pressured into signing in 1969. More recently, this same fear of entrapment has been reflected in proposals for a NATO "no-first-use" policy from many of the same people who directed U.S. strategic policy in the 1960s. Meanwhile, the Reagan administration has also been strongly attracted to the idea of collaborating with the U.S.S.R. to denuclearize Europe.

However, neither a bipolar nuclear cartel nor denuclearization can be reconciled with a genuine policy of devolution in NATO, which requires some kind of independent European nuclear deterrent. Adequate deterrence for Europe remains America's vital interest and, indeed, principal strategic problem. Given plans for removing European-based U.S. intermediate-range nuclear forces (INF), American policy should show solicitous concern both for the British and French nuclear forces and for some NATO or European entity capable of providing a reliable deterrent for the rest of the alliance. In the INF talks Washington did end up taking a firm line on preserving the British and French nuclear forces, in particular, on preserving their freedom to upgrade their forces, but only after sending some confusing early signals.

In general, recent U.S. strategic concepts seem to have been framed without serious thought to their consequences for West European defense. President Ronald Reagan's pursuit of the Strategic Defense Initiative (SDI) stirs doubts about the ultimate U.S. commitment to Western Europe by raising the specter of an isolationist America withdrawn to the shelter of some antimissile shield. At the October 1986 U.S.-Soviet summit meeting in Reykjavík, Iceland, Reagan's preoccupation with SDI led him to suggest to Soviet leader Mikhail Gorbachev that all ballistic missiles, if not all nuclear weapons, be eliminated.

America's arms control diplomacy has grown so accident-prone because it has failed to grasp the realities of a plural strategic environment. Now lost in the self-indulgent technological fantasies of SDI, American strategic thinking never has focused on the positive possibilities and implications of multiple deterrence.

As the French have argued since the 1950s, extended deterrence alone lacks plausibility because no country can reasonably be expected to commit suicide on behalf of another. But when a country is defending its own life or planning to avenge its own imminent death, even a small nuclear force poised at an opponent's largest cities can offer successful deterrence. A multiplicity of national deterrents, moreover, can augment the effectiveness of a general extended deterrent because two or more retaliatory triggers add greatly to the uncertainty or complexity of the risk faced by any would-be aggressor. In today's multipolar world, a national deterrent strategy like France's addresses rather than denies reality. The superpowers are increasingly overextended; the plural trend in nuclear arms is not some anomalous technological fluke but reflects the overall political and economic direction of the world system.

Undoubtedly, a world of several nuclear powers creates new worries of war by accident or miscalculation. But it is far from self-evident, contrary to the view of many political scientists, that more deterrent forces automatically increase the overall risk of nuclear war. War is an existential, not a statistical, phenomenon. Assessing its probability requires a situational, not an actuarial, analysis.

The newer nuclear powers—France, Great Britain, and the People's Republic of China—are, if anything, less pugnacious than the old ones. The new multiple strategic balance is inherently more stable than a system that relies exclusively on extended deterrence. That Britain or France or any other European power would be more likely to start a nuclear war than the United States or the U.S.S.R. seems improbable. The superpowers, after all, can imagine themselves surviving a nuclear war in some fashion, but no European country can nourish such illusions.

An increasingly fashionable analogy compares the dangers of nuclear escalation in Europe to the spiral of automatic mobilizations that led to World War I. But as long as European defense remains robustly nuclear, the parallel seems far-fetched. While no government exactly wanted the war in 1914, most vastly underestimated its destructive consequences, and all of them hoped to win it. Today no country in Europe is likely to expect victory in a nuclear war. Even Soviet leaders would never run the risk unless convinced they could somehow escape largely unscathed. And they would be far less likely to reach such a conclusion if faced by an array of indigenous and secure European deterrents, supported by an American guarantee, rather than only a devalued American promise to sacrifice itself for Western Europe. Insofar as West European deterrents firmly restore the balance of terror, the risk of nuclear war is negligible.

In summary, while America's vital interest in European independence from Soviet hegemony remains the same, the relative capacity of Americans and West Europeans to maintain the continental military balance, especially the nuclear balance, has changed radically. Devolution is the obvious solution, which means a NATO structure that accommodates mutually reinforcing U.S. European deterrents. Trying to avoid the obvious pushes American policy toward the idea of a denuclearized Europe—the misbegotten offspring of the hegemony-or-nothing mentality, crossed with its twin, the bipolar imagination of the 1960s.

Such a mentality cannot be a reliable guide in a plural world, where interdependence grows ever more pervasive and complex. An isolated American imagination, mired in nostalgia for hegemony, will find it increasingly difficult to keep up with the changing realities. Pragmatism used to be thought a particularly American trait. Twenty years of deterioration in NATO ought to be enough to prompt a new direction for American policy. NATO, the critical coalition for shaping the postwar system, should be the place to begin its rejuvenation.

NATO: Time To Call It a Day?

Colin S. Gray

It is fair to say that NATO [North Atlantic Treaty Organization] is living on borrowed time. The material basis (or lack thereof) of its present strategy reflects a very different era of assumptions about the military balance. The theories of deterrence that undergird flexible response and controlled escalation resolved the dilemma the United States came to face in the early 1960s, namely, the assumption of risks to its survival on behalf of merely vital, as opposed to existential, interests. But these theories did so by presuming, wrongly as it turns out, a permanent margin of U.S. strategic nuclear superiority. The failure to reform NATO's force structure means that the mismatch between plans and expectations, on the one hand, and prospective crisis or wartime reality, on the other, grows ever wider. If the Alliance does not manage a process of purposeful change, it is likely to find itself the victim of a process of rapid change that it neither endorsed, nor could easily survive.

It is a premise of what follows that containment of Soviet power is a geopolitical necessity for the United States. A Soviet Union no longer contained in a landlocked condition by severe balance-of-power distractions within Eurasia, would pose a very severe threat to U.S. interests in the wider world.[1] The Soviet Union is a distressingly acquisitive, if anachronistic, *imperial power*, by contemporary Western standards. Neither emerging conventional weapon technologies nor new strategic defensive devices will magically exorcise the Soviet military threat. There are no panaceas to the U.S.–Soviet problem—the Soviet Union will not evolve rapidly into an ordinary *status quo* power.

Geopolitically, containment is the correct guiding concept for U.S. national security policy. The concept of containment, and the ideas underpinning it, have not been overtaken by changes in weapon technologies or by the limited Soviet geostrategic success in establishing a handful of outposts in Africa, the Middle East, South East Asia, the Caribbean and Central America. However, containment as a policy, rather than as a concept, is in serious danger of being overtaken by political, economic and military change. What is at issue is the political viability under stress, and the plain military feasibility, of U.S. military strategy as an expression and implementation of containment.

Two concepts have been offered as an alternative to containment: devolution and fortress America. These two concepts of disengagement, presented and analyzed here, enjoy support on the Left and the Right of the American political spectrum. Either could become policy over the next several decades, by purposeful political design, or under the pressure of events.

DEVOLUTION

Devolution is intended strictly to describe a process of major restructuring of the terms of U.S. alliance ties. It is consistent with the basic concept of containment, but if pursued rigorously it could very easily amount, *de facto*, to a change in concept and a major shift among policy means. The central idea of devolution is that the United States would devolve upon its principal security partners many, and perhaps most, of the forward military power-balancing duties that are currently U.S. responsibility. It

Colin S. Gray, "NATO: Time To Call It a Day?" *National Interest*, no. 10 (Winter 1987–88), pp. 14–20. Reprinted by permission of *The National Interest*.

[1] See Colin S. Gray, "Keeping the Soviets Landlocked: Geostrategy for a Maritime America," *The National Interest*, No. 4 (Summer 1986), pp. 24–36.

is important to identify the probable motives behind such a hypothetical shift in U.S. policy.

First, devolution would restore flexibility, or freedom of action, to U.S. foreign policy that long has been absent. Depending upon the variant of devolved posture, the United States would continue to be an ally of countries in Europe and Asia. But as in the case of Great Britain with respect to France in 1914 and again in the late 1930s, those allies would not be able to assume any automaticity of direct U.S. military involvement in their local defense.

Second, the United States would change the terms of alliance to a condition wherein its more or less full, and certainly immediate, military support could not be taken for granted. NATO-Europeans always have assumed that the United States has no practical security alternative to having its military frontier in Central Europe. Devolution would correct this (allegedly false) assumption. It would say, and mean, that U.S. support of a kind that carried very high risks to the American homeland would have to be *deserved* by local countries and would be considered as an option in Washington in light of global security factors.

Third, devolution would transform security dependents into true allies and security partners. Security dependency is a fundamentally unhealthy relationship which places undue burdens on all parties to the relationship.

Fourth, devolution would mark a U.S. determination to effect a more accurate match between risk and the calculated worth of foreign interests. The terms of the NATO Alliance, as interpreted over the years, require the United States to regard an attack upon any of its members as an attack upon the United States. This formula rests upon very shaky geopolitical grounds. NATO's strategy is a compromise among its geopolitically distinct members who define their survival and vital interests differently. As a result, NATO is incapable of designing and effecting a defense strategy which makes much operational sense.

Fifth, devolution would express an American determination no longer to subsidize the preferences of others. U.S. defense expenditure, strategy and force structure are affected very significantly by the military mission of containing Soviet military power in and around Europe. NATO-European countries are able to indulge in extravagant social welfare provisions because the United States has agreed to function as their security blanket. NATO-European countries have also chosen to strengthen their domestic economies by trading with Warsaw Pact states, a pattern creating a dual cost for the United States. The Pact states partially finance their anti-NATO military preparations from the benefits of their trading relations with Western Europe. The United States shoulders the lion's share of countering these preparations. NATO-European countries increasingly become political hostages to the domestic economic benefits that flow from these trading relations, thereby greatly complicating the U.S. task as alliance leader in proposing, coordinating, and effecting Western security policy.

A potentially very serious, even terminal, political problem in alliance relations lurks in the realm of "burden-sharing." The U.S. has chosen to live for more than three decades with the perception, accurate or not, that its European allies are persistent underachievers.[2]

---

[2] For a carefully reasoned and computed analysis challenging this perception, see Klaus Knorr, "Burden-Sharing in NATO: Aspects of U.S. Policy," *Orbis*, Vol. 29, No. 3 (Fall 1985), pp. 517–36. Knorr finds that: "With one exception (extended nuclear deterrence), any careful analysis will find it hard to conclude that the United States has been carrying, relative to national economic capacity, an inequitable share of the burdens that the major members of NATO (Class I and II) have assumed for purposes of military deterrence and defense vis-à-vis the U.S.S.R. Even a comparison limited to budgetary data cannot show

European politicians and officials probably believe that in company with death and taxes, American complaints about allies' defense contributions are a permanent feature of the human condition. To date, the results of American complaints and exhortations have been very modest. Declarations of good faith, promises to do better in the future, and, above all else, deft maneuvering by Atlanticists in Washington, have sufficed to keep U.S. irritation within manageable bounds.

American critics of NATO-European countries' defense efforts notice that apparent European under-achievement has practical implications for the quality of risks the United States runs in Europe. Those critics, however, rarely notice that free riding, if such it be, is the logical expression of a quite rational perspective upon security. European governments do not simply choose to "pass (some of) the buck" of security production to the United States in order to liberate national resources for more attractive purposes, such as domestic welfare. These governments believe that their national security is maximized by purposeful underinvestment in regional defense. The combination of European underinvestment and dependence on the U.S. makes Soviet leaders confront a NATO that lacks a plausible regional defense capability, except the essential abilities to deny options for *coups de mains*, but has the ability to compel an invader to wage war on a very large scale.

Finally, devolution would require that the U.S.'s NATO allies take what many American, and some European, commentators view as a more mature and responsible view of their own security needs. In the context of devolu-

tion, those allies who failed to make adequate provisions for their national security would know that they could not count on somebody else to step in to take up the slack. Free goods are rarely appreciated appropriately. NATO-European countries would be likely to place a correct value upon their security if they had to provide it and pay for it almost entirely themselves. Moreover, the help the United States would provide in time of dire need would also be assayed accurately in the new security context.

The arguments specified above contain a measure of truth. They reflect a generally dormant American attitude that few NATO-Europeans have elected to take very seriously to date. It may be argued that because contemporary variants of isolationist sentiment are likely one day to achieve political dominance in Washington, it is preferable that that event be anticipated, if it cannot totally be precluded, by means of a careful and deliberate restructuring of the terms of the Atlantic Alliance in the direction of greater local self-reliance. Such a restructuring could defuse American isolationist impulses and prevent a wholesale American withdrawal, conducted in such a way that no security arrangement worthy of the name would be available to help manage a transition.

But while these arguments for devolution are not without merit, they are still fatally flawed. First, the present structure and defensive arrangements of the Western Alliance work well enough in peacetime, although the quality of their likely performance in time of crisis and war should be improved. Second, there is no credible alternative structure for the security of the Eurasian Rimlands to an alliance led by the United States. Third, the United States cannot be a full-fledged member, let alone the leader, of the Western Alliance unless it is present militarily in the zones of Soviet pressure. Finally, it is a geopolitical fallacy to believe that the United States can en-

---

inequity once allowance is made for the high cost of military manpower in the United States, and for the proportion of American forces earmarked for missions outside Europe and the Atlantic," p. 534. For the contrary view, see Melvyn Krauss, *How NATO Weakens the West* (New York: Simon and Schuster, 1986).

hance its security either by washing its hands of its current Eurasian security responsibilities, or by altering dramatically the military terms of many of those responsibilities.

Although devolution is not intended to be a near-synonym for the concept of an isolationist fortress America, in practice it would be likely to precipitate political circumstances in the United States and abroad that would lead inexorably to an isolated stance. In principle, however, devolution, or alliance restructuring, certainly is intellectually compatible with the proposition that the United States should be altering its strategy and military posture, but not its basic national security concept. If the idea of devolution were to guide U.S. policy, it would not mean that the United States had decided it was no longer concerned to contain Soviet power and influence. Rather, it would mean that the United States had decided that in the future containment would be effected differently. A wide variety of policy options could be accommodated by devolution.

For example, the United States could announce that it would withdraw all of its armed forces from current forward deployment in and around Eurasia on a set schedule. The schedule could be protracted over a five to ten year period. The United States would offer to remain politically allied, as at present, but it would regain freedom of action with respect to the level and nature of future military involvement in foreign conflict. In conception, this would be American Gaullism. As with France today, the United States would proclaim simultaneously its steadiness as a firm ally and its determination to control its own destiny and protect its own interests.

This most rigorous variant of devolution would express a determination not to have a large fraction of the U.S. armed forces locked into an overseas garrison status, or tied to the need to sustain, reinforce, and, if need be, rescue garrisons in particular predetermined lo-

cations. In conception, at least, the United States would not be retreating; it would not be analogous to Constantine's legions leaving Britain to its fate in 407 A.D. America would rather be recognizing that the potential for regional self-help in general purpose forces can never be tapped appropriately so long as she continues to assume the burden of regional defense to the extent that she has in the postwar period. The U.S. armed forces would be organized, equipped, and trained so as to pose a more formidable global threat to Soviet power and influence. Those forces would emphasize maritime/air strength for amphibious flexibility, against the backcloth of a first-class strategic forces posture.

An all-too-obvious prerequisite for this form of devolution would have to be a U.S. determination to carry through its military redeployment design regardless of regional consequences.[3] Devolution would be a gamble that the allies would choose to accept the additional regional security responsibilities that the United States would be relinquishing. It would be the American hope that these duties would devolve upon regional powers, but the risk that the allies might decline to pick up the baton that the United States would be laying down would have to be recognized.

A second possibility would be a very substantial thinning out of U.S. forces deployed in and about Western Europe, Korea, and Japan, short of a total withdrawal. The U.S. force withdrawals would be sufficiently large (on the scale of a half or perhaps two-thirds) to make a noteworthy adverse difference—absent local compensation—in the strength of the allied order of battle. This second possibility, however, might produce the worst of all security worlds for the United States. Rather

---

[3] This is not strictly true, but if the United States resolved to experiment on a "try it and see" basis with military disengagement, the allies would be motivated strongly to ensure that the experiment failed.

than responding by filling the preparedness gap left by the large U.S. force withdrawals, the forward-placed allies might prefer to believe that the residual American military deployment would be sufficiently large that the extant military strategy and tactics of the Alliance could still obtain, even with no European (or Japanese) gap-filling. NATO's defenses would be thinner, but that fact may not trouble Europeans who have never defined their security in relation to the putative ability of the Alliance actually to defend their territory. As we mentioned earlier, NATO-European governments have opted for a combination of regional weakness and dependence on the U.S. This combination, and its appeal to NATO-European governments, might not be jeopardized by the thinning out of U.S. forces.

West Germany would argue that its manpower pool for military service is shrinking and that it cannot provide additional standing forces (though it is certainly the case that it could greatly increase the effectiveness of its reserves). France, apart from being predictably unenthusiastic about any large-scale increase in the size and effectiveness of the *Bundeswebr,* would respond to partial U.S. devolution by reaffirming its current defense policy, particularly the nuclear theme in that policy. Britain could fill a part of the gap left by the devolving Americans, but only by reintroducing the draft and shifting resources from social welfare to security functions. In practice, it is very likely that Britain, far from assuming new continental burdens, would prefer to follow the American example and begin a process of continental disengagement. Rather than send additional forces to Germany, Britain probably would prefer to invest in the modernization of its national nuclear deterrent, in the revitalization of its grossly inadequate home air defenses, and in the strengthening of its navy.

The arguments presented above merely skirt the field of probable developments that would not meet with American favor. However, a potentially very important point has been omitted from the discussion so far. In contrast to a condition of total military withdrawal from Western Europe, a United States that retained as many as half its current military assets in that region would have those assets as a large bargaining chip for leverage over the allies. Furthermore, the fact that perhaps half of the U.S. garrison had been withdrawn, would demonstrate a determination to restructure the military arrangements of the Alliance that could not be matched by any number of speeches.

NATO-Europe has come very much to take the United States for granted as a net security guarantor. If the United States ever should decide to proceed down the path of measured devolution, it will be able to persuade the allies that they do need to assume additional regional duties only by actually withdrawing forces on a non-token scale. With half or so of its forces remaining, the United States could link the continued forward deployment of those forces to the actions taken, or not taken, by the European allies.

A third possibility would comprise U.S. retention of strictly token force elements in Western Europe and Northeast Asia. They would symbolize American commitment, and hence should have a deterrent value out of all proportion to their military significance. But they would be sufficiently small (some tactical air squadrons, an armored brigade or two, and a small permanent naval presence) to free the hands of U.S. defense planners to design a truly global strategy that would emphasize the American long suits of maritime and air power.

The potential benefits to the United States of devolution options cannot be doubted. Clearly, it would be very desirable for Americans if the local defense of Western Europe were to repose almost entirely in Western European hands. It would be in the U.S. interest for its military commitments to NATO-Europe to be so modest that a military defeat in that theater would not compromise fatally the ability of the United States to wage war effectively elsewhere, and so on. However, the United States cannot select a particular national security concept unless it believes that it could live tolerably well with its failure.

The dissolution of the Western Alliance would be a highly plausible consequence of total, or even substantial, U.S. force withdrawals from Western Europe and North East Asia. Furthermore, the degree of local confidence in the strength of U.S. security commitments is a large barrier to nuclear proliferation. A NATO-Europe deprived of the support of a U.S. security commitment could evolve in three basic directions: "superpower Europe"; "*Europe des patries*"; or "accommodationist Europe," contracting what Walter Laqueur has termed the malady of "Hollanditis."

The evidence favoring the proposition that a "superpower Europe" is lurking in the wings waiting to be born once the United States removes the security blanket, is less than overwhelming. "Superpower Europe" is certainly feasible in terms of resources, but history suggests that Europe lacks the creative political assets and sense of essential common interests to reorganize in its own defense. The second direction, "*Europe des patries*," is security nonsense. The idea that a non-communist Europe comprising proud, well-armed (meaning *nuclear* armed) states, willing and able to resist Soviet intimidation on an individual basis, is sheer fantasy.

In addition, the nuclear armament of West Germany is problematic. Very few events plausibly might provoke a deliberate Soviet military lunge into West Germany, but a whole range of scenarios can be composed for such an eventuality should Bonn announce an intention to acquire truly national nuclear forces.

"Accommodationist Europe" is the most likely outcome of total or very substantial U.S. military withdrawal. The real action in the Soviet-American rivalry in Europe is taking place in the minds of Europeans. Faced with the realities of American military withdrawal, French material weakness and rigorous self-regard, German anxiety concerning its military vulnerability and dreams of reunification, and British weakness and insular yearnings, it is not too difficult to conclude that the policy preference of an average European would be *sauve qui peut*. There would be no principal guardian to organize and direct the Western end of the European security order.

Some, perhaps many, Americans will not be unduly disturbed by this analysis. They believe that should a U.S. troop withdrawal reveal a NATO-European willingness to accommodate the Soviet Union, then it is better that Americans discover this now rather than in the midst of some terrible military crisis. But Western Europe does not have sufficient political assets to organize itself as a unitary state or regional security pact with sufficient military muscle to withstand Soviet intimidation.

Proponents of the variants of devolution have to consider the meaning for security of trends in contemporary European political culture. Overall, it is by no means obvious that the societies of Western Europe have the moral vitality necessary to sustain themselves in a condition of political independence *vis-à-vis* Soviet hegemonism.

The experience of a sustained prosperity in the wake of two devastating protracted wars, set against the backdrop of nuclear fears, may have so completely debellicized the welfare democracies of Western Europe that they no longer possess the cultural attributes necessary for self-defense. European countries adhere to NATO not because the function of NATO is preparation for war in the service of deterrence, order, and peace. Instead, the mere existence of NATO, and particularly the generally comforting security connection to the off-shore superpower, is itself viewed as a guarantee of peace.

The major immediate source of popular anxiety in Western Europe over its security condition is a local mirror image of the principal neoisolationist concern in the United States. A trans-Atlantic difference is that in some European countries alienation has attained the character of a mass movement, whereas in the United States alienation from the NATO enterprise is largely confined to a handful of intellectuals and policy commentators. The European peace movements express both the belief that Europe has a right to peace, and the perception that the current U.S. direction of Alliance security policies comprises a threat to the exercise of that right.

It is certainly true that nuclear defense questions have been the catalysts for popular protest in Western European countries. But one should not neglect the implications of the fact that some of the societies of the NATO allies have come to reject war as an instrument of policy, possibly even in the strictest conditions of self-defense. Prosperity and an understandable nuclear dread have completed the process of debellicization that was far advanced by the nightmares of 1914–18 and 1939–45. By this logic, war has become unacceptable and unthinkable for the complex, densely populated, and enormously vulnerable societies of Western Europe.

The visible trends concerning the capacity for sufficient collective action in self-defense on the part of Western Europe are not comforting. If it is true that NATO-Europe at the popular level is more disturbed by its perceptions of U.S. belligerence than by the course of Soviet imperialism, there have to be serious grounds for doubt concerning the European political ability to effect functional substitutes for the American legions that could be recalled.

For the near-term future at least, this author believes that the societies, and certainly the governments, of NATO-Europe prefer to live with what they discern as their American problem rather than to launch the bold venture of trying to live without that problem. Americans, secure in their political and strategic culture, and, one hopes, clear-eyed about the geopolitical realities of the global contest with the Soviet empire, understandably fail adequately to see themselves as others see them. American policy-makers should recognize the potential for damage of a politically significant, strongly negative strain in European attitudes towards the United States.

These attitudes are not really a rejection of distasteful and allegedly dangerous American policy traits, but rather a rejection of the distasteful and certainly dangerous enduring facts of international politics. By virtue of its power position in the international system the United States has been inoculated by responsibility against rejection of power politics in favor of fantasies of perpetual peace. Devolution, as a conceptual guide for national security policy, must meet one or two requirements. The first is that European, and perhaps Japanese, societies respond to a far more conditional, and certainly less locally visible, *Pax Americana* by meeting regional security challenges with suitable regional effort. No amount of careful historical research, however, can reveal beyond a reasonable doubt just how Western Europe and Japan would behave with respect to regional organization and provision for military security, in the face of a cumulatively dramatic shift in U.S. strategy along one or another of the devolutionary tracks identified here. If this first requirement is not met, then there has to be a persuasive theory explaining how vital American interests can be protected in the context of a security-defaulting Eurasian Rimland.

Analysis of the concept of devolution suggests that it has some merit as a means for the

United States to effect some desirable changes in its national military strategy, changes designed to secure a better fit between means and ends within the ambit of containment. But in some key respects devolution, or military withdrawal, is puzzling in the context of an intended continuation of containment. A United States liberated from very heavy garrison duties in the direct defense of Western Europe should indeed have regained much of its freedom of strategic action. But what would a United States so liberated wish to accomplish? Certainly, it would be better prepared to conduct an essentially maritime strategy, but where and to what purpose would U.S. military power be applied in the event of a military conflict in Europe? Would it be the U.S. intention to rush forces to Europe in the event of an acute crisis there? Is it the idea that a United States free, or substantially free, of European defense burdens would enjoy freedom of action to threaten the Soviet Union elsewhere? In which case where, and for what purpose?

There is a sensible case to be made for the United States to seek some substantial relief from those forward defense duties in Europe that could be assumed by continental European allies, and adopt a national military strategy more suitable for the prosecution of a genuinely global conflict. The benefits of a greater freedom to act strongly in regions aside from Central-Western Europe, however, would be purchased too dearly if the geostrategic advantages conferred upon the United States by the current security structure supporting non-Soviet controlled Eurasia were to be placed at very severe risk as a consequence. Devolution is sensible to the degree to which it points to the desirability of strategy adjustment and postural evolution, rather than to the merit in wholesale change.

In debating the future course of U.S. national security policy, one should not permit confusion to emerge between means and ends. To debate the desirability and feasibility of the United States devolving some of its forward defense duties upon regional allies is to debate policy instrumentalities. The ultimate purpose of the policy is not to seek relief from unwanted burdens, but to contain Soviet power and influence.

FORTRESS AMERICA

Proponents of strategic withdrawal from containment concerns to a fortress America have to address the question of how the vital interests of the United States should be defined in geographical terms. Would the U.S. defense perimeter be strictly the coastal defense of U.S. territory? Would fortress America embrace the "quartersphere" of the United States, Canada, Central America and the Caribbean? Or, would the United States view as its security domain the bicontinental hemisphere from the Drake Passage to the Arctic Ocean? An expansive definition of the domain of fortress America most likely would include Greenland, Iceland and the Azores, as well as the Marshall and Mariana Islands in the Western Pacific. The core of the idea of fortress America is plain enough, but operational questions concerning its prudent implementation in defense policy raise a host of practical difficulties. For example, in terms of U.S. military security, the current "barrier allies" of Eurasia—preeminently Norway, Britain, Turkey, and Japan—are vastly more important and worth supporting against Soviet hegemonic pressure than are the countries of South America below the equator.

The concept of fortress America, however, should not be dismissed too lightly as an archaic idea that has been overtaken by a new American maturity as well as by the alleged facts of global security interdependence. Its proponents contend that although the interests of the United States inevitably are impacted by shifts in the security structures of

Eurasia, the United States cannot, should not, and fortunately need not attempt to afford to pay the price of global guardianship. They argue that U.S. forward military diplomacy around the Rimland of Eurasia has generated threat perception in the Soviet Union that belies the true, defensive character of U.S. foreign policy; has reduced vastly the local European and Asian incentives to construct and pay for security structures and policies well adapted to local needs; and, most important of all, has generated potentially fatal dangers to U.S. survival interests.[4]

The core features of the fortress America concept comprise these principles: First, the United States should protect the survival interests of the American people, if need be at the expense of vital and lesser interests. Second, the United States explicitly would eschew a global, indeed any extra-hemispheric, military guardianship role on behalf of international order. Third, the United States would have no alliance ties beyond the Hemisphere of a kind that carry, or might encourage, expectations that military assistance would be provided. Fourth, the United States would be moved by a determination to achieve the maximum feasible measure of freedom of international action (or inaction). Fifth, a critical corollary to the others, the United States would be determined not to play any security role, unilaterally or in bilateral and multilateral contexts, outside the Western Hemisphere that would be likely to generate or fuel political antagonism towards itself.

A United States seeking to practice the fortress America concept as policy need not foreswear all political or military interests in Eurasia. Indeed, given the values of the American people, the cultural and sentimental ties that many feel for the homelands of their forebears, and the facts of economic interdependence, such denial would be unrealistic. Fortress America need not resemble very closely an isolated, let alone an isolationist, America. The United States could remain militarily a very strong power and could state its willingness, indeed its determination, to defend its most important interests when and where those interests might be threatened. However, those interests would not include the territorial integrity of countries around the Rimland of Eurasia from Norway to South Korea, or the security of oil supply from the Persian Gulf to Western Europe and the Far East.

The term *fortress* America is probably as misleading as the term isolationism. A United States embarking upon this policy course need not evolve a siege economy, nor would the American people need to be mobilized and regimented after the fashion of a beleaguered garrison. Even in the event of Soviet domination of virtually the whole of the "World-Island" of Eurasia-Africa, in Mackinder's conception, the United States would be protected by vast oceanic distances from the newly expanded base of Soviet power. A very heavily nuclear-armed United States need have no fear of Soviet invasion.

It has been argued that an interventionist geopolitical logic spoke more to the constraints imposed by U.S. political culture and national ethos than to strategic realities, that the domestic debate in the United States in 1940–41 was constrained culturally to the all-or-nothing choice between global interventionism to "save" the Old World, or a very muscular defense of the New World (and its trans-Pacific holdings) after the Monroe Doctrine. Geostrategically, though not culturally, the United States could have considered very seriously the policy option of permitting the

---

[4] A forceful discussion of the actual and potential costs of global containment policy is Robert W. Tucker, *The Purposes of American Power: An Essay on National Security* (New York: Praeger, 1981). Tucker has a discomforting knack of framing questions that threaten the jugular of orthodox thinking. For example: "Why should we persist in commitments whose sacrifice would not risk our physical survival but whose retention does?" p. 121.

wars in Eurasia to run their courses. It is thus probably true to claim that in theory the United States had policy options intermediate between a hemispheric fortress America and a crusade of intervention to defeat the Axis powers in Eurasia. In practice, however, the intermediate options would have required the United States to behave imperially in a very un-American manner, moved by considerations of prudential strategic advantage (or disadvantage to be avoided).

The debate over isolation and intervention in 1940–41 is of some enduring significance in that it showed American democracy capable of contemplating seriously only two concepts for national security policy. There was a missing middle to the debate. American political culture today is not different in its essentials, and the same tendencies are evident. This means that strategically more rewarding options than the stark policy alternatives of global forward (and multilateral) containment and what would amount to fortress America may not find support in the reality of domestic political environment. Americans can understand and empathize with a mission of global resistance to Soviet hegemony, as they can the concept of the United States standing aside from the sullying disputes of unworthy foreigners. The idea of the United States intervening very selectively, on an as-needed basis, to protect strictly vital U.S. interests, simply would be to ask too much, or too little, of the American people.

At root, a United States opting for a national security concept of fortress America would be saying that henceforth it would accept the most dire of risks only on behalf of the most important of its national interests. In practice, though not in principle, a rigorous policy of forward security–duty devolution and fortress America could be close to indistinguishable. A pure application of fortress America would have no formal U.S. security connections whatsoever in Eurasia. It could be

argued that the security shock of U.S. military withdrawal would be softened were political alliance connections to remain in place. Such a diplomatic lifeline could affect negatively the determination likely to be shown locally to design and pay for a new security framework. According to this line of thought, the only security shock likely to be sufficient to trigger the creation of local defense communities plausibly capable of resisting Soviet intimidation would be local recognition that Europeans and Asians unambiguously were on their own.

Several major uncertainties pertain to fortress America: Would the former allies of the United States attempt to organize themselves in such a way that Soviet hegemony could be prevented? If the attempt were made to organize regionally for defense, would it be likely to succeed? Could the American people live with the distinct possibility that the unintended consequence of such a radical shift in their national security policy would be to donate the whole of Eurasia to Soviet imperialism?

How strong a case can be presented for the concept of fortress America?

The adoption of a fortress America concept could not fairly be characterized as an American retreat, or as evidence of an American failure of will or nerve. On the contrary, adoption of a fortress America concept would constitute a return to the traditional and most genuinely American national security policy, the policy pursued from the time of George Washington until Franklin D. Roosevelt's third term of office. The most probable consequences of a fortress America policy would be consistent with the underlying U.S. foreign policy intention in the early years of the NATO Alliance. Adoption of the concept of fortress America would not be so much a rejection of the global guardian role of the past forty years, but rather long overdue action in recognition of the substantial success of that policy. People today tend to forget that the U.S. military commitment to, and in, Europe was not intended to be permanent. U.S. allies in Eurasia now have all the economic and political assets needed to evolve from a security adolescent to a security adult.

The forward security commitments of the United States in Europe and East Asia also have the quality of long familiarity about them. But is it really a very radical suggestion to propose that the United States should not deploy well in excess of 400,000 military personnel abroad *prospectively forever?* Do opponents of the several variants of fortress America propose that the American taxpayer should subsidize the national security of Western European countries and of Japan forever? What is the ethical, political, economic, or military basis for the proposition that wealthy Europeans and Japanese should not foot the full bill for their own defense?

The United States needs freedom of action in order to define and protect its own interests in the world. NATO-Europe perennially is distressed by the consequences of the fact that the United States is a power that has truly global security roles to play. For example, European officials have been very critical of what they discern as a "Pacific tilt" to U.S. grand strategy in the 1980's. The difficulty lies in the structure of the situation. On the one hand the United States is a global power which faces security problems close to its own border to the South, projects power across two oceans, and has inherited guardianship duties from Britain in South Asia and the Middle East. On the other hand, the European allies of the United States are regional powers who do not want the political stability achieved in Europe to be threatened by the consequences of tensions elsewhere in the world. It is a geopolitical fact, however, that alliance with the United States provides an unwanted connection with security problems in distant parts of the world. The burden of this argument is that NATO-European countries should be released to de-

sign and conduct the security policies for Europe that they believe best meet their local needs.

Proponents of fortress America need not profess indifference to the security of Europeans and Asians, though many undoubtedly would. They need say only that their concern stops short of a willingness to commit the United States, in advance, to go to war on behalf of other countries. Also, they could argue that Western Europe is more likely to design and sustain a lasting and effective regional security structure than is a NATO Alliance permanently riven with political tensions among its current, geopolitically unduly diverse, members. The opinion could be offered that the Germans, Frenchmen, Britons, Spaniards, Norwegians, and others, are not exactly natural candidates for appeasement roles on the evidence of their histories. Once the first shock of being cast adrift had worn off, these old, socially and ethnically homogeneous countries would realize that they had ample resources with which to thwart Soviet hegemonial ambitions.

Some Western Europeans may believe that although the United States has been both their last line of defense and even a notable contributor to their first line of defense, it also may well have been an important part of the European security problem. Some part of the Soviet motive for its ever-renewed political offensive against the coherence of NATO may have had less to do with any desire to dominate Western Europe for its own sake, than with the ambition to separate the United States from its European allies. While it is not in the nature of Soviet/Russian political culture to be a good neighbor, the Soviet Union may adopt a more relaxed defense posture towards a Western Europe that was no longer a Trojan horse for the real enemy across the Atlantic. Indeed, it is possible that the Soviet Union would ask of a Western Europe bereft of plausible American military support, only that it stand on the sidelines with respect to the Soviet-American competition.

The United States would like Western Europe and East Asia to continue to provide continental military distraction on a major scale for Soviet imperialism. Americans attracted to disengagement concepts should recognize that while it may be beyond the ambition and political strength of Western Europe to create a superpower quality of defense capability, some widespread functional analogue of Swiss, Yugoslav, and Swedish deterrence may well be entirely feasible. Provided its neutrality were not unduly benign towards the Soviet Union, a relatively militarily weak, though nuclear-armed, Western Europe that would not add its economic strength or its strategic geography to the Soviet imperium, would be distinctly tolerable for a fortress or otherwise thoroughly disengaged America.[5]

Finally, people of a fortress-America persuasion may argue that even should the pessimists be proved correct, in that the Rimland countries of Eurasia would fail to reorganize effectively to provide alternative security structures to a defunct NATO, the consequences need not be so terrible. It could be argued that the Soviet Union lacks the material strength to achieve hegemony over all of Eurasia. As they expand, empires acquire more and more of the seeds of their own destruction. While the Soviet Union could intimidate and even physically coerce any country or countries in Eurasia that it found to be unac-

---

[5] This author is not persuaded that even a well-armed and neutral-intending, or neutralist, multinational Western Europe, would be able over the long run to avoid functional cooperation as an agent of Soviet *Weltpolitik*. The Soviet Union could not venture forth on the high seas in quest of a greater and greater measure of imperial security, leaving a powerful and potentially hostile Western European garrison in its rear. While a Western Europe independent of direct Soviet control must always have some considerable continental-distraction value, one should assume that the Soviet Union would strive to achieve the necessary degree of *contrôle*.

ceptably uncooperative, it could not possibly occupy Western Europe, and/or China, and so on, *and profit by the deed.* Even if the Soviet Union enjoyed substantially unchallenged strategic primacy throughout Eurasia, the value of that primacy as an asset would be far less than might be supposed in the correlation of forces with a United States strategically excluded from the "World-Island."

POLICY APPRAISAL

There is some abstract merit in the fortress America argument, but not enough to warrant very serious public interest. For six major reasons fortress America and its close affiliates should be rejected.

First, a U.S. withdrawal on the scale and of the quality under discussion here would constitute a geopolitical revolution in the structure of international security in favor of the Soviets. Although the Soviet Union defines the United States as its principal enemy, as it must on grounds of capability, Soviet strategy appears to have the proximate goal of expelling U.S. power and influence from the Rimland of Eurasia and, *ipso facto,* isolating the United States from potential sources of support. Devolution or fortress America, while it would pose the Soviet Union some difficult problems to solve, plainly would provide Soviet leaders with strategic opportunities of historic dimensions. The United States would be withdrawing voluntarily from many of the fields of greatest economic and strategic significance, and effectively would be inviting the Soviet Union to exploit the newly created imbalance of power in Eurasia to strengthen itself for the long-term struggle against a United States that chose to stand alone.

Second, it is not at all obvious that the United States would want to remain militarily isolated under all circumstances. Far from purchasing peace, and nuclear peace in particular, through disengagement, the United States instead would be encouraging an upheaval in Eurasian security structures of a kind that quite plausibly could lead to war. A responsible proponent of fortress America is unlikely to be totally indifferent to the prospect of *après moi le deluge*. Repeatedly in this century the United States has permitted events to teach that it does have interests in Europe and Asia worth fighting to protect. There is good reason for anxiety that a United States which disengaged, through a thoroughgoing devolution or through adoption of the fortress America concept, could trigger sequences of events in Eurasia which would greatly reduce deterrent effect in Soviet minds and hence would place vital U.S. interests at severe risk. Moreover, one can predict that the United States would still want to intervene militarily, if and when traditional friends and former allies were subject to aggression or even to severe political pressure. However, the United States would be intervening late, it would lack a regional logistics infrastructure, and it might confront a military task more of an offensive-liberation than of a defensive character.[6]

It should be recalled that there has not been a resolution of the German problem. The dilemma posed by Germany is that, united, it would be too powerful for the peace of mind of most of its neighbors and near-neighbors, while divided, it constitutes the major item of unresolved security business in Europe. The prospect of West Germany bereft of American,

and probably British, military deployments or commitments, essentially let loose from the NATO framework to see to its own security, has potentially catastrophic implications for the peace of Europe.

Third, the geopolitical realities of Eurasian security are such that the security-producing potential of NATO-Europe is far less than is the sum of its several columns of national assets. This is not just a matter of will, let alone courage; it is a matter of history and particularly of the strong national particularisms that have matured over the centuries. NATO without the United States would have no leader, and there are no likely European candidates to play that role effectively. The degree of Franco-German reconciliation has been remarkable, but neither country could accept a clear leadership role for the other. Similarly, Britain would veto either French or German leadership, yet would lack the strength, not to mention the confidence and trust of others, to assert leadership itself.

Fourth, disengagement on one of the fortress-America models would not be viable as a policy theme in American political culture today. An American politician usually can secure a hearing for claims that Uncle Sam is being exploited by free-riding, overly self-regarding and ungrateful foreigners. Also, an American politician probably could attract a following for the proposition that the United States should declare peace with the outside world and retire to its well-defended island continent, or bi-continent *à la* James Monroe, to pursue virtuous American pursuits. Day by day in normal times these sentiments could well dominate policy consideration. But how well would these sentiments play if and when South Korea were overrun by North Korea? Or if Israel faced a military catastrophe? Or if Soviet forces intervened in West Germany?

Interventionism in truly worthy causes and security guardianship overseas has taken sufficiently deep root in the U.S. world-view and in Americans' views of themselves, that firm and

---

[6] In 1914 Germany was encouraged by the absence of formal alliance ties between Britain and France to hope, if not quite believe, that the former would stand aside. In 1940 the absence of alliance ties between the United States and Britain, France, or the Netherlands, fed a belief in Tokyo that Japan might have a Southeast Asian option for expansion that would not require the conduct of war with the United States. Fortunately for Western civilization, Japan decided not to gamble on the possibility of U.S. neutrality in the event of an attack confined to British and Dutch possessions in Southeast Asia. The point is that while the existence of formal commitments can never guarantee a sufficiency of deterrence—witness Hitler's invasion of Poland—the absence of such commitments must function to breed hope in the minds of statesmen considering adventure, that one will choose to stand aside.

truly rigorous disengagement is simply not viable in U.S. domestic politics, at least once the consequences of that policy were brought home. The United States has been changed as a country by the events and trends of the twentieth century. Although an isolationist and certainly a unilateralist impulse remains, and should not be dismissed lightly by foreigners, in practice Americans would demand that their government *do something* were Soviet and North Korean tanks to celebrate the American departure from Rimland Eurasia in a traditional Soviet or North Korean manner.

Fifth, trite though it may sound, history does teach that predatory countries abhor a power vacuum. It is as certain as anything in politics can be that the Soviet Union would hasten to exploit the American withdrawal. There would be good reason for haste on the Soviet part. The U.S. policy action would be so foolish in geopolitical terms that Soviet leaders probably would anticipate a U.S. policy reversal following the next general election. Any proponent of any of the variants of fortress America whose position rests on the belief that the Soviet Union would behave in a more benign fashion towards its regional neighbors in the absence of local U.S. security complications, should be reminded of the enduring cultural and stylistic features of the Soviet imperial system. All that would change in the geopolitical structure of Soviet security policy as a consequence of American disengagement would be the absence of the only power capable of organizing effective collective resistance to Soviet ambitions around the periphery of Eurasia.

One is reminded of the security arguments that were advanced retrospectively in defense of appeasement of Hitler over Czechoslovakia in 1938. American disengagement would be a retreat from the dangers of war which are believed to lurk in foreign entanglements. The United States today, as with Britain in 1938–39, cannot achieve "real peace," because such a condition, requiring a general and possibly lasting settlement of political differences, is not possible with the character of adversary that we face in the Soviet Union. In 1938 Britain chose to buy peace, meaning a postponement of war, by abandoning a well armed friend. As the *Leitmotiv* for policy, fortress America would not achieve peace, because the United States affronts the Soviet Union by its very independent political existence. What it would achieve would be the deletion from the American column of a large number of wealthy and, in many cases, heavily armed allies. The pertinent question is whether or not these allies contribute more to American insecurity than security.

Sixth, in fact fortress America, devolution, disengagement, America First—whatever rhetorical preference is exercised—would be a policy rooted in fear and would constitute an historically unprecedented American defeat in geostrategic terms. If a fortress America concept truly were implemented as a policy on the terms advocated by its more logically rigorous proponents, it would amount to the United States granting the Soviet Union a free hand in Eurasia.

The central geostrategic point is that the United States is locked into a long-term, potentially deadly struggle with the Soviet Union, and it is not in the U.S. interest vastly to simplify Soviet security problems in Eurasia. Furthermore, it cannot be in the U.S. interest knowingly to risk creating an insecurity condition in Europe and East Asia, which virtually would invite the Soviet Union to press for unilateral advantage over the economically well-endowed former security clients of the United States.

Some readers may wonder why the family of disengagement concepts discussed here under the headings of devolution and fortress America have been analyzed in such detail, given the strength of judgment expressed in their disfavor. The reasons are that these concepts can be presented with a superficially acceptable face; they are enjoying a resurgence of public attention (if not widespread popularity) at the present time; they do have an enduring appeal to some deeply American cultural traits; and they are very dangerous. Fortress America merits serious discussion for much the same set of reasons that a study of U.S. security problems must focus more than passing attention upon the prospects for general nuclear war. The low probability of occurrence is more than counterbalanced by the prospective horrors of the hypothetical, if admittedly unlikely, event.

QUESTIONS FOR DISCUSSION

1. Have NATO nations maintained their security because of NATO or in spite of NATO? What are the reasons for your answer?
2. Can U.S. and Western European interests be reconciled? What are the reasons for your answer?
3. What are the advantages and disadvantages of disengagement by the United States from Europe?
4. What effect would a gradual reduction of U.S. forces in Europe have on the defense expenditures of other NATO nations?
5. How has NATO changed from 1949 to the present? Why has it changed?

SUGGESTED READINGS

Baumann, Carol Edler, ed. *Europe in NATO: Deterrence, Defense, and Arms Control.* New York: Praeger, 1987.

Cohen, Eliot A. "Do We Still Need Europe?" *Commentary*, 81 (Jan. 1986), pp. 28–35.

DeYoung, Karen. "NATO Fears U.S. Cost Cutting." *Washington Post*, Apr. 25, 1988, pp. A1, A19.

Freedman, Lawrence. "Managing Alliances." *Foreign Policy*, no. 71 (Summer 1988), pp. 65–85.

Joffe, Josef. *The Limited Partnership: Europe, the United States, and the Burdens of Alliance.* Cambridge, Mass.: Ballinger, 1987.

Kaplan, Lawrence S. *NATO and the United States: The Enduring Alliance.* Boston: Twayne Publishers, 1988.

Krauss, Melvyn. *How NATO Weakens the West.* New York: Simon and Schuster, 1986.

Layne, Christopher. "Atlanticism without NATO." *Foreign Policy*, no. 67 (Summer 1987), pp. 22–45.

Palmer, John. *Europe without America? The Crisis in Atlantic Relations.* New York: Oxford University Press, 1987.

Rogers, Bernard W. "Why NATO Continues To Need American Troops." *Wall Street Journal*, July 8, 1987, p. 19.

21 Is Free Trade Good for the United States?

YES

Steven E. Daskal

Free Trade and Prosperity: A Global Approach

NO

John M. Culbertson

The Folly of Free Trade

Free Trade and Prosperity: A Global Approach

by Steven E. Daskal

Americans are especially prone to feel obligated to help others on a global scale. Whether it is the unfortunate plight of our fellows in the underdeveloped nations, often known as the "Third World," or the difficulties and unemployment facing some Americans at home, we care. Within that context, free trade is a vital issue, because it is one of the primary means by which the market economy helps create global prosperity.

When surveying the world economic situation, some Americans feel guilt over our comparative wealth and comfort in contrast to the millions living at the subsistence level. Our size, power, and wealth appear to some as being of little value unless we use that wealth to help the less fortunate. We send food, money, training advisors, educators, and missionaries around the world in a sincere effort to help others. These efforts have been undertaken by individuals, religious and social organizations, charitable associations, and the government. As believers in voluntarism and limited government, it is inappropriate for us to criticize how individuals freely spend their money. However, when the government coerces us through taxation to send aid overseas, we often have cause to object to the way our involuntary contribution is being spent on activities that appear unnecessary, wasteful, or even counterproductive.

Sometimes efforts to feed the starving prove well-intentioned, but sadly ineffectual.

Steven E. Daskal, "Free Trade and Prosperity: A Global Approach," *Freeman*, 36 (Feb. 1986), pp. 66–72. Reprinted with permission of the Foundation for Economic Education, Inc.

Even if the entire U.S. budget were directly distributed to the poorer half of the world's population, it would amount to less than $1,000 per person, certainly not enough to cure global poverty. Of course, with both our own bureaucracy and that of the recipient nation serving as intermediaries, a lot of that $1,000 would never reach the poor, but would instead support a small army of administrators, investigators, analysts, and auditors in both countries. If the recipient country's government were less than scrupulously honest, as is all too often the case, the poor would wind up with a couple of cups of milk and grain, while the U.S. government would be bankrupt. After decades of receiving such aid, the recipient country would still be poor, and in fact there would be more poor people to feed in the future. One would hope that a better way to help these people would have been discovered by now.

While we continue to be concerned about the poor overseas, we also feel an obligation to ensure maximum employment of our own citizens. Unemployment is generally recognized as a significant problem, for both personal and social reasons. Given current law, the financial drain the unemployed place upon society through the wide range of "compensation" and support programs is also of growing concern. While in most cases, the value of the welfare benefits an individual can receive is less than working wages, welfare pays well enough to support many people for extended periods of time. As government regulations and compensation plans directly and indirectly increase the cost of labor, and commensurately decrease the average worker's net pay, more and more businesses find it less profitable and more difficult to hire workers. Thus, unemployment, like global poverty, seems unlikely to disappear, despite the growing expenditures attempting to combat it. The more the government spends and regulates, the fewer people can be hired by private enterprise.

A popular scapegoat for unemployment in the United States (and in many other "industrialized" nations) is the "trade deficit." Many people, especially manufacturers and unionized workers, see imported vehicles, electronics, machine tools, and textiles flooding our markets and "taking away" sales from American manufacturers. These lost sales translate, they contend, into reduced production requirements, and ultimately lost American jobs. The fact that imported goods create sales, financing, service, and other related employment is generally ignored, because domestic industrial workers and manufacturers are far better organized, have more political clout, and are much more vocal. The result is a periodic frenzy of proposals to "protect American jobs and industry" through tariffs and quotas intended to limit or eliminate imports. As natural and unavoidable consequences of such moves:

- the cost of a given item to the American consumer rises due to the higher cost of producing the American product and the loss of competitive pressure on prices;
- consumers have less choice and fewer products available for purchase, reducing the incentive to increase earnings;
- the overall strength of the American economy falters as consumer spending drops in response to rising prices;
- Americans involved in buying and selling imported goods would be faced with significant losses and possibly unemployment;
- foreign manufacturers lose business, resulting in higher unemployment, lower tax revenues, and higher government spending in foreign countries;
- foreign individuals, corporations, and governments have fewer dollars to buy U.S. goods and services, or to pay off their heavy debt burdens; and
- growing economic problems in foreign nations often lead to political instability and increased anti-Americanism, increasing require-

ments for non-productive defense spending both overseas and in the United States.

Protectionism, like any other form of government intervention in economic life, has a cost. Government tariffs and quotas transfer money to certain people who have invested in, manage, or work for, industries that aren't competitive on their own merits. This forced transfer guarantees these firms that they will have a greater market share than they would have had without protection from competition. Without facing the pressures of the free market, they can continue to produce more expensive, less desirable goods, knowing their market cannot be taken by foreign competitors. Thus, the consumers (which often include the people benefiting from the protection) pay for protection—they get less, and pay more.

How much do we pay, as consumers, for protection of a few industries? Michael Munger, in "The Costs of Protectionism," estimates the total burden (in 1980 dollars) to be over $58 billion, and it is probably even greater today. Nearly a third of that cost was in the textile and apparel market, a burden that fell most heavily on the poor, who tend to buy the least expensive clothing that doesn't look cheap. They tended to favor foreign-made goods because they looked good, and didn't cost as much as American-made items. This value differential existed despite the tariffs and quotas involved, but it was greatly reduced. While the more affluent could afford the higher prices or even switch to American products, the poor were faced with buying less.

Six billion dollars worth of tariffs and other barriers were applied to agricultural products, another area where the poor pay the cost for protectionism. On the other hand, protecting the jobs of highly-paid auto, steel and machinery production workers (and their employers) accounted for $26 billion in added protection costs. These costs affect all of us in a myriad of ways, because higher-priced transportation and manufacturing equipment raises the cost of all commodities to the consumer. Since these indirect costs are not included in the $26 billion, the true cost of protectionism in this segment of the economy could in fact be far higher.

Despite the "chance to modernize and catch up" that protection was supposed to offer these industries, most of them have chronically cried for protection against imports for decades. Only the threat of protection being phased out forced automakers and some steel manufacturers to begin modernizing. Some still haven't, and are slowly crumbling despite protection. The loss of employment in various aspects of importing and exporting goods is another unknown cost.

Another common cause of pleas for protection is the accusation that foreign states are selling goods in the U.S. at a price lower than it costs the foreign manufacturer to produce it. This practice, known as "dumping," is more often a reflection of some economist's incorrect analysis of the cost of production of a given item, rather than an example of some competing nation's attempts to undermine our economy. True "dumping" results in the "dumper" losing money on every piece sold, while the recipient, an American consumer, has saved money that can be invested elsewhere. True "dumping" will ultimately bankrupt the "dumper."

Even when Communist bloc nations with their controlled economies "dump" goods in the West to obtain hard currency, they are doing even more damage to their already inefficient, stifled economies. If they manage to temporarily "corner" a market, they will still have to provide equivalent goods at the same low prices, or face the re-entry of Western firms into competition with them. Despite the rock-bottom pricing structure subsidized by the various Eastern European governments,

Russian "Ladas," "Polski Fiats," and Czech "Skodas" have not cornered the relatively open automobile market in Canada or Switzerland. Due to their greater economic efficiency, the Japanese and South Koreans provide far better cars for only a little more money. All "dumping" provided the Communists was a chance to subsidize the poorest segment of the Canadian auto market.

The French economist and legislator Frederic Bastiat recognized the fallacy of protectionism in the 1840s. He often resorted to satire to illustrate the absurdity of being preoccupied with maintaining a "favorable balance of trade." One of these was so believable that many thought it was a good example of the benefits of protection!

> A French merchant shipped $50,000 worth of goods to New Orleans and sold them for a profit of $17,000. He invested the entire $67,000 in American cotton and shipped it back to France. Thus, the customhouse record showed that the French nation had imported more than it had exported—an *unfavorable* balance of trade. Very bad.
>
> At a later date, the merchant decided to repeat the personally profitable transaction. But just outside the harbor his ship was sunk in a storm. Thus, the customhouse record showed that the French nation had exported more products than it had imported—a *favorable* balance of trade. Very good. Additionally, more jobs were thereby created for shipbuilders.
>
> Since storms at sea are undependable, perhaps the safest government policy would be to record the exports at the custom-house and then throw the goods into the ocean. In that way, the nation could guarantee to itself the profit that results from a favorable balance of trade.

That economic disaster results from trade restriction and protectionism is not just theoretical speculation, however. The events of the period between 1922 and World War II illustrate them very graphically. The mid-1920s was a period of generally increasing prosperity. However, then as now, the rapid changes in economic organization, management and technology had severe impact on a few outdated industries that relied heavily on manual labor, and hurt those farmers who were still using nineteenth-century techniques.

Jude Wanniski, a former member of the *Wall Street Journal*'s editorial staff, wrote a book entitled *The Way the World Works*. He describes the manner in which the beleaguered "low-tech" manufacturers and farm lobbyists pushed through the infamous Smoot-Hawley tariff act. The idea of keeping out foreign competition sounded good to the news media, but it terrified the bankers and investors of Wall Street. When it appeared certain the bill would be passed, the stock market panicked. The result was the stock market crash of the autumn of 1929, followed by the Depression that was fueled by the general collapse of world trade. Consumers in America and the rest of the world were forced to buy inefficiently produced domestic goods, or pay extortionate prices for foreign ones. Foreign governments of course retaliated in kind, many having already begun economic warfare against the rest of the world. Markets for American goods dried up, investment collapsed, businesses failed, jobs disappeared.

Despite the popular belief that laws passed since 1929 could prevent another Great Depression, it *could* happen again. America is far more dependent upon imports and exports today than it was in the 1920s. A global trade war would have disastrous consequences at home, and could create enormous security problems for us abroad. As reliant as we are upon free trade, the rest of the world is even more dependent upon it, even though they may not recognize it. A collapse of world trade would hurt virtually all of our allies, and threaten the survival of many developing nations barely able to avoid default on their debts.

If one looks at things from a sufficiently broad perspective, one begins to see a major

contradiction in our foreign policy. On the one hand, we want to help the poor overseas, and try to do so at great expense, but with limited success. We spend great sums of money to help defend foreign nations from present and potential enemies. Yet, on the other hand, we are willing to threaten the economic and political stability of these same nations (and our own) by creating insurmountable walls against their ability to freely sell goods in the world's richest market—the United States. This is a significant and costly inconsistency.

We have sent aid money to strengthen the economies of countries such as Japan, Thailand, Israel, Italy, Turkey, South Korea, and West Germany (to name a few). If these nations are to develop strong economies, they will naturally try to export goods to the United States and other nations. Yet, our response is to consider tariffs to shut out their products—threatening the same economies we ostensibly wanted to develop. The consumer ultimately pays the bill for all of this. They pay taxes to support efforts aimed at creating productive enterprises overseas, and pay higher prices (and have less free choice) because of attempts to protect American businesses against competition from overseas. And, as the ultimate blow to the budget and good sense, we pay to defend the same nations that supposedly "threaten" American jobs and profits.

Americans sincerely want to help people overseas. The question has become *how* to help them to the greatest extent while spending the least of our own hard-earned money. We also care about the health of our economy. Once again, the question is *how* to help preserve U.S. economic prosperity without disrupting international trade and causing ever-higher prices. The best method for accomplishing both goals is through free trade!

Why free trade? A basic economic reality—buying the best goods at the lowest prices—makes free trade more economical than closing our markets to foreign competitors. American consumers (all of us, including businesses and unionized labor) benefit by obtaining more goods for less money, while the foreign manufacturers and workers benefit by having jobs, making profits, and paying taxes to governments which then have a better chance to pay off their enormous debts. This, in turn, will make American banks more secure.

Free trade allows consumers around the world to buy more for less, which in turn creates more revenue for businesses. Governments have less call to provide tax-supported benefits to individuals or businesses, thus relieving the need to continue increasing taxes, inflation, or deficits. Ultimately, free trade will allow all but the poorest, least educated, and least diligent nations to get ahead. Examples of this are easy to find.

The most successful of the developing countries, states such as Singapore, the Republic of Korea, Republic of China (Taiwan), and Hong Kong, have built themselves up from illiteracy and poverty largely due to their respect for the power of free trade and relative economic freedom. Potentially wealthy developing nations, such as China, Brazil, Argentina, Nigeria, and Mexico, have stifled their own economic development through confused myriads of protective tariffs, import quotas, and centralized government manipulation of the economy.

Free trade also helps Americans and our trading partners overseas increase national security against both invasion and subversion. Open trade tends to improve the economic health of all trading nations. These nations tend to be more stable internally, since strong economies generally result in reduced unemployment, greater availability and affordability of food, clothing, and other commodities, and relief from the sense of desperation felt by people barely able to survive—a desperation that often leads to disorder and revolution. These increasingly self-sufficient nations also are better able to defend themselves against invasion. Their industries are strong, their people are more confident, and they are able to obtain necessary imported supplies easily. Thus, nations dedicated to free trade tend to be more valuable as friends and allies, and less of a liability needing continuous costly support and military assistance.

If this sounds too easy, too good to be true, just reflect on the benefits we gained in our own country by the elimination of trade restrictions between the colonies/states after the adoption of the Constitution. Free trade allowed for better direction of local economic activity. New Englanders didn't have to struggle to be self-sufficient in agriculture on their rocky soil, while Southerners could freely purchase better, less costly tools and machinery built in large New England and mid-Atlantic factories. Entire new industries developed to support this commerce, as evidenced by the growth of banks and by the flurry of railroad, steamship, and canal companies that were formed in the 19th century. While inflexible individuals and businesses may have suffered, the overall prosperity of all of the states increased dramatically, and employment grew rapidly despite the destruction of the Civil War and the influx of impoverished immigrants from around the world.

Free trade works, both in the context of international development and in ensuring greater domestic prosperity. It helps the poor and at the same time helps the working class, the middle class, and the wealthy. It works because it represents efficiency—from each according to his ability, to each according to his work (work in the scientific sense of energy expended that has a tangible result). Money is not wasted administering complex trade agreements, monitoring the "fairness" of international trade practices, or buying overpriced goods. Money is not involuntarily taken from taxpayers to subsidize inefficient American businesses or the poor overseas.

Open international trading relations, especially between private individuals and businesses, facilitates peaceful relations between nations. Warfare is often a costly, destructive, and unsuccessful means to acquire another nation's goods and services—trade is a far more efficient and mutually beneficial way to obtain the desired goal. Free trade is a sound basis for relations between free nations. It is the best type of foreign aid. And it is good for American consumers and investors.

The Folly of Free Trade

John M. Culbertson

Any manager who tries to create a strategy out of worn-out clichés and unexamined nostrums is dismissed. Yet in the United States and other Western countries we have grown comfortable with the government following outworn nostrums about free trade. We have elevated the economic theory of free trade to the status of a national theology, and we follow its simple dictums as if they were immutable laws. We appear prepared to follow the precepts of free trade wherever they lead us, even if that means plunging lemminglike to our economic ruin.

Today the evidence should be clear to anyone who wants to look at it: our blind allegiance to free trade threatens our national standard of living and our economic future. By sacrificing our home market on the altar of free trade, we are condemning ourselves and our children to a future of fewer competitive businesses, fewer good jobs, less opportunity, and a lower standard of living. These unacceptable outcomes threaten us in ways that are all related to our practice of free trade.

American business's stake in these matters is clear. If we do not wish to live with these outcomes, then we must construct a new and effective way to think about trade that will serve the interests of both business and the nation.

John M. Culbertson, "The Folly of Free Trade," *Harvard Business Review*, 64 (Sept.–Oct. 1986), pp. 122–28. Reprinted by permission of the *Harvard Business Review*. Copyright © 1986 by the President and Fellows of Harvard College; all rights reserved.

THREATS OF FREE TRADE

As we practice it, free trade has profoundly destructive results for the United States and other Western nations. First, nations that do not play by our rules practice unequal competition. Second, free trade puts us in direct competition with low-wage nations, countries that have a lower standard of living than the United States. Third, by allowing these nations to take over big sectors of our market, we permit the permanent interruption of an important relationship between demand and supply that has been the main engine of economic growth in American history.

Unequal National Competition

Classical economics teaches us that free exchange works to produce the best results for all, whether the exchange takes place within one nation or across national boundaries. But this concept works only when the exchange is an equal one that occurs within a common framework of laws, customs, rules, and regulations. Economic competition conducted under the law of the jungle leads to chaos and failure. The price system becomes a guide to nothing that is sensible or tolerable.

The laissez-faire approach to economics fashionable in the United States permits distorted outcomes precisely because it neglects the essential role of rules and regulations in preventing destructive competition. When each nation creates self-serving rules, free trade across national boundaries becomes destructive—an unequal competition under inconsistent and inharmonious rules.

Most American companies facing international competition have encountered the problem. Most governments are playing a simple game: they use their myriad powers—subsidies, favorable banking practices, local content requirements, exchange control, and the like—to win jobs and gain higher incomes for their people or to achieve a favorable national balance of payments.

American companies, therefore, end up competing not with foreign companies but with sovereign foreign states—states intent on winning jobs and sometimes whole industries for themselves. Foreign competitors are able to beat out a U.S. company not because of superior economic efficiency but because of subsidies. Japan grants favorable credit terms to certain industries, and many countries give cheap export-finance loans. European nations have special treatment for the value-added tax on exported goods. Most of the Pacific rim nations have weak or nonexistent environmental regulations, and Taiwan often fails to enforce its patent and copyright laws. Laborers in places like China lack the rights of U.S. workers.

Wage Competition among Nations

Among nations, competition over wages causes desirable industries and jobs to move from countries with higher standards of living and higher wages to countries with lower standards of living and lower wages. It is an unequal form of competition that explains much of the recent movement of industries and jobs out of the United States, undercutting our production.

Low-wage nations can raise their standards of living at the expense of ours in two ways: export their people to the United States or import U.S. jobs to their people. The result of either approach would be the same—our wages and standard of living would fall to match the level of the lower-wage nation while, at least temporarily, those of the lower-wage nation would rise.

If there were free immigration and truly open borders, workers from the lower-wage countries would stream into the higher-wage countries. These new arrivals would compete for jobs, accept work for lower pay, and force the existing jobholders to accept either lower wages or unemployment. Precisely for this reason, of course, no one accepts or supports the notion of free immigration.

We do, however, accept and support the notion of free trade, which has the same effect. Instead of exporting workers to the United States, lower-wage countries simply import our jobs and industries to their workers. As the higher-wage nation suffers cutbacks in production, failures of companies, and losses of jobs, the market dictates that workers accept lower wages and a reduced standard of living to match the lower-wage foreign competition.

For example, Japan, Taiwan, and, most recently, South Korea have had rapid increases in desirable jobs in major industries and in their standards of living. Through unbalanced exports to us, they have taken over U.S. markets and jobs. They have gained industries and jobs that we have lost. These countries could not have risen so rapidly if they had based their advance on their home markets or on balanced and mutually beneficial trade with other nations.

Under either free immigration or free trade, however, the lower-wage nation enjoys only a short-term benefit. Rapid economic advance based on taking over the markets, the industries, and the jobs of high-income nations is likely to be a blind alley. Gradually, the higher-wage nation, deprived of its economic base, becomes poorer and its market shrinks—or it belatedly begins protecting itself from one-sided imports. The low-wage nation then may wish it had followed a pattern of economic growth that was sustainable and not parasitic.

Either free migration or free trade would work to turn the world into a "population commune," drifting into global poverty, pulled down by the negative-sum game of international wage competition.

Demand and Markets

Our present-day economics fails to recognize the importance of demand and markets—and thus exaggerates what production alone can accomplish. Yet a nation's productive capabilities are decisively limited by the levels and kinds of its domestic demand and its access to foreign markets. But in the United States, we persistently fail to see the importance of our vast, prosperous, and accessible domestic market. We don't appreciate the key role that the demand side of our domestic market has played in generating economic growth for our country. As a result, we are now about to give away our great advantage to our foreign competitors.

America's rise to economic preeminence was based on the interaction between the market's demand and the pace-setting industries that developed to meet that demand. The process was self-feeding. Favorable circumstances—the size of the U.S. market, extraordinary resources, freedom from over-population, a favorable position in the two world wars—gave the U.S. market a unique richness and diversity. This market was the magnet that drew forth the new industries that, in turn, created even more wealth. In the interaction of demand and supply, the U.S. economy became the pathbreaker for the world.

But recently this self-feeding interaction has been interrupted, as Japan and other countries of the Pacific rim have taken over large shares of the U.S. market. These nations have recognized the role of demand in fostering industrial growth and, by using government subsidies and lower-wage workers, have simply substituted their industries for American industries in the demand-supply relationship. With the U.S. market switched over to fueling the meteoric advance of foreign industries, U.S. industry has begun to decline.

Unlike the historical demand-and-supply relationship between market and industry, the new relationship that substitutes foreign industry for American industry represents an economic blind alley. The domestic markets of these foreign producers have neither the size nor the wealth to support their own indus-

tries. As they undercut U.S. production, however, they will gradually weaken the American economic base that they have come to depend on. Rather than a self-sustaining, self-reinforcing process, this new relationship becomes self-liquidating.

UNDERLYING MYTHS OF FREE TRADE

Much of the debate over trade today is conducted within a narrow range of thinking, a set of ideas dictated by classical economics. If the United States is to develop a realistic trade policy, we first need to examine these underlying notions, recognize them for the myths that they are, and then substitute more practical attitudes toward the role of trade in our economy. Seven myths in particular dominate conventional thinking about trade.

Comparative Advantage Governs International Trade   To justify free trade, laissez-faire economists from Adam Smith to the present have claimed that international trade and competition work totally differently from trade within one nation's borders. They argue that international trade and competition are not based on price comparisons—that is, that trade is not subject to the rule that low-priced goods undercut high-priced goods and that low-priced labor undercuts high-priced labor. Rather, they say, international trade is governed by comparative advantage. It depends on differences in the internal structures of prices in the trading countries and is not affected by differences in their absolute levels of costs and prices.

To support this contention, economists offer an example in which two nations with different wage and cost levels nevertheless have a pattern of trade that is balanced and mutually beneficial. They then say that the example shows how free trade will result in balanced and mutually beneficial international trade and competition. What it actually illustrates is that if the two nations require their trade to be in balance, then the trade will be governed by comparative advantage and absolute price levels will not matter. When trading nations require their trade to be in balance, the low-wage, low-price nation cannot pull away the industries and jobs of the other nation. Under this condition, differences in the nations' absolute costs will not matter.

Most of international trade is not governed by comparative advantage. Rather, it reflects wage and price competition on the part of countries seeking jobs and economic growth.

Exchange Rate Adjustments Automatically Keep Foreign Trade in Balance According to our classical economics, the huge U.S. trade deficit and the export of American industries and jobs indicate only the need for an adjustment in the exchange rate: a decline in the international value of the dollar would make everything all right again. The implicit argument is that a decline in the dollar would balance U.S. trade and improve the competitiveness of U.S. industries without forcing a domestic decline in real wages and the standard of living.

Again, this argument is fallacious. A decline in the dollar is simply a way for the United States to become poorer. It is a way for the American economy to accede to the inevitable results of competition from lower-wage and lower-standard-of-living nations by becoming itself a lower-wage, lower-standard-of-living nation. A devalued dollar is, quite simply, worth less. By reducing the value of the dollar we cut real wages, diminish U.S. buying power, and bring the U.S. economy more in line with the lower-standard-of-living countries against which free trade has pitted us.

U.S. Companies Can Become Competitive through Cost Cutting Others argue that the way to bring U.S. trade into balance is for American companies to compete by cutting costs. But in global competition, there is no way U.S. production at wages of $10 an hour can become competitive with efficient foreign production at wages of $1 an hour. Efforts to compete by cutting costs are suicidal.

Frantic cost cutting to accomplish what is impossible destroys the future capabilities of companies as well as the nation. Abandoning research and development, chopping investment, decimating staff is a formula for self-destruction. The U.S. oil industry is warning the nation that it is being forced to cripple its future capabilities by lowering costs to survive the flood of cheap foreign oil. Many other industries are also going through massive cuts in future-oriented expenditures.

First, they can find ways to economize within their companies—always a useful measure at the start. But the company that chooses to go this route will eventually find itself faced with deeper and deeper cuts. Almost inevitably, the process changes from cutting fat to cutting meat to cutting close to the bone. Some American companies have already reached the last steps—firing skilled people, abandoning research and development, scaling back investment. These actions, taken in the name of achieving competitiveness, will only destroy the company's capabilities.

The second path is more direct but leads to the same outcome: to lower costs, American companies can turn to offshore sources and buy components or finished products from lower-cost foreign companies. If begun on a small enough scale, this approach can delude an American business into thinking it has restored its competitiveness. In fact, it is an admission of defeat—one that the foreign source will understand and gradually exploit by capturing more and more of the product's value-added and eventually discarding the empty shell of the American business. Companies that shift production abroad through outsourcing, closing U.S. factories, building new ones abroad, establishing joint ventures with foreign companies, and giving up products become essentially importers of foreign goods. Such a shift has been prevalent in automobiles, apparel, footwear, computers, telephone equipment—perhaps in most manufacturing industries. It does not take much imagination to see what lies at the end of this road.

Low-Cost Goods Are Efficiently Produced Goods Economists often assert that the production of something more cheaply in one country than in another is evidence that it is produced there more efficiently and therefore should be produced in the cheaper country. In the United States, this argument is used to support the conclusion that goods that can be made abroad more cheaply—and presumably more efficiently—should be made abroad.

This argument is based on a false assumption. Lower cost is linked with efficiency only when the goods under examination are of equal quality and the producers are all operating under the same rules, including government and labor policies that reflect accepted social and environmental values. To shift production from the United States to low-wage foreign labor may cut costs but does not necessarily raise efficiency. This is because low-cost labor, by definition, means a lower standard of living. If the standard of living in a low-labor-cost economy is low, how can anyone sensibly call that economy efficient?

In shifting production to countries with low wage rates, with large government production subsidies, or with lax production regulations, free trade actually *reduces* economic efficiency—as does producing goods for the American market on the opposite side of the world in order to take advantage of cheap labor. In international trade, the price system works perversely. Low cost does not imply efficiency.

All It Takes to Make Free Trade Work Is a Level Playing Field A popular argument designed to deal with the rising flood of foreign imports is the notion of the level playing field: since most of our foreign competitors do not play by the same trade rules as the United States, these countries must admit our goods to make things fair. Then we will be playing by the same rules—our rules.

Two things are wrong with this argument. First, since many other nations do not suffer from our delusions about free trade, they will not be threatened, cajoled, or pressured into adopting our rules against their self-interest. Second, since they generally have cheaper labor and yet increasingly use more of the advanced technologies of advanced nations, our foreign competitors will actually exploit the U.S. market even more under universal free trade. Our trade would not be brought into balance—certainly not at any acceptable standard of living—by other countries adopting free trade. We would only suffer more broadly the destructive consequences of free trade.

The United States Should Give LDCs Unlimited Market Access The argument that the United States has a responsibility to help less developed countries [LDCs] by granting them free access to its market has a humanitarian ring. For two reasons, however, such a position is good neither for us nor the LDCs.

First, granting unlimited access to our market is like signing a blank check—which nobody should ever do. Moreover, while less developed countries could cumulatively cause serious erosion in the U.S. standard of living, for each of them the benefits could be so small as to produce no marked improvement in their standard of living. Also, their basic economic underpinnings would remain unchanged.

Second, in encouraging LDCs to base their economic advancement on exploitation of the U.S. market, we are guiding these nations into a blind alley. The experiment can only fail, either because the United States belatedly wakes up to the ruinous effects of this approach and limits imports or because the wage competition causes the U.S. economy to decline and the U.S. market to shrink. A far more humanitarian approach would be for the United States to advise these nations to tie their economic programs into a pattern that would prove workable and sustainable over the long run.

The Change to a Global Economy Is Inevitable and Desirable These days it is increasingly fashionable for Americans to say that the separate national economies must inexorably evolve into a global economy. This is simply the latest version of the kind of wave-of-the-future rhetoric that economists and others have applied to many movements now dead and forgotten.

The proposition is that the spread of free trade and international economic integration will proceed because all nations approve and desire it and because it will be successful. Put this way, the argument falls of its own weight. It is not true that all nations desire thoroughgoing international economic integration, with its implied override of national economic objectives, interests, and policies. For example, Japan—a model of realism and success in so many recent competitive undertakings—is hardly rushing to submerge itself in a one-world economic commune. And the destructive effects of free trade are now so obvious that at some point the United States and other high-income nations will wake up before worldwide economic integration drags them down into worldwide poverty. Rather than blithely assuming that a world economy is inevitable, we should expect worldwide economic integration to stop before it spreads much further. No nation is willing to preside over its own economic ruin.

Despite its fashionable ring, this one-world doctrine is dangerous. It simply reinforces the folly of free trade. The correct course is for nations to get their own economic affairs and their own international trade under control and to use the only functional structure that works—a world of effective national economies, engaged with one another in mutually beneficial trade and constructive competition.

A REALISTIC TRADE POLICY

With imports pushing them against the wall, American companies in many industries have seen only a narrow choice: leave the industry or move production overseas. The decision of AT&T to give in to foreign competition and shift production of telephones from Shreveport, Louisiana to a new factory in Singapore typifies one reaction to these inexorable pressures. Given this choice, which leaves out the prospect of a constructive U.S. trade policy opening a third option—remaining competitive at home—most companies, preferring foreign production to corporate failure, are moving their production abroad or buying foreign production for resale. But while it may be hopeless for these companies to try to compete from their U.S. production base under existing trade policy, managers choosing to move overseas should realize that there is no guarantee of success abroad. In fact, the American exodus to foreign production bases may bring about the very circumstances that will undermine that move.

From pressure in Congress to a new pragmatism about trade in the Reagan administration, the signs are clear: America's willingness to play victim to the free-trade doctrine is unlikely to continue much longer. At some point in the not-too-distant future, the United States will put limitations on foreign imports to balance America's trade. When that happens, companies that have moved abroad will find themselves on the wrong side of the fence. As a more reasonable U.S. trade policy begins to reconnect the powerful domestic market with U.S. companies—restoring the self-reinforcing process of economic growth in this country—American companies that have gone abroad will be on the outside looking in.

Moreover, in a world in which nations generally will be hard-pressed to meet domestic demands, the operations of American companies in other countries are unlikely to receive favorable treatment or political support. American companies will be the natural target of frustration and disappointment. The prospect of operating in such an environment—with but limited access to a rehabilitated U.S. economy and a flourishing U.S. market—should give American executives pause before they leap over the fence. Under U.S. trade policy, they are being asked to choose between two losing strategies: they can cease production now in the face of unfettered importation or they can move abroad and find themselves on the wrong side of the fence when the change in U.S. trade policy finally comes. The solution, of course, is for American business leaders to support a change in trade policy now, before it is too late.

A realistic trade policy would end the general underselling of American production by foreign production. It would set limits on the proportions of U.S. markets that could be taken by imports and ensure for U.S. industry a market on which it could rebuild and resume its advance. The new policy would put U.S. exports on a strong foundation by tying them to U.S. imports as in the principle of comparative advantage rather than by allowing low-wage foreign producers to generally undercut U.S. exporters through their absolute cost advantage.

These accomplishments will be possible only if we move beyond the slogans that dominate the trade debate: "Free trade is good." "Protectionism is bad." A revolution in ideas that replaces sloganeering with pragmatic analysis must underlie the revolution in accomplishments. American business must play the decisive leadership role.

A number of principles should guide this effort at understanding and shaping a new and pragmatic U.S. trade policy:

1. In a world of diverse nations, free trade works perversely, causing destructive competition among nations, including wage competition that tends to reduce all nations to a lowest-common-denominator standard of living.

2. Making trade among diverse nations constructive means balancing it and preventing destructive shifts of industries between nations. Just as they need a fiscal budget to keep expenditures in line with incomes, nations need a trade budget to keep imports in line with exports.

3. To balance its trade and continue its economic growth, a nation with a high standard of living and an attractive market will find permanent limitations on imports necessary, just as limitations on immigration are.

4. In balancing its trade, the high-income, high-cost nation will tie its exports to its imports through trade packages or through exports subsidized from the proceeds of import licenses. These arrangements could bring about balanced international trade that would correspond to comparative advantage.

5. Import limitations supposed to be nondiscriminatory—such as tariffs—are actually very discriminatory. For example, uniform U.S. tariff rates high enough to balance U.S. trade with low-wage nations would virtually exclude imports from other high-income nations and would thus discriminate against those with high incomes.

6. Countries must manage their trade in ways that meet their particular needs and capabilities. National differences in circumstances, ideologies, administrative capabilities, and other factors are too important to

permit any uniform and general system for arranging international trade.

7. National governments have a legitimate and necessary role in arranging constructive international trade. Government is the only agency that can assume the responsibility for managing a nation's trade budget in a way beneficial to the interests of the nation. The interest of the nation in balanced trade is in concert with the interest of American business in guaranteed access to the American market.

BALANCING U.S. TRADE

The U.S. economy urgently needs immediate action to stop unfairly advantaged imports from undercutting U.S. production. Month by month, American companies are sinking, failing, or giving up on U.S. production and moving their operations offshore. The once mighty U.S. automobile industry, located in the nation with the world's greatest market for automobiles, is being liquidated through joint ventures with Japanese companies, shifting the design and production of its cars abroad, producing American cars largely with foreign-made components, abandoning the small-car market to imports, and shifting its capital to secondary industries. The longer we allow this process to go on unchallenged, the dimmer our economic future will be.

Two kinds of trade policies, therefore, need to be put into place: some first steps to hold the line, halt the erosion of the American economy, and begin to move in the direction of balanced trade and some permanent measures that will ensure balanced and mutually advantageous trade among nations.

To hold the line, we should immediately impose quotas on certain goods, at least halting their increase in market share and, in some cases, reversing recent rapid growth. The inadequate quotas on autos, steel, textiles, apparel, footwear, and machinery can serve as a point of departure. The goal is a comprehensive trade policy that protects and defends the interests and future of the United States—that protects the nation rather than any special interest. The imposition of quotas would be a step in the direction of import limitations to balance our trade; quotas would begin the process of designing a system of mutually beneficial trade between us and our trading partners.

The United States should quickly establish provisional targets for the maximum share of its market available to various foreign-made products. Over time these targets would be tied to a balanced pattern of trade. In establishing the targets, we would send foreign producers a clear signal of what to expect in the way of access to our market. Even more important, the targets would tell American producers how much of the domestic market would be reserved for them so that they could begin gearing up for U.S. production and at the same time spell out the clear dangers of moving more production overseas.

Some quotas should be based on existing legislation and on the findings of the U.S. International Trade Organization [ITO] regarding the economic injury that foreign competition has inflicted on such U.S. industries as footwear, textiles, and apparel. But we should reject the notion—on which ITO is based—that quotas are only a temporary remedy designed to give domestic industries time to shrink or become competitive.

Our new trade policy should make it clear that we want permanent limitations on imports to the American market. The basis of a realistic U.S. trade policy is a permanent system of limitations on imports to the American market, coupled with the promotion of desired exports within the framework of balanced and mutually advantageous trade with other nations. A trade policy that tries to force free trade on the world is doomed to failure—and would ruin us if adopted.

A permanent system limiting imports to the U.S. market and maintaining balanced trade should eventually replace these temporary measures. Such a system must serve a number of goals. It must:

- Preserve the United States as a high-income nation with a great market for advanced goods.
- Produce balanced and mutually advantageous trade plus debt dealings with each nation, nation-group, and the world.
- Produce an industrial composition of trade that serves U.S. interests and reserves a defined share of the home market for U.S. producers by taking into account factors like the defense implications, the development of breakthrough technology, the kinds of jobs produced, and the kinds of jobs required.

Creating and administering a trade policy that meets these goals is a demanding task—but so is running a corporation in today's world. In either case, simple slogans that promise easy success are unrealistic. A successful trade policy requires foresight, realism, judgment, honesty, knowledge, administrative effectiveness, and toughness in enforcing rules and regulations, just as the operations of large companies do. At both organizational levels, that of the company and that of the nation, adapting successfully to a complex, uncertain, and changing economic environment is a hard-won achievement. The hope of the United States lies in recognizing and tackling this difficult task rather than in waiting for Providence or free trade to bring us success on a platter.

The permanent system of balanced trade should be based on the inherent value of the U.S. market. Its size and wealth give it great value to foreign producers and other nations. We should capture this value for the benefit of all Americans through two mechanisms: quid pro quo trade packages arranged with other nations and the sale at market price of a limited number of import licenses. We should use part or all of the revenue generated by these sales to support particular U.S. industries whose products we want to export to further national interests.

The United States should enforce these import-limiting arrangements rigorously and promptly—not in the way that the government now handles these matters. We should strive to detect trade violations quickly and take immediate action. Moreover, punishment must provide real remedies rather than the long-delayed hand slaps delivered now. We must treat the import limitation program as a set of serious business contracts between nations—not as a theater for acts of political symbolism.

A TIME TO RETHINK

In touting free trade to other nations, the United States has not only invited its own economic destruction but also misled other countries in their expectations from international trade. It is time for America to reject this false god and accept the blame for preaching an unrealistic doctrine. We must repudiate the notion that the rest of the world can achieve economic growth by unbalanced sales to the U.S. market.

Mutually beneficial and balanced international trade is the only trade policy that makes sense. Apart from transition problems, it would do no violence to any nation's valid claims. By moving to such a policy we would be helping low-income nations develop sustainable economic programs and safeguarding the living standards of high-income nations. We owe it to all countries of the world to put to an end the unrealistic idea that more countries can emulate Japan and achieve economic advance through a parasitic relationship with the American market.

The delusion that free trade is the road to worldwide affluence has influenced many countries; the delusion will hurt many of them. We need to escape from this belief and build a new system of international trade—one that rests on realism and mutual benefit for all nations.

QUESTIONS FOR DISCUSSION

1. How should the United States respond to protectionism by other countries?
2. What effect does protectionism have on jobs in the nations engaging in protectionist measures?
3. Who benefits and who is hurt by U.S. protectionism?
4. What effect does protectionism have on competition?
5. What evidence is available to evaluate the case for free trade?

SUGGESTED READINGS

Bhagwati, Jagdish A. *Protectionism.* Cambridge, Mass.: MIT Press, 1988.

Bovard, James. "U.S. Trade Laws Are a National Disgrace." *USA Magazine,* 116 (Jan. 1988), pp. 29–31.

Gall, Norman. "Does Anyone Really Believe in Free Trade?" *Forbes,* 138 (Dec. 15, 1986), pp. 115–20.

Dobbelmann, Pierre F. "The Perils of Protectionism." *Vital Speeches of the Day,* 53 (July 15, 1987), pp. 590–94.

Lawrence, Robert Z., and Robert E. Litan. "The Protectionist Prescription: Errors in Diagnosis and Cure." In *Brookings Papers on Economic Activity,* 1, ed. William C. Brainard and George L. Perry. Washington, D.C.: Brookings Institution, 1987. Pp. 289–310.

McFadden, Michael. "Protectionism Can't Protect Jobs." *Fortune,* 115 (May 11, 1987), pp. 121, 124–26, 128.

Nivola, Pietro S. "The New Protectionism: U.S. Trade Policy in Historical Perspective." *Political Science Quarterly,* 101, no. 4 (1986), pp. 577–600.

"Proposed Foreign Trade Legislation: Pro and Con." *Congressional Digest,* 65 (Aug.–Sept. 1986), entire issue.

U.S. Cong., House of Representatives. *Comprehensive Trade Legislation.* Hearings before the Subcommittee on Trade of the Ways and Means Committee, 100th Cong., 1st Sess., 1987.

"U.S. Foreign Trade Policy: Pro and Con." *Congressional Digest,* 66 (June–July 1987), entire issue.

22 Should the United States Take Active Measures Against All Dictatorships?

YES

Roy Lechtreck

Let's Treat All Dictators Alike

NO

Ted Galen Carpenter

The United States and Third World Dictatorships: A Case for Benign Detachment

Let's Treat All Dictators Alike

Roy Lechtreck

The controversy over our foreign policy toward right-wing dictatorships like South Africa and Chile and left-wing dictatorships like Russia and Cuba reveals an amazing divergence of opinion concerning dictatorships and how we should deal with them. Some people want us to come down hard on the right-wing dictatorships while being friendly to communist regimes. Others want us to come down hard on the communist regimes while being friendly to the others. Very few seem to feel we ought to come down hard on *all* dictatorships. Most people seem to think a double standard is justifiable.

Two reasons primarily have been given to explain the double standard. One is that there is supposedly a basic difference between authoritarian (right-wing) and totalitarian (left-wing) regimes. The first type of regime, it is argued, is not as great a threat to world peace as is the second. (However, there is no evidence that the authoritarian regime violates human rights any less, as is evident when comparing, for instance, South Africa or Chile with Russia or China.) The second reason is that it allows our government to favor those countries that are cooperative with our business interests, which have an inordinate say in the shaping of our foreign policy.

The Reagan Administration strongly supports the idea that the distinctions between these two forms of dictatorship are valid. Upon investigation, though, the distinctions

Roy Lechtreck, "Let's Treat All Dictators Alike," *USA Today Magazine,* 116 (Mar. 1988), pp. 71–73. Reprinted from *USA Today Magazine.* Copyright 1988 by the Society for the Advancement of Education.

are almost worthless. We must remember that one of the most aggressive countries in the world in the colonial period was England, an authoritarian (or semi-authoritarian) regime, and right-wing dictatorships started both world wars. Although the left-wing countries probably still wish to dominate the world, so far they have caused less turbulence in the world than have their opposites.

Will they cause more turbulence in the future? Is Russia's presence in Afghanistan a sign that they soon will go into Turkey or Finland? While we can not predict the future from the past, a look at the last half-century of Soviet foreign policy does give us some clues. Russian expansion in that period has not been as reckless or as imperialistic as some have assumed. In the early 1920's, the Russians tried to stir up revolutions in Europe and Asia, but failed. They learned a lesson. Lenin's "world revolution now" theory was replaced by a much more cautious Stalinist policy which continues today.

Several patterns emerge. Communism will try to move in when a nearby country is in disarray because of the aftermath of war; realign its borders after a war; establish satellite states along its new borders; fight to defend what it has acquired; unite countries which have been split into communist and non-communist halves and where agreed-upon elections to reunite the country have not taken place; help rebels in a right-wing regime overthrow their American-supported dictator, thereby taking over that country, as in China, Cuba, and Vietnam; and, through trade, aid, and arms sales, induce hostile countries to become neutral, neutral countries to become friendly, and friendly countries to be satellites.

In no sense are totalitarian governments peace-loving, but their successes have come about by grasping opportunities that they seldom, if ever, have created, not by any well-thought-out design. If non-communist countries behaved differently toward each other, and toward their own citizens, Russia and Cuba today would not be totalitarian governments hostile to the West. If the free world had adopted more humane policies in the past, left-wing dictatorships would not exist, and if the West began to adopt a more humane policy today, these dictatorships would be stopped in their tracks. More blood has been shed in ordinary wars and acts of terrorism since World War II between non-communist countries, or groups fighting other non-communist countries or groups, than has been shed between communist nations fighting non-communist nations.

Since right-wing and left-wing regimes both have been aggressive, we can say that the first reason for treating such regimes differently (that one is more dangerous than the other) is false. Both systems are basically similar. They are both chauvinistic and, as many scholars have pointed out, there is very little difference internally between right-wing Nazism and left-wing communism.

The second argument for justifying the double standard was that we should give preferential treatment to countries that give preferential treatment to our multinational conglomerates. Yet, if these corporations, as many do, exploit their workers, damage the environment, waste national resources, or manufacture unsafe products, they can not build up good will for America. If a right-wing regime supports such businesses, there is all the more reason to oppose, not support, that regime.

Even if there were legitimate distinctions between these two types of tyrannies, the consequences of maintaining a double standard have been ignored. The double standard is also counterproductive. It is unfortunate that the ethical arguments are ignored, but it is against our own national security to ignore the pragmatic arguments. The most obvious methods of supporting dictatorships are trading with them, lending or giving them money,

and selling them arms. Trade between two countries having different levels of economic development helps the less developed country the most. There is ample evidence that, without trade, the non-industrialized countries would have remained non-industrialized. Moreover, trade with the communist bloc and the right-wing bloc strengthens the ruling elites in both types of regimes, since economic benefits do not trickle down to the common man in dictatorships; the gap between the rich and the poor widens.

The sale of computers to Russia, for instance, does not get us anything of equal value in return. The price we charge for a product of advanced technology is not the true worth of that product. If there are a thousand items produced, the research and development [R and D] costs are divided by a thousand, and the Russian purchase of one item (to tear apart and duplicate), or their purchase of many items because they do not have the trained manpower or equipment to make the products themselves, allows them to feed off American R and D. Moreover, sale of grain to the Soviets at cheap prices allows them to use rubles for their military program, rather than to overhaul their inefficient farm system. The average Russian citizen's life is no better.

The purchase of coffee, bananas, copper, and oil did not help the peasants in Latin America or Iran either, but only the planter-business-military alliance. High-tech dictatorships are certainly more of a threat to world peace than low-tech dictatorships, but the free-world sale of military hardware to the Third World makes them, relatively speaking, just as warlike as their bigger brothers, as is obvious in the raids of Argentina on the Falklands and the Indonesians on East Timor, in opposition to the wishes of the peaceful people being invaded. This hardware also makes it easier for the police and army to brutalize the people, as has been obvious in the past in Argentina, Brazil, Chile, El Salvador, and Guatemala. If trade made countries more prosperous and therefore less aggressive, wars would be getting fewer and fewer and less and less bloody. Since it hasn't happened that way, the theory behind détente with any type of dictatorship is fallacious. Our trade with authoritarian and totalitarian nations, in fact, weakens us and makes us increase our defense spending to counteract the increased strength of the enemy. Western technology was used in producing equipment for the invasion of Afghanistan *and* the Falklands!

Just as trade strengthens the regime we trade with, so do aid and arms sales. In the Truman Administration, most aid was economic. Today, most aid is military—money to buy weapons and feed and train soldiers. This obviously strengthens the dictatorships we deal with. Further, if such a dictatorship is overthrown, the arms then fall into the hands of forces hostile to the U.S. This has happened in Vietnam, Nicaragua, and Iran.

There is no denying that the chief threat to the peace of the world is the U.S.S.R. Yet, the Soviets have not become a world power because of open warfare with big powers. The spread of communism has been due almost exclusively to its support of "freedom fighters" in countries where human rights have been violated flagrantly. Since World War II, no country has gone communist that has had several decades of uninterrupted democratic government. All of the Eastern European satellites of the Soviet Union had been under Nazi control and "liberated" by the Russians; Indochina was a colony of France; China was governed by warlords; Cuba was ruled by the dictator Batista; Afghanistan was an Islamic authoritarian regime; and so it goes with Nicaragua, Angola, South Yemen, Ethiopia, etc. Not all countries go communist where human rights are violated, but all countries that are communist became communist as a direct or indirect result of human rights violations.

Such violations give communists a foothold. Therefore, democracy is the best antidote to totalitarianism.

NO TRADE, NO AID

American foreign policy, then, must not align itself with dictators just because they are the anti-communist variety. Our support of authoritarian dictators inevitably leads the oppressed to seek the support of totalitarian dictators, and, if the oppressed win their freedom, they naturally join the totalitarian bloc. We must not strengthen the communist bloc either. A no-trade, no-aid policy toward all is necessary.

Of course, a no-trade, no-aid policy on our part alone might not be enough to topple dictatorships. If, however, our "allies" try to take up the slack and seem to be filling the dictators' demands, then we ought to apply our no-trade, no-aid policy to them also. Our new policy would be to isolate the dictators *and* those who support dictators.

Can anyone doubt that this policy would bring dictators to their knees? It certainly would impose hardships on America, but the hardships would not be as great as some fear. The idea that they or our "allies" could do without America is absurd. The Japanese and West Germans may be hard-working and smart, but they both need American goods and markets. Obviously, some American businesses would be hurt, but employment in American auto and steel plants would rise, and we would turn out our own VCR's [video cassette recorders] and other hardware we now import. Farmers, who no longer would be able to sell wheat to Russia, might find jobs in the cities, and we greatly would slow down our own soil erosion, water pollution, and depletion of underground water supplies. Inflation might go up, but this would be a small price to pay. In five or 10 years, we could have low inflation rates again, drastically curtail our defense expenditures, and cut taxes or pay off the debt.

In the last 40 years, our position *vis-a-vis* Russia has been slipping. It has not stopped slipping just because Ronald Reagan is in the White House, even though the arms race goes on. Despite the recent INF [intermediate-range nuclear forces] treaty, we won't abandon the Star Wars plan for fear we will not come out ahead. However, if we adopted the policy outlined above, we would not have to worry about whether Russia would be a danger to world peace if total nuclear disarmament occurred. It wouldn't be—it would be too weak. Russia would not go to war and be totally destroyed just to prevent this policy from being applied.

Critics may condemn this policy as too ruthless, saying we have no right to tell other countries what to do, but it is less ruthless than overthrowing the governments of Iran and Guatemala and propping up authoritarian governments throughout the world. We have supported almost every authoritarian dictatorship in the world, against the best interest of the downtrodden in those countries. The proposed policy would substitute rational power diplomacy for irrational power diplomacy. The communists started the Cold War, but it is wrong to think we must arm to the teeth to remain free. A change in our foreign-economic policy would be more effective and cheaper than a continuous arms race.

Since we have had a policy of supporting right-wing dictators for so long, it is only natural to assume that, in the near future, an authoritarian government will be overthrown by a group hostile to the U.S. If we then turn hostile to the new rulers, we certainly will lose that nation. It will immediately, or in a few years, be a totalitarian regime. To prevent this from happening, the American government must give it the trade and aid it needs to recover from the economic ravages of a dictatorship and to give the people hope that their

children will have at least a slightly better standard of living than they now have.

It already might be too late to save the Philippines. Corazon Aquino may not be able to prevent the country from sliding into economic disaster, may not be able to win over the communist guerrillas, and may be unwilling to grant the U.S. continued use of our military bases there. The situation under her predecessor, Ferdinand Marcos, may have deteriorated into a state beyond repair. Only time will tell. However, we surely can still save South Africa, Guatemala, South Korea, and scores of other countries from going communist.

SENDING WRONG SIGNALS

Our support for the contra rebels in (and around) Nicaragua has not only been ineffective, but it sends wrong signals to people in other countries, just as does our continued support for the apartheid regime in South Africa. The Reagan Administration may think that we have better leverage over the dictatorships if we remain friendly with them, but that is like saying children have leverage with a neighborhood bully only so long as they don't make the bully mad, or that the proper way for government to handle a bank embezzler is to tell him that he shouldn't do it in such large amounts in the future or he may be locked up.

Moreover, the freedom fighters in dictatorships may even need outside help at times—over and above our refusing to help the tyrants any more. If so, we actually should send the rebels arms and money. We should remember that the main reason for our forefathers' drafting of the Declaration of Independence was to gain European support for our cause. If the French (and other European countries) took the attitude toward us in the 1770's that we now take toward the freedom fighters in other lands (and took toward the

Hungarian freedom fighters in 1956), we probably still would be a colony of England. Our support of the Afghan rebels (through indirect means, of course) may be too little, but at least it can be justified. How can we then justify our failure to support the blacks in South Africa? Again, we see an example of the double standard.

Many people inside and outside our country feel a double standard is un-American. The Declaration of Independence said that people had a right to overthrow tyrants and establish a new government which would promote their "safety and happiness." We said that the inalienable rights of the people must be interpreted and applied by the people, not by monarchs. Yet, George III was far less a tyrant than the current ruler of Chile, and all of George's ministers were fairer to the colonials than the Botha government is to the blacks in South Africa or the Soviet regime to the Baltic peoples who were forced into "voluntary" membership in the U.S.S.R.

The preamble of our Constitution states the goals of government: justice, domestic tranquility, defense, general welfare, and liberty. What dictatorship comes close to granting more than one of these? Yet, we are friendlier to the tyrants than to the dissidents.

World peace can come about only when the dictators are no longer able to cause trouble for others, and world prosperity can come about only when we have world peace. From a humanitarian and a pragmatic point of view, we must oppose all left-wing and right-wing dictatorships. Our foreign policy is obviously a failure when we spend hundreds of billions of dollars on defense and see no end in sight. A greater number of people today are under the control of tyrants than ever before in the history of the world. An arms race has not weakened them. We must, therefore, adopt an economic policy of no trade or aid to dictators or those who assist dictators.

In the past, we have adopted policies of containment, brinkmanship, massive retaliation, limited war, and détente. Still, we have not stopped the advance of totalitarianism. Our diplomatic and military policies have failed, so what is left but economic measures or all-out war? The Strategic Defense Initiative (Star Wars) may not be operable. Even if, by some miracle, it does work, it will not stop the advance of dictatorships. It would not have prevented the Russian invasion of Afghanistan and would not prevent the Russian invasion of Pakistan (to wipe out Afghan rebel bases), Greece kicking U.S. military bases out of its country, or the complete conquest of Angola, to mention just a few possible scenarios.

Economic measures against dictatorships hit them at their weakest spot. We could begin the policy outlined above by saying we no longer will sell high-tech and medium-tech equipment to Russia, and we will cut back 50 percent on imports from countries which try to take up the slack. We also would announce, in this first stage, that all military aid to right-wing dictatorships will cease immediately. In stage two, we would cut off grain supplies to Russia, and tell American firms in authoritarian countries that they must leave those countries. If stage two doesn't bring about substantial changes in the policies of the dictatorships, then we would move on to stage three—complete economic isolation of these nations.

Prior to the implementation of stage one, we would tell the rest of the world what our future policy would be and the reasons for it. We would say that we no longer see any significant difference between dictatorships, and that both types are threats to peace and world prosperity. We also would say that past anti-communist policies have failed, and we must develop more effective policies. Then, after, say, six months, we go to stage one.

The United States and Third World Dictatorships: A Case for Benign Detachment

Ted Galen Carpenter

It is a central dilemma of contemporary American foreign policy that the world's leading capitalist democracy must confront an environment in which a majority of nations are neither capitalist nor democratic. U.S. leaders have rarely exhibited ingenuity or grace in handling this delicate and often frustrating situation.

The current turmoil in Central America is illustrative of a larger problem. American officials assert that this vital region is under assault from doctrinaire communist revolutionaries trained, funded, and controlled by the Soviet Union. Danger to the well-being of the United States is immediate and serious, administration spokesmen argue, and it is imperative that the Marxist-Leninist tide be prevented from engulfing Central America. Accomplishing this objective requires a confrontational posture toward the communist beachhead (Nicaragua) combined with massive support for all "friendly" regimes, ranging from democratic Costa Rica to autocratic Guatemala. Washington's Central American policy displays in microcosm most of the faulty assumptions underlying America's approach to the entire Third World.

The current strategy of the United States betrays a virtual siege mentality. It was not always thus. Throughout the nineteenth cen-

tury U.S. policymakers exuded confidence that the rest of the world would emulate America's political and economic system, seeing the United States as a "beacon on the hill" guiding humanity to a better future.[1] As late as the 1940s, most Americans and their political representatives still believed that democracy would triumph as a universal system. The prospective breakup of the European colonial empires throughout Asia and Africa was generally viewed as an opportunity, not a calamity. Scores of new nations would emerge from that process, and Americans were confident that most would choose the path of democracy and free enterprise, thus isolating the Soviet Union and its coterie of Marxist-Leninist dictatorships in Eastern Europe.

The actual results were acutely disappointing. No wave of new democracies occurred in this "Third World"; instead, decolonization produced a plethora of dictatorships, some of which appeared distressingly friendly to Moscow. This development was especially disturbing to Washington since it took place at a time when America's cold war confrontation with the U.S.S.R. was at its most virulent. The nature and magnitude of that struggle caused American leaders to view the Third World primarily as another arena in the conflict. Consequently, the proliferation of left-wing revolutionary movements and governments seemed to undermine America's own security and well-being.

COLD WAR FACTORS

Washington's response to this adversity has been a particularly simplistic and unfortunate

---

Ted Galen Carpenter, "The United States and Third World Dictatorships: A Case for Benign Detachment," *Cato Institute Policy Analysis*, 58 (Washington, D.C.: Cato Institute, Aug. 15, 1985). Reprinted by permission of the Cato Institute.

[1] In his farewell address, President Andrew Jackson expressed the prevailing sentiments of his countrymen when he said that Providence had selected the American people to be "the guardians of freedom to preserve it for the benefit of the human race." See James D. Richardson, ed., *Messages and Papers of the Presidents*, vol. 3 (Washington: Government Printing Office, 1896), p. 308.

one. American leaders increasingly regarded any anticommunist regime, however repressive and undemocratic it might be at home, as an "ally," a "force for stability," and even a "friend." At the same time, they viewed leftist governments—even those elected under democratic procedures—as little more than Soviet surrogates, or at least targets of opportunity for communist machinations.

A portent of this mind-set among U.S. policymakers surfaced during the earliest stages of the cold war. President Harry Truman's enunciation of the so-called Truman Doctrine in 1947 proclaimed the willingness of the United States to assist friendly governments resisting not only external aggression but also "armed minorities" in their own midst.[2] It was an ominous passage, for the United States was arrogating the right to intervene in the internal affairs of other nations to help preserve regimes deemed friendly to American interests. Although Washington had engaged in such conduct throughout Central America and the Caribbean for several decades, those incidents were a geographical aberration in what was otherwise a noninterventionist foreign policy. The Truman Doctrine raised the specter that America's meddlesome paternalism in one region might now be applied on a global basis.

Although President Truman stressed that the status quo was not "sacred," his doctrine soon made the United States a patron of repressive, reactionary regimes around the world. It was a measure of how far that trend had developed by 1961 that President John F. Kennedy could proclaim in his inaugural address America's determination to "support any friend, oppose any foe" in the battle against world communism. Today, leading foreign policy spokesmen such as Henry Kissinger, Alexander Haig, and Jeane Kirkpatrick express a fondness for "friendly"

authoritarian regimes that would have seemed incomprehensible to most Americans only a few decades ago.[3]

A false realism as well as moral insensitivity characterizes American policy toward Third World dictatorships. There is a disturbing tendency to view such regimes in caricature, regarding right-wing governments as valuable friends whose repressive excesses must be ignored or excused, while perceiving leftist insurgent movements and governments as mortal threats to America's national interest, justifying a posture of unrelenting hostility.[4] For example, the Reagan administration pursues a confrontational policy toward the Marxist government of Nicaragua, terminating all aid programs, imposing a trade embargo, and supporting rebel guerrillas. At the same time, Washington lavishes economic and military aid upon equally repressive "allies" in South Korea, the Philippines, Zaire, and elsewhere.

The consequences of this simplistic and morally inconsistent strategy are highly unfortunate. America finds itself involved far too often in futile or mutually destructive confrontations with left-wing regimes. Even worse is the evolution of a cozy relationship between Washington and a host of right-wing authoritarian governments. A pervasive perception of the United States as the sponsor and protector of such dictatorships has undermined America's credibility as a spokesman for democracy,

---

[2] *Public Papers of the Presidents of the United States: Harry S. Truman, 1947* (Washington: Government Printing Office, 1963), pp. 178–79.

[3] For examples of such sentiments, see Henry A. Kissinger, *Years of Upheaval* (Boston: Little, Brown and Co., 1982), especially pp. 409–13, 667–74, 676; Alexander M. Haig, Jr., *Caveat: Realism, Reagan and Foreign Policy* (New York: Macmillan, 1984), pp. 30, 90, 96, 126, 268–70, 275, 278, 298; and Jeane Kirkpatrick, *Dictatorships and Double Standards* (New York: Simon and Schuster, 1982), especially pp. 23–25, 32–33, 44, 49–51, 65–67, 70–71, 80, 86, 133–134. An even more blatant apologia can be found in Richard Nixon, *No More Vietnams* (New York: Arbor House, 1985), pp. 13, 20–21, 218–19, 225.

[4] A concise analysis of such thinking is provided in Melvyn P. Leffler, "From the Truman Doctrine to the Carter Doctrine: Lessons and Dilemmas of the Cold War," *Diplomatic History* (Fall 1983): 245–66.

caused Third World peoples to equate both capitalism and democracy with U.S. hegemony, and established a milieu for rabidly anti-American revolutions.[5] It is an approach that creates a massive reservoir of ill will and, in the long run, weakens rather than strengthens America's national security.

Washington's policy toward Third World dictatorships is seriously flawed in several respects. One fundamental defect is the tendency to view largely internal struggles exclusively through the prism of America's ongoing cold war with the Soviet Union. Secretary of State John Foster Dulles was an early practitioner of this parochial viewpoint during the 1950s when he insisted that the emerging nations of Asia and Africa "choose sides" in that conflict. Nonalignment or neutralism Dulles viewed as moral cowardice or tacit support for the U.S.S.R. Such an attitude only antagonized nonaligned leaders who were concerned primarily with charting a postcolonial political and economic course for their new nations and cared little about an acrimonious competition between two alien superpowers. The chilly relationship between India, the Third World's leading democracy, and the United States throughout this period was due in large part to Washington's hostility toward Prime Minister Jawaharlal Nehru's policy of nonalignment.

American policymakers have learned few lessons from Dulles's errors in the subsequent quarter-century. During the 1960s, Washington still saw internal political conflicts in nations as diverse as Vietnam and the Dominican Republic exclusively as skirmishes in the larger cold war. A decade after the victory of one faction in the complex tribal, linguistic, and economic struggle in Angola, former sec-

retary of state Henry Kissinger describes that war as part of "an unprecedented Soviet geopolitical offensive" on a global scale.[6] Kissinger's former boss, Gerald Ford, likewise interprets the episode purely as a struggle between "pro-Communist" and "pro-West" forces.[7] Former U.N. ambassador Jeane Kirkpatrick views such countries as Mozambique and Nicaragua not as nations in their own right, but as components of the Soviet empire.[8] Similarly, President Reagan's bipartisan commission on Central America describes the multifaceted conflicts of that troubled region as part of a Soviet-Cuban "geo-strategic challenge" to the United States.[9]

RIGHT-WING EMBRACE

This failure to understand the complexities and ambiguities of Third World power rivalries has impelled the United States to adopt misguided and counterproductive strategies. One manifestation is an uncritical willingness to embrace repressive regimes if they possess sufficient anticommunist credentials.

At times this tendency has proven more than a trifle embarrassing. During a toast to the shah of Iran on New Year's Eve 1977, President Jimmy Carter lavished praise on that autocratic monarch: "Iran, because of the great leadership of the Shah, is an island of stability in one of the more troubled areas of the world. This is a great tribute to you, Your Majesty, and to your leadership, and to the respect and admiration and love which your people give

---

[5] An excellent discussion of that process can be found in Jonathan Kwitny, *Endless Enemies: The Making of an Unfriendly World* (New York: Congdon and Weed, 1984), pp. 48, 106–8, 264–68, 389–90, 394.

[6] Kissinger, p. 28.

[7] Gerald R. Ford, *A Time to Heal* (New York: Berkley Books, 1980), p. 334.

[8] Kirkpatrick, p. 123; see also her speech before the Dallas Council on World Affairs, April 12, 1985, quoted in Mark Miller, "Kirkpatrick Urges Support for U.S. Aid to Contras," *Dallas Morning News*, April 13, 1985.

[9] *The Report of the President's National Bipartisan Commission on Central America* (New York: Macmillan, 1984), p. 14. For additional expressions of the same thesis, see pp. 16, 102–3, 105, 109–12.

to you." Apparently concluding that America's vocal enthusiasm for the shah and his policies during the previous quarter-century did not link the United States sufficiently to his fate, the president emphasized: "We have no other nation on earth who [sic] is closer to us in planning for our mutual military security."[10]

Barely a year later the shah's regime lay in ruins, soon to be replaced by a virulently anti-American government. President Carter's assumption that the shah was loved by the Iranian people was a classic case of wishful thinking. CIA [Central Intelligence Agency] operatives in the field warned their superiors that the American perception was a delusion, but those reports were ignored because they did not reflect established policy.[11] Blind to reality, the administration identified itself and American security interests with a regime that was already careening toward oblivion.

One might think that American leaders would have gained some humility from the wreckage of Iranian policy and at least learned to curb vocal expressions of support for right-wing autocrats. Unfortunately, that has not been the case. Less than four years after Carter's gaffe, Vice President George Bush fawned over Philippine dictator Ferdinand Marcos: "We stand with you sir. . . . We love your adherence to democratic principle [sic] and to the democratic processes. And we will not leave you in isolation."[12]

It is a considerable understatement to suggest that the burgeoning Philippine opposition (which contains many legitimate democrats, such as Salvador Laurel and Butz Aquino) did not appreciate effusive praise for the man who suspended the national constitution, declared martial law, governed by decree, and imprisoned political opponents to perpetuate his own power. From the standpoint of long-term American interests (not to mention common decency and historical accuracy), Vice President Bush should have considered how a successor Philippine government might perceive his enthusiasm for Marcos. Instead of acting prudently, the Reagan administration seems determined to antagonize the opposition forces. During his second presidential campaign debate with Walter Mondale, President Reagan not only defended this nation's intimate relationship with the current Manila regime but also implied that the only alternative to Marcos was a communist takeover—a gross distortion of reality.[13]

Ill-considered hyperbole with respect to right-wing autocratic governments places the United States in an awkward, even hypocritical posture. Equally unfortunate is the extensive and at times highly visible material assistance that Washington gives such regimes. For more than three decades, the United States helped train and equip the military force that the Somoza family used to dominate Nicaragua and systematically loot that nation. Similarly, the American government provided lavish military hardware to the shah of Iran as well as "security" and "counter insurgency" training to SAVAK, the monarch's infamous secret police. Throughout the same period Washington gave similar assistance to a succession of Brazilian military governments, a parade of Guatemalan dictatorships, the junta that ruled Greece from 1967 to 1974, and several other repressive governments. Most recently, the United States gave the Marcos re-

---

[10] *Public Papers of the Presidents of the United States: Jimmy Carter, 1977* (Washington: Government Printing Office, 1978), pp. 2221–22.

[11] Jesse Leaf, "Iran: A Blind Spot in U.S. Intelligence," *Washington Post*, January 18, 1979; Barry Rubin, *Paved with Good Intentions: The American Experience and Iran* (New York: Oxford University Press, 1980), p. 201.

[12] Department of State, *Department of State Bulletin* 81, no. 2053 (August 1981): 30.

[13] "A Tie Goes to the Gipper," *Time*, October 29, 1984, pp. 24–25.

gime economic and military aid totaling more than $227 million, plus millions more in payments for the military installations at Clark Field and Subic Bay. Despite ample signs of that government's increasingly shaky tenure, the Reagan administration asked Congress to increase aid by nearly 20 percent. Congress exhibited little enthusiasm for that approach, approving instead a significantly smaller sum and attaching various "human rights" restrictions.[14]

Warm public endorsements of autocratic regimes combined with substantial (at times lavish) material support produce an explosive mixture that repeatedly damages American prestige and credibility. Many of those governments retain only the most precarious hold on power, lacking significant popular support and depending heavily upon the use of terror to intimidate opponents. When repressive tactics no longer prove sufficient, the dictatorships can collapse with dramatic suddenness—as in Iran. American patronage thus causes the United States to become closely identified with hated governments and their policies. The domestic populations see those regimes as little more than American clients—extensions of U.S. power. Consequently, they do not view the ouster of a repressive autocrat as merely an internal political change, but as the eradication of American domination.

Moreover, there is a virtual reflex action to repudiate everything American—including capitalist economics and Western-style democ-racy. The United States unwittingly contributes to that process. By portraying corrupt, autocratic rulers as symbols of the "free world," we risk having long-suffering populations take us at our word. They do not see capitalism and democracy as those systems operate in the West, enabling people to achieve prosperity and individual freedom. Instead, Third World people identify free enterprise and democratic values with the corruption and repression they have endured. Historian Walter LaFeber describes how that reasoning has worked in Central America: "U.S. citizens see [capitalist democracy] as having given them the highest standard of living and the most open society in the world. Many Central Americans have increasingly associated capitalism with a brutal oligarchy-military complex that has been supported by U.S. policies—and armies."[15]

An attitude eventually emerges that if Ferdinand Marcos, Augusto Pinochet, or Chun Doo Hwan represents democratic capitalism, then any alternative, even communism, might be preferable. It is a dangerous delusion, and Washington justifiably urges Third World populations to recognize Marxism as a lethal snare. But the suspicion engendered by America's myopic foreign policy inclines them to reject such warnings as self-serving propaganda.

The explosion of emotional, often hysterical, anti-Americanism in Iran cannot be understood apart from the context of Washington's massive and highly visible sponsorship of the shah during the preceding quarter-century. The same relationship exists in Nicaragua, where a more sedate, but still pervasive, anti-Americanism is directly attributable to America's long-standing connection with the detested Somoza family. Other caldrons are now

---

[14] Greg Jones, "Anti-U.S. Sentiment Grows in Philippines," *Dallas Morning News,* April 4, 1985; "House Approves Two-Year $25.4 Billion Foreign Aid Bill," *Dallas Morning News,* August 1, 1985. A Senate Foreign Relations Committee staff report, prepared by Carl Ford and Frederick Brown following lengthy visits to the Philippines, warned of the increasingly precarious position of the Marcos government. Even officials within the State Department and Defense Department reportedly urged that the United States begin to "distance itself" from Marcos. "Downsiders vs. Optimists," *Newsweek,* October 22, 1984, p. 51.

[15] Walter LaFeber, *Inevitable Revolutions* (New York: W. W. Norton, 1984), p. 14; Kwitny, pp. 5–6, 105–8, 203–4, 302–6, 389–90, 394.

boiling in Zaire, Guatemala, South Korea, and the Philippines. Ramon Mitra, an opposition member of the Philippine National Assembly, underscores the danger inherent in America's sponsorship of repressive regimes, warning that once Marcos is overthrown, "this will become one of the most bitter, anti-American countries in this part of the world."[16] As a recipe for breeding antagonism and ill will, it would be difficult to surpass existing U.S. foreign policy.

HOSTILITY TO THE LEFT

The flip side of Washington's promiscuous enthusiasm for right-wing autocrats is an equally pervasive hostility toward leftist Third World regimes and insurgent movements. There have been occasional exceptions to this rule throughout the cold war era. For example, the United States developed a cordial relationship with communist Yugoslavia after Premier Josef Tito broke with the Soviet Union in 1948. A similar process occurred during the early 1970s, when the Nixon administration engineered a rapprochement with China, ending more than two decades of frigid hostility. These achievements are instructive and should have demonstrated to American policymakers that it is possible for the United States to coexist with Marxist regimes. But that lesson has not been learned, and such incidents of enlightenment stand as graphic exceptions to an otherwise dreary record.

More typical of America's posture is the ongoing feud with the Cuban government of Fidel Castro, now in its 27th year. The campaign to oust Castro or, failing that, to make him a hemispheric pariah, was shortsighted, futile, and counterproductive from the outset. It served only to give him a largely undeserved status as a principled, courageous revolutionary and to drive his government into Moscow's willing embrace. Soviet defector Arkady Shevchenko recalls a 1960 conversation with Nikita Khrushchev in which the latter viewed America's hostility toward Cuba with undisguised glee. Describing U.S. efforts to "drive Castro to the wall" instead of establishing normal relations as "stupid," Khrushchev concluded: "Castro will have to gravitate to us like an iron filing to a magnet."[17] It was an accurate prediction.

Apparently having learned little from the Cuban experience, the Reagan administration seems determined to make the same errors with the Sandinista government of Nicaragua. Washington's attempts to isolate the Managua regime diplomatically, the imposition of economic sanctions, the "covert" funding of the *contra* guerrillas, and the use of apocalyptic rhetoric to describe the internal struggle for power in that country all seem like an eerie case of *deja vu*. President Reagan's depiction of the *contras* as "the moral equal" of America's own founding fathers constitutes ample evidence that U.S. policy-makers have not learned to view Third World power struggles with even modest sophistication.[18] One need not romanticize the Sandinista regime, excuse its suppression of political dissent, or rationalize its acts of brutality (e.g., the treatment of the Miskito Indians), as the American political left is prone to do, to advocate a more restrained and detached policy. Administration leaders fear that Nicaragua will become a Soviet satellite in Central America; Washington's current belligerent course virtually guarantees

---

[16] Greg Jones, "Communists Reported Gaining in Philippines," *Dallas Morning News,* March 13, 1985. A concise discussion of the growing turmoil in the Philippines and its potential consequences for the United States is found in Robert A. Manning, "The Philippines in Crisis," *Foreign Affairs* (Winter 1984–85): 392–410.

[17] Arkady N. Shevchenko, *Breaking with Moscow* (New York: Alfred A. Knopf, 1985), p. 105.

[18] Gerald M. Boyd, "Reagan Terms Nicaragua Rebels 'Moral Equal' of Founding Fathers," *New York Times,* March 2, 1985.

that outcome. As in the case of Cuba nearly three decades ago, the United States is creating a self-fulfilling prophecy.

The American government's hostility toward left-wing regimes in the Third World has even extended to *democratic* governments with a leftist slant. An early victim of this antipathy was Iranian prime minister Mohammed Mossadegh. Evidence now clearly shows extensive CIA involvement (including planning and funding) in the 1953 royalist coup that enabled the shah to establish himself as an absolute monarch.[19] Mossadegh's "crime" was not that he was communist, but that he depended on communist elements for some of his support and advocated policies inimical to powerful Anglo-American economic interests. A year later, the left-leaning reformist government of Jacobo Arbenz in Guatemala suffered the same fate. This time American complicity in the overthrow of a democratically elected government was even more blatant. The U.S. ambassador to Guatemala reportedly boasted that he had brought the counterrevolution to a successful conclusion barely "forty-five minutes behind schedule."[20] Even President Reagan's bipartisan commission on Central America concedes U.S. assistance in the coup, and Washington's role has been amply documented elsewhere.[21]

Buoyed by such successes, the United States helped oust Patrice Lumumba, the first elected prime minister of the Congo (now Zaire), in 1960.[22] Like Mossadegh and Arbenz, Lumumba had committed the unpardonable sin of soliciting communist support. There is also some evidence of American complicity in the 1973 military coup that toppled the government of Chilean president Salvador Allende. We do know that the Nixon administration sought to thwart Allende's election in 1970, discussed a coup with disgruntled elements of the military immediately following that election, and ordered steps to isolate and destabilize the new government economically.[23] No less a figure than Henry Kissinger, then serving as national security adviser, concedes that the United States authorized covert payments of more than $8.8 million to opponents of the Allende government during the three years preceding the coup.[24] Given the relatively modest size of the Chilean economy and population, an infusion of $8.8 million certainly created a considerable political impact, but Kissinger and Nixon both blame Allende's downfall entirely on internal factors. The Marxist president's pursuit of disastrous economic programs together with his systematic attempts to undercut the conservative middle class and harass political opponents undoubtedly galvanized the opposition, weakening his already precarious political position. Nevertheless, it would be naive to accept at face value the Nixon administration's protestations of innocence regarding the coup, especially in light of Kissinger's ominous assertion that Allende was "not merely an economic nuisance or a political critic but a geopolitical challenge."[25]

It is reprehensible for a government that preaches the virtues of noninterference in the internal affairs of other nations to have

---

[19] Kwitny, pp. 164–77; Richard and Gladys Harkness, "The Mysterious Doings of the CIA," *Saturday Evening Post*, November 6, 1954, pp. 34–35; Rubin, pp. 77–90.

[20] Quoted in Richard H. Immerman, *The CIA in Guatemala* (Austin: University of Texas Press, 1982), p. 141.

[21] *Commission on Central America Report*, p. 25. Accounts of the CIA operation include Immerman, passim; LaFeber, pp. 119–25; Blanche Wiesen Cook, *The Declassified Eisenhower* (Garden City, N.Y.: Doubleday, 1981), pp. 218–19, 233–89; Stephen Schlesinger and Stephen Kinzer, *Bitter Fruit: The Untold Story of America's Coup in Guatemala* (New York: Doubleday, 1982), passim.

[22] Madeleine G. Kalb, *The Congo Cables* (New York: Macmillan, 1982), pp. 50–55, 63–67, 77–83, 89–104, 129–39, 144–52, 157–79, 184–96; Kwitny, pp. 52–70.

[23] Henry A. Kissinger, *White House Years* (Boston: Little, Brown and Co., 1979), pp. 673–77, 681.

[24] Kissinger, *Years of Upheaval*, pp. 382, 395, 403.

[25] Ibid., p. 376.

amassed such a record of interference. The level of shame mounts when American meddling undermines a sister democracy and helps install a repressive autocracy. Yet in Iran, Guatemala, Zaire, and Chile that was precisely what happened. Post-Mossadegh Iran endured the shah's corrupt authoritarianism for 25 years before desperately embracing the fanaticism of the Ayatollah Khomeini. Guatemala after Arbenz has witnessed a dreary succession of military dictatorships, each one rivaling its predecessor in brutality.[26] The ouster of Patrice Lumumba facilitated the rise to power of Mobutu Sese Seko (nee Joseph Mobutu) in Zaire. Mobutu's regime is regarded as one of the most corrupt and repressive on any continent.

Perhaps Chile is the saddest case of all. Although deified by Western liberals, Salvador Allende had his unsavory qualities. His enthusiasm for Marxist economic bromides pushed his nation to the brink of disaster. He also exhibited a nasty authoritarian streak of his own, including an intolerance of political critics. Nevertheless, his actions remained (although sometimes just barely) within constitutional bounds. Moreover, he was the last in an unbroken series of democratically elected rulers stretching back more than four decades—an impressive record in Latin America. The Pinochet dictatorship that replaced Allende nearly 12 years ago is conspicuous for its brutal and systematic violation of individual liberties. Yet Henry Kissinger can assert that the "change in government in Chile was on balance favorable— even from the point of view of human

rights."[27] Such a view reflects either willful blindness or an astounding cynicism.

OFFICIAL JUSTIFICATIONS

Those individuals who justify America's existing policy toward the Third World cite strategic, economic, and ideological considerations. On the strategic level, they argue that the United States must prevent geographically important regions from falling under the sway of regimes subservient to the Soviet Union. Otherwise, a shift in the balance of global military power could jeopardize American security interests, perhaps even imperil the nation's continued existence. Economically, the United States must maintain access to vital supplies of raw materials and keep markets open for American products and investments. It is not possible, this argument holds, for an economy based upon free enterprise to endure if the world is dominated by state-run Marxist systems. Finally, beyond questions of strategic and economic self-interest, the United States must thwart communist expansionism in the Third World to ensure that America and its democratic allies do not become islands in a global sea of hostile, totalitarian dictatorships.

All these arguments possess a certain facile appeal, but they hold up only if one accepts some very dubious conceptions of America's strategic, economic, and ideological interests. Moreover, proponents have often employed these arguments as transparent rationalizations for questionable foreign policy initiatives.

Strategic Considerations

The notion that the United States must assist and defend right-wing regimes while opposing leftist insurgencies or governments for its

---

[26] Even President Reagan's commission on Central America conceded that after the ouster of Arbenz, Guatemalan politics became especially "divisive, violent and polarized." *Commission on Central America Report*, p. 25. See also John A. Booth, "A Guatemalan Nightmare: Levels of Political Violence," *Journal of Interamerican Studies* (May 1980): especially 199–200, 218–20.

[27] Kissinger, *Years of Upheaval*, p. 411.

own strategic self-interest depends on several important subsidiary assumptions. Those who justify America's Third World policy on this basis generally define "strategic interests" in a most expansive manner. In its crudest form, this approach regards Third World states as little more than bases or forward staging areas for American military power. Reagan administration officials defend continued support of the Marcos dictatorship, for example, because otherwise the United States might lose its installations at Clark Field and Subic Bay, complicating the defense of other Far Eastern allies.[28]

A more subtle argument is to portray a particular regime as a "keystone" or "force for stability" in a particular region. This thesis featured prominently in Washington's support for the shah of Iran with respect to the Persian Gulf, Mobutu Sese Seko with respect to Central Africa, and a succession of Brazilian military governments with respect to South America. Such a rationale is convincing only if one assumes that the United States truly possesses "vital" strategic interests in regions as diverse as Southeast Asia, the Persian Gulf, Central Africa, and South America, and that successor regimes in regional "keystone" nations would be hostile to those interests.

One can and should question whether the United States actually has strategic interests, vital or otherwise, in areas thousands of miles removed from its own shores. Moreover, Washington's current approach assumes that the presence of authoritarian Third World allies somehow enhances America's own security. It is a curious belief. How a plethora of small, often militarily insignificant nations, governed by unpopular and unstable regimes, could augment U.S. strength in a showdown with the Soviet Union is a mystery. One could

make a more plausible argument that attempts to prop up tottering allies *weaken* America's security. These efforts drain U.S. financial resources and stretch defense forces dangerously thin. Worst of all is the risk that a crumbling Third World ally could become an arena for ill-advised American military adventures. As we saw in Vietnam, the entrance to such quagmires is easier to find than the exit.

The inordinate fear of successor governments is equally dubious, for it assumes that such regimes would inevitably be left-wing and subservient to Moscow. Neither assumption is necessarily warranted. The ouster of a right-wing autocracy does not lead ineluctably to a radical leftist government. Vigorous democracies succeeded rightist dictatorships in Portugal and Greece, and there is a reasonable possibility of a similar occurrence in the Philippines once Marcos passes from the scene. Moreover, even in cases where a staunchly leftist government does emerge, subservience to Moscow cannot be assumed. Such pessimism may have had some validity in the bipolar ideological environment of the late 1940s and early 1950s, but given the diffusion of power away from both Moscow and Washington in the past 30 years, it is now dangerously obsolete. When China and the U.S.S.R. are mortal adversaries, Yugoslavia charts a consistently independent course, and such a country as Rumania—in Moscow's own geopolitical "backyard"—dares exhibit maverick tendencies on selected foreign policy issues, the assumption that a Marxist Third World state will be merely a Soviet stooge is clearly unwarranted.

There is no doubt that the Soviet Union exploits local crises to further its own foreign policy objectives and that the Kremlin often supports, equips, and funds radical insurgencies. But there is a vast difference between assisting a revolutionary movement and *controlling* it. The mere fact that leftist forces accept Soviet money and military

---

[28] See the comments of Richard L. Armitage, assistant secretary of defense for international security affairs. "The Carrot and the Stick," *Newsweek*, March 25, 1985, p. 66.

hardware does not mean that once in power they would tamely submit to dictation from Moscow. Yet this distinction has escaped two generations of American foreign policy officials. They habitually equate support with control—regarding any acceptance of Soviet aid as a "mark of Cain" justifying unrelenting U.S. hostility.[29]

Otherwise sophisticated foreign policy spokesmen spin elaborate theories about the supposed strategic dangers posed to the United States if "friendly" autocratic regimes fall. At times this attitude verges on paranoia. The report of President Reagan's bipartisan commission on Central America, for example, concludes that a proliferation of Marxist governments in Central America would threaten U.S. shipping lanes in the Caribbean, interdicting vital supply lines in the event of a Middle East or European war.[30] How the nations of Central America could accomplish such a feat against the world's foremost military power the commission sages do not say. As it is doubtful that the Central American states could muster more than minuscule naval and air power contingents of their own, the only plausible theory is that they would allow their homelands to be used as bases for Soviet strikeforces. Such action would make sense only if the regimes all had suicide complexes, since U.S. retaliation would be inevitable, swift, and devastating. Yet commission members brazenly cite such a strategic "threat" as an imperative reason for the United States to defend Central American autocracies against "destabilizing" insurgencies.

The Economic Dimension

The economic thesis for current U.S. foreign policy is no more persuasive than the strategic rationale. Assumptions that rightist governments serve as pliant instruments of American economic objectives or that left-wing regimes become commercial adversaries cannot be sustained as a general rule. It is true that countries ruled by right-wing autocrats tend to be friendlier arenas for U.S. investment, but the price in bureaucratic restrictions and "commissions" (i.e., bribes) to key officials is often very high. Moreover, governments of whatever ideological stripe usually operate according to principles of economic self-interest, which may or may not correspond to American desires.

Washington received a rude awakening on that score in the 1970s, when its closest Middle East allies—Iran and Saudi Arabia—helped engineer OPEC's [Organization of Petroleum Exporting Countries] massive oil price hikes. Neither U.S. client was willing to forgo financial gain out of any sense of gratitude for political and military support. Much the same situation occurred in 1980, when the Carter administration invoked a grain embargo against the Soviet Union for the latter's invasion of Afghanistan. The United States encouraged, even pressured, its allies to cooperate in that boycott. Nevertheless, the Argentine military junta, a regime that the United States had routinely counted upon to stem the tide of leftist insurgency in Latin America, promptly seized the opportunity to boost its grain sales to the U.S.S.R.[31]

Just as right-wing regimes exhibit a stubborn independence on economic matters, revolutionary leftist governments are not inher-

---

[29] For examples, see *Commission on Central America Report*, pp. 31–32, 103–9; Haig, pp. 26–27, 32, 122–23, 125, 129, 135; Department of State, *Communist Interference in El Salvador: Documents Demonstrating Communist Support of El Salvador Insurgency* (Washington: Government Printing Office, 1981), passim.

[30] *Commission on Central America Report*, pp. 109–11.

[31] "Argentina's Silent Partner," *New York Times*, March 26, 1980; Edward Schumacher, "Argentina and Soviet Are No Longer Just Business Partners," *New York Times*, July 12, 1981.

ent commercial enemies. When the United States has allowed trade with leftist countries to occur, that trade has usually flourished. The lucrative oil and mineral commerce with the Marxist government of Angola is a case in point.[32] Similarly, once the emotional feud with mainland China ceased in the 1970s, commercial and investment opportunities for the United States also began to emerge. Although a Marxist state dominating the global market in some vital commodity might conceivably attempt to blackmail the United States, that danger is both remote and theoretical. Indeed, as several scholars have shown, the entire notion of the democratic West's "resource dependency" is overblown.[33]

Economic realities exert a powerful influence that often transcends purely political considerations. Most Third World governments, whether right-wing or left-wing, benefit from extensive commercial ties with the industrialized West, particularly the United States. America is often the principal market for their exports and is a vital source of developmental capital.[34] Revolutionary rhetoric, even when sincerely believed, cannot change that fundamental equation. It is no coincidence that Third World governments have rarely instituted economic boycotts; most embargoes originate as a deliberate U.S. policy to punish perceived political misdeeds.

As in the case of political and military bellicosity, a confrontational approach to commerce is unproductive. The Reagan administration's trade embargo against Nicaragua is designed ostensibly to deflect the Sandinista government from a pro-Soviet course. It will likely produce the opposite effect. External pressures strengthen doctrinaire elements, like Interior Minister Tomas Borge, who want to chart an uncompromising Marxist-Leninist course. Under the pretext of national unity, Borge and his cohorts can now promote greater economic regimentation and equate even mild dissent with treason. Trade sanctions also injure Nicaragua's fragile private sector, already under siege from collectivist forces in the government. Worst of all, America's withdrawal as a trading partner offers the Soviet bloc a superb opportunity to fill that void, thus integrating Nicaragua into a global socialist system.

Rather than adopting economic sanctions as a device for political intimidation, the United States should relish the prospect of promoting commercial connections to the greatest extent possible. Nothing would more readily provide evidence to left-wing leaders that a system based on private property and incentives is vastly superior to the lumbering inefficiencies of Marxist central planning. On those rare occasions when the United States has pursued a conciliatory rather than a truculent and confrontational approach, the results have been gratifying. The Marxist regime in Mozambique, for instance, first looked to the Soviet bloc for economic as well as ideological guidance, only to confront arrogant Russian imperialism and a recipe for economic disaster. The disillusioned leadership now has begun to turn away from the U.S.S.R. and open its country to Western trade and investment, a process that is likely to accelerate in the coming years.[35]

---

[32] Terence Smith, "Companies Resisting U.S. Foreign Policy," *New York Times*, June 27, 1981; Kwitny, pp. 149–50; James Brooke, "Inside the East Bloc's African Outpost," *New York Times*, January 13, 1985.

[33] See, for example, Michael Shafer, "Mineral Myths," *Foreign Policy* (Summer 1982): 154–71.

[34] For a discussion of this point, see Kwitny, pp. 18, 75–76, 149–50.

[35] Anthony Lewis, "Mozambique Seeks Western Investment," *New York Times*, February 5, 1983; "Mozambique Dismisses 3 Cabinet Ministers," *New York Times*, June 17, 1984; Jeff Trimble, "Mozambique's Marxists Turn to the Left," *U.S. News and World Report*, February 25, 1985, pp. 37–38.

Ideological Biases

The most misguided justification for America's attachment to right-wing Third World states lies in the realm of politics and ideology. Proponents assume an underlying ideological affinity between authoritarian systems and Western democracies. They insist that while rightist regimes may be repressive, such governments are natural U.S. allies in the struggle against world communism. Conversely, revolutionary leftist movements are "totalitarian" in origin and constitute accretions to the power of that global menace.

No one has advanced this thesis more passionately and at greater length than former U.S. ambassador to the United Nations Jeane Kirkpatrick. While conceding that "traditional" autocracies sometimes engage in practices that offend American "sensibilities," Kirkpatrick clearly finds those regimes more palatable than their leftist adversaries. She asserts that "traditional authoritarian governments are less repressive than revolutionary autocracies," are "more susceptible to liberalization," and are "more compatible with U.S. interests."[36] That being the case, American aid to keep such friendly regimes in power is not only justified but becomes something akin to a moral imperative.

Kirkpatrick's thesis is flawed in several respects. Her assertion that rightist autocracies are less repressive than their left-wing counterparts is only partially valid. If one selects an extreme example, like the murderous Pol Pot government of Cambodia in the mid- and late 1970s, even the worst rightist regimes compare favorably. Moreover, Marxist dictatorships do tend to be more systematic in eradicating all competing power centers, thus rendering it more difficult for a political opposition to coalesce. In other words, "totalitarian" regimes are usually more efficient in institutionalizing their repression. Nevertheless, it is pertinent to observe that several former and current U.S. allies in the Third World have amassed appalling human rights records. Their brutality may be less efficient, but in many cases it is scarcely less severe.

Even if one concedes that the repression practiced by leftist dictatorships is more pervasive and severe than that of right-wing dictatorships, a more fundamental issue still exists—American complicity. The United States has neither the power nor the requisite moral mandate to eradicate injustice and oppression in the world. At the same time, as the most powerful and visible symbol of democracy, America does have an obligation not to become a participant in acts of repression and brutality. Our sponsorship of right-wing autocracies violates that crucial responsibility. Assisting dictatorial regimes makes the U.S. government (and by extension the public that elects it) an accomplice in the suppression of other peoples' liberty. In a profound way, such complicity constitutes a stain on our democratic heritage.

Kirkpatrick's contention that traditional autocracies are more susceptible to liberalization likewise misses a fundamental point. She asserts that autocratic regimes sometimes "evolve" into more democratic forms, whereas no analogous case exists with respect to revolutionary socialist governments. Yet her own examples—Spain, Greece, and Brazil—do not involve evolutionary transformations, but rather the *restoration* of democratic systems that right-wing elements had destroyed. History demonstrates that while communist revolutionaries oust competing repressive systems, rightist insurgents habitually overthrow democratically elected governments. There is only one instance of a successful communist uprising against an established democracy: the takeover of

---

[36] Kirkpatrick, pp. 44, 49.

Czechoslovakia in March 1948. Conversely, right-wing coups and revolutions have erased numerous democratic regimes. Spain (1936), Guatemala (1954), Brazil (1964), Greece (1967), the Philippines (1972), Chile (1973), and Argentina (1976) represent only the most prominent examples. It may be more difficult to eradicate leftist (especially totalitarian) systems than it is to replace rightist regimes, but right-wing autocratic movements pose the more lethal threat to functioning democracies. No fact more effectively demolishes the naive notion of an underlying affinity between democracies and rightist dictatorships. The two systems are not allies; they are inherent adversaries.

Those who embrace Kirkpatrick's thesis accuse American liberals, with some justification, of applying a "double standard" toward Third World dictatorships. Liberals have indeed exhibited selective morality on a score of occasions. Some who condemned the repressive policies of U.S. allies in Southeast Asia during the late 1960s and early 1970s remained strangely silent when Hanoi created a flood of refugees and violated the sovereignty of neighboring nations. Today, it is fashionable for liberals to advocate sanctions against South Africa and Chile while supporting expanded contacts with Cuba and the Soviet Union, nations with equally abysmal human rights records. Many leftists conveniently ignore atrocities committed by revolutionary socialist regimes, even when, as in the case of Pol Pot, those acts reach genocidal proportions.

But Kirkpatrick and her cohorts also employ an obnoxious double standard. For example, the Reagan administration denounced the November elections in Nicaragua as a "farce" because of restrictions the Sandinistas placed on their opponents. Yet administration officials praised the balloting in South Korea three months later as an important and positive step to-

ward full democracy, even though opposition parties labored under onerous restraints comparable to those in Nicaragua.[37] We have already seen examples of Washington's enthusiasm for Marcos-style "democracy" in the Philippines.

An even more blatant application of a double standard is the attitude of American conservatives toward the practices of right-wing autocrats. While excoriating Marxist dictators, Jeane Kirkpatrick fairly gushes with enthusiasm for the likes of Somoza and the shah. Those leaders were "positively friendly" to the United States. They sent their sons to be educated at American universities and voted with America at the U.N., and their embassies were active in Washington social life![38] Perhaps Kirkpatrick believes that such behavior should have impressed the inmates languishing in the political prisons of Managua and Teheran. What she finds inconvenient to recognize—a point equally true of Henry Kissinger, Alexander Haig, and George Shultz—is that the autocratic "friends" who seem so charming during periodic Washington visits are the same individuals who routinely order the imprisonment, torture, or murder of political opponents at home. Only a pervasive double standard allows American conservatives to condemn Marxist repression while acting as apologists for the brutal excesses of right-wing "allies."

JIMMY CARTER AND HUMAN RIGHTS

Unfortunately, indiscriminate support for "traditional" autocrats combined with pervasive hostility toward Marxist regimes has been a staple of American policy in the Third World for the past 35 years. The most notable devia-

---

[37] "U.S. Official Calls Vote in Nicaragua a 'Farce,'" *Dallas Morning News*, November 6, 1984; "A Challenge for President Chun," *Time*, February 25, 1985, p. 37.
[38] Kirkpatrick, p. 25.

tion from this dreary record occurred during Jimmy Carter's administration. President Carter's approach to Third World affairs began with an apparent sophistication that had eluded his predecessors entirely. In May 1977 Carter stated: "Being confident of our future, we are now free of that inordinate fear of communism which once led us to embrace any dictator who joined us in that fear."[39] He made it clear that human rights considerations would play a significant role in determining whether U.S. military and economic aid would flow to other nations.

It seemed a gratifying departure from previous policy, but the Carter approach contained two fundamental flaws, both of which contributed to its ultimate failure. In his memoirs, the former president unwittingly underscored one weakness himself: "I was determined to combine support for our more authoritarian allies and friends with the promotion of human rights within their countries."[40] This conception produced a constant "balancing act" between perceived American security interests and human rights considerations. As one scholar of the period has observed, Carter's foreign policy became "whipsawed" between those conflicting objectives. By 1980 "the president's human rights policies had been hopelessly compromised by exceptions made for security reasons."[41]

Moreover, Carter defined human rights in such an expansive manner as to include issues of education, nutrition, housing, and so on.[42]

Thus armed, the administration assumed a right to meddle in the internal affairs of numerous nations, provoking resentment on all sides. The results were predictable. President Carter's seemingly noble objectives degenerated into a hypocritical hodgepodge that left America's policy toward the Third World in near chaos.

The fundamental weakness of the Carter approach was its attempt to graft concern about human rights to an existing interventionist foreign policy rather than reassessing the underlying elements of that policy. Administration leaders should have viewed human rights considerations as a rationale for reducing the level of American political and military involvement in the Third World. But to adopt such a course would have meant evaluating whether the preservation of various right-wing autocracies was actually vital to American security, indeed, whether important American interests were involved at all in regions remote from our own homeland. Neither the president nor his subordinates were willing or able to make such a drastic reassessment. Consequently, the human rights issue became a vehicle for more rather than less intervention.

AN ALTERNATIVE: BENIGN DETACHMENT

This central defect in the Carter administration's foreign policy should serve as a cautionary reminder regarding efforts to structure a more equitable and coherent approach to Third World affairs. A new policy must eschew inconsistent moral posturing as well as amoral geopolitics. The most constructive alternative would stress "benign detachment" toward *all* Third World dictatorships, whatever their ideological orientation.

The concept of benign detachment is grounded in the indisputable reality that, for the foreseeable future, the United States will

---

[39] *Public Papers of the Presidents: Jimmy Carter, 1977*, p. 956.

[40] Jimmy Carter, *Keeping Faith* (New York: Bantam Books, 1982), p. 143.

[41] Walter LaFeber, "From Confusion to Cold War: The Memoirs of the Carter Administration," *Diplomatic History* (Winter 1984): 6. See also the views of former secretary of state Cyrus Vance on the need to "balance" security and human rights concerns. Cyrus Vance, *Hard Choices: Critical Years in America's Foreign Policy* (New York: Simon and Schuster, 1983), pp. 32–33, 127–28, 516.

[42] Carter, p. 144.

confront a Third World environment in which a majority of nations are undemocratic. It would unquestionably prove easier to function in a community of capitalist democracies, but we do not have that luxury. Democracy and capitalism may emerge as powerful doctrines throughout the Third World, but such a transformation would be long-term, reflecting indigenous historical experiences. We certainly cannot hasten that process by abandoning our own ideals and embracing reactionary autocrats. In the interim, the United States must learn to coexist with a variety of dictatorships. Benign detachment represents the most productive and least intrusive method of achieving that objective.

This approach would reject the simplistic categorization of right-wing regimes as friends and Marxist governments as enemies. It would require redefining America's national interests in a more circumspect manner. No longer should Washington conclude that the survival of a reactionary dictatorship, no matter how repressive, corrupt, and unstable it might be, somehow enhances the security of the United States. A policy of benign detachment would likewise repudiate the notion that there is an underlying kinship between rightist autocracies and Western democracies. Right-wing dictatorships are just as alien to our values as their left-wing counterparts.

America's primary objective should be a more restrained and even-handed policy toward repressive Third World regimes. Cordial diplomatic and economic relations should be encouraged with *all* governments that are willing to reciprocate, be they democratic, authoritarian, royalist, or Marxist. This would require normalizing diplomatic and commercial relations with such states as Cuba, Nicaragua, and Vietnam while curtailing aid to so-called allies.

Conservatives invariably protest that this position is a manifestation of a liberal double standard.[43] It is not. In fact, conservatives ignore the actual effects such policies have had in the past. Take the case of mainland China. Throughout the 1950s and 1960s, Washington's attempts to isolate the People's Republic of China only caused that nation to turn inward and fester, producing a particularly oppressive and regimented system. Since the United States abandoned its misguided strategy in the early 1970s, China has become a far more open and progressive nation. Deng Xiaoping and his followers now eagerly welcome Western trade and investment, particularly in the field of high technology. Equally important are the changes sweeping the domestic economy. Chinese officials are dismantling crucial elements of Marxist central planning, decentralizing production, creating incentives, and even legalizing certain forms of private property. All those developments should be gratifying to Americans who believe in the virtues of a market economy. Moreover, the first, albeit hesitant, signs of political liberalization in China are beginning to emerge. Prominent Chinese spokesmen even assert publicly that Karl Marx was not infallible and that many of his ideas are irrelevant in the modern era—sentiments that would have merited the death sentence only a few years ago.[44]

While the U.S. initiative in establishing cordial political and economic relations with China cannot account entirely for this movement toward liberalization, there is no ques-

---

[43] See, for example, Kirkpatrick, pp. 41–42, 46–47, 69; and Gerald Ford, p. xvii. Implicit in their arguments is the notion that U.S. taxpayers are obligated to continue funding right-wing dictators in the manner to which they have become accustomed.

[44] "China Repudiates Orthodox Marxism as Obsolete Theories," *Dallas Morning News*, December 8, 1984. On Chinese economic reforms, see George C. Wang, ed. and trans., *Economic Reform in the PRC* (Boulder, Colo.: Westview Press, 1982), passim; and A. Doak Barnett, *China's Economy in Global Perspective* (Washington: Brookings Institution, 1981), especially pp. 34–37, 45–55, 86–98, 506–39.

tion that it helps facilitate progressive trends. Conservatives who advocate isolating Cuba, Vietnam, Nicaragua, and other Marxist states would do well to ponder that point. Liberals who endorse economic sanctions against South Africa should consider whether their suggested strategy is not counterproductive as well.

Encouraging diplomatic and commercial relations with all nations is a beneficial strategy, but aid programs and security training are another matter entirely. Economist Peter T. Bauer has shown how foreign aid inherently undermines the values of capitalism and democracy throughout the Third World. Developmental funds promote distressingly little economic progress and help entrench corrupt political elites. "Since official wealth transfers go to governments and not to the people at large, they promote the disastrous politicization of life in the Third World," Bauer observes. Moreover, aid "increases the power, resources and patronage of governments compared to the rest of society and therefore their power over it."[45]

The tragic results of military assistance and security training are even more apparent. Both help repressive regimes maintain authority through acts of terrorism directed against ideological opponents and the public. Incentives for essential reforms and liberalization are diminished because the governments believe that U.S. material aid and political support will prove sufficient to perpetuate their power. Even worse, military aid implicates the United States in the atrocities those governments commit, thus creating extensive and potentially disastrous entanglements.

An even-handed policy should avoid involvement in Third World quarrels not directly pertinent to America's own security requirements, however crucial they might seem to the immediate participants. The United States has no holy writ to destabilize the governments of Cuba or Nicaragua because it finds them repugnant, nor to preserve autocratic systems in South Korea or Zaire because it considers them congenial. By the same token, America has not been anointed to overthrow the Pinochet regime in Chile or reform the South African government, even though zealous liberals might think such actions would promote human progress.

A policy of benign detachment is not isolationist—at least insofar as that term is used to describe a xenophobic, "storm shelter" approach to world affairs. Quite the contrary, it adopts a tolerant and optimistic outlook, seeing Third World states not merely as pawns in America's cold war with the Soviet Union, but as unique and diverse entities. Extensive economic relations are not merely acceptable, they are essential to enhancing the ultimate appeal of capitalism and democracy. There is even room for American mediation efforts to help resolve internecine or regional conflicts, provided that all parties to a dispute desire such assistance and our role harbors no danger of political or military entanglements. The United States need not practice a surly isolation. America can be an active participant in Third World affairs, but the nature of such interaction must be limited, consistent, and nonintrusive.

A policy of benign detachment would bring numerous benefits to the United States. No longer would America be perceived as the patron of repressive, decaying dictatorships, or as the principal obstacle to indigenous change in the Third World. Our current policy tragically identifies the United States and—even worse—its capitalist democratic system with the most reactionary elements around the globe. This foolish posture enables the Soviet Union to pose as the champion of both democracy and Third World nationalism. It is time

---

[45] Peter T. Bauer, *Equality, the Third World and Economic Delusion* (Cambridge: Harvard University Press, 1981), pp. 103–4.

that America recaptured that moral high ground. If the United States allowed the people of Third World nations to work out their own destinies instead of trying to enlist them as unwilling combatants in the cold war, Russia's hypocritical, grasping imperialism would soon stand exposed. Moscow, not Washington, might well become the principal target of nationalistic wrath throughout Asia, Africa, and Latin America. Moreover, the inherent inequities and inefficiencies of Marxist economics would soon become evident to all but the most rabid ideologues.

Equally important, a conciliatory noninterventionist posture toward the Third World would reduce the risk of U.S. military involvement in complex quarrels generally not relevant to American security. Savings in terms of both dollars and lives could be enormous. Our current policy threatens to foment a plethora of "brush fire" conflicts with all the attendant expense, bitterness, and divisiveness that characterized the Vietnam war.

Finally, and not the least important, reducing our Third World commitments would put an end to the hypocrisy that has pervaded U.S. relations with countries in the Third World. It is debilitating for a society that honors democracy and fundamental human rights to embrace regimes that scorn both values. A nation that believes in human liberty has no need for, and should not want, "friends" who routinely practice the worst forms of repression. A policy of detachment would restore a badly needed sense of honor and consistency to American foreign policy.

QUESTIONS FOR DISCUSSION

1. Should the kind of political system that a country possesses matter to U.S. foreign policy makers?

2. Should the fact that some dictatorships are much more harsh on their people than other dictatorships make a difference in considering the relationship between the United States and dictatorships in general?

3. What effect would an active, but nonmilitary, policy by the United States have on the quality of life for the ordinary people who suffer in dictatorships?

4. What are the military and foreign policy consequences of Roy Lechtreck's proposals?

5. How would the Soviet Union respond to a U.S. policy based on Roy Lechtreck's proposals?

SUGGESTED READINGS

Carleton, David. "The Role of Human Rights in U.S. Foreign Assistance Policy: A Critique and Reappraisal." *American Journal of Political Science*, 31 (Nov. 1987), pp. 1001–18.

Forsythe, David P. *Human Rights and U.S. Foreign Policy: Congress Reconsidered.* Gainesville, Fla.: University of Florida Press, 1988.

Hoffmann, Stanley. "Reaching for the Most Difficult: Human Rights As a Foreign Policy Goal." *Daedalus*, 112 (Fall 1983), pp. 19–49.

Kagan, Donald. "Human Rights, Moralism, and Foreign Policy." *Washington Quarterly*, 6 (Winter 1983), pp. 86–95.

Kristol, Irving. "'Human Rights': The Hidden Agenda." *National Interest*, no. 6 (Winter 1986–87), pp. 3–11.

Mower, A. Glenn, Jr. *Human Rights and American Foreign Policy: The Carter and Reagan Experiences.* New York: Greenwood, 1987.

Novak, Michael. *Human Rights and the New Realism: Strategic Thinking in a New Age.* New York: Freedom House, 1986.

Tyagi, Yogesh K. "National Security and Human Rights: Some Reflections." *International Studies*, 22 (Oct.–Dec. 1985), pp. 319–35.

Vance, Cyrus R. "The Human Rights Imperative." *Foreign Policy*, no. 63 (Summer 1986), pp. 3–19.

Vincent, R.J., ed. *Foreign Policy and Human Rights: Issues and Responses.* Cambridge, Eng.: Cambridge University Press, 1986.

23 Is the United States in Relative Decline?

YES

Paul Kennedy

The (Relative) Decline of America

NO

Joseph S. Nye, Jr.

Understating U.S. Strength

The (Relative) Decline of America

Paul Kennedy

THE EROSION OF U.S. GRAND STRATEGY

In February of 1941, when Henry Luce's *Life* magazine announced that this was the "American century," the claim accorded well with the economic realities of power. Even before the United States entered the Second World War, it produced about a third of the world's manufactures, which was more than twice the production of Nazi Germany and almost ten times that of Japan. By 1945, with the Fascist states defeated and America's wartime allies economically exhausted, the U.S. share of world manufacturing output was closer to half—a proportion never before or since attained by a single nation. More than any of the great world empires—Rome, Imperial Spain, or Victorian Britain—the United States appeared destined to dominate international politics for decades, if not centuries, to come.

In such circumstances it seemed to American decision-makers natural (if occasionally awkward) to extend U.S. military protection to those countries pleading for help in the turbulent years after 1945. First came involvement in Greece and Turkey; and then, from 1949 onward, the extraordinarily wide-ranging commitment to NATO [North Atlantic Treaty Organization]; the special relationship with Israel and, often contrarily, with Saudi Arabia, Jordan, Egypt, and lesser Arab states; and obligations to the partners in such regional defense organizations as SEATO [South East Asia

Treaty Organization], CENTO [Central Treaty Organization], and ANZUS [Australia–New Zealand–United States]. Closer to home, there was the Rio Pact and the special hemispheric defense arrangements with Canada. By early 1970, as Ronald Steel has pointed out, the United States "had more than 1,000,000 soldiers in 30 countries, was a member of 4 regional defense alliances and an active participant in a fifth, had mutual defense treaties with 42 nations, was a member of 53 international organizations, and was furnishing military or economic aid to nearly 100 nations across the face of the globe." Although the end of the Vietnam War significantly reduced the number of American troops overseas, the global array of U.S. obligations that remained would have astonished the Founding Fathers.

Yet while America's commitments steadily increased after 1945, its share of world manufacturing and of world gross national product began to decline, at first rather slowly, and then with increasing speed. In one sense, it could be argued, such a decline is irrelevant: this country is nowadays far richer, absolutely, than it was in 1945 or 1950, and most of its citizens are much better off *in absolute terms.* In another sense, however, the shrinking of America's share of world production is alarming because of the implications for American grand strategy—which is measured not by military forces alone but by their integration with all those other elements (economic, social, political, and diplomatic) that contribute toward a successful long-term national policy.

The gradual erosion of the economic foundations of America's power has been of several kinds. In the first place, there is the country's industrial decline relative to overall world production, not only in older manufactures, such as textiles, iron and steel, shipbuilding, and basic chemicals, but also—though it is harder to judge the final outcome at this stage of industrial-technological combat—in robotics, aerospace technology, automobiles, ma-

Paul Kennedy, "The (Relative) Decline of America," *Atlantic Monthly,* 260 (Aug. 1987), pp. 29–34, 36–38. Reprinted by permission of Random House and Unwin Hyman.

chine tools, and computers. Both areas pose immense problems: in traditional and basic manufacturing the gap in wage scales between the United States and newly industrializing countries is probably such that no efficiency measures will close it; but to lose out in the competition in future technologies, if that indeed should occur, would be even more disastrous.

The second, and in many ways less expected, sector of decline is agriculture. Only a decade ago experts were predicting a frightening global imbalance between food requirements and farming output. But the scenarios of famine and disaster stimulated two powerful responses: the first was a tremendous investment in American farming from the 1970s onward, fueled by the prospect of ever larger overseas food sales; the second was a large-scale investigation, funded by the West, into scientific means of increasing Third World crop outputs. These have been so successful as to turn growing numbers of Third World countries into food exporters, and thus competitors of the United States. At the same time, the European Economic Community [EEC] has become a major producer of agricultural surpluses, owing to its price-support system. In consequence, experts now refer to a "world awash in food," and this state of affairs in turn has led to sharp declines in agricultural prices and in American food exports—and has driven many farmers out of business.

Like mid-Victorian Britons, Americans after 1945 favored free trade and open competition, not just because they held that global commerce and prosperity would be advanced in the process but also because they knew that they were most likely to benefit from a lack of protectionism. Forty years later, with that confidence ebbing, there is a predictable shift of opinion in favor of protecting the domestic market and the domestic producer. And, just as in Edwardian Britain, defenders of the existing system point out that higher tariffs not

only might make domestic products *less* competitive internationally but also might have other undesirable repercussions—a global tariff war, blows against American exports, the undermining of the currencies of certain newly industrializing countries, and an economic crisis like that of the 1930s.

Along with these difficulties affecting American manufacturing and agriculture has come great turbulence in the nation's finances. The uncompetitiveness of U.S. industrial products abroad and the declining sales of agricultural exports have together produced staggering deficits in visible trade—$160 billion in the twelve months ending with April of 1986—but what is more alarming is that such a gap can no longer be covered by American earnings on "invisibles," which are the traditional recourse of a mature economy. On the contrary, the United States has been able to pay its way in the world only by importing ever larger amounts of capital. This has, of course, transformed it from the world's largest creditor to the world's largest debtor nation in the space of a few years.

Compounding this problem—in the view of many critics, causing this problem—have been the budgetary policies of the U.S. government itself.

FEDERAL DEFICIT, DEBT, AND INTEREST (IN BILLIONS)

	Deficit	Debt	Interest on Debt
1980	$ 59.6	$ 914.3	$ 52.5
1983	$195.4	$1,381.9	$ 87.8
1985	$202.8	$1,823.1	$129.0

A continuation of this trend, alarmed voices have pointed out, would push the U.S. national debt to around $13 *trillion* by the year 2000 (fourteen times the debt in 1980) and the interest payments on the debt to $1.5 *trillion* (twenty-nine times the 1980 payments). In fact a lowering of interest rates could make those estimates too high, but the overall trend is still very unhealthy. Even if federal deficits could be reduced to a "mere" $100 billion annually, the compounding of national debt and interest payments by the early twenty-first century would still cause unprecedented sums of money to be diverted in that direction. The only historical examples that come to mind of Great Powers so increasing their indebtedness *in peacetime* are France in the 1780s, where the fiscal crisis finally led to revolution, and Russia early in this century.

Indeed, it is difficult to imagine how the American economy could have got by without the inflow of foreign funds in the early 1980s, even if that had the awkward consequence of inflating the dollar and thereby further hurting U.S. agricultural and manufacturing exports. But, one wonders, what might happen if those funds are pulled out of the dollar, causing its value to drop precipitously?

Some say that alarmist voices are exaggerating the gravity of what is happening to the U.S. economy and failing to note the "naturalness" of most of these developments. For example, the midwestern farm belt would be much less badly off if so many farmers had not bought land at inflated prices and excessive interest rates in the late 1970s. The move from manufacturing into services is understandable, and is occurring in all advanced countries. And U.S. manufacturing *output* has been rising in absolute terms, even if employment (especially blue-collar employment) in manufacturing has been falling—but that too is a "natural" trend, as the world increasingly moves from material-based to knowledge-based production. Similarly, there is nothing wrong in the metamorphosis of American financial institutions into world financial institutions, with bases in Tokyo and London as well as New York, to handle (and profit from) the heavy flow of capital; that can only increase the nation's earnings from services. Even the large annual federal deficits and the mounting national debt are sometimes de-

scribed as being not very serious, after allowance is made for inflation; and there exists in some quarters a belief that the economy will "grow its way out" of these deficits, or that government measures will close the gap, whether by increasing taxes or cutting spending or both. A too hasty attempt to slash the deficit, it is pointed out, could well trigger a major recession.

The positive signs of growth in the American economy are said to be even more reassuring. Because of the boom in the service sector, the United States has been creating jobs over the past decade faster than it has done at any time in its peacetime history—and certainly a lot faster than Western Europe has been. America's far greater degree of labor mobility eases such transformations in the job market. Furthermore, the enormous American commitment to high technology—not just in California and New England but also in Virginia, Arizona, and many other places—promises ever greater production, and thus national wealth (as well as ensuring a strategic edge over the Soviet Union). Indeed, it is precisely because of the opportunities existing in the American economy that the nation continues to attract millions of immigrants and to generate thousands of new entrepreneurs, and the capital that pours into the country can be tapped for further investment, especially in research and development. Finally, if long-term shifts in the global terms of trade are, as economists suspect, leading to steadily lower prices for foodstuffs and raw materials, that ought to benefit an economy that still imports enormous amounts of oil, metal ores, and so on (even if it hurts particular American interests, such as farmers and oilmen).

Many of these points may be valid. Since the American economy is so large and diverse, some sectors and regions are likely to be growing while others are in decline—and to characterize the whole with generalizations about "crisis" or "boom" is therefore inappropriate.

Given the decline in the price of raw materials, the ebbing of the dollar's unsustainably high exchange value since early 1985, the reduction that has occurred in interest rates, and the impact of all three trends on inflation and on business confidence, it is not surprising that some professional economists are optimistic about the future.

Nevertheless, from the viewpoint of American grand strategy, and of the economic foundation necessary to an effective long-term strategy, the picture is much less rosy. In the first place, America's capacity to carry the burden of military liabilities that it has assumed since 1945 is obviously less than it was several decades ago, when its shares of global manufacturing and GNP [gross national product] were much larger, its agriculture was secure, its balance of payments was far healthier, the government budget was in balance, and it was not in debt to the rest of the world. From that larger viewpoint there is something in the analogy that is made by certain political scientists between America's position today and that of previous "declining hegemons." Here again it is instructive to note the uncanny similarity between the growing mood of anxiety in thoughtful circles in the United States today and that which pervaded all political parties in Edwardian Britain and led to what has been termed the national efficiency movement—a broad-based debate among the nation's decision-making, business, and educational elites over ways to reverse a growing uncompetitiveness with other advanced societies. In terms of commercial expertise, levels of training and education, efficiency of production, and standards of income and (among the less well off) living, health, and housing, the number-one power of 1900 seemed to be losing its superiority, with dire implications for its long-term *strategic* position. Hence the calls for "renewal" and "reorganization" came as much from the right as from the left. Such campaigns usually do lead to reforms here

and there, but their very existence is, ironically, a confirmation of decline. When a Great Power is strong and unchallenged, it will be much less likely to debate its capacity to meet its obligations than when it is relatively weaker.

In particular, there could be serious implications for American grand strategy if the U.S. industrial base continues to shrink. If there were ever in the future to be a large-scale war that remained conventional (because of the belligerents' fear of triggering a nuclear holocaust), one must wonder, would America's productive capacities be adequate after years of decline in certain key industries, the erosion of blue-collar employment, and so on? One is reminded of the warning cry of the British nationalist economist Professor W. A. S. Hewins in 1904 about the impact of British industrial decay upon that country's power:

> Suppose an industry which is threatened [by foreign competition] is one which lies at the very root of your system of National defense, where are you then? You could not get on without an iron industry, a great Engineering trade, because in modern warfare you would not have the means of producing, and maintaining in a state of efficiency, your fleets and armies.

It is hard to imagine that the decline in American industrial capacity could be so severe: America's manufacturing base is simply much broader than Edwardian Britain's was, and—an important point—the so-called defense-related industries not only have been sustained by Pentagon procurement but also have taken part in the shift from materials-intensive to knowledge-intensive (high-tech) manufacturing, which over the long term will also reduce the West's reliance on critical raw materials. Even so, the expatriation from the United States of, say, semiconductor assembly, the erosion of the American shipping and ship-building industry, and the closing down of so many American mines and oil fields represent trends that cannot but be damaging in the event of another long, Great Power, coalition war. If, moreover, historical precedents have any validity at all, the most critical constraint upon any surge in wartime production will be the number of skilled craftsmen— which causes one to wonder about the huge long-term decline in American blue-collar employment, including the employment of skilled craftsmen.

A problem quite different but equally important for sustaining a proper grand strategy concerns the impact of slow economic growth on the American social-political consensus. To a degree that amazes most Europeans, the United States in the twentieth century has managed to avoid overt "class" politics. This, one imagines, is a result of America's unique history. Many of its immigrants had fled from socially rigid circumstances elsewhere; the sheer size of the country had long allowed those who were disillusioned with their economic position to escape to the West, and also made the organization of labor much more difficult than in, say, France or Britain; and those same geographic dimensions, and the entrepreneurial opportunities within them, encouraged the development of a largely unreconstructed form of laissez-faire capitalism that has dominated the political culture of the nation (despite occasional counterattacks from the left). In consequence, the earnings gap between rich and poor is significantly larger in the United States than in any other advanced industrial society, and state expenditures on social services claim a lower share of GNP than in comparable countries except Japan, whose family-based support system for the poor and the aged appears much stronger.

This lack of class politics despite obvious socio-economic disparities has been possible because the nation's overall growth since the 1930s has offered the prospect of individual betterment to a majority of the population, and, disturbingly, because the poorest third of American society has not been mobilized to vote regularly. But given the different birthrates of whites on the one hand and blacks and Hispanics on the other, given the changing composition of the flow of immigrants into the United States, given also the economic metamorphosis that is leading to the loss of millions of relatively high-paying jobs in manufacturing, and the creation of millions of poorly paid jobs in services, it may be unwise to assume that the prevailing norms of the American political economy (such as low government social expenditures and low taxes on the rich) would be maintained if the nation entered a period of sustained economic difficulty caused by a plunging dollar and slow growth. An American polity that responds to external challenges by increasing defense expenditures, and reacts to the budgetary crisis by cutting existing social expenditures, runs the risk of provoking an eventual political backlash. There are no easy answers in dealing with the constant three-way tension between defense, consumption, and investment as national priorities.

IMPERIAL OVERSTRETCH

This brings us, inevitably, to the delicate relationship between slow economic growth and high defense spending. The debate over the economics of defense spending is a heated one and—bearing in mind the size and variety of the American economy, the stimulus that can come from large government contracts, and the technological spin-offs from weapons research—the evidence does not point simply in one direction. But what is significant for our purposes is the comparative dimension. Although (as is often pointed out) defense expenditures amounted to ten percent of GNP under President Eisenhower and nine percent under President Kennedy, America's shares of global production and wealth were at that time around twice what they are today, and, more particularly, the American economy was not then facing challenges to either its traditional or its high-technology manufactures. The United States now devotes about seven percent of its GNP to defense spending, while its major economic rivals, especially Japan, allocate a far smaller proportion. If this situation continues, then America's rivals will have more funds free for civilian investment. If the United States continues to direct a huge proportion of its research and development activities toward military-related production while the Japanese and West Germans concentrate on commercial research and development, and if the Pentagon drains off the ablest of the country's scientists and engineers from the design and production of goods for the world market, while similar personnel in other countries are bringing out better consumer products, then it seems inevitable that the American share of world manufacturing will decline steadily, and likely that American economic growth rates will be slower than those of countries dedicated to the marketplace and less eager to channel resources into defense.

It is almost superfluous to say that these tendencies place the United States on the horns of a most acute, if long-term, dilemma. Simply because it is *the* global superpower, with military commitments far more extensive than those of a regional power like Japan or West Germany, it requires much larger defense forces. Furthermore, since the U.S.S.R. is seen to be the major military threat to American interests around the globe, and is clearly devoting a far greater proportion of its GNP to defense, American decision-makers are inevitably worried about "losing" the arms race with Russia. Yet the more sensible among the decision-makers can also perceive that the burden of armaments is debilitating the Soviet economy, and that if the two superpowers continue to allocate ever larger shares of their national wealth to the unproductive field of armaments, the critical question might soon

be, Whose economy will decline *fastest*, relative to the economies of such expanding states as Japan, China, and so forth? A small investment in armaments may leave a globally overstretched power like the United States feeling vulnerable everywhere, but a very heavy investment in them, while bringing greater security in the short term, may so erode the commercial competitiveness of the American economy that the nation will be less secure in the long term.

Here, too, the historical precedents are not encouraging. Past experience shows that even as the relative economic strength of number-one countries has ebbed, the growing foreign challenges to their position have compelled them to allocate more and more of their resources to the military sector, which in turn has squeezed out productive investment and, over time, led to a downward spiral of slower growth, heavier taxes, deepening domestic splits over spending priorities, and a weakening capacity to bear the burdens of defense. If this, indeed, is the pattern of history, one is tempted to paraphrase Shaw's deadly serious quip and say: "Rome fell. Babylon fell. Scarsdale's turn will come."

How is one to interpret what is going on? And what, if anything, can be done about these problems? Far too many of the remarks made in political speeches suggest that while politicians worry more than they did about the nation's economic future, they tend to believe that the problems have quick and simple-minded solutions. For example, some call for tariffs—but they fail to address the charge that whenever industry and agriculture are protected, they become less productive. Others urge "competitiveness"—but they fail to explain how, say, American textile workers are to compete with textile workers earning only a twentieth of American wages. Still others put the blame for the decline of American efficiency on the government, which they say takes too much of the national income—but they fail to explain how the Swiss and the Germans, with their far higher tax rates, remain competitive on the world market. There are those who want to increase defense spending to meet perceived threats overseas—but they rarely concede that such a policy would further unbalance the economy. And there are those who want to reduce defense spending—but they rarely suggest which commitments (Israel? Korea? Egypt? Europe?) should go, in order to balance means and ends.

Above all, there is rarely any sense of the long-term context in which this American dilemma must be seen, or of the blindingly obvious point that the problem is not new. The study of world history might be the most useful endeavor for today's decision-makers. Such study would free politicians from the ethnocentric and temporal blinkers that so often restrict vision, allowing them to perceive some of the larger facts about international affairs.

The first of these is that the relative strengths of the leading nations have never remained constant, because the uneven rates of growth of different societies and technological and organizational breakthroughs bring greater advantage to one society than to another. For example, the coming of the long-range-gunned sailing ship and the rise of Atlantic trade after 1500 were not uniformly beneficial to the states of Europe—they benefited some much more than others. In the same way, the later development of steam power, and of the coal and metal resources upon which it relied, drastically increased the relative power of certain nations. Once their productive capacity was enhanced, countries would normally find it easier to sustain the burdens of spending heavily on armaments in peacetime, and of maintaining and supplying large armies and fleets in wartime. It sounds crudely mercantilistic to express it this way, but wealth is usually needed to underpin military power, and military power is usually

needed to acquire and protect wealth. If, however, too large a proportion of a state's resources is diverted from the creation of wealth and allocated instead to military purposes, that is likely to lead to a weakening of national power over the long term. And if a state overextends itself strategically, by, say, conquering extensive territories or waging costly wars, it runs the risk that the benefits ultimately gained from external expansion may be outweighed by the great expense—a problem that becomes acute if the nation concerned has entered a period of relative economic decline. The history of the rise and fall of the leading countries since the advance of Western Europe in the sixteenth century—that is, of nations such as Spain, the Netherlands, France, Great Britain, and, currently, the United States—shows a significant correlation over the long term between productive and revenue-raising capacity on the one hand and military strength on the other.

Of course, both wealth *and* power are always relative. Three hundred years ago the German mercantilistic writer Philip von Hornigk observed that "whether a nation be today mighty and rich or not depends not on the abundance or security of its power or riches, but principally on whether its neighbors possess more or less of it."

The Netherlands in the mid-eighteenth century was richer in absolute terms than it had been a hundred years earlier, but by that stage it was much less of a Great Power, because neighbors like France and Britain had more power and riches. The France of 1914 was, absolutely, more powerful than the one of 1850—but that was little consolation when France was being eclipsed by a much stronger Germany. Britain has far greater wealth today than it had in its mid-Victorian prime, and its armed forces possess far more powerful weapons, but its share of world product has shrunk from about 25 percent to about three percent. If a nation has "more of it" than its contemporaries, things are fine; if not, there are problems.

This does not mean, however, that a nation's relative economic and military power will rise and fall in parallel. Most of the historical examples suggest that the trajectory of a state's military-territorial influence lags noticeably behind the trajectory of its relative economic strength. The reason for this is not difficult to grasp. An economically expanding power—Britain in the 1860s, the United States in the 1890s, Japan today—may well choose to become rich rather than to spend heavily on armaments. A half century later priorities may well have altered. The earlier economic expansion has brought with it overseas obligations: dependence on foreign markets and raw materials, military alliances, perhaps bases and colonies. Other, rival powers are now expanding economically at a faster rate, and wish in their turn to extend their influence abroad. The world has become a more competitive place, and the country's market shares are being eroded. Pessimistic observers talk of decline; patriotic statesmen call for "renewal."

In these more troubled circumstances the Great Power is likely to spend much more on defense than it did two generations earlier and yet still find the world to be less secure—simply because other powers have grown faster, and are becoming stronger. Imperial Spain spent much more money on its army in the troubled 1630s and 1640s than it had in the 1580s, when the Castilian economy was healthier. Britain's defense expenditures were far greater in 1910 than they were, say, at the time of Palmerston's death, in 1865, when the British economy was at its relative peak; but did any Britons at the later date feel more secure? The same problem appears to confront both the United States and the Soviet Union today. Great Powers in relative decline instinctively respond by spending more on security, thereby diverting potential resources from investment and compounding their long-term dilemma.

After the Second World War the position of the United States and the U.S.S.R. as powers in a class by themselves appeared to be reinforced by the advent of nuclear weapons and delivery systems. The strategic and diplomatic landscape was now entirely different from that of 1900, let alone 1800. And yet the process of rise and fall among Great Powers had not ceased. Militarily, the United States and the U.S.S.R. stayed in the forefront as the 1960s gave way to the 1970s and 1980s. Indeed, because they both interpret international problems in bipolar, and often Manichean, terms, their rivalry has driven them into an ever-escalating arms race that no other powers feel capable of joining. Over the same few decades, however, the global productive balances have been changing faster than ever before. The Third World's share of total manufacturing output and GNP, which was depressed to an all-time low in the decade after 1945, has steadily expanded. Europe has recovered from its wartime batterings and, in the form of the EEC, become the world's largest trading unit. The People's Republic of China is leaping forward at an impressive rate. Japan's postwar economic growth has been so phenomenal that, according to some measures, Japan recently overtook the Soviet Union in total GNP. Meanwhile, growth rates in both the United States and the U.S.S.R. have become more sluggish, and those countries' shares of global production and wealth have shrunk dramatically since the 1960s.

It is worth bearing the Soviet Union's difficulties in mind when one analyzes the present and future circumstances of the United States, because of two important distinctions. The first is that while it can be argued that the U.S. share of world power has been declining faster than the Soviet share over the past few decades, the problems of the United States are probably nowhere near as great as those of the

Soviet Union. Moreover, America's absolute strength (especially in industrial and technological fields) is still much greater than that of the U.S.S.R. The second is that the very unstructured, laissez-faire nature of American society (while not without its weaknesses) probably gives the United States a better chance of readjusting to changing circumstances than a rigid and *dirigiste* power has. But its potential in turn depends upon a national leadership that can understand the larger processes at work in the world today and perceives both the strong and the weak points of the country's position as the United States seeks to adjust to the changing global environment.

Although the United States is at present still pre-eminent economically and perhaps even militarily, it cannot avoid the two great tests that challenge the longevity of every major power that occupies the number-one position in world affairs. First, in the military-strategic realm, can it preserve a reasonable balance between the nation's perceived defense commitments and the means it possesses to maintain those commitments? And second, as an intimately related question, can it preserve the technological and economic bases of its power from relative erosion in the face of the ever-shifting patterns of global production? This test of American abilities will be the greater because America, like Imperial Spain around 1600 or the British Empire around 1900, bears a heavy burden of strategic commitments, made decades earlier, when the nation's political, economic, and military capacity to influence world affairs seemed so much more assured. The United States now runs the risk, so familiar to historians of the rise and fall of Great Powers, of what might be called "imperial overstretch": that is to say, decision-makers in Washington must face the awkward and enduring fact that the total of the United States's global interests

and obligations is nowadays far too large for the country to be able to defend them all simultaneously.

To be sure, it is hardly likely that the United States would be called upon to defend all of its overseas interests simultaneously and unilaterally, unaided by the NATO members in Western Europe, Israel in the Middle East, or Japan, Australia, and possibly China in the Pacific. Nor are all the regional trends unfavorable to the United States with respect to defense. For example, while aggression by the unpredictable North Korean regime is always possible, it would hardly be welcomed by Beijing—furthermore, South Korea has grown to have more than twice the population and four times the GNP of the North. Also, while the expansion of Soviet forces in the Far East is alarming to Washington, it is balanced by the growing threat that China poses to the U.S.S.R.'s land and sea lines of communication in that area. The recent sober admission by Secretary of Defense Caspar Weinberger that "we can never afford to buy the capabilities sufficient to meet all of our commitments with one hundred percent confidence" is surely true; but it is also true that the potential anti-Soviet resources in the world (the United States, Western Europe, Japan, China, Australasia) are far greater than the resources lined up on the U.S.S.R.'s side.

Despite such consolations, the fundamental grand-strategic problem remains: the United States today has roughly the same enormous array of military obligations across the globe that it had a quarter century ago, when its shares of world GNP, manufacturing production, military spending, and armed-forces personnel were much larger than they are now. In 1985, forty years after America's triumph in the Second World War and more than a decade after its pull-out from Vietnam, 526,000 members of the U.S. armed forces were abroad (including 64,000 afloat). That total is substantially more than the overseas deployments in peacetime of the military and naval forces of the British Empire at the height of its power. Nevertheless, in the opinion of the Joint Chiefs of Staff, and of many civilian experts, it is simply not enough. Despite a near-trebling of the American defense budget since the late 1970s, the numerical size of the armed forces on active duty has increased by just five percent. As the British and the French military found in their time, a nation with extensive overseas obligations will always have a more difficult manpower problem than a state that keeps its armed forces solely for home defense, and a politically liberal and economically laissez-faire society sensitive to the unpopularity of conscription will have a greater problem than most.

MANAGING RELATIVE DECLINE

Ultimately, the only answer to whether the United States can preserve its position is *no*—for it simply has not been given to any one society to remain permanently ahead of all the others, freezing the patterns of different growth rates, technological advance, and military development that have existed since time immemorial. But historical precedents do not imply that the United States is destined to shrink to the relative obscurity of former leading powers like Spain and the Netherlands, or to disintegrate like the Roman and Austro-Hungarian empires; it is too large to do the former, and probably too homogeneous to do the latter. Even the British analogy, much favored in the current political-science literature, is not a good one if it ignores the differences in scale. The geographic size, population, and natural resources of Great Britain suggest that it ought to possess roughly three or four percent of the world's wealth and power, all other things being equal. But precisely because all other things are never equal, a peculiar set of historical and technological circumstances permitted Great

Britain to possess, say, 25 percent of the world's wealth and power in its prime. Since those favorable circumstances have disappeared, all that it has been doing is returning to its more "natural" size. In the same way, it may be argued, the geographic extent, population, and natural resources of the United States suggest that it ought to possess 16 or 18 percent of the world's wealth and power. But because of historical and technological circumstances favorable to it, that share rose to 40 percent or more by 1945, and what we are witnessing today is the ebbing away from that extraordinarily high figure to a more natural share. That decline is being masked by the country's enormous military capability at present, and also by its success in internationalizing American capitalism and culture. Yet even when it has declined to the position of occupying no more than its natural share of the world's wealth and power, a long time into the future, the United States will still be a very significant power in a multipolar world, simply because of its size.

The task facing American statesmen over the next decades, therefore, is to recognize that broad trends are under way, and that there is a need to manage affairs so that the relative erosion of America's position takes place slowly and smoothly, unaided by policies that bring short-term advantage but long-term disadvantage. Among the realities that statesmen, from the President down, must be alert to are these: that technological and therefore socio-economic change is occurring in the world faster than it has ever before; that the international community is much more politically and culturally diverse than has been assumed, and is defiant of simplistic remedies offered by either Washington or Moscow for its problems; that the economic and productive power balances are no longer tilted as favorably in America's direction as they were in 1945. Even in the military realm there are signs of a certain redistribution of the balances, away from a bipolar and toward a multipolar system, in which American economic and military strength is likely to remain greater than that of any other individual country but will cease to be as disproportionate as it was in the decades immediately after the Second World War. In all the discussions about the erosion of American leadership it needs to be repeated again and again that the decline is relative, not absolute, and is therefore perfectly natural, and that a serious threat to the real interests of the United States can come only from a failure to adjust sensibly to the new world order.

Just how well can the American system adjust to a state of relative decline? Already, a growing awareness of the gap between U.S. obligations and U.S. power has led to questions by gloomier critics about the overall political culture in which Washington decision-makers have to operate. It has been suggested with increasing frequency that a country needing to reformulate its grand strategy in the light of the larger, uncontrollable changes taking place in world affairs may be ill served by an electoral system that seems to paralyze foreign-policy decision-making every two years. Foreign policy may be undercut by the extraordinary pressures applied by lobbyists, political-action committees, and other interest groups, all of whom, by definition, are prejudiced in favor of this or that policy change, and by the simplification of vital but complex international and strategic issues, inherent to mass media whose time and space for such things are limited and whose raison d'être is chiefly to make money and only secondarily to inform. It may also be undercut by the still powerful escapist urges in the American social culture, which are perhaps understandable in terms of the nation's frontier past but hinder its coming to terms with today's complex, integrated world and with other cultures and ideologies. Finally, the country may not al-

ways be helped by the division of decision-making powers that was deliberately created when it was geographically and strategically isolated from the rest of the world, two centuries ago, and had time to find a consensus on the few issues that actually concerned foreign policy. This division may be less serviceable now that the United States is a global superpower, often called upon to make swift decisions vis-à-vis countries that enjoy far fewer constraints. No one of these obstacles prevents the execution of a coherent, long-term American grand strategy. However, their cumulative effect is to make it difficult to carry out policy changes that seem to hurt special interests and occur in an election year. It may therefore be here, in the cultural and political realms, that the evolution of an overall American policy to meet the twenty-first century will be subjected to the greatest test.

Nevertheless, given the considerable array of strengths still possessed by the United States, it ought not in theory to be beyond the talents of successive Administrations to orchestrate this readjustment so as, in Walter Lippmann's classic phrase, to bring "into balance... the nation's commitments and the nation's power." Although there is no single state obviously preparing to take over America's global burdens, in the way that the United States assumed Britain's role in the 1940s, the country has fewer problems than had Imperial Spain, besieged by enemies on all fronts, or the Netherlands, squeezed between France and England, or the British Empire, facing numerous challengers. The tests before the United States as it heads toward the twenty-first century are certainly daunting, perhaps especially in the economic sphere; but the nation's resources remain considerable, *if* they can be properly utilized and *if* there is a judicious recognition of both the limitations and the opportunities of American power.

Understating U.S. Strength

Joseph S. Nye, Jr.

Many Americans see the end of the Reagan administration as the end of an era. The popular press reports regularly on the decline of American power. The historian Paul Kennedy's 1988 book *The Rise and Fall of the Great Powers* became an unexpected best seller. Foreign-policy experts quote Walter Lippmann about the need to adjust the country's commitments to fit the country's strength. Public-opinion polls reveal increased anxiety over economic security, and congressional resolutions press the allies to relieve the United States of some of its defense burdens.

American concern about decline is nothing new. As Arthur Schlesinger, Jr., pointed out in his book *The Cycles of American History* (1986), such anxieties have arisen from time to time since the earliest days of the Republic. History also suggests that concern among countries about their rise and fall can produce political instability. For centuries historians and political scientists have drawn lessons from Thucydides' conclusion that not merely the rise of Athenian power, but also the fear it created in Sparta, led to the Peloponnesian War, which was so fatal for ancient Greece. At the beginning of this century Great Britain was concerned about the rise of Germany, which in turn worried about the expansion of Russia. The resulting anxieties contributed to the start of World War I.

As the end of the Reagan administration and the end of the century approach, it is important to develop an accurate understanding

Joseph S. Nye, Jr., "Understating U.S. Strength," *Foreign Policy,* no. 72 (Fall 1988), pp. 105–29. Reprinted by permission of *Foreign Policy.*

of America's world position. Clearly, major changes in American power have taken place since the 1950s. Depending on the base year chosen, the United States then represented one-third to two-fifths of world product and world military expenditure, whereas today it is responsible for a little more than one-fifth of both measures. But the notion of American decline confuses different times and causes. There has been a relative decline since the 1950s but less decline in America's share of world product if the 1930s or the late 1960s is taken as the base line. From a longer perspective, the century that began in the 1870s, when the United States became the world's largest economy, may be the first of several to come.

Moreover, the decline of America's position from the artificial high of the 1950s could have several causes. One is an absolute decline stemming from society's loss of cohesion and inventiveness generally. A second cause might be the external rise of a new economic and military power that surpasses the previous great power. A third cause combines both internal and external factors: The efforts to stave off a rising power might sap the internal strength of an older power.

None of these theories fits the United States well. It has not experienced an absolute decline, and relative decline is in large part an artifact of the extraordinary base line of the 1950s. The United States is not being challenged by a rising military power. Nor are external commitments sapping America's internal strength. And, with certain domestic reforms, the United States will be better placed than most societies to adapt to the new dimensions of power in the information age.

Although the United States must adjust to a new era of multipolarity and interdependence in world politics, Americans should not understate U.S. strength. Misleading historical analogies and false anxieties might prompt Americans to adopt policies of retrenchment that, ironically, could produce the results they are supposed to forestall.

The theme of American decline ran like a dark thread through the 1980 presidential election. Images from the 1970s, such as gas-ration queues, Soviet troops in Afghanistan, and revolutionaries in Iran burning American flags, brought about fears in the early 1980s that reflected real problems. But these problems were exaggerated. One fear was expressed in the self-limiting inclinations on foreign affairs after the Vietnam War. U.S. foreign policy long has been characterized by cycles of inward- and outward-oriented attitudes. Thus it is not surprising that the reaction against the U.S. involvement in Vietnam limited the use of American power in other areas, such as Angola in 1975.

Similarly, the military dimensions of the U.S.-Soviet balance shifted during the 1960s and early 1970s. The Soviet Union had established rough strategic nuclear parity and an improved ability to support conventional and proxy forces far from its homeland. But many Americans overreacted in believing that these changes indicated Soviet superiority. They failed to discern the stagnation that clearly has constrained Soviet power in the 1980s.

Also in the 1970s, the United States grew dependent on imports for nearly one-half of its oil consumption. However, the degree of disruption was partly the result of inept domestic policies that controlled oil prices and failed to develop an adequate strategic petroleum reserve. The ensuing economic slowdown was typical of all of the big capitalist economies.

Two other changes in the American world position have deeper roots. One is that power in the global economy increasingly has spread among other countries, particularly U.S. allies. This was in large part the result of postwar American policy. Rather than seeking hegemony over its allies, the United States opted to stimulate their economic revival and create a strategic partnership in balancing Soviet power.

To the extent that the United States has had a grand strategy for foreign policy over the past 40 years, it has been to promote economic prosperity and political stability in Western Europe and Japan and a close alliance with them. As George Kennan, then a U.S. diplomat, pointed out after World War II, only a few areas in the world have the industrial and technological creativity to affect the global balance of power deeply: the United States, the Soviet Union, Western Europe, and Japan. Of these, Europe and Japan are close geographically to the Soviet Union. That they are close to America politically is profoundly important. The diffusion of economic growth was a deliberate U.S. foreign-policy goal and a wise one.

The other long-term cause of America's changed global position is the increased complexity of international interdependence, which has reduced the potential for any country to exercise decisive influence over the whole system. Complexity derives from more actors, more issues, greater interactions, and less hierarchy in international politics. The role of military force has changed in subtle ways. Force remains the most effective form of power in some situations: Witness U.S. actions against Grenada and Libya. But in general, force has become more costly for great powers to apply effectively, as the Americans found in Vietnam and the Soviets discovered in Afghanistan.

The Soviet experience in Afghanistan illustrates that the increased costliness of force does not constrain only democracies. But modern technologies, including cheap and reliable means of destroying planes and ships, may ease the way for both lesser states involved in regional rivalries and terrorist groups to employ force. The net effect of these changes eats away the international hierarchy traditionally based on military power. Other power resources, such as economic vitality, diplomatic skill, attractive cultural values, and a society attuned to an open flow of information, all become more important.

This erosion of international hierarchy is sometimes portrayed as the decline of America, as though the causes lie with its own internal processes. But with more than one-fifth of world military expenditures and global economic product, the United States still is the most powerful state in the world and will very likely remain that way far into the future. To understand what has happened, the distinction must be made between influence over other countries and influence over outcomes in the international system as a whole. The United States still carries more leverage than other countries. However, it has less leverage than in the past because the heightened complexity of interdependence makes extracting the outcomes it prefers more difficult. In addition, all of the major powers have less power than in the past over nationalistically awakened populations.

Thus the task of reversing the decline of American power that the Reagan administration accepted in 1981 was both easier and more difficult than it thought. It was easier because some of the causes of apparent decline reflected the particular conditions of the 1970s and had been exaggerated in public debate. It was harder because some of the factors in America's changing global position reflected not decline in the United States but historical trends in world politics. Trying to reverse those deeper external causes—incipient multipolarity and the increased complexity of interdependence—is like trying to turn back the tide. The American position of the 1950s cannot be recaptured. The relevant question is how a broader range of power resources can be used to meet American goals in this changed world.

By and large, the Reagan administration coped well with the short-term, self-inflicted causes of the relative decline of U.S. power in the 1970s. Despite the wasteful manner in which some of it was spent, the unprecedented real increase in the defense budget over the first 5 years of the Reagan presidency sent a strong signal both to the allies and to the U.S.S.R. Ronald Reagan's "get tough" attitude reinforced the message. Since perceptions of what the Soviets call the "correlation of forces" are influenced heavily by psychological factors, these actions went a long way toward reversing the effects of the inward orientation that followed the Vietnam War. Reagan in effect relaxed some of the "Vietnam syndrome" constraints on American foreign policy.

Reagan restored confidence in the institution of the presidency by following Dwight Eisenhower's example and realizing its monarchical potential. Alas, unlike Eisenhower, he was inattentive to the prime ministerial aspects of the job, and the Iran-*contra* scandal subsequently squandered many of the beneficial aspects of his public posture. If Reagan had quit after his first term, he could have been remembered widely as the man who restored American power and confidence after the pessimistic 1970s.

The larger question, however, is how well the Reagan administration responded to the longer-term trends in the diffusion of economic growth among the allies, to the emergence of multipolar dimensions in the nonmilitary aspects of world politics, and to the increasing complexity of interdependence that complicates the application of American power. In these areas the Reagan record has been less satisfying. Michael Howard, an astute British observer, argues that 1987 "saw relations between the governments of the United States and its European allies reach a nadir" because of the inept handling of the nuclear guarantee at the superpower summit meeting in Reykjavík, Iceland, the Iran-*contra* affair, and the budget deficit. The Princeton University political scientist Robert Gilpin argued in the Summer 1987 issue of *Daedalus* that

> the Reagan years have masked the profound developments that have occurred and the challenges they have posed. The United States has been living on borrowed time—and borrowed money—for much of the last decade; this has enabled the United States to postpone the inevitable and painful adjustments to the new realities in global diplomatic, economic, and strategic relationships.

BACK TO THE CENTER

In 1981 the new administration reflected the diversity of a victorious coalition. It included traditional internationalist Republicans, disaffected neoconservative Democrats, and unilateralists descended in part from the old isolationist wing of the Republican party. They agreed on an increased defense budget, a greater willingness to use force, hostility toward the Soviet Union, and a diminished role for arms control. Initially the Reagan coalition downgraded the role of international institutions and global issues such as human rights and nonproliferation.

In retrospect, two things are particularly striking about this 1981 world view. First, it differs considerably from Reagan administration policies in 1988. In some ways there is a greater difference between the views at the beginning and the end of the Reagan era than there is between Reagan and the Democratic opposition in 1988. Conservatives such as Howard Phillips ended up calling Reagan "a useful idiot for Soviet propaganda"; neoconservatives such as Irving Kristol complained that Reagan's "most dismaying performance has been in foreign affairs"; and the *Wall Street Journal* predicted that "the U.S. will lapse into a position of strategic inferiority, as the result of trends started in the last year of the Reagan Administration."

The second striking thing about the 1981 approach was its deviation from traditional Republican views of containment. In surveying postwar strategies of containment, the historian John Lewis Gaddis noted that the Democrats (Harry Truman, John Kennedy, and Lyndon Johnson) were fiscal liberals willing to tax and spend. They tended to take a broader view of containment because they were optimistic about the means of U.S. power. Republican fiscal conservatives (Eisenhower, Richard Nixon, and Gerald Ford) were more reluctant to tax and spend and thus chose more selective goals and methods of containment.[1] Not only did Reagan take an expansive view of containment, but his supply-side fiscal unorthodoxy broke the postwar partisan pattern. On security issues, he spent like a Democrat but taxed like a Republican. Reagan was drawn back toward the mainstream of postwar American foreign policy, but he refused to raise taxes to finance his strategy. Both points are important in judging Reagan's legacy for America's global position.

The most dramatic changes came in Reagan's rhetoric and policies toward the Soviet Union. Some explain the new approach as a response to changes in the Soviet Union that Reagan brought about. Talking and acting tough had helped bring the Soviets to the bargaining table. Reagan's defense build-up and the successful deployment of the intermediate-range nuclear missiles in 1983 certainly contributed to the Soviet view that their 1970s estimation of a favorable correlation of forces no longer held in the 1980s.

Yet there is a danger that Americans might learn lessons from the recent U.S.-Soviet relationship that are too simple. Economic problems in the Soviet Union and the client socialist countries, as well as a series of dying leaders, helped to persuade the Soviets that

---

[1] John Lewis Gaddis, "Containment and the Logic of Strategy," *National Interest,* no. 10 (Winter 1987–88): 27–38. See also Gaddis, *Strategies of Containment* (New York: Oxford University Press, 1982).

the correlation of forces had turned against them. The changes in Soviet policy under Mikhail Gorbachev have come in response not only to American pressure, but also to structurally rooted internal Soviet problems that would have existed whether or not Reagan came to power or Jimmy Carter had been re-elected.

Moreover, that Reagan began to soften his rhetoric in 1984, an election year, suggests that changes in the Soviet Union were not the only cause of the new U.S. policy. As an astute politician faced with growing congressional resistance to his nuclear modernization program, Reagan made adjustments.

By making the adjustments in 1984, Reagan deprived his Democratic opponent of a major campaign issue, the charge that he was the only postwar president not to meet with his Soviet counterpart. Now Reagan has taken part in more U.S.-Soviet summits than any other postwar leader. As the political scientist Samuel Huntington wrote: "By talking like Ronald Reagan, in short, Ronald Reagan may end up acting the way Jimmy Carter wanted to act but could not. Moderation, especially in practice, may be the child of extremism, particularly in rhetoric."[2] Although the causation is more complex than officials like to admit, Reagan has left U.S.-Soviet relations in better shape than he found them. In the management of the basic East-West balance, Reagan, so heavily criticized in his first term, deserves credit for these improvements.

Reagan's modification of the traditional Republican strategy of containment, however, has had less happy consequences. The so-called Reagan Doctrine of rolling back Soviet advances in the Third World has had mixed success. In one case, providing arms to the anticommunist rebels in Afghanistan, Reagan

enjoyed broad popular and congressional support, and the policy scored an impressive success. But other cases have been more controversial at home and less successful abroad. Support for the anti-Sandinista *contra* forces in Nicaragua proved to be a major source of contention; Reagan failed to couple diplomacy with force, and administration efforts to bypass congressional restraints severely damaged Reagan's presidency.

Even greater damage was done, however, by abandoning the traditional Republican approach to financing security policy. The Reagan administration succeeded in shifting resources into defense with a 50 per cent increase in real terms over the first 5 years. The share of gross national product (GNP) devoted to defense rose from slightly more than 5.2 per cent to 6.3 per cent. But Reagan failed to provide additional financing for this increase. Instead, the national debt rose by almost $1 trillion. In a sense, the tax reductions of 1981 gave away the revenue base that could have financed much of the increase in defense spending. As Senator Bill Bradley (D.-New Jersey) wrote in the Spring 1988 issue of *New Perspectives Quarterly:*

> In 1981, the government was defunded. This was a decision...that was taken by a small group of ideologues whose real objective was to eliminate government from many areas of American life. They chose to accomplish this goal by causing a crisis—the enormous deficits—which they assumed would force massive cuts in social programs.

Although the deficits put congressional Democrats on the defensive, they did not force major social cuts.

The administration turned to financing its deficits through foreign borrowing, and to attract foreign funds it raised interest rates. Not only did the United States become the world's largest debtor country but also the influx of capital pushed up the value of the dollar, en-

---

[2] Samuel P. Huntington, "Renewed Hostility," in *The Making of America's Soviet Policy*, ed. Joseph S. Nye, Jr. (New Haven: Yale University Press, 1984), 289.

couraging imports and discouraging exports. That, in turn, contributed to massive trade deficits, the erosion of the U.S. manufacturing sector, and rising domestic protectionist pressures. Federal spending's share of GNP rose from 20.5 per cent in 1979 to 23.8 per cent in 1986; the increase was financed by borrowing an average of 3.4 per cent of GNP each year. This borrowing from other countries and against America's future will have to be serviced. In the future Americans will have to cut consumption and increase savings to defray the Reagan debt. The adjustment may be painful, but it is well within the capacity of the American economy over the next decade.

The twin deficits have created an uneasiness about the economic future. But some observers read more into America's economic problems at the end of the Reagan era. The analyst David Calleo, writing in the Spring 1988 *New Perspectives Quarterly*, believes that "thanks to economic strain and mismanagement, relative decline has begun to turn absolute." A particularly popular theory of decline has been Paul Kennedy's theory of imperial overstretch. In his formulation, economic change shifts productive capabilities and interests among countries. Growing countries project military power to protect their interests, but eventually the cost of projecting military power saps their strength. Then they are replaced by another rising economic power.

Kennedy's history is impressive and certainly correct about the importance of the economic foundations of power. But his theory of imperial overstretch does not fit the American case. In Kennedy's words, "The difficulties experienced by contemporary societies which are militarily top-heavy merely repeat those which, in their time, affected Philip II's Spain, Nicholas II's Russia and Hitler's Germany."[3]

But the United States is nothing like Philip II's empire, where, as Kennedy shows, three-fourths of all government expenditures were "devoted to war or to debt repayments for previous wars." In the United States today, approximately 29 per cent of the federal budget is spent on defense and veterans' benefits.

Even after Reagan's build-up, the current U.S. defense outlay is about 6 per cent of GNP and is lower than those of the Eisenhower and Kennedy administrations, which spent about 10 per cent. Those who wish to rescue the theory of imperial overstretch sometimes argue that the net burden today is greater because the United States has a lower share of world product than it had previously. They liken the United States to an aging man carrying a pack up a hill. He has become less able to carry the burden. But the facts still do not fit the theory. The ratio between the defense share of U.S. national product and the American share of world product has changed little since the 1950s.

Alternatively, theorists of imperial overstretch sometimes simply assume that defense spending is bad for the economy. They cite Japan's spending a bit more than 1 per cent of its GNP on defense and its higher economic growth rate than the United States. Such simple correlations are misleading. South Korea and the People's Republic of China (PRC) spend a much higher proportion of their GNP on defense than Japan does; yet they have higher economic growth rates than Japan. Moreover, it is difficult to find careful and balanced economic studies that show that defense spending has a negative net impact on the economy. The myriad effects of defense spending are very complex, and the net effect is difficult to sort out.[4]

Cutting defense expenditures and withdrawing from global commitments might do

---

[3] Paul Kennedy, *The Rise and Fall of the Great Powers: Economic Change and Military Conflict from 1500 to 2000* (New York: Random House, 1987), 444.

[4] See Gordon Adams and David Gold, *Defense Spending and the Economy: Does the Defense Dollar Make a Difference?* (Washington, D.C.: Defense Budget Project, 1987).

little to solve U.S. economic problems, but it very likely would exacerbate America's international situation. Providing for the defense of other countries is a source of American influence and regional stability. It affects the way Western Europe and Japan respond to U.S. interests in the economic as well as the military and political arenas. For example, defense ties with the United States helped persuade Japan to rely on an American plane rather than developing a new fighter aircraft by itself. Further, Japanese business and government leaders appear to see no substitute for U.S. global leadership.

The Persian Gulf offers another example of the problems with backing away from foreign commitments. Although the United States receives only 7 per cent of its oil from the gulf while Japan receives nearly 60 per cent, a loss of gulf oil would severely damage the U.S. economy. The interdependence of world oil markets would spread a price rise equally for all oil imports regardless of source. The United States is in the gulf to defend its own as well as its allies' interests. America's influence there rests in part on the defense it provides for conservative oil-producing states. Power in the gulf does not come only out of the barrel of a gun, but neither does it come only from a barrel of oil.

Curtailing international commitments would leave the United States less able to influence other governments in areas such as cooperating against terrorism, slowing the rate of nuclear proliferation, restricting arms supplies, and managing regional balances. Pulling out of defense commitments would add to America's vulnerability rather than restore its strength.

Another fashionable analogy is drawn between the United States at the end of the 20th century and Great Britain at the end of the 19th century. Those who question the theory of decline are likened to the conservatives of Edwardian England who did not want to face change.

Yet important differences exist between the British and American positions. Britain was a small island country governing a vast territorial empire and was heavily dependent on trade. Imports represented 25 per cent of British GNP in 1914. The comparable U.S. figure in 1985 was 10 per cent. Moreover, America already has allies that include the most significant countries in the world economy. The challenge is not to seek new allies but to maintain relations with those America already has. Cutting back on defense commitments to those allies would reduce U.S. influence with them over the broad agenda of common interests, as well as benefit the Soviet adversary in the East-West military balance.

Most important, Britain faced rising contenders in Germany, the United States, and Russia. The nearest of those contenders, Germany, not only had surpassed Britain in economic strength but also was en route to becoming militarily dominant on the European continent and a threat to Britain's supremacy. America's external situation today is very different. Its principal military adversary, the Soviet Union, is the power suffering from imperial overstretch. Not only does the U.S.S.R dominate an unstable East European empire, but also its economy has suffered a serious deceleration of the growth rates that previously allowed Soviet expansionism. In addition, Soviet defense is estimated to be at least 15 per cent of GNP, and some estimates place the costs of defense and empire generally at more than 20 per cent of GNP—some three times higher than the relative burden on the U.S. economy.

It is not surprising, then, that Gorbachev seeks a period of external calm in order to concentrate on restructuring the Soviet economy. His task is monumental and may not be accomplished at all. Even over the long run it may prove impossible without major internal political changes. The proper analogy would be if Emperor William II's Germany, rather than passing Britain in economic and military strength, had been declining and searching for a breathing spell from its military build-up.

When the other major world powers identified by Kennan some four decades ago are studied, it is difficult to say that any of them are overtaking the United States in both military and economic power. Western Europe has the skilled population and GNP but not the political unity to play a powerful defense or political role in the world. Despite the plan to reduce barriers within the Common Market by 1992, few observers predict that European integration will progress soon to a single government or a single security policy. In short, Western Europe lacks the necessary cohesion to play a great-power role.

Similarly, the PRC is a potential rival of the United States over a much longer term. Chinese economic growth has maintained the high annual rate of nearly 9 per cent for much of the 1980s, and Beijing, of course, possesses a growing force of nuclear weapons. But the PRC remains a country whose human and technological infrastructure is developed to an extent far below that of the United States or even the Soviet Union. And in any case, the prospect is slight that the PRC will become an equal contender on a global scale in the next half century.

THE JAPANESE CHALLENGE

Thus the question of external challenge from rising powers boils down to the American relationship with Japan. Although Japan's economy is roughly one-half the size of America's, it has kept its political cohesion and its ability to grow consistently through the fat years of the 1960s, the lean years of the 1970s, and the mixed years of the 1980s. In addition, Japan has taken the lead from the United States in certain areas of high technology and has challenged the United States in markets long dominated by the Americans.

An increasing number of Americans believe that Japanese economic strength is a greater

national challenge than Soviet military power. But economic competition is not a zero-sum game where one country's gain is its competitor's loss. Japan has chosen the strategy of a trading state rather than of a military power. In this role Japanese growth not only challenges the United States but also benefits it through greater choice for American consumers and competition that keeps American industry on its toes. For example, the rise of Japanese competition has had both a useful and a painful effect on the American automobile industry. Of course, the competition should be fair; governmental help and hard bargaining will be necessary to prevent the erosion of certain strategic industries, such as semiconductors. But such a government role should not expand into broad protectionism.

Is it inevitable that Japan will develop military power commensurate with its economic power? Not necessarily. Military posture does not always closely follow economic power. It took 70 years from the time America became the world's foremost economic power to fully project its military strength and become a dominant factor in the global military balance.

An American strategy that forced Japan to spend more of its GNP on defense or closed U.S. markets might push Japanese nationalism into full-blown independence from the United States. A tolerable situation could become a true threat. Spending 1 per cent of its GNP on defense has allowed Japan to develop a military capability on the scale of the major West European countries. Those who would press Japan to triple its defense spending should realize that the probable consequences include frightening the PRC, South Korea, and the Southeast Asian countries into increasing their defense expenditures and perhaps pressuring the United States to increase its military spending in the area.

The balance of power in East Asia illustrates the complexity of the situation America now faces. Twenty years ago the United States squandered lives, resources, and prestige in a futile effort to contain communism in Southeast Asia. The prevailing image was the domino theory. A more realistic metaphor would have been the game checkers. As the West should have learned from the Yugoslavian experience, the nationalism of one communist country can be used to check another. The current pattern of relations among communist states in East Asia follows the realist adage that "the enemy of my enemy is my friend." If the Soviet Union is colored red, the PRC black, Vietnam red, and Cambodia black, the pattern of the larger Asian game outside Indochina is not dominoes at all. Thus despite the American defeat in Vietnam and Vietnam's occupation of Cambodia, East Asia is an area of relative tranquility where American security interests are well protected.

In fact, the American position is unique in the East Asian balance. Only the United States is both an economic and a military superpower. As a result the United States has more influence in the area than any other country. Both the PRC and Japan want the United States involved in diplomatic events. The U.S. naval presence and alliances are an important source of American strength. East Asia is a balance of asymmetries in economic and military strength, with the United States best placed to moderate among them. A sensible U.S. strategy for Asia must build upon a complex view of power that includes military and economic dimensions and uses America's unique diplomatic position.

The economic dimensions of power require another look at the sources of American strength. In his article in the Summer 1987 issue of *Daedalus*, Gilpin says that

> the economic crisis of the American System is a consequence of the long-term relative decline of the American economy and, more immediately, the policies of the Reagan Administration....At the same time that the United States has assumed

the largest portion of the burden of financing the American System and of confronting the growth of Soviet power, the American people have demanded both an ever-rising standard of living and improved government services.

The issue of American competitiveness in the international economy has touched a raw nerve. It is noted often that America's share of global exports of manufactured products declined from 21.3 per cent in 1957 to 13.9 per cent in 1983. Part of that decline resulted from the ill-conceived fiscal policies described above; but part had deeper roots. The American economy has a much lower rate of saving than do those of its major industrial competitors, leaving fewer resources for investment. While the American economy has been more successful in creating jobs in the 1980s than those of the West European states, most have come in the service sector where measured rates of productivity growth are lower than in manufacturing. Annual U.S. gains in productivity have averaged 1.4 per cent in the 1980s, down from 2.7 per cent between 1947 and 1968.

The United States will need to invest more in human resources, particularly in education. American test scores in mathematics and the sciences compare poorly with those of other industrial countries. The United States does not produce enough engineers to meet its needs. Fully one-fifth of American engineers are foreign or foreign-born. America's global share of new patents has been declining as Japan's has been rising.

These problems are serious, but they are not irremediable if Americans develop an effective political consensus. Americans should be cautious about overinterpreting such problems as symptomatic of long-term declines in the work ethic or American management. Rather than a diminishment of the work ethic, a large part of the export problem was the overvaluation of the dollar. With a fall in the value of the dollar, exports began to increase.

Other changes reflect the evolving nature of the international economy. For example, the evolution of manufacturing by transnational corporations demonstrates their ability to shift production from place to place in the global market. Such transnational flows create problems, but they can also offer rewards for the national economy. While domestic manufacturing matters, it would be a mistake to use indexes of manufacturing exports as the sole criterion for judging America's economic role in the world.

Throughout the centuries statesmen and other observers have made mistakes in perceiving the metric of economic power. For example, in the 17th century, mercantilist theorists who focused on Spain's reserves of gold bullion would not have understood the rise of France with its stronger administrative and commercial structure, or later, Britain with its conditions favorable to political stability and the industrial revolution. At the turn of the century, when the historian Brooks Adams used the control of metals and minerals as the predictive index of future military and economic power, he was led to expect the ascendancy of Russia and China. But as the Harvard University social scientist Daniel Bell has pointed out, the core of postindustrial societies lies in the professional and technical services, and in that realm the United States and Japan are the two leading countries.

In Bell's ordering, the first technological revolution came 200 years ago with the application of steam power to transportation and factory machine production. The second technological revolution arrived a century ago with the spread of electricity and chemistry that allowed the production of synthetics and plastics. The third technological revolution, under way today, is joining computers and telecommunications to produce such technologies as television imagery, voice telephone, digital computer data, and facsimile. These technologies in turn offer a single though differentiated system of services from interlinked computers and electronic mail

to information storage and retrieval. This revolution is changing the notion of markets from geographic places to global networks.[5] So the United States remains at the forefront of new sources of economic power, even though it shares that position with Japan. The United States should exploit its competitive advantage in information-based production processes, an advantage that is directly related to the openness, decentralization, and democracy of the American system. This is precisely where the communist societies are at their weakest. As Gorbachev realizes, a closed system could prevent the Soviet Union from remaining a first-rate global power in the information age.

The principal danger at the conclusion of the Reagan era is that misunderstood causes and nationalistic impulses will lead to inappropriate responses. A *Newsweek* poll published on February 22, 1988, showed economic nationalism rising in the United States, with one-half of the respondents favoring trade barriers to reduce the flow of foreign products into the country. In fact, protectionism in America is on the rise; the percentage of U.S. imports that are protected rose from 8 per cent in 1975 to 21 per cent in 1985.[6] But inward-turning and protectionist responses would cut the United States off from the open flow of goods, talents, and information that are sources of its strength; they allow the United States to draw upon global resources in its periodic surges of self-renewal. For example, while Americans are properly concerned that the American education system does not yield enough engineers, the other side of the coin is that few societies remain so open that they are able to cope with a shortage of talent by importing and absorbing it. The openness of American society, as manifested in the success of new im-

---

[5] See Daniel Bell, "The World and the United States in 2013," *Daedalus*, Summer 1987, 1–31.

[6] Alan Murray, "As Free-Trade Bastion, U.S. Isn't Half as Pure as Many People Think," *Wall Street Journal*, 1 November 1985, 1.

migrants, is a great source of strength not shared by the Soviet Union or Japan.

At a more general level, the economist Mancur Olson, in his study *The Rise and Decline of Nations* (1982), found that falling productivity and growth are linked to declining domestic competition. Advanced societies face the danger of domestic sclerosis as interest groups use government to protect their privileges and thereby curb national competitiveness. The best remedy for such institutional and group sclerosis is maintaining an open attitude to international competition and talents.

Seen in this perspective, the appropriate U.S. strategy is not to withdraw from international commitments in the illusory hope of protecting America from interdependence or arresting the change in its relative power position. On the contrary, such measures would contribute to, rather than arrest, the relative decline of American power because the sources of that change are mainly outside the United States. Instead, Americans must face the fact that they have to transfer resources from consumption to investment. At home, they need to invest in new technologies, infrastructure, and human resources. Abroad, they need to invest in defense, aid, and institutions that afford leverage with the international system on the many issues in which the United States is heavily interdependent.

Recent polls suggest that Americans are increasingly concerned about international economic security. The next decade may see a considerable shift in the foreign-policy agenda, particularly if a Soviet preoccupation with domestic matters leads to a period of quiescence in East-West relations. Still, Americans must remember that the balance of military power will remain crucial so long as there are great powers. Domestically, America must rebuild the economic foundation of its power by reasserting a balanced fiscal policy; providing incentives for saving; investing in education, research, and development; and using

government judiciously to smooth the process of adjustment. If America is to compete in a global information economy, it cannot afford its current waste of human resources. Enhancing its competitive position will also require hard bargaining to develop international cooperation, as well as stronger support for international economic institutions. Similarly, the United States must strengthen the structure of the postwar alliances whereby two of the five major centers of global power are allied with America rather than the Soviet Union. This will require a better sharing of alliance burdens, for Western Europe and Japan can do more. But the United States should avoid escalating friction and pullbacks over burden sharing that could rupture the alliances and thus diminish U.S. power.

Such a strategy will also require a strong conventional and naval presence along with a backdrop of credible nuclear deterrence. Certainly domestic reforms are needed to reduce wasteful military expenditure. At the same time, the United States can explore opportunities created by internal Soviet problems for reducing the level of armament at which the balance of power is maintained. Although arms control has not saved money in the past, it may in the future if U.S.-Soviet relations continue to improve. Finally, in a world where transnational communications are the basis for economic and social strength, the United States needs to be forthright in asserting its values of openness and human rights, for American influence rests not only on military and economic might but also on values. The attractiveness and global spread of American culture in the information age is a subtle yet important source of influence that few other countries possess.

A GAIN FOR BOTH SIDES

Of the two major sources of long-term change in America's position in the world, the emergence of multipolarity is less difficult to deal with than the increased complexity of interdependence. America will remain a preponderant power in a multipolar structure if it wisely maintains its alliance relationships. No other state is likely to surpass the United States in both economic and military power in the next few decades unless America follows foolish policies. As the United States struggles with Japan over how to distribute the mutual gains of interdependence in trade and investment, Americans must remember that both sides can, in fact, gain. Japan should be encouraged to accelerate the internal economic expansion suggested in the report of its own Advisory Group on Economic Structural Adjustment for International Harmony, also known as the Maekawa report. It can be asked to play a larger role—in return for a larger voice—in maintaining international institutions. Japan should be pressed not to increase military expenditures but to boost assistance to strategically important developing countries such as the Philippines and to help relieve the enormous burden of Third World debt. Japan will soon replace the United States as the largest aid donor in the world.

Similarly, in America's struggle with its European allies over defense burden sharing, Americans have to avoid the use of tendentious measurements of percentages of GNP because they fail to reveal major European contributions—60 per cent of NATO's active forces (partly by draft) and 80 per cent of alliance force reserves. The size of American defense budgets reflects broader defense interests than West Europeans have. It is in part the price of being the preponderant global power. Moreover, unilaterally withdrawing U.S. troops from Europe would not save money unless the army's overall size were cut. Over the coming decade adjustments will be made in the NATO alliance, but they should come through consensus among the allies and arms control with the East, not from unilateral measures. Otherwise the Soviets would simply receive a gift.

It will be crucial not to let the politics of petulance blind the United States to its long-term interest. After all, the U.S. involvement in European defense is not a matter of charity. It is a matter of self-interest in maintaining a global balance of power and stability in a region that has led the way into two world wars. Even in a period of reduced Soviet threat, the American presence remains a stabilizing force in Europe. Gradually, with further European integration, including enhanced defense cooperation, the American presence may become less central. But the U.S. interest in European stability will continue.

In the coming years the greater problem for the United States and other countries will be the complexity of interdependence and the difficulty of maintaining world order in the face of such issues as the spread of technology for nuclear-armed ballistic missiles and bio-chemical warfare, the rise of fundamentalist religious and nationalist movements, terrorism, environmental pollution, and the maintenance of the international economic and financial system. The United States will be the leading state in an era when, in contrast to the 1800s or the 1950s, the conditions for economic hegemony no longer obtain. As a great power, America will not be helpless, but it will face considerable frustration in trying to move others toward sharing the burdens of leadership. Leadership by unilateral example will be important, but the United States will have to coordinate its positions with those of other states more closely than it did in the extraordinary period immediately following World War II. In that sense, the problem will not be solely the challenge that the growing multipolarity of major states will pose for American power, but also what might be called entropy, or the notion that the major states will not be able to maintain order as easily as in the past.

It is safe to predict that some places in the Third World will always be experiencing turmoil. Communication advances and social modernization stir populations from old patterns and lead to strong pressures on weak political institutions. The best approach will be to have nationalism work for, rather than against, America. Nationalism is the most effective counter to Soviet expansionism even though nationalist regimes are sometimes anti-American as well. The United States is bound to be confronted with governments that refer to themselves as Latin American Marxists, African socialists, and Asian communists. With some exceptions, the United States can be relaxed about the domestic social changes that such regimes proclaim so long as those changes do not ally them with the Soviet opponent in ways that alter the world balance of power or contribute to the problems of disorder, terrorism, and proliferation. The dividing line between what is domestic and what is international can never be absolute, and America cannot be indifferent to gross violations of human rights abroad. Nonetheless, the broad distinction can help the United States to thread its way through social complexity and Third World change without backing itself into a corner that benefits the U.S.S.R.

The capacity of major powers to control affairs is further constrained by the increase in the number of foreign-policy issues that has accompanied growing economic and social interdependence. As a great power with a stake in world order, the United States has a strong interest in developing and supporting international regimes—sets of rules and institutions that govern areas of interdependence. Such regimes vary greatly in their scope and membership. They deal with everything from monetary issues, international trade, and management of natural resources to cooperation against terrorism, control of armaments, environmental pollution, and the management of particular geographic areas.

Orderly processes allow the pursuit of multiple national interests in a way that reduces their mutual interference, the cost of trade-offs, and the degree of risk. Thus even an imperfect nonproliferation regime reduces some uncertainties and insecurities. The treaties and institutions that govern international nuclear energy are not perfect, but they do create a presumption against proliferation that slows the spread of nuclear weaponry and thus enables the United States to cope better with potential destabilizing effects. Certainly it does not follow that all international regimes are in the U.S. interest. Some may be beyond repair. For one, the United Nations Educational, Scientific and Cultural Organization may be too politicized to serve American interests in scientific and educational cooperation. In some cases the United States may want to establish smaller groups with higher standards. Some trading partners may be willing to agree to a greater reduction of nontariff barriers than could be agreed upon by all members of the General Agreement on Tariffs and Trade. Sorting out U.S. interests as they relate to each international organization certainly will require more attention in the future.

Importantly, the dichotomy between unilateral and multilateral action is not as sharp as it first appears. That may seem paradoxical, but unilateral action can play an important role in building up international regimes. Exercising leadership often calls for someone to go first. Nonetheless, the unilateral action should not prevent others from joining in, and the action should be consistent with the long-term goals the United States has for international organizations.

A special form of unilateral action, of course, is the use of military force. Judiciously used, or threatened, military force can play a critical role in maintaining international order. For example, the knowledge that great powers can, at least in principle, assert their right of passage through contested waters is certainly a useful background to American bargaining over the law of the sea. Indiscriminate use of force, however, can prove too costly in relation to the particular interests pursued. Trying to seize oil fields as a response to an oil crisis could bring about an economic crisis. In some cases, such as environmental pollution and international monetary issues, force is largely irrelevant, and diplomatic hints of force may generate resentment that interferes with American objectives. A key consideration is always the coupling of force with legitimacy. If a military action is regarded broadly as justifiable at home and abroad, the cost of employing force can be reduced. In contrast to its rhetoric, the Reagan administration's practice was more cautious in the direct use of American force and thus kept the costs within manageable bounds.

In sum, Americans are right to be concerned about the changing position of the United States in world politics. But portraying the problem as American decline is misleading. For it directs attention away from the real causes, which lie in long-term changes in world politics, and suggests remedies that would weaken rather than strengthen American standing. Withdrawal from international commitments would reduce U.S. influence without necessarily strengthening the domestic economy.

Although the next decade will require Americans to cope with Reagan's debts, there is no reason why the world's wealthiest country cannot pay for both its international commitments and its domestic investments. Americans can afford both social security and international security. The ultimate irony of the Reagan legacy would be if Americans perceived the short-term

problems he has bequeathed as indicators of long-term decline and responded by cutting themselves off from the sources of their international influence. In short, it is important not to mistake the short-term problems arising from the Reagan period's borrowed prosperity for a symptom of long-term American decline. The latter need not be the case unless Americans react inappropriately to global changes and inflict the wounds upon themselves.

QUESTIONS FOR DISCUSSION

1. What constitutes power in foreign policy?
2. What role does a nation's economic strength play in the conduct of foreign policy?
3. What criteria should be used in determining whether the United States is in decline?
4. What changes should the United States make in its overseas commitments if Paul Kennedy's analysis is correct?
5. What effect do increased defense expenditures have on a nation's economy?

SUGGESTED READINGS

Calleo, David P. *Beyond American Hegemony: The Future of the Western Alliance.* New York: Basic Books, 1987.

Garten, Jeffrey. "Is American Decline Inevitable?" *World Policy Journal,* 5 (Winter 1987–88), pp. 151–74.

Gilpin, Robert. *The Political Economy of International Relations.* Princeton, N.J.: Princeton University Press, 1987.

Harries, Owen. "The Rise of American Decline." *Commentary,* 85 (May 1988), pp. 32–36.

Kennedy, Paul M. *The Rise and Fall of the Great Powers: Economic Change and Military Conflict from 1500 to 2000.* New York: Random House, 1987.

Mead, Walter Russell. *Mortal Splendor: The American Empire in Transition.* Boston: Houghton Mifflin, 1987.

Moynihan, Daniel Patrick. "Debunking the Myth of Decline." *New York Times Magazine,* June 19, 1988, pp. 34, 52–53.

Olson, Mancur. *The Rise and Decline of Nations: Eco-*

nomic Growth, Stagflation, and Social Rigidities. New Haven: Yale University Press, 1982.

Peters, Peter. "The Morning After." *Atlantic Monthly*, 260 (Oct. 1987), pp. 43–69.

Prestowitz, Clyde V., Jr. *Trading Places: How We Allowed Japan To Take the Lead*. New York: Basic Books, 1988.

Schlesinger, James R. "Debunking the Myth of Decline." *New York Times Magazine*, June 19, 1988, pp. 35–36.

Schmeisser, Peter. "Taking Stock: Is America in Decline?" *New York Times Magazine*, Apr. 17, 1988, pp. 24–27, 66–68, 96.

Tuchman, Barbara W. "A Nation in Decline?" *New York Times Magazine*, Sept. 20, 1987, pp. 52, 54–55, 57, 142, 145.